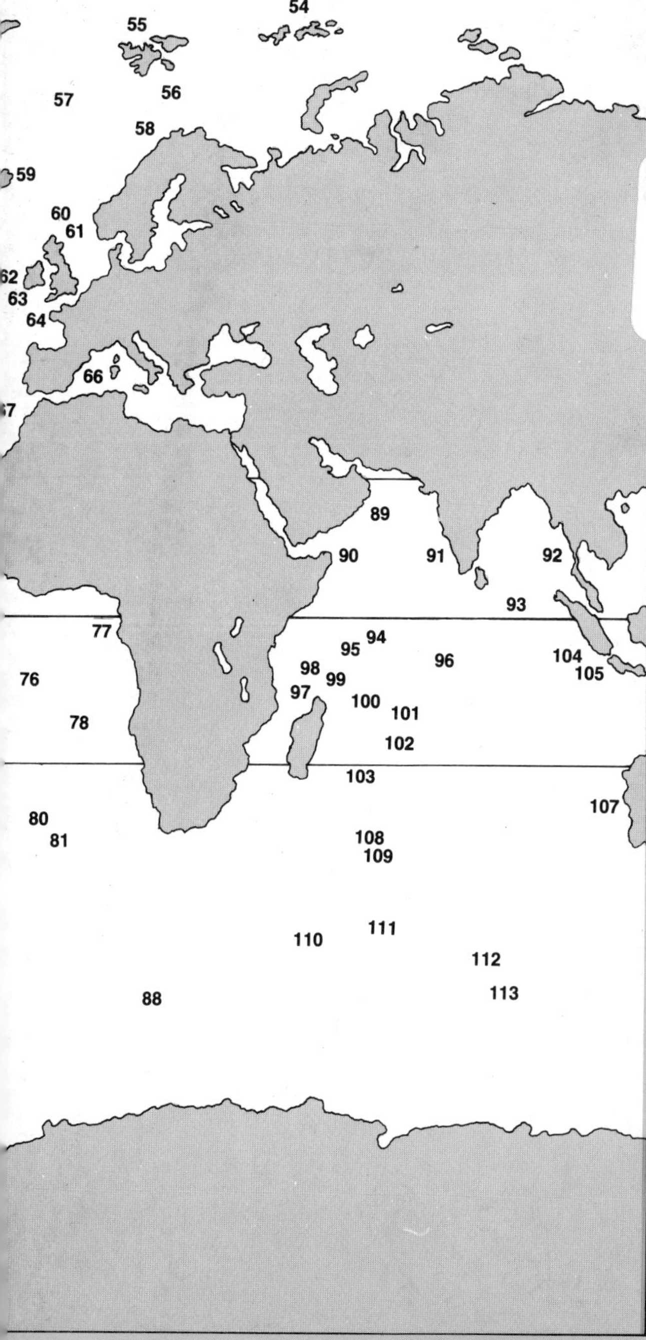

34 Three Kings Is.
35 Kermadec Is.
36 Chatham Is.
37 Bounty Is.
38 Antipodes.
39 Solander Rock.
40 Snares Is.
41 Stewart I.
42 Aukland Is.
43 Campbell I.
44 Macquarie I.
45 Austral Is.
46 Oneno I.
47 Henderson I.
48 Pitcairn I.
49 Ducie I.
50 Easter I.
51 Juan Fernandez Is.
52 Mocha I.
53 Cape Horn.

Arctic and North Atlantic.

54 Franz Joseph Land.
55 Spitzbergen.

62 South West Ireland.
63 Stokholm and Skomer.
64 Channel Is.
65 Azores.
66 Balearic Is.
67 Madeira.
68 Salvage.
69 Canary Is.
70 Bermuda.
71 Bahama Is.
72 Hispanola I.
73 Cape Verde Is.
74 St Pauls Rocks.

South Atlantic Ocean.

75 Fernando de Noronha.
76 Ascension I.
77 Sao Tome I.
78 St Helena.
79 Trinidad – Martin Vas.
80 Tristan da Cunha.
81 Gough I.
82 Staten I.
83 Falkland I.
84 South Georgia.
85 South Sandwich Is.
86 South Orkney Is.
87 South Shetland.
88 Bouvet I.

Northern Indian Ocean

89 Kuria Muria Is.
90 Socotra I.
91 Laccadive Is.
92 Andaman Is.
93 Maldive Is.

Southern Indian Ocean.

94 Seychelles.
95 Amirantes.
96 Chagos Archipelago.
97 Comoro Is.
98 Aldabra Is.
99 Providence I.
100 Alegela I.
101 Cargados Carajos I.
102 Mauritius.
103 Reunion.
104 Cocus Keeling Is.
105 Christmas I.
106 Lacapede Is.
107 Abrolhos Is.
108 Amsterdam.
109 St Paul.
110 Marion and Prince Edward Is.
111 Crozet Is.
112 Kerguelen Is.
113 Heard.
114 Antarctic Peninsula.

SEABIRDS
an identification guide

Margaret A. Kelly
27 Van Buren Avenue
East Greenbush
New York
12061
477-9016 } (518)
465-3833 }

SEABIRDS

an identification guide

by Peter Harrison

illustrated by the author

Houghton Mifflin Company
Boston 1983

Library of Congress Cataloging in Publication Data

Harrison, Peter.
Seabirds, an identification guide.

Bibliography: p.
Includes index.
1. Seabirds—Identification. 2. Birds—Identification.
I. Title.
QL673.H29 1983 598.29′24 82-15564

ISBN 0-395-33253-2

Printed and bound in Great Britain

CONTENTS

ACKNOWLEDGEMENTS

My interest in seabirds began some 20 years ago during a fierce northwest gale. Ten birders, myself the youngest, were crouched in the lee of the coastguard lookout at St Ives Island. Below us the Atlantic roared inwards, dashing itself against the Cornish coast. The bay was a maelstrom of foaming white caps and black watery hollows; above the troughs, with contemptuous mastery the Gannets rode out the storm, rising and falling in long white lines, thousands upon thousands escaping the storm like retreating troops. Hardly a minute passed without the shout of 'bonxie', 'skua', or 'petrel'. Until then most of my birding had been with terrestrial species, but that gale converted me to seabirds. I have been hooked on them ever since.

During my teens, Laurie Williams, a local Cornish birder, spent many hours coaxing and encouraging my interest in seabirds. From him and the other St Ives watchers came the inspiration to write this guide. In 1973 my wife Carol and I set out on a seven-year research-gathering expedition. Our travels took us from the Arctic to the Antarctic through the continents of Europe, Africa, Australia and the Americas. During those years we received generous support and help from local birders the world over. To all those people, too numerous to mention here, I record my thanks. Drafts of species accounts were sent to leading seabird experts in several countries. Without exception the following people offered constructive advice and helpful suggestions for improvements; to them go my grateful thanks: Richard Brooke (taxonomy), Dr Peter Fullagar (*Sphenisciformes*, *Procellariiformes*, *Pelecaniformes*, *Stercorariidae* and southern *Laridae*), Peter Grant (gulls and terns), Dr JR Jehl, Jnr (Pacific seabirds), Ron Naveen (storm-petrels and North American seabirds), Dr Bryan Nelson (frigatebirds), Ian Sinclair (Southern Oceans seabirds), Richard Stallcup (North American west coast seabirds), Peter Stewart (Mediterranean seabirds), Dr Jerry van Tets (*Sphenisciformes*, *Procellariiformes*, *Pelecaniformes*, *Stercorariidae* and southern *Laridae*), Dr John Warham (*Sphenisciformes* and *Procellariiformes*). Especial thanks go also to Mr Galbraith at the birdroom, British Museum (Natural History), and to Mrs Vale, the chief librarian. Grateful thanks also go to David Christie, copy-editor, who provided much helpful advice and suggestions for improvements to the text. My thanks also go to Croom Helm Ltd for their part in producing this guide, especially to Christopher Helm, Mike Conway and to Jo Hemmings, Natural History Editor, and her American counterpart Harry Foster at Houghton Mifflin. My thanks also go to the Consultant Editors concerned—Mark Beaman at Croom Helm and Peter Alden at Houghton Mifflin.

There are two people who deserve especial mention and without whose help this guide could not have been written in its present form. Victor Tucker, a lifelong friend, has given much of his spare time over several years in the gathering of information and proofreading. His suggestions and acute criticisms, on both text and artwork, delivered with much dry humour, were invaluable. For all those long evenings and weekends when I kept him at home, making copious suggestions for improvements to the text instead of out birding, I offer my sincere and grateful thanks.

Finally my greatest thanks go to my wife, Carol, without whose help and encouragement this guide would not have been completed. Acting as a wife, mother and secretary, she endured hardships that would have routed the best of men. Her courage and resolve during adventure and crisis were a constant example. In the later stages of this project she typed and re-typed drafts and revisions with a cheerful silence. Only the people that know her will appreciate how much she has contributed to this guide and, without her, how little I would have achieved.

FOREWORD

The sea is now the great frontier for those birders who have mastered the identification of land-based birds. Although regional field guides usually include brief accounts of offshore and pelagic birds, there has always been a need for a more extensive guide such as this which caters for those travellers and far-ranging binocular addicts who spend time at the shiprail. The pioneer work, WB Alexander's *Birds of the Ocean*, first published in 1928, filled the niche for many years. It was rather rudimentary by today's standards but the patternistic treatment of the illustrations was valid, a forerunner of field guides to come.

In 1953, about 25 years after the initial publication of Alexander, James Fisher and I laid plans to write and illustrate our own field guide to the world's seabirds. Fisher with his usual sensitivity felt that we should not publish our effort while his friend Alexander, many years his senior, was still living. At that time, Fisher, who had just completed his monograph on the Fulmar, had an encyclopedic knowledge of seabirds equalled by few ornithologists, among whom would have to be mentioned Dr Robert Cushman Murphy of the American Museum of Natural History and Dr William Bourne of England. Dr Bourne expressed doubts that we could handle the various dark petrels critically, and I suspect he may have been right. After many years of travel, in every ocean of the world, mainly on the *Lindblad Explorer*, I am still puzzled by some of the 'odd jobs' that I see scaling over the waves.

In 1970 James Fisher died in a motor accident while driving home from London. He had not gone very far with his dream of a comprehensive seabird guide, having allowed too many other projects to gain priority. I had no intention of going it alone without the benefit of Fisher's scholarship, even though I then had field experience with a majority of the world's seabirds. To meet the growing need, other authors soon published guides: Watson and Hines (Antarctic); Tuck and Heinzel (World); Harper and Kinsky (Albatrosses and Petrels); etc.

Because of the burgeoning interest in pelagic birds, offshore trips are now scheduled regularly, departing from at least eight or ten ports on the Atlantic and Pacific coasts of North America. At Monterey, in California, boatloads of birders are organised almost every weekend. Similarly, from the Florida Keys to the Gulf of Maine, and from Baja California and San Diego to the offshore waters of Oregon and Washington, the seabirds are receiving a scrutiny that they had not known previously. Pelagic species that were formerly regarded as casual or accidental are now spotted with some regularity. The situation is much the same in the North Sea and around the coasts of the British Isles.

Birds flying over the sea won't stay still while you train your glass on them and, of course, using a telescope on boatdeck or shipdeck is out of the question without a gyroscopic stabiliser. Although a few species of pelagic birds are ship followers, the majority are not; they pass abeam or across the bow, often at a distance, and must be imprinted on the mind quickly before they disappear over the featureless sea.

The publication of this new and very complete guide to the world's seabirds is a red-letter event for the field glass fraternity. The book should accompany every transoceanic traveller and every intrepid birder who ventures offshore in small fishing boats. Through its use we should all become more sophisticated in our ability to recognise challenging seabirds, not only by their field marks and their 'jizz', to use the British term, but also by their flight and other behaviour. The illustrations usually show several plumages or several views of a species, often giving us visual information hitherto unavailable in other reference works.

Peter Harrison, who laboured for eleven years on this guide, has doubled as author and artist, a fortunate combination because everyone sees things a bit differently. It is frustrating for an author to try to convey to an illustrator exactly the way he sees the bird in his mind's eye. To bridge this gulf Peter Harrison set out to learn the craft of bird illustration, and by so doing he has given his seabirds the stamp of authenticity. Whereas a photograph is a record of a split second in the life of a bird, subject to all the vagaries of light, angle and chance, a drawing can be more informative because it is a composite of the artist's field knowledge of the bird.

For the first time some difficult groups have been made to seem less difficult; for example, the notoriously difficult-to-identify prions. These small grey-backed petrels often go unidentified as they dart and dash over the waves of the Southern Oceans. The seafaring birder tentatively identifies the various prion species mainly by the part of the ocean in which he finds them. But in their wanderings all the forms might mingle, as Peter Harrison found during his years as a fisherman and deckhand on trawlers. He has sorted them out visually for us.

It is doubtful whether any other ornithologist or birder can match the number of seabirds that Harrison has actually seen in life. Of the approximately 312 species, he has had field experience with all but 30. We salute him for his industry and artistry in producing this book which will give us much instruction and pleasure.

Roger Tory Peterson

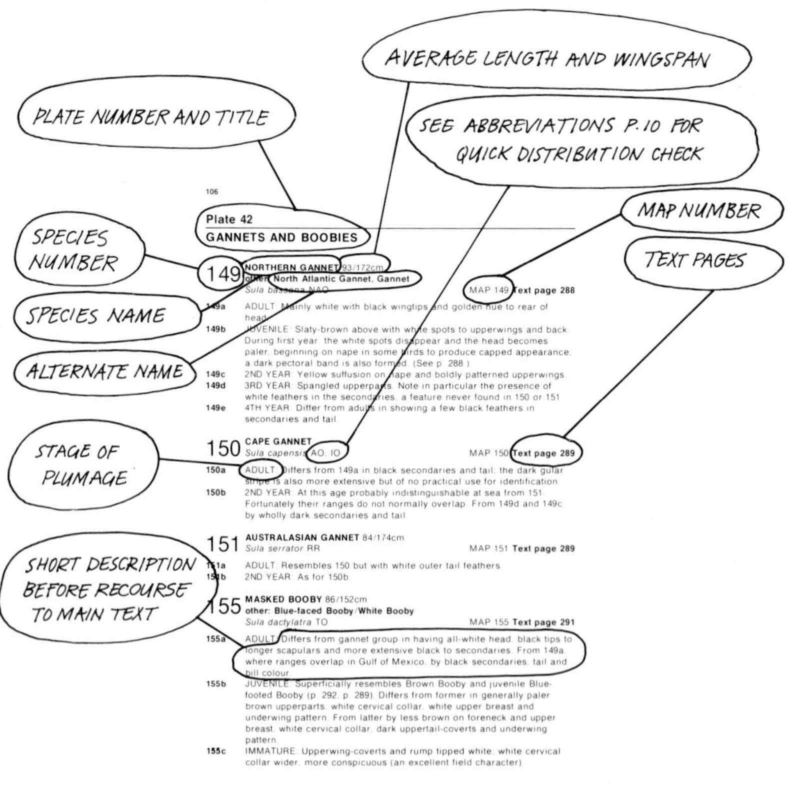

106

Plate 42
GANNETS AND BOOBIES

149 **NORTHERN GANNET** 93/172cm
other: North Atlantic Gannet, Gannet
Sula bassana NAO — MAP 149 **Text page 288**

149a ADULT: Mainly white with black wingtips and golden hue to rear of head.
149b JUVENILE: Slaty-brown above with white spots to upperwings and back. During first year, the white spots disappear and the head becomes paler, beginning on nape in some birds to produce capped appearance; a dark pectoral band is also formed. (See p. 288.)
149c 2ND YEAR: Yellow suffusion on nape and boldly patterned upperwings.
149d 3RD YEAR: Spangled upperparts. Note in particular the presence of white feathers in the secondaries, a feature never found in 150 or 151.
149e 4TH YEAR: Differ from adults in showing a few black feathers in secondaries and tail.

150 **CAPE GANNET**
Sula capensis AO, IO — MAP 150 **Text page 289**

150a ADULT: Differs from 149a in black secondaries and tail; the dark gular stripe is also more extensive but of no practical use for identification.
150b 2ND YEAR: At this age probably indistinguishable at sea from 151. Fortunately their ranges do not normally overlap. From 149d and 149c by wholly dark secondaries and tail.

151 **AUSTRALASIAN GANNET** 84/174cm
Sula serrator RR — MAP 151 **Text page 289**

151a ADULT: Resembles 150 but with white outer tail feathers.
151b 2ND YEAR: As for 150b.

155 **MASKED BOOBY** 86/152cm
other: Blue-faced Booby/White Booby
Sula dactylatra TO — MAP 155 **Text page 291**

155a ADULT: Differs from gannet group in having all-white head, black tips to longer scapulars and more extensive black to secondaries. From 149a, where ranges overlap in Gulf of Mexico, by black secondaries, tail and bill colour.
155b JUVENILE: Superficially resembles Brown Booby and juvenile Blue-footed Booby (p. 292, p. 289). Differs from former in generally paler brown upperparts, white cervical collar, white upper breast and underwing pattern. From latter by less brown on foreneck and upper breast, white cervical collar, dark uppertail-coverts and underwing pattern.
155c IMMATURE: Upperwing-coverts and rump tipped white; white cervical collar wider, more conspicuous (an excellent field character).

HOW TO USE THIS GUIDE

The recent trend in field guides to adopt a text facing art plate format, whilst aesthetically pleasing, imposes far too many restrictions on the treatment of the more difficult species. The format adopted in this guide is thus divided into six basic sections so that the more problematic species can be treated in depth.

SECTION 1

INTRODUCTION

Deals mainly with seabird identification characters and some of the problems likely to be encountered whilst observing birds at sea. Fig. 1 shows the topography of a gannet. These terms are used throughout the text and, if not already known, should be memorised. They will help you to recognise and describe unfamiliar birds more accurately and quickly.

SECTION 2

ART PLATES AND FACING CAPTIONS

The 88 art plates reproduced in full colour have been painted over a period of four years. They have been drawn almost exclusively from field notes and my personal collection of several thousand photographs taken throughout an eleven-year study period. Shrewd observers will see these plates as no more than an interpretation of known facts upon which to build further knowledge by careful field observation. They are as accurate as my artistic ability allowed at the time of completion. The main figures on each art plate are drawn to the same scale; smaller thumbnail sketches are used to enforce other characters or features raised in the text. The diverse sizes between such groups as albatrosses and storm-petrels have prevented the use of a standardised scale on each of the art plates, but this deficiency has been redressed on the facing caption pages by following the preferred common name of each species with its average length and wingspan in centimetres. Where possible birds which look alike and share similar ranges have been grouped together to save needless time thumbing through pages of illustrations. This has dictated that the species numbers, which have been arranged systematically, often appear out of numerical order on the facing caption pages. The facing captions text should not be used as the main source of reference. It contains but a few brief points taken from the main text to facilitate identification. The facing caption layout is as on the left.

SECTION 3

SYSTEMATIC LIST AND MAIN TEXT

Seabird taxonomy is continually being evaluated. The nomenclature adopted for *Sphenisciformes* and *Procellariiformes* is based on the recent 2nd edition of Peters's *Birds of the World* (Mayr, E, & Cottrell, GW, 1979), although I have not followed the new sequence of orders and families. The nomenclature for *Charadriiformes* is based on Howard & Moore's *A Complete Checklist of the Birds of the World* (1980). In a number of cases I have 'split' or 'lumped' species following more recent revisions by various authorities. In this respect I record my grateful thanks to Richard Brooke who steered me through unknown waters with suggestions on taxonomic treatment. In many cases complete texts are included for distinct, isolated subspecies. Where it seems likely that distinct forms will be split into two or more full species, I have given each 'form' the same species number but with a different suffix to allow for easy reference or possible future changes in status. Wherever possible throughout the text I have disclosed my reference sources so that the reader can be directed to more thorough or complementary articles on identification or taxonomy.

The main text covers 312 species and all subspecies which can be distinguished at sea are described. Each species has an individual account summarised as follows.

1 Species Number and Name
Alternative names of importance; plate and map numbers, dimensions and bare parts colours of adults during breeding season. Where marked geographical variation occurs bare parts colours of the nominate race only are given.

2 Introductory paragraph which highlights the information found in the main text, beginning with the species' range, brief notes on similar species found within that range and differences to look for. Sexual and seasonal differences are discussed with notes on juveniles, subspecies and, if appropriate, albinism, melanism, genetic variation and incidence of hybrids.

3 Plumage Description
Beginning with juvenile stage at fledging, or, in the case of certain alcids, departure from their ledges; and all other subsequent plumages where known. The term 'adult breeding' is used in this section simply to describe the plumage acquired during the nuptial period and does not infer that the bird is actively engaged in a reproductive cycle. Space considerations have dictated that the style adopted for these descriptions is sequential and telegraphic. On the other hand, the space gained from tight editing and small print has been used for vignettes and identification keys to amplify points mentioned in text or on the art plates. Note: The term 'no specimens examined/available' indicates that

no museum specimens or field notes were available to the author for that particular stage of plumage.

4 Flight, Habits and Jizz
These are discussed under the heading **FHJ**. This section mentions only those points pertaining to field identification and, where necessary, plumage points are discussed to force home points raised in section 3.

5 Distribution and Movements
These are discussed under the heading **DM**. Generally the order in which a species' breeding range is described begins from the Bering Sea area and proceeds from north to south and then in an easterly direction. Principal breeding areas/islands can be located on the end-papers. Egg-dates and fledging dates are given, plus, where appropriate, the times of exodus from colonies, range of post-breeding pelagic dispersal and dates of return to colonies. Treated on a world scale, this section is not always as full as one would wish but it far exceeds the information found in any of the standard field guides.

6 Similar Species
These are discussed under the heading **SS**. All species which have similar plumage and are likely to occur within the same area as the species under discussion are listed and the key identification points for their separation discussed.

SECTION 4

DISTRIBUTION MAPS

The maps are arranged ten per page. All map numbers coincide with each species' number to enable speedy cross-referencing between art plates, text and maps. The distribution of all species and distinct subspecies is shown in 2-colour maps to indicate breeding, non-breeding and migratory distribution. The dispersal of the more pelagic species remains largely unknown and, as such, these maps should be regarded only as a basic summary of our incomplete knowledge. An asterisk on the map denotes some, but not all, of the occurrences outside the species' normal range. A question mark indicates that a species' range may extend to that area. Refer to p. 442 for map key.

SECTION 5

SELECTED BIBLIOGRAPHY

This section is fully cross-referenced to the main text. It has been included to allow progressive birders to expand their research peripheries on special topics beyond the scope of this book.

SECTION 6

INDEX

Fully cross-referenced to preferred English names and commonly used synonyms and scientific names.

ABBREVIATIONS

On the facing captions text immediately following the scientific name and preceding the map reference number, abbreviations are used to convey a quick distribution reference. This key has been used only for the more pelagic species so that readers can check, at a glance, in which ocean the species under scrutiny normally occurs. Some species may be restricted to one ocean but have been recorded elsewhere and may be suspected of being circumpolar in Southern Oceans (e.g. Buller's Albatross). In such cases only the ocean in which the species is known to occur regularly is listed under the quick distributional reference; a fuller treatment of its range will be found in the main text under DM and by referring to the species map. To avoid possible confusion the abbreviations have been kept to a minimum and are as follows:

WR = Wide-ranging (likely to be met with in Pacific, Atlantic and Indian Oceans).
PO = Pacific Ocean.
AO = Atlantic Ocean.
IO = Indian Ocean.
AR = Arctic Ocean and region.
AN = Antarctic region.
SO = Southern Oceans (higher latitudes of Pacific, Atlantic and Indian Oceans forming circumpolar water mass between Antarctic Continent and the major land masses of South America, Africa and Australia).
RR = Restricted range.

The prefixes **N**, **S** and **T** are used to denote North, South and Tropical respectively. Thus NPO and TPO read: North Pacific Ocean and Tropical Pacific Ocean.

Throughout the main text north, south, east and west have been abbreviated to **N**, **S**, **E** and **W** respectively. Thus 'occasionally wanders S to N Pacific Ocean' reads: 'occasionally wanders south to North Pacific Ocean'. Within the main text months are abbreviated to three letters. Thus **Apr** reads April. Islands are noted simply with '**I.**' whilst groups of islands are denoted '**Is**'.

As previously mentioned, **FHJ** indicates flight, habits and jizz, **DM** distribution and movements, and **SS** similar species.

GLOSSARY

JUVENILE
Used here to refer to the plumage at point of fledging or, as in the case of some alcids, departure from ledges.

JUVENILE (FIRST-STAGE) (SECOND STAGE) (ETC.)
In larger birds, especially frigatebirds, several years elapse before full maturity is attained. For convenience, headings such as 'Juvenile (first stage)' are used to catalogue the small changes in the basic juvenile plumage during the first months or perhaps years at sea. The terms are not meant to imply known ages, rather stages in a slow and perhaps arbitrary sequence of plumage patterns in which subsequent stages are described under immature and sub-adult headings.

FIRST-WINTER
Refers mainly to gull plumages in northern hemisphere. Juveniles undergo a moult of head and body feathers starting about August. This plumage is retained until March, when first-summer plumage is attained.

FIRST-SUMMER
Refers mainly to gull plumages in northern hemisphere. First-winter birds acquire first-summer plumage by undergoing head and body moult during March and April. This plumage is retained until about September, when second-winter plumage is attained.

SECOND-WINTER
Refers mainly to gull plumages in northern hemisphere. First-summer birds undergo a complete moult beginning about September. This plumage is retained until about March, when second-summer plumage is acquired.

SECOND-SUMMER
Refers mainly to gull plumages in northern hemisphere. Second-winter birds undergo head and body moult beginning about March. This plumage is retained until about September, when third-winter plumage is attained.

THIRD-WINTER
Refers mainly to gull plumages in northern hemisphere. Second-summer birds undergo a complete moult beginning about September. This plumage is retained until about March, when third-summer plumage is attained.

THIRD-SUMMER
Refers mainly to gull plumages in northern hemisphere. Third-winter birds undergo head and body moult beginning about March. This plumage is retained until about September, when a complete moult occurs to produce fourth-winter or adult non-breeding plumage. In smaller gulls adult non-breeding plumage is usually acquired after second-summer plumage.

IMMATURE
An arbitrary term used to describe any plumage between juvenile and sub-adult stages.

SUB-ADULT
A plumage stage resembling adult but bearing some signs of immaturity.

ADULT NON-BREEDING
Term used to describe the plumage of adults during winter or non-breeding period for those species whose plumage varies seasonally. Normally acquired by post-nuptial moult each autumn.

ADULT BREEDING
Term used to describe plumage worn by a bird during reproductive or nuptial period but not necessarily the plumage of a bird actively engaged in reproduction.

ABERRANT
Diverging from the normal, e.g. in plumage colour or pattern, usually due to a genetic malfunction.

ALBINISM
A total or partial absence of pigment in feathers and bare parts normally coloured, i.e. white.

ALLOPATRIC
A term used to designate closely allied species or families of birds living in different geographical areas.

CULMEN
Term used for the top ridge or plate of a bird's bill. See Fig. 4, p. 221.

CULMINICORN
One of the horny plates making up the bill. See p. 221 for Fig.

GONYS
The prominent ridge/angle formed by the fusion of two halves of the lower mandible towards the tip; especially noticeable in gulls and marked in some larger species by a red spot.

HYBRID
The result of interbreeding by two different species. Most show characters intermediate between the parental species.

INNER WING
That portion of the wing extending from innermost primary to the body, i.e. proximal portion.

LATERICORN
A horny plate running along the cutting edge of the upper mandible. See p. 221 for Fig.

LEUCISM
Allied to albinism. A dilution of the normal plumage pigmentation.

MELANISM
The opposite of albinism. An excess of dark pigment in the plumage or bare parts.

MORPH
Coined by JS Huxley to denote any one of the colour forms, i.e. dark morph, intermediate morph, pale morph, of a species' population subject to polymorphism.

OUTER WING
That portion of the wing including all the primaries, their coverts and alula, i.e. distal portion.

PLATES
Parts of the bill, several horny plates, viz. culminicorn, latericorn, separated by distinct grooves.

POLYMORPHISM
Showing greater differences than the usual level of individual variation within a population.

POST-OCULAR
Area on sides of face behind the eye; the upper ear-coverts.

RAMICORN
A horny plate running along the cutting edge of the lower mandible. See p. 221 for Fig.

SADDLE
Term used to describe the area on upperparts formed by combination of mantle, scapulars and back. Used mainly in gull and tern descriptions.

SEXUAL DIMORPHISM
A difference in size or plumage between males and females of the same species.

SPECIES
The basic category into which living things are divided. An interbreeding group (of birds) that does not interbreed with other groups, or, if some individuals do, they do not do so significantly enough to break down their specific identity.

SUBSPECIES
A race or population distinguishable from the members of other populations within the species to which they belong.

SUPERSPECIES
A term for two or more species or kinds (of birds) separated geographically and so similar in form and habits that without a geographical barrier they would probably interbreed and produce fertile young, viz. the allopatric gannets (p. 288).

SULCUS
Lateral groove on lower mandible filled with coloured membrane.

SYMPATRIC
Term used for related species which breed within the same geographical area.

TOMIUM
The cutting edge of the bill.

UPPERPARTS
Collective term used to describe mantle, scapulars, back, rump and uppertail-coverts.

Fig. 1. Topography of a Seabird

1 Upper mandible
2 Lower mandible
3 Iris
4 Legs/feet
5 Forehead
6 Crown
7 Nape
8 Hindneck
9 Ear-coverts/cheek
10 Chin
11 Gular stripe
12 Throat
13 Foreneck
14 Mantle
15 Back
16 Rump
17 Uppertail-coverts
18 Breast
19 Belly
20 Flank/side
21 Thigh
22 Ventral area
23 Undertail-coverts
24 Primaries
25 Secondaries
26 Primary-coverts
27 Alula
28 Greater coverts
29 Median coverts
30 Lesser coverts
31 Marginal coverts
32 Carpal joint
33 Underwing-coverts
34 Axillaries
35 Scapulars
36 Tail

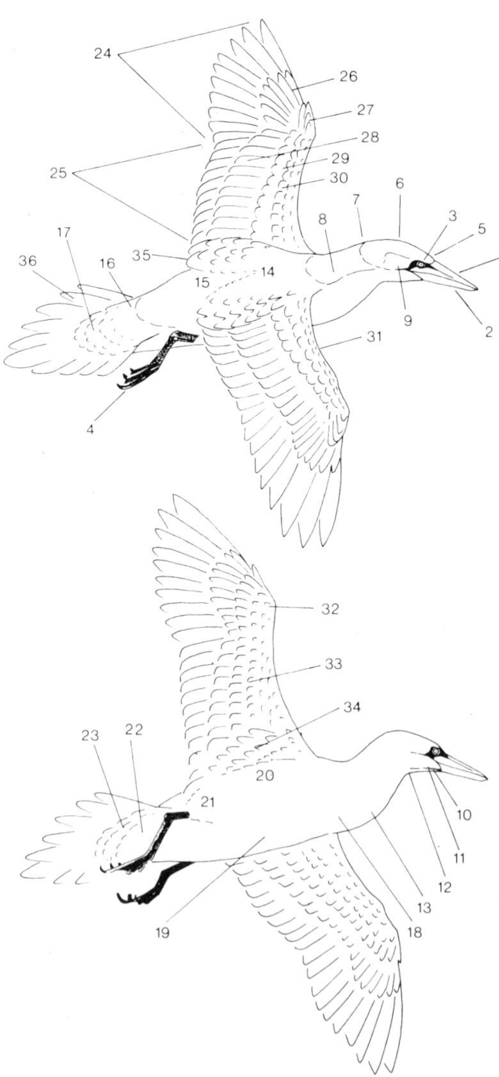

INTRODUCTION

This book is intended to help scientists, mariners and amateur birders identify seabirds. The text and illustrations concentrate on plumage sequences and distribution, rather than on their biology, or pertinent oceanography. This has enabled the production of a guide at a cost which should be within the reach of both amateur and professional ornithologists alike.

Seabirds are defined here as those species whose normal habitat and food source is the sea, whether they be coastal, offshore or pelagic. Certain fringe orders, notably divers/loons, grebes and pelicans, have been included because at certain times of the year the sea provides some members of their group with their habitat choice and principal source of food. Regrettably, the necessary division of the *Anatidae* to define 'seaducks' including those species which visit bays and coasts during the winter is somewhat arbitrary. Most ducks may visit the coast at some stage of the year, and to include the 140 or so species would be outside the scope of this book. Line drawings of seaducks, and certain geese, however, follow the main text on p. 406, with suggestions for further reading for different continents, most of which have adequate field guide publications covering these groups.

Modern-day research of seabirds can be defined as starting with the publication of *Birds of the Ocean* by WB Alexander in 1928. Since then many researchers have helped to expand the peripheries of our seabird knowledge. Moreover, there has been a dramatic increase in the number of amateur birdwatchers actively participating in seabird research during the last 30 years. This has been responsible in part for the appearance of several seabird groups around the world (p. 22). The recent spate of activity among birders has produced a flood of research material, so much so that it is often impossible to be fully aware of the total material now being published.

It would be wrong to conclude, however, that we know a good deal about seabirds. Present-day research has barely scratched the surface. We know practically nothing of the pelagic dispersal, biology or even breeding areas of some of the species contained in this work. The identification of seabirds can be far more complex than the identification of terrestrial species, which often oblige observers by sitting or perching long enough to enable an accurate identification or, at worst, a hurried note and a sketch. Seabirds are rarely so co-operative. Most are seen from an unstable deck or wind-torn headland, as often as not disappearing behind a moderate swell, reappearing fleetingly and at increasing range. At sea, observations are, therefore, normally far from ideal and many birds cannot be identified specifically. The 'odd job' among a flock of known species usually allows no time for on-the-spot recourse to a reference work and the observer can only record as many characters as possible and hope that later research will yield a positive identification. One should never guess at a bird's identity. Mystery birds will always occur, identification being thwarted by a combination of range, light and often basic inexperience. My own list of personal odd jobs is quite extensive.

Fortunately not all seabirds are seen so briefly. The less pelagic species offer easier opportunities. Gulls especially are dependent to some extent on the activities of man, whilst divers/loons can often be found in sheltered bays of the northern hemisphere during the winter. Those observers fortunate enough to visit the bird islands of the Southern Oceans cannot fail to be impressed by the vast penguin rookeries or by their almost total disregard of the presence of human forms within their ranks. Clearly then it is the fleeting glance of the more pelagic species which will cause most problems to an observer, and to facilitate identification one should be aware of the recognised terms used for describing the parts of a bird (Fig. 1).

SEABIRD IDENTIFICATION CHARACTERS

The following discussion is concerned with those characters which enable an observer to identify a bird in the field. In any identification it is important to know what to look for so that in a brief sighting valuable time is not lost looking at unimportant detail. Confronted by one of the smaller albatrosses, for instance, it is quite pointless to spend time deciding whether the upperwings are dark brown or slate-black, or whether the tail is greyer than the mantle. The colour of the bill and the underwing are the key points to get down on paper; if these two points are not recorded an accurate identification is impossible. Many key points can be memorised from books for most of the plumage stages likely to be encountered, but no book (and this one is certainly no exception) can cover all the plumage variations and the tricks that light, distance and incomplete views can play on an observer. These factors which limit our capabilities can be appreciated only through field experience. Once they are known it is possible to compensate for them, because all identifications take several factors into account. If the range of the aforementioned albatross is extreme and the bill colour vague, then the underwing pattern will be the only key identification point on which an identification can be based. An observer must examine critically, therefore, the differences in width of the leading and trailing edges or dark wedge-shaped incursions into the white underwing-coverts.

This guide is concerned with identification at sea but in exceptional cases, e.g. diving-petrels and *Fregetta* storm-petrels, additional material has been included within the text for identification in the hand. Observers who require more detailed measurements should consult Murphy (1936), Palmer (1962), Alexander (1955), Serventy *et al*. (1971) and Cramp & Simmons (1977). The following notes are intended as an introduction to the species accounts given in the main text, and the headings used follow that of the text sequence.

Size: Distance at sea is difficult to judge. Inexperienced observers are more likely to overestimate distance and consequently underestimate the size of a bird. In all cases the dimensions of a bird are most easily judged by comparison with a species of a known size. The relative jizz, discussed below, is also easier to determine in this manner.

Bare parts: In the *Laridae* and *Spheniscidae* the colour of eyes, legs and bill should be one of the first points noted. Bill and leg colour can also be of importance in certain shearwaters, petrels and albatrosses, but the problem here, of course, is that many species fail to approach closely enough to allow such critical examination. Cormorants often have colourful facial skin. In flight the projection of feet beyond the tail point can also be of value in separating similarly-plumaged species. It should be noted that only feet which project sufficiently to be regularly noted are mentioned in the text. For example Wilson's Storm-petrel has feet which project well beyond the tail in flight, whereas the feet of Leach's Storm-petrel also project but by such a small amount that they are rarely, if ever, noted as doing so in the field. Consequently, the main text places little importance on the projecting feet of Leach's Storm-petrel. The bill of any bird tells an evolutionary story and, with a little practice, can be used to classify birds into their different groups or families. Bills are tools, and as such have been modified to suit particular purposes. Each of the main bill types is shown below and observers should familiarise themselves with each type to allow prompt and accurate generic classification of birds sighted.

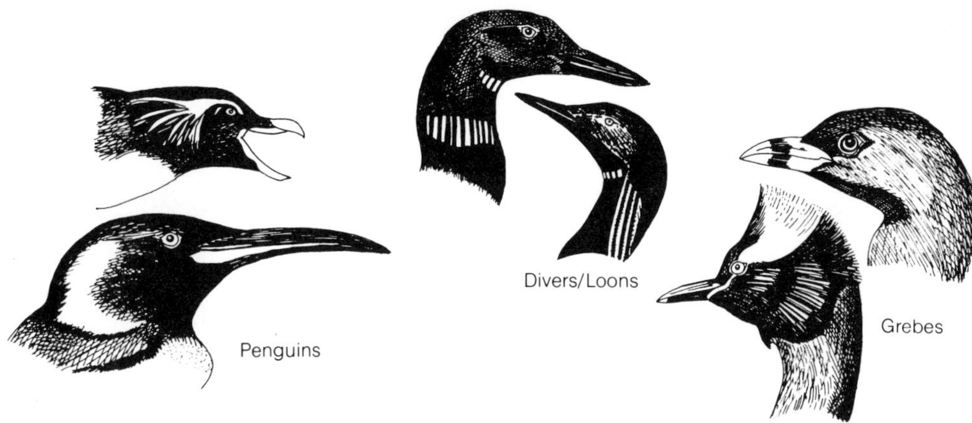
Penguins
Divers/Loons
Grebes

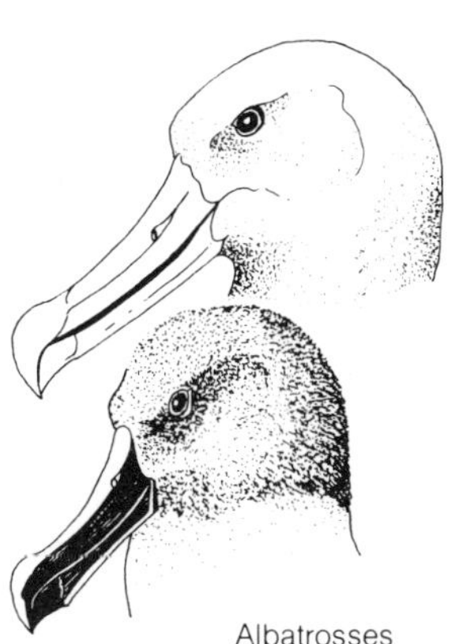
Albatrosses

Penguins, known to all, have a variety of bill shapes but all are stout and covered with several coalesced horny plates. To enable prey to be grasped and held they have caruncles on both tongue and palate.
Divers/loons have sturdy pointed bills, with narrow nostrils. The four species have bills which differ in weight and in angle of tilt, as discussed in the main text.
In grebes bill shape varies from rather diver-like, as in the Slavonian Grebe, to short and sturdy, as found in the Pied-billed Grebe of America.
Albatrosses have long, robust bills which are strongly hooked at the tip, an adaptation for dealing with their principal food, slippery cephalopods. They are unique in that the external nostrils are separate and placed on either side of the culminicorn (see Fig. 4, p. 221), not joined together ovcr thc culmen as in petrels and shearwaters. Bill colour in adult albatrosses is diagnostic.
Petrels show a wide variety of bill shapes, from that of the massive giant petrels to the smaller *Pterodroma* petrels, but all have the nostrils united in a single tube over the top of the bill, as do the shearwaters. Petrels, however, have stouter bills which are hooked at the tip, and, with the thicker-set head and neck, are readily separated from the often similarly-plumaged shearwaters.
Prions have a variety of bill shapes. All are hooked, weakly so in some cases, but unlike other birds they have a row of comb-like lamellae on the inside of the upper mandible's cutting edge which is used to strain off plankton. At sea identification is problematic but not impossible.
Shearwaters, probably the best known of all the tubenoses, have long, slender bills. Several species have coloured legs and bills which can be diagnostic.
Storm-petrels, the smallest of all seabirds, have hooked bills with a proportionately conspicuous nostril tube.
Diving-petrels, the southern counterpart of the alcids, have rather squat bills with the nostril tubes separated on top of the culmen. Sketches on p. 278 deal with identification in the hand, based on bill shapes of the four species.

Petrels

Prions

Diving-Petrels

Storm-Petrels

Shear waters

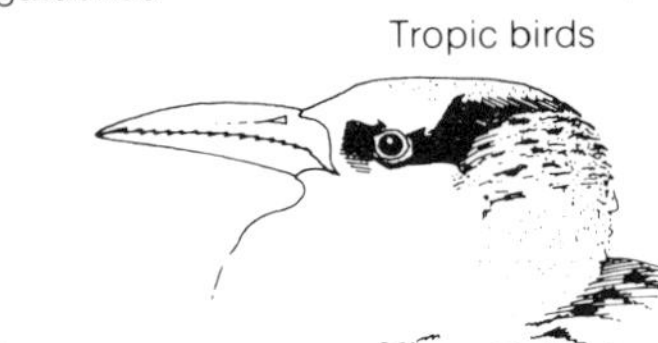

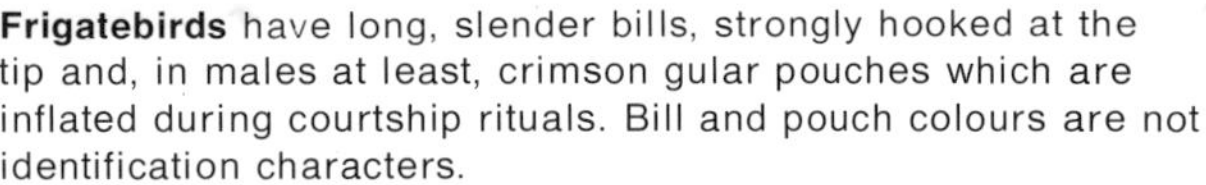

Frigatebirds have long, slender bills, strongly hooked at the tip and, in males at least, crimson gular pouches which are inflated during courtship rituals. Bill and pouch colours are not identification characters.

Tropicbirds have robust dagger-like bills with serrated edges. This is an indication of their feeding habits: they dive from heights of 15 metres in the manner of a gannet.

Cormorants, a cosmopolitan group, are well known to most people. Bill shape is long, slender and strongly hooked at the tip. For identification purposes the colour of the caruncles and naked skin on the face are useful characters.

Boobies and gannets have long dagger-like bills and often plunge from considerable heights to secure their prey. As in the tropicbirds their external nostrils are closed, but secondary external nostrils have evolved at the angle of the mouth, the opening being sealed off with flexible flaps by water pressure when plunging.

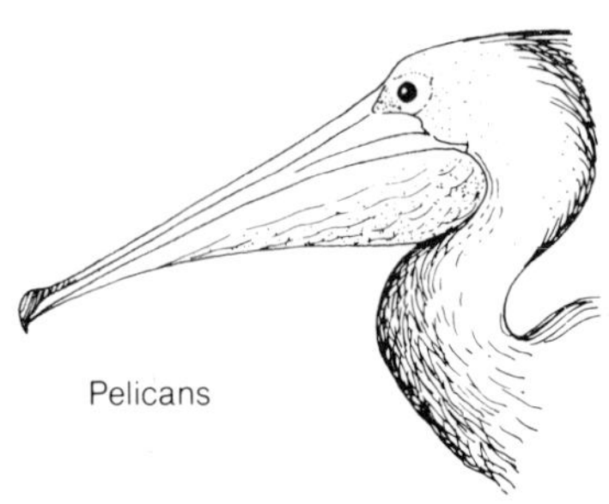

Pelicans need no introduction; their extensible pouches, which can hold up to 3 gallons (13·6 litres) of water, and broad beaks render them instantly recognisable.

Phalaropes are an offshoot of the wader group. Two of the three species are pelagic outside their breeding season. Their long, thin bills differ proportionately each from the others' and can be a useful means for separating the three species. (See main text, p. 318.)

Sheathbills, as their name implies, have a horny, saddle-like sheath which extends over the base of the upper bill and partly shields the nostrils. They have fleshy wattles at the base of the bill and below the eyes. Bill coloration is diagnostic.

Skuas, piratical and aggressive, have robust, hooked bills and differ from gulls in having a fleshy cere across the base of the upper mandible.

Gulls are well-known, conspicuous birds. Bill shape varies from the robust Pacific Gull to the more slender form found in the European Black-headed Gull. Unlike the skuas, whose bills are made up of four horny plates, gulls have undivided beaks. Bill and leg coloration are important field characters and can simplify identification problems.

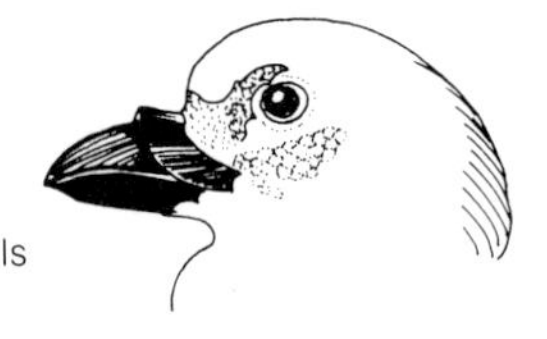

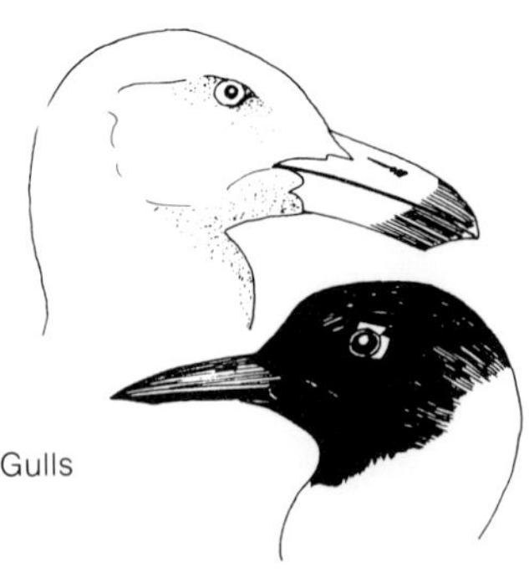

Terns

Skimmers

Auks

Terns are graceful gull-like birds with proportionately longer, more pointed bills than gulls, but size and shape do vary. **Skimmers** have one of the most remarkable bills of all birds. They are the only group of birds having a longer lower mandible than the upper. Fishing methods are discussed in the main text. **Auks** have a variety of bill shapes, some brightly coloured. Puffins have a series of backward-projecting spines on their tongues enabling them to carry several small fish at a time.

Plumage With very few exceptions seabirds are black, white, brown or admixtures of these. The preponderance of black or brown in the plumage of many pelagic birds (e.g. shearwaters and storm-petrels) may be for anti-abrasive reasons, as melanin (dark pigment) is thought to strengthen feathers. Despite (or perhaps because of) this restricted palette the complexity of plumages is often bewildering, as can be seen in the subtle diversity of northern hemisphere gull plumages. Whilst colour is certainly important to note, it is the patterns formed within a seabird's plumage that are the more helpful. Brown birds at a distance normally appear black, whilst white birds can often appear grey, particularly the underwings if in shadow. Dark tips or leading edges on the other hand, whether brown or black, if accurately noted can often clinch an identification. The plumage patterns normally found can be classified under the following headings.

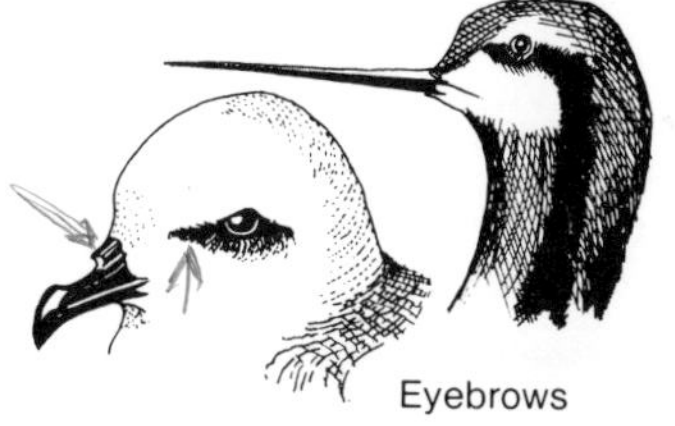
Eyebrows

Dark Caps Do they reach the eye as in Manx Shearwater, or just above as in the Little Shearwater? Perhaps the forehead is white as in some *Pterodroma* petrels and the Little Tern. Alternatively, the distant impression of a dark cap may be that of a complete hood as found in some gulls, the extent of which can be diagnostic.

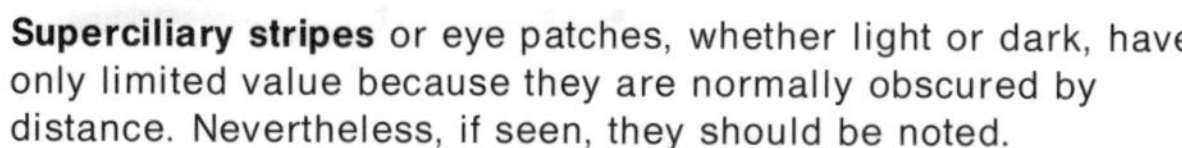

Superciliary stripes or eye patches, whether light or dark, have only limited value because they are normally obscured by distance. Nevertheless, if seen, they should be noted.

Dark caps

Collars

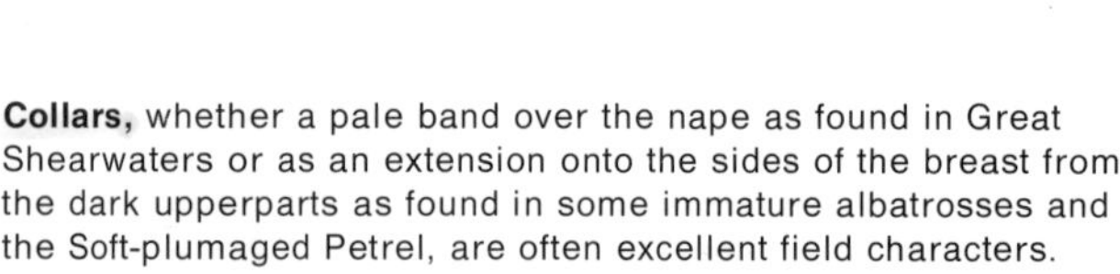

Wing Patterns

Collars, whether a pale band over the nape as found in Great Shearwaters or as an extension onto the sides of the breast from the dark upperparts as found in some immature albatrosses and the Soft-plumaged Petrel, are often excellent field characters.

Wing patterns occur on the upper and lower surfaces in several ways and can be diagnostic. Where age, and consequently moult, affects pattern stability, as in juvenile and immature gulls and some albatrosses, caution must always be exercised. Adult gulls can be identified on wing pattern, particularly the tips of the primaries, and albatrosses by the shape and extent of white on the underwing; whilst some *Pterodroma* petrels, prions and the Blue Petrel show an open M mark extending from wingtip to wingtip and joining across the lower back. The axillary colour can also be diagnostic, as in the Chatham Island Petrel which also has a bold underwing pattern. Penguins can be identified by underflipper pattern.

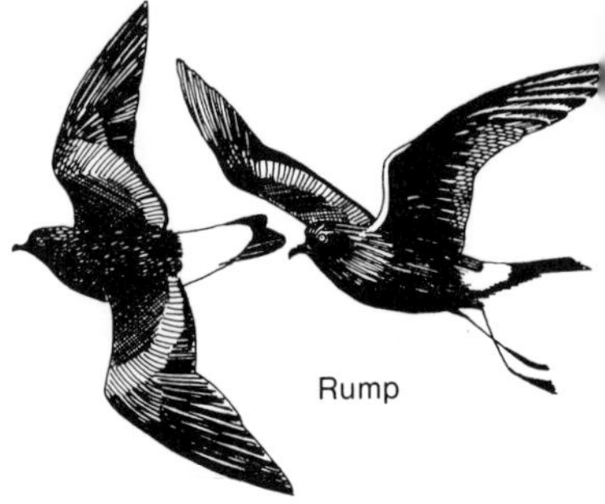

Rump

Rump colour is also important, particularly if dealing with otherwise dark species as in certain storm-petrels. The extent of white on the rump can be diagnostic, as in the Galapagos Storm-petrel.

Tail patterns are useful when dealing with certain gulls. Normally only juveniles and sub-adults display tail bands, but there are exceptions as found in adult Pacific and Band-tailed Gulls. The Blue Petrel is unique among petrels in having a white tip to the tail.

Tail

The foregoing patterns are by no means definitive and, moreover, there are obvious complications to consider. The maturing of most birds is often shown in a definite and orderly sequence of plumage patterns caused either by the appearance of new feathers or by the effects of abrasion and bleaching on the older feathers. This can be helpful in determining the approximate age of a bird. Sexual dimorphism is rarely encountered in seabirds, but some species have definite breeding and non-breeding plumages and care may be needed during the transitional stages. Birds renew worn feathers or acquire nuptial dress by periodically moulting their feathers. The modes of moult of flight feathers in albatrosses and related species have recently been discussed by Brooke (1981), who is recommended for further reading. He shows that feather replacement occurs in several different ways and these can vary not only between species, but also between different ages of the same species. Thus, an adult albatross will show a wave moult but an immature a simple descending moult. Breeding or migration requirements often cause what is termed interrupted or arrested moult in many seabirds, and this may cause problems in ageing or even identifying a bird at sea. Furthermore, wing moult is not necessarily symmetrical in both wings, although, apparently, the deviation is small. In some species, e.g. diving-petrels and certain alcids, the loss of old feathers is so rapid and complete that flight is impossible. The disadvantages are obvious. Migratory birds like the Australasian Short-tailed Shearwater migrate to contra-nuptial quarters off North America before moulting.

Gulls, terns and cormorants moult twice a year, normally one complete one after breeding and a pre-nuptial moult of body and head feathers. Consequently, the non-breeding or winter appearance of gulls and terns can be quite different from that of their summer or breeding plumage. Divers/loons and phalaropes also have markedly different plumages in winter and summer. Whilst most birds undergo a complete moult each year, the great albatrosses have a more or less continuous moult of wing feathers, some of which may not be replaced annually.

Observers should note that in mainly brown-plumaged birds the difference between fresh and old plumage can be quite marked. Fresh plumage normally appears blacker, worn plumage browner, whilst bleaching from the sun and abrasion can accentuate pale bars on the wing-coverts of some petrels. It is important to realise, therefore, that the stability of plumage patterns is influenced by moult and the effects of abrasion and bleaching.

Flight, Habits and Jizz, although lumped together under the heading FHJ in the text, are treated separately in this discussion of seabird characters.

Flight The way in which a bird propels itself through the air is another useful character to look for. Does the bird under scrutiny glide on stiff, outstretched wings with only occasional flaps, soaring in broad arcs, like an albatross, or does it flap and glide, shearing the waves and banking and twisting, like a shearwater? Perhaps it flies like a gadfly-petrel, rising and falling in what is termed pendulum motion progression as it towers above the horizon, only to disappear from view on its downward stroke. Is it high above the ship, like a gull, or pattering a few inches from the surface, like a storm-petrel? Some species fly in a direct and purposeful manner; others, the prions for instance, are very erratic, circling and zigzagging over the waves. The relative height of flight can also be of use, as well as the looseness, stiffness and frequency of wing strokes. Are the wings constantly moving, as they do in a diving-petrel, or stiff and mainly motionless, as in the albatrosses?

Habits within the context of this guide refer to characters useful for identification purposes and need not necessarily be related to breeding, display mechanisms or the biology of the species. Of prime consideration are its social habits. Does it occur in huge flocks at sea, like the erratic twisting prions, or only as individuals or pairs, as in the tropicbirds? The feeding habits of a bird are of especial help in any identification process. Does it pursue and harry other birds, like the piratical skuas/jaegers and frigatebirds, or spin like a top on the water, like a phalarope? Perhaps the birds are scavengers, hanging off the stern for galley scraps, like gulls, albatrosses and giant petrels. Some birds follow ships, others fly off at their approach. During trawling operations, however, many birds which otherwise would show little or no interest may approach more closely, and such factors should always be taken into consideration.

Gannets, boobies and tropicbirds plunge head first, often from a considerable height, to capture their prey. Others—grebes, alcids, divers/loons and cormorants—dive from the surface, propelling themselves underwater by either wings or feet, often to great depths. Many pelagic species associate with cetaceans and shoaling fish, whilst gulls mass in dense ranks at refuse tips and fishmeal plants. Whether a species is pelagic, offshore, inshore or coastal is also a useful character. Storms can, of course, upset this order.

Observers should, therefore, look for the methods of food acquisition, whether the bird occurs singly or in flocks, whether it associates with cetaceans, and the distance it occurs from the shore. All of these habits can be helpful.

Jizz is not created by any particular feature of plumage, nor by behavioural traits or even by shape, though much does depend on shape. Jizz is rather a combination of ill-defined elements which allows a bird to be labelled as 'elegant', 'powerful', 'impressive' etc. Despite its abstract connotations, jizz can enable a bird to be recognised instantly without recourse to critical examination of such things as wingtips etc., and this is one of the most important characters of all to look for.

Correct identification often begins not with colour or pattern, but with the appreciation of jizz and shape, the mixture of proportions which enables an observer to categorise a species within an order. The fact that you have decided that it is an albatross means that, from the 312 species covered in this guide, you have reduced the limit of error to a choice of 13 species. Conversely, if you are wrong on the initial generic identification and the large long-winged bird is in fact a giant petrel, no amount of searching (hopefully!) should enable an observer to find it among the albatross plates. In this respect only field experience can give you the knowledge to class birds into an order at a glance. Like most things, the more you practise and test your own ability, the further you will push the limits of your identification capabilities.

Shape definitely has a lot to do with jizz, and observers should remember that a species' shape depends on the individual body components' relative proportions to one another. Look in particular for whether wings are held stiffly or loosely, whether they are long, broad, slender, pointed or rounded. Do they cause the body to look large or small? The same consideration should also be given to the tail, and its shape noted. Fig. 2 shows the diversity of tail shapes within seabirds. Whilst on the rear end, do the feet project beyond the tail? With experience, these considerations become second nature.

Voice and display are noted only for those species where it is an aid to identification, such as terns. Most pelagic species rarely utter a note except when competing for food and offal, but there are exceptions. The Black-winged Petrel, for instance, towers high above the horizon, often in groups, piping shrilly during spectacular aerial chases; because this is unusual in seabirds away from natal islands, and thus an identification character, it is discussed in the main text. The courtship dance, bill-clapping and tail-fanning of some albatrosses is, however, not mentioned, bill colour at close range being diagnostic.

Distribution and movements of many pelagic species are imperfectly known and the text and maps should be regarded as an indication only. Despite this handicap, a species' known distribution can be regarded as a probability factor when considering the identity of a species, and consequently an aid to identification. An all-black storm-petrel off California is more likely to be a Black Storm-petrel breeding at the San Benito Islands than the similar Markham's Storm-petrel, which occurs further south in the Humboldt Current region. The Black Storm-petrel's non-breeding range, however, overlaps that of Markham's Storm-petrel and off Ecuador and Peru probability factors cannot, therefore, be employed. Conversely, if birdwatching in Britain, it would be wiser to consider European Black-headed Gull possibilities than some of its Asiatic counterparts.

Never forget, however, that seabirds, particularly pelagic species, are capable of long journeys. The Arctic Tern is a prime example, and some albatrosses have even been found foraging over 3,200 kilometres from their chicks. Storms can also push a bird far from its normal range; non-adults in all species are more prone to being driven off course or simply wandering.

In ending this discussion on the characters which enable a bird to be identified, I would state that most birds can be identified in the field under the right conditions. We simply have to learn the right set of rules for each group. The main problem, however, is that prevailing conditions often limit our capabilities. Many birds, even when viewed closely, will be found to be impossible to identify—despite books of this nature: binoculars fog up, the ship suddenly lurches at the point of critical analysis, the activities of curious fellow passengers etc.; the pitfalls are numerous. The more distinctive species can be recognised a mile or more distant, of course, but the all-brown types, storm-petrels, prions and gadfly-petrels require careful treatment even under optimum conditions.

Fig. 2. Tail Shapes of Some Seabirds

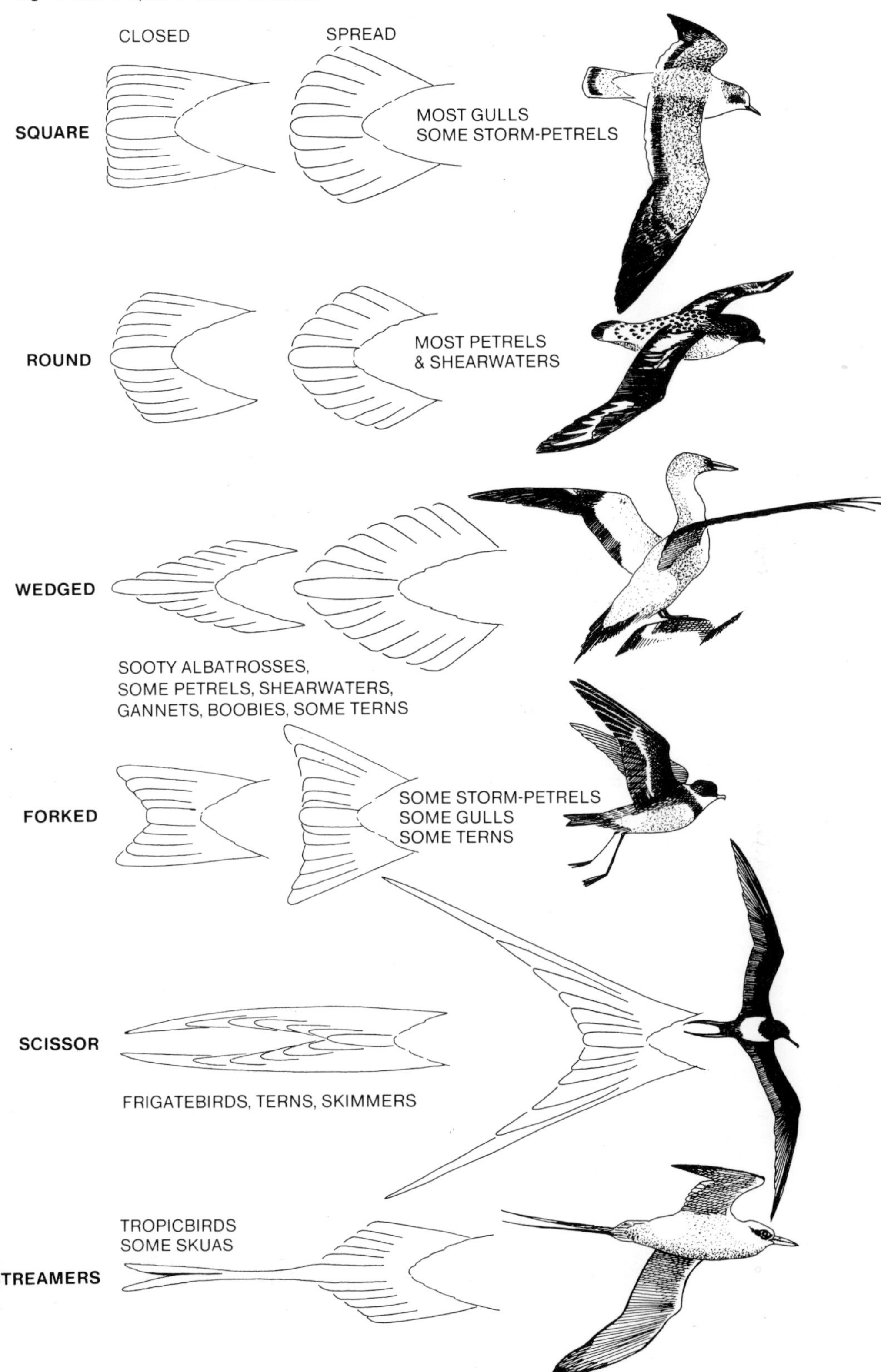

RECORDING OBSERVATIONS OF SEABIRDS

The observation of all seabirds, but particularly of pelagic species, is useful only if properly and accurately recorded and subsequently made available to further our knowledge and understanding. It is important, therefore, that each observer records observations systematically.

Date, Location and Time

All entries into a field notebook should be dated, with each observation prefixed by the time of day. When on a voyage and long periods of observations are undertaken, it is becoming normal practice to make a 180° scan of the sea immediately ahead of the ship at ten-minute intervals; all other sightings between scans are recorded, including hourly counts of species in the wake. The location is obviously important, usually recorded as a noonday position in cruise ships and placed on the passengers' information board. If a bird is observed well outside its known range, the ship's navigational officer will normally supply an accurate chart position.

Meteorological Conditions

Following date and location the weather should be noted, starting with wind direction and strength, cloud cover and precipitation, i.e. mist, fog, rain, hail or snow. Sea temperature, if available, is more important than air temperature. Should conditions change, line squalls pass, cloud banks lift, wind strength increase etc., these should of course be entered, plus the sighting of islands etc.

Notes and Sketches

Sketches, however rudimentary, should be important features of every notebook as they allow an observer quickly to record jizz, shape and plumage patterns without recourse to time-consuming descriptive notes. Observations should include the degree of certainty of each identification, or as many characters as possible to enable later research. The number, or estimated numbers if in larger flocks, flight direction if moving purposefully, feeding behaviour, and a description of the flight progression—'direct', 'erratic', 'high and looping' etc.—should all be recorded.

Many researchers now use pocket dictaphones for notes, and cameras fitted with telephoto lenses to enable birds to be photographed at sea. The benefits of both should be obvious. We owe our thanks to people like John Warham, who has published a wealth of seabird photographs, as well as writing books on the subject, that artists are at last getting the correct shape and jizz to their seabird illustrations.

Finally, having noted your observations, with or without photographs, make sure that they find use. Most countries have bird societies which publish annual reports; a visit to the local museum or library should produce the address of a local birder who can give you further information. Notes on seabirds recorded during voyages should be sent to the editors of the appropriate seabird groups:

PACIFIC SEABIRD GROUP:
Wildlife Research Field Station, Humboldt State University, Arcata, California, 95521, USA.

SEABIRD GROUP:
c/o Zoology Dept, Tillydrone Avenue, Aberdeen, AB9 2TN, Scotland.

SOUTH AFRICAN SEABIRD GROUP:
c/o Percy Fitzpatrick Institute of African Ornithology, University of Cape Town, Rondebosch, 7700 South Africa.

AUSTRALASIAN SEABIRD GROUP:
PO Box 65, Civic Square, ACT. 2608, Australia.

ROYAL NAVAL BIRDWATCHING SOCIETY:
Hon. Sec. RNBWS, Melrose, 23 St David's Road, Southsea, Hants, England.

It is hoped that the eleven years required to compile and research this guide, seven of which were spent travelling the globe, working at times at such jobs as deckhand, penguin-catcher, apple-picker, designer and travel courier, have produced a book which will be of real and definite value to the fieldworker. Alas, it is not definitive, so much remains to be solved; there are large gaps in both distribution and identification knowledge in many species, but if this guide helps promote interest and participation these gaps will one day be filled.

Suggested amendments to the text, illustrations or maps would be welcome for possible inclusion in future editions of this book. They should be sent c/o Croom Helm Ltd, Provident House, Burrell Row, Beckenham, Kent BR3 1AT, England, marked for the attention of Peter Harrison. All correspondence will be answered.

PLATES 1-88

Plate 1

LARGE AND MEDIUM-SIZED PENGUINS

1 **KING PENGUIN** 94cm
Aptenodytes patagonicus SO MAP 1 **Text page 200**

1a ADULT: Distinctive at colonies; differs from Emperor Penguin in smaller size, browner head, colour and shape of auricular patches.

1b JUVENILE: Much as adult except for greyish tips to crown feathers and pale yellow auricular patches. See 2b below.

1c CHICK: Dense woolly-brown.

2 **EMPEROR PENGUIN** 112cm
Aptenodytes forsteri AN MAP 2 **Text page 200**

2a ADULT: Distinctive at colonies; differs from King Penguin in larger size, blacker head, colour and shape of auricular patches.

2b JUVENILE: Much as adult except for whitish auricular patches and whiter chin and throat. In worn plumage (shown swimming) head and upperparts much browner; differs from 1b at this stage in whiter auricular patches.

2c CHICK: Silver-grey plumage combined with black head and white face mask diagnostic.

3 **GENTOO PENGUIN** 76cm
Pygoscelis papua SO MAP 3 **Text page 201**

3a ADULT: Easily recognised by white patches over eye joined across crown by narrow white bar.

3b JUVENILE: Much as adult except white patch over eyes less extensive; bill weaker and duller.

3c CHICK: Brownish-grey above, white below.

1a
1b
1c
1a
2a
2b
2a
2c
3a
3a
3b
3c

Plate 2

MEDIUM-SIZED PENGUINS

11 **YELLOW-EYED PENGUIN** 76cm
Megadyptes antipodes RR MAP 11 **Text page 205**

11a ADULT: Confined to seas off SE New Zealand and its sub-antarctic islands. Thin yellow band from eyes across nape diagnostic.
11b IMMATURE: Much as adult except for incomplete yellow band on head and white chin and throat.
11c CHICK: Wholly chocolate-brown.

5 **CHINSTRAP PENGUIN** 77cm
other: Bearded Penguin
Pygoscelis antarctica AN MAP 5 **Text page 202**

5a ADULT: White sides of face, chin and throat broken by narrow black 'chinstrap' diagnostic.
5b JUVENILE/IMMATURE: As 5a except for blackish tips to chin and throat feathers.
5c CHICK: Silvery-grey or brown above, head and underparts paler.

4 **ADELIE PENGUIN** 71cm
Pygoscelis adeliae AN MAP 4 **Text page 201**

4a ADULT: Uncrested black and white penguin with comical, button-eyed appearance.
4b JUVENILE: Much as adult except for white chin and throat. Demarcation between black and white occurs well below the eye, a useful character at sea when separating from any stage of 5.
4c CHICK: Wholly grey-brown.

11a
11b
11c
11a
5b
5a
5c
5a
4a
4b
4c
4a

Plate 3

CRESTED PENGUINS

9 **ROCKHOPPER PENGUIN** 61cm
Eudyptes chrysocome SO MAP 9 **Text page 204**

9a ADULT: Unlike 10a below, the head plumes are not joined on the forehead and it has a black occipital crest, and a smaller bill.

9b IMMATURE: As 9a except for less developed superciliary and weaker bill. Chin and throat sometimes paler.

9c JUVENILE: Much as 9b except chin and throat mottled with white.

10 **MACARONI PENGUIN** 71cm
Eudyptes chrysolophus SAO, SIO MAP 10 **Text page 204**

10a ADULT: Larger than 9a above. Head plumes are joined in solid patch on forehead; fleshy margin at gape usually more extensive.

10b IMMATURE: As adult except for shorter, tuft-like head plumes. Differs from 9b above in larger size; heavier bill with larger fleshy margin at gape; and head plumes.

10c JUVENILE: As 10b but head plumes less extensive, chin and throat greyer.

10X **ROYAL PENGUIN** 73cm
Eudyptes c. schlegeli RR MAP 10 **Text page 204**

10Xa ADULT: As 10 above but generally larger with heavier bill and grey or white sides of face, chin and throat. See notes p. 205 regarding status.

10Xb IMMATURE: As ault except for reduced head plumes and weaker bill.

9c
9b
9a
10b
10c
10a
10Xa
10Xb

Plate 4

CRESTED PENGUINS

6 **FIORDLAND CRESTED PENGUIN** 67cm
other: Thick-billed/Victoria/New Zealand Crested Penguin
Eudyptes pachyrhynchus RR MAP 6 **Text page 202**

6a ADULT: Differs from 8a below in absence of fleshy margins at base of bill; note parallel white stripes across black cheeks.

6b IMMATURE: As adult except for shorter head plumes, white chin and throat, greyish cheeks.

8 **SNARES ISLAND PENGUIN** 73cm
other: Snares Penguin/Snares Crested Penguin
Eudyptes robustus RR MAP 8 **Text page 203**

8a ADULT: Resembles 6a but bill larger with prominent pink, fleshy margin at base of mandible, and lacks white parallel streaks across cheeks of that species.

8b IMMATURE: Differs from 6b in darker cheeks and throat, and pink, fleshy margin at base of mandible; at sea these differences would be of little use.

7 **ERECT CRESTED PENGUIN** 68cm
Eudyptes sclateri RR MAP 7 **Text page 203**

7a ADULT: Differs from smaller Rockhopper Penguin (p. 204) in brush-like crest, prominent pink fleshy margin at gape and underflipper pattern (Fig. 3, p. 202).

7b IMMATURE: Differs from immature Rockhopper Penguin in white chin, eyebrow and underflipper pattern.

12 **LITTLE PENGUIN** 40cm
other: Fairy/Blue or Little Blue Penguin
Eudyptula minor RR MAP 12 **Text page 205**

Smallest penguin; occurs commonly on coasts of southern Australia, Tasmania and New Zealand. Distinctive blue-grey upperparts, lack of crest and size enable straightforward identification.

12X **WHITE-FLIPPERED PENGUIN** 42cm
Eudyptula (minor) albosignata RR MAP 12 **Text page 206**

Slightly larger than nominate race with paler back and whiter margins to flipper. Restricted to Canterbury region of South Island, New Zealand.

8a
8b
6a
6b
6a
8a
7a
12X
12
12
7a
7b

Plate 5

Spheniscus PENGUINS

13 **JACKASS PENGUIN** 68cm
Spheniscus demersus RR MAP 13 **Text page 206**

13a ADULT: The only penguin regularly occurring off coasts of South Africa; once abundant, now seriously threatened. Unmistakable, but Rockhopper and Macaroni Penguins (p. 204, p. 204) occasionally occur within range.
13b ADULT: Some individuals (mutants) show two black bands over upper breast suggesting 15a below.
13c JUVENILE: Lacks conspicuous head pattern of adult.
13d IMMATURE: As juvenile except for ghost-image of adult's head pattern.

14 **HUMBOLDT PENGUIN** 70cm
other: Peruvian Penguin
Spheniscus humboldti RR MAP 14 **Text page 206**

14a ADULT: Range overlaps with 15 in southern Chile. It differs in narrower white stripe over head and only a single black breast band.
14b JUVENILE/IMMATURE: Differs from similar 15b in wholly brownish-grey head and prominent fleshy margins at base of bill.

15 **MAGELLANIC PENGUIN** 71cm
Spheniscus magellanicus RR MAP 15 **Text page 207**

15a ADULT: Differs from 14a above in smaller bill, wider white band over head and two black bands across breast.
15b JUVENILE/IMMATURE: Differs from 14b above in slightly capped apearance, with whitish or grey cheeks and partial breast band.

16 **GALAPAGOS PENGUIN** 48cm
Spheniscus mendiculus RR MAP 16 **Text page 207**

16a ADULT: Unmistakable; the only penguin at Galapagos Islands.
16b JUVENILE/IMMATURE: Lacks adult's head pattern.

13d
13a
13d
13a
13c
13b
13a
14a
14b
14b
14a
14b
14a
15a
15b
15a
15b
15b
15a
16a
16b
16b
16a
16b
16a

Plate 6

DIVERS/LOONS

20 **WHITE-BILLED DIVER** 83/147cm
other: Yellow-billed Loon
Gavia adamsii AR, NPO, NAO MAP 20 **Text page 210**

20a ADULT BREEDING: Blackish head and neck, white necklace and ivory bill diagnostic.

20b ADULT NON-BREEDING: Bill pale ivory-white. Unlike 19b, head much paler than upperparts, an excellent field character.

20c FIRST-WINTER: Resembles 20b but sides of face whiter. Upperparts more heavily scaled than in 19c.

19 **GREAT NORTHERN DIVER** 76/137cm
other: Common Loon
Gavia immer AR, NPO, NAO MAP 19 **Text page 210**

19a ADULT BREEDING: Blackish head and neck, white necklace and blackish bill diagnostic.

19b ADULT NON-BREEDING: Smaller than 20 above, differing in steeply angled crown, dark culmen, head colour and horizontal carriage of head and bill. Confusion also possible with larger examples of 18.

19c FIRST-WINTER: As 19b but upperparts scaled with buffish-white.

18 **BLACK-THROATED DIVER** 68/120cm
other: Arctic Loon (includes Pacific Loon, 18X)
Gavia arctica AR, NPO, NAO MAP 18 **Text page 209**

18a ADULT BREEDING: Combination of grey head, black throat patch and spotted upperparts diagnostic (but see notes on status of 18X, p. 209).

18X ADULT BREEDING (PACIFIC DIVER *G.a. pacificus*): Status under review. Smaller than nominate race with proportionately smaller head, shorter bill and rich purple iridescence on throat patch.

18b ADULT NON-BREEDING: Best separated from 17b by straighter, dagger-like bill held horizontally, lack of noticeable white spotting on upperparts, and distinctive white flank patch.

18c FIRST-WINTER: Resembles 18b but upperparts indistinctly scaled with buffish-white.

17 **RED-THROATED DIVER** 61/110cm
other: Red-throated Loon
Gavia stellata AR, NPO, NAO MAP 17 **Text page 208**

17a ADULT BREEDING: Differs from all other adult divers in unspotted upperparts. Combination of greyish-brown head and reddish patch on foreneck diagnostic.

17b ADULT NON-BREEDING: Upperparts spotted with white, appearing paler, more greyish-brown, than in 18b above and differs further in upwards tilt of head and bill and lack of white flank patch.

17c FIRST-WINTER: As 17b but spots on upperparts greyer and longer, forming V-shaped marks on scapulars.

20c
20a
20b
20a
20b
19b
19a
19a
19b
19c
18c
18X
18a
18b
18b
18a
17b
17a
17b
17a
17c

Plate 7

GREBES

34 **GREAT CRESTED GREBE** 49/87cm
other: Crested Grebe
Podiceps cristatus MAP 34 **Text page 218**

34a ADULT BREEDING: Unmistakable.
34b ADULT NON-BREEDING: Crown black with white stripe over eye and blackish stripe from eye to pinkish-yellow bill. Sides of face, foreneck and underparts white.
34c JUVENILE: Resembles non-breeding adult but sides of face and neck striped with black (moult to first-winter plumage begins as early as Jul/Aug).

33 **RED-NECKED GREBE** 45/80cm
other: Holböll's Grebe
Podiceps grisegena MAP 33 **Text page 217**

33a ADULT BREEDING: Unmistakable.
33b ADULT NON-BREEDING: Greyer foreneck and ear-coverts than Great Crested Grebe; bill proportionately deeper, shorter, with diagnostic yellow base.
33c JUVENILE: Resembles non-breeding adult but sides of face and upper neck striped black and white. Differs from 34c in chestnut sides of neck and tawny-buff foreneck.

35 **HORNED GREBE** 33/60cm
other: Slavonian Grebe
Podiceps auritus MAP 35 **Text page 218**

35a ADULT BREEDING: Unmistakable. At distance head plumes extend slightly past nape.
35b ADULT NON-BREEDING: Whiter-faced than 36b. Upper lores with grey spot. Head proportionately larger and flatter, neck thicker. In flight, marginal and lesser upperwing-coverts white, upperparts slightly browner in hue than in 35a.
35c JUVENILE: As non-breeding adult except: division between dark cap and paler ear-coverts diffuse, suggesting Black-necked Grebe, but lacks dusky band at base of neck; crown and bill shape as adult.

36 **BLACK-NECKED GREBE** 30/57cm
other: Eared Grebe
Podiceps nigricollis MAP 36 **Text page 219**

36a ADULT BREEDING: Unmistakable. At distance head plumes reach only to ear-coverts.
36b ADULT NON-BREEDING: Appears darker than 35b with diffuse division between dark crown and sides of face and indistinct white patch behind ear-coverts; foreneck and upperparts duskier.
36c JUVENILE: Resembles non-breeding adult but with duskier cheeks and buffish cast to sides of upper neck; dusky band across base of neck.

34a
34a
34b
34b
34c
33b
33b
33a
33a
33c
35a
35b
35a
35b
35c
36a
36b
36b
36c
36a

Plate 8

SOUTH AMERICAN GREBES

32 **GREAT GREBE** 61/?cm
Podiceps major MAP 32 **Text page 216**

32a ADULT BREEDING: Mostly blackish above, foreneck deep chestnut.
32b ADULT NON-BREEDING: As 32a but upperparts greyer; face whiter, foreneck pale chestnut tipped with white.

28 **WHITE-TUFTED GREBE** 32/?cm
Rollandia rolland MAP 28 **Text page 215**

28a ADULT BREEDING: Mostly black above except for conspicuous patch of white plumes, streaked with black, springing from sides of face. Underparts mainly deep chestnut.
28b ADULT NON-BREEDING: Upperparts and foreneck dull reddish-brown, chin, throat and most of underparts white.

29 **SHORT-WINGED GREBE** 28/?cm
Rollandia micropterum MAP 29 **Text page 215**

29a ADULT BREEDING: Crown and upperparts blackish, nape chestnut, chin and foreneck white. Underparts mostly white peppered with chestnut.
29b ADULT NON-BREEDING: As 29a but crown pale chestnut, hindneck cinnamon-brown, upperparts browner. Underparts mostly white.

38 **JUNIN GREBE** 35/?cm
other: Puna Grebe
Podiceps taczanowskii MAP 38 **Text page 220**

38a ADULT BREEDING: Mostly soft greyish-brown above, white below.
38b ADULT NON-BREEDING: As 38a but lacks crest and lacks black on nape and hindneck.

32b
32b
32a
32a
28b
28b
28a
28a
29a
29b
38a
38a
38b
38b

Plate 9

AMERICAN GREBES

26 **PIED-BILLED GREBE** 34/59cm
Podilymbus podiceps MAP 26 **Text page 214**

26a ADULT BREEDING: Small; stocky jizz and banded bill diagnostic.
26b ADULT NON-BREEDING: Band on bill faint or absent; throat whitish. See 25b below.
26c JUVENILE: As 26b but sides of head striped (retained by some until Oct in North America).

25 **LEAST GREBE** 25/35cm
other: American Dabchick/Least Dabchick
Tachybaptus dominicus RR MAP 25 **Text page 213**

25a ADULT BREEDING: Differs from 26a in smaller size, orange iris, dark bill and, in flight, prominent upperwing stripe. Males average darker.
25b ADULT NON-BREEDING (sexes alike): As 25b but duller with white chin and whiter flanks.

39 **WESTERN GREBE** 65/90cm
Aechmophorus occidentalis MAP 39 **Text page 220**

Note: Refer to p. 220 for status of *A.o clarkii* which may be a good species.
39a ADULT BREEDING: The largest North American grebe; swan-necked jizz unmistakable.
39b ADULT NON-BREEDING: Much as 39a except crown and hindneck duller, merging more with white face and foreneck.
39c DOWNY YOUNG: Unique; all other grebes have boldly striped young.

Main Selection

Seabirds

OF EASTERN NORTH PACIFIC AND ARCTIC WATERS

Edited by Delphine Haley

"Against the illimitable blue of the sky, over the unfathomable blue of the ocean, the sea birds of the Pacific wing the cycle of their lives. For them the ocean is a larder: the islands and atolls their mating ground and nurseries."

—George C. Munro, *Birds of Hawaii*

Birding Book Society
July 1984

Main Selection

Seabirds of Eastern North Pacific and Arctic Waters

Edited by Delphine Haley

Long an inspiration for poets and mariners alike, seabirds have found their way into human lives through ornamentation and ceremony, myth and legend. Their impact on culture ranges from the symbolic to the practical, gracing the prose of Milton and Shakespeare and attracting the keen interest and dedication of naturalists and ornithologists.

"In the following chapters," writes Delphine Haley in the preface to this volume, "thirteen scientists present the results of their interest in marine birds, totaling more than two hundred years of research on land and at sea . . . Each author has approached his subject in his own way, in an effort to convey firsthand interest and enthusiasm, as well as firsthand knowledge and experience.

"The geographical boundaries for this book have been established from the Gulf of California (lat 22° N) west across the top of Baja California to the outermost Northwestern Hawaiian Islands (long 180°), thence north to the Arctic Ocean, including the Bering Sea, and east to the border of Alaska and Canada (long 120° W)."

In her introductory chapters, the editor describes the physical setting of the birds and their adaptations to and tenuous truce with the sea. Each author then offers his expertise in providing details of the most recent research on the birds' life cycles. The cacophonous din of shearwater colonies, the comic parades of courting boobies, the boundless world in which seagulls glide—all are evoked in the authors' recounting of feeding habits, mating rituals, and nesting strategies. Providing such details, as well as insight into future conservation, these authors also point to a larger life cycle—that of sea and coastal land.

Richly illustrated with color photographs, line drawings, and maps, SEABIRDS OF EASTERN NORTH PACIFIC AND ARCTIC WATERS is a felicitous blend of visual and scholarly efforts that will invite both the lay person and the informed expert to explore further the remarkable world of these elegant winged creatures.

"The sea is now the great frontier for the serious birder. This beautiful book does for the eastern North Pacific and the Arctic what Robert Cushman Murphy's classic did for seabirds of South America a generation ago. It is beautifully written by a baker's dozen of top authorities who know how to use words without resorting to academic jargon. The illustrations are superb and the maps set a new standard."

—Roger Tory Peterson

"*Seabirds of Eastern North Pacific and Arctic Waters* provides a fine summary of current knowledge about these distinctive and fascinating birds. The illustrations are superb and the very readable text, largely concentrating on breeding biology, has been prepared by authors highly knowledgeable about the respective species groups. The book should prove a valuable addition to any bird lover's library."

—Roger B. Clapp
U.S. Fish and Wildlife Service,
Smithsonian Institution

"A state-of-the-science review of the natural history of eastern North Pacific (west coast) seabirds by thirteen people most competent to write about them—field biologists whose lives' work has focused on them and who are also able to share their insights and understanding in an informative and readable manner.

This is a book for professional biologists, amateur naturalists, and other serious ponderers of the sea, and for west coast birders squinting westward."

—John Dillon, *Oceans*

Contents

- Outsized Volume, 9¼" x 12¼"
- 214 pages
- 90 full-color photographs
- Numerous line drawings and maps

(Pacific Search Press, 1984)

(95064)

Publisher's Price $39.95

Member's Price $29.95

Earns **two** bonus credits toward the four required for your next Bonus Selection

Additional Selections

Please remember we cannot sell a book at the Bonus Price unless your order comes on a Bonus Certificate!

94075. **THE BREEDING BIRDS OF EUROPE—VOLUMES 1 & 2,** *by Manfred Pforr and Alfred Limbrunner/translated by Richard Stoneman/ edited by Iain Robertson.* These two photographic handbooks offer some of the most remarkable photos available anywhere. Each volume also contains essential information on the habitat, food, reproductive biology and migration of over 330 different species. *Earns* ***two*** *bonus credits.*
• Handsome Slipcased Set, each book 8½" x 8" • 721 pages • over 900 color photographs • 330 colored distribution maps (Croom Helm/Tanager Books, 1982)
Publisher's Price $48.00
Member's Price $33.50 **A 35% Discount!**
Bonus Price $16.80

94056. **THE BIRDWATCHER'S COMPANION: AN ENCYCLOPEDIC HANDBOOK OF NORTH AMERICAN BIRDLIFE,** *by Christopher Leahy/ illustrated by Gordon Morrison.* "Birders whose shelves have reached carrying capacity must now be looking for a synthesis that gives, in readily accessible format, all the information they really want. For me, (this book) is the answer."—Roger Pasquier, *International Council for Bird Preservation. Earns* ***two*** *bonus credits.*
• 917 pages • Color plates and drawings
(Hill and Wang, 1982)
Publisher's Price $29.50 **Member's Price $21.95**
Bonus Price $9.95

36290. **BIRDS AS BUILDERS,** *by Peter Goodfellow.* A compelling and scientific survey of how birds build nests and tend their young. "Excellent."—*American Birds*
• 168 pages • Striking photographs in full-color and black-and-white (Arco Publishing Co., 1977)
Publisher's Price $15.95 **Member's Price $11.95**
Bonus Price $5.65

95282. **WADING BIRDS OF THE WORLD,** *by Eric and Richard Soothill.* Describing over 300 species of waders, including the Charadrii (snipes, oyster-catchers, plovers, dotterels, sandpipers, avocets, stilts, phalaropes, etc.) and the Ciconiiformes and Gruiformes (among them herons, bitterns, storks, ibises, flamingos, cranes, and limpkins). Details are given of each bird's characteristics and behavior, voice, distribution, habitat, food, breeding, and display. *Earns* ***two*** *bonus credits.*
• 6¼" x 9¾" • 334 pages • 96 color photographs • 70 line drawings (Sterling, 1982)
Publisher's Price $29.95 **Member's Price $22.50**
Bonus Price $10.48

94408. **HOW BIRDS WORK: A GUIDE TO BIRD BIOLOGY,** *by Ron Freethy.* A straight-forward introduction to the science of bird biology, the author provides basic information enabling the amateur birdwatcher to better understand his "quarry", distinguish its individual characteristics, and appreciate its behavior.
• 232 pages • 12 color and 40 black-and-white photographs • 80 line drawings and tables
(Blandford Press, 1982)
Publisher's Price $15.95 **Member's Price $11.95**
Bonus Price $5.58

41305. **THE CUCKOO,** *by Ian Wyllie.* Describes in detail the habits of a bird which puzzles and fascinates ornithologists and amateur bird-watchers alike. Totally absorbing. *Earns* ***two*** *bonus credits.*
• 176 pages • Beautiful photographs
(Universe Books, 1981)
Publisher's Price $30.00 **Member's Price $22.50**
Bonus Price $9.75

94409. **HOW LIFE LEARNED TO LIVE: ADAPTATION IN NATURE,** *by Helmut Tributsch.* Simply written and well illustrated, this is an account of the world of biophysics—the ingenious means plants and animals have devised to turn the principles of physics and engineering to their advantage in the struggle to adapt and survive.
• 217 pages • Numerous photographs and drawings (MIT Press, 1982—First published in 1976 as *Wie das Leben leben lernte*)
Publisher's Price $19.95 **Member's Price $13.95**
Bonus Price $6.98

94057. **BIRDS IN THE GARDEN,** *by Mike Mockler.* Details of the different species to be found in various town and city habitats, the everyday activities of garden birds, what they do at night and during the winter, and the breeding cycle of courtship, mating, nesting, laying and raising of the young. (Blandford Press, 1982)
• 160 pages • Filled with full-color photographs
Publisher's Price $19.95 **Member's Price $14.95**
Bonus Price $6.98

87058. **WHERE TO FIND BIRDS IN NEW YORK STATE,** *by Susan Roney Drennan.* Filled with up-to-date information and maps, this impeccably accurate volume is the first and only guide ever published covering more than 500 of the best birding spots in the entire state of New York. *Earns* ***two*** *bonus credits.*
• 700 pages • 106 maps
(Syracuse University Press, 1981)
Publisher's Price $38.00 **Member's Price $26.50**
Bonus Price $11.40

87190. **WILD GEESE OF THE WORLD: THEIR LIFE HISTORY AND ECOLOGY,** *by Myrfyn Owen.* Draws on the latest findings for one of the most superlative references ever published on the 15 species of true geese. *Earns* ***two*** *bonus credits.*
• 236 pages • 8 color plates and 25 line drawings • 25 distribution maps and 30 charts
(B. T. Batsford Ltd., 1980)
Publisher's Price $34.95 **Member's Price $24.45**
Bonus Price $10.48

94055. **BIRDS OF TROPICAL AMERICA,** *by Alexander F. Skutch/drawings by Dana Gardner.* The vivid and intimate biographies of 34 species of some scarcely known, curious and brilliantly feathered American birds including the only comprehensive studies now available of the Wood-quail, the Jacamar, and the New World Barbet. Written by an ornithologist who might easily be dubbed the Sherlock Holmes of the tropical bird world. *Earns* ***two*** *bonus credits.*
• 320 pages • 32 black-and-white photographs • 37 line drawings (University of Texas Press, 1983)
Publisher's Price $29.95 **Member's Price $22.50**
Bonus Price $9.98

Call Toll Free
1-(800)-343-9444

26a
26a
26b
26b
26c
25b
25a
25a
39a
25b
39b
39a
39c

Plate 10

DABCHICKS

21 **LITTLE GREBE** 27/42cm
other: Red-throated Little Grebe/Dabchick
Tachybaptus ruficollis MAP 21 **Text page 212**

21a ADULT BREEDING: Mostly blackish above, sides of face and foreneck dark chestnut, flanks and thighs browner.

21b ADULT NON-BREEDING: Dark olive-brown on crown, hindneck and upperparts; sides of face and flanks sandy-brown, ventral area pale grey or white.

21c JUVENILE: Resembles adult non-breeding but with striped face, tawny-brown foreneck and breast (retained in some until Nov/Dec).

22 **AUSTRALASIAN LITTLE GREBE** 28/?cm
other: Black-throated Little Grebe/Australasian Dabchick
Tachybaptus novaehollandiae MAP 22 **Text page 212**

22a ADULT BREEDING: Resembles the cosmopolitan Little Grebe above except for black, not rufous, ear-coverts, throat and foreneck.

22b ADULT (TRANSITIONAL): Resembles non-breeding adult but sides of face and neck rufous.

22c ADULT NON-BREEDING: Upperparts mostly dull greyish-brown, underparts silvery-grey. Yellow spot at base of bill separates from 30b below.

22d JUVENILE: As non-breeding adult except for blackish streaks to side of face.

30 **HOARY-HEADED GREBE** 30/?cm
Poliocephalus poliocephalus MAP 30 **Text page 215**

30a ADULT BREEDING: Mostly brownish-grey above, sides of face finely streaked white, hindcrown and nape black, foreneck grey or dun-white.

30b ADULT NON-BREEDING: As 30a but duller grey above, lacks black on hindcrown and nape; mostly white on underparts.

30c JUVENILE: As 30b except for blackish streaks to face.

31 **NEW ZEALAND DABCHICK** 28/?cm
Poliocephalus rufopectus MAP 31 **Text page 216**

31a ADULT BREEDING: Forehead and crown black, glossed green, sides of face streaked white; foreneck and breast rufous. Lacks yellow spot at base of bill found in 22.

31b ADULT NON-BREEDING: Upperparts mostly fawn-brown, crown and hindneck darker, underparts mostly white.

31c JUVENILE: As non-breeding adult except sides of face streaked black.

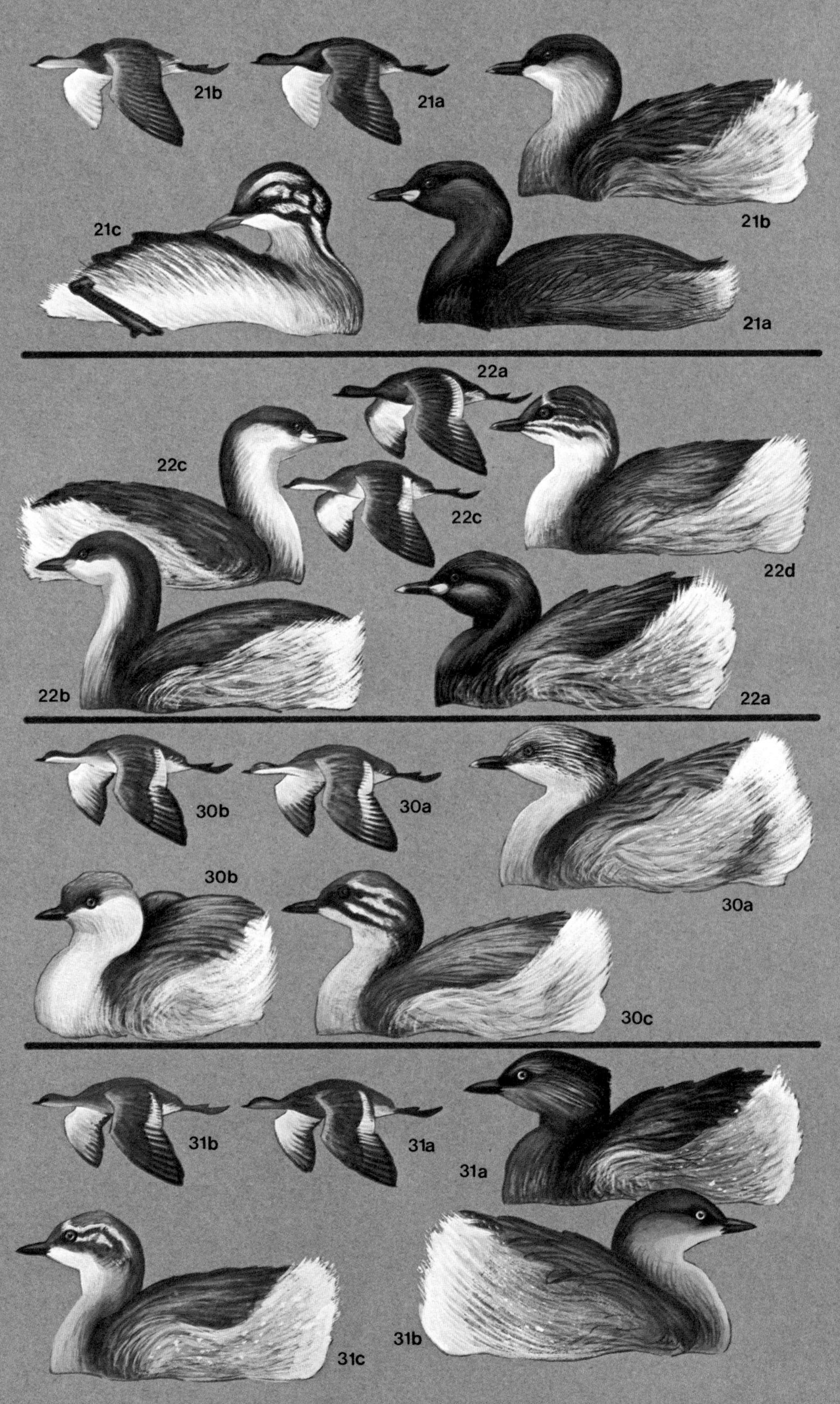
21b
21a
21b
21c
21a
22a
22c
22c
22d
22b
22a
30b
30a
30b
30a
30c
31b
31a
31a
31c
31b

Plate 11

GREBES

24 **DELACOUR'S LITTLE GREBE** 25/?cm
other: Aloatra Dabchick
Tachybaptus rufolavatus RR MAP 24 **Text page 213**

24a ADULT BREEDING: Separated from 23a by extensive cinnamon wash on foreneck and upper breast.

24b ADULT NON-BREEDING: Separated from 23b by browner upperparts and more mottled breast, flanks and thighs.

24c JUVENILE: Resembles non-breeding adult except head and sides of neck striped white and cinnamon.

23 **MADAGASCAR LITTLE GREBE** 25/?cm
other: Madagascar Dabchick
Tachybaptus pelzelnii RR MAP 23 **Text page 213**

23a ADULT BREEDING: Separated from 24a above by rufous sides of neck.

23b ADULT NON-BREEDING: Greyer in tone than 24b above with whiter lower breast, belly and ventral area.

23c JUVENILE: Resembles non-breeding adult except sides of face and neck striped white and grey-brown.

37 **SILVERY GREBE** 28/?cm
Podiceps occipitalis MAP 37 **Text page 219**

37 ADULT BREEDING: Distinguished from White-tufted Grebe (p. 215) by white foreneck and conspicuously black nape and hindneck.

27 **ATITLAN GREBE** 48/?cm
Podilymbus gigas RR MAP 27 **Text page 214**

27a ADULT BREEDING: Half as large again as Pied-billed Grebe (p. 214), which it resembles in appearance; practically flightless, restricted to Lake Atitlan.

27b JUVENILE: As adult except for browner tone and whitish stripes to sides of head and neck.

24a
24b
24b
24c
24a
23a
23b
23b
23a
23c
37
27b
27a

Plate 12

WHITE-BACKED (GREAT) ALBATROSSES

40 **WANDERING ALBATROSS** 115/300cm

Diomedea exulans SO MAP 40 **Text page 222**

40a STAGE 1 (JUVENILE): Wholly chocolate-brown except for conspicuous white face mask; underwing white, tipped black, narrowly margined black on trailing edge as in adult but with small brownish area on axillaries.

40b STAGE 2: As juvenile except upperparts flecked with white; underparts mostly white with conspicuous brown breast band.

40c STAGE 3: Head, body and upperwing patch become progressively whiter. Differs from any stage of 41 in indistinct breast band and blackish tail.

40d STAGE 4: Head and body mostly white except for indistinct mottling on crown and greyish breast band. White inner wing patch more noticeable.

40e STAGE 5: White inner wing patches link with back to form diagnostic white wedge into otherwise dark upperwing. Upperwing thus whitens from the centre outwards to leading edge. By comparison, the upperwing of nominate Royal whitens from the leading edge inwards (see 41e/f).

40f STAGE 6: Upperwing continues to whiten. Tail of most individuals retains black sides.

40g STAGE 7: Older birds of both species (40 & 41) are difficult to separate; fortunately they probably represent less than 1 in 20 of all sightings (pers. obs.). At close range dark cutting edges and rather yellower bill would indicate a Royal, black in the tail a Wanderer.

41 **ROYAL ALBATROSS** 114/330cm

Diomedea epomophora SO MAP 41 **Text page 224**

The two subspecies are separable at sea and are thus described separately below. Neither race undergoes the complex immature stages of the Wandering Albatross: they fledge with head, body and tail mostly white.

D.e. sanfordi

41a JUVENILE: As adult except crown and lower back mottled or tipped brownish-black; tail white with small black tips. (A Wanderer with such dark upperwings would show a mostly black tail and pronounced mottling on head, saddle and breast.)

41b ADULT: Combination of white head and tail with mostly black upperwing diagnostic. The underwing also has a diagnostic mark near the carpal joint (see Fig. 6, p. 224).

D.e. epomophora

41c STAGE 1 (JUVENILE): Much as 41a except head usually wholly white; upperwing with faint white midwing patch.

41d STAGE 2: As 41c except white inner wing patch more pronounced; leading edge narrowly white.

41e/f STAGES 3 & 4: Upperwing becomes progressively whiter from the leading edge inwards (see 40e). Tail white.

41g STAGE 5: See 40g above.

40g
40c
40b
40a
40c
40a
40g
40f
40e
40d
41b
41a
41a
41b
41g
41f
41e
41d
41c

Plate 13

ALBATROSSES

46 **BLACK-BROWED ALBATROSS** 88/240cm
other: Black-browed Mollymawk
Diomedea melanophris SO — MAP 46 **Text page 228**

46a ADULT: Bears superficial resemblance to a very large black-backed gull; dark saddle and upperwings contrast strongly with white head, rump and underparts. Underwing white, broadly and irregularly margined black. (It has the widest leading margin of any albatross.) At closer range dark eyebrow and bright yellowish-orange bill are diagnostic.

46b ADULT: *D.m. impavida* breeding in New Zealand area is similar except for honey-coloured iris, more extensive eyebrow and usually a darker underwing. Juvenile *impavida* have underwings as dark as juvenile Grey-headed Albatrosses and require careful treatment. See Fig. 7, p. 228, for *impavida* underwing patterns.

46c SUB-ADULT: Diagnostic horn-coloured bill with black tip. Head white; most show decomposed breast band. Underwing resembles that of adult but paler areas greyer in tone.

46d JUVENILE: Bill greyish or dark horn with black tip and darker ridges (most reliable character to separate from 50d below).

46e Between juvenile and immature stages bill shows a paler central area, the tip, upper and lower ridges remaining dark. It is important to note the distinct difference in acquisition of adult bill coloration between this species and the Grey-headed Albatross. In present species bill is first greyish or dark horn with dark tip and ridges; then latericorn and ramicorn (Fig. 4, p. 221) become horn-yellow, the upper and lower ridges plus tips remaining dark; in the following stage the ridges become yellowish to produce bill colour as in 46c. By comparison Grey-headed fledges with wholly blackish bill (never appears dark-tipped); the tip is first to show yellow (50c) followed by upper and lower ridges (50b), the latericorn and ramicorn remaining black.

50 **GREY-HEADED ALBATROSS** 81/220cm
other: Grey-headed Mollymawk
Diomedea chrysostoma SO — MAP 50 **Text page 231**

50a ADULT: Bill glossy black, upper and lower ridges bright yellow, tipped orange; at long range appears wholly black. Combination of dark bill, grey head and whiter underwing should prevent confusion with 46a. Compared with 46a leading edge of underwing is narrower, but is wider than in White-capped, Yellow-nosed or Buller's Albatrosses (p. 229, p. 230, p. 228). More likely to be confused with equally dark-headed adults of nominate Yellow-nosed in S. Atlantic but that species has different jizz, bill and underwing pattern.

50b SUB-ADULT: As adult but bill duller, head paler; scattered greyish tips across underwing-coverts.

50c IMMATURE: Bill blackish, tip faintly yellow. Extent of grey on head, breast and underwing-coverts variable; some may show white foreheads and sides of face (little different from some Black-browed). Bill colour most reliable character to look for.

50d JUVENILE: Bill black. During first year at sea, head darker than in adult (some wholly grey). The underwing is the darkest of any southern *Diomedea* albatross at this age (but see juveniles of 46b above).

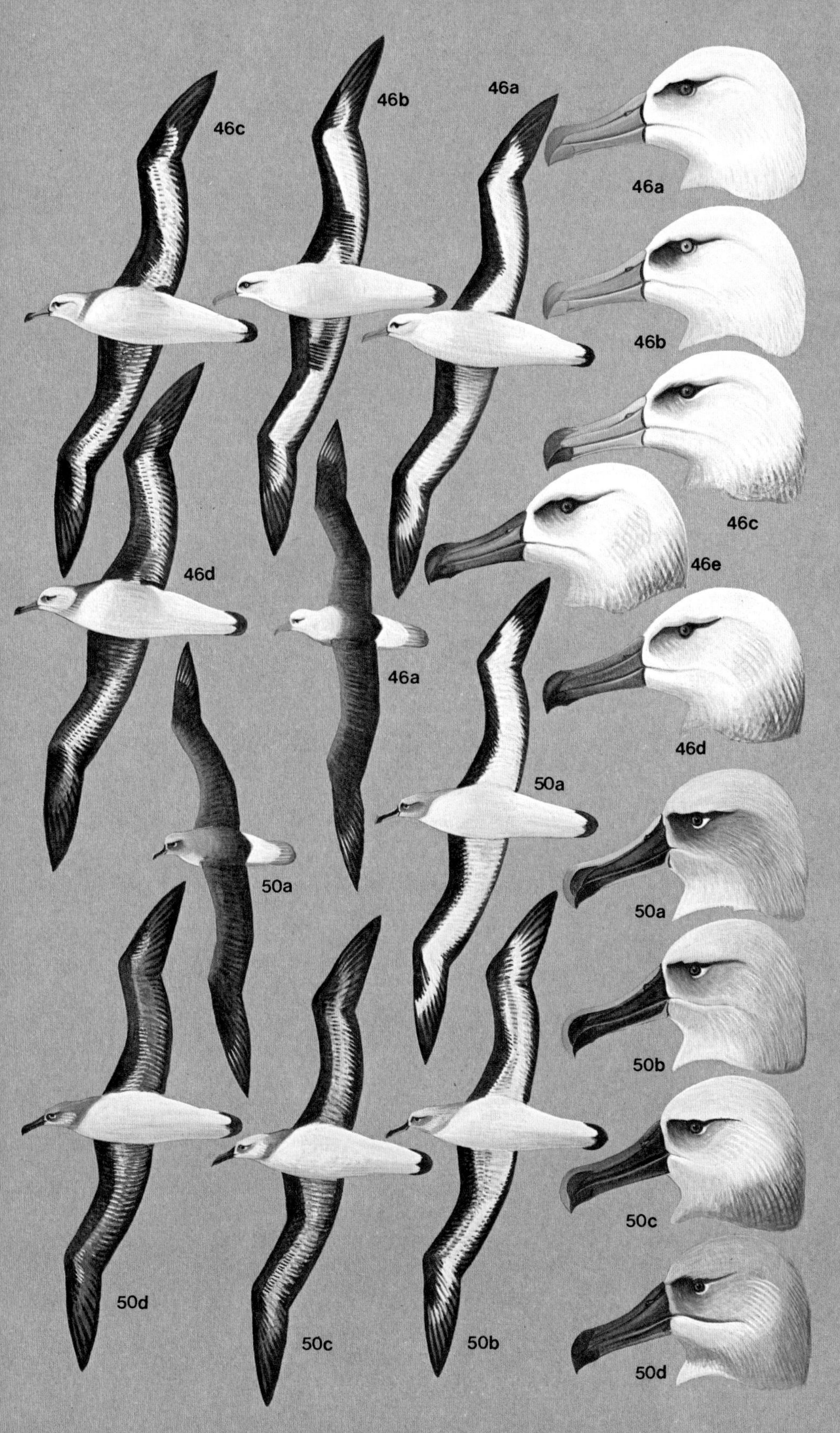

46c
46b
46a
46a
46b
46c
46d
46e
46a
46d
50a
50a
50a
50b
50c
50d
50c
50b
50d

Plate 14

ALBATROSSES

49 **YELLOW-NOSED ALBATROSS** 76/191cm
other: Yellow-nosed Mollymawk
Diomedea chlororhynchos SAO, SIO MAP 49 **Text page 230**

49a ADULT (*D.c. bassi*): Combination of narrow black margins on underwing and bill colour diagnostic. At close range greyish suffusion over cheeks and nape usually visible; at long range appears wholly white-headed with black bill.

49b ADULT (*D.c. chlororhynchos*): As 49a except head mostly grey; beware more southerly Grey-headed Albatross (p. 231).

49c JUVENILE: As adult except head white (both races) with wholly black bill.

48 **WHITE-CAPPED ALBATROSS**
(Includes Salvin's and Chatham Island Albatrosses, 48X and 48Y)

The three subspecies of *Diomedea cauta* are the largest of the Southern Oceans 'mollymawks'. They differ from all other albatrosses in having white underwings with narrow black margins and a diagnostic 'thumbmark' at the base of the leading edge. They are described separately below.

WHITE-CAPPED ALBATROSS 99/256cm
other: Shy Albatross/Mollymawk
Diomedea cauta cauta SO MAP 48 **Text page 229**

48a ADULT: Differs from *salvini* in white head, grey cheeks and smaller but blacker tip to underwing.

48b JUVENILE: In worn plumage head often white with partial collar (beware immature Black-browed and Grey-headed Albatrosses, p. 228, p. 231).

48X **SALVIN'S ALBATROSS** 93/250cm
other: Salvin's Mollymawk
Diomedea cauta salvini SO MAP 48X **Text page 229**

48Xa ADULT: Differs from *cauta* in pronounced greyish-brown or brown head contrasting with white forehead and upper breast; paler grey-brown mantle and larger, though greyer, tip to underwing. (See Buller's and Grey-headed Albatrosses, p. 228, p. 231.)

48Xb JUVENILE: Differs from juvenile *cauta* only in underwing tip colour.

48Y **CHATHAM ISLAND ALBATROSS/MOLLYMAWK** 90/220cm
Diomedea cauta eremita RR MAP 48Y **Text page 229**

48Y ADULT: Resembles *salvini* in plumage but smaller, head darker, without white cap; bill yellowish with dark mark on lower nail.

47 **BULLER'S ALBATROSS** 78/210cm
other: Buller's Mollymawk
Diomedea bulleri SPO MAP 47 **Text page 228**

47a ADULT: Differs from Grey-headed Albatross (p. 231) in contrasting white forehead, narrower underwing margins and bill colour.

47b JUVENILE: Underwing identical to adult; bill brownish-horn with dark mark on nails.

47c IMMATURE: As 47b but culminicorn and ramicorn gradually turn horn-coloured, then yellow.

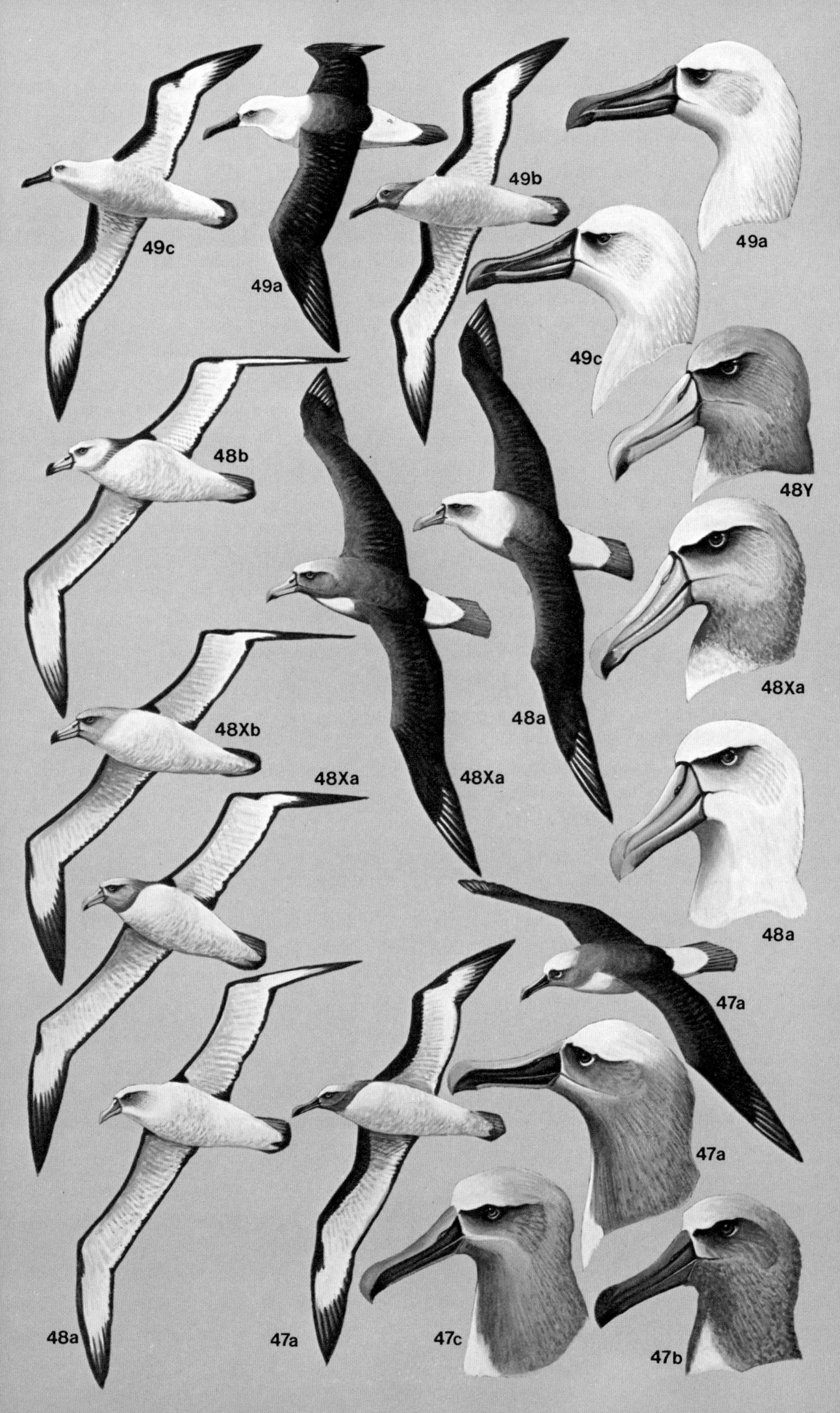
49c
49a
49b
49a
49c
48b
48Y
48Xa
48a
48Xb
48Xa
48Xa
48a
47a
47a
48a
47a
47c
47b

Plate 15

ALBATROSSES

45 **LAYSAN ALBATROSS** 80/199cm
Diomedea immutabilis NPO MAP 45 **Text page 227**

45 ADULT and JUVENILE: Alike, latter differing only in greyer bill. In fresh plumage, upperwings, mantle and back blackish-grey, head, rump and underparts white. Underwing mainly white with narrow dark margins and irregular blackish streaks on coverts (much individual variation). Dark eye patch visible at close range.

51 **SOOTY ALBATROSS** 86/203cm
other: Dark-mantled Sooty Albatross
Phoebetria fusca SAO, SIO MAP 51 **Text page 231**

51a ADULT: Wholly sooty-brown, darker on head, slightly paler across nape, with white or yellowish shafts to primaries and tail. At close range, bill black with yellow or orange sulcus along lower mandible.

51b JUVENILE: In fresh plumage closely resembles adult except for slightly paler head and mantle; grey sulcus and eye crescents. Primaries and tail lack pale shafts.

51c IMMATURE: During first year at sea body feathers wear quickly, most birds showing buffish-grey (sometimes white) collar and nape extending onto mantle and upper back. Adults in worn plumage (Apr/May) show similar plumage characters but with bright sulcus and whitish primary shafts. These types superficially resemble Light-mantled Sooty, but usually differ in darker brown lower back and rump.

52 **LIGHT-MANTLED SOOTY ALBATROSS** 84/215cm
Phoebetria palpebrata SO MAP 52 **Text page 232**

52a ADULT: Differs from Sooty Albatross in distinctive frosty-grey mantle extending to lower back and rump, and contrasting with dark brown head and wings. At close range, bill black with blue or purple sulcus along lower mandible.

52b JUVENILE: Best separated from 51b by extent of paleness on back and rump. In 51b this normally confined to mantle and upper back, whereas in present species it extends to lower back and rump.

52c IMMATURE: Much as adult but mantle and upper breast often show buff tips. See notes under 52b for separation from Sooty Albatross.

45
45
45
51a
51c
51a
51b
52c
52a
52a
52b
52a

Plate 16

PACIFIC ALBATROSSES

43 **SHORT-TAILED ALBATROSS** 89/221cm
other: Steller's Albatross
Diomedea albatrus NPO MAP 43 **Text page 226**

43a ADULT: Largest and only white-bodied albatross of the N. Pacific.
43b JUVENILE (FIRST STAGE): Closely resembles smaller juvenile Black-footed Albatross (44c). Differs in large pink bill, pale legs and lack of white at base of bill.
43c JUVENILE (SECOND STAGE): As 43b but whitish chin divided from buff-brown or off-white underparts by conspicuous dark collar. Thumbnail shows start of diagnostic white upperwing patches, which, combined with pink bill and feet, are excellent in-flight characters never found in any stage of 44 below.
43d IMMATURE (FIRST STAGE): Plumage generally whiter; head shows conspicuous white forehead and dark cap. Upperwing mostly sepia-brown, but note start of second white patch.
Underwing-coverts begin to show whitish tips at this stage.
43e IMMATURE (SECOND STAGE): Some may breed in this plumage. Dark cervical collar combined with whitish body and white upperwing patches produces distinctly different appearance from any stage of 44 below.
43f SUB-ADULT: Resembles adult but with brownish cervical collar; corresponding white areas variably sullied with brownish tips.

44 **BLACK-FOOTED ALBATROSS** 71/203cm
Diomedea nigripes NPO MAP 44 **Text page 227**

NOTE: Plumage sequences poorly understood and complicated by some variance in colour of uppertail-coverts, ventral area and undertail-coverts of adult.
44a ADULT: Mostly dusky-brown except narrow whitish area at base of bill, over base of tail and, normally, whitish undertail-coverts and ventral area.
44b ADULT (aberrant or aged): Superficially resembles 'immature' stages of Short-tailed Albatross but bill and legs darker, size smaller. Head lacks conspicuous dark cervical collar or golden hue, and wings, whilst paler than in typical form, lack diagnostic white patches found in the Short-tailed Albatross.
44c JUVENILE: Bill and legs dark. Plumage wholly sooty-brown except for faintly white area at base of bill. See 43b above.

43e
43f
43a
43b
43c
43e
43a
43d
43c
43b
44c
44a
44b
44a

Plate 17

ALBATROSSES AND LARGE PETRELS

42 **WAVED ALBATROSS** 89/235cm
other: Galapagos Albatross
Diomedea irrorata RR — MAP 42 **Text page 225**

42 ADULT: The only albatross of the Galapagos region, unlikely to be confused with other species if seen properly. Range overlaps with 54 off Peruvian coast and perhaps also with 53.

53 **NORTHERN GIANT PETREL** 87/190cm
other: Northern Giant Fulmar
Macronectes halli SO — MAP 53 **Text page 233**

53a ADULT: Head never as pale as in Southern Giant Petrel, from which best distinguished by slightly capped appearance and (usually) reddish, dark-tipped bill. Whole of underparts generally paler than upperparts, thus lacking white-breasted impression of 54b below. Leading edge of wing dark.

53b JUVENILE (FIRST STAGE): Wholly glossy black to begin with, as in 54c, but soon fades to dark blackish-brown. Bill colour in most populations would seem to be the only way of separating juveniles of the two species at this stage, although further work may show some overlap. (See discussion in main text.)

53c JUVENILE (SECOND STAGE): As first stage except scattered whitish feather tips at base of bill and on sides of face, chin and throat.

53d IMMATURE: Resembles adult but capped appearance more pronounced. Separated from immature Southern Giant Petrel by darker crown and bill colour, which at this age diagnostic. Underparts also normally paler than 54e with slight collar effect across throat.

54 **SOUTHERN GIANT PETREL** 87/195cm
other: Southern Giant Fulmar
Macronectes giganteus SO — MAP 54 **Text page 234**

54a ADULT (WHITE MORPH): Unique to Southern Giant Petrel; occur as nestlings and remain white throughout life without transitional plumage stages.

54b ADULT (DARK MORPH): Resembles 53a but head and upper breast almost white, tip of bill pale green. Upperparts and remainder of underparts normally greyish-brown without the contrast found in 53a. Leading edge of wing pale.

54c JUVENILE (FIRST STAGE): Shown in blackish plumage, but soon fades to blackish-brown as depicted in 53b above.

54d JUVENILE (SECOND STAGE): As first stage except for scattered white tips at base of bill and on sides of face, chin and throat.

54e IMMATURE: Resembles 53d with more or less identical freckling on crown (though rather greyer, less blackish-brown, and therefore not so prominently capped). Main distinction lies in bill colour, darker lower breast and underparts.

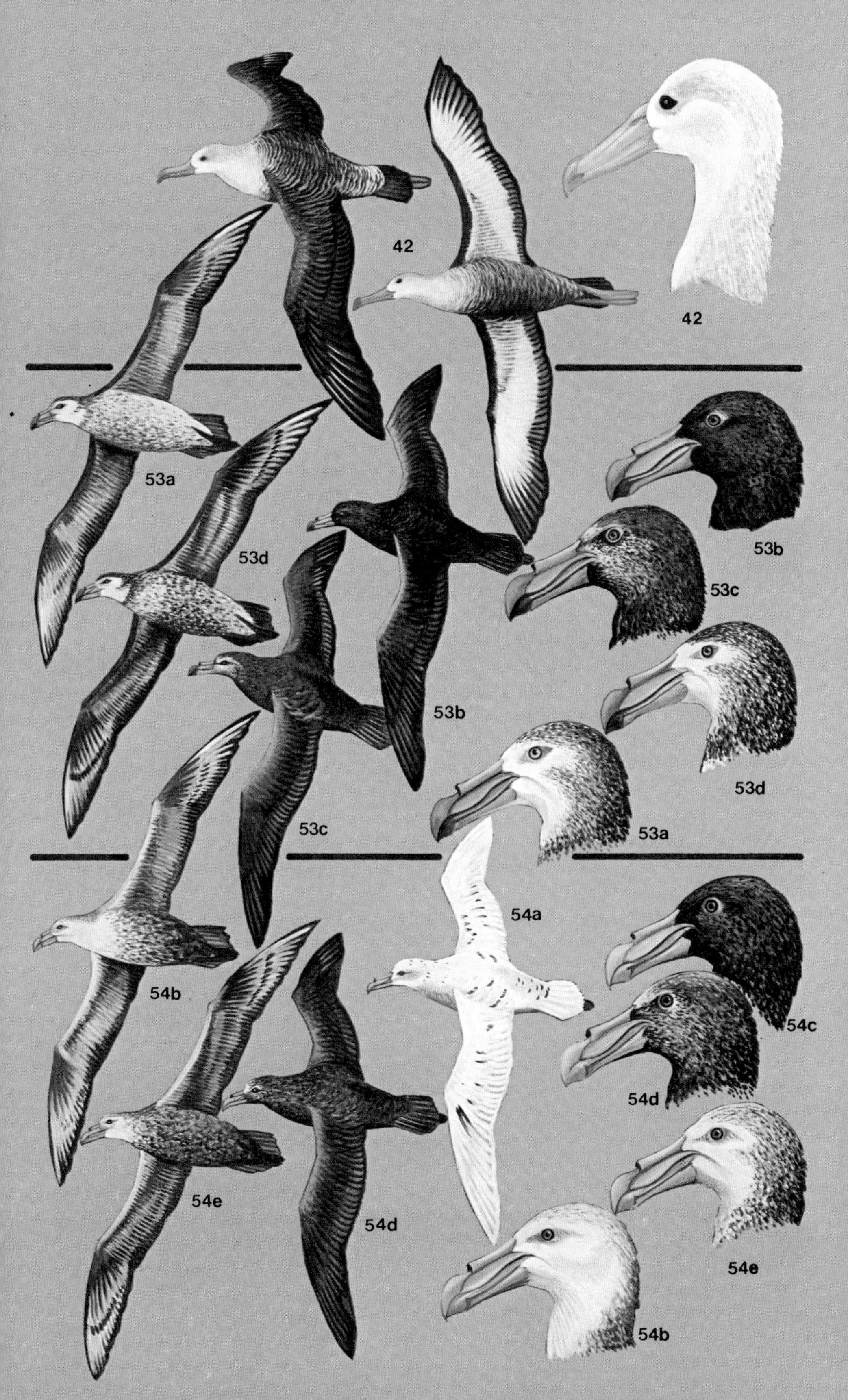
42
42
53a
53d
53b
53b
53c
53c
53d
53a
54a
54b
54c
54d
54e
54d
54e
54b

Plate 18

SOUTHERN PETRELS

57 **ANTARCTIC PETREL** 43/102cm
Thalassoica antarctica AN MAP 57 **Text page 236**

57a FRESH PLUMAGE: Recognised by combination of brown upperparts contrasting with broad white subterminal trailing edges of wings.

57b WORN PLUMAGE: As 57a but brown areas bleached and worn paler to tan-brown, hindneck sometimes white.

58 **CAPE PETREL** 39/86cm
other: Pintado Petrel, Cape Pigeon
Daption capense SO MAP 58 **Text page 236**

58a *D.c. capense*: Larger than 58b with whiter upperparts, although in worn plumage difference often negligible.

58b *D.c. australe*: Australasian region. When seen together with nominate race appears decidedly smaller and darker.

59 **SNOW PETREL** 32/78cm
Pagodroma nivea AN MAP 59 **Text page 237**

59 Distinctive; the world's only small, wholly white petrel. Rarely strays far from icefloes and icebergs.

86 **BLUE PETREL** 29/62cm
Halobaena caerulea SO MAP 86 **Text page 250**

86 Without comparative experience, or under poor conditions, difficult to separate from prions (p. 251). Differs from all forms of that genus in white forehead with blackish crown and hindneck extending as partial but obvious collar across sides of breast. If seen, white-tipped tail with black subterminal band diagnostic. Flight less erratic than that of prions, with more frequent gliding on stiff bowed wings.

57a
57a
58b
57b
58a
58b
58a
59
59
86
86
86

Plate 19

FULMARS AND SHEATHBILLS

55 **NORTHERN FULMAR** 48/107cm
other: Fulmar, Arctic Fulmar
Fulmarus glacialis NAO, NPO MAP 55 **Text page 235**

55a DOUBLE LIGHT MORPH: Superficially resembles gull species; differs in stubby bill, bull-necked jizz and distinctive flap-and-glide flight, soaring effortlessly over waves, often in high bounding arcs.

55b DOUBLE DARK MORPH: At close range structural differences separate from immature gulls and shearwaters. At long range, however, wheeling flight suggestive of larger shearwaters; beware especially of confusing *F.g. rodgersii* with Pink-footed Shearwater (p. 257) in North Pacific. NOTE: Intermediates between 55a and 55b occur in continuous gradation.

56 **ANTARCTIC FULMAR** 48/117cm
other: Silver-grey/Southern Fulmar
Fulmarus glacialoides SO MAP 56 **Text page 235**

56a TYPICAL: There are few grey and white petrels in the Southern Oceans and none with a combination of white head, white underwing and gull-like proportions. See White-headed and Grey Petrels (p. 238, p. 254).

56b ATYPICAL: The amount of black on the tip of the upperwing varies considerably, possibly due to moult/wear. (The example opposite is the darkest that I have on record, photographed off New Zealand.)

193 **AMERICAN SHEATHBILL** 40/79cm
other: Snowy Sheathbill/Paddy
Chionis alba RR MAP 193 **Text page 320**

193 The only white terrestrial shorebird of the Antarctic region. Confined to the Antarctic Peninsula and the Scotia Arc; migrates N to Falklands, Tierra del Fuego and Patagonia during austral winter.

194 **LESSER SHEATHBILL** 39/76cm
other: Black-faced Sheathbill/Paddy
Chionis minor RR MAP 194 **Text page 320**

194 Confined to sub-antarctic islands of Indian Ocean; sedentary, unlikely to be seen at sea (unlike 193).

55b
55a
55a
55a
55b
56a
56b
56a
56a
193
194

Plate 20

PRIONS (Whalebirds)

Taxonomy not fully agreed upon. Cox (1980) is followed in this guide but an alternative treatment is that of Harper (1980).

87 **BROAD-BILLED PRION** 27/61cm
(Includes Salvin's and Antarctic Prions)
Pachyptila vittata SO MAP 87 **Text page 251**

87a *P.v. vittata*: Differs from Fairy Prion in darker, more definite, head pattern and narrower, less extensive, tail band.

87b *P.(v.) desolata*: Much as nominate *vittata* but with more extensive mottling on sides of breast extending as partial but distinctive collar. When viewed from the side, or elevated position, foreshortening imparts distinctive 'white-chinned' appearance, rendering it the easiest of all prions to identify at sea.

88 **FAIRY PRION** 26/58cm
(Includes Fulmar Prion)
Pachyptila turtur SO MAP 88 **Text page 252**

88a *P.t. turtur*: Differs from Broad-billed Prion group in lack of distinctive head pattern and more extensive, broad, black tip to tail.

88b *P.(t.) crassirostris*: Much as nominate *turtur* except for brighter blue upperparts, broader, more defined open M mark and more noticeable tail band. See 'Flight' in main text.

89 **THIN-BILLED PRION** 26/56cm
other: Slender-billed Prion
Pachyptila belcheri SO MAP 89 **Text page 253**

89 Differs from all other prions in distinctive long, white superciliary, highlighted by dark grey streak through eye. Differs from Fairy Prion in distinctive facial pattern; narrower, incomplete tail band. Viewed from below, undertail shows long dark central streak; by comparison Fairy Prions show only a blackish terminal band.

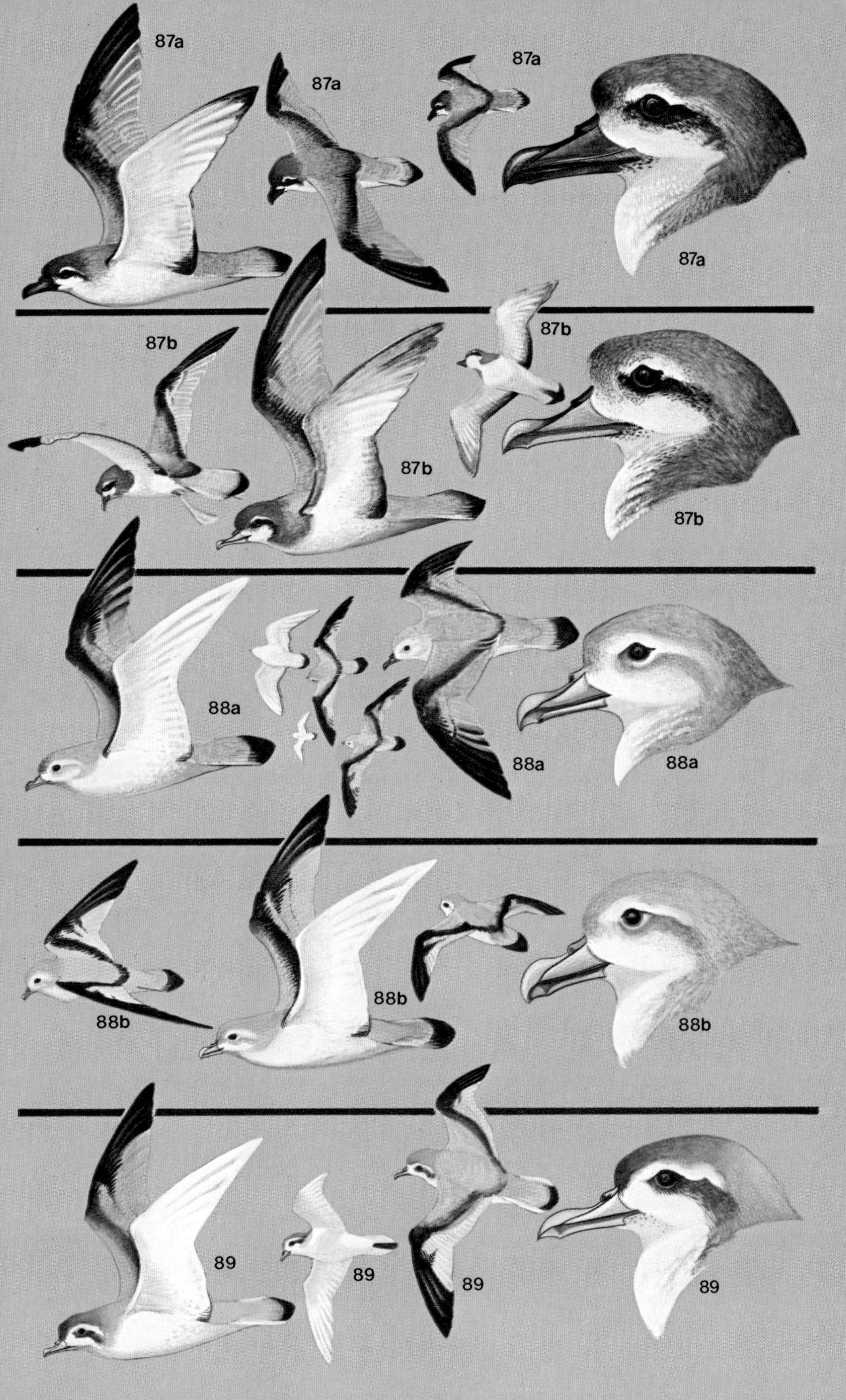
87a
87a
87a
87a
87b
87b
87b
87b
88a
88a
88a
88b
88b
88b
89
89
89
89

Plate 21

LARGER PETRELS AND GADFLY-PETRELS

60 **GREAT-WINGED PETREL** 41/97cm
other: Grey-faced Petrel
Pterodroma macroptera SO — MAP 60 **Text page 237**

60a ADULT (*P.m. macroptera*): Differs from Sooty and Short-tailed Shearwaters in stubby black bill, stocky, bull-necked jizz, darker underwing and impetuous flight. Juveniles have greyer faces and are probably indistinguishable at sea from 60b.

60b **GREY-FACED PETREL** (*P.m. gouldi*): As 60a but with greyer face and chin.

70 **KERGUELEN PETREL** 36/81cm
Pterodroma brevirostris SO — MAP 70 **Text page 242**

Wholly slate-grey; in strong sunshine, plumage highly reflective with silvery flashes, particularly on underwing. Flight rapid, wheeling and bounding; frequently hangs high above waves on motionless wings. See 75b.

75 **SOFT-PLUMAGED PETREL** 34/89cm
Pterodroma mollis AO, SIO — MAP 75 **Text page 245**

Four subspecies, some separable at sea under optimum conditions. All races distinctive in combination of dark face mask; white underbody and breast band of variable extent; dusky grey underwings. The two northern subspecies (*P.m. feae* and *P.m. madeira*) are generally paler and greyer than southern races, lacking pronounced face mask and breast band.

75a *P.m. feae*: Confined to North Atlantic (*P.m. madeira* similar but more heavily mottled on flanks).

75b *P.m. mollis*: Central South Atlantic. Differs from *P.m. dubia* in paler, greyer upperparts; less pronounced face mask and breast band; whiter outer tail feathers.

75c *P.m. dubia*: Sub-antarctic Indian Ocean north to South Africa and east to New Zealand.

75d DARK MORPH: Differs from Kerguelen Petrel in browner cast to plumage, lack of silvery highlights and lack of white leading edge to wing. Flight and jizz also different.

94 **PARKINSON'S PETREL** 46/115cm
other: Black Petrel
Procellaria parkinsoni PO — MAP 94 **Text page 255**

A large, wholly blackish-brown petrel with paler primary shafts to underwing. Pale bill with dark tip also shared by larger, but otherwise similar, Westland Petrel (p. 256). See also White-chinned Petrel (p. 255).

70
60b
60a
75d
60a
75b
75a
75c
94
75c

Plate 22

GADFLY-PETRELS

65 **ATLANTIC PETREL** 44/104cm
other: Schlegel's Petrel
Pterodroma incerta SAO, SIO MAP 65 **Text page 240**

65a FRESH PLUMAGE: Head and upperparts dark brown, sharply demarcated across upper breast from white underparts. Underwing wholly dark brown.
65b WORN PLUMAGE: Similar but chin and throat paler. Greyer tips to upperparts and wings. Nape grey, sometimes white, forming partial collar.

69 **PROVIDENCE PETREL** 40/94cm
other: Solander's Petrel
Pterodroma solandri PO MAP 69 **Text page 242**

69 FRESH PLUMAGE: Head darker in tone than body, unlike 72b which it closely resembles. Best told by darker underwing and greyer cast to mantle, back and upperwings. Upperwing lacks white shafts. Legs and feet grey.

72 **KERMADEC PETREL** 38/92cm
Pterodroma neglecta PO MAP 72 **Text page 243**

72a LIGHT MORPH: White head and underparts contrast with mainly brown upperparts, wings and tail.
72b DARK MORPH: Closely resembles 74c and 69. Differs from former in white shafts on upperwing and darker underwing; from 69 in white shafts on upperwing and whiter face.

74 **HERALD PETREL** 37/95cm
other: Trinidade Petrel, Trinidad Petrel (error)
Pterodroma arminjoniana AO, IO, PO MAP 74 **Text page 244**

74a PALE MORPH: Ashy-brown head (never white as in 72a). Upperparts mostly ashy-brown with paler feather edges enhanced by wear; primaries, secondaries and tertials darker, forming faint M mark. Underparts mainly white with dusky breast band.
74b INTERMEDIATE MORPH: Various types occur, complicated by partial albinism in some birds (Murphy 1936). Most show dark underparts with irregular white tips concentrated on chin, throat, lower breast and belly. Others (not illustrated) show partial albinism on head, sometimes on mantle.
74c DARK MORPH: Head and underparts dark brown.

65a
65b
69
65a
72a
69
72b
72a
72b
74a
74a
74b
74c
74c

Plate 23

LARGER GADFLY-PETRELS

78 **WHITE-NECKED PETREL** 43/95cm
(Includes Juan Fernandez Petrel)
Pterodroma externa TPO MAP 78 **Text page 246**

78a *P.e. externa*: Range overlaps with darker Hawaiian Petrel during northwards migration. Present species differs in paler upperparts and underwing pattern.

78b *P.e. cervicalis*: Resembles nominate except for white hindcollar, paler head and greyer tail. Migrates northwards past Fiji towards Japan. See Buller's Shearwater (p. 260).

63 **BLACK-CAPPED PETREL** 40/95cm
other: Diablotin (includes Jamaica Petrel)
Pterodroma hasitata RR MAP 63 **Text page 239**

63a TYPICAL: Differs from Bermuda Petrel (p. 239) in white hindcollar and conspicuous white rump. See also Great Shearwater (p. 258) which has different flight and jizz, less white on hindneck and rump.

63b ATYPICAL: Plumage variable; lacks white hindcollar and/or white rump. Darkest individuals would closely resemble Bermuda Petrel at sea.

63c **JAMAICA PETREL:** Now thought to be extinct; is generally regarded as a melanistic race of *P.h. hasitata* which formerly bred on Jamaica but, as with both Bermuda and Magenta Petrels (p. 239, p. 244), a few may still exist.

64 **BERMUDA PETREL** 38/89cm
other: Cahow
Pterodroma cahow RR MAP 64 **Text page 239**

64 Differs from typical Black-capped Petrel (p. 239) in lack of both white hindneck and broad white rump. Beware of darker examples of that species, which may lack white hindneck and/or rump. See also Great Shearwater (p. 258).

77 **HAWAIIAN PETREL** 43/91cm
other: Dark-rumped Petrel
Pterodroma phaeopygia TPO MAP 77 **Text page 246**

77 Differs from 78a in darker sides to face, underwing pattern and small dusky spot on axillaries. Some examples show whitish patches on sides of rump. Note long-winged jizz.

78b
78b
78a
78a
63a
63c
64
63a
64
63b
77
77
77

Plate 24

GADFLY-PETRELS

62 **WHITE-HEADED PETREL** 43/109cm
Pterodroma lessonii SO MAP 62 **Text page 238**

62 Unlikely to be seen north of 30°S, unlike 66, 67 and 76 below whose ranges are more tropical. Combination of white head and tail with wholly dark underwing diagnostic. See also Soft-plumaged and Grey Petrels (p. 245, p. 254), which also have grey underwings and white bodies but differ in darker head and, in latter, dark undertail-coverts.

67 **PHOENIX PETREL** 35/83cm
Pterodroma alba TPO MAP 67 **Text page 241**

67 Resembles 66 below but slightly smaller with less robust jizz, and whitish chin and throat. These differences are not easy to discern at sea. Several other Pacific gadfly-petrels have similar colour patterns, e.g. intermediate colour phases of Kermadec and Herald Petrels (p. 243, p. 244). Present species differs from these in dark underwing lacking white at base of primaries.

66 **TAHITI PETREL** 39/84cm
(Includes Beck's Petrel)
Pterodroma rostrata TPO MAP 66 **Text page 240**

66 Closely resembles 67 but differs in slightly larger size, heavier jizz, dark chin and throat. At sea appears as a medium-sized white-bellied gadfly-petrel with an entirely dark head and upper breast. The dark underwing often appears to have a narrow, pale line through the centre.

76 **BARAU'S PETREL** 38/?cm
Pterodroma baraui TIO MAP 76 **Text page 245**

76 Unlike any other gadfly of the Tropical Indian Ocean. Underwing pattern separates it from Herald, Soft-plumaged, Atlantic and Mascarene Petrels, all of which regularly occur S of Reunion I.

62
62
62
67
67
67
66
66
66
76
76
76

Plate 25

GADFLY-PETRELS

71 **MURPHY'S PETREL** 39/97cm
Pterodroma ultima TPO MAP 71 **Text page 243**

71 Little-known central South Pacific species. Differs from all other dark gadfly-petrels of the area in wholly dark underwings. See Providence Petrel (p. 242) and dark morph Herald Petrel (p. 244).

73 **MAGENTA PETREL** ?/?cm
Pterodroma magentae MAP 73 **Text page 244**

73 Recently discovered at Chatham Is near New Zealand but status unknown. May only be a form of Phoenix Petrel from SW Pacific. (Fullagar, pers. comm.)

81 **BONIN PETREL** 30/67cm
Pterodroma hypoleuca TPO MAP 81 **Text page 248**

81 Tropical North Pacific from Bonins E to Hawaiian Is. Differs from Hawaiian Petrel (p. 246) in smaller size, darker forecrown and sides of face, greyer back and distinctly different underwing pattern. See also transient Black-winged and Cook's Petrels (p. 249, p. 247).

82 **BLACK-WINGED PETREL** 30/67cm
Pterodroma nigripennis TPO MAP 82 **Text page 249**

82 Differs from other Pacific gadfly-petrels in combination of grey head and upperparts extending to sides of breast as partial collar (an excellent character), and broad blackish margin and diagonal bar extending from carpal inwards across coverts. Bonin Petrel (81) has darker head and carpal patch. (See 83.)

83 **CHATHAM ISLAND PETREL** 30/67cm
Pterodroma axillaris RR MAP 83 **Text page 249**

83 Restricted to Chatham Is, near New Zealand, and adjacent seas. Differs from all small/medium gadfly-petrels in diagnostic underwing pattern. Beware of 82.

71
73
73
81
81
82
82
83
83

Plate 26

GADFLY-PETRELS

68 **MOTTLED PETREL** 34/74cm
other: Scaled/Peale's Petrel
Pterodroma inexpectata PO MAP 68 **Text page 241**

68a Medium-sized gadfly-petrel, readily separable from congeners by combination of broad, blackish diagonal stripe on underwing and dark grey belly patch.

68b Some, perhaps in fresh plumage, lack dark cap, crown appearing frosty-grey with conspicuous eye patch. (Usually occurs in winter quarters.)

79 **COOK'S PETREL** 26/66cm
Pterodroma cooki PO MAP 79 **Text page 247**

79 Differs from similar Pycroft's and Stejneger's Petrels (84X and 84), which also have mostly white underwings, in lack of darker cap, paler upperparts with more distinct M mark and whitish outer tail feathers.

84X **PYCROFT'S PETREL** 26/66cm
Pterodroma (longirostris) pycrofti RR MAP 84X **Text page 250**

84X Closely resembles Cook's Petrel, differing only in darker cap, generally browner upperparts and less white on outer tail feathers.

84 **STEJNEGER'S PETREL** 26/66cm
Pterodroma longirostris PO MAP 84 **Text page 249**

84 Differs from Cook's Petrel (p. 247) in distinctly darker upperparts with pronounced dark cap, usually clearly demarcated from mantle, and uniformly dark tail. Gould's Petrel (80), which also has a dark cap, has darker upperparts with more distinctly margined underwings.

80 **GOULD'S PETREL** 30/71cm
other: White-winged Petrel
Pterodroma leucoptera RR MAP 80 **Text page 247**

80 The darkest of all Tasman Sea 'cookilarias' petrels. Combination of sooty-brown head, dark upperparts and an underwing pattern intermediate between Cook's and Black-winged Petrels (p. 247, p. 249) diagnostic.

80X **COLLARED PETREL** 30/71cm
Pterodroma (leucoptera) brevipes RR MAP 80X **Text page 248**

80X Generally regarded as a melanistic race of Gould's Petrel. Occurs in various plumages ranging from partial breast band; diffuse breast band separating white throat from white belly, to wholly grey underparts except for white chin and throat.

68a
68b
79
84X
80
84
80X
80X

Plate 27

DARK PETRELS

61 **MASCARENE PETREL** 36/?cm
other: Reunion Petrel
Pterodroma aterrima IO MAP 61 **Text page 238**

61 Recently discovered on Reunion I, this medium-sized gadfly-petrel has a heavy bill and a wholly dark plumage. Flight swift and impetuous. Differs from 90 in larger size, heavier bill and shorter, squarer tail. See also dark phase Herald Petrel (p. 244).

90 **BULWER'S PETREL** 26/67cm
Bulweria bulwerii AO, PO, IO MAP 90 **Text page 244**

90a Size intermediate between storm-petrels and smaller gadfly-petrels. In good light and at close range, upperwing shows a pale diagonal bar across coverts. In normal flight, tail is long and carried in a tapering point (not, as popularly depicted, in a broad wedge-shape).

90b During flight manoeuvres tail is *briefly* fanned to show distinctive wedge-shape.

90c At even moderate range appears wholly dark, but low-level flight, size and jizz separate it from 91 (range may overlap in Indian Ocean).

91 **JOUANIN'S PETREL** 31/79cm
Bulweria fallax IO MAP 91 **Text page 254**

91a Resembles 90 but larger with heavier head, larger bill, and a faster swooping flight, bounding in high, zigzagging arcs 15–20m above waves.

91b In worn plumage some may show pale upperwing diagonals as in Bulwer's Petrel.

85 **MACGILLIVRAY'S PETREL** 30/?cm
Pterodroma macgillivrayi SPO MAP 85 **Text page 250**

85 Apparently lacks the pale underwing diagonals of 90. Differs in more robust bill and slightly larger size. Known only from one specimen taken at the Fiji group, but recent sightings of dark petrels offshore suggest that it may still occur there.

61
61
61
61
90a
90c
90a
90a
90b
90a
91a
91a
91a
91a
91b
85
85
85
85
85

Plate 28

LARGER SHEARWATERS AND PETRELS

102 **BULLER'S SHEARWATER** 46/97cm
other: New Zealand/Grey-backed Shearwater
Puffinus bulleri PO MAP 102 **Text page 260**

102 Large, slender-bodied shearwater with striking upperparts pattern; unlike any other Pacific shearwater. Beware of *Pterodroma externa* group (p. 246).

92 **GREY PETREL** 48/120cm
other: Brown Petrel, Pediunker, Great Grey Shearwater
Procellaria cinerea SO MAP 92 **Text page 254**

92 Large; combination of ash-brown upperparts and white underparts with grey underwings and undertail-coverts diagnostic. See also Cory's Shearwater, Atlantic and White-headed Petrels (p. 257, p. 240, p. 238).

93 **WHITE-CHINNED PETREL** 55/140cm
other: Shoemaker/Cape Hen
Procellaria aequinoctialis SO MAP 93 **Text page 255**

93a *P.a. aequinoctialis*: Large, blackish-brown petrel; unmarked ivory-coloured bill and whitish chin diagnostic. Readily identifiable throughout most of range, but beware of 95 in Australasian region.

93b *P.a. conspicillata*: Southern Atlantic; differs in more extensive white on sides of face.

95 **WESTLAND PETREL** 51/137cm
other: Westland Black Petrel
Procellaria westlandica RR MAP 95 **Text page 256**

95 Resembles 93a in all respects except for black tip to bill; obviously this is hard to ascertain at sea. Parkinson's Petrel (p. 255) is smaller with more delicate bill.

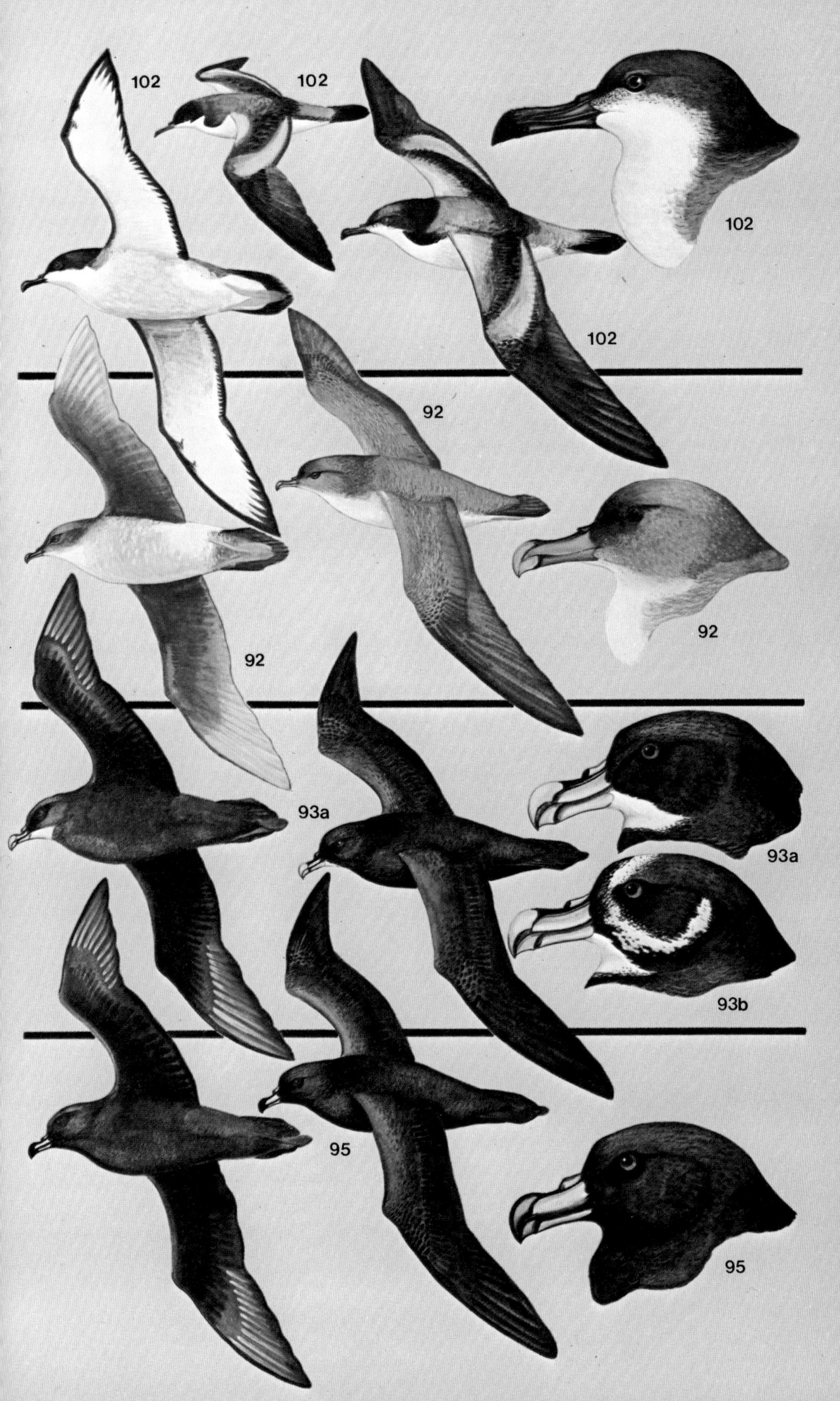
102
102
102
102
92
92
92
93a
93a
93b
95
95

Plate 29

LARGER SHEARWATERS

100 **GREAT SHEARWATER** 49/105cm
other: Greater Shearwater
Puffinus gravis AO MAP 100 **Text page 258**

100a Differs from 97 in distinct capped appearance and prominent white band over tail. The dark belly patch is an excellent diagnostic character but surprisingly hard to see at sea, being more apparent when the bird banks sharply towards the observer.

100b During rapid moult in North Atlantic (Jul/Aug), white bands on wing often formed where missing coverts expose white bases of secondaries and greater primary coverts.

97 **CORY'S SHEARWATER** 49/111cm
other: Mediterranean Shearwater
Calonectris diomedea AO, IO MAP 97 **Text page 257**

97 Lacks the obvious contrast between head and upperparts of 100. In winter quarters off southern Africa beware of Grey Petrel (p. 254), which has grey underwings and undertail-coverts.

98 **PINK-FOOTED SHEARWATER** 48/109cm
Puffinus creatopus PO MAP 98 **Text page 257**

98 Combination of greyish-brown upperparts, white underparts, mottled underwings and dark-tipped pinkish bill diagnostic throughout much of range. Beware of pale morph Wedge-tailed Shearwaters (p. 259) off west Mexico.

96 **STREAKED SHEARWATER**
other: White-faced Shearwater
Calonectris leucomelas PO MAP 96 **Text page 256**

96 Differs from 97 in white-faced aspect with dark streaking on hindcrown and nape; scaly upperparts and whiter underwing; some may show pronounced white over uppertail-coverts.

100b
100a
100a
100a
97
97
97
97
98
98
98
96
96
96
96

Plate 30

DARK SHEARWATERS

99 **FLESH-FOOTED SHEARWATER** 43/103cm
other: Pale-footed Shearwater
Puffinus carneipes PO, IO MAP 99 **Text page 258**

99 Large, wholly blackish-brown shearwater slightly larger than 101 below; wings held straighter, not bowed and well forward. In good light, bases of primaries on underwing silvery (Fig. 8, p. 259). Bill colour diagnostic.

101 **WEDGE-TAILED SHEARWATER** 43/101cm
Puffinus pacificus TPO, TIO MAP 101 **Text page 259**

101a DARK MORPH: Large, wholly blackish-brown shearwater with distinctive buoyant flight; broad-based wings held bowed and well forward. Wedge-shaped tail often hard to discern at sea except when fanned, but appears longer-tailed than 99.

101b PALE MORPH: Paler brown above; underparts and underwing mostly white; sides of breast, flanks, inner underwing-coverts and undertail coverts mottled with brown.

101c DARK MORPH (worn plumage): Upperwing coverts paler forming pale bands across inner wing.

103 **SOOTY SHEARWATER** 44/99cm
Puffinus griseus PO, AO, SO MAP 103 **Text page 260**

103 Medium-sized, sooty-brown shearwater with white underwing, variable in extent, normally appearing as a white flash when at distance. Wings proportionately long, rather narrow and swept back, contrasting with small head and heavy body. Flight swift, wing action stiff, often fast.

104 **SHORT-TAILED SHEARWATER** 42/98cm
other: Slender-billed Shearwater
Puffinus tenuirostris PO MAP 104 **Text page 261**

104 Closely resembles 103; slightly smaller size apparent only if seen together. Underwing normally greyer without white coverts but variable. Main distinction is shorter bill. In winter quarters some short-tailed appear to have indistinct caps, whitish chins and average darker, more velvety-brown on upperparts than 103.

101c
101a
99
101a
103
101b
103
104
103
104
104
103

Plate 31

SMALLER SHEARWATERS

105 **HEINROTH'S SHEARWATER** 27/?cm
Puffinus (lherminieri) heinrothi RR MAP 105 **Text page 261**

105 Known only from seas off New Britain. Marked individual variation: some with wholly brown underparts but others with white oblong-shaped patch from lower breast to belly. NOTE: Considered a race of Audubon's Shearwater (p. 266) by some authors.

106 **CHRISTMAS SHEARWATER** 36/76cm
Puffinus nativitatis PO MAP 106 **Text page 262**

106 Separated from sympatric Wedge-tailed Shearwater (p. 259) by much smaller size, short, rounded tail and rather fast, stiff wingbeats during low-level flap-and-glide flight. See also transient Sooty and Short-tailed Shearwaters, which have paler underwings (p. 260, p. 261).

113 **LITTLE SHEARWATER** 27/62cm
other: Dusky Shearwater
Puffinus assimilis WR MAP 113 **Text page 265**

113a *P.a. assimilis* (SW Pacific): Small, black and white shearwater with distinctive 'aukish' jizz and low-level flutter-and-glide flight. Differs from larger Manx Shearwater (p. 262) in shorter bill, whiter face, proportionately shorter wings and different flight.

113b *P.a. elegans* (Southern Oceans): Differs from other races in blackish sides of head extending well below level of eye.

113c *P.(a.) boydi* (Cape Verde Is, Atlantic Ocean): Status under review; perhaps better placed with Audubon's Shearwater group. Note brownish upperparts and undertail-coverts.

114 **AUDUBON'S SHEARWATER** 30/69cm
(Includes Persian Shearwater)
Puffinus lherminieri TPO, TAO, TIO MAP 114 **Text page 266**

114a *Puffinus lherminieri*: Prefers warmer waters than 113 although their pelagic ranges occasionally overlap. It differs in browner upperparts and dark undertail-coverts (but see 113c), wider margins and tip to underwing, and greater extent of brown on head and sides of breast. See main text for structural differences.

114b *Puffinus lherminieri persicus* (Persian Shearwater): Persian Gulf. Differs from nominate in slightly larger size, longer bill, darker underwing, and mottling to flanks and axillaries.

105
105
106
106
113a
113c
113b
113a
114b
114a
114a

Plate 32

'MANX' SHEARWATER GROUP

107 **MANX SHEARWATER** 34/82cm
Puffinus puffinus puffinus AO MAP 107 **Text page 262**

107 Differs from other Atlantic 'forms' in blackish upperparts contrasting with white underparts; note pure white underwing-coverts and mostly white undertail-coverts. Little Shearwater (p. 265) is smaller with different flight and whiter sides of face.

107X **MANX SHEARWATER (Balearic Race)** 38/87cm
Puffinus p. mauretanicus NAO MAP 107X **Text page 263**

Lacks sharp demarcation between dark brown upperparts and whitish underparts. Underwing more extensively marked than in nominate, undertail-coverts brown; darkest examples may recall larger Sooty Shearwater (p. 260).

107Y **MANX SHEARWATER (Levantine Race)** 34/82cm
Puffinus p. yelkouan RR MAP 107Y **Text page 263**

Resembles nominate form but upperparts brownish, not black.

108 **FLUTTERING SHEARWATER** 33/76cm
Puffinus gavia RR MAP 108 **Text page 263**

Differs from Hutton's Shearwater in browner upperparts, which become increasingly rusty in tone with wear; whiter underparts and underwing. See also Little Shearwater (p. 265).

109 **HUTTON'S SHEARWATER** 38/90cm
Puffinus huttoni RR MAP 109 **Text page 264**

Remains uniformly blackish-brown throughout year (unlike Fluttering Shearwater). Differs further from that form in darker head and throat; underwing with smudgy brownish tip, trailing edge and axillaries. See also Little Shearwater (p. 265).

110 **NEWELL'S SHEARWATER** 32/82cm
other: Manx Shearwater (Hawaiian race of)
Puffinus (p) newelli RR MAP 110 **Text page 264**

Differs from nominate Manx Shearwater in conspicuous white sides of rump which, in flight, form distinctive patches above black tail.

111 **BLACK-VENTED SHEARWATER** 34/82cm
Puffinus opisthomelas RR MAP 111 **Text page 264**

Differs from Townsend's Shearwater below in lack of definite demarcation between brown upperparts and whitish underparts. Underwing dull white with smudgy borders and axillaries; pattern may thus suggest Pink-footed Shearwater (p. 257), but that species is larger, heavier and has a different flight.

112 **TOWNSEND'S SHEARWATER** 33/76cm
Puffinus auricularis RR MAP 112 **Text page 265**

Differs from 110 in less white on sides of rump and blackish undertail-coverts; sides of breast also usually darker. Black-vented Shearwater is much browner above, lacks definite demarcation between upper- and underparts, and has smudgy brown wing margins and axillaries.

107
107X
107X
107Y
107
107X
107Y
109
108
108
109
111
112
110
110
111
112

Plate 33

WHITE-RUMPED STORM-PETRELS

115 **WILSON'S STORM-PETREL** 17/40cm

Oceanites oceanicus WR MAP 115 **Text page 267**

115a TYPICAL *O.o. exasperatus*: Resembles a large, broad-winged British Storm-petrel (122) but with different upper/underwing pattern and, usually, a distinctly different flight. Compared with 127, smaller with more extensive white on rump which extends considerably to lateral undertail-coverts; sometimes shows projecting feet with yellow webs; wings broader and shorter, lacking definite angles on leading and trailing edges. See flight in text.

115b FRESH PLUMAGE: Darker sooty-brown with less pronounced diagonal bar on upperwing.

115c WORN PLUMAGE: Browner and duller; diagonal bar almost as prominent as in some 127.

115d Cape Horn race (*O.o. oceanicus*) is smaller than more migratory Antarctic race *O.o. exasperatus* and may have white on vent (beware Elliot's Storm-petrel, p. 268).

122 **BRITISH STORM-PETREL** 15/37cm

other: Storm-petrel, European Storm-petrel

Hydrobates pelagicus AO MAP 122 **Text page 272**

122 Smallest and darkest Atlantic storm-petrel, with only a narrow diagonal bar on upperwing and a weak, fluttering, bat-like flight. Underwing stripe diagnostic.

125 **MADEIRAN STORM-PETREL** 20/43cm

other: Harcourt's/Band-rumped Storm-petrel

Oceanodroma castro TPO, TAO MAP 125 **Text page 273**

125 Differs from 127a in shorter, somewhat broader wings with evenly-cut white rump band; jizz thus intermediate between Wilson's and Leach's Storm-petrels. Flight usually buoyant, relatively shallow wingbeats and shearwater-like glides producing steady zigzag progression.

127 **LEACH'S STORM-PETREL** 21/47cm

Oceanodroma leucorhoa AO, PO, IO MAP 127 **Text page 274**

127a TYPICAL: Long-winged storm-petrel usually with erratic, bounding flight, and utilising fewer wingbeats than 115 or 122. Compared with 115, wing shape long and rather narrow with obvious angle at the carpal and more pointed tip. Forked tail and grey line down white rump difficult to observe at sea.

127b ATYPICAL: In autumn some (perhaps juveniles in fresh plumage?) show a broader diagonal bar on upperwing.

127c DARK-RUMPED FORMS: In NE Pacific, nominate *O.l. leucorhoa* show continuous gradation from northern white-rumped forms to wholly dark-rumped individuals in southern colonies.

115b
115d
115a
115a
115a
115c
122
122
122
125
125
127b
127c
127a
127a
127a
127c

Plate 34
SOUTHERN STORM-PETRELS

117 **GREY-BACKED STORM-PETREL** 17/39cm
Garrodia nereis SAO, SIO, SPO MAP 117 **Text page 269**

117 A small grey and white species readily identified by grey upperparts, lack of white rump, and blackish head. Secondary-coverts often show pale bar across upperwing. In fresh plumage juveniles and adults have paler feather tips to mantle, back and wing-coverts. In direct flight feet usually extend beyond tail.

118 **WHITE-FACED STORM-PETREL** 20/42cm
other: Frigate-petrel
Pelagodroma marina AO, IO, SPO MAP 118 **Text page 269**

118a ADULT (fresh plumage): Combination of patterned face, brownish-grey upperparts and white underparts diagnostic. See flight in main text.
118b ADULT (worn plumage): Differs from 118a in paler tips to greater coverts forming pale upperwing bar.
118c ADULT (*P.m. eadesi*): Cape Verde Is race has whiter forehead and whitish hindcollar (variable).
118d Some may show whiter rump.

Fregetta storm-petrels
A complex group generally regarded as two sibling species, each of which is usually credited with two colour morphs plus intermediates. Variants, however, probably rare; most sightings can be specifically identified given reasonable views.

119 **BLACK-BELLIED STORM-PETREL** 20/46cm
Fregetta tropica SAO, SPO, IO MAP 119 **Text page 270**

119 TYPICAL MORPH: Differs from 120 in slightly darker upperparts and blackish line extending down centre of belly to unite, usually, with dark undertail-coverts.

120 **WHITE-BELLIED STORM-PETREL** 18/44cm
Fregetta grallaria SPO, SAO, SIO MAP 120 **Text page 270**

120 TYPICAL MORPH: Lacks mid-ventral stripe of 119, but pattern of underparts often difficult to ascertain at sea, particularly from high, unstable vantage.

117
117
117
118b
118a
118a
118d
118c
119
119
119
120
120
120

Plate 35

PACIFIC STORM-PETRELS

123 **LEAST STORM-PETREL** 14/32cm
Halocyptena microsoma NPO MAP 123 **Text page 272**

123 Smallest Pacific storm-petrel, with proportionately short, rounded wings and wedge-shaped tail. Differs from 132 in dark underwing-coverts and more fluttery flight with deeper wingbeats.

130 **BLACK STORM-PETREL** 23/49cm
Oceanodroma melania NPO MAP 130 **Text page 276**

130 Slightly browner in tone than 132 with darker underwing-coverts and more vigorous wing action, the wings rising and falling well above and below line of body. When seen together, the larger size and proportionately longer wings of present species are usually obvious. Beware Markham's Storm-petrel (p. 275) off western South America and dark Leach's off western North America.

132 **ASHY STORM-PETREL** 19/?cm
Oceanodroma homochroa RR MAP 132 **Text page 277**

132 Smaller than 130, with proportionately shorter wings imparting chunkier outline. Differs in pale suffusion on underwing-coverts and more fluttering flight; wingbeats not so high or deep (except when gaining flight).

134 **FORK-TAILED STORM-PETREL** 21/46cm
Oceanodroma furcata NPO MAP 134 **Text page 278**

134 The only pale grey storm-petrel in N Pacific; beware phalarope spp. (p. 318).

123
123
123
130
130
130
132
132
134
134
134

Plate 36

PACIFIC STORM-PETRELS

116 **ELLIOT'S STORM-PETREL** 16/?cm
other: White-vented Storm-petrel
Oceanites gracilis RR MAP 116 **Text page 268**

116 Resembles miniature Wilson's Storm-petrel (p. 267); differs in white belly and pale suffusion on underwing. Habitually 'walks on water'; follows ships.

124 **WEDGE-RUMPED STORM-PETREL** 19/?cm
other: Galapagos Storm-petrel
Oceanodroma tethys RR MAP 124 **Text page 273**

124 Has the largest white rump of any storm-petrel, often appearing white-tailed at sea. Compared with 116, appears blacker at sea with distinctly different, forceful, direct flight.

128 **MARKHAM'S STORM-PETREL** 23/?cm
other: Sooty Storm-petrel
Oceanodroma markhami RR MAP 128 **Text page 275**

128 Closely resembles Black Storm-petrel (p. 276). Differs in more extensive upperwing bar (reaching to carpal), slower and shallower wingbeats with more prolonged gliding and, perhaps most importantly, preference for cooler water.

133 **HORNBY'S STORM-PETREL** 22/?cm
other: Ringed Storm-petrel
Oceanodroma hornbyi RR MAP 133 **Text page 277**

133 Distinctive, the only grey-backed storm-petrel within its range; note whitish underparts, dark breast band and forked tail.

116
116
116
124
124
124
124
128
128
133
133

Plate 37

STORM-PETRELS

121 **WHITE-THROATED STORM-PETREL** 26/?cm
Nesofregetta fuliginosa TPO MAP 121 **Text page 271**

121a TYPICAL MORPH: Distinctive; largest of the storm-petrels, with narrow white bar over rump, white underparts and dark breast band. See 'Flight' in main text.

121b INTERMEDIATE MORPH: Underparts variable, showing continuous gradation between 121a and 121c.

121c DARK MORPH: Wholly dark except for paler upperwing-coverts. Differs from smaller Tristram's Storm-petrel in distinctive wing shape, deeply forked tail and 'leap-and-glide' flight progression (see details in main text).

126 **SWINHOE'S STORM-PETREL** 20/45cm
Oceanodroma monorhis NPO, NIO MAP 126 **Text page 274**

126 Difficult to separate from Tristram's Storm-petrel; differs in smaller size, shallower notched tail, less pronounced upperwing bar and generally browner cast to plumage (beware worn Tristram's).

129 **TRISTRAM'S STORM-PETREL** 25/56cm
other: Sooty Storm-petrel
Oceanodroma tristrami TPO MAP 129 **Text page 276**

129 Larger than Swinhoe's Storm-petrel, with bluish or greyish cast to plumage (when fresh), more prominent upperwing bar and more deeply forked tail. See Matsudaira's Storm-petrel.

131 **MATSUDAIRA'S STORM-PETREL** 25/56cm
Oceanodroma matsudairae TPO, TIO MAP 131 **Text page 276**

131 Appreciably larger than Swinhoe's Storm-petrel, with broader-based wings and white forewing patch; flight slower. Tristram's Storm-petrel lacks white on outer wing and has a more pronounced upperwing bar.

121a
126
126
121b
121a
129
121c
129
131
131
131
131
131

Plate 38

DIVING-PETRELS

135 **GEORGIAN DIVING-PETREL** 19/31cm
Pelecanoides georgicus SAO, SIO MAP 135 **Text page 279**

135 Closely resembles Common Diving-petrel, differing only in variable grey tips to scapulars, white tips of secondaries, blacker upperwings and white (not grey) underwing-coverts. These differences are rarely discernible at sea, even when viewed closely, due to small size and fast, whirring flight (wings are normally in constant motion). The pale tips to scapulars and secondaries are often reduced with wear. See Fig. 10 for separation in the hand (p. 278).

136 **COMMON DIVING-PETREL** 22/35cm
other: Sub-antarctic Diving-petrel
Pelecanoides urinatrix SO MAP 136 **Text page 279**

136a Southern Oceans. Several races are recognised, varying in size of bill and extent of mottling on throat and foreneck, although latter can vary between individuals of the same population. Safely separated from 135 only in the hand (Fig. 10), although lack of white stripe across scapulars, browner upperwings and grey underwing-coverts may be of use at close range.

136b Darker examples have greyish collars across foreneck and throat.

137 **PERUVIAN DIVING-PETREL** 22/?cm
Pelecanoides garnoti RR MAP 137 **Text page 280**

137 Restricted to Humboldt Current, breeding on islands off coasts of Peru and northern Chile. Locality is normally sufficient clue to identity, but in southern part of range overlaps with Magellan Diving-petrel, which, however, has distinctive plumage. Formerly numerous, has decreased rapidly since turn of the century.

138 **MAGELLAN DIVING-PETREL** 20/?cm
Pelecanoides magellani RR MAP 138 **Text page 280**

A distinctive species, safely distinguished from other diving-petrels at close range, though distance and conditions can negate differences. Unlike other members of the family, juveniles distinguishable from adults.

138a ADULT (fresh plumage, Jul onwards): Glossy black upperparts; scapulars, lower back, rump and wing-coverts fringed with white. Diagnostic half-collar extends from throat across sides of neck to hindcrown; foreneck white, never mottled grey.

138b ADULT (worn plumage, Mar): Similar to 138a but lacks whitish fringes to wing-coverts; white tips to secondaries reduced or absent.

138c JUVENILE: As adult except scapulars, lower back and rump lack white fringes.

135
135
136a
136a
136b
136a
137
137
137
138b
138c
138b
138a
138a
138a

Plate 39

TROPICBIRDS

139 **RED-BILLED TROPICBIRD** 48/105cm
Phaethon aethereus TPO, TAO, TIO MAP 139 **Text page 281**

139a ADULT: Combination of red bill, barred upperparts and long white streamers diagnostic.

139b JUVENILE: Bill yellowish, tip black. Differs from other juvenile/immature tropicbirds in finer, denser barring on upperparts and broad eye-stripe extending across hindneck as a nuchal collar.

140 **RED-TAILED TROPICBIRD** 46/104cm
Phaethon rubricauda TPO, TIO MAP 140 **Text page 282**

140a ADULT: Whitest of all the tropicbirds, often with rosy tint on body and wings. Red bill and red tail streamers diagnostic.

140b JUVENILE: Resembles juvenile Red-billed but lacks both nuchal collar and barred secondaries on underwing.

141 **WHITE-TAILED TROPICBIRD** 39/92cm
Phaethon lepturus PO, AO, IO MAP 141 **Text page 282**

141a ADULT (typical): When upperparts can be seen, combination of yellowish or orange bill, diagnostic upperwing pattern and long white streamers enables straightforward identification. When soaring, translucent underwings show 'shadows' of black tertials and secondary coverts of upperwing, which, together with structure and jizz, are useful characters.

141b ADULT (*P.l. fulvus*): Christmas Island, Indian Ocean. Differs from 141a in golden-apricot wash over white plumage.

141c JUVENILE: Differs from juvenile Red-billed in lack of distinct nuchal collar and coarser, more widespread barring on upperparts. Juvenile Red-tailed Tropicbird has less black on outer primaries.

139a
139a
139b
140a
140a
139a
140b
140a
141b
141c
141a
141a
141a
141a

Plate 40
PELICANS

142 **EASTERN WHITE PELICAN** 157/315cm
other: White Pelican
Pelecanus onocrotalus MAP 142 **Text page 283**

142a ADULT BREEDING: Mainly white, with black primaries shading to grey on inner secondaries. Underwing pattern diagnostic when separating from 145a. Bare parts coloration useful when swimming or perched, but difficult to determine at long range.
142b ADULT NON-BREEDING: Plumage similar to 142a, but greyer in tone with brownish cast to coverts. Lacks crest and yellow base of foreneck; bill and pouch duller.
142c JUVENILE: Mainly ash-brown above with paler edges on mantle, coverts and scapulars. The wing appears much browner than 143d, 144c or 145c, with pale rump and underwing stripe.

145 **DALMATIAN PELICAN** 170/328cm
Pelecanus crispus MAP 145 **Text page 285**

145a ADULT BREEDING: Silvery-white above, greyer below, with different underwing pattern from any stage of 142. Lead-grey legs/feet diagnostic (but see immature and some adult-winter Spot-billed Pelicans, p. 284).
145b ADULT NON-BREEDING: Greyer than 145a, with reduced crest and duller-coloured bare parts.
145c JUVENILE: Greyer in tone than 142c, more closely resembling adult Pink-backed Pelican, which is smaller, with different underwing and bare parts coloration.

144 **SPOT-BILLED PELICAN** 140/?cm
other: Grey Pelican
Pelecanus philippensis MAP 144 **Text page 284**

144a ADULT BREEDING: Mainly white, with brown crest and hindneck. Lower back, rump, flanks and undertail-coverts vinaceous-pink. Tail ashy-brown.
144b ADULT NON-BREEDING: As 144a but browner on nape, mantle, back and wing-coverts. Some birds occasionally show greyish legs (beware much larger Dalmatian Pelican, p. 285).
144c JUVENILE: Legs grey. Resembles 144b, but nape, hindneck, mantle, back and upperwing-coverts browner.

143 **PINK-BACKED PELICAN** 127/277cm
Pelecanus rufescens MAP 143 **Text page 284**

143a ADULT BREEDING: Differs from 142a in much smaller size, bill/leg colours, and underwing pattern.
143b ADULT NON-BREEDING: Similar to 143a but lacks pink cast. Mantle, scapulars, back and upperwing-coverts sullied with brown.
143c IMMATURE: As 143b but hindneck, mantle, scapulars and back with brownish cast. Upperwing-coverts and secondaries edged with brown.
143d JUVENILE: Whiter rump than adult; ash-brown wings show paler flight feathers which darken towards maturity.

142c
142c
142a
142a
142b
142c
142b
145b
145c
145c
145b
145a
145b
145a
144c
144b
144c
144a
144a
144b
144a
143b
143b
143a
143b
143a
143c
143d

Plate 41

PELICANS

146 AUSTRALIAN PELICAN 167/252cm
Pelecanus conspicillatus MAP 146 **Text page 285**

146a ADULT BREEDING: The only pelican of the region. Mostly black and white, with small yellow plumes on foreneck.

146b ADULT NON-BREEDING: As 146a but with grey or black tips to nape feathers.

146c JUVENILE: Resembles non-breeding adult, but brown where adults are black.

147 AMERICAN WHITE PELICAN 152/271cm
Pelecanus erythrorhynchos MAP 147 **Text page 286**

147a ADULT BREEDING: The only 'white' pelican of the region.

147b ADULT NON-BREEDING: As 147a but lacks knob on upper mandible. Nape grey.

147c JUVENILE: Resembles 147b but with brown wash to crown and hindneck; primaries and secondaries browner.

148 BROWN PELICAN 114/203cm
Pelecanus occidentalis MAP 148 **Text page 286**

148a ADULT BREEDING: Unmistakable throughout much of range, though if 148X is treated as a separate species care is required to separate the two. Present form is smaller, with smaller crest and, in most races, browner belly without white streaks.

148b ADULT NON-BREEDING: As 148a except head and neck mostly white with yellowish cast on crown (see 148Xb below).

148c JUVENILE: Mostly brown on upperparts, merging into white on breast.

148d Brown Pelicans, including 148X below, are unique among pelicans, preferring a marine habitat and executing spectacular plunge-dives.

148X PERUVIAN PELICAN 152/228cm
other: Chilean Pelican
Pelecanus (occidentalis) thagus MAP 148X **Text page 287**

148Xa ADULT BREEDING: As 148a above but bill pinkish with grey gular pouch. Size much larger, with more pronounced straw-coloured crest on head. Underparts greyer with white streaks on belly.

148Xb ADULT NON-BREEDING: Generally appears much whiter on head, mantle, scapulars, back and upperwing-coverts than 148b above. NOTE: Juveniles not illustrated, but probably differ from 148c above only in size.

146a
146b
146a
146b
146c
146c
147a
147a
147c
147a
147c
147b
148d
148c
148a
148b
148a
148c
148Xa
148a
148Xa
148Xb
148Xa

Plate 42

GANNETS AND BOOBIES

149 **NORTHERN GANNET** 93/172cm
other: North Atlantic Gannet, Gannet
Sula bassana NAO MAP 149 **Text page 288**

149a ADULT: Mainly white with black wingtips and golden hue to rear of head.

149b JUVENILE: Slaty-brown above with white spots to upperwings and back. During first year, the white spots disappear and the head becomes paler, beginning on nape in some birds to produce capped appearance; a dark pectoral band is also formed. (See p. 288.)

149c 2ND YEAR: Yellow suffusion on nape and boldly patterned upperwings.

149d 3RD YEAR: Spangled upperparts. Note in particular the presence of white feathers in the secondaries, a feature never found in 150 or 151.

149e 4TH YEAR: Differ from adults in showing a few black feathers in secondaries and tail.

150 **CAPE GANNET**
Sula capensis AO, IO MAP 150 **Text page 289**

150a ADULT: Differs from 149a in black secondaries and tail; the dark gular stripe is also more extensive but of no practical use for identification.

150b 2ND YEAR: At this age probably indistinguishable at sea from 151. Fortunately their ranges do not normally overlap. From 149d and 149c by wholly dark secondaries and tail.

151 **AUSTRALASIAN GANNET** 84/174cm
Sula serrator RR MAP 151 **Text page 289**

151a ADULT: Resembles 150 but with white outer tail feathers.

151b 2ND YEAR: As for 150b.

155 **MASKED BOOBY** 86/152cm
other: Blue-faced Booby/White Booby
Sula dactylatra TO MAP 155 **Text page 291**

155a ADULT: Differs from gannet group in having all-white head, black tips to longer scapulars and more extensive black to secondaries. From 149a, where ranges overlap in Gulf of Mexico, by black secondaries, tail and bill colour.

155b JUVENILE: Superficially resembles Brown Booby and juvenile Blue-footed Booby (p. 292, p. 289). Differs from former in generally paler brown upperparts, white cervical collar, white upper breast and underwing pattern. From latter by less brown on foreneck and upper breast, white cervical collar, dark uppertail-coverts and underwing pattern.

155c IMMATURE: Upperwing-coverts and rump tipped white; white cervical collar wider, more conspicuous (an excellent field character).

157 **BROWN BOOBY** 69/141cm
Sula leucogaster TO MAP 157 **Text page 292**

157a ADULT: Dark chocolate-brown above, terminating at upper breast in clear-cut division.

157b ADULT MALE: *S.l. brewsteri* in eastern Pacific have pale grey, almost white, heads and grey bills.

157c JUVENILE: Shows ghost-image of adult's pattern but with duller brown upperparts. White underparts are lightly mottled with brown. Juvenile and immature gannets show white-spotted or spangled upperparts, pale chins and throats.

149a
149d
149b
149e
149c
149a
150a
150b
150a
151a
151b
151a
155a
155b
155b
155c
155b
155a
155a
157a
157a
157c
157b
157c
157a
157a

Plate 43

BOOBIES

152 BLUE-FOOTED BOOBY 80/152cm
Sula nebouxii RR MAP 152 **Text page 289**

152a ADULT: Blue feet diagnostic. Differs further from 153a in darker head, different upper- and underwing pattern; note white rectangular patch on axillaries.

152b JUVENILE: Easily confused with juvenile Masked and Brown Boobies (p. 291, p. 292). Differs from former in more extensive brown on head and neck; white uppertail-coverts forming narrow horseshoe over base of tail; and different underwing pattern. At all ages Brown Booby lacks white at junction of hindneck and mantle, and has wholly brown rump and uppertail-coverts; underwing also differs.

153 PERUVIAN BOOBY 74/?cm
Sula variegata RR MAP 153 **Text page 290**

153a ADULT: Differs from 152a in white head, black face mask and different underwing pattern.

153b JUVENILE: Resembles adult, but shows yellow or brown cast to head and underparts with darker upperwings.

156 RED-FOOTED BOOBY 71/96cm
Sula sula WR MAP 156 **Text page 291**

156a WHITE MORPH (typical): Mainly white, with yellowish wash on crown and hindneck; primaries and secondaries black. Underwing has diagnostic black carpal patch.

156b WHITE MORPH (Galapagos form): As 156a but tail blackish-brown (beware of larger Masked Booby, which has black scapulars and lacks carpal patch on underwing).

156c WHITE MORPH (Christmas Is form): As 156a but with variable, usually pronounced, golden cast to white plumage.

156d BROWN MORPH: Wholly greyish-brown.

156e WHITE-TAILED BROWN MORPH: As 156d but lower back, rump, lower belly, tail-coverts and tail white or yellowish-white.

156f WHITE-TAILED AND WHITE-HEADED BROWN MORPH: As 156e but with white head.

156g JUVENILE: Wholly brown or blackish-grey with yellowish-grey legs. (All morphs fledge in this plumage.)

156h INTERMEDIATE: Transitional plumage types occur throughout range. Patchy underwing without definite pattern, red or brownish-red legs, and small size separate it from all other sulids.

154 ABBOTT'S BOOBY 71/?cm
Sula abbotti RR MAP 154 **Text page 290**

154a ADULT FEMALE: Differs from male in pinkish bill.

154b ADULT MALE: Bill pinkish-grey, otherwise as female.

154c ADULT, WORN PLUMAGE (Male shown): Upperparts bleached browner; virtually indistinguishable from juveniles at sea.

154d JUVENILE: Generally as adult in bleached/worn plumage but with grey bill.

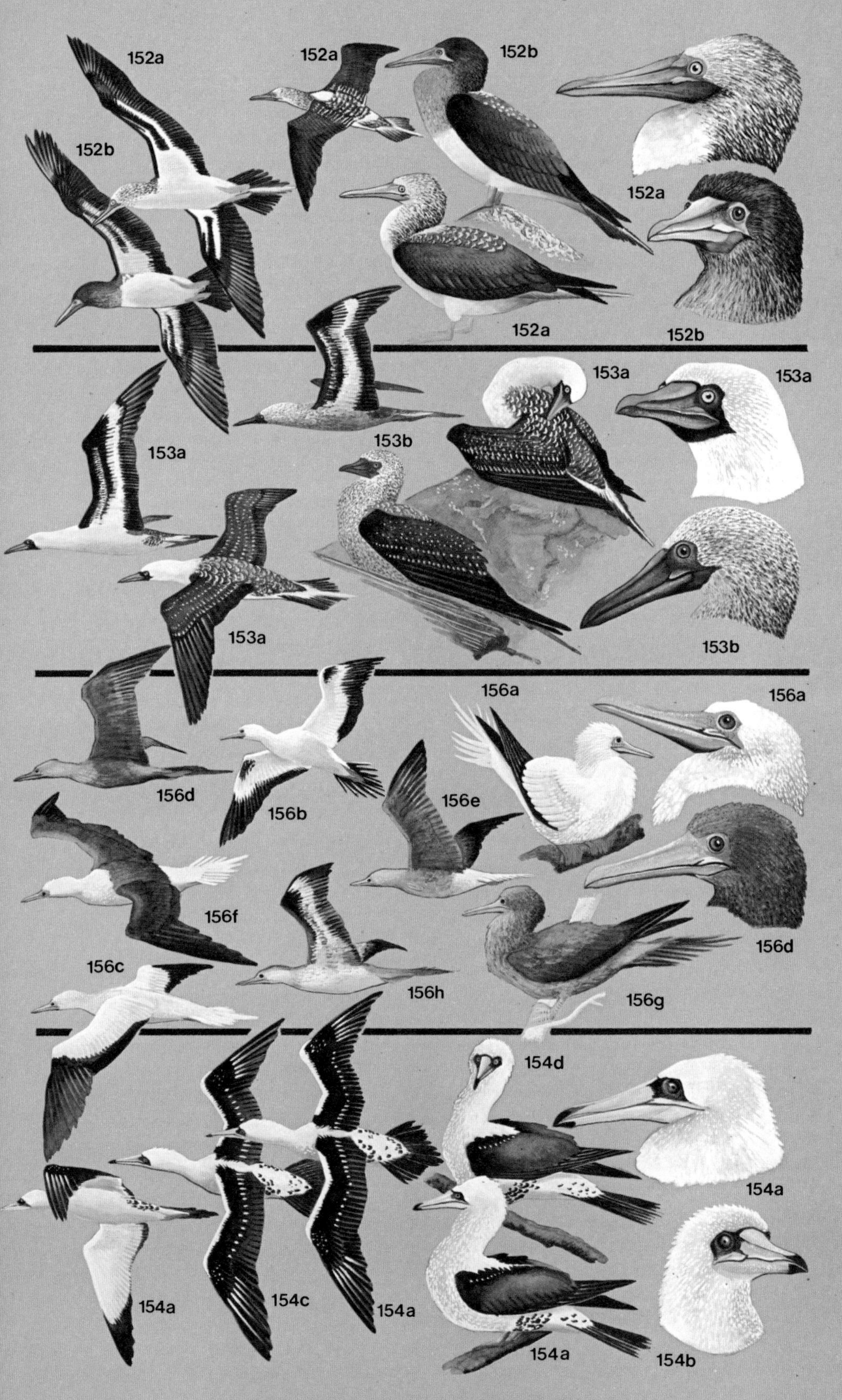

152a
152a
152b
152b
152a
152a
152a
152b
153a
153a
153a
153b
153a
153b
156a
156a
156d
156b
156e
156f
156d
156c
156h
156g
154d
154a
154a
154c
154a
154a
154b

Plate 44

CORMORANTS

161 **GREAT CORMORANT** 90/140cm
other: Common Cormorant (includes White-breasted Cormorant)
Phalacrocorax carbo WR MAP 161 **Text page 295**

161a ADULT BREEDING (*P.c. carbo*): Differs from sympatric 168a in larger size, thicker, longer neck and diagnostic white thigh patch.
161b ADULT NON-BREEDING (*P.c. carbo*). Looks white on head and thigh.
161c JUVENILE (*P.c. carbo*): Much as 161b but browner above with dirty-white underparts.
161d IMMATURE (*P.c. carbo*): As 161c but upperparts and belly become progressively darker.

Subspecies
161e ADULT BREEDING (*P.c. sinensis*): Southern Europe E to central Asia.
161f ADULT BREEDING (*P.c. maroccanus*): NW Africa. As 161e but white throat extends to upper breast.
161g ADULT BREEDING WHITE-BREASTED CORMORANT (*P.c. lucidus*): Africa S of the Sahara. Most distinctive subspecies, usually with white foreneck and breast throughout year (in NE Africa some have dark necks).

168 **SHAG** 72/97cm
Phalacrocorax aristotelis RR MAP 168 **Text page 298**

168a ADULT BREEDING: Smaller and darker than 161a, with recurved wispy crest and dark thighs. See text for structural differences.
168b ADULT NON-BREEDING: Differs from 168a in lack of crest and browner, duller plumage.
168c JUVENILE (nominate): Mostly dull brown, with whitish chin, throat and foreneck.
168d JUVENILE (*P.a. desmarestii*): Usually shows whiter belly than nominate (though subject to individual variation).

183 **PYGMY CORMORANT** 50/85cm
Phalacrocorax pygmeus RR MAP 183 **Text page 306**

183a ADULT BREEDING: At start of breeding season, head mostly black with dense white filoplumes on sides of crown and head.
183b ADULT BREEDING: As season progresses head becomes browner.
183c ADULT NON-BREEDING: Differs from 183b in duller and browner upperparts with paler feather edges and whitish chin, throat and foreneck.
183d JUVENILE: Much as non-breeding adult except underparts mostly white.

181 **LONG-TAILED CORMORANT** 52/85cm
other: Reed Cormorant (includes Crowned Cormorant, 181X)
Phalacrocorax africanus RR MAP 181 **Text page 305**

181a ADULT BREEDING: Mostly blackish, with short crest, conspicuous silvery wing-coverts and scapulars edged and tipped black.
181b ADULT NON-BREEDING: Browner above, including head, with whitish chin and throat merging into brownish-white breast and belly.
181c JUVENILE: As 181b but upperparts browner, less scaly; underparts whiter.

181X **CROWNED CORMORANT**
P.(a.) coronatus RR MAP 181X **Text page 306**

ADULT BREEDING: Confined to coasts of Namibia and South Africa. Differs from 181a in retaining a crest the year round, darker upperparts, shorter tail and longer legs. Habits almost exclusively marine.

161c
161a
161a
161f
161d
161g
161e
161c
161b
168d
168b
168c
168a
168a
183b
183a
183d
183d
183c
183b
181a
181X
181c
181b
181a

Plate 45

CORMORANTS

164 **SOCOTRA CORMORANT** 80/106cm
Phalacrocorax nigrogularis RR MAP 164 **Text page 296**

164a ADULT BREEDING: Endemic to Persian Gulf area, where range overlaps with larger Great Cormorant (p. 295) and freshwater Pygmy Cormorant (p. 306). Often encountered in large flocks; breeds in vast colonies.

164b ADULT NON-BREEDING: Generally duller than 164a, without white eye tuft and fewer filoplumes.

164c JUVENILE: Generally brown above, whitish below.

164d IMMATURE: Differs from 164c in darker spots on mantle and browner underparts.

165 **BANK CORMORANT** 76/132cm
Phalacrocorax neglectus RR MAP 165 **Text page 297**

165a ADULT BREEDING: Separated from sympatric White-breasted (161g) and Cape Cormorants (p. 295, p. 296) by mostly black plumage, black facial skin, and diagnostic white rump (retained for short period only).

165b ADULT NON-BREEDING: Much as 165a but browner and duller (woolly-looking); lacks white rump and flecking on head.

165c ATYPICAL: Leucistic individuals, showing variable amounts of white on face and foreneck, are frequently met with.

163 **CAPE CORMORANT** 62/109cm
Phalacrocorax capensis RR MAP 163 **Text page 296**

163a ADULT BREEDING: Most abundant cormorant off Namibia and South Africa; huge numbers form characteristic extended skeins. Differs from larger, sympatric, Bank and White-breasted Cormorants in wholly blackish-bronze plumage with bright yellow facial skin.

163b ADULT NON-BREEDING: Mostly dull blackish-brown, paler on chin, foreneck and upper breast; facial skin dull brown.

163c JUVENILE: As 163b but chin, foreneck and upper breast whiter.

162 **INDIAN CORMORANT** 65/?cm
other: Indian Shag
Phalacrocorax fuscicollis RR MAP 162 **Text page 295**

162a ADULT BREEDING: Asiatic, frequents marine and freshwater locations. Larger, more slender than Javanese Cormorant (p. 306), with noticeable white tuft behind eye.

162b ADULT NON-BREEDING: As 162a but duller and browner with whitish cheeks, chin and throat. Differs from similar Javanese Cormorant in proportionately slenderer, longer bill and more scaly upperparts.

162c JUVENILE: Much as 162b but duller above, dingy-white below.

164a
164a
164c
164a
164c
164d
164b
165b
165a
165c
165b
165b
165b
165c
163a
163c
163c
163b
163a
162b
162c
162b
162b
162a
162b

Plate 46

AUSTRALASIAN CORMORANTS

173 **PIED CORMORANT** 75/121cm
Phalacrocorax varius RR MAP 173 **Text page 301**

173a ADULT BREEDING: Differs from 174 in brighter facial skin and demarcation between black and white occurring well above eye.

173b JUVENILE: Resembles 174c but facial skin yellowish; brownish wash across foreneck and upper breast wears rapidly, imparting mostly white-fronted appearance. (Some immatures in New Zealand virtually all brown below.)

180 **LITTLE PIED CORMORANT** 60/87cm
other: Little/White-throated Shag
Phalacrocorax melanoleucos RR MAP 180 **Text page 305**

Polymorphic; occurs in three phases in New Zealand, with light morph occurring from Australia N to New Guinea and Malay Archipelago. Pale morphs in all populations may show black mottling on upper breast (not illustrated).

180a ADULT PALE MORPH (typical): Differs from all other Australasian cormorants in compressed yellow bill, brownish eyes, long tail and white thighs.

180b JUVENILE PALE MORPH: Much as 180a but brownish crown extends to level of eye; thighs mottled black and white.

180c ADULT DARK MORPH (*P.m. brevirostris*): Commonest morph in New Zealand; distinctive, no other cormorant is black with white sides to face.

180d INTERMEDIATE MORPH: As 180c except white extends to upper breast.

180e JUVENILE DARK MORPH: Differs from sympatric 160 in compressed yellow bill.

160 **LITTLE BLACK CORMORANT** 61/81cm
Phalacrocorax sulcirostris RR MAP 160 **Text page 294**

160a ADULT BREEDING: Differs from 180e and much larger Great Cormorant (p. 295) in mostly dark plumage and facial skin. See also Javanese Cormorant (p. 306).

160b ADULT NON-BREEDING: As 160a but browner; lacks white filoplumes.

160c JUVENILE: Much as non-breeding adult but mostly silky dark or rusty brown.

174 **BLACK-FACED CORMORANT** 65/107cm
Phalacrocorax fuscescens RR MAP 174 **Text page 301**

174a ADULT BREEDING: Differs from 173a in more extensive black on face and white filoplumes on hindneck, rump and thighs.

174b ADULT NON-BREEDING: As 174a but lacks white filoplumes. See 173a.

174c JUVENILE: Differs from 173b in generally darker face and foreneck with grey (not yellow) skin before eye.

173a
173a
173b
180a
180e
180c
180d
180a
180b
160b
160a
160b
160c
174c
174b
174b
174c
174a

Plate 47
SOUTHERN CORMORANTS

175 NEW ZEALAND KING CORMORANT 76/?cm
(Includes Stewart and Chatham Island Cormorants, 175X and 175Y)
Phalacrocorax carunculatus RR MAP 175 **Text page 302**

175a ADULT BREEDING: Restricted to Marlborough Sounds, New Zealand. Differs from Pied Cormorant (p. 301) in blacker face, pink legs/feet, white alar bar and dorsal patch.
175b JUVENILE: As non-breeding adult but duller, lacks caruncles.
175Xa ADULT BREEDING, PALE MORPH (*P.c. chalconotus*): Restricted to southern New Zealand.
175Xb ADULT BREEDING, DARK MORPH (*P.c. chalconotus*): Wholly blackish with bronze-green lustre.
175Xc ADULT BREEDING, INTERMEDIATE MORPH (*P.c. chalconotus*).
175Y ADULT BREEDING (*P.c. onslowi*): Restricted to Chatham Is, off New Zealand, where Pitt Island Shag and Great Cormorant (p. 305, p. 295) also occur.

176 CAMPBELL ISLAND CORMORANT 63/105cm
(Includes Auckland and Bounty Island Cormorants, 176X and 176Y)
Phalacrocorax campbelli RR MAP 176 **Text page 303**

176a ADULT BREEDING: Restricted to Campbell I., where Little Pied Cormorant also breeds.
176b ADULT NON-BREEDING: As 176a but lacks crest.
176c JUVENILE: Resembles non-breeding adult; upperparts brown, chin dark.
176X ADULT BREEDING (*P.c. colensoi*): Restricted to Auckland Is.
176Y ADULT BREEDING (*P.c. ranfurlyi*): Restricted to Bounty Is.

177 IMPERIAL SHAG 72/124cm
(Formerly Blue-eyed and King Cormorants)
Phalacrocorax atriceps SO MAP 177 **Text page 303**

177a ADULT BREEDING: Coasts of southern South America; polymorphic, darker individuals indistinguishable from 177Ya.
177b ADULT NON-BREEDING: Lacks crest of breeding adult; alar bar and dorsal patch reduced or lacking; caruncles duller.
177c JUVENILE: Pattern as non-breeding adult but duller and browner.
177d ADULT BREEDING (*P.a. nivalis*): Restricted to Heard Is, southern Indian Ocean. Larger, with whiter cheeks than other subspecies.
177X ADULT BREEDING (atypical): Individuals with intermediate cheek patterns occur on South American mainland.
177Ya ADULT BREEDING (*P.a. albiventor*): Differs from typical examples of 177a in darker cheeks and lack of dorsal bar. Restricted to Falkland Is.
177Yb ADULT NON-BREEDING (*P.a. albiventor*): Lacks crest of 177Ya, alar bar reduced or lacking; caruncles duller.
177Yc JUVENILE (*P.a. albiventor*): Pattern as non-breeding adult but duller and browner above.
177Z ADULT BREEDING (*P.a. verrucosus*): Restricted to Kerguelen Is, southern Indian Ocean. May be a good species. Smaller, with shorter bill and darker cheeks than 177a.

175b
175Xc
175Xb
175a
175Xa
175a
175Y
175Xb
175Xa
175Y
176X
176c
176b
176Y
176a
176Y
176a
176X
177Ya
177Ya
177Ya
177Yb
177Z
177Yc
177Yc
177a
177b
177X
177a
177a
177c
177c
177d

Plate 48
CORMORANTS

179 **SPOTTED SHAG** 69/?cm
other: Spotted Cormorant/Blue Shag/Pitt Island Shag
Phalacrocorax punctatus RR MAP 179 **Text page 304**

There are two distinct races of this colourful species. They are described separately below.

179a ADULT BREEDING (*P.p. punctatus*): Boldly patterned head, upperparts greyish-green with darker spots.

179b ADULT NON-BREEDING: Similar to 179a but lacks double crest, white stripe over eye and filoplumes to head and neck.

179c JUVENILE: Upperparts mouse-brown. Underparts mostly off-white except for brownish breast, and darker flanks, thighs and undertail-coverts.

179d ADULT BREEDING (*P.p. featherstoni*): Lacks the white stripe over eye of nominate race; sides of face and neck liberally streaked with white filoplumes. Remainder of plumage as nominate but darker in tone.

182 **JAVANESE CORMORANT** 56/90cm
other: Little Cormorant
Phalacrocorax niger RR MAP 182 **Text page 306**

182a ADULT BREEDING: Mainly blackish-green, scattered white filoplumes to head and neck; wing-coverts paler. See Indian Cormorant (p. 295), which is larger with more scaly appearance to upperparts in both winter and summer plumage.

182b ADULT NON-BREEDING: Largely blackish-brown with variable amounts of white to chin and throat.

182c JUVENILE: Similar to 182b but upperparts duller brown. Paler throat and breast.

166 **JAPANESE CORMORANT** 92/152cm
other: Temminck's Cormorant
Phalacrocorax capillatus (=*P. filamentosus*) RR MAP 166 **Text page 297**

166a ADULT BREEDING: Closely resembles Great Cormorant (p. 295), from which it can be separated at close range by greener cast and extent of white on throat (see Fig. 12, p. 297).

166b ADULT NON-BREEDING: Similar to 166a except head lacks short crest and white filoplumes; thigh patch absent.

166c JUVENILE: Mainly brown above, brownish-white below.

184 **GALAPAGOS CORMORANT** 95/—cm
Nannopterum (=*Phalocrocorax*) *harrisi* RR MAP 184 **Text page 307**

Restricted to two Galapagos islands; sedentary, unlikely to be seen even at other islands in the group. No similar species within range.

184a ADULT: Blackish-brown above, greyer on wing-coverts; underparts browner, often with ochre hue.

184b JUVENILE: Blackish-brown above and below.

179d
179c
179d
179a
179a
179b
182a
182b
182b
182c
182a
182c
166b
166a
166c
166a
166b
184a
184a
184b
184a

Plate 49

PACIFIC CORMORANTS

158 **DOUBLE-CRESTED CORMORANT** 84/134cm
Phalacrocorax auritus NPO, NAO MAP 158 **Text page 293**

158a ADULT BREEDING: Differs from Brandt's Cormorant in slightly larger size and bright orange facial skin and gular pouch. See Olivaceous Cormorant (p. 294).

158b ADULT NON-BREEDING: As 158a but duller and browner; lacks crest.

158c JUVENILE: Differs from similarly aged Brandt's Cormorant in paler chin, throat, foreneck and upper breast, latter usually whitish, scaled with brown.

167 **BRANDT'S CORMORANT** 85/118cm
Phalacrocorax penicillatus NPO MAP 167 **Text page 298**

167a ADULT BREEDING: Differs from Double-crested Cormorant in dark facial skin, brilliant sky-blue gular with yellowish border, and white, hair-like filoplumes; head lacks crest.

167b ADULT NON-BREEDING: As 167a but lacks white filoplumes and blue gular; generally appears blackish with brownish or yellowish-tan border to gular.

167c JUVENILE: Uniform brown, underparts slightly paler with indistinct paler V across upper breast.

169 **PELAGIC CORMORANT** 68/96cm
Phalacrocorax pelagicus NPO MAP 169 **Text page 299**

169a ADULT BREEDING: Differs from larger Brandt's and Double-crested Cormorants in reddish facial skin (hard to see), double crest, white flank patches and rich greenish lustre.

169b ADULT NON-BREEDING: Appears wholly blackish with variable greenish gloss and greyish or yellowish bill.

169c JUVENILE: Mostly uniform brown, underparts slightly paler, but never shows the contrast found in Brandt's and Double-crested Cormorants. See Red-faced Cormorant (170c).

170 **RED-FACED CORMORANT** 84/116cm
Phalacrocorax urile RR MAP 170 **Text page 299**

170a ADULT BREEDING: Larger than Pelagic Cormorant, differing mainly in proportionately larger head, longer bill, thicker neck, and brighter red facial skin extending further across unfeathered forehead. In flight flat-brown upperwings contrast with iridescent body.

170b ADULT NON-BREEDING: As 170a but duller; lacks crests and white flank patch.

170c JUVENILE: Differs from juvenile Pelagic Cormorant in size, structure, and brighter facial skin united across forehead.

158a
158b
158c
158b
167b
167a
167b
167c
169a
169b
170a
170c
170b
169c

Plate 50

SOUTH AMERICAN CORMORANTS

159 **OLIVACEOUS CORMORANT** 65/101cm
other: Neotropic Cormorant/Bigua Cormorant
Phalacrocorax olivaceus RR MAP 159 **Text page 294**

159a ADULT BREEDING: Mainly dark with blue-green lustre and white tufts to sides of head. White border to gular pouch diagnostic.

159b ADULT NON-BREEDING: Duller, lacking white tufts, though retaining border to gular pouch.

159c JUVENILE: Wholly brown at first, lacking white border to gular. Feather tips on throat, foreneck and belly quickly abrade to reveal brownish-white bases as in 159d below.

159d IMMATURE: As 159c but with white border to gular pouch and brownish-white underparts. During transition to adult plumage, underparts become spotted with brown and black.

171 **ROCK SHAG** 66/92cm
other: Magellan Shag
Phalacrocorax magellanicus RR MAP 171 **Text page 300**

171a ADULT BREEDING: Upperparts mainly dark bronze-green, with red eye patch, white tufts in post-auricular region, and scattered white filoplumes to head, neck and mantle. Lower breast and belly white, thigh patch black.

171b ADULT TRANSITIONAL: Upperparts browner, throat whiter with irregular blackish spots.

171c ADULT NON-BREEDING: Brown above, white below. Distinguished from 172b below by size, black bill and white foreneck.

171d IMMATURE: Upperparts, including head and foreneck, mainly brown. Underparts mostly brown with white tips to belly and vent. (Juveniles have similar upperparts but belly and vent are white.)

172 **GUANAY CORMORANT** 76/?cm
Phalacrocorax bougainvillii RR MAP 172 **Text page 300**

172a ADULT BREEDING: Upperparts mainly blue-black; short crest on crown with white tuft over eye and scattered filoplumes on neck. White chin separated from white underparts by black throat band.

172b ADULT NON-BREEDING: As 172a but upperparts dull brown; head lacks crest.

172c IMMATURE: As adult non-breeding but underparts with brownish cast, bare parts duller.

178 **RED-LEGGED SHAG** 76/?cm
Phalacrocorax gaimardi RR MAP 178 **Text page 304**

178a ADULT BREEDING: At distance upperparts appear grey, with paler grey underparts. At closer range, white patches to sides of head and silvery wing-coverts are easily seen. Note red feet.

178b ADULT NON-BREEDING: As 178a but lacks white filoplumes to head. Upperparts marginally darker.

178c IMMATURE: Resembles 178b but brownish-grey above, with white chin, grey-brown breast and white underparts.

159b
159c
159d
159b
159a
159a
159d
171c
171b
171a
171a
171d
171d
172a
172b
172b
172c
172b
172c
172b
172b
178c
178c
178b
178a
178b
178c

Plate 51

FRIGATEBIRDS
(see also Figs 15 and 16, pp. 312 and 315)

187 **MAGNIFICENT FRIGATEBIRD** 101/238cm
Fregata magnificens TPO, TAO MAP 187 **Text page 310**

187a ADULT MALE: Usually differs from adult male Great Frigatebird in blackish feet and lack of pronounced bar on upperwing, but some overlap of these characters occurs; separation at sea perhaps impossible. See also adult male Ascension Frigatebird (p. 308).

187b ADULT FEMALE: Differs from adult female Great Frigatebird in black chin and throat, and narrow white tips across axillaries forming three or four diagnostic wavy lines on underwing. This useful character is present to some degree in all plumages except first- and second-stage juveniles and adult males.

187c JUVENILE (FIRST STAGE): Head and underparts white, with narrow incomplete breast band enclosing triangular-shaped belly patch.

187d JUVENILE (SECOND STAGE): Probably indistinguishable from 'second-stage' juvenile white-breasted Great Frigatebirds, but at Galapagos Is, one of the few places where two are sympatric, the tawny-breasted form of Great occurs and thus they are separable. All subsequent stages, except adult males, have diagnostic pale tips on axillaries as noted in 187b.

187e SUB-ADULT MALE: Legs dull red. Differs from 188e below in shape of mottled white horseshoe on breast and diagnostic pale tips to axillaries.

187f SUB-ADULT FEMALE: As adult female except belly mottled with white.

188 **GREAT FRIGATEBIRD** 93/218cm
Fregata minor TPO, TAO, TIO MAP 188 **Text page 313**

188a ADULT MALE: Typical examples differ from most 187a in pronounced alar bar and reddish or brown legs (see also adult male Ascension Frigatebird).

188b ADULT FEMALE: Differs from adult female Lesser, Christmas and Magnificent Frigatebirds in whitish-grey chin and throat and wholly dark axillaries, a character present in both sexes at all ages.

188c JUVENILE (FIRST STAGE): Head and upper breast tawny or white (varies between populations), divided from white belly by variable brownish breast band. Differs from similar first-stage juvenile Lesser Frigatebird in dark axillaries and whiter belly. See also juvenile Christmas Frigatebird (p. 310), which has indistinct white 'spur' on underwing.

188d JUVENILE (SECOND STAGE): As first-stage juvenile but lacks breast band. Tawny-breasted forms, the more commonplace type, are safely distinguishable from second-stage Magnificent Frigatebirds, which have white heads and upper breasts. White-breasted form, however, is probably indistinguishable until white spurs of Magnificent appear on axillaries.

188e SUB-ADULT MALE: Mostly black except for inverted whitish horseshoe across lower breast. Differs from corresponding male Magnificent and Lesser Frigatebirds in wholly black axillaries.

188f SUB-ADULT FEMALE: As adult female except for mottled white belly patch.

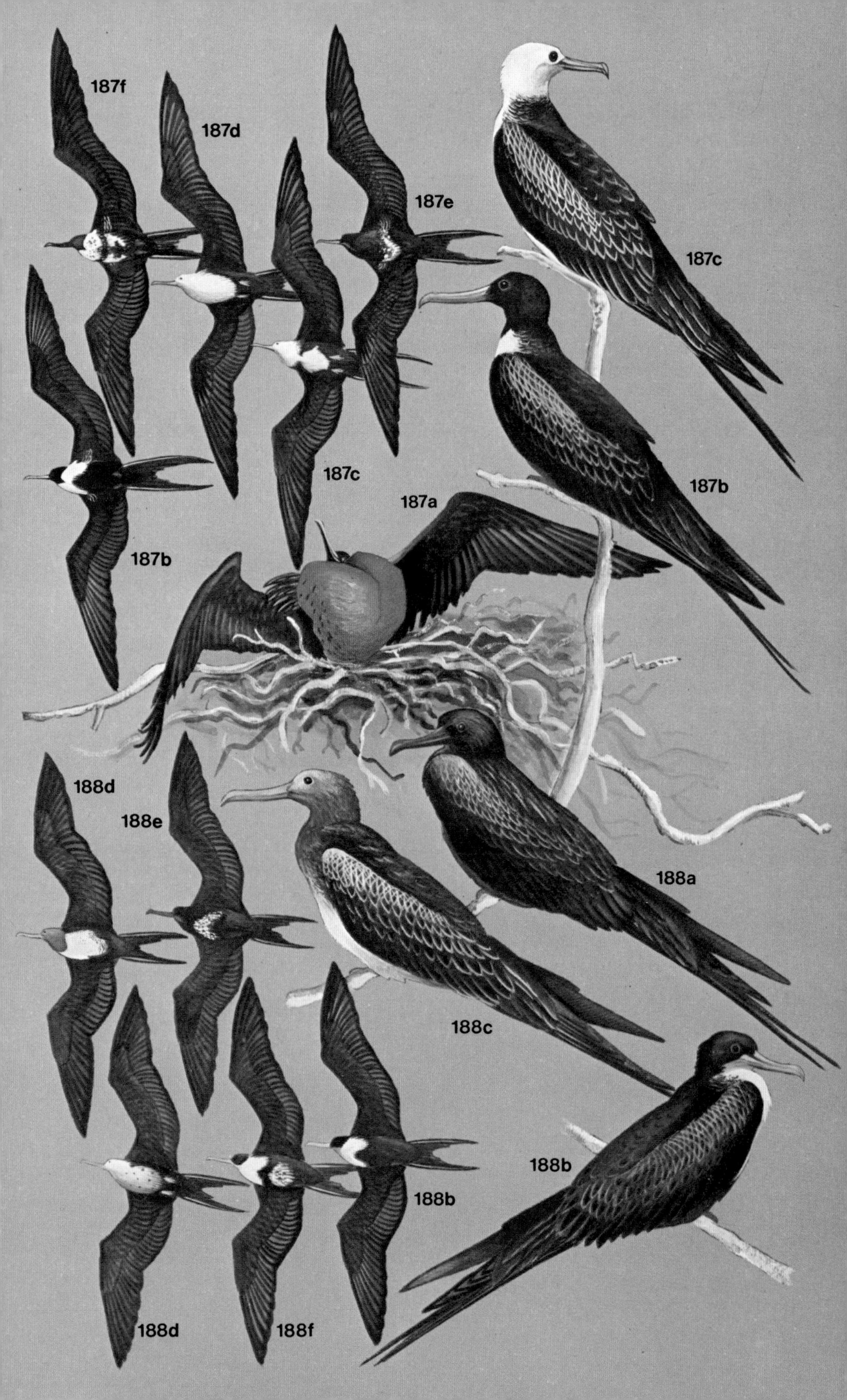
187f
187d
187e
187c
187c
187b
187a
187b
188d
188e
188a
188c
188b
188b
188d
188f

Plate 52

FRIGATEBIRDS
(see also Figs 17, 13, 14, pp. 316, 309, 311)

189 LESSER FRIGATEBIRD 76/184cm
Fregata ariel TO MAP 189 **Text page 315**

189a ADULT MALE: Easiest of all frigatebirds to identify; wholly blackish except for white flank patch and 'spur' across axillaries.

189b ADULT FEMALE: Safely separable from female Great Frigatebird (p. 313) by black chin and throat and white 'spur' across axillaries. See also Christmas Frigatebird (p. 310).

189c JUVENILE (FIRST STAGE): Differs from corresponding Great Frigatebird (p. 313) in darker tawny head and white 'spur' on underwing.

189d JUVENILE (SECOND STAGE): Closely resembles juvenile Great Frigatebird (p. 313); differs in white 'spur' on axillaries and blacker belly. Differs from juvenile Christmas Frigatebird (186c below) in more extensive black on belly, terminating at lower breast in inverted V.

189e SUB-ADULT MALE: As adult male except white flank and 'spur' are linked across mottled black and white breast.

189f SUB-ADULT FEMALE: Separated from corresponding Great Frigatebird (p. 313) by darker chin and throat, white 'spur' across axillaries. From similar-stage Christmas Frigatebird (p. 310) by shorter white 'spur' on underwing and blacker belly, terminating at lower breast in inverted V.

185 ASCENSION FRIGATEBIRD 91/198cm
Fregata aquila TAO MAP 185 **Text page 308**

185a ADULT MALE (DARK MORPH): Probably indistinguishable from adult male Magnificent Frigatebird (p. 310) at sea, although ranges not known to overlap.

185b ADULT FEMALE (DARK MORPH): Plumage mostly blackish, except for brownish hindcollar extending broadly across upper breast as continuous band and pale alar bar on upperwing.

185c ADULT FEMALE (PALE MORPH): As dark morph except for white lower breast, belly and 'spur' on axillaries. (It is not known whether birds breeding in this plumage represent polymorphic phase, rare mutant or simply transitional stage in the slow and gradual darkening of plumage, with some birds breeding before 'adult' plumage attained.)

185d JUVENILE (SECOND STAGE): White head divided from white lower breast by broad brown band; note white rectangular 'spur' on axillaries.

186 CHRISTMAS FRIGATEBIRD 94/218cm
other: Andrews's Frigatebird
Fregata andrewsi RR MAP 186 **Text page 310**

186a ADULT MALE: Unique; mostly black except for diagnostic belly patch.

186b ADULT FEMALE: Differs from corresponding Great Frigatebird (p. 313) in black chin and throat and white 'spur' on underwing. See notes above under 189b; note in particular extensive white belly.

186c JUVENILE: Differs from first-stage juvenile Lesser Frigatebird (p. 315) in white belly and broader breast band. Separation from juvenile Great Frigatebird (p. 313) more difficult, but that species lacks white on axillaries.

186d SUB-ADULT MALE: As adult male but lower breast scaled black and white.

189d
189f
189b
189a
189e
189c
189b
189a
185b
185d
185d
185c
185b
185a
186d
186b
186c
186b
186a
186c
186a

Plate 53

PHALAROPES

192 WILSON'S PHALAROPE 22/36cm
Phalaropus tricolor WR

MAP 192 **Text page 319**

192a ADULT FEMALE BREEDING: Unmistakable; boldly patterned head, neck and upperparts, underparts mostly white.

192b ADULT MALE BREEDING: Similar to 192a but much duller.

192c ADULT NON-BREEDING: Sexes alike. Upperparts pale grey, rump white; underparts mostly white. Distinguished from 190 or 191 by larger size, longer, thinner bill and lack of white in wing.

192d JUVENILE: As 192c but upperparts buffer, sides of breast often duskier.

191 RED-NECKED PHALAROPE 17/34cm
other: Northern Phalarope
Phalaropus lobatus WR

MAP 191 **Text page 318**

191a ADULT FEMALE BREEDING: Head mostly blackish-slate with bright chestnut patches on sides of neck and breast; chin white. Dark upperparts distinctly striped with buff. Underparts mostly white.

191b ADULT MALE BREEDING: Similar to 191a but duller.

191c ADULT NON-BREEDING: Sexes alike, differs from 190b in much darker upperparts. In autumn beware of moulting and juvenile Red (Grey) Phalaropes, which can have atypical upperparts (190c below).

191d JUVENILE: Resembles adult non-breeding but back and scapulars broadly edged tawny-buff.

190 RED PHALAROPE 20/37cm
other: Grey Phalarope
Phalaropus fulicarius WR

MAP 190 **Text page 318**

190a ADULT FEMALE BREEDING: Crown and chin black, sides of face white. Dark upperparts broadly edged tawny-buff; underparts wholly brick-red.

190b ADULT NON-BREEDING: Sexes alike. Bill black. Upperparts mostly grey, without the pronounced blackish streaks found in 191c. Underparts mostly white.

190c ADULT LATE SUMMER/AUTUMN: Bill blackish. Darker-backed than 190b, sides of rump rusty. Underparts mostly white, upper breast buff or grey. These darker-backed individuals occurring on passage during Sept–Oct are likely to be mistaken for 191c above. See also p. 318 for description of juveniles, which have dark backs with buff streaks.

192c
192a
192d
192b
192a
191a
191d
191b
191c
191c
191a
190b
190b
190c
190a
190a

Plate 54

SKUAS/JAEGERS

199 POMARINE SKUA 54/124cm
other: Pomarine Jaeger
Stercorarius pomarinus WR MAP 199 **Text page 324**

199a ADULT BREEDING (LIGHT MORPH): Differs from smaller, rather falcon-like Arctic Skua in heavier, more powerful jizz and twisted, spoon-shaped, tail streamers.
199b ADULT (DARK MORPH): Mostly dark brown.
199c JUVENILE (LIGHT MORPH): Differs from Arctic Skua in jizz and barring on rump and uppertail-coverts. Note blunt tail tips.
199d IMMATURE (LIGHT MORPH): Differs from adult in barred axillaries, underwing- and tail-coverts. Note short, blunt streamers.
199e ADULT NON-BREEDING: Much as immature but underwing-coverts uniformly dark.

195 GREAT SKUA 58/150cm
other: Bonxie
Catharacta skua NAO MAP 195 **Text page 321**

195a ADULT: Unlike South Polar Skua, there is little contrast between upperparts and head; many lack dark cap.
195b JUVENILE: Duller than adult; underparts usually more tawny.

197 SOUTH POLAR SKUA 53/127cm
other: McCormick's Skua
Catharacta maccormicki WR MAP 197 **Text page 322**

197a ADULT (LIGHT MORPH): Obvious contrast between uniform upperparts and paler head and underparts.
197b ADULT (INTERMEDIATE MORPH): As light morph but head and underbody straw or buff-brown; note uniform hindcollar.
197c ADULT (DARK MORPH): Closely resembles juvenile Great Skua but nape paler, forming indistinct collar; most show paler area at base of bill. See structure in FHJ (p. 322).
197d JUVENILE (PALE MORPH): Bill blue, tip black. Plumage much as adult but with head and underbody greyer, upperparts uniform or with paler edges as illustrated opposite.

196 CHILEAN SKUA 58/?cm
Catharacta chilensis RR MAP 196 **Text page 321**

196 ADULT: Combination of dark cap, and cinnamon underbody and underwing-coverts diagnostic.

198 ANTARCTIC SKUA 63/?cm
Catharacta antarctica SO MAP 198 **Text page 323**

198 ADULT (*C.a. lonnbergi*): Resembles northern *C. skua* but colouration more uniform; head lacks dark cap. See main text for other sub-species.

199a
199b
199d
199e
199c
199e
199a
195a
195b
195a
197d
197a
198
197b
197c
196

Plate 55

SKUAS/JAEGERS

200 **ARCTIC SKUA** 45/105cm
other: Parasitic Jaeger
Stercorarius parasiticus WR MAP 200 **Text page 325**

200a ADULT BREEDING (LIGHT MORPH): Differs from Long-tailed Skua in more diffuse cap, lack of distinct trailing edge on upperwing, brown (not greyish-brown) plumage. Note overall structure.

200b ADULT BREEDING (DARK MORPH): Mostly dark fulvous-brown.

200c ADULT BREEDING (INTERMEDIATE MORPH): Variable; almost continuous gradation between 200a and 200b; note breast band, a feature never found in breeding Long-tailed Skua.

200d ADULT NON-BREEDING (LIGHT MORPH): Resembles immature but underwing-coverts and axillaries lack barring.

200e JUVENILE (INTERMEDIATE MORPH): Differs from corresponding Long-tailed Skua in less pronounced barring on tail-coverts and underwing. Note four white primary shafts' overall structure and pointed tail projections.

200f JUVENILE (LIGHT MORPH): Much as 200e but paler.

200g SUB-ADULT (INTERMEDIATE MORPH): Differs from non-breeding adult in shorter tail projections and barred underwing-coverts.

201 **LONG-TAILED SKUA** 54/80cm
other: Long-tailed Jaeger
Stercorarius longicaudus WR MAP 201 **Text page 326**

201a ADULT BREEDING: Differs from light morph Arctic Skua in neater cap, greyer tone, distinct trailing edge on upperwing.

201b ADULT (MOULTING FROM BREEDING TO NON-BREEDING, late Aug–Nov): Differs from 201a in dusky sides to face and neck, paler edges and darker feather centres to upperparts, barring on underparts, and conspicuous white bars on tail-coverts.

JUVENILES: The three morphs differ from corresponding Arctic Skuas in pale legs, only two white primary shafts in upperwing, and blunt tail projections. Each morph further differs in:

201c JUVENILE (LIGHT MORPH): Distinctive; combination of whitish head, and conspicuously barred undertail-coverts and underwing-coverts diagnostic.

201d JUVENILE (DARK MORPH): Upper- and undertail-coverts usually conspicuously barred in equal black and white divisions; note also distinctive barring on underwing-coverts and axillaries.

201e JUVENILE (INTERMEDIATE MORPH): Much as 201d but with partial breast band and indistinct cap.

201f ADULT BREEDING (DARK MORPH): Differs from 200b in less white in upperwing and overall structure.

200d
200g
200c
200a
200a
200e
200b
200e
200f
201d
201b
201a
201e
201c
201f

Plate 56

DARK-BACKED GULLS

202 **PACIFIC GULL** 62/147cm
Larus pacificus RR MAP 202 **Text page 328**

202a ADULT BREEDING: The only adult black-backed gull in Australia with dark tail band. Note massive bill.

202b JUVENILE: Resembles 219b below but, if seen clearly, massive bill with pink base and dark tip diagnostic.

202c THIRD-WINTER: White head shows dusky streaks; saddle and upperwings blackish with brownish cast; dusky markings on breast. Tail band ill-defined.

219 **KELP GULL** 58/135cm
other: Dominican/Southern Black-backed Gull
Larus dominicanus SO MAP 219 **Text page 343**

219a ADULT BREEDING: The only large, black-backed and wholly white-tailed gull breeding in the southern hemisphere.

219b JUVENILE: Differs from 202b in smaller size and smaller, blackish bill (ranges overlap in Australia).

219c THIRD-WINTER: Differs from 202c in smaller unbanded bill and white tail. See also Band-tailed Gull (p. 333).

210 **BLACK-TAILED GULL** 47/?cm
other: Japanese/Temminck's Gull
Larus crassirostris RR MAP 210 **Text page 333**

210a ADULT BREEDING: Saddle and upperwings blackish-grey, primaries appearing wholly dark without white mirrors. Tail shows prominent black band.

210b JUVENILE: Mostly rich brown above, whiter below, with almost wholly black tail and a flesh-coloured bill with black tip.

210c SECOND-WINTER: Bill yellow with black subterminal tip. Resembles breeding adult, but saddle and upperwing somewhat browner with faint streaking on head and full-width tail band.

202b
202c
202b
202a
202a
219c
219c
219b
219a
219b
219a
210b
210c
210b
210c
210a
210a

Plate 57

DARK-BACKED PACIFIC GULLS

218 WESTERN GULL 64/137cm
(Includes Yellow-footed Gull *L.o. livens*)
Larus occidentalis NPO MAP 218 **Text page 342**

218a ADULT BREEDING (*L.o. occidentalis*): Differs from Herring and California Gulls (p. 337, p. 341) in darker mantle, different wingtip pattern and dusky trailing edge to underwing. (Non-breeders similar except for very faint streaking on nape and sides of head.) See also Glaucous-winged Gull (p. 345).

218b ADULT BREEDING (*L.o. wymani*): Darker-mantled than nominate, showing little contrast between wingtip and mantle.

218c ADULT NON-BREEDING: Typical examples differ little from breeding adults. Those with dense streaking on head and nape, with proportionately larger eye (as illustrated opposite), may be nominate Western × Glaucous-winged hybrids (non-breeding *L.o. wymani* have some grey nape streaks but are not sympatric with Glaucous-winged) (Stallcup, pers. comm.).

218d FIRST-WINTER: Difficult to separate from similar-stage Herring Gull (p. 337). Differs mainly in bulk and jizz with generally darker grey-brown plumage; mantle, scapulars and back appear spotted. In flight inner primaries usually lack conspicuously paler 'window' found in Herring Gull.

218e THIRD-WINTER: Differs from second-winter Herring Gull (p. 337) in darker grey saddle and mostly black tail.

220 SLATY-BACKED GULL 64/137cm
Larus schistisagus NPO MAP 220 **Text page 343**

220a ADULT BREEDING: Differs from Western Gull in darker saddle and upperwings, and broader, more conspicuous white trailing edge to wing and tertials. The blackish tips to outer 4–5 primaries usually separated from slate-grey upperwing by an indistinct whitish band. See also Herring Gull *L.a. vagae* (p. 337).

220b ADULT NON-BREEDING: As 220a but head and hindneck streaked grey-brown.

220c FIRST-WINTER: Differs from corresponding Western Gull in whiter head and paler underparts, with pale 'window' on inner primaries and broader dark band along trailing edge of upperwing.

220d FIRST-SUMMER: Resembles more closely a large, bleached-out Herring Gull (p. 337), thus much greyer and paler than any stage of Western Gull.

218d
218e
218b
218c
218a
218b
218e
220b
218d
220d
220c
220d
220a

Plate 58

HERRING GULL
(see also Plate 62, Fig. 214a)

214 **HERRING GULL** 61/139cm
Larus argentatus NPO, NAO MAP 214 **Text page 337**

NOTE: Unless otherwise stated, following descriptions refer to *L.a. argenteus.*

214a ADULT BREEDING: The most familiar large gull of the North Atlantic. Could be confused with much smaller Common Gull (p. 336) but wingtip pattern and bare parts different. Thumbnail shows difference in underwing pattern of all Herring Gull races from Lesser Black-backed Gull (a useful field character for separating dark-backed races from paler-backed races of Lesser Black-backed).

214b ADULT NON-BREEDING: Head and sides of breast streaked brownish-grey (varies individually but normally heavy).

214c JUVENILE: Differs from similar Lesser Black-backed Gull (p. 340) in pale 'window' on inner primaries and narrower, less dark, subterminal band along trailing edge of wing.

214d FIRST-SUMMER: Upperparts and upperwings much paler and lighter grey than any stage of Lesser Black-backed (p. 340).

214e SECOND-WINTER: Mantle, scapulars and back more or less clear grey, giving 'saddle' effect. Wings and tail resemble first-summer but paler.

214f THIRD-WINTER: Resembles non-breeding adult but more extensive black on wingtips extends to primary-coverts and alula. Inner secondaries, tertials and tail often sullied with brown.

214g ADULT NON-BREEDING (*L.a. taimyrensis*): Legs pink or yellowish. Head only faintly streaked greyish-brown; grey upperparts intermediate in tone between *L.a. vagae* and *L.a. heuglini.*

214h ADULT NON-BREEDING (*L.a. heuglini*): Legs yellow. Upperparts and upperwing colour almost as dark as *L.f. graellsii* (p. 340) but winter ranges do not normally overlap. Likely to be confused with *L.f. fuscus* in wintering quarters, but in latter head is almost white with different underwing pattern (see thumbnails opposite).

216 **LESSER BLACK-BACKED GULL** 56/124cm
Larus fuscus NAO MAP 216 **Text page 340**

216a ADULT BREEDING: Underwing differs from 214a in dusky subterminal band along secondaries. See also Great Black-backed Gull (p. 344).

216a
214a
214a
214a
214a
214b
214f
214d
214e
214g
214d
214c
214h

Plate 59

BLACK-BACKED GULLS

216 LESSER BLACK-BACKED GULL 56/124cm
Larus fuscus NAO

MAP 216 **Text page 340**

216b ADULT NON-BREEDING (*L.f. fuscus*): Winters mainly Red Sea S to Kenya. White head, blackish saddle and upperwings, and underwing pattern enable ready separation from dark races of Herring Gull (p. 337). Smaller size, different wingtip pattern and yellow legs distinguish it from 221a below.

216c ADULT NON-BREEDING (*L.f. graellsii*): Winters mainly NW Europe S to western Mediterranean and Nigeria. Colour of saddle and upperwing enables ready separation from 221b below. Beware dark races of Herring Gull (p. 337) (see Fig. 216a, Plate 58, for underwing pattern comparison).

216d JUVENILE (races probably not distinguishable): Differs from both 221c below and juvenile Herring Gull in generally darker upperparts and upperwing. Innermost primaries lack paler 'windows' of those species, and the darker greater coverts form broader dark trailing edge to upperwing; with practice, these are excellent flight characters.

216e FIRST-SUMMER (*L.f. graellsii*): Differs from 221 below in smaller size. Upperparts and upperwings lack distinct contrast of that species, with rather darker head and sides of breast. In flight differs in broader trailing edge and lack of paler 'window' on innermost primaries.

216f SECOND-SUMMER (*L.f. graellsii*): Saddle usually clear slate-grey (black in *L.f. fuscus*) with inner wing-coverts fading to rich sepia-brown; rump conspicuously white.

221 GREAT BLACK-BACKED GULL 75/160cm
other: Greater Black-backed Gull
Larus marinus NAO

MAP 221 **Text page 344**

221a ADULT BREEDING: Differs from breeding *L.f. fuscus* in larger size pink legs and wingtip pattern.

221b ADULT NON-BREEDING: Differs from *L.f. graellsii* and *L.f. intermedius* (p. 340) in diagnostic 'mirror' pattern, blackish saddle and upperwings, whiter head and pink (not yellow) legs.

221c JUVENILE: See notes under 216d above. Differs from similar but smaller juvenile Herring Gull (p. 337) in whiter head and chequered saddle contrasting with paler rump and base of tail.

221d FIRST-WINTER: Head whiter and upperparts and upperwing-coverts more distinctly chequered black and white than in either first-winter Herring or Lesser Black-backed Gulls (p. 337, p. 340).

221e SECOND-WINTER: Resembles the darker-headed second-winter Herring Gull, but has darker saddle with heavy brown subterminal tips forming more contrasting pattern. At all ages proportionately larger head and bill are useful field characters.

216d
216d
216f
216b
216c
216e
221a
221d
221e
221c
221b

Plate 60

NORTH AMERICAN GULLS

206 **HEERMANN'S GULL** 49/120cm
Larus heermannii RR — MAP 206 **Text page 331**

206a ADULT BREEDING: Unmistakable; the only gull within its range which has white head, dusky underparts, black tail and red bill.

206b ADULT NON-BREEDING: As breeding adult except for ill-defined dusky hood.

206c FIRST-WINTER: Mostly dusky-brown with paler, olive or tawny-brown, wing-coverts. At long range, flight shape and colour can suggest skua spp. (p. 320).

206d SECOND-WINTER: Much as non-breeding adult except bill more orange, plumage browner in tone; some show white in primary-coverts.

215 **THAYER'S GULL** 59/?cm
Larus thayeri RR — MAP 215 **Text page 339**

215a ADULT BREEDING: Differs from Herring Gull in combination of dark iris and less extensive and blackish-grey wingtip with whitish outer primaries to underwing. Legs, saddle and upperwings usually darker than Herring; structure differs in slighter bill and longer-winged, more delicate jizz. See Kumlien's Gull (p. 348).

215b ADULT NON-BREEDING: Head, sides of neck and upper breast streaked grey-brown.

215c FIRST-WINTER: Differs from similarly-aged Herring Gull in uniform grey-brown or chocolate-brown primaries and less contrasting mantle, scapulars and back; underside of outer primaries whitish. Kumlien's Gull (p. 348) can approach Thayer's in darkness of primaries, but mantle, scapulars and back usually more contrasting with whitish tips and barring (greyer in Thayer's).

217 **CALIFORNIA GULL** 54/131cm
Larus californicus RR — MAP 217 **Text page 341**

217a ADULT BREEDING: Smaller than Herring Gull (p. 337) with yellowish legs and darker saddle and upperwings; bill usually with black and red spot on lower mandible. Ring-billed Gull (p. 335) is smaller, with shorter, banded bill and paler saddle and upperwings.

217b ADULT NON-BREEDING: As 217a but with conspicuous necklace of dusky spots on nape, quite unlike the smudgy nape and head of Herring Gull (p. 337). Recalls smaller Ring-billed Gull (p. 335) but that species lacks red on bill, has brighter yellow legs, pale eye and paler grey saddle and upperwings.

217c FIRST-WINTER: Black-tipped pink bill and structure separate it from both Herring and Western Gulls (p. 337, p. 342). Ring-billed Gulls of similar age have different upperwing and white tail with narrower black subterminal band.

206a
206b
206d
206a
206d
206c
206c
215c
215a
215b
215c
215c
217c
217a
217c
217b

Plate 61

GULLS

212 RING-BILLED GULL 49/124cm
Larus delawarensis MAP 212 **Text page 335**

212a ADULT BREEDING: Differs from 213 below in banded bill, paler upperparts and upperwings, smaller white 'mirrors', and more angled crown giving 'fiercer' expression, a characteristic present at all ages. Bill usually longer, more robust, with 'heavy' tip.

212b ADULT NON-BREEDING: Differs from 213b below in banded bill, heavier spots (not streaks) on nape, paler upperparts and upperwings, and smaller white 'mirrors'.

212c FIRST-WINTER: Differs from 213c in more defined markings on nape, sides of breast and flanks, more pronounced wing pattern, paler saddle and less clear-cut tail band. When perched, heavy tipped bill, and darker tertials lacking prominent pale fringes, are additional characters.

212d FIRST-SUMMER: Banded bill pink or yellowish. Nape and sides of breast lightly spotted. Tertials show ragged buffish edges, particularly lowermost on closed wing, but never as prominent as in Common Gull. This feature coupled with paler mantle and scapulars an excellent character when searching through perched flocks.

212e SECOND-WINTER: Differs from 213d in banded bill, heavier spots (not clouding) on nape and paler mantle, scapulars and back. In flight, best characters are one 'mirror' (not two) on outer primaries and partial tail band. (In western North America beware of 213f.)

213 COMMON GULL 43/120cm
other: Mew Gull
Larus canus MAP 213 **Text page 336**

213a ADULT BREEDING: Legs and bill yellowish-green, iris dark. Crown more rounded than 212a above, imparting more gentle expression; bill usually smaller, less robust, with tapered tip.

213b ADULT NON-BREEDING: Differs from 212b in dark iris, clouded head and nape, darker upperparts and upperwings, larger white 'mirrors' and more prominent white tertial fringe when perched.

213c FIRST-WINTER: Head and underparts less marked than 212c; rump lacks obvious spots; saddle darker, tertials paler with broader fringes, and more clear-cut tail band.

213d SECOND-WINTER: Differs from 212d above in paler nape, darker saddle, two white 'mirrors' on outer primaries and wholly white tail.

L.c. brachyrhynchus: Confined to western North America, adult (not illustrated) is smaller and darker-mantled than either nominate or Ring-billed Gull.

213e FIRST-WINTER (*L.c. brachyrhynchus*): Confined to western North America. Much browner and darker than either nominate or 212c.

213f SECOND-WINTER (*L.c. brachyrhynchus*): As 213d but saddle darker; partial tail band. Differs from local Ring-billed Gulls of same age in two (not one) 'mirrors' and darker saddle. See structure in main text.

244 SABINE'S GULL 34/89cm
Larus sabini PO, AO MAP 244 **Text page 361**

244a ADULT BREEDING: Unmistakable. Dark grey hood can appear black; striking tri-coloured upperwings.

244b ADULT NON-BREEDING: As 244a but black on head restricted to patch or half-collar over nape, sometimes extending to ear-coverts.

244c JUVENILE: Head appears wholly dark at long range; distinctive tri-coloured upperwing pattern. Dusky bar on underwing varies considerably, but if present diagnostic.

212b
212c
212d
212a
212c
212e
213d
213c
213c
213a
213b
213e
213e
213f
244b
244a
244c
244c

Plate 62

WHITE-WINGED GULLS

223 **GLAUCOUS GULL** 71/137cm
Larus hyperboreus AR, NPO, NAO MAP 223 **Text page 346**

223a ADULT BREEDING: A large, powerful species distinguished from 224a below by larger size, bill proportions and, at close range, yellow eye-ring. Lacks black on wing tips.

223b ADULT NON-BREEDING: Head, neck and sides of breast clouded and streaked, often densely, with brownish-grey.

223c FIRST-WINTER: Bill colour diagnostic in large gulls. Plumage possibly browner or more gingery in tone than 224c, but there is much individual variation. See also Glaucous-winged Gull (p. 345).

223d THIRD-WINTER: Yellow bill usually has indistinct dusky marks near tip. Mantle, scapulars and back pale grey with pale brown or whitish tips.

224 **ICELAND GULL** 61/127cm
(Includes Kumlien's Gull, 224X)
Larus glaucoides NAO MAP 224 **Text page 347**

224a ADULT BREEDING: Differs from 223a in red orbital ring (difficult to see at any range). Otherwise similar except for smaller size, lighter jizz and perhaps in more silvery-white appearance on saddle. Wings project well past tail when perched.

224b ADULT NON-BREEDING: As 223b above but usually smaller with proportionately smaller bill.

224c FIRST-WINTER: Differs from 223c above in darker bill. Plumage similar but perhaps with finer barring and, usually, more distinct whitish terminal band.

224d THIRD-WINTER: Mantle, scapulars and back pale grey, rump and tail mostly white; underparts faintly clouded grey-brown. Upperwing greyer, particularly median coverts.

224X KUMLIEN'S GULL: Differs from 224a in variable grey or brown outer webs and subterminal bars on outer 5 primaries. See main text for differences at other ages.

246 **IVORY GULL** 43/110cm
Pagophila eburnea AR MAP 246 **Text page 363**

246a ADULT BREEDING: Wholly ivory-white; unmistakable.

246b FIRST-WINTER: Appears white at distance. Amount of black on face and upperparts varies individually; all have dark tips to primaries and tail.

NOTE: Whilst typical Glaucous and Iceland Gulls are relatively straightforward to separate (given comparative experience), hybrids and albinos present obvious complications. The two anomalous plumages shown opposite (214X and 214a) are by no means typical.

214X HERRING GULL × GLAUCOUS GULL HYBRID: Superficially resembles both 223 and 224 but note darker tail band. All hybrids retain darker ear-coverts, faint secondary bars, darker primaries, banded tails or combinations of these characters.

214a HERRING GULL (albino): Pure white birds are almost certainly albinos, which normally retain typical bare parts colours; this first-winter Herring Gull has a wholly dark bill. Adults are more difficult, perhaps impossible, to separate, although crown shape and bill proportions should be useful.

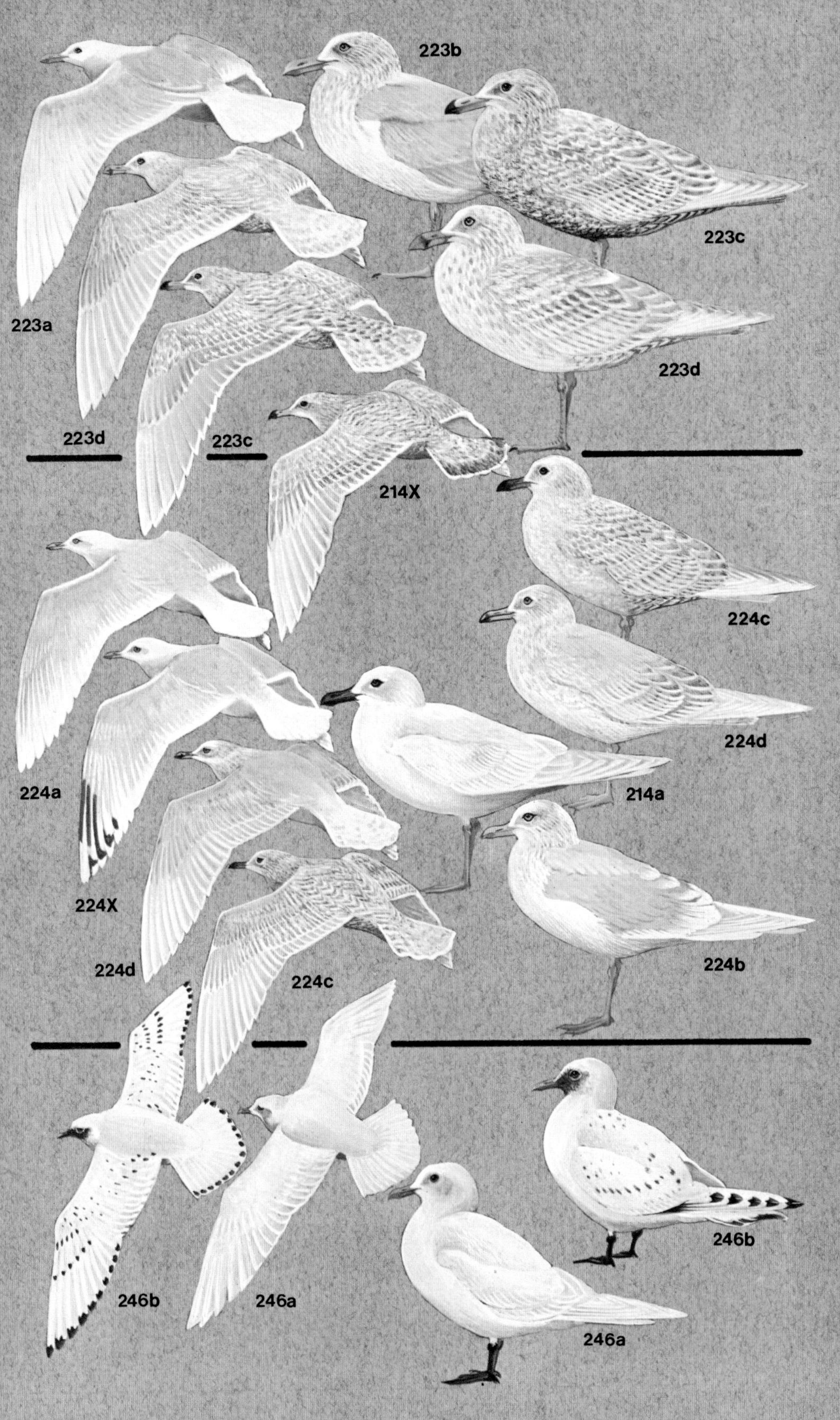

223a
223b
223c
223d
223d
223c
214X
224c
224a
224d
214a
224X
224b
224d
224c
246b
246a
246b
246a

Plate 63

GULLS

236 **BLACK-HEADED GULL** 40/92cm
Larus ridibundus MAP 236 **Text page 356**

236a ADULT SUMMER: Only European gull with dark brown hood (extends only to hindcrown).

236b ADULT NON-BREEDING: As 236a except head white with blackish ear spot. Underwing differs from all stages of 238 in dusky inner primaries.

236c FIRST-WINTER: Differs from 238c mainly in larger size, bill and underwing pattern.

236d FIRST-SUMMER: As 236c but with partial brown hood; wing and tail patterns faded.

238 **BONAPARTE'S GULL** 35/82cm
Larus philadelphia MAP 238 **Text page 357**

238a ADULT BREEDING: Smaller than other North American hooded gulls, and has white leading edge to outer wing.

238b ADULT NON-BREEDING: Resembles miniature 236b; differs in black bill and black-tipped white primaries on underwing.

238c FIRST-WINTER: Differs from 236c mainly in underwing pattern, grey nape, deeper grey mantle, scapulars and back and darker carpal bar.

238d FIRST-SUMMER: Resembles 238c but with partial blackish-grey hood.

239 **LITTLE GULL** 27/64cm
Larus minutus MAP 239 **Text page 357**

239a ADULT BREEDING: Smallest gull. Combination of size, black hood and blackish underwing diagnostic.

239b ADULT NON-BREEDING: Small size, unmarked upperwing and blackish underwing with broad, white trailing edge diagnostic.

239c FIRST-WINTER: Small size and blackish M across upper surfaces distinguish this species from all other gulls except Ross's (p. 361), which however has distinctive jizz and much whiter head.

239d FIRST-SUMMER: Generally as 239c but with partial hood, broken tail band and much faded upperwing pattern.

236d
236b
236c
236a
236d
236c
238c
238c
238d
238b
238d
238a
239a
239c
239a
239c
239b
239d

Plate 64

AMERICAN GULLS

226 LAUGHING GULL 40/103cm
Larus atricilla AO, PO MAP 226 **Text page 349**

226a ADULT BREEDING: See notes in main text on structural differences between this and Franklin's Gull (p. 352), which allow any age to be separated. Present stage differs from 230a in blacker wingtip without prominent white apical spots or white dividing band.

226b ADULT NON-BREEDING: Differs from 230b in less pronounced partial hood and wingtip pattern.

226c FIRST-WINTER: Differs from 230c in less pronounced partial hood, dusky breast and flanks, and more extensive tail band.

230 FRANKLIN'S GULL 35/90cm
Larus pipixcan MAP 230 **Text page 352**

230a ADULT BREEDING: Differs from larger, more rakish Laughing Gull in prominent white tips to primaries; black subterminal tips separated from grey upperwing by whitish band.

230b ADULT NON-BREEDING: Differs from Laughing Gull in wingtip pattern and more pronounced, partial hood.

230c FIRST-WINTER: Has more defined partial hood than Laughing Gull with whiter breast and flanks; tail band less extensive (note white outer feathers).

222 GLAUCOUS-WINGED GULL 65/134cm
Larus glaucescens NPO MAP 222 **Text page 345**

222a ADULT BREEDING: Differs from congeners in grey primary tips. See Glaucous, Herring and Western Gulls (p. 346, p. 337, p. 342).

222b ADULT NON-BREEDING: As breeding adult except for streaking on head.

222c FIRST-WINTER: Differs from first-winter Glaucous Gull (p. 346) in black bill and uniform tail. Like that species has characteristic 'blunt end' when perched, wings hardly projecting beyond tail.

226c
226c
226c
226b
226a
230a
230b
230c
230c
222b
222a
222c

Plate 65

GULLS

234 **BLACK-BILLED GULL** 37/?cm
other: Buller's Gull
Larus bulleri RR — MAP 234 **Text page 355**

234a ADULT: Sympatric with 231 in New Zealand. Present species is much paler in general appearance with white leading edge to outer wing; pale eye and blackish bill.

234b JUVENILE: Often confused with 231b due to black-tipped pinkish bill. Head pattern, however, shows distinct dusky bar over crown and dusky ear spot, characters never found in 231b; wing pattern also different.

234c FIRST-WINTER: As 234b but nape whiter, saddle mostly clear grey.

231 **SILVER GULL** 41/93cm
other: Red-billed Gull (includes Hartlaub's Gull, 231X)
Larus novaehollandiae — MAP 231 **Text page 352**

231a ADULT (*L.n.novaehollandiae*): The only small gull in Australia. Range overlaps with 234 in New Zealand but separable by differences in upperwing pattern.

231X ADULT BREEDING (*L.n. hartlaubii*): Probably a separate species. Restricted to Namibia and Western Cape Province, South Africa, where range overlaps with Grey-headed Gull. During breeding has pale lavender-grey hood and darker necklace; note dark iris. Limited hybridisation occurs at mixed colonies with Grey-headed.

231b JUVENILE: See 234b above. Differs from 228b in whiter head and tail.

231c FIRST-WINTER: Unlike 234c and 228c, white head lacks ear spot. (In South Africa *L.n. hartlaubii* differs further from 228c in bill colour and whiter tail.)

228 **GREY-HEADED GULL** 42/102cm
Larus cirrocephalus — MAP 228 **Text page 351**

228a ADULT BREEDING: Grey hood, concentrated along posterior margin, coupled with wing pattern diagnostic throughout most of range; beware breeding 231X in South Africa.

228b JUVENILE: Differs from 231b in bill colour, darker head, wider tail band and heavier markings on wing-coverts.

228c FIRST-WINTER: Differs from 231c above in bill colour, ear spot and wider tail band.

228d FIRST-SUMMER: Partial grey hood; wings and tail as 228c but faded and worn.

228e SECOND-WINTER: Resembles non-breeding adult (not illustrated) but with indistinct trailing edge along secondaries and smaller 'mirrors' on outermost primaries.

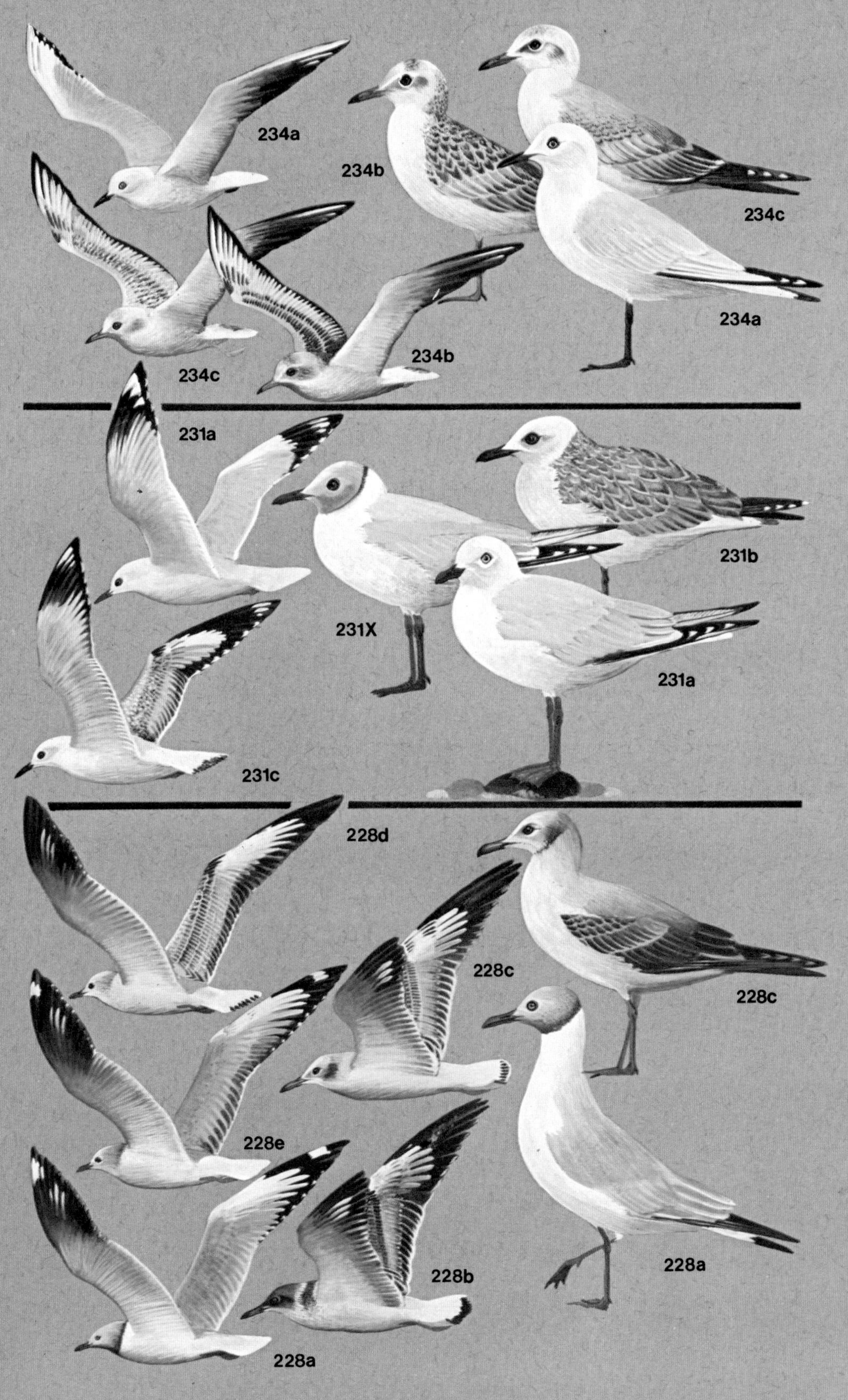
234a
234b
234c
234c
234b
234a
231a
231b
231X
231a
231c
228d
228c
228c
228e
228b
228a
228a

Plate 66

SOUTH AMERICAN GULLS

243 SWALLOW-TAILED GULL 57/131cm

Larus furcatus RR MAP 243 **Text page 360**

243a ADULT BREEDING: Unmistakable at the Galapagos Is.
243b ADULT NON-BREEDING: As 243a but head mostly white; dusky eye patch, partial grey breast band.
243c JUVENILE: Head mainly white; dark eye-crescent and ear spot. Upperparts 'scaled' brown and white. Forked tail has black terminal band.
243d FIRST-SUMMER: Much as 243c except for partial hood and grey saddle. Wings and tail unmoulted, faded through wear.

204 LAVA GULL 53/?cm
other: Dusky Gull

Larus fuliginosus RR MAP 204 **Text page 330**

204a ADULT BREEDING: Endemic to Galapagos Is; unlikely to be mistaken.
204b JUVENILE: Distinctly different from 243c, the only other gull of the region.
204c FIRST-WINTER: Intermediate between adult and juvenile; head rather dark with admixture of brown and grey on saddle, coverts and breast.
204d FIRST-SUMMER: As 204b but head, body and wings greyer.

229 ANDEAN GULL 48/?cm
other: Mountain Gull

Larus serranus RR MAP 229 **Text page 351**

229a ADULT BREEDING: Unlikely to be mistaken in the high Andes, where it breeds, but also occurs along Peruvian coast.
229b ADULT NON-BREEDING: Some move to coast during winter. Wing pattern distinctive, but see Franklin's and Grey-headed Gulls (p. 352, p. 351), which also occur along coasts of Ecuador and Peru.
229c JUVENILE: Distinctive in high Andes. On the coast juvenile Franklin's and Laughing Gulls also occur (p. 352, p. 349) but have distinctly different upperwing patterns. See also Grey-headed Gull (p. 351).
229d FIRST-SUMMER: On coasts of Ecuador, Peru and Chile could be confused with first-summer/second-winter Grey-headed Gull (p. 351), but that species lacks the three large, elongated 'mirrors' on outer primaries of present species.

243a
243c
243d
243b
243a
243c
204d
204b
204c
204a
204a
204b
229b
229d
229a
229b
229c

Plate 67

SOUTH AMERICAN GULLS

205 **GREY GULL** 46/?cm
other: Gray Gull
Larus modestus RR MAP 205 **Text page 330**

205a ADULT BREEDING: Plumage mainly lead-grey with whitish-grey hood and white trailing edge to wing.
205b ADULT NON-BREEDING: As 205a but with brown hood.
205c JUVENILE: Mainly pale brownish-grey with paler feather edges, particularly on lesser and median coverts which form a pale area on closed wing (enhanced by wear).
205d SECOND-WINTER: As 205b but head darker, plumage generally browner.

209 **BAND-TAILED GULL** 51/124cm
other: Belcher's/Simeon Gull
Larus belcheri RR MAP 209 **Text page 333**

209a ADULT BREEDING: Resembles Kelp Gull (p. 343) but smaller with banded bill and tail; outer primaries lack white tips of that species.
209b ADULT NON-BREEDING: As 209a but with brown hood.
209c JUVENILE: Dark brown hood extends to breast; saddle brownish with broad, buff edges. Scaly plumage fades rapidly, becoming generally greyer with larger, less defined edges to saddle and upperwing-coverts.
209d SECOND-WINTER: Much as 209b but grizzled hood extends to upper breast; upperparts and underparts browner in tone.

203 **DOLPHIN GULL** 44/104cm
other: Magellan/Scoresby's Gull
Larus scoresbii RR MAP 203 **Text page 329**

203a ADULT BREEDING: Resembles Kelp Gull (p. 343) but smaller with stout red bill and red legs; underparts greyer.
203b ADULT NON-BREEDING: As 203a but with grey hood.
203c JUVENILE: As 203b but browner hood, saddle, upperwings and breast; tail banded.
203d SECOND-WINTER: As 203b except darker hood, indistinct streaking on breast, decomposed tail band and banded bill.

205a
205d
205b
205d
205c
205c
205a
209b
209d
209c
209b
209a
209c
209d
209a
203d
203c
203c
203d
203a
203a
203b
203b

Plate 68

HOODED GULLS

227 INDIAN BLACK-HEADED GULL 42/?cm
other: Brown-headed Gull
Larus brunnicephalus RR MAP 227 **Text page 350**

227a ADULT BREEDING: Separated from European Black-headed Gull (p. 356) by larger size and different wingtip pattern.

227b ADULT NON-BREEDING: Range overlaps with European Black-headed Gull (p. 356) in parts of Asia, but can be separated by pale iris, heavier bill, larger size and different wingtip pattern.

227c FIRST-WINTER: Resembles 227b except for lack of prominent 'mirrors', brownish secondaries, carpal bar and upperwing-coverts. Separated from similar-stage European Black-headed Gull (p. 356) by heavier bill, larger size and upperwing pattern.

233 RELICT GULL ?/?cm
other: Mongolian Gull
Larus relictus RR MAP 233 **Text page 354**

233 ADULT BREEDING: Slightly larger and heavier-billed than Mediterranean Gull (p. 353); differs in blackish subterminal crescent across outer primaries, recalling much larger Great Black-headed Gull (p. 348). NOTE: Plumage stages not fully known, hence only breeding adult shown opposite. Refer to p. 354 for further sketches.

240 CHINESE BLACK-HEADED GULL 32/?cm
other: Saunders's Gull
Larus saundersi RR MAP 240 **Text page 358**

240a ADULT BREEDING: Recalls Bonaparte's Gull (p. 357) but bill heavier; black 'windows' on underwing diagnostic.

240b ADULT NON-BREEDING: Smaller, with darker saddle than other Asiatic hooded gulls; underwing pattern diagnostic.

240c FIRST-WINTER: Recalls similar-stage Bonaparte's Gull (p. 357); separated by stouter bill, wholly white outer primary, and narrower tail band.

235 BROWN-HOODED GULL 37/?cm
other: Patagonian Black-headed Gull
Larus maculipennis RR MAP 235 **Text page 355**

235a ADULT BREEDING: Size and jizz recall European Black-headed Gull (p. 356), but outer primaries normally lack black tips of that species. (Some retarded second-year birds often retain blackish subterminal tips to outer primaries, see Fig. 24, p. 355.)

235b ADULT NON-BREEDING: Differs from Grey-headed Gull (p. 351), which also occurs in South America, in darker head markings and wingtip pattern.

235c JUVENILE: Differs from similar-stage Grey-headed Gull (p. 351) mainly in head markings and whitish 'mirrors' on outermost two primaries.

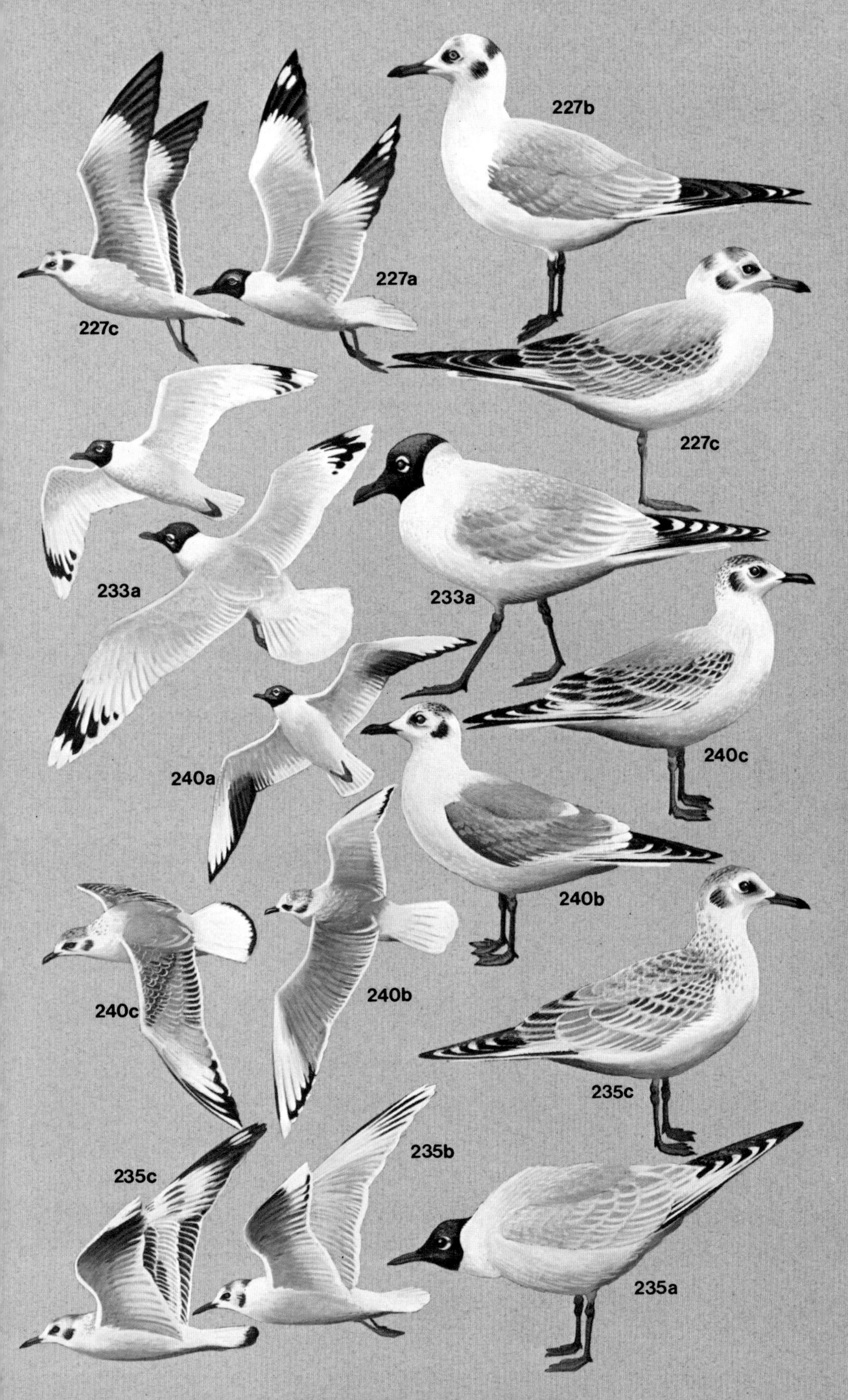
227b
227a
227c
227c
233a
233a
240c
240a
240b
240c
240b
235c
235b
235c
235a

Plate 69

GULLS

232 MEDITERRANEAN GULL 41/91cm
Larus melanocephalus RR MAP 232 **Text page 353**

232a ADULT BREEDING: Combination of extensive jet-black hood, crimson bare parts and unmarked wings diagnostic.
232b ADULT NON-BREEDING: As 232a but hood replaced by dark eye-crescent and dusky ear-coverts extending diffusely over crown.
232c FIRST-WINTER: Differs from Common Gull (p. 336) in structure, bare parts colours, ill-defined partial hood, more contrasting upperwing pattern and narrower tail band. See also European Black-headed Gull (p. 356).
232d SECOND-WINTER: As 232b but with black subterminal marks on outer primaries.

237 SLENDER-BILLED GULL 42/94cm
Larus genei RR MAP 237 **Text page 356**

237a ADULT BREEDING: Upperwing pattern recalls European Black-headed Gull (p. 356), but head and iris white with longer, more slender bill and pink flush to underparts. Jizz distinctly different from that species.
237b ADULT NON-BREEDING: As 237a but usually with faint grey ear spot (never as pronounced as in European Black-headed Gull, p. 356).
237c FIRST WINTER: Differs from corresponding European Black-headed Gull in lack of prominent ear spot and paler, less distinct markings on upperwing.
237d FIRST-SUMMER: As 237c but head white, wing and tail pattern further faded through wear.

211 AUDOUIN'S GULL 51/?cm
Larus audouinii RR MAP 211 **Text page 334**

211a ADULT BREEDING: Superficially resembles Herring Gull (p. 337), but smaller with more slender jizz and different coloured bare parts. (At long range appears paler above on upperparts and upperwings than Herring Gull, with dark bill and eye giving distinctive facial expression.)
211b FIRST-WINTER: Differs from corresponding local race of Herring Gull in lack of pronounced streaking on ear-coverts, different upperwing and tail patterns (see Fig. 20, p. 335) and grey, not pink, legs.
211c SECOND-WINTER: Differs from corresponding local race of Herring Gull in lack of prominent pale 'window' on innermost primaries, paler grey upperparts and upperwings and neater tail pattern. Bare parts also differ.

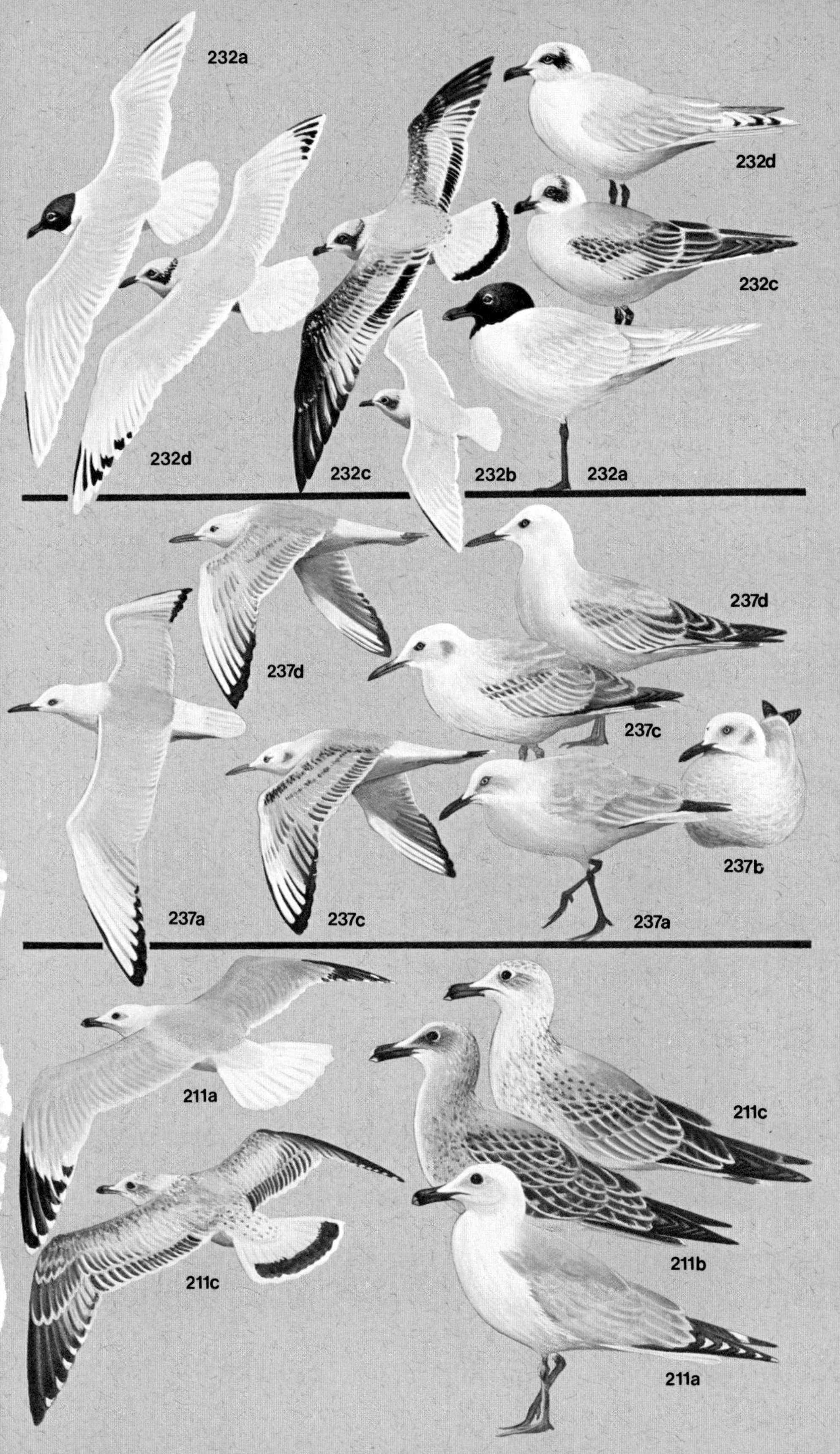
232a
232d
232c
232d
232c
232b
232a
237d
237d
237c
237b
237a
237c
237a
211a
211c
211b
211c
211a

Plate 70

GULLS

207 **WHITE-EYED GULL** 39/?cm
other: Red Sea Black-headed Gull
Larus leucophthalmus RR MAP 207 **Text page 331**

207a ADULT BREEDING: Differs from 208a in smaller size, lighter jizz, bill colour, jet-black hood, prominent white crescents above and below eye, and greyer plumage.

207b FIRST-WINTER: Darker above than 208c, particularly head, with distinct white crescents above and below eye. Some stages of 208, however, equally as dark and brown. Separation best based on smaller size, lighter jizz and finer, darker bill.

207c SECOND-SUMMER: Differs from 207a in brownish cast to upperwings, more prominent secondary bar, and partial tail band.

208 **SOOTY GULL** 46/?cm
other: Aden/Hemprich's Gull
Larus hemprichi RR MAP 208 **Text page 332**

208a ADULT BREEDING: Resembles 207a; upperparts sometimes as grey but usually rather browner. Larger size, diagnostic bill and duller yellow legs are safest characters to look for.

208b JUVENILE: Paler-headed than juveniles of 207, with prominent pale feather edges to upperparts. Heavier blue-grey bill with black tip diagnostic.

208c FIRST-WINTER: Pale fringes on upperwing-coverts give scaly pattern not found in any stage of 207.

208d SECOND-WINTER: Bill dull greenish-yellow with black subterminal band and reddish tip. Head uniform pale fawn-brown, extending to breast. Mantle and upperwings grey with fawn cast. In flight appears rather pale with prominent dark bar along secondaries.

208e ADULT NON-BREEDING: Much browner than 208a with white cervical collar reduced or lacking. Easily separated from 207 by size, colour of bill, brownish hood and upperparts.

225 **GREAT BLACK-HEADED GULL** 69/?cm
Larus ichthyaetus NIO MAP 225 **Text page 348**

225a ADULT BREEDING: Unmistakable; the only large gull with a black hood and banded bill.

225b ADULT NON-BREEDING: Differs from corresponding Herring Gull in banded bill, darker ear-coverts and overall structure.

225c FIRST-WINTER: Differs from Herring Gull (p. 337) in overall larger size, banded bill, darker ear-coverts and, in flight, by clear white rump and distinct tail band.

225d FIRST-SUMMER: Differs from Herring Gull (p. 337) in partial hood, white rump and tail band. Midwing panel on upperwing often paler, sometimes whitish.

225e SECOND-SUMMER: Differs from Herring Gull (p. 337) in partial or full hood, and upperwing pattern.

207a
207a
207c
207b
208d
208d
208e
208a
208b
208c
225b
225d
225c
225e
225a

Plate 71

SMALL GULLS

241 **KITTIWAKE** 41/91cm
other: Black-legged Kittiwake
Larus tridactyla NPO, AR, NAO MAP 241 **Text page 359**

241a ADULT BREEDING: Differs from most other gulls in combination of yellow bill, black legs and wholly black wingtips. NOTE: *L.t. pollicaris* in Pacific has slightly darker upperparts and more black on wingtips.

241b ADULT NON-BREEDING: Similar to 241a but with dusky eye-crescent, and variable blackish ear spot which sometimes extends to hindneck.

241c FIRST-WINTER: Combination of whitish head, dark cervical collar and striking M mark across upperwings should prevent confusion with most other species. See also Sabine's, Little and Ross's Gulls (p. 361, p. 357, p. 361).

241d FIRST-SUMMER: Plumage highly variable; some resemble first-winter but others, especially during late summer/autumn, may lack extensive black on outer wing. (See main text.)

242 **RED-LEGGED KITTIWAKE** 37/91cm
Larus brevirostris NPO MAP 242 **Text page 359**

242a ADULT BREEDING: Resembles 241a but upperparts slightly darker and more uniform grey, without silvery bases to primaries. Underwing mostly grey. Legs red.

242b ADULT NON-BREEDING: As for 242a but with dusky eye-crescent and ear spot; crown and nape washed blue-grey.

242c JUVENILE: Differs from juvenile Black-legged Kittiwake in fewer black spots over nape, lack of black on tail, and absence of carpal bar.

242d FIRST-WINTER: Dark spots on nape usually absent; differs further from 241c in lack of black on tail and absence of carpal bar.

245 **ROSS'S GULL** 31/?cm
Rhodostethia rosea AR MAP 245 **Text page 361**

245a ADULT BREEDING: Unmistakable; pale grey upperparts, narrow black neck-ring and variable pinkish cast to white underparts.

245b ADULT NON-BREEDING: Legs dull orange. Upperparts much paler than European Black-headed or Bonaparte's Gulls (p. 356, p. 357), with pronounced dusky eye-crescent and ear spot. In flight, from below, grey secondaries and inner primaries broadly tipped white form conspicuous trailing edge recalling Little Gull (p. 357), but underwing usually paler than that species. Some show variable pinkish cast to underparts.

245c FIRST-WINTER: Resembles non-breeding adult but with striking M mark across upper surfaces; secondaries white, central tail feathers subterminally tipped black. See also Kittiwake and Little Gull (p. 359, p. 357).

245d FIRST-SUMMER: As 245c but with partial or complete neck-ring decomposed and faded; longer central tail feathers sometimes broken, creating squarer-tailed jizz.

241a
241c
241c
241d
241b
241d
241a
242d
242a
242a
242b
242c
245c
245b
245c
245d
245b
245a

Plate 72

NODDIES

285 **BROWN NODDY** 42/83cm
other: Common Noddy
Anous stolidus TO MAP 285 **Text page 388**

285a ADULT: White forehead sharply demarcated from black lores. Remainder of plumage brown, darker on primaries and tail. Pale underwing shows darker margins. Unlike 286a appears two-toned at sea.

285b JUVENILE: As adult but has dark forehead and crown with whitish tips to saddle, upperwing-coverts and secondaries.

285c IMMATURE: As adult but usually lacks well-defined cap.

286 **LESSER NODDY** 32/60cm
Anous tenuirostris TIO MAP 286 **Text page 389**

286a ADULT: As for 285a, but the more extensive ash-grey crown and forehead normally merge evenly on the lores without sharp demarcation. Bill proportionately longer and finer than in 285. Unlike 285a appears mostly blackish at sea.

286b ATYPICAL: Some adults of the race *melanops* show sharply demarcated lores; whether simply aberrant or linked to moult/age factors is not known.

286X **BLACK NODDY** 37/69cm
other: White-capped Noddy
Anous t. minutus TAO, TPO MAP 286X **Text page 389**

286Xa ADULT: Appears blacker than 285 or 286, with whiter and more extensive cap, sharply demarcated lores and longer bill. Underwing differs from sympatric 285 in uniform colour without darker margins.

286Xb JUVENILE: Has less white on crown, which is sharply demarcated from blackish nape. Upperwing-coverts and secondaries tipped with buff.

286Xc IMMATURE: Similar to juvenile but without pale feather tips to secondaries and coverts.

284 **GREY NODDY** 27/48cm
other: Blue-grey Noddy
Procelsterna cerulea TPO MAP 284 **Text page 387**

284a PALE MORPH: Whitish head and underparts, greyer wings and tail.

284b DARK MORPH: Darker head and underparts. Underwing differs from 284a in grey, not white, coverts.

284c IMMATURE PALE MORPH: Shows dark primaries with brownish cast to saddle, wings and tail.

285a
285a
285a
285a
285c
285a
285c
285b
286a
286a
286a
286b
286a
286b
286b
286Xa
286Xa
286Xa
286Xc
286Xb
284c
284a
284a
284a
284c
284b
284b
284b

Plate 73

TERNS

269 **SOOTY TERN** 44/90cm
other: Wideawake
Sterna fuscata TO MAP 269 **Text page 378**

Wide-ranging black and white tern of subtropical and tropical seas; often encountered in huge flocks, appearing at distance as clouds of smoke. Frequently soars high over ocean to locate shoaling fish or flocks of feeding seabirds.

269a ADULT: Broad white forehead extends only to eye; upperparts wholly black without pale cervical collar. Underparts white.

269b JUVENILE: Distinct from 268b below. Mostly sooty-brown, including head; feathers of saddle, upperwing-coverts and belly tipped with white; ventral area and undertail-coverts white.

269c FIRST-SUMMER: Resembles 269a but underparts variably dark, some with solid black chin, throat and breast, others (perhaps older birds) mostly white below with dusky wash on chin, throat and upper breast.

268 **BRIDLED TERN** 36/76cm
other: Brown-winged Tern
Sterna anaethetus TO MAP 268 **Text page 378**

Resembles Sooty Tern but less pelagic, more inshore, although often seen many miles from landfall.

268a ADULT: Differs from Sooty Tern in narrow white forehead extending over and beyond eye as a narrow white supercilium; black crown and nape normally separated from upperparts by greyish cervical collar. Upperparts browner, not black; more white on outer tail feathers, underparts greyer.

268b JUVENILE: Resembles adult but saddle and upperwings tipped buff and white, less spotted than in juvenile Sooty Tern, with underparts mostly white, sides of breast and flanks washed with grey.

267 **GREY-BACKED TERN** 36/74cm
other: Spectacled Tern
Sterna lunata TPO MAP 267 **Text page 377**

Resembles Bridled Tern but saddle greyer, underparts whiter.

267a ADULT BREEDING: As Bridled Tern but upperparts, particularly saddle, greyer resembling more northerly Aleutian Tern, but rump dark with underparts wholly white.

267b JUVENILE: As adult but head pattern less defined, upperparts grey tipped with brown and buff; sides of breast grey.

266 **ALEUTIAN TERN** 36/78cm
Sterna aleutica RR MAP 266 **Text page 376**

Distinctive in North Pacific, where it occurs alongside Arctic and Common Terns. Complete plumages unknown; non-breeding adults may have whiter crowns and underparts.

266a ADULT BREEDING: Mostly lead-grey above, contrasting with white rump and deeply forked tail; forehead broadly white, cap and streak through eye black. Underparts slightly paler grey than upperparts, ventral area and undertail-coverts white.

266b JUVENILE: Head mostly fawn-brown, saddle sepia-brown tipped buff-brown, rump and tail grey. Underparts white, strongly washed fawn-brown on sides of breast, less so on flanks and belly. How long this plumage remains is unknown; presumably during first winter upperparts mostly clear grey, underparts whiter.

269c
269a
269a
269a
269b
268b
268b
268a
268a
268a
267a
267b
267a
267a
266a
266a
266a
266b

Plate 74

LARGE TERNS

252 **CASPIAN TERN** 53/134cm
Sterna caspia WR MAP 252 **Text page 368**

252a ADULT BREEDING: Enormous. Confusion possible only with smaller 277a. Combination of dusky-tipped, blood-red bill and wholly dark outer primaries of underwing diagnostic.

252b ADULT NON-BREEDING: Separated from 277b by bill colour, darker head and underwing.

252c FIRST-WINTER: Cap darkest of any large juvenile tern; differs further from 277c in underwing and in leg colour.

277 **ROYAL TERN** 49/109cm
Sterna maxima AO, PO MAP 277 **Text page 383**

277a ADULT BREEDING: Differs from larger 252a in more orange, unmarked bill and in underwing pattern. Most retain full black cap only for a short period and, whilst Caspian retains a dark cap until late in nesting season, most Royals show white foreheads before eggs are hatched.

277b ADULT NON-BREEDING: Head and underwing much whiter than in 252b.

277c FIRST-WINTER: Head pattern, conspicuous dark carpal bar, pale midwing panel, tail, and leg colour should prevent confusion with 252c.

281 **ELEGANT TERN** 41/?cm
Sterna elegans RR MAP 281 **Text page 386**

281a ADULT BREEDING: Resembles 277a but smaller, with proportionately longer, finer, drooping bill.

281b ADULT NON-BREEDING: As 281a except forehead and crown white, latter freckled with black.

250 **LARGE-BILLED TERN** 37/92cm
Phaetusa simplex RR MAP 250 **Text page 366**

250a ADULT BREEDING: Unmistakable. Confined mainly to freshwater locations; unlikely to be seen at sea.

250b ADULT NON-BREEDING: As 250a but forehead and crown paler.

252b
252c
252a
252c
252a
277b
277b
277a
277a
277c
281a
250b
281b
250a

Plate 75

TERNS

261 **ROSEATE TERN** 39/78cm
Sterna dougallii WR MAP 261 **Text page 373**

261a ADULT BREEDING: Upperparts appear almost white in flight. When perched, legs slightly longer than in 255, tail streamers project well past wingtip.

261b ADULT NON-BREEDING: As 261a except for brownish-orange legs, white forehead, and shorter tail streamers. Pale upperparts and white underwing separate this from any stage of 255, 256 or 259.

261c JUVENILE/FIRST-WINTER: Differs from both 256 and 255 in much darker head and brownish saddle. Upperwing shows carpal bar of 255 and whitish secondaries of 256.

261d JUVENILE/FLEDGLING: Much as 261c but upperparts more golden-brown with larger, darker tips.

256 **ARCTIC TERN** 36/80cm
Sterna paradisaea WR MAP 256 **Text page 370**

256a ADULT BREEDING: Differs from 255a in slimmer, more attenuated jizz, more uniform outer primaries on upperwing, and narrower black trailing edge on underwing. When perched, legs shorter than 255, tail streamers project beyond wingtip.

256b ADULT NON-BREEDING: Bill blackish, legs blackish-red. Forehead and underparts white; lacks long tail streamers. Differs from 255b in head and bill shape, and underwing pattern.

256c JUVENILE/FIRST-WINTER: Separated from 255c by darker grey upper surfaces contrasting with white secondaries and pure white rump (lacks prominent dark carpal bar and dusky secondaries of 255c). Underwing as adult.

256d JUVENILE/FLEDGLING: Lacks brownish appearance of both 255 and 261, with only a faint carpal bar. Underwing distinctly different from any stage of 255.

255 **COMMON TERN** 36/80cm
Sterna hirundo WR MAP 255 **Text page 370**

255a ADULT BREEDING: Differs from 256a in dark wedge on upperwing and broader, smudgy black trailing edge on outer underwing. When perched, tips of wings and tail more or less equal.

255b ADULT NON-BREEDING: As 255a except for blackish bill, and white forehead and underparts. See White-cheeked Tern (p. 375).

255c JUVENILE/FIRST-WINTER: Differs from others on this plate in pronounced carpal bar and dusky-grey secondaries.

255d JUVENILE: As 255c, but typically with stronger ginger-brown cast to upperparts and heavier scaling on mantle (but not usually as pronounced as in darker-headed juvenile Roseate Tern).

259 **FORSTER'S TERN** 37/80cm
Sterna forsteri RR MAP 259 **Text page 372**

259a ADULT BREEDING: Recalls 255a but bill heavier, more orange-red, legs noticeably longer. In flight, bases of inner primaries distinctly silvery-white.

259b ADULT NON-BREEDING: Recalls dainty Sandwich Tern (p. 386). Head mostly white, with conspicuous black eye patches.

259c FIRST-WINTER: Much as 259b except black eye patch usually more extensive, nape greyer. Tail shows narrow black border along inner fork.

259d JUVENILE/FLEDGLING: Differs from 255d in browner head and lack of pronounced carpal bar on upperwing.

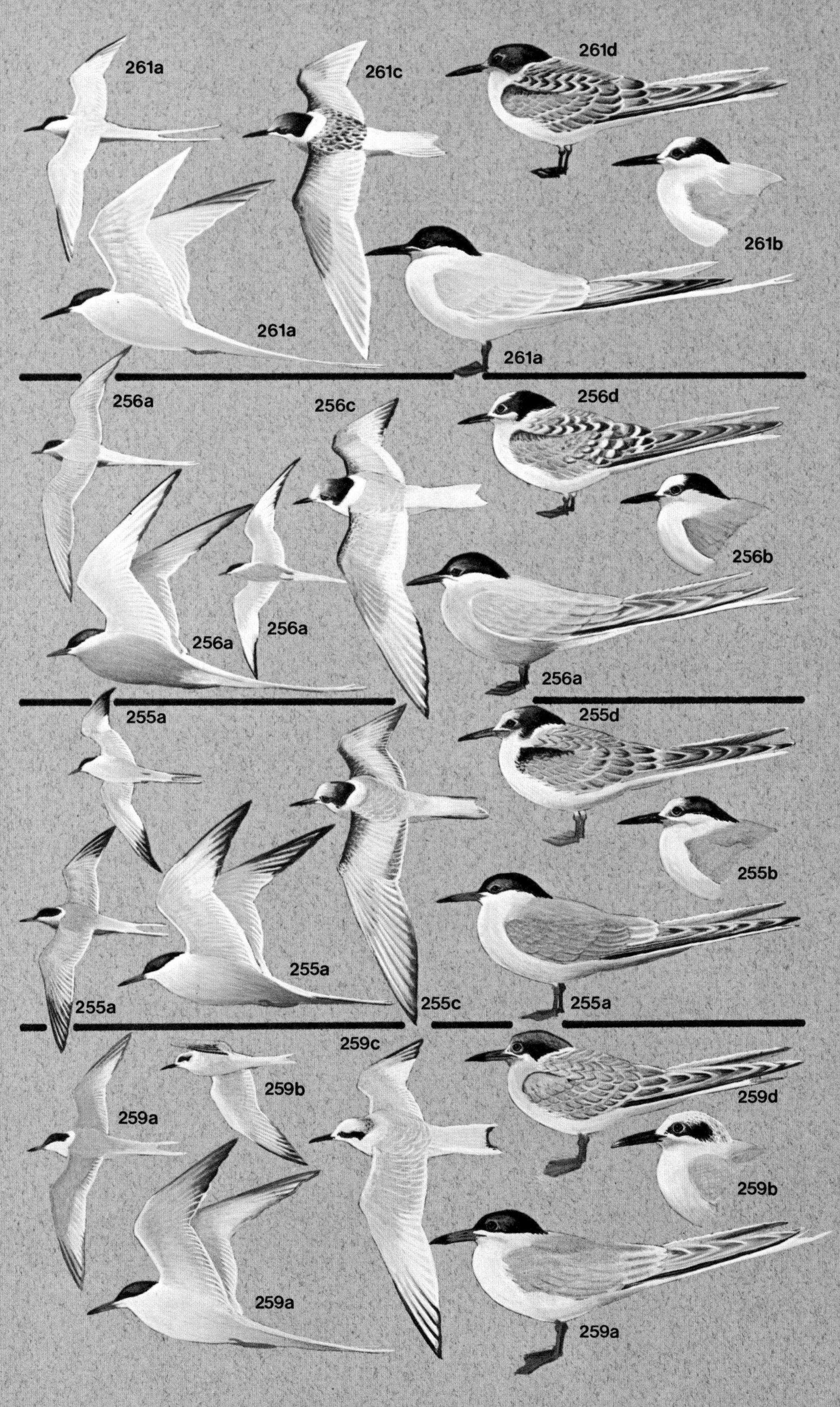

261a
261c
261d
261b
261a
261a
256a
256c
256d
256b
256a
256a
256a
255a
255d
255b
255a
255a
255c
255a
259c
259b
259d
259a
259b
259a
259a

Plate 76

MEDIUM AND LARGE TERNS

251 **GULL-BILLED TERN** 39/94cm
Sterna nilotica WR MAP 251 **Text page 367**

251a ADULT BREEDING: Appears mainly white in the field with black, gull-like bill, uncrested cap and dusky-grey trailing edge to primaries.
251b ADULT NON-BREEDING: As breeding adult except for dark eye patch and deeper grey outer primaries.
251c JUVENILE: As 251b except rear of crown and nape have brownish cast. Upperparts broadly tipped brown, primaries darker.
251d FIRST-WINTER: As 251c but brown tips to upperparts reduced or lacking.

282 **SANDWICH TERN** 42/92cm
Sterna sandvicensis AO, NIO MAP 282 **Text page 386**

282a ADULT BREEDING: Appears mainly white in the field. Differs from 251a above in slender bill with pale yellow tip, more graceful jizz and feeding habits.
282b ADULT NON-BREEDING: As 282a but forehead and lores white; black crown streaked with white.
282c JUVENILE: As 282b but grey upperparts broadly tipped with brown.
282d FIRST-WINTER: Much as non-breeding adult except for brownish tips to saddle and upperwing-coverts.

276 **CRESTED TERN** 46/104cm
other: Swift Tern, Great Crested Tern
Sterna bergii IO, PO MAP 276 **Text page 383**

276a ADULT BREEDING: A large tern with massive, drooping bill, long wings and powerful flight.
276b ADULT NON-BREEDING: As 276a except forehead, lores and forecrown white (not as extensive as in 278b below). Saddle and upperwings lose their even greyness.
276c JUVENILE: Resembles 276b but with dusky markings on throat and sides of face. Saddle and upperwings deeper grey and heavily tipped with brown.

278 **LESSER CRESTED TERN** 40/91cm
Sterna bengalensis IO, PO MAP 278 **Text page 384**

278a ADULT BREEDING (*S.b. bengalensis*): Smaller, more delicately proportioned than 276a, with bright orange bill. Unlike that species, black cap not so shaggy and normally extends to base of bill (though this may be a variable character). In Red Sea area saddle and upperwings bluer and paler than local race of 276.
278b ADULT NON-BREEDING (*S.b. bengalensis*): White forehead and crown more extensive than in 276b, reaching almost to nape, giving distinctly different facial expression.
278c ADULT NON-BREEDING (*S.b. torrestii*): Darker saddle and upperwings than nominate race, appearing much darker above than Australian race of larger Crested Tern.
278d JUVENILE: Bill greyish-yellow. As 278b except saddle and upperwing-coverts tipped with brown. Upperwing shows dark outer primaries and dusky band along secondaries. Unlike 276c, lacks pronounced carpal bar; upperparts more uniform grey.
278e FIRST-WINTER: As 278d but saddle and upperwing-coverts clearer grey.

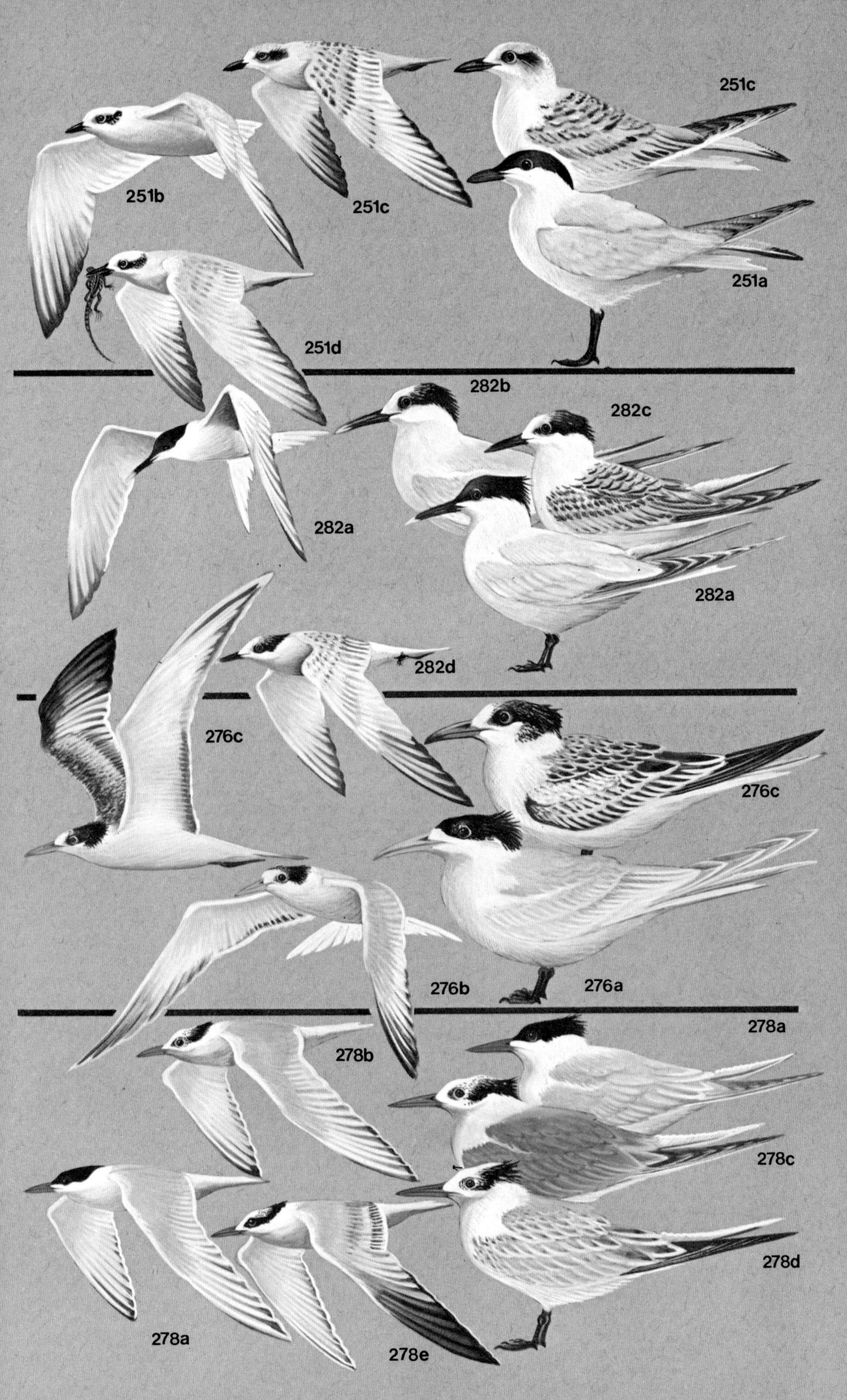
251c
251b
251c
251a
251d
282b
282c
282a
282a
282d
276c
276c
276b
276a
278a
278b
278c
278d
278a
278e

Plate 77

TERNS

253 **INDIAN RIVER TERN** 40/?cm
Sterna aurantia RR — MAP 253 **Text page 369**

253a ADULT BREEDING: Asiatic freshwater species, unlikely to be seen at sea. In flight, black cap, dark grey upperparts, white underparts and streamered tail impart distinctive jizz.

253b ADULT NON-BREEDING: Dusky tip to bill. Confusion likely with smaller, shorter-tailed Black-bellied Tern (p. 376), but that species normally shows some dark mottling on belly.

260 **TRUDEAU'S TERN** 33/77cm
other: Snowy-crowned Tern
Sterna trudeaui RR — MAP 260 **Text page 373**

260a ADULT BREEDING: Mostly grey; white crown and nape contrast with black eye patch.

260b ADULT NON-BREEDING: As 260a but post-ocular eye patch greyer, underparts white. (Closely resembles Forster's Tern, p. 372, in appearance, though ranges do not normally overlap.)

260c JUVENILE: Unlike many juvenile terns, lacks a dark carpal bar. Plumage generally as 260b, but eye patch more extensive with faint brownish mottling on crown and grey wash on nape. Upperparts and upperwing-coverts lightly tipped brown, heaviest on tertials.

263 **WHITE-CHEEKED TERN** 32/?cm
Sterna repressa RR — MAP 263 **Text page 375**

263a ADULT BREEDING: Colour pattern suggests Arctic Tern but jizz much closer to *Chlidonias* than *Sterna*.

263b ADULT WINTER: Similar to non-breeding Common Tern (p. 370), which winters within present species' range; differs in darker grey upperwing, lack of dark wedge in primaries and greyer rump and tail.

263c FIRST-WINTER: As 263b but with carpal bar and dusky-grey primaries and secondaries. Juvenile Common Tern (p. 370) has paler grey upperparts, whiter rump and tail and smaller carpal bar.

279 **CHINESE CRESTED TERN** 38/?cm
Sterna bernsteini RR — MAP 279 **Text page 385**

279a ADULT BREEDING: Resembles Crested Tern (p. 383) but much smaller, with prominent black tip to bill, full cap, paler upperparts and longer tail streamers.

279b ADULT NON-BREEDING: As 279a but forehead and crown white; bill tip yellow.

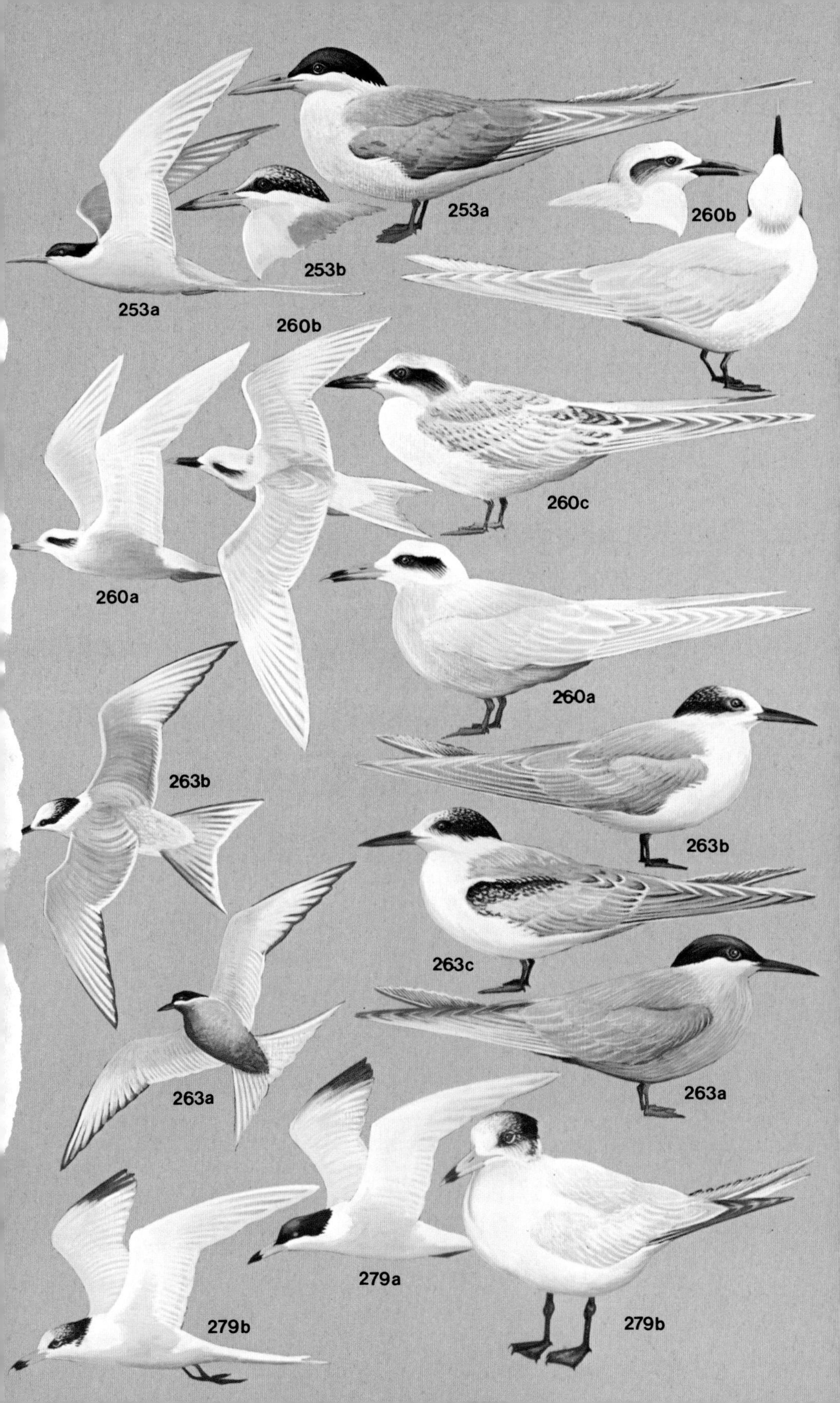

253a
253b
253a
260b
260b
260c
260a
260a
263b
263b
263c
263a
263a
279a
279b
279b

Plate 78

SOUTH AMERICAN TERNS

283 **INCA TERN** 41/?cm
Larosterna inca RR MAP 283 **Text page 387**

283a ADULT: Mostly blue-grey except for indistinct blackish cap, white moustache-like facial plumes, and white trailing edge of wing.
283b JUVENILE: Wholly purplish-brown, upperparts lightly scaled with grey.
283c IMMATURE: Resembles adult but mostly brownish-grey; shorter moustache-like facial plumes, trailing edge of wing ash-grey.

254 **SOUTH AMERICAN TERN** 42/85cm
Sterna hirundinacea RR MAP 254 **Text page 369**

254a ADULT BREEDING: Black cap contrasts with pale pearl-grey upperparts and white rump. In southern parts of range overlaps with smaller Antarctic Tern (p. 371), which has a smaller bill and darker overall plumage. These differences are not always easy to discern at sea.
254b ADULT NON-BREEDING: As breeding adult except forehead and forecrown mostly white; underparts mainly white. Differs from non-breeding Antarctic Tern (p. 371) in paler grey upperparts and bill proportions.
254c JUVENILE: Rather dark, plover-like plumage.
254d FIRST-WINTER: As non-breeding adult except for scattered brownish tips to upperparts and noticeable carpal bar.

272 **AMAZON TERN** 23/?cm
other: Yellow-billed Tern
Sterna superciliaris RR MAP 272 **Text page 380**

272a ADULT BREEDING: Forehead narrowly white, extending over eye in narrow supercilium; crown and nape black. Upperparts grey, underparts white. Upperwing has outer 3–4 primaries black.
272b ADULT NON-BREEDING: As breeding adult except crown and lores largely white, flecked with black.
272c JUVENILE: Head mainly greyish-brown; eye-crescent, streak through eye and nape blackish-brown. Upperparts grey, tipped with brown, underparts mostly white, sides of breast washed with brownish-grey.

280 **CAYENNE TERN**
other: Sandwich Tern (race of)
Sterna (sandvicensis) eurygnatha MAP 280 **Text page 385**

280a ADULT BREEDING: Crested black cap; upperparts pale grey, outer primaries dusky-grey, rump and underparts white. Bill and leg colour varies.
280b ADULT NON-BREEDING: As breeding adult except forehead and lores white; crown mottled with black and white.
280c JUVENILE: Differs from non-breeding adult in brown tips to upperparts and noticeable carpal bar on upperwing.

283c
283a
283a
283b
283a
254c
283c
254a
254b
254d
272b
272c
272a
272b
272b
272a
280b
280a
280c
280c

Plate 79
TERNS

262 **WHITE-FRONTED TERN** 41/?cm
Sterna striata RR MAP 262 **Text page 374**

262a ADULT BREEDING: Most likely to be confused with migrant Common Terns (p. 370) in SE Australia. Separated by heavier black bill, white band over base of bill, whiter upperparts and lack of pronounced dusky trailing edge along underside of primaries.
262b ADULT NON-BREEDING: Superficially resembles non-breeding Common Tern (p. 370), but bill larger and heavier giving 'large-headed' appearance. Underwing as 262a; once this character is learnt, identification is straightforward.
262c FIRST-SUMMER: As 262b but with dark carpal bar and darker grey primaries.
262d JUVENILE: Upperparts heavily marked with brown; upperwing shows distinct carpal bar.

265 **BLACK-BELLIED TERN** 31/?cm
Sterna melanogastra RR MAP 265 **Text page 376**

265a ADULT BREEDING: Asiatic freshwater species unlikely to be seen at sea. Black belly combined with yellow-orange bill diagnostic.
265b ADULT NON-BREEDING: Confusion possible only with much larger Indian River Tern (p. 369), which also has a yellowish bill. Most individuals of present species, however, retain some dark mottling on belly.

271 **BLACK-FRONTED TERN** 32/?cm
Sterna albostriata RR MAP 271 **Text page 380**

271a ADULT BREEDING: Unmistakable. Restricted to New Zealand. Habits and appearance recall Eurasian Whiskered Tern (p. 364).
271b ADULT NON-BREEDING: Smaller size and 'marsh-tern' jizz should prevent confusion with larger, paler, black-billed White-fronted Tern (p. 374).

257 **ANTARCTIC TERN** 41/79cm
other: Wreathed Tern
Sterna vittata SO MAP 257 **Text page 371**

257a ADULT BREEDING: Distinguished from 258 by larger size, heavier bill, paler upperparts, and white underwing and tail. NOTE: Depth of grey on upper- and underparts varies between different populations and individually.
257b ADULT NON-BREEDING: Separated from both Arctic and Common Terns (p. 370, p. 370) by larger size, heavier brighter bill, red legs, and heavier jizz. At close range lores usually whiter than in either of those species.
257c ADULT TRANSITIONAL: As non-breeding adult but with smoky-grey band across lower breast (useful character when searching through 'commic' tern roosts in southern hemisphere).
257d JUVENILE: Black bill smaller and finer than in adult. Juvenile Kerguelen Tern (not illustrated) is similar but much darker, especially chin, throat and breast.

258 **KERGUELEN TERN** 33/75cm
Sterna virgata RR, IO MAP 258 **Text page 372**

258 ADULT BREEDING: Resembles 257a but smaller and darker. White rump contrasts with grey upperparts and tail. From below, underwing grey, not white. See main text for differences in other plumage stages.

262d
262c
262b
262a
271b
265b
271a
265a
257a
257a
257d
257a
257c
258
257b
258
258

Plate 80

SMALLER TERNS

264 **BLACK-NAPED TERN** 31/61cm
Sterna sumatrana IO, PO MAP 264 **Text page 375**

264a ADULT: Appears almost white in the field, with a characteristic black band running from each eye to join on nape.

264b JUVENILE: Bill dusky-yellow, legs blackish. Crown streaked grey-brown; upperparts and upperwing-coverts tipped brown. Size and jizz readily separate it from all juveniles of species shown below.

275 **LITTLE TERN** 24/52cm
other: Least Tern (includes Saunders's Tern, 275X)
Sterna albifrons WR MAP 275 **Text page 382**

275a ADULT BREEDING: Size and hurried flight, during which it often hovers, usually sufficient to clinch identification in northern hemisphere. See main text for overlap with 270, 273 and 274 below in southern hemisphere.

275X ADULT BREEDING (*S.a. saundersi*): Treated as separate species by some authors. Differs from nominate race in darker wingtips, rump and tail. Restricted to Red Sea and NW Indian Ocean.

275b JUVENILE: Bill dusky, legs dull yellow. Size distinguishes it from other terns throughout northern hemisphere. Probably indistinguishable from juveniles of 275X; see main text for further details.

275c ADULT NON-BREEDING: As breeding adult except bill almost blackish; crown mottled with white.

270 **FAIRY TERN** 24/50cm
other: Nereis Tern
Sterna nereis RR MAP 270 **Text page 379**

270a ADULT BREEDING: From Little Tern by paler underparts, unmarked orange bill and white lores.

270b ADULT NON-BREEDING: Head pattern resembles Black-naped Tern (p. 375) but bill, leg colour, size and jizz enable ready separation. Difficult to distinguish from Little Tern (p. 382) where ranges overlap in Australia, but paler upperparts and whiter crown helpful.

270c FIRST-SUMMER: As non-breeding adult but bill and legs black. Faint carpal bar.

274 **PERUVIAN TERN** 23/?cm
other: Chilean Tern
Sterna lorata RR MAP 274 **Text page 382**

274a ADULT BREEDING: Head pattern recalls breeding Little Tern (p. 382), which may reach northern Peru in non-breeding dress during austral summer. Greyish plumage, including rump, tail and underparts, enables ready separation.

274b ADULT NON-BREEDING: As breeding adult except crown streaked with white, underparts paler.

273 **DAMARA TERN** 23/51cm
Sterna balaenarum RR MAP 273 **Text page 381**

273a ADULT BREEDING: Size, wholly black cap and bill diagnostic.

273b ADULT NON-BREEDING: Differs from Little Tern (p. 382) by proportionately longer, slightly decurved black bill and generally paler plumage, appearing, at distance, like miniature Sandwich Tern.

264b
264a
264a
275a
275c
275b
275X
270a
275a
270a
270c
270b
274a
274b
274a
273b
273a
273b
273a

Plate 81

MARSH TERNS

247 **WHISKERED TERN** 26/69cm
Chlidonias hybridus MAP 247 **Text page 364**

247a ADULT BREEDING: Unmistakable within range and habitat.

247b ADULT NON-BREEDING: Resembles 248b below in general coloration but rump never white and, when perched, bill and head shape longer recalling *Sterna* terns. Jizz also different: wings proportionately longer, narrower at base, more pointed at tips, with longer, and more evidently forked, tail.

247c JUVENILE: Apart from jizz, differs from 249c in longer bill, paler cap, paler upperwing lacking carpal bar, and distinctive saddle effect; from 248c by longer bill, richer brown saddle, grey (not white) rump and paler leading edge to upperwing.

247d FIRST-WINTER: In northern hemisphere most examples have mainly grey saddle by Nov/Dec but otherwise resemble 247c.

247e MOULTING ADULTS: These show a continuous gradation between 247a and 247b.

249 **BLACK TERN** 23/66cm
Chlidonias niger MAP 249 **Text page 365**

249a ADULT BREEDING: Unmistakable within range and habitat.

249b ADULT NON-BREEDING: Resembles 248b; differs in darker, more extensive cap, longer bill, darker legs, grey (not white) rump and blackish marks on sides of breast.

249c JUVENILE: Separable from 248c by longer bill, darker legs, darker more extensive cap, lack of pronounced saddle and of white rump, and by dark smudge on sides of breast at base of forewing.

249d FIRST-WINTER: Saddle mostly clear grey; otherwise as 249c.

249e MOULTING ADULTS: These show continuous gradation from 249a to 249b.

248 **WHITE-WINGED BLACK TERN** 23/66cm
Chlidonias leucopterus MAP 248 **Text page 364**

248a ADULT BREEDING: Unmistakable within range and habitat.

248b ADULT NON-BREEDING: Resembles 247b above but jizz different, that species resembling more closely *Sterna* terns. Plumage differs from 247b in whiter hindcollar, and obvious contrast between grey upperparts and white or very pale grey rump.

248c JUVENILE: Resembles 247c, but combination of dark saddle, pale midwing panel, whitish rump and lack of dark mark on side of breast diagnostic.

248d FIRST-WINTER: In Europe many examples attain more or less clear grey saddle by late Oct/Nov (timing varies according to individual age); rump also becomes slightly greyer in tone but always shows obvious contrast with grey upperparts.

248e MOULTING ADULTS: Whilst many individuals attain a wholly white underwing, some retain blackish tips to the larger underwing-coverts.

247c
247b
247e
247a
247b
247a
247d
247a
249b
249a
249b
249c
249d
249a
249e
249a
248b
248d
248a
248c
248a
248e
248a
248b

Plate 82

TERNS AND SKIMMERS

287 **WHITE TERN** 30/78cm
other: Fairy Tern
Gygis alba TO — MAP 287 **Text page 390**
(Drawn to same scale as perched skimmers)

287a ADULT: Unmistakable; the only wholly white tern.
287b JUVENILE: Combination of dark ear spot, rounded wings, greyish-brown saddle and upperwings, dark primary shafts and short tail may impart gull-like quality, but size, bill and eye should prevent confusion with any other tropical species.

288 **BLACK SKIMMER** 45/117cm
Rynchops niger RR — MAP 288 **Text page 391**

288a ADULT BREEDING: Unmistakable within range.
288b ADULT NON-BREEDING: As breeding adult but bill duller, upperparts browner, with whitish collar across lower hindneck.
288c JUVENILE: Bill dusky-red with blackish tip. Upperparts boldly patterned brown and white, later fading to dingy mottled effect; underparts white.

289 **AFRICAN SKIMMER** 38/106cm
Rynchops flavirostris RR — MAP 289 **Text page 391**

289a ADULT BREEDING: Unmistakable within range. Resembles larger Black Skimmer, differs mainly in unmarked bill.
289b ADULT NON-BREEDING: As breeding adult except upperparts paler and browner, with broad whitish collar across lower hindneck.

290 **INDIAN SKIMMER** 43/102cm
Rynchops albicollis RR — MAP 290 **Text page 392**

290 ADULT BREEDING: Unmistakable within range. Differs from 288a and 289a in broad white collar across hindneck, giving distinct capped effect.

288a
287b
287a
288c
288b
288a
289a
289a
289b
289b
290
290

Plate 83

ATLANTIC AUKS

295 **BLACK GUILLEMOT** 33/58cm
other: Tystie
Cepphus grylle AR, NPO, NAO MAP 295 **Text page 396**

295a ADULT BREEDING: Unmistakable throughout most of range; wholly blackish except for conspicuous white upperwing patches. In flight underwing shows white axillaries and coverts.

295b ADULT NON-BREEDING: Head mostly white, duskier on crown and around eye. Upperparts barred grey and white; underparts mostly white. Wings and tail of breeding adult unmoulted though browner through abrasion.

295c JUVENILE/FIRST-AUTUMN: Darker on forehead and crown than non-breeding adult. White upperwing patch broken by brown tips.

292 **RAZORBILL** 41/64cm
Alca torda AR, NAO MAP 292 **Text page 393**

292a ADULT BREEDING: Head and upperparts mostly black, contrasting with white sides of lower back and narrow trailing edge of secondaries in flight. Underparts mostly white. Bill diagnostic.

292b ADULT NON-BREEDING: Similar to 292a but chin, throat and ear-coverts white, extending upwards behind eye. Distinguished from similarly-patterned Guillemot (p. 395) by blacker upperparts, larger head and bill, thickset jizz.

292c IMMATURE/FIRST-SUMMER: Similar to 292b but ear-coverts and sides of breast duskier. Bill slimmer with ill-defined band.

310 **ATLANTIC PUFFIN** 29/56cm
other: Puffin
Fratercula arctica NAO MAP 310 **Text page 404**

310a ADULT BREEDING: Unmistakable at close range.

310b ADULT NON-BREEDING: Bill yellower distally, face duskier. Small examples could be confused with Little Auk (p. 392), although jizz, size and bill readily separate if seen well.

310c IMMATURE: Resembles 310b but bill smaller, reddish at tip, face duskier.

291 **LITTLE AUK** 22/32cm
other: Dovekie
Alle alle AR, NAO MAP 291 **Text page 392**

291a ADULT BREEDING: Unlike any other bird of the high Arctic; some penetrate north to 82°N. Blackish head and upperparts contrast with white underparts. Small dumpy jizz and whirring wings characteristic.

291b ADULT NON-BREEDING: Resembles 291a but chin, throat, upper breast and ear-coverts white.

295a
295a
295c
295b
292a
292a
292c
292b
292a
310a
310a
310c
310a
310b
291a
291b
291a
291a
291b

Plate 84

AUKS

293 **BRÜNNICH'S GUILLEMOT** 46/76cm
other: Thick-billed Murre
Uria lomvia AR, NAO, NPO MAP 293 **Text page 394**

293a ADULT BREEDING: Differs from 294a in shorter, heavier bill with white tomium stripe; white upper breast extends upwards in sharply pointed, inverted V (rounded in Guillemot). Post-nuptial head moult occurs later than in Guillemot; any dark-headed alcid during autumn or winter should be fully investigated, particularly in Pacific where Razorbills (p. 393) do not occur.

293b ADULT TRANSITIONAL: As breeding adult except for white border at base of lower mandible. Likely to occur during Nov, and May/Jul.

293c ADULT NON-BREEDING: Resembles breeding adult except blackish-brown cap merges evenly under eye into white chin and throat. Differs from Guillemot in darker-headed aspect and lack of post-ocular streak across white ear-coverts.

294 **GUILLEMOT** 42/71cm
other: Common Murre
Uria aalge AR, NAO, NPO MAP 294 **Text page 395**

294a ADULT BREEDING: Differs from Brünnich's Guillemot in longer, finer bill and white breast terminating on throat in rounded, inverted V. Southern *U.a. albionis* is also browner in tone than that species.

294b ADULT TRANSITIONAL (bridled form shown, see p. 395): During Jul/Aug dark ear-coverts, chin and throat break down to show mottled brown and white areas. See notes above and in main text on differences in timing of post- and pre-nuptial head moults in Brünnich's and Common Guillemots.

294c ADULT NON-BREEDING: Foreneck, chin and throat white with diagnostic post-ocular stripe across white ear-coverts.

294d JUVENILE: Departs from ledges 18–25 days after hatching. (Beware Little Auk, p. 392.)

294e FIRST-WINTER: Head darker than 294c, bill proportionately shorter.

311 **HORNED PUFFIN** 38/57cm
Fratercula corniculata NPO MAP 311 **Text page 405**

311a ADULT BREEDING: Unmistakable within range.

311b ADULT NON-BREEDING: Bill-sheath shed to reveal dusky bill with reddish tip; sides of face greyer.

293c
293a
293c
293a
293b
294c
294a
294c
294e
294b
294d
311b
311a
311a
311a

Plate 85

PACIFIC ALCIDS

296 **PIGEON GUILLEMOT** 32/?cm
Cepphus columba NPO — MAP 296 **Text page 396**

296a ADULT BREEDING: Unmistakable throughout much of range. Separated from similar Black Guillemot (p. 396) by black wedge in white upperwing-coverts and brownish-grey underwing-coverts (white in Black Guillemot).

296b ADULT NON-BREEDING: Plumage variable due to prolonged moult sequences. As first-winter Black Guillemot also has a broken white upperwing patch, colour of underwing-coverts is probably most reliable character to look for.

296c TRANSITIONAL ADULT (Jan–Apr): Pattern can suggest winter-plumage Marbled Murrelet, but present species larger with white coverts (not scapulars) and different jizz.

296d JUVENILE: Distinctive throughout much of range, but where Black Guillemots also likely to occur brownish-grey (not white) underwing-coverts most reliable character.

296e ADULT BREEDING (*C.c. snowi*): Resembles larger 297a but lacks white 'spectacles', some show wholly dark upperwings.

296f ADULT TRANSITIONAL (*C.c. snowi*): Beware of confusing with larger, heavier-billed 297.

297 **SPECTACLED GUILLEMOT** 37/?cm
other: Sooty Guillemot
Cepphus carbo RR — MAP 297 **Text page 397**

297a ADULT BREEDING: Distinctive; mostly dull sooty-black except for conspicuous white 'spectacles'.

297b ADULT NON-BREEDING: As 297a but underparts white, uniformly tipped very pale grey-brown.

297c ADULT TRANSITIONAL: As 297a except underparts scaled with white.

312 **TUFTED PUFFIN** 38/?cm
Lunda cirrhata NPO — MAP 312 **Text page 406**

312a ADULT BREEDING: Unmistakable.

312b ADULT NON-BREEDING: Bill-sheath, white sides of face, and plumes lost. Generally appears blackish above, merging without demarcation into brownish-grey underparts; at close range, paler superciliary over eye. Non-breeding Rhinoceros Auklet (p. 404) similarly patterned, but head and bill shape distinctly different.

312c JUVENILE: Much as 312b. Beware of confusing with Rhinoceros Auklet (p. 404), which has different bill and more pointed wings.

296a
296d
296a
296b
296c
296e
297c
296f
297b
297a
312a
312c
312b
312a
312a
312c

Plate 86

PACIFIC ALCIDS

306 **CRESTED AUKLET** 23/?cm
Aethia cristatella NPO MAP 306 **Text page 402**

306a ADULT BREEDING: Larger than Whiskered Auklet with only one, not three, facial streaks.

306b ADULT NON-BREEDING: Bill-sheath shed; crest and auricular stripe retained but somewhat reduced.

306c JUVENILE: Differs from juvenile Whiskered Auklet in darker head without stripes, and larger size. Cassin's Auklet (p. 401) similar but with dark bill and, in flight, a whiter belly.

308 **WHISKERED AUKLET** 17/?cm
Aethia pygmaea NPO MAP 308 **Text page 403**

308a ADULT BREEDING: Smaller than Crested Auklet with proportionately smaller bill and three white facial streaks on face, two of which fork outwards from gape. (Non-breeding adults similar but with shorter crest and less defined white facial streaks.)

308b JUVENILE: Differs from both Crested and Cassin's Auklets in three, whitish, indistinct streaks on sides of face; Cassin's also has darker bill.

307 **LEAST AUKLET** 15/?cm
Aethia pusilla NPO MAP 307 **Text page 403**

307a ADULT BREEDING: Tiny; white throat and ill-defined breast band diagnostic.

307b ADULT NON-BREEDING: Superficially resembles non-breeding Marbled and Kittlitz's Murrelets (p. 398, p. 398), which also have whitish scapulars. Present species however smaller, with dark cap extending well below eye-level and broken with white auricular streak. (Juveniles similar but lack white auricular streak, Bent 1919.)

309 **RHINOCEROS AUKLET** 36/?cm
Cerorhinca monocerata NPO MAP 309 **Text page 404**

309a ADULT BREEDING: Large brownish alcid with whitish belly; more closely related to puffins than to auklets. Yellowish-orange bill with erect horn diagnostic.

309b ADULT NON-BREEDING: Bill-sheath shed, white facial streaks reduced. Superficially resembles immature Tufted Puffin (p. 406), but wings more pointed with smaller, more pointed bill.

309c JUVENILE: As non-breeding adult except bill smaller and finer, head lacks facial streaks.

306b
306a
306a
306c
308a
308b
308a
307b
307b
307a
307a
309b
309a
309c
309b

Plate 87

PACIFIC ALCIDS

300 **XANTUS' MURRELET** 25/?cm
Endomychura hypoleuca RR MAP 300 **Text page 399**

300a *E.h. scrippsi*: Differs from Craveri's Murrelet in slightly larger size, shorter bill, greyer cast to upperparts and black cap extending only to line of gape. In flight, present species has whiter sides of breast and mostly white underwing (although latter often hard to ascertain due to whirring wings).

300b *E.h. hypoleuca*: As 300a but has prominent white crescents above and below eye (both *scrippsi* and Craveri's Murrelet have only indistinct whitish crescents).

301 **CRAVERI'S MURRELET** 21/?cm
Endomychura craveri RR MAP 301 **Text page 400**

301 Differs from both races of Xantus' Murrelet in slightly longer bill; black cap extending to bottom edge of lower mandible; darker upperparts; more extensive, blackish 'spurs' on sides of breast; and dusky grey and white underwing-coverts.

303 **CRESTED MURRELET** 26/?cm
other: Japanese Murrelet
Synthliboramphus wumizusume RR MAP 303 **Text page 401**

303 ADULT BREEDING: Resembles better-known Ancient Murrelet (p. 400), but with short black crest and less extensive black on chin and throat.

304 **CASSIN'S AUKLET** 21/?cm
Ptychoramphus aleuticus NPO MAP 304 **Text page 401**

304 Small, plump alcid with dusky plumage at all seasons. Much larger Rhinoceros Auklet (p. 404) has yellowish bill. In north of range beware immature Crested and Whiskered Auklets (p. 402, p. 403). See also breeding Marbled Murrelet (p. 398).

300a
300a
300a
300b
301
301
301
303
303
304
304

Plate 88

PACIFIC ALCIDS

298 **MARBLED MURRELET** 24/?cm
Brachyramphus marmoratus NPO MAP 298 **Text page 398**

298a ADULT BREEDING: Differs from Kittlitz's Murrelet in browner, less cryptic upperparts, slightly capped appearance and darker belly. At close range, bill longer and more slender.

298b ADULT NON-BREEDING: The only alcid with pale scapulars regularly occurring S of Alaska. Differs from Kittlitz's Murrelet, where ranges overlap, by blacker upperparts, darker cap extending below eye and dark outer tail feathers.

299 **KITTLITZ'S MURRELET** 23/?cm
Brachyramphus brevirostris NPO MAP 299 **Text page 398**

299a ADULT BREEDING: Differs from Marbled Murrelet in much shorter bill and more cryptic, sandy-brown, upperparts. At distance, lacks both indistinct capped effect and dark brown back of that species.

299b ADULT NON-BREEDING: Differs from both Marbled Murrelet and Least Auklet (p. 398, p. 403) in white of face extending upwards above eye, imparting white-faced aspect; upperparts greyer, outer tail feathers white.

302 **ANCIENT MURRELET** 26/?cm
Synthliboramphus antiquum NPO MAP 302 **Text page 400**

302a ADULT BREEDING: Uncrested black head contrasting with blue-grey back and white underparts diagnostic. See also Crested Murrelet (p. 401) off Japan.

302b ADULT NON-BREEDING: Only the much smaller and generally darker Cassin's Auklet (p. 401) appears grey-backed at sea (but see Crested Murrelet, p. 401). The pale bill and black head with white underparts extending upwards on sides of neck to form partial collar are useful field characters, visible at some distance.

302c JUVENILE: Precocial; joins adults at sea within a few days of hatching, swimming and diving readily but unable to fly.

305 **PARAKEET AUKLET** 24/?cm
Cyclorrhynchus psittacula NPO MAP 305 **Text page 402**

305a ADULT BREEDING: Differs from much smaller Least Auklet (p. 403) in dark chin and throat and proportionately larger bill.

305b ADULT NON-BREEDING: Stout brownish-red bill, size and clear white breast enable ready separation from congeners. Beware some Rhinoceros Auklets (p. 404), which may show orange-red bill but differ in dark breast and flanks.

298b
298a
298a
298b
299a
299a
299b
299b
302b
302a
302c
302a
302b
305a
305b
305a

SYSTEMATIC SECTION

Order *SPHENISCIFORMES*

Family *SPHENISCIDAE* penguins

Six genera comprising 16 species, all flightless, stocky, aquatic birds with dark upperparts and white underparts. Although most closely related to petrels and shearwaters (*Procellariidae*), they are highly specialised. They differ from most seabirds in their layer of blubber, thick pile of modified feathers, moult process and their physiology associated with pursuit-diving, during which Emperor Penguins can reach depths of 265m and remain submerged for up to 9 minutes. The Emperor is the largest, standing over 1m high; smallest is the Little Blue Penguin, only 40cm high. Sexes outwardly similar, males average slightly larger; in both *Eudyptula* and *Eudyptes*, there are minor differences in the bill structure of the sexes.

On land penguins are clumsy, progressing with obvious difficulty in waddling gait or short hops. The more southern forms toboggan over ice and snow on their belly, using feet and flippers for rapid propulsion. By contrast penguins are ideally suited to a marine environment, literally flying through the water, often at great speed, when they porpoise out of the water to breathe. They float on the surface with head and back exposed, their tails occasionally held cocked.

Penguins are seldom seen during sea voyages in Southern Oceans, their low profile and cryptic colouring rendering them almost invisible; they also dive at the approach of ships. This has greatly compounded the problems of plotting the pelagic distribution of many species during the austral winter.

Identification at colonies is usually straightforward; at sea it is often impossible. In all cases identification should be based on size; proportion and colour of bill; pattern and colour of head. In worn plumage all species appear browner.

Genus *APTENODYTES*

Two species. Largest of the penguins, each with diagnostic head pattern. Their breeding ranges do not usually overlap. During austral winter pelagic ranges may, however, overlap, especially off southern South America.

1 KING PENGUIN
Aptenodytes patagonicus

PLATE 1 Figs 1a-1c
MAP 1

Length 95cm (37½in.). Iris brown. Bill blackish, inner two-thirds of lower mandible pink or orange. Legs/feet dark grey.

Sub-antarctic islands and adjacent seas; range may occasionally overlap with larger Emperor Penguin (p. 200). Sexes outwardly alike; no seasonal variation. Juveniles separable from adults. Two subspecies listed.

CHICK: Wholly greyish-brown at first then dense woolly-brown.

JUVENILE: Smaller than adult; lower mandible only faintly marked pink. Overall plumage much as adult except for greyish tips to crown feathers and pale yellow auricular patches.

ADULT: Head Blackish-brown except for bright orange auricular patches. **Body** Upperparts silvery-grey with blackish border extending from throat along flanks. Underparts mostly white; upper breast faintly yellowish. **Flipper** Upperside as upperparts; underside white, broadly tipped blue-grey. **Tail** Blackish-grey, short.

HJ: Smaller and more brightly coloured than more southerly Emperor Penguin (p. 200). Unusual in that breeding occurs only twice every three years (Stonehouse 1960).

DM: Circumpolar. *A.p. patagonicus* breeds South Georgia; those breeding on Falklands usually assigned to this subspecies. Status on islands off Cape Horn (Staten and Horn Is) requires clarification. *A.p. halli* breeds Marion, Prince Edward, Crozet, Kerguelen, Heard and Macquarie Is. Early breeders return to colonies Sep, late breeders Nov. Egg-dates Nov–Mar; fledging and departure Nov to Apr of following year depending on month of hatching. Pelagic range not fully known; juveniles and non-breeders probably wander more extensively. Vagrants have occured N to Gough I., South Africa and southern Australia.

SS: See notes under Emperor Penguin (p. 200).

2 EMPEROR PENGUIN
Aptenodytes forsteri

PLATE 1 Figs 2a-2c
MAP 2

Length 115cm (42in.). Iris brown. Bill blackish, inner two-thirds of lower mandible coral-pink to lilac. Legs/feet dark grey.

Antarctic; range may overlap with smaller King Penguin (p. 200) off southern tip of South America. Sexes alike; no seasonal variation. Juveniles separable from adults. No subspecies.

Wader topography II:

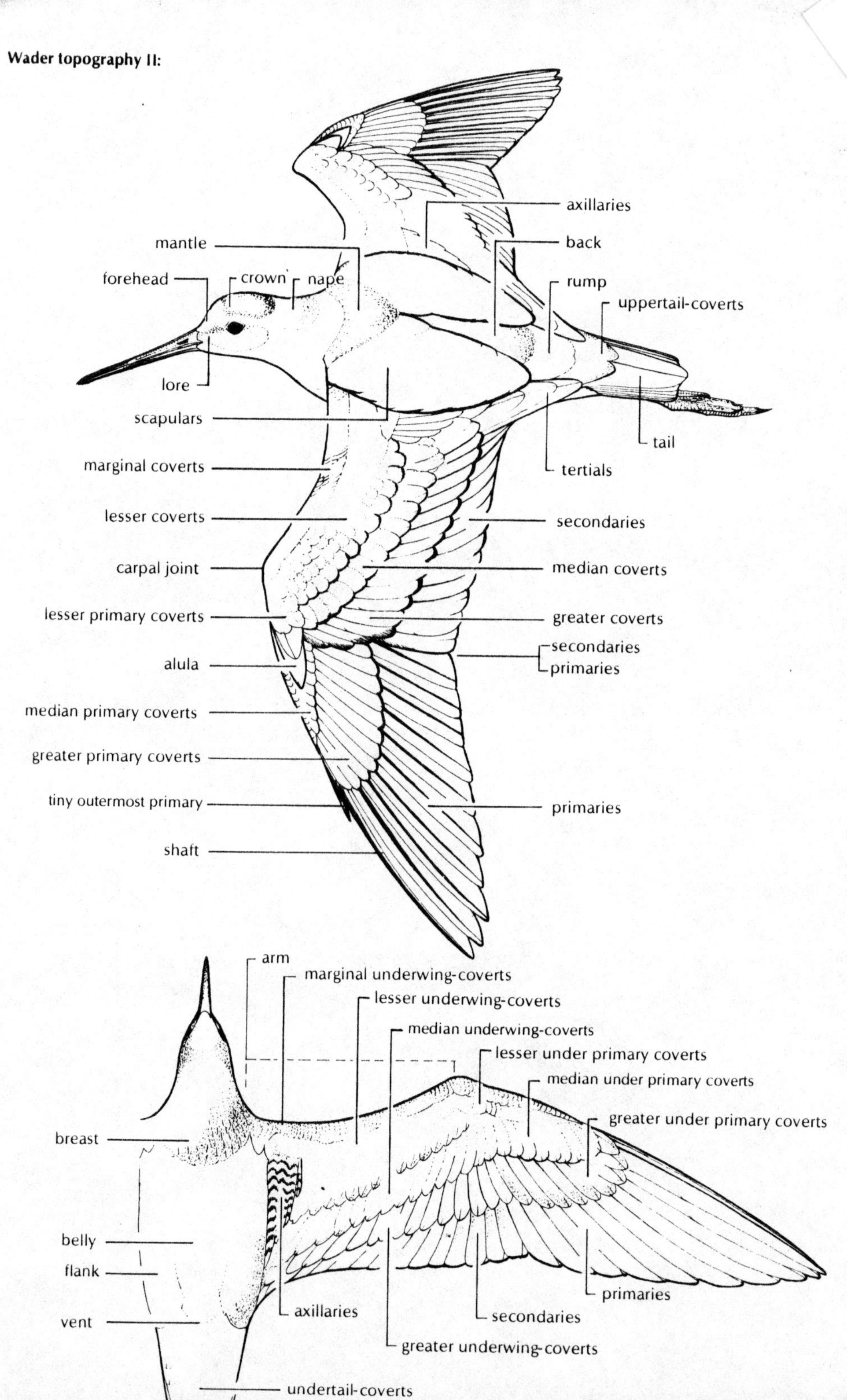

CHICK: Mostly silvery- to darkish grey with conspicuous white face mask and blackish head.
JUVENILE: Smaller than adult; inner two-thirds of lower mandible dull pinkish-orange. Overall pattern much as adult except for whitish auricular patches on sides of head and whitish chin and throat. During first year at sea auricular patches become more pronounced, head and upperparts area browner.
ADULT: Head Blackish-blue except for large yellow and white auricular patches. **Body** Upperparts light blue-grey with blackish border extending downwards from sides of neck to flanks. Underparts mostly white; upper breast faintly yellowish. **Flipper** Upperside as upperparts, underside white. **Tail** Blackish-grey, short. NOTE In worn plumage auricular patches whiter.
HJ: Largest of all penguins. Unique in incubating its egg during dark Antarctic winter.
DM: Breeds at about 30 localities around Antarctic continent and at the Dion Is off the southern Antarctic Peninsula. Returns to colonies Mar/Apr; egg-dates May/Jun; fledging and departure begins Dec. Pelagic range not fully known: formerly thought confined to open pack ice in Antarctic zone; recent sightings off southern South America, particularly those of Rumboll (1977) at 40°30′S, 54°34′W, off Argentina, indicate that juveniles or non-breeders may wander more extensively than currently realised.
SS: Adults distinctive at colonies but, at sea, brown-headed juveniles with pinkish-orange stripes on lower mandibles would be extremely difficult to separate from juvenile King Penguins (p. 200), although auricular patches are white, not yellowish.

Genus *PYGOSCELIS*

Three species. Moderately large, two without head ornaments; the third, Gentoo Penguin, with white band over the crown from eye to eye, easily separated from both Chinstrap and Adélie Penguins. Latter two separated by critical examination of head pattern; beware especially confusing white-chinned juvenile Adélie with whiter-faced Chinstrap.

3 GENTOO PENGUIN
Pygoscelis papua

PLATE 1 Figs 3a-3c
MAP 3

Length 81cm (31in.). Iris brown or dull red. Bill orange-red, ridge of culmen black. Legs/feet yellow-orange.

Circumpolar in sub-antarctic regions; distinctive head pattern should prevent confusion with other species. Sexes alike; no seasonal variation though appears browner in worn plumage. Juveniles separable from adults. Two subspecies listed, differing mainly in bill, flipper and foot measurements. Partial albinism reported (Stonehouse 1972).
CHICK: Silvery-grey below with dark grey head and greyish back. In secondary down, head and upperparts light grey-brown; underparts, including chin, white.
JUVENILE: Smaller than adult; bill weaker and duller. Overall plumage much as adult except white bar over crown duller, less extensive; chin and throat sometimes greyer.
ADULT: Head Mostly blue-black except for variable white patch above eye linked by narrow bar over crown. **Body** Upperparts blue-black. Underparts mostly white. **Flipper** Upperside as upperparts with broad, white trailing edge; underside white; tip blackish. **Tail** Blue-black, base often whitish.
HJ: Large black and white penguin with distinctive head pattern. Rather timid, breeds in small colonies.
DM: Circumpolar in sub-antarctic zone. *P.p. papua* breeds Falkland, Staten, Prince Edward, Marion, Crozet, Kerguelen and Macquarie Is; and S to Antarctic Convergence on South Georgia and Heard Is. *P.p. ellsworthii* breeds Antarctic zone on South Sandwich, South Orkney and South Shetlands Is, and on Antarctic Peninsula S to about 65°S. Returns to colonies Aug–Oct; egg-dates Aug–Nov; fledging and departure of juveniles Dec–Mar; adults depart after moult during Mar–Jun. Pelagic range not fully known; northern populations probably disperse to adjacent seas, whilst southern population more strongly migratory. Some winter N to about 43°S on coast of Argentina; vagrants occur N to Tasmania and New Zealand.
SS: Large size and distinctive head pattern should prevent confusion with other species.

4 ADÉLIE PENGUIN
Pygoscelis adeliae

PLATE 2 Figs 4a-4c
MAP 4

Length 70cm ($27\frac{1}{2}$in.). Iris white. Bill reddish, tipped black (feathered for half its length). Legs/feet pink, soles black.

Antarctic seas; range overlaps with Chinstrap (p. 202). Sexes alike; no seasonal variation. Juveniles separable from adults. No subspecies.
CHICK: First down: head sooty-grey, remainder silvery-grey. Secondary down: wholly greyish-brown.
JUVENILE: Smaller and slimmer than adult with weaker bill. Plumage as adult except for darker eye-ring and white chin and throat.
IMMATURE: Eye-ring becomes white at about 1 year of age, followed in Feb by moult to adult plumage.
ADULT: Head Blue-black. **Body** Upperparts blue-black. Underparts white. **Flipper** Upperside as upperparts with narrow white trailing edge; underside white, narrowly margined with black along leading edge. **Tail** Blue-black.
HJ: Medium- to small-sized, uncrested penguin with dark head and comical button-eyed appearance. Bold and inquisitive.

DM: Circumpolar; breeds in large colonies, some exceeding 1 million, on South Shetland, South Orkney (?), South Sandwich and Bouvet Is, and along coasts and islands of Antarctic continent. Returns to colonies Oct; egg-dates Nov; fledging and departure of juveniles Jan/Feb. Adults moult mostly on sea ice during Feb–Mar before returning to open pack ice. Migratory but range not fully known; probably circumpolar S of 60°S. Vagrants have occurred N to Falklands, South Georgia, Kerguelen, Heard and Macquarie Is. Two records from Australia are suspect (Serventy *et al.* 1971).
SS: See notes under Chinstrap Penguin (p. 202).

5 CHINSTRAP PENGUIN
other: Bearded Penguin
Pygoscelis antarctica

PLATE 2 Figs 5a-5c

MAP 5

Length 68cm (27in.). Iris red, orbital ring black. Bill black. Legs/feet pinkish.

Antarctic seas; range overlaps with Adélie Penguin (p. 201). Sexes alike, no seasonal variation. Juveniles separable from adults. No subspecies.
CHICK: First down: wholly silvery-white. Secondary down: mostly silvery-grey or brown above, head and underparts paler.
JUVENILE/IMMATURE: As adult but smaller and slimmer with weaker bill and scattered dark feather tips on chin and cheeks.
ADULT: Head Uncrested; forehead, crown and nape blue-black with white cheeks, chin and throat crossed by a thin black line. **Body** Upperparts blue-black. Underparts white. **Flipper** Upperside as upperparts with narrow white trailing edge; underside white; small black tip. **Tail** Blue-black.
HJ: About same size as Adélie (p. 201) but with conspicuous white sides to face. Gregarious and pugnacious (Beware!). Often porpoises, frequently cocks tail when swimming (as do all *Pygoscelis* penguins).
DM: Breeds mainly at South Orkney, South Shetland, South Georgia, South Sandwich and on Antarctic Peninsula as far S as Anvers I. Smaller numbers breed Bouvet, Peter First, Heard and Balleny Is. Sladen (1964) suggested numbers and range increasing concurrently with slaughter of whales, with whom penguins share a common food resource (krill). Returns to colonies Nov; egg-dates Nov/Dec, fledging and departure of juveniles Feb/Mar. Adults finally depart Mar–Jun. Winter movements largely unknown, presumably to open sea bordering pack ice. Stragglers occasionally reported far from land in lower latitudes of Southern Oceans; vagrants have reached Macquarie I. and Tasmania (Serventy *et al.* 1971).
SS: Immature Adélie Penguins (p. 201) also have white chins but demarcation between black and white lies well below eye and apparent bill length is much shorter.

Genus *EUDYPTES*

Five species. Moderate to moderately large; all adults have head ornaments in form of yellow superciliary crests; juveniles and immatures have only poorly developed crests. Crested penguins are hardest of all penguin groups to identify specifically. Adults at colonies distinguished from each other primarily by shape and distribution of their crests, particularly the point at which they start, and whether they are joined across forehead. Shape and proportion of bill plus presence of fleshy margins at gape also important characters to note down. Failure to record these characters accurately will prevent positive identification. Juveniles require careful treatment.

At sea the crests normally lie flat and compressed when wet, and specific identification unlikely unless at close range. The difficulties of identifying crested penguins at sea should not be underestimated.

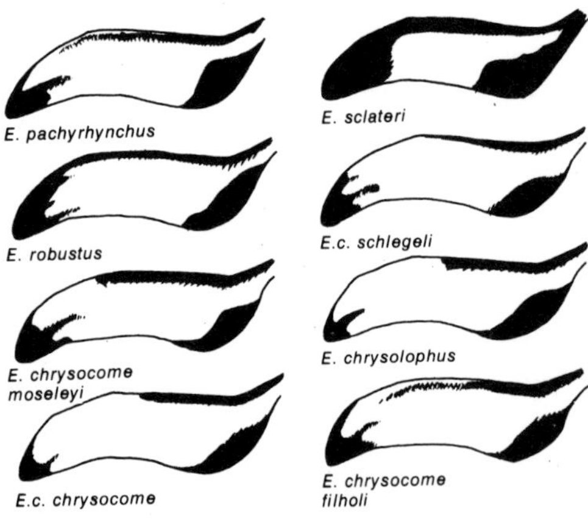

Fig. 3. Underside of *Eudyptes* flippers

6 FIORDLAND CRESTED PENGUIN
others: Thick-billed/Victoria/New Zealand Crested Penguin
Eudyptes pachyrhynchus

PLATE 4 Figs 6a-6b

MAP 6

Length 55cm (21½in.). Iris claret. Bill reddish-brown, without pink fleshy margins at base. Legs/feet pink, soles brown.

New Zealand and its offshore islands; range overlaps with Snares Island, and with wandering Rockhopper and Erect-crested Penguins (p. 203, p. 204, p. 203). Sexes outwardly alike, males average larger with more robust bills and broader superciliary stripes (Warham, pers. comm.). Juveniles

separable from adults. No subspecies.
CHICK: Secondary down: head and upperparts sooty-brown, underparts dirty-white.
JUVENILE: Smaller than adult with weaker, brownish bill. Plumage much as adult except for short yellow crest, white chin and throat, and cheeks more or less suffused or streaked with grey.
IMMATURE: Much as adult except for shorter crest.
ADULT: Head Mostly blue-black, with broad yellow crest beginning in recess formed by culminicorn and latericorn and sweeping over eye to lie flat on nape. The black cheek feathers are usually parted to show their white bases as two to five short, parallel streaks. **Body** Upperparts blue-black. Underparts white. **Flipper** Upperside as upperparts with narrow white trailing edge; underside, see Fig. 3, p. 202. **Tail** Blackish-blue.
HJ: Medium-sized crested penguin differing from most other members of genus in lack of pink fleshy margins at base of bill. Breeds in rather loose colonies near the sea, usually in temperate rain forest on headlands and islands. Frequently encountered in small parties off breeding islands; they sit fairly low in water, often with tail cocked
DM: Breeds mainland New Zealand along W and SE coasts of South Island from southern Westland to Solander and Stewart Is. Returns to colonies Jul; egg-dates Aug; fledging and departure of juveniles Nov. Adults return to breeding areas to moult during Jan–Feb with departure to pelagic habitat during early Mar (see especially Warham 1974). Movements not known but probably wanders extensively, occuring regularly W to seas off southern Australia and Tasmania and S to the Snares Is, where it is a visitor during moult periods.
SS: Adults and immatures differ from those of Snares Island Penguin (p. 203) in smaller bill, absence of fleshy margins at base of bill and white streaks across cheek feathers. Juveniles and immatures difficult, perhaps impossible, to separate at sea. See also Erect-crested Penguin (p. 203).

---

7 ERECT-CRESTED PENGUIN — PLATE 4 Figs 7a-7b
Eudyptes sclateri — MAP 7

Length 67cm (26½in.). Iris brown. Bill reddish-brown, pink fleshy margins at base. Legs/feet pink, soles black.

Islands S of New Zealand; range overlaps with Rockhopper Penguin (p. 204) and, during winter or dispersal, with Snares and Fiordland Penguins (p. 203, p. 202). Sexes outwardly alike; males average larger with more robust bills. No seasonal variation. Juveniles separable from adults. No subspecies.
CHICK: Secondary down: head and upperparts sooty-black, underparts white.
JUVENILE: Much as adult except eyebrows less developed, chin and throat whitish.
IMMATURE: As juvenile except chin and throat blackish.
ADULT: Head Mostly blackish; a golden-yellow, brush-like crest begins at base of bill close to gape and extends backwards over eye. **Body** Upperparts blackish. Underparts white. **Flipper** Upperside as upperparts with narrow, white trailing edge; underside mostly white with broad blackish anterior margin and tip. **Tail** Blackish; long.
HJ: Medium-sized crested penguin with brush-like crests although at sea, when wet, crests often flattened (Warham, pers. comm.). Nests in large colonies on rocky coasts (unlike Snares and Fiordland Penguins, p. 203, p. 202).
DM: Huge breeding colonies at Bounty and Antipodes Is, New Zealand. A few pairs breed at Campbell and Auckland Is. Returns to colonies Sep; egg-dates Oct; fledging date unknown. During winter months disperses to pelagic habitat but precise movements unknown; some occur N to coasts of Canterbury and Cook Strait. Stragglers, usually immatures or moulting birds, have occurred S to Macquarie I. (Falla *et al.* 1975), W to the Snares Is and N to Tasmania and southern Australia (Serventy *et al.* 1971). These records indicate a wide dispersal area. One straggler has reached Falkland Is.
SS: Brush-like crest and underflipper pattern separate present species at all ages from all other penguins. Juveniles differ from those of smaller Rockhopper in white chin and throat, and underflipper pattern. See also Fiordland and Snares Penguins (p. 202, p. 203).

---

8 SNARES ISLAND PENGUIN — PLATE 4 Figs 8a-8b
other: Snares Penguin, Snares Crested Penguin
Eudyptes robustus — MAP 8

Length 56cm (22in.). Iris claret. Bill reddish-brown, pink fleshy margin at base. Legs/feet pink, soles black.

Snares Islands, SE of New Zealand; range overlaps with Fiordland Crested Penguin (p. 202). Sexes outwardly alike, males average larger with more robust bills. Juveniles separable from adults. No subspecies.
CHICK: Secondary down: head and upperparts smoky-brown; underparts white.
JUVENILE: Smaller than adult with weaker, brownish bill. Plumage as adult except crest shorter; chin and throat white with blackish feather tips, becoming darker, more mottled, with age.
IMMATURE: As adult except for shorter crest.
ADULT: Head Mostly blue-black except for yellow crest beginning in recess formed by culminicorn and latericorn, sweeping over eye to nape and becoming bushy. **Body** Upperparts blue-black. Underparts white. **Flipper** Upperside as upperparts with narrow, white trailing edge; underside pattern shown in Fig. 3 (p. 202). **Tail** Blackish-blue.
HJ: Much as Fiordland Penguin but bill heavier, rear of crest somewhat bushier, and prominent pink fleshy margin at base of bill.
DM: Breeding restricted to Snares Is, SE of New Zealand. Returns to colonies Aug; egg-dates

Sep/Oct; fledging and departure of juveniles Jan. Adults moult Feb/Mar with most birds at sea by late Apr (see especially Warham 1974). Pelagic range and movements largely unknown, but has occurred Australia (Warham, pers. comm.).

SS: See notes under Fiordland Crested Penguin (p. 202).

9 ROCKHOPPER PENGUIN

Eudyptes chrysocome

PLATE 3 Figs 9a-9c
MAP 9

Length 55cm (21½in.). Iris red. Bill reddish-brown, narrow fleshy margin at base of bill varies from black to pinkish. Legs/feet pink, soles black.

Sub-antarctic islands; range overlaps with Macaroni, Royal, Snares and Erect-crested Penguins (p. 204, p. 205, p. 203, p. 203). Sexes outwardly alike; males generally larger with more robust bills; no seasonal variation. Juveniles separable from adults. Three subspecies listed; northern race *E.c. moseleyi* averages larger with fuller crest and darker underflipper pattern (Fig. 3). Fleshy margin at base of bill may be a further subspecific character. (See Watson 1975; Carins 1974.)

CHICK: First down: head and upperparts grey-brown; underparts and tip of black bill white. Secondary down: similar but head darker than upperparts.

JUVENILE: Smaller than adult, bill dull brownish-red. Plumage pattern much as adult but with only a faint crest and white mottling on chin and throat.

IMMATURE: As adult except for shorter, more erect head tassels; paler chin and throat.

ADULT: Head Mostly black with occipital crest and glossy yellow crest culminating in drooping, tasselled plumes on sides of head. **Body** Upperparts blue-black. Underparts mostly white. **Flipper** Upperside as upperparts with narrow white trailing edge; underside varies between races (see Fig. 3). **Tail** Blue-black above.

HJ: Small black and white crested penguin; noisy and quarrelsome, often breeding in huge colonies. Adept at climbing steep cliffs and, true to name, usually progresses on land in series of stiff, feet-together hops.

DM: Circumpolar in sub-antarctic zone: *E.c. chrysocome* breeds islands off Cape Horn and the Falklands; *E.c. moseleyi* at Tristan da Cunha, Gough, St Paul and Amsterdam Is; *E.c. filholi* at Prince Edward, Marion, Crozet, Kerguelen, Heard, Macquarie, Campbell, Auckland, and Antipodes. Returns to colonies Oct/Nov; egg-dates Nov/Dec. Fledging and departure of juveniles Mar/Apr; adults depart after moulting during Apr–May, though schedule on Tristan da Cunha group 6–8 weeks earlier. All populations desert natal islands in winter for pelagic habitat, but movements unknown. Some winter N to about 35°S off Argentina. A frequent straggler to coasts of South Africa and Australia, especially during moult periods.

SS: At colonies all penguins are easily identified. Present species differs from other adult crested penguins in smaller size, black occipital crest (unique) and that the drooping, golden head plumes neither reach the bill nor join together across forehead. Sinclair (pers. comm.) notes that at sea the fleshy base to Macaroni's bill appears as bright pale area, even at long range, and thus distinguishes it from Rockhopper. Immature Rockhopper and Macaroni Penguins can be separated by size, head and underflipper patterns.

10 MACARONI PENGUIN (Includes Royal Penguin)

Eudyptes chrysolophus

PLATE 3 Figs 10a-10c
PLATE 3 Figs 10Xa-10Xb
MAP 10

Length 70cm (27½in.). Iris reddish-brown. Bill reddish-brown with pinkish fleshy margin at gape. Legs/feet pink, soles black.

Sub-antarctic islands of southern Atlantic and Indian Oceans, where range overlaps with smaller Rockhopper Penguin (p. 204). Sexes outwardly alike, males average larger with more robust bills; no seasonal variation. Juveniles separable from adults. Although recognised as a valid race, Royal Penguin *E.c. schlegeli* is probably better regarded as colour phase of a binomially-treated species which is commonest at Macquarie I.; readily separable from typical *E.c. chrysolophus* but intermediates between the two forms occur at Macquarie I. (Shaughnessy 1975), and occurs among Macaroni populations elsewhere (Barre *et al.* 1976). See also Berruti (1981). *E.c. schlegeli* is described separately below (10X).

CHICK: First down: head and upperparts grey, underparts white. Secondary down: similar but head darker than back.

JUVENILE: Smaller than adult, bill dull brownish-red. Plumage much as adult except head plumes reduced to broken yellow wisps on forehead and behind eye; chin and throat dark grey.

IMMATURE: Much as adult except head plumes less developed, often appearing as dense yellow mat on forehead with wispy strands behind eye.

ADULT: Head Mostly blue-black terminating on upper breast in V-shaped junction; a patch of rich golden feathers on forehead extends backwards, drooping over eyes. **Body** Upperparts blue-black except for whitish uppertail-coverts. Underparts white. **Flipper** Upperside as upperparts with narrow white trailing edge; underside, see Fig. 3. **Tail** Blue-black above.

HJ: Compared with Rockhopper, present species about a third as large again with proportionately larger, more robust bill and fleshy gape. Unlike that species, head plumes are joined across forehead and, due to lack of pronounced occipital crest, head

shape appears more rounded.
DM: *E.c. chrysolophus* breeds at South Georgia, South Sandwich, South Orkney, South Shetland Is and on the Antarctic Peninsula. Further E it breeds on Bouvet, Prince Edward, Marion, Crozet, Kerguelen and Heard Is. Small numbers also breed in the Falkland group and possibly at Isla Noir, off Chile. Returns to colonies Sep–Nov; egg-dates Oct–Dec. Fledging and departure of juveniles Feb/Mar. Adults go to sea for about 5 weeks before returning to breeding grounds to moult; final departure Apr/May. Nothing is known of its movements during austral winter, but it seems likely that it remains in cold sub-antarctic seas between 45°S and 65°S. Vagrants have occurred N to South Africa.
SS: See notes under Rockhopper Penguin (p. 204).

10X ROYAL PENGUIN
Eudyptes chrysolophus schlegeli

ADULT: Generally as nominate race except for white or grey sides to face, chin and throat. Overall size and proportions of bill average larger.

DM: Confined to Macquarie I. but birds with these characters also occur in other populations. See especially Berruti (1981).

Genus *MEGADYPTES*

One species. Moderately large, restricted to coasts and islands of New Zealand. Separation from sympatric crested penguins straightforward.

11 YELLOW-EYED PENGUIN
Megadyptes antipodes

PLATE 2 Figs 11a-11c
MAP 11

Length 66cm (26in.). Iris yellow. Bill mostly dull pinkish-red, culmen and subterminal band reddish-brown. Legs/feet pinkish.

Confined to South Island, New Zealand, and Campbell and Auckland Is. Size and colour distinctive. Sexes alike; no seasonal variation. Juveniles separable from adults. No subspecies.
CHICK: Wholly cocoa-brown.
JUVENILE/IMMATURE: Much as adult except yellow band confined to sides of head; chin and throat mostly white.
ADULT: Head Forehead and crown pale, golden-yellow, with blackish shaft-streaks; sides of face, chin and throat similar but with brownish hue; nape slate-grey. A band of yellow feathers beginning above eye encircles hindcrown. **Body** Upperparts slate-grey. Underparts white. **Flipper** Upperside as upperparts with moderately broad white trailing edge; underside mostly white. **Tail** Slate-grey.
HJ: A distinctive species. Nests singly or in loose colonies in temperate forest or on grassy coastal cliffs. Returns to land at dusk, normally congregating in small groups offshore.
DM: Confined to SE corner of South Island, New Zealand, from about Oamaru S to Stewart I., also Auckland and Campbell Is. Returns to nest-sites Aug; egg-dates Sep/Oct. Fledging and departure Feb/Mar. Sedentary, occasionally wanders N to Cook Strait.
SS: White-faced Royal Penguin (p. 205) could occasionally occur within seas off southern New Zealand. Differs from all crested penguins by having a longer narrower bill and no crest.

Genus *EUDYPTULA*

One species although some authors recognise *E.(m.) albosignata* as separate species. Smallest penguin, restricted to Australasian region; separation from sympatric crested penguins in areas of overlap straightforward.

12 LITTLE PENGUIN
other: Fairy, Blue or Little Blue Penguin (includes White-flippered Penguin, 12X)
Eudyptula minor

PLATE 4 Fig. 12
MAP 12

Length 40cm (16in.). Iris silvery-grey, pupil black. Bill blackish-grey. Legs/feet flesh-white.

Australia and New Zealand; small size and blue-grey plumage distinctive. Sexes outwardly alike; males average larger with heavier bill. No seasonal variation, but in old or worn plumage upperparts often wear to greyish-brown. Juveniles differ from adults only in size of bill. Three subspecies listed, of which *E.(m.) albosignata* separable at sea and thus described separately below (12X).
CHICK: First down: chocolate-brown, paling with age. Secondary down: light, greyish-chocolate above, whitish below.
PLUMAGE: Head Mostly metallic blue-grey, paler on sides of face; chin and throat white. **Body** Upperparts metallic blue-grey of rather variable hue becoming increasingly browner with wear. Underparts white. **Flipper** Upperside as upperparts with narrow white trailing edge; underside mostly white; tip dusky. **Tail** Short; blue- or silvery-grey.
HJ: Smallest penguin; distinctive due to blue-grey

upperparts and lack of crest. Gregarious, often seen in small groups offshore; returns to landfall at night.

DM: (After Kinsky & Falla 1976) Australasian region. *E.m. novaehollandiae* breeds coasts and islands of southern Australia and Tasmania from Fremantle E to Port Stephens; *E.m. minor* breeds coasts of North Island, and some coasts of South Island, New Zealand, also Stewart and Chatham Is; *E.(m.) albosignata* breeds Banks Peninsula, South Island, New Zealand. Egg-dates Jul–Jan. Non-migratory.

SS: Unmistakable; much smaller and paler than other penguins; lacks crest.

12X WHITE-FLIPPERED PENGUIN
E.(m.) albosignata

PLATE 4 Fig. 12X
MAP 12

Treated as full species by some authors. Differs from nominate form in slightly larger size, paler upperparts and broad white margins to both leading and trailing edges of upperflipper which, in males, may link across centre of flipper. Restricted to region of Banks Peninsula, near Canterbury, on E coast of South Island, New Zealand.

Genus *SPHENISCUS*

Four species. Moderately large, uncrested black and white penguins with representatives on coasts of Africa and South America. Both Galapagos and South African Jackass Penguins are geographically isolated, ensuring straightforward identification. The ranges of Humboldt and Magellanic Penguins overlap in southern Chile; separation of adults straightforward if head and breast patterns critically examined; juveniles require more care.

13 JACKASS PENGUIN
Spheniscus demersus

PLATE 5 Figs 13a-13d
MAP 13

Length 70cm (27½in.). Iris dark with pink skin at base of upper mandible and encircling eye. Bill stout, black with grey transverse bar. Legs/feet black.

Coasts of South Africa and Namibia; no other penguin occurs regularly within range. Sexes alike, no seasonal variation. Juveniles separable from adults. No subspecies.

CHICK: Secondary down: head and upperparts brown, underparts whitish.

JUVENILE: Head and upperparts blackish-grey merging on upper breast into white underparts. Thus lacks both white head stripes and inverted black horseshoe on breast of adult.

IMMATURE: Much as juvenile except throat and band over eye become increasingly white, imparting ghost-image of adult's pattern.

ADULT: Head Mostly blackish except for white band on each side of crown, looping over eye and behind cheeks to meet with white upper breast. **Body** Upperparts blackish-grey. Underparts mostly white with inverted black horseshoe extending down flank to thigh; some show partial or complete second breast band. **Flipper** Upperside as upperparts with narrow white trailing edge; underside mostly white, margins dusky. **Tail** Blackish.

HJ: Swims low in water, often in small groups; rarely encountered more than 8km from islands or mainland.

DM: Confined to southern Africa, breeding offshore islands of Namibia and South Africa E to eastern Cape Province. Non-breeders occasionally wander N to Angola and Mozambique. Numbers declining due to oil spillage and destruction of/interference with nesting islands; ultimate survival threatened.

SS: Only penguin likely to be encountered at sea off southern Africa, although both Rockhopper and Macaroni Penguins (p. 204, p. 204) occasionally occur.

14 HUMBOLDT PENGUIN
other: Peruvian Penguin
Spheniscus humboldti

PLATE 5 Figs 14a-14b
MAP 14

Length 65cm (25½in.). Iris reddish-brown, eye-ring pink. Bill black with grey transverse bar and prominent fleshy margins at base. Legs/feet black.

Humboldt Current region off western South America; range overlaps with Magellanic Penguin (p. 207) for 10° of latitude between Valdivia and Coquimbo, Chile (Murphy 1936). Sexes alike; no seasonal variation. Juveniles separable from adults. No subspecies.

CHICK: Secondary down: head and upperparts grey, white below.

JUVENILE/IMMATURE: Head rather brown in tone with greyer cheeks, thus lacking white stripe of adult. Underparts white.

ADULT: Head Mostly black except for narrow white stripe on each side of crown, looping over eye and broadening at junction with white upper breast. **Body** Upperparts blackish-grey. Underparts mostly white with inverted black horseshoe extending down flank to thigh. **Flipper** Upperside as upperparts with whitish trailing edge; underside mostly white. **Tail** Blackish.

HJ: Compared with Magellanic Penguin (p. 207)

present species has narrower white crown stripe, imparting darker-headed appearance; breast has only one cross band. Seen closely, stout bill is also larger with more extensive fleshy margins at base. Gregarious, often met with in small groups at sea; on land rather timid.

DM: Breeds coast of Peru and Chile from about 5°S southwards to about 33°S near Valparaiso, Chile, but exact limits obscured by presence of Magellanic Penguin (p. 207). Egg-dates throughout year; nests in burrows or caves. Non-breeders may occasionally wander N to Gulf of Guayaquil and S to about 37°S.

SS: See notes under Magellanic Penguin (p. 207).

15 MAGELLANIC PENGUIN
Spheniscus magellanicus

PLATE 5 Figs 15a-15b
MAP 15

Length 70cm (27½in.). Iris brown, eye-ring pink. Bill stout, black with grey transverse bar and narrow fleshy margins at base. Legs/feet black.

Pacific and Atlantic coasts of southern South America; range overlaps with Humboldt Penguin (p. 206) between Valdivia and Coquimbo, Chile (Murphy 1936). Sexes alike; no seasonal variation. Juveniles separable from adults. No subspecies.

CHICK: Secondary down: head and upperparts brown, underparts whitish.

JUVENILE/IMMATURE: Differs from adult in whitish-grey sides of face, chin and throat, and indistinct greyish band across upper breast; thus lacks adult's striking head pattern and black bands across breast.

ADULT: Head Mostly blackish except for broad white band on each side of crown, looping over eye and joining on throat. **Body** Upperparts blackish-grey. Underparts mostly white except for inverted black horseshoe extending down flank to thigh; a second, wider, band crosses upper breast. **Flipper:** Upperside as upperparts with narrow white trailing edge; underside white with dusky margins. **Tail** Blackish-grey.

HJ: Bill stout but smaller than similarly-sized Humboldt Penguin (p. 206). Head has more contrasting pattern due to much wider white band on crown and sides of head; also two, not one, black bands across upper breast. Gregarious, often met with in small parties at sea.

DM: Atlantic and Pacific coasts of southern South America. Breeds at Falkland Is and along Patagonian coast from about 43°S southwards to Cape Horn and its outlying islands, then N along Pacific coast to Santa Maria I. (37°S); also at Juan Fernandez Is (32°S) off Chile. Returns to colonies about Sep, egg-dates Sep/Oct, fledging and dispersal Mar/Apr. Winter range extends N to southern Brazil, occasionally N to Rio de Janeiro (23°S) on Atlantic coast and to about 30°S on Pacific coast. At the Falklands a few seen throughout winter months. Vagrants have reached New Zealand and South Georgia (Watson 1975).

SS: Adults separated from those of the larger-billed Humboldt Penguin (p. 206) by wider white bands on head and two black bands across breast. Juveniles more difficult to separate: those of Magellanic have whitish-grey cheeks and throat with partial or complete grey breast band; by comparison juvenile Humboldt have generally dark brownish or grey head colour extending to upper breast.

16 GALAPAGOS PENGUIN
Spheniscus mendiculus

PLATE 5 Figs 16a-16b
MAP 16

Length 53cm (21in.). Iris dark, narrow pink eye-ring. Bill short; upper mandible black, base of lower pinkish-yellow. Legs/feet black.

Restricted to Galapagos Is, Pacific Ocean; unmistakable within range. Sexes alike, no seasonal variation. Juveniles separable from adults. No subspecies.

CHICK: No information available.

JUVENILE/IMMATURE: Differs from adult in wholly dark head; cheeks and chin greyer, thus lacks narrow supercilium and breast band of adult.

ADULT: Head Mostly blackish with narrow white line from eye curving behind cheeks to join on throat. **Body** Upperparts blackish-grey. Underparts mostly white; two indistinct bands across upper breast, the lower extending narrowly down flanks to thigh (at distance appears as one wide band). **Flipper** Upperside as upperparts; underside white with wide black margin at base. **Tail** Blackish.

HJ: A small penguin. Loosely colonial, small family groups often seen offshore; swims low in water with dorsal area awash but tail often elevated.

DM: Endemic to Galapagos Is, where a few thousand pairs breed around coasts of Fernandina and Isabela (see Harris 1974). Small parties often seen at James, Santa Cruz and Floreana. One straggler captured on Pacific coast of Panama.

SS: Unmistakable.

Order *GAVIIFORMES*

Family *GAVIIDAE* divers/loons

Single genus containing four species; status of *G.a. pacifica* currently under review, in time may be elevated to a full species. Divers, or loons as they are affectionately termed in North America, are large, mainly fish-eating, foot-propelled diving birds inhabiting fresh- and saltwater locations in northern Holarctic area. They bear a superficial resemblance to cormorants; bodies are sleek, with thick-set necks and dagger-like bills. Unlike the grebes, which have only tail tufts, divers have short but well-developed tails of 16–20 feathers. They dive from the surface, normally without springing clear, and are capable of reaching depths of about 75m. Sexes outwardly alike. All species breed on fresh water from tiny ponds to slow-flowing rivers. Their long, wailing cries, and mournful laughter, are a characteristic sound of the Arctic wilderness areas. Highly migratory. All except Red-throated Diver require a long run to become airborne from both land and water but, once aloft, flight is swif and powerful with neck extended forward anc down, imparting characteristic hump-backed jiz with feet projecting well beyond tail and hel together sole to sole.

Genus *GAVIA*

Four species, restricted to northern hemisphere. Identification during breeding season straightforward. In non-breeding plumage separation more difficult but, when seen under good conditions, should present few problems to experienced observer. Key points are bill size, shape and colour; head shape and colour, and whether lighter or darker than upperparts; overall jizz. For further reading see Burn & Mather (1974) and Binford & Remsen (1974).

17 RED-THROATED DIVER
other: Red-throated Loon
Gavia stellata

PLATE 6 Figs 17a-17c

MAP 17

Length 53–69cm (21–27in.). Wingspan 106–116cm (42–45½in.). Males average larger. Iris reddish. Bill blue-grey, culmen blackish. Legs/feet blackish, webs pink.

Circumpolar, most widespread diver, breeding Arctic and sub-arctic tundra. Migrates S in winter, range overlaps with other divers. Distinguished at all ages by smaller size, slender, uptilted bill and distinctive plumage. Sexes alike; marked seasonal variation. Juveniles and first-winter birds separable from adults. No subspecies.

JUVENILE/FIRST-WINTER: Bill pale brownish-grey, culmen darker. As non-breeding adult except: **Head** Forehead and sides of neck darker. **Body** Upperparts duller and browner, less spotted. Underparts washed with brown, particularly flanks. **Wings** Upperwing: primaries and secondaries blackish-brown, remainder greyish-brown, coverts faintly tipped white. Underwing: primaries and secondaries blackish, remainder white, **Tail** Brownish; undertail white.

ADULT NON-BREEDING: Bill pale grey, culmen dark grey. **Head** Forehead, crown and hindneck brownish-grey lightly peppered white and merging evenly into white sides of face, chin, throat and foreneck. **Body** Upperparts pale brownish-grey finely spotted with white, scapulars streaked white. Underparts mainly white, flanks and undertail-coverts washed brownish-grey. **Wings** As adult breeding except greyer. **Tail** Brownish.

ADULT BREEDING: Head Mostly grey, rear of crown indistinctly striped black and white and becoming heavier, more distinct, at base of hindneck; lower foreneck dull reddish (appearing black in dull light or at distance). **Body** Upperparts dark brownish-grey, faintly green in good light. Underparts mainly white, sides of breast striped black and white, flanks and undertail-coverts mixed brown and white. **Wings** Upperwing: primaries, their coverts, and secondaries dark brown, remainder paler brown. Underwing: primaries and secondaries brownish-grey, coverts white. **Tail** Brown, narrowly tipped paler brown.

FHJ: Smallest diver although size often not noticeably different from Black-throated (p. 209) in the field. Often sits very low in water with head and bill carried in characteristic upwards tilt of about 20°. Upperparts throughout year appear paler and browner than in congeners. In flight wings appear rather short and pointed with faster, higher, wing strokes than in Black-throated Diver. Red-throated is only diver which can take off directly from water; all others require a running start.

DM: Most northerly of the divers, breeding in western N America from Aleutians and Alaska S to British Columbia on Pacific coast, then E across Arctic Canada and Greenland S to Hudson Bay and Newfoundland on Atlantic coast; also Iceland and northern Europe E across USSR to Kamchatka and Commander Is, mostly above 60°N although S to about 55°N in Scotland and Sea of Okhotsk (USSR). Returns to breeding areas late May/Jun; egg-dates Jun/Jul. Dispersal begins Aug/Sep. In N America peak counts on Great Lakes over 1,200 before flight to American Atlantic coast, where peak passage over 1,000 off Townsend's Inlet, New Jersey, during Nov, extending S to Florida, occasionally Gulf States. Less numerous on N American Pacific coast wintering S to NW Mexico and, although regarded as 'uncommon', Sauppe (1979) recorded over 33,000 moving N off California between 7 Mar and 24 May during spring migration. In W Europe the most numerous diver, wintering in coastal areas from about 67°N in Norway southward to Iberia, though numbers much less impressive than in N America; few aggregations number over 200 birds; some flocks occasionally peak at 500.

SS: See notes under Black-throated Diver (p. 209). Beware also distant views of Shags (p. 298) and cormorant species, particularly first-winter or immature types with pale breasts.

---

18 BLACK-THROATED DIVER
other: Arctic Loon (includes Pacific Loon, 18X)
Gavia arctica

PLATE 6 Figs 18a-18c

MAP 18

Length 58–73cm (23–29in.). Wingspan 110–130cm ($43\frac{1}{2}$–51in.). Iris reddish. Bill black. Legs/feet blackish, webs pinker.

Almost circumpolar in Arctic tundra regions though absent from Greenland. Migrates S in winter where range overlaps with other divers. Most confusion likely to arise with larger non-breeding Great Northern Diver, but bill more slender with crown and hindneck paler than blackish back. Best character, ignored by many guides, is whitish flank patch. Sexes alike, marked seasonal variation. Juveniles and first-winter types separable from adults. Three subspecies listed, of which status of Pacific Diver (*G.a. pacifica*) is currently under review; further work may show that this form is specifically distinct as it is apparently sympatric with *G.a. viridigularis* in NE Siberia (Vaurie, in Cramp & Simmons 1977). Unless stated, the following notes refer to *G.a. arctica* and *G.a. viridigularis*. Gray (1958) reported a presumed Black-throated × Great Northern Diver hybrid.

JUVENILE/FIRST-WINTER: Iris brownish; bill grey, culmen and tip blackish. As non-breeding adult except: **Head:** Forehead blackish. **Body** Upperparts browner, all feathers faintly edged with light grey, giving scaly appearance. **Wings** Browner, coverts lacking white spots. **Tail** Browner, tip whitish.

ADULT NON-BREEDING: Bill grey, culmen blackish. **Head** Forehead very dark brown shading to greyish-brown on crown, hindneck, sides of face, chin and throat. Foreneck and sides of neck white, some with indistinct mottling across base of lower foreneck. **Body** Upperparts mostly dark brown, with indistinct white subterminal spots on scapulars; appears blackish above at distance or in poor light. Underparts mainly white, sides of breast streaked with grey, thigh dark brown with indistinct brown bar across ventral area, and mixed brown/white undertail-coverts. **Wings** Upperwing: primaries and secondaries blackish, remainder blackish-brown, coverts faintly spotted with white. Underwing: primaries and secondaries blackish-brown, remainder white, axillaries streaked brown. **Tail** Blackish-brown, tip white.

ADULT BREEDING: Head Mostly grey, paler on hindneck, shading into blackish chin, throat and foreneck, latter with five narrow white stripes. **Body** Upperparts blackish with rectangular white blocking, heaviest on scapulars, smaller and fainter on rump. Underparts: sides of upper breast streaked black and white, remainder mainly white except blackish thighs and line across ventral area. **Wings and Tail** As non-breeding adult but with whiter spots across coverts.

18X PACIFIC DIVER
G.a. pacifica

Smaller than nominate race, with proportionately shorter bill. In breeding plumage nape and hindneck paler grey with rich purple iridescence on throat. Non-breeding plumage characters probably as nominate.

FHJ: Compared with Red-throated Diver (p. 208), it is slightly larger and stockier with proportionately larger, straighter and thicker bill held horizontally when swimming, not angled up at 20°. In flight wingbeats slower and shallower.

DM: Almost circumpolar. *G.a. pacifica* breeds from eastern Siberia and Alaska E to Hudson Bay and Baffin Island; *G.a. arctica* breeds northern Europe E to Lena River, USSR; *G.a. viridigularis* from Lena River eastwards, a few occasionally reported breeding western Alaska. Returns to breeding areas late Apr/May; egg-dates May–Jul. Dispersal begins Aug but protracted. American *G.a. pacifica* winters almost exclusively along N American Pacific coast S to Mexico; casual inland and E to Atlantic coasts. Eurasian *G.a. arctica* winters coasts of western Europe S to Biscay, although main wintering area appears to be Baltic Sea with SE flightway to Black and Caspian Seas; occasionally S to Elat, northern Red Sea (Krabbe 1979). Asiatic *G.a. viridigularis* migrates SE to western Pacific to winter off Japan, where abundant visitor to Seto (inland) Sea. Return passage in all populations begins Mar/Apr. Most notable numbers recorded by Sauppe (1979): over 1 million flying northwards past Pigeon Point, California, N America, between 7 Mar and 24 May 1979 with daily peak of 72,680 on 21 Apr.

SS: Breeding adults distinctive. In winter best separated from Red-throated Diver (p. 208) by more robust appearance, straighter bill, white flank patch and, at close range, lack of distinctive white spots on upperparts. See also larger Great Northern Diver (p. 210), which has crown and hindneck darker than upperparts (paler than upperparts in present species) and also lacks white flank patch of Black-throated. See also Shag (p. 298) and cormorant species, particularly white-breasted juveniles/immatures.

19 GREAT NORTHERN DIVER
other: Common Loon
Gavia immer

PLATE 6 Figs 19a-19c

MAP 19

Length 61–91cm (24–36in.). Wingspan 127–147cm (50–58in.). Iris red. Bill black. Legs/feet blackish, webs pink.

Northern hemisphere, breeding Arctic and subarctic regions of N America, Iceland and Greenland. Migrates S in winter, when range overlaps with other divers. Separation of the four straightforward if viewed closely but distance or poor conditions often negate differences. Sexes alike, marked seasonal difference. Juveniles, first-winter and first-summer types separable. Gray (1958) reported a presumed Great Northern × Black-throated hybrid. No subspecies.

JUVENILE/FIRST-WINTER: Bill blue-grey in juveniles tending to greyish-white by autumn, but culmen always black. Plumage resembles non-breeding adult except: **Head** Division between brownish hindneck and white foreneck less distinct, sides of neck finely streaked with brown. **Body** Upperparts browner, distinctly scalloped pale grey, giving pronounced transverse barring visible at some distance. Underparts mostly white except for brownish flanks and greyish-brown undertail-coverts. **Wings** Upperwing browner, lacks white spots on wing-coverts and inner secondaries.

ADULT NON-BREEDING: Bill greyish, culmen brown or blackish. **Head** Forehead and crown dark greyish-brown extending to ear-coverts; narrow area around eye, lower lores, chin and throat white. Hindneck as crown, extending diffusely to sides of neck and forming indistinct half-collar at base of otherwise white foreneck. **Body** Upperparts dark brownish-grey with ghost-image of breeding adult's white blocking, heaviest on scapulars. Underparts mostly white, sides of breast, flanks and undertail-coverts variably marked with brown. **Wings** As adult breeding, but duller.

ADULT BREEDING: Head Including upper neck mostly blackish with purple-green lustre, except for six to eight short white streaks across throat and about 15 white streaks in half-collar on each side of neck. **Body** Upperparts blackish, spotted white, with larger blocking on scapulars becoming small and rounded on rump. Underparts mainly white, sides of breast striped black and white; flanks spotted black and white, with a dark bar across vent and mixed black/white on undertail-coverts. **Wings** Upperwing: primaries and most secondaries brownish-black with dark shafts, primary-coverts wholly black, remainder of coverts and inner secondaries spotted with white. Underwing: coverts white shading to brown on primaries and secondaries, axillaries streaked with brown. **Tail** Blackish.

FHJ: Size can overlap with largest Black-throated (p. 209) but usually much larger, with proportionately heavier body, straighter, more robust bill; neck also shorter and thicker but not always discernible. When swimming looks obviously bulky, and often sits high, head held horizontally with rather angular head shape, the forehead rising steeply from base of bill, though this is at times also apparent in some Black-throated Divers. Typical hunch-backed jizz in flight, wingbeats noticeably slower than in the two smaller divers and shallower than those of White-billed Diver. Winters mainly along coasts, occasionally inland, ice permitting. Less tendency towards forming large, lasting flocks than the two smaller divers.

DM: Northern hemisphere, breeds in N America from Aleutian Is and Bering Sea coasts E throughout lake country to southern Baffin I., Canada, and S to Great Lakes and Newfoundland. Northern limits of range poorly known; regarded primarily as a migrant in Beaufort Sea (Johnson *et al*. 1975). Also breeds Iceland and Greenland, occasionally Scotland, perhaps regularly Bear I., USSR. Returns to breeding areas May/Jun; egg-dates May/Jun; dispersal begins Aug, most Sep/Oct, but exact routes little known. In western N America winters along Pacific coast from S Alaska to Baja California. In eastern N America many gather on Great Lakes during late autumn, often forming flocks of up to 700 or 800, before dispersal southwards with coastal migration and broad-front passage (but particularly SE to Maryland and Chesapeake Bay). Winter range extends from Newfoundland to Florida and Gulf States. In E Atlantic winters along shores of western Europe from Scandinavia S to Brittany, France, occasionally Biscay; most off SW Britain, rarer off E and SE shores of England. Stragglers occur S to Turkey, Algeria and Azores. Spring migration begins Apr/May.

SS: See notes under White-billed Diver (p. 210). Refer also to Great Cormorant (p. 295), which has same bulk as this species; beware especially distant views of white-breasted juveniles/immatures.

20 WHITE-BILLED DIVER
other: Yellow-billed Loon
Gavia adamsii

PLATE 6 Figs 20a-20c

MAP 20

Length 76–91cm (30–36in.). Wingspan 137–152cm (54–60in.). Iris red. Bill pale yellow to ivory-white. Legs/feet brownish-grey.

Northern hemisphere, breeding above tree-line in N America and Eurasia. Migrates S in winter, when range overlaps with Great Northern Diver (p. 210), with which confusion always possible. Viewed under optimum conditions, white culmen, paler head (winter) and white primary shafts diagnostic. Bill generally larger, often with upper mandible projecting over lower mandible and held at slight upwards tilt, accentuating angle of gonys. Sexes alike, marked seasonal variation. Juveniles, first-winter and first-summer types separable. No subspecies.

JUVENILE/FIRST-WINTER: Iris brown, bill smaller than in adult but similarly coloured, angled gonys sometimes poorly developed. Resembles non-breeding adult except: **Head** Paler brown; area around eye whiter, extending to include most of lores and ear-coverts to form whitish crescent on sides of face. Sides of neck more peppered greyish-brown. **Body** Upperparts paler brown, mantle, back and scapulars broadly edged buffish-white, imparting distinctive scalloped appearance; rump finely spotted with white. Underparts mostly white, sides of breast, flanks and undertail-coverts variably marked with brown. **Wings and Tail** As adult non-breeding except browner; upperwing-coverts and inner secondaries wholly brown.

ADULT NON-BREEDING: Bill always ivory-white to cream, including the culmen, but base occasionally darker and accentuated by feathering from crown to nasal groove. Thus at longer range basal third of culmen can appear dark. **Head** Forehead and crown brownish; area around and below eye paler, sometimes white as in first-winter, extending upwards behind ear-coverts towards nape and becoming spotted, merging into pale brownish nape. Hindneck paler brown, middle portion liberally flecked white but darker at base. Foreneck white, base lightly peppered with brown often forming collar. **Body** Upperparts darker than head, mostly blackish-brown, faintly 'oily', with ghost-image of breeding adult's white rectangular blocking, heaviest on scapulars. Underparts mostly white; sides of breast, flanks and undertail-coverts variably marked with brown. **Wings** As breeding adult but duller. **Tail** Brownish.

ADULT BREEDING: Head Including upper neck mostly blackish with purple sheen, except for four short white streaks across throat and about ten white vertical streaks in half-collar on each side of neck. **Body** Upperparts blackish, spotted white, larger rectangular blocking on scapulars becoming smaller, more rounded, on rump, none on lower back. Underparts mainly white except black stripes on sides of upper breast, blackish flanks, and mixed black/white undertail-coverts. **Wings** Primaries and their coverts blackish-brown, the shafts ivory or yellowish-brown (diagnostic). Secondaries brownish-black, innermost tipped with white; coverts brownish-black, all tipped white. Underwing: white coverts, greyer on primaries and secondaries, axillaries streaked black. **Tail** Blackish above, white below.

FHJ: Largest diver, characteristic upwards tilt of bill and head recalling much smaller Red-throated Diver. Bill shape can vary, but generally larger and deeper at base than in Great Northern Diver with almost straight culmen and sharp upwards angle from gonys to tip. These differences less apparent in first-year birds. Heavier jizz not always apparent unless seen alongside Great Northern; in flight, wingbeats deeper than in that species. Does not appear to flock at any time.

DM: High Arctic. Breeds in N America from Alaska, north of tree-line, from Cape Prince of Wales S to Salmon River, the Mackenzie River delta and Arctic coasts of NW Canada. In Eurasia breeds from Murmansk and Novaya Zemlya eastwards across Arctic shores of USSR to Siberia. Exact distribution throughout range poorly documented. Returns to breeding areas May/Jun; egg-dates Jun/Jul; dispersal begins Aug/Sep. All except western Russian population appear to move E towards Chukchi Sea and then S through Bering Straits to N Pacific, wintering off S Alaska S to British Columbia, rarely S to California, Japan and China. Those W of Laptev Sea move W to winter mainly off Norway, with a few regularly reaching northern coasts of Britain. Recent sightings of first-winter birds in Baltic Sea S to Holland may indicate a winter 'nursery area' (Madge, pers. comm.). Casual in winter to N American Atlantic coast and S to Caspian Sea and Poland.

SS: White bill of breeding adult diagnostic. In non-breeding and immature plumages confusion likely with Great Northern Diver (p. 210). Present species differs in slightly larger size, flatter crown and diagnostic ivory-white culmen and primary shafts. Most previous literature has placed too much importance on bill shape differences between the two species and, whilst the present species has a generally larger bill with straighter culmen and sharply angled gonys, there is some overlap. White-billed Divers in winter months best separated at all ages by white culmen, and distinct pale-headed appearance—an excellent field character visible at considerable range. By comparison non-breeding Great Northern usually have a black culmen with darker head and neck markings extending well below level of eye. Any large diver in non-breeding plumage with hindcrown much paler in tone than back more likely to be White-billed and should be carefully scrutinised.

Order *PODICIPEDIFORMES*

Family *PODICIPEDIDAE* grebes

Cosmopolitan, one or more species occurring on all major land masses except Antarctica. Fifty distinct forms have been described, usually reduced to about 20 species in six genera. All breed on fresh water. Rather weak fliers, although some are migratory, dispersing to coastal waters in winter (hence the inclusion of the whole family in this guide). They bear a superficial resemblance to ducks but their necks are usually long and slender, bills pointed, never flattened. All have dense plumage and lack a functional tail. They steer in water and air with their feet, the toes of which are lobed. A few species are flightless. The remainder fly with rapid wingbeats, the neck extended and held lower than the back, giving a hump-backed jizz. When swimming they prefer to dive to escape danger. Most have elaborate courtship displays; sexes normally alike but may differ in size.

Identification in summer plumage usually straightforward, as many species have distinctive plumes or colours on head and neck. In winter or non-breeding plumage, when colours largely grey, brown and white, jizz, length/thickness of neck, and bill are as important as colour patterns. It should be appreciated that, as grebes can alter their buoyancy by expelling air from their bodies, the jizz of a bird floating high will be very different from that of an alarmed bird which would tend to sink lower into the water; under such conditions some species show only bill and eyes above water. The apparent length of the neck can also vary and depends on conditions or the bird's activity.

Genus *TACHYBAPTUS*

Five species; small, mainly freshwater grebes (commonly referred to as dabchicks) distributed in America, Eurasia, Africa and Australasia.

21 LITTLE GREBE
other: Red-throated Little Grebe, Dabchick
Tachybaptus ruficollis

PLATE 10 Figs 21a-21c

MAP 21

Length 25–29cm (10–$11\frac{1}{2}$in.). Wingspan 40–45cm (16–18in.). Iris brownish-red. Bill black, tip white, face spot yellow. Legs/feet dusky olive-green.

Rare on sea; occurs widely throughout Old World. Sexes alike, marked seasonal variation. Juveniles separable from adults. Nine subspecies listed, some separable, but ranges do not normally overlap. Interbreeds with Delacour's Little Grebe.

JUVENILE: As non-breeding adult except: **Head** Crown and hindneck dark brown, sides of face and neck variably striped with white, some with tawny suffusion. Chin and throat white merging into tawny-brown foreneck.

ADULT NON-BREEDING: Head Crown and hindneck dark olive-brown, chin and throat white, remainder, including foreneck, sandy-buff. **Body** Upperparts dark olive-brown. Underparts mostly white, sides and flanks pale sandy-brown. **Wings** As breeding adult.

ADULT BREEDING: Head Forehead, crown and hindneck black; throat, ear-coverts, sides and foreneck chestnut merging into dark brown lower foreneck. **Body** Upperparts blackish-brown, sides of rump tawny-brown. Underparts blackish-brown mottled with white, heaviest on belly; ventral area grey. **Wings** Upperwing mainly dark brown, inner webs of secondaries variably white, nominate race showing little if any white in flight but in *T.r. capensis* and *T.r. iraquensis* white inner webs often show an indistinct wing bar. Underwing mostly white. **Tail** (tuft) Blackish-brown above, whitish below.

FHJ: Small freshwater grebe occurring throughout much of the Old World on small ponds and vegetated fringes of larger lakes and reservoirs. Some sedentary, but others move to winter along tidal estuaries and sheltered coastal bays.

DM: *T.r. ruficollis* breeds throughout much of Europe, northwest Africa, Turkey and Israel; *T.r. capensis* Africa south of Sahara, Caucasus, Transcaucasia, Armenia, Egypt, and southern Asia east to Burma; *T.r. iraquensis* Iraq and southwest Iran; *T.r. poggei* eastern Asia from central Manchuria S through Japan, Taiwan and Malay Peninsula; *T.r. philippensis* some Philippine islands; *T.r. cotabato* Mindanao Is, Philippine Is; *T.r. tricolor* Celebes, Moluccas and northern New Guinea; *T.r. vulcanorum* Java, Bali, Lombok, Sumba, Flores, Timor and the Kai Is; *T.r. collaris* Solomons, New Ireland, New Britain and parts of New Guinea. Northern populations dispersive.

SS: See non-breeding Black-necked and Horned Grebes (p. 219, p. 218). Also Delacour's and Madagascar Little Grebes (p. 213, p. 213).

22 AUSTRALASIAN LITTLE GREBE
other: Black-throated Little Grebe/Australian Dabchick
Tachybaptus novaehollandiae

PLATE 10 Figs 22a-22d

MAP 22

Length 28cm (11in.). Wingspan 39cm ($15\frac{1}{2}$in.). Iris varies, red, orange or white, pupil black. Bill black, tip ivory, face spot yellow. Legs/feet olive-green.

Not on ocean; breeds in Indonesia and Australasia, where range overlaps with Little, Hoary-headed and New Zealand Grebes (p. 212, p. 215, p. 216). Sexes alike, marked seasonal variation. Juveniles separable from adults. Seven subspecies.

JUVENILE: As non-breeding adult except for blackish stripes from gape across whitish ear-coverts.

ADULT NON-BREEDING: As breeding adult except: **Head** Including hindneck mostly dull greyish-brown, chin, throat and foreneck white, shading to brownish at base of foreneck. **Body** Upperparts greyish-brown. Underparts mostly white except greyish-brown upper breast, flanks and thighs.

ADULT BREEDING: Head Including chin and throat mostly black except for rufous stripe running from eye to sides of neck and greyish-black foreneck. **Body** Upperparts blackish-grey. Underparts mostly silver-grey, breast, flanks, thighs and ventral area mottled with brown. **Wings** Upperwing: outer primaries brown, bases of innermost white increasing inwards and uniting with white secondaries; remainder as upperparts. **Tail** (tuft) Blackish-grey

above, whitish below.
FHJ: Small freshwater grebe frequenting ponds, small areas of open water in swamps, and slow, winding rivers.
DM: *T.n. novaehollandiae* breeds New Guinea, Australia and Tasmania (vagrants have bred in New Zealand); *T.n. leucosternos* New Hebrides and New Caledonia; *T.n. rennellianus* Rennel I., Solomon Is; *T.n. javanicus* Java; *T.n. timorensis* Timor; *T.n. fomosus* Great Sangi I., Talaud Is; *T.n. incola* northern New Guinea.
SS: Yellow spot at base of bill separates adults from both Hoary-headed Grebe and New Zealand Grebe (p. 215, p. 216); see also plumage differences in main text.

23 MADAGASCAR LITTLE GREBE
other: Madagascar Dabchick
Tachybaptus pelzelnii

PLATE 11 Figs 23a-23c
MAP 23

Length 25cm (10in.). Wingspan not recorded. Iris brown or dull red. Bill black with pale tip. Legs/feet olive-grey

Not on ocean; confined to Madagascar, resembles Little Grebe (p. 212) but rufous restricted to sides of neck. Sexes alike; marked seasonal difference. Juveniles separable.
JUVENILE: As non-breeding adult except sides of head and neck variably striped brownish-grey; foreneck whiter.
ADULT NON-BREEDING: As breeding adult except: **Head:** Cap dull brown, sides of face and foreneck dull grey-brown. **Body** Underparts white (conspicuous in flight).
ADULT BREEDING: Head Oily-black cap extends from base of bill to nape; chin, throat and ear-coverts fawn-grey. Hindneck and foreneck dark brownish-grey, sides of neck rufous. **Body** Upperparts dark brownish-grey. Underparts: upper breast dark brownish-grey, remainder mostly white except for greyish mottling on flanks, thighs and ventral area. **Wings** Upperwing: mostly brown, inner webs of inner primaries and all of secondaries white, forming narrow wing bar in flight. **Tail** (tuft) Brownish-grey.
FHJ: Jizz as Little Grebe; habits unrecorded.
DM: Confined to Madagascar, Indian Ocean.
SS: Separated from Delacour's Little Grebe (p. 213), also endemic to Madagascar, by greyer sides of face, rufous sides of neck, and whiter underparts. In non-breeding plumage upperparts and upper breast paler, without rufous mottling.

24 DELACOUR'S LITTLE GREBE
other: Aloatra Dabchick
Tachybaptus rufolavatus

PLATE 11 Figs 24a-24c
MAP 24

Length 25cm (10in.). Wingspan not recorded. Iris brown or dull red. Bill black with pale tip. Legs/feet olive-grey.

Not on ocean; confined to Madagascar, treated as separate species by most authors but apparently hybridises with African race of Little Grebe (p. 212) (Cramp & Simmons 1977). Sexes alike; marked seasonal difference. Juveniles separable.
JUVENILE: As adult non-breeding except sides of face and neck striped with white.
ADULT NON-BREEDING: As breeding adult except: **Head** Cap dull brown; chin, throat and ear-coverts faintly washed cinnamon. **Body** Upperparts browner.
ADULT BREEDING: Head Oily-black cap extends from base of bill to nape then narrowly down hindneck; chin whitish becoming pale cinnamon on throat, ear-coverts, sides of neck and foreneck. **Body** Upperparts dark sepia. Underparts mottled cinnamon, white and grey, darkest on upper breast and flanks. **Wings** Mostly brown except for whitish secondaries and inner webs of inner primaries. **Tail** (tuft) Sepia.
FHJ: Probably as Little Grebe (p. 212).
DM: Confined to Lake Aloatra, Madagascar.
SS: See notes under Madagascar Little Grebe (p. 213).

25 LEAST GREBE
other: American Dabchick, Least Dabchick
Tachybaptus dominicus

PLATE 9 Figs 25a-25b
MAP 25

Length 23–26cm (9–10½in.). Wingspan 35cm (14in.). Iris golden-orange, pupil black. Bill black, extreme tip white. Legs/feet brownish-olive.

Not on ocean, occurs from southern North America to Argentina. Sexes vary: males have proportionately larger heads, thicker necks and longer bills, with slightly darker overall plumage. Juveniles separable from adults. Four subspecies listed differing mainly in size and the tone of upperparts. *P.d. brachypterus* is described below.
Note: sometimes placed within *Podiceps*.
JUVENILE: Much as non-breeding adult except for white stripes on sides of head.
ADULT NON-BREEDING: As breeding adult except plumage generally duller with white chin and whiter flanks.
ADULT BREEDING: Head Crown and chin blackish, remainder mostly dark lead-brown shading to brownish on lower foreneck. **Body** Upperparts slaty-brown with greenish sheen. Underparts: centre of belly and undertail-coverts white; breast, flanks and thighs barred buffish-grey. **Wings** Upperwing as upperparts except bases of primaries and most of secondaries whitish forming uninterrupted wing bar. **Tail** (tuft) Undertail white.

FHJ: Smallest American grebe. Drab plumage, dark bill and conspicuous orange eye impart distinctive appearance. In flight shows conspicuous wing bar. Frequents freshwater locations.
DM: *T.d. brachypterus* breeds locally southern Texas and Sinaloa S to Panama; *T.d. bangsi* southern Baja California; *T.d. dominicus* Bahama Is, Greater Antilles, Virgin Is, and Cozumel Is; *T.d. brachyrhynchus* tropical South America S to Peru, Bolivia, Argentina, Paraguay and southern Brazil. Mostly sedentary. Egg-dates throughout year, subject to local conditions.
SS: Differs from Pied-billed Grebe (p. 214) in shape and colour of bill, eye colour, jizz and prominent white wing bar in flight.

Genus *PODILYMBUS*

Two species, one endangered. Both confined to New World.

26 PIED-BILLED GREBE
Podilymbus podiceps

PLATE 9 Figs 26a-26c
MAP 26

Length 30–38cm (12–15in.). Wingspan 56–64cm (22–25in.). Iris reddish-brown. Bill bluish-white with black subterminal band. Legs/feet slate-grey.

Rare on ocean, most widespread American grebe; northern populations migrate S to ice-free localities during winter. Slight sexual variation; males average larger with more clear-cut plumage pattern. Juveniles separable from adults. Three subspecies listed, varying in size, size of bill and subterminal band, extent of throat patch, and tone of upperparts. Nominate race is described below. Weller (1959) recorded one albino.
JUVENILE: Much as non-breeding adult except for whitish stripes on sides of face and slightly darker grey upperparts.
ADULT NON-BREEDING: Much as breeding adult except band on bill faint or absent; throat whitish or brown. Remainder of plumage more tawny in tone; undertail-coverts whiter.
ADULT BREEDING: Head Mostly blackish or greyish-brown, sides of face and neck paler; chin and throat black. **Body** Upperparts dark greyish-brown. Underparts: centre of belly and undertail-coverts white; breast, flanks and thighs barred and tipped grey-brown. **Wings** Upperwing dark greyish-brown except for indistinct variable whitish bar across secondaries. **Tail** (tuft) Underside whitish.
FHJ: Small, stocky grebe with short neck, large head and chicken-like bill. Shy, skulking and rather solitary in habits, though at staging points during migration peaks of 20,000 sometimes recorded (Salton Sea, California). In flight lacks a clearly defined wing bar.
DM: Throughout most of North, Central and South America, mainly on weed-fringed ponds, streams, etc. *P.p. podiceps* breeds from British Columbia E to Quebec, New Brunswick and Atlantic coast states S to southern Baja California and Mexico; *P.p. antillarum* breeds throughout West Indies; *P.p. antarcticus* breeds throughout much of South America S to Argentina. *P.p. podiceps* returns to nesting areas Mar/Apr; egg-dates Apr/May. Fledging and dispersal Aug onwards. Extreme northern populations vacate breeding areas by mid Nov; elsewhere winters from within breeding range (ice permitting) S to Baja California and Mexico. Prefers mainly freshwater localities but occasionally in estuaries and bays, especially in hard weather. Vagrants to Hawaii and western Europe.
SS: Stocky jizz and banded 'chicken-bill' should rule out confusion with other American grebes.

27 ATITLAN GREBE
other: Giant Grebe
Podilymbus gigas

PLATE 11 Figs 27a-27b
MAP 27

Length 48cm (19in.). Wingspan not recorded (practically flightless). Iris black, eye-ring and facial skin whitish. Bill ivory with broad black subterminal band. Legs/feet olive-grey.

Not on ocean, resembles giant Pied-billed Grebe; restricted to Guatemalan highlands, Central America. Sexes alike, seasonal variation not recorded but probably marked as in similar Pied-billed Grebe. Juveniles separable.
JUVENILE: As non-breeding adult except sides of face and neck striped black and white; upperparts browner.
ADULT BREEDING: Head Including neck, mostly dark blackish-grey, crown and hindneck darker, chin and throat blackish. **Body** Upperparts blackish-brown faintly glossed green. Underparts: upper breast speckled black and grey, extending to sides and flanks; thighs mottled fawn-brown, belly and ventral area white. **Wings** As upperparts. **Tail** (tuft) Blackish above, white below.
FHJ: Half as large again as Pied-billed Grebe; practically flightless.
DM: Sole population restricted to Lake Atitlan, in the highlands of southwest Guatemala, Central America; survival threatened.

Genus *ROLLANDIA*

Two species; medium-sized grebes confined to South America.

28 WHITE-TUFTED GREBE
Rollandia rolland

PLATE 8 Figs 28a-28b
MAP 28

Length 28–36cm (11–14in.) (includes geographical variation). Wingspan not recorded. Iris red, pupil black. Bill, legs/feet blackish.

Confined to South America, some move to creeks and bays during winter. Sexes alike; seasonal variation. Juveniles separable from adults. Three subspecies listed differing from each other mainly in size.

JUVENILE: As adult non-breeding except: Bill brown, feet yellowish. **Head** Including neck mostly dull reddish-brown, chin, throat and sides of face white with two irregular blackish streaks across cheeks. **Body** Upperparts blackish-brown. Underparts mostly white, upper breast as foreneck; flanks, sides and vent vinaceous-grey.

ADULT NON-BREEDING: As breeding adult except: **Head** Lacks crest, foreneck crown and whole of neck dull reddish-brown; chin, thoat and lower ear-coverts white. **Body** Upperparts brown; underparts mostly white.

ADULT BREEDING: Head Crested; mostly black, including neck, except for narrow white streak over eye broadening to conspicuous white tufts on ear-coverts. **Body** Upperparts blackish-brown, glossed green, shading to russet on rump. Underparts mainly chestnut, sides and flanks mottled blackish-brown, ventral area white. **Wings** Upperwing: blackish-brown, inner webs and tips of secondaries white, showing as a wing bar in flight. Underwing-coverts white, primaries and secondaries brown. **Tail** (tuft) Blackish-brown above, white below.

FHJ: Small/medium-sized grebe frequenting ponds, streams and rivers; some move to creeks and inshore marine habitat in non-breeding season.

DM: Confined to South America. *R.r. rolland* breeds Falkland Is; *R.r. chilensis* lowlands of South America from about 10°S in Peru southwards and from Paraguay and southern Brazil southwards to Tierra del Fuego; *R.r. morrisoni* breeds highlands of Peru and Bolivia.

SS: Silvery Grebe (p. 219) in breeding plumage has golden plumes on sides of head, with grey forehead and crown and blackish nape and white foreneck. In non-breeding plumage uptilted bill and gleaming white foreneck of that species facilitates easy separation from present species.

29 SHORT-WINGED GREBE
Rollandia micropterum

PLATE 8 Figs 29a-29b
MAP 29

Length 28cm (11in.). Flightless. Iris brown. Bill reddish-brown. Legs/feet black (in skin).

Confined to South America; flightless, restricted to two lakes in the high Andes. Sexes alike. No specimens of juveniles or first-winter types available for examination. No subspecies.

ADULT NON-BREEDING: As breeding adult except: **Head** Lacks plumes. Crown, lores, nape and ear-coverts pale chestnut, hindneck pale cinnamon-brown. **Body** Upperparts brown. Underparts mostly white, sides of breast and flanks lightly peppered with rufous-brown.

ADULT BREEDING: Head Crested, forehead and crown blackish, feathers basally chestnut, lores and ear-coverts black, springing from sides of face in short plumes; chin, throat and foreneck white, nape chestnut, hindneck brown. **Body** Upperparts dark brown, highlighted with scattered black streaks shading to chestnut on rump and tail tuft. Underparts satin-white, peppered with chestnut and brown, heaviest on sides of breast, flanks and vent **Wings** Upperwing: primaries brown, secondaries white; outer webs dusted brown, heaviest on innermost feathers; coverts as upperparts.

FHJ: Flightless, medium-sized grebe. Often runs across water for considerable distance, futilely flapping its wings (Alden, pers. comm.).

DM: Restricted to Lakes Umayo, Titicaca and Poopo in Peruvian and Bolivian Andes.

Genus *POLIOCEPHALUS*

Two species; small-sized grebes confined to Australasia.

30 HOARY-HEADED GREBE
Poliocephalus poliocephalus

PLATE 10 Figs 30a-30c
MAP 30

Length 30cm (12in.). Wingspan 46cm (18in). Iris varies, brown, yellow or white. Bill black, tip ivory. Legs/feet olive-green.

Rare on ocean; breeds Australia and New Zealand; range overlaps with Australasian Little Grebe and New Zealand Grebe (p. 212, p. 216). Breeding adults distinctive but more care required to separate non-breeders. Sexes alike, marked seasonal variation. Juveniles separable from adults. No subspecies.

JUVENILE: As non-breeding adult except for variable black streaks on sides of face.

ADULT NON-BREEDING: As breeding adult except: **Head** Lacks black nape patch. White hair-streaks on ear-coverts and sides of neck reduced or absent. **Body** Upperparts duller and greyer.

ADULT BREEDING: Head Forehead fawn-brown streaked with white shading to almost black on hindcrown and nape; lores and ear-coverts densely streaked white. Hindneck narrowly brown,

sides and foreneck grey or dun-white. **Body** Upperparts brownish-grey. Underparts mostly white, upper breast grey or dun-white, flanks and thighs mottled with brownish-grey. **Wings** Upperwing: outer three primaries mostly brownish-grey, remainder white, tipped brown, decreasing inwards, secondaries white; coverts and tertials as upperparts. Underwing-coverts white, primaries and secondaries brown. **Tail** (tuft) Brownish-grey above, whitish below.
FHJ: Frequents larger areas of open water, swamps, lakes and estuaries, also sheltered coastal bays and creeks.
DM: Breeds in Western Australia from Perth to Esperance and further E in New South Wales, Victoria, Tasmania and eastern South Australia. Since 1976 has bred in Southland, New Zealand (Fullagar and Van Tets, pers. comm.).
SS: In non-breeding plumage best separated from Australasian Little Grebe by lack of white spot at base of bill.

31 NEW ZEALAND GREBE
other: New Zealand Dabchick
Poliocephalus rufopectus

PLATE 10 Figs 31a-31c
MAP 31

Length 28cm (11in.). Wingspan not recorded. Iris white, pupil black. Bill, legs/feet black (in skins).

Breeds New Zealand where a few Hoary-headed and Australasian Dabchicks also occur and breed. Sexes alike; seasonal variation. Juveniles separable from adults. No subspecies.
JUVENILE: As non-breeding adult except: **Head** Two variable blackish streaks across cheeks, foreneck paler fawn-brown.
ADULT NON-BREEDING: As breeding adult except: **Head** Crown and hindneck dark brown, sides of face, chin, throat, sides and foreneck dull fawn-brown. **Body** Upperparts paler and browner; underparts mostly white. Sides of breast and flanks mottled with fawn-brown.
ADULT BREEDING: Head Forehead and crown black, glossed green, lores and ear-coverts similar but paler with greyish hair-like streaks; chin and throat brown, hindneck blackish-brown, shading to rufous on foreneck. **Body** Upperparts blackish-brown. Underparts mostly white, breast rufous, flanks, thighs and ventral area barred cinnamon and brown. **Wings** Upperwing as upperparts except secondaries white, tipped brown, increasing in extent inwards. **Tail** (tuft) Blackish-brown above, white below.
FHJ: Small freshwater grebe inhabiting ponds etc. from sea-level up to about 910m. Mainly sedentary, occasionally forms small flocks during winter.
DM: Confined to New Zealand, mainly North Island (commonest near Rotorua); now scarce South Island (Falla *et al.* 1970).
SS: See Australasian Little and Hoary-headed Grebes (p. 212, p. 215).

Genus *PODICEPS*

Eight species, medium- to large-sized grebes confined to Americas and Eurasia. One species, the Hooded Grebe *P. gallardoi*, was discovered only in 1974 (Rumboll 1974). Extensive studies on the breeding biology of this species, including competition and losses to aggressive coots, have been conducted at the only known breeding lake, Laguna Las Escarchados, Santa Cruz Province, Argentina. Publication of these studies received too late for inclusion in this work.

32 GREAT GREBE
Podiceps major

PLATE 8 Figs 32a-32b
MAP 32

Length 61cm (24in.). Wingspan unrecorded. Iris dark claret-brown, narrow inner ring silvery-white. Bill black. Legs/feet black and grey.

Confined to southern South America. The only large, long-necked grebe in coastal South America. Sexes alike; seasonal variation. Juveniles separable from adults. No subspecies.
JUVENILE: (in down) Bill smaller than adult. **Head** Mostly white, forehead and crown brown, sides of face and foreneck variably and indistinctly striped with brownish-grey. **Body** Upperparts brownish-grey, edged paler; underparts mostly white, flanks washed with grey. **Wings** As upperparts (quills not yet fully developed).
FIRST-WINTER: No specimens available. Reynolds (in Humphrey *et al.* 1970) noted considerable difference in upperparts of Tierra del Fuego birds, some, perhaps young, being much paler.
ADULT NON-BREEDING: As breeding adult except: **Head** Forehead and crown dull greyish-black; sides of face, chin and throat whiter. Sides of neck and foreneck dull chestnut, variably mottled white, hindneck dull grey. **Body** Upperparts greyish-brown, each feather indistinctly fringed pale grey. Underparts mainly white, flanks and ventral area faintly mottled with grey.
ADULT BREEDING: Head Mostly black, glossed green, ear-coverts, lores, chin and throat greyer giving slightly capped effect; hindneck as crown, sides and foreneck chestnut. **Body** Upperparts blackish-brown, glossed green. Underparts mostly white, upper breast and flanks chestnut. **Wings** Upperwings: primaries mostly brown with white bases increasing in extent inwards and uniting with whitish secondaries, innermost of which have

brownish edges. Coverts as upperparts. Underwing mainly white, primaries dusky, scattered chestnut tips along marginal and lesser coverts. Tail (tuft) Blackish-brown above, whitish below.
FHJ: Large, long-necked grebe with massive bill. Frequents low-altitude lakes and lagoons, moving to estuaries and coastal waters during non-breeding season.
DM: Confined to shores of South America from Piura, Peru (5°S), S to Pisco (14°S), and again in Chile from Coquimbo S to Tierra del Fuego. On eastern littoral from Rio Grande do Sul, Brazil (30°S), S through Paraguay, Uruguay and Argentina except Andean region. Has occurred Falklands (Woods 1975).
SS: Large size and massive bill should prevent confusion with other South American grebes.

---

33 RED-NECKED GREBE
other: Holböll's Grebe
Podiceps grisegena

PLATE 7 Figs 33a-33c

MAP 33

Length 40–50cm (16–19½in.). Wingspan 77–85cm (30–33½in.). Iris dark brown. Bill black, base bright yellow. Legs/feet blackish or olive-grey.

Wide-ranging in northern hemisphere, the largest N American grebe. In Eurasia range overlaps with larger Great Crested Grebe (p. 218). Summer adults easily separated but in winter, under poor conditions or at long range, care needed. Yellow base to bill diagnostic at all seasons. Sexes alike; marked seasonal variation in head and neck pattern. Juveniles separable from adults. Two subspecies. Albinism occasionally reported.
JUVENILE: Iris yellow, bill duller than adult. **Head** Forehead and crown dark brown or slaty, sides of face white, streaked with black, chin and throat white; hindneck brownish-grey, rusty on sides, tawny-buff on foreneck. **Body** Upperparts dark brown with indistinct pale edges. Underparts mostly white except tawny-buff breast, greyish flanks and vent. **Wings** As adult summer, perhaps less white in secondaries. **Tail** As adult non-breeding.
FIRST-WINTER: Probably indistinguishable from non-breeding adult, although iris may be yellow, bill paler (Cramp & Simmons 1977).
ADULT NON-BREEDING: Bill greyish, base dull yellow. **Head** Forehead and crown black, slightly crested, ear-coverts mouse-grey, chin and throat white extending in short crescent towards nape. Hindneck greyish-brown extending variably across upper neck. **Body** Upperparts dark blackish-brown indistinctly edged with grey. Underparts variably greyish-white, mottled grey on breast, belly and flanks. **Wings** As breeding adult.
ADULT BREEDING: Head Slightly crested; forehead and crown black, chin, throat and cheeks french-grey, bordered white. Hindneck narrowly dark brown, sides and foreneck chestnut. **Body** Upperparts brownish-black indistinctly edged with grey. Underparts: sides of breast and flanks chestnut, mottled brown, shading to white on belly and vent. **Wings** Primaries, their coverts and most of remaining coverts brownish-grey, secondaries, lesser and marginal coverts white. Underwing mostly white except for brownish primaries and inner secondaries. **Tail** (tuft) Blackish above, white below.
FHJ: Largest N American grebe. In Europe, compared with Great Crested Grebe (p. 218) smaller, more compact with shorter thicker neck; shorter, stouter bill, proportionately larger head, more rounded crown. In flight bulkier body, shorter neck, wider and shorter wings also evident. Breeds inland, dispersing to coasts in winter. See Davis & Vinicombe (1980) on possible differences in winter diving technique between this species and Great Crested Grebe.
DM: Migratory and dispersive, nominate race breeds central and southeast Europe including Denmark, southern Sweden, Finland, West Germany, Hungary, Poland and USSR, east to Volga basin and west Siberia. *P.g. holboellii* breeds southeast Asia from Kamchatka south to Hokkaido, Japan, and west to Mongolia. Also in N America from Alaska, western and central Canada south to Washington and east to Minnesota. Egg-dates May/Jun. Migratory, principal European wintering areas North and Baltic Seas from Norway, Sweden and Denmark, south to Holland; smaller numbers S to England and France, occasionally W to Ireland. Some S to Adriatic, Black and Caspian Seas, straggler to southern Mediterranean; old records off Morocco require confirmation. Occasionally winters inland. Asiatic stock winters from Japan S to East China Sea. In N America winters along Pacific coast from Pribiloff Is and southern Alaska S to British Columbia, occasionally southern California. On Atlantic coast from Newfoundland and Nova Scotia S to Georgia and Florida; some remain on Great Lakes (ice permitting), Gregarious at migratory staging points in N America; peak figures off Cape Cod during Apr often exceed 2,000.
SS: In winter differs from Great Crested Grebe (p. 218) in shorter thicker neck, proportionately larger head, stouter bill and more compact body, less long and flat, imparting distinctive jizz. Yellow base of bill diagnostic. At long range jizz can resemble that of Horned Grebe (p. 218).

34 GREAT CRESTED GREBE
other: Crested Grebe
Podiceps cristatus

PLATE 7 Figs 34a-34c

MAP 34

Length 46–51cm (18–20in.). Wingspan 85–90cm (33–35½in.). Iris crimson, pupil black. Bill: culmen and cutting edges dark horn, sides pinkish-grey. Legs/feet olive-yellow.

Largest Old World grebe; range overlaps with Red-necked (p. 217). Breeding adults distinctive; during winter months care needed to separate the two species, but with practice or at closer range identification straightforward. Sexes alike; marked seasonal variation of head and neck pattern. Juveniles separable from adults. Three subspecies listed.

JUVENILE: Iris orange, pupil black; bill pinker on sides than adult; legs/feet brownish-grey. Resembles non-breeding adult except: **Head** Faint white tips to crown with blackish streaks on sides of face and neck (retained until late autumn). **Wings** Upperwing: greyer on secondaries; outer greater coverts dark grey.

ADULT NON-BREEDING: As breeding adult except: **Head** Crown dark grey, short crest at rear, cheeks, throat and chin white. **Body** Upperparts mostly blackish-grey, indistinctly edged pale grey. Underparts mainly white, flanks mottled dusky. **Wings** As breeding adult.

ADULT BREEDING: Head Crown glossy black, crested at rear; base of frill and nape chestnut, tip of frill black; supercilium, cheeks, chin and throat white. Hindneck glossy black, shading to grey at base, sides variably rufous, foreneck white. **Body** Upperparts blackish-brown with indistinct grey edges, scapulars variably white. Underparts mostly white, flanks rufous mottled dusky. **Wings** Primaries dark brownish-grey, whiter at base, innermost tipped white; secondaries mainly white, outermost brownish-grey. Marginal and lesser coverts white, remainder brownish-grey except whitish inner webs of outer greater coverts. Underwing white below. NOTE: African and Australasian races differ little between non-breeding and breeding plumages, unlike nominate which sheds crest and frill, becoming generally whiter.

FHJ: Largest Old World grebe, unmistakable in summer, frequenting lakes, reservoirs etc. Typical grebe flight: hump-backed jizz, trailing legs and feet, rapid wingbeats. In summer head shape often distinctly triangular. During winter many disperse to estuaries and coasts.

DM: Dispersive and migratory. Nominate breeds much of Europe, E across Asia to Mongolia and China with scattered localities in North Africa, Turkey and Iran; *P.c. infuscatus* East and South Africa; *P.c. australis* Australia and New Zealand. In Europe returns breeding areas Mar/Apr; disperses Jul/Aug to moult on larger waters before prolonged movement to coast during autumn/winter, though many winter on lakes of central Europe. More strongly migratory in northern parts of range. Winters S to Morocco, heavy concentrations Black and Caspian Seas.

SS: See Red-necked Grebe (p. 217).

35 HORNED GREBE
other: Slavonian Grebe
Podiceps auritus

PLATE 7 Figs 35a-35c

MAP 35

Length 31–38cm (12–15in.). Wingspan 59–65cm (23–25½in.). Iris red, eye-ring white. Bill black, whitish-yellow tip. Legs/feet blackish-blue or grey.

Wide-ranging in northern hemisphere; range overlaps with Black-necked Grebe (p. 219). Breeding adults distinctive but care required to separate the two species in winter. Sexes alike; seasonal variation of head and neck pattern. Juveniles separable from adults. Two subspecies. Albinism occasionally reported.

JUVENILE: Bill brown, tip grey. Resembles non-breeding adult except diffuse division between dark cap and white cheeks, latter variably tipped brownish-grey. Upperparts browner.

ADULT NON-BREEDING: Bill dusky, iris pink or red. **Head** Forehead and crown blackish-grey, extending to level of eye, upper lores grey, chin, throat and sides of face white. Hindneck narrowly blackish-grey, often broken with white, particularly on upper neck, forming indistinct white collar; sides and foreneck white, variably washed grey on sides and base. **Body** Upperparts brownish-grey. Underparts mainly white, flanks mottled grey with grey wash to vent and undertail-coverts. **Wings and Tail** As breeding adult.

ADULT BREEDING: Head Mostly black; lores chestnut, continuing over eye towards nape in broad, yellow plume. Hindneck dark brown, sides and foreneck chestnut. **Body** Upperparts glossy black with indistinct grey edges. Underparts: breast and flanks chestnut, remainder white. **Wings** Upperwing: primaries blackish-brown, secondaries mostly white. Underwing white. **Tail** (tuft) Blackish above, white below.

FHJ: Although largest of the three smaller European grebes, size difference almost useless as field character. In winter closely resembles Black-necked Grebe (p. 219); differs in proportionately larger, flatter head and thicker neck. At closer range, bill deeper and rather stubby without upwards tilt. Breeds inland, winters both inshore coastal waters and freshwater locations.

DM: *P.a. auritus* breeds from Iceland, the Faeroes and northern Scotland E to Kamchatka, mostly between 63°N and 50°N. Returns to Icelandic colonies Apr/May; egg-dates Apr–Jun; departure begins Aug. Winters from ice-free parts of breeding range S to Iberian Peninsula, Black, Caspian and Aral Seas, and SE Iran, and in the east to China and Japan. *P.a. cornutus* breeds in North America from central and southern Alaska and Canada S to

Idaho, northern South Dakota and central Minnesota. Winters along Pacific coast from Aleutians to southern California, and on Atlantic coast from Nova Scotia to southern Texas.
SS: Differs from breeding Black-necked Grebe (p. 219) in head pattern and chestnut foreneck. In winter by somewhat different jizz, head and bill shape and distribution of black on head and neck, sides of face always whiter even at distance, but beware transitional plumage. From distant Red-necked Grebe (p. 217) by smaller, slimmer jizz, smaller bill.

36 BLACK-NECKED GREBE
other: Eared Grebe
Podiceps nigricollis

PLATE 7 Figs 36a-36c

MAP 36

Length 28–34cm (11–13½in.). Wingspan 56–60cm (22–23½in.). Iris red, eye-ring white. Bill black. Legs/feet blackish-grey.

Wide-ranging in northern hemisphere; range overlaps with Horned Grebe (p. 218). Breeding adults distinctive but care required to separate the two species in winter. Sexes alike; seasonal variation of head and neck pattern. Juveniles separable from adults. Four subspecies described. Albinism occasionally reported.
JUVENILE: Resembles non-breeding adult except: **Head** Crown and hindneck browner, cheeks and neck tinged buff, dusky collar at base of foreneck. **Body** Upperparts paler and browner, indistinctly edged grey, flanks paler.
ADULT NON-BREEDING: Bill blue-grey, culmen black. **Head** Forehead, lores and crown blackish extending well below eye and merging with greyish ear-coverts; chin and throat white. Hindneck blackish-grey, small white patch on sides of upper neck, remainder greyish-white washed grey. **Body** Upperparts greyish-black. Underparts: flanks mottled grey, otherwise white. **Wings and Tail** As breeding adult.
ADULT BREEDING: Head Mostly black, crown slightly crested, tuft of long golden feathers springing from behind eye and drooping over ear-coverts. Neck black. **Body** Upperparts mostly black, merging to brown on rump. Underparts: breast black, flanks mottled rufous and black, remainder white. **Wings** Upperwing: outer primaries blackish-brown, innermost white uniting with white secondaries, innermost of which edged blackish-grey; coverts blackish-grey. Underwing mostly white, axillaries grey.
FHJ: Compared with Horned Grebe (p. 218) in winter, has slighter build with steeply rising forecrown, more rounded nape and slightly upturned bill; head and bill often tilted upwards when swimming. Breeds inland; winters both inland and along coasts, gregarious, forms large flocks.
DM: Widespread. In North America *P.n. californicus* breeds from SW Canada S to Baja California, central Arizona, northern New Mexico and southern Texas. In South America *P.n. andinus* breeds on scattered lakes N of Bogota in temperate Andes. In Europe *P.n. nigricollis* breeds sporadically throughout many European countries from Scotland and Finland S to Spain and E to Albania, Bulgaria, Turkey, and then E across Asia between about 57°N and 45°N including Caspian and Aral Seas, Lake Balkash and western Mongolia; also SE China. *P.n. gurneyi* breeds at scattered localities in tropical and southern Africa, including S Angola, S Ethiopia, Namibia and South Africa. Egg-dates Apr–Jun in northern populations. Most populations migratory and dispersive in winter. North American population winters mainly in southwestern region on inland lakes, where daily winter peak on Salton Sea, California, may reach half a million; some extend S to Colombia in South America; regular but rare on Atlantic coast of N America from Massachusetts S to Long I. and New Jersey; casual Florida. In Europe small numbers winter English Channel coasts, less commonly in southwest, S to Iberia and on ice-free lakes of central Europe. Main Eurasian wintering area Caspian and Black Seas and lakes of Turkey, where daily peak around 18,000 on Lake Bordur, Dec (*Turkish Bird Report*, 1970–73); also winters Turkestan, Pakistan, north India, Japan.
SS: See notes under Horned Grebe (p. 218).

37 SILVERY GREBE
Podiceps occipitalis

PLATE 11 Fig. 37
MAP 37

Length 28cm (11in.). Wingspan not recorded. Iris crimson. Bill, legs/feet black.

Confined to South America. Sexes alike; seasonal variation. Juveniles separable from adults. Two subspecies listed.
JUVENILE: No information.
ADULT NON-BREEDING: As breeding adult except head lacks facial plumes.
ADULT BREEDING: Head Mostly soft coffee-grey with conspicuously black nape and hindneck and large frill of dull yellowish plumes springing from sides of head; chin, throat and foreneck white. **Body** Upperparts dark grey-brown. Underparts white, flanks streaked black. **Wings** Dark grey-brown with white wing bar.
FHJ: Slightly smaller than White-tufted Grebe.
DM: Confined to South America. *P.o. occipitalis* breeds from Tierra del Fuego N to about 25°N in Argentina and Chile; *P.o. juninensis* in Andean regions of northern Chile and Argentina N to Peru, Ecuador and Colombia. Egg-dates probably Oct–Dec on Falkland Is (Woods 1975). Partial migrant (see Humphrey *et al.* 1970).
SS: Differs from White-tufted Grebe (p. 215) in white foreneck and black nape and hindneck.

38 JUNÍN GREBE
other: Puna Grebe
Podiceps taczanowskii

PLATE 8 Figs 38a-38b
MAP 38

Length 35cm (14in.). Wingspan not recorded. Iris red. Bill black. Legs/feet yellowish-brown (in skin).

Never on ocean; restricted to Lake Junín, Peru. Sexes alike; seasonal variation. No specimens of juveniles or first-winter types available for examination. No subspecies.

ADULT NON-BREEDING: As breeding adult except: **Head** Lacks crest and black on nape and hindneck.

ADULT BREEDING: Head Short crest. Forehead and crown soft greyish-brown, nape black; hindneck narrowly blackish-brown; remainder, including foreneck, white. **Body** Upperparts brownish-grey paling to white or grey on rump. Underparts mostly white, flanks and ventral area mottled with grey-brown. **Wings** Upperwing: primaries and coverts greyish-brown, secondaries similar except inner webs white forming wing bar. Underwing mainly white.

FHJ: Medium/large-sized grebe appearing grey above, white below; lower mandible sharply angled from gonys to tip, giving distinct upwards tilt when swimming.

DM: South America, known only from Lake Junín, Peru.

SS: See Silvery Grebe (p. 219).

Genus *AECHMOPHORUS*

One species; confined to North America.

39 WESTERN GREBE
Aechmophorus occidentalis

PLATE 9 Figs 39a-39c
MAP 39

Length 56–74cm (22–29in.). Wingspan 76–102cm (30–40in.). Iris red. Bill mostly dusky with yellow base or sides. Legs/feet yellowish-grey.

Western North America; a common visitor to sea coasts during winter. Sexes outwardly alike, males average larger with more robust bills. Juveniles differ from most young grebes in unstriped heads. Two subspecies (differing in extent of black on head) which may prove to be good species. They are sympatric in most areas of overlap although hybridisation occurs at one location in Mexico. (See *Western Birds* 12: 41–46).

JUVENILE (FIRST-AUTUMN): Much as non-breeding adult except crown and hindneck rather greyer and merging more with white sides of face and foreneck. Upperparts usually have more distinct greyish edges.

ADULT NON-BREEDING: Head Crown, nape and hindneck dull blackish-brown, lores greyish; remainder satin-white. **Body** Upperparts slaty-brown with indistinct greyish edges. Underparts mostly white; greyish barring along flanks. **Wings** Upperwing mainly slate-brown except for white wing bar extending across secondaries to primaries. Underwing dusky-grey. **Tail** (tuft) as upperparts, whiter below.

BREEDING ADULT: Generally as non-breeding adult except crown, nape and hindneck blacker and more clearly demarcated from white sides of face and foreneck.

FHJ: Largest and longest-necked North American grebe, with rather long, thin slightly upturned bill. Gregarious, both at inland breeding locations and during winter on sea coasts.

DM: Colonial; hundreds, even thousands, at favoured localities. *A.o. occidentalis* breeds from central British Columbia S to southern California, West Mexico and E to Lake Winnipeg. Returns to colonies Apr/May; egg-dates May/Jun. Dispersal begins Sep with most moving W to saltwater locations; flocks of several thousand not uncommon at staging points. Winters mainly along Pacific coast on salt water from SE Alaska and British Columbia S to Baja California and Mexico. Smaller numbers winter inland freshwater locations E to Nevada. Stragglers have reached NW to Aleutian Is and E to Atlantic and Gulf coasts S to Tampa Bay, Florida. *A.o. clarkii* breeds lakes of Mexican Plateau and western USA.

SS: Unmistakable but see Red-necked Grebe (p. 217).

Order *PROCELLARIIFORMES*

albatrosses, petrels and shearwaters, storm-petrels, diving-petrels

Four families comprising 23 genera and about 93 species, ranging in size from albatrosses to diminutive storm-petrels. All have the external nostrils placed in tubes on top or sides of upper mandible; nasal sense organ highly developed. Bill always hooked and divided into plates separated by grooves.

Most return to land only to breed, and are thus seabirds in the true pelagic sense. Sexes outwardly alike (except in Wandering Albatross); in some species males average larger with more robust bills. No seasonal variation of plumage but some species polymorphic; albinism and melanism recorded. Separation at sea often problematical; see notes below in genera sections.

Family *DIOMEDEIDAE* albatrosses

Two genera comprising 13 species; differs from *Procellariidae* group of petrels in having external nostrils displaced on either side of culminicorn. Sexes outwardly alike except in Wandering Albatross *Diomedea exulans*, females of which resemble immature males. Three species in North Pacific, nine in Southern Oceans and one, the Waved Albatross *D. irrorata*, confined to seas off the Galapagos Is and equatorial western South America. An indication of the Southern Oceans origins of the family is that even the three North Pacific albatrosses nest during the southern hemisphere spring and summer (Oct–Apr).

Albatrosses mature slowly, the great albatrosses not breeding until their ninth or tenth year, whilst the smaller 'mollymawks' probably begin in their sixth or seventh year. They enjoy a long life, and some have recorded ages of over 50 years. All species normally mate for life, the pair-bond being reinforced by elaborate courtship dances. In the event of one bird being killed, however, it seems likely that the surviving bird will find a new mate. Most species nest annually, but the two great albatrosses have incubation and fledging periods lasting nearly eleven months and thus reproduce only biennially. Only one egg is laid, a feature common to all *Procellariiformes*. In Southern Oceans representatives the mainly white egg is laid on a concave mound of mud or soil lined with grass or feathers. In Pacific Ocean species the nest is little more than a hollow scraped in the ground. Both birds incubate and feed the chick, on a rich oily substance regurgitated from the stomach. The ability of the parents to convert food and store it in this way, without fear of deterioration, is a tremendous advantage and gives them an immense foraging range. Some parent birds have been found over 3,200km from their chicks, who can take up to 1.8kg (4lb) of regurgitated oil in one sitting.

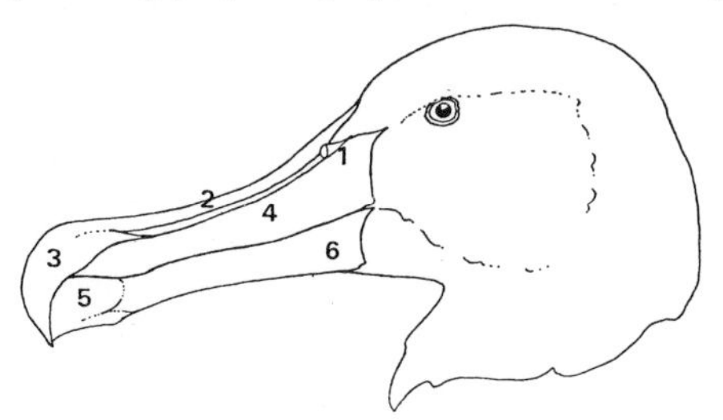

1. NOSTRILS (displaced on either side of culminicorn)
2. CULMINICORN
3. MAXILLARY UNGUIS
4. LATERICORN
5. MANDIBULAR UNGUIS
6. RAMICORN

Fig. 4. The bill of an albatross (diagrammatic).

All the albatrosses have large hooked bills made up of a number of horny plates (Fig. 4). They feed mainly on squid, but most species will join other seabirds at trawling grounds to participate in the mêlée for offal. Food is usually taken from the surface, although birds have been seen to submerge completely in an effort to retrieve scraps. Many species follow in ship's wake for long periods, alighting with wings raised in characteristic threat-posture to inspect galley waste.

Albatrosses are easily recognised by combination of great size (but see also giant petrels, p. 233) and peerless, characteristic soaring flight on bowed, motionless wings. In wind up to about 30 knots the wings of the eleven *Diomedea* species are usually held straight, slightly flexed at the carpal joint, and noticeably bowed. In higher winds wings are drawn towards body and strongly flexed to enable effortless high-speed flight. The two species of primitive, dusky-brown *Phoebetria* albatrosses have more slender wings, which are usually held bowed and flexed giving impression of greater gracefulness and agility. In reality both genera are equally accomplished at dynamic soaring. Air currents are essential for albatrosses to maintain sustained flight; in low wind speeds they usually roost on water until more favourable conditions prevail. All species require moderate run along water's surface into wind to become airborne.

The calm conditions prevailing in both Tropical Pacific and Tropical Atlantic Oceans effectively prevent the nine species of southern albatrosses from regularly penetrating into northern hemisphere. Recent sightings of both Yellow-nosed and Black-browed Albatrosses in North Atlantic suggest that some at least reach northern latitudes, although assisted passage cannot be ruled out.

For identification purposes it is helpful to split the 13 species into four groups, which are discussed separately below.

1 GREAT ALBATROSSES

There are two species of great albatross, the Wandering Albatross and the Royal Albatross *D. epomophora*. Both occur in the southern hemisphere. They are at once recognised by their huge size, some specimens having a wingspan in excess of 3.51m (138in.). The average wingspan, however, is probably in the region of 3m (118in.). General plumage black and white, differing from smaller albatrosses (mollymawks) in having white backs and mainly white underwings. Separation of the two great albatrosses at sea reasonably straightforward once the whitening sequence of the upperwings, which occurs in distinctly different ways, is learnt (see Fig. 5, p. 223). At close range bill coloration diagnostic.

2 MOLLYMAWKS

The smaller species of albatross are usually referred to as mollymawks by seafarers in the southern hemisphere. The term is retained here for simplicity, conveniently separating the smaller, Southern Oceans dark-backed albatrosses from the two larger species of white-backed albatrosses. The term mollymawk originates from the Dutch word 'mallemowk', meaning foolish gull. Their plumage pattern resembles that of a large black-backed gull but they have a wingspan of approximately 2.2m (86in.). Unlike the great albatrosses, their feet do not project beyond the tail when in flight.

Identification of the five species of mollymawks at sea is often considered problematical. Although bill coloration of adults diagnostic, of little practical importance for medium- or long-range observations, particularly when observer standing on an unstable deck. Underwing pattern a better guide to identification under such conditions, and with comparative experience most individuals can be accurately identified even at extreme ranges. Whenever possible, bill and head coloration should be used to confirm long-range identification.

3 PACIFIC ALBATROSSES
Typical examples of the four adult North Pacific albatrosses have distinctly different plumage patterns which should minimise identification problems. The dark-backed Laysan Albatross *D. immutabilis* resembles a Southern Oceans mollymawk in colour pattern. The Waved Albatross is the only albatross found in seas off equatorial western South America. Most confusion occurs when separating atypical Black-footed *D. nigripes* from juvenile and immature Short-tailed Albatrosses *D. albatrus*. The latter species is one of the world's rarest birds.

4 SOOTY ALBATROSSES
The light-mantled Sooty Albatross *P. palpebrata* and the Sooty Albatross *P. fusca* are mainly dark-plumaged birds with blackish bills, slender wings and comparatively long tails. They have a wingspan of about 2.2m (86in.). Separation of the two at sea is problematical in the juvenile stages, and in certain cases may be impossible, some birds possessing characters of both species. Further research is required before firm conclusions can be reached on the separation of these earlier plumage stages.

Genus *DIOMEDEA*

Eleven species; huge to large pelagic seabirds. In all identification processes it is essential to record accurately width and extent of underwing margins; head markings; and, if possible, bill and leg colour. In the great albatrosses and for separation of atypical Black-footed from Short-tailed Albatrosses, upperwing pattern, head markings and tail patterns are further details to record.

40 WANDERING ALBATROSS
Diomedea exulans

PLATE 12 Figs 40a-40g
MAP 40

Length 107–135cm (42–53in.). Wingspan 254–351cm (100–138in.). Iris brown, orbital ring blue or pink. Bill flesh-white to pinkish with horn-coloured nails. Legs/feet pinkish to bluish-white.

Circumpolar in Southern Oceans; confusion possible only with Royal Albatross, particularly southern race of latter *D.e. epomophora*. Most stages readily separable however due to differences in sequence of progressive whitening of upperwing (Harrison, P, 1979). In all races females average smaller and usually retain some black, brown or grey on head, body and tail, with white area on wings less extensive than in the larger, whiter-plumaged males. No seasonal variation, juveniles separable from adults. Two subspecies listed differing mainly in size and whiteness of plumage; the smallest and darkest examples usually breed in north of range. The following notes describe plumage stages from juvenile through to the so-called 'snowy' stage, which probably represents old males of the more southerly *D.e. chionoptera*. It should be appreciated that different populations have different end points in plumage maturity; males pass through a phase similar to that of adult female before reaching their final plumage stage.

STAGE 1 (JUVENILE): Wholly chocolate-brown except for conspicuous white face mask; underwing at this and all subsequent stages resembles stage 7. (Beware giant petrels and sooty albatrosses, p. 233, p. 231.)

STAGE 2: Much as juvenile on head and upperparts but with white feather tips appearing on saddle, rump and centre of upperwing. Underparts: belly and flanks mostly white, with conspicuous brown breast band and undertail-coverts.

STAGE 3: (some females, e.g. at Gough and Campbell Is, breed in this or stage 2 plumage). **Head** Mostly white except for brownish crown and mottling on sides of neck. **Body** Mostly white with brown and grey vermiculations on saddle and flanks, and indistinct breast band. **Wings** Upperwing mainly blackish-brown with small whitish patch on inner wing. **Tail** White, sides and tip blackish.

STAGE 4: As stage 3 except head and body whiter. White patches on inner wing increase in area, becoming conspicuous field marks. Tail generally whiter but dark sides and tips of outermost feathers usually retained.

STAGE 5: As stage 4 except head and body mostly white. White patches on inner wing link with back, forming conspicuous and diagnostic wedge into otherwise dark upperwing. Tail mostly white; most retain dark outer tail feathers.

STAGE 6: As stage 5 except white wedge extends *outwards* towards leading edge. Tail usually retains some dusky markings; only 6% of over 600 examined by Gibson (1964) showed wholly white tails.

STAGE 7: Head White (at breeding islands both sexes often have pinkish stain on head). **Body** White. **Wings** Upperwing mostly white except for black primaries and narrow margin along secondaries. Underwing white with blackish primaries

Fig. 5. Schematic upperparts pattern of Wandering and Royal Albatrosses (p. 222, p. 224).

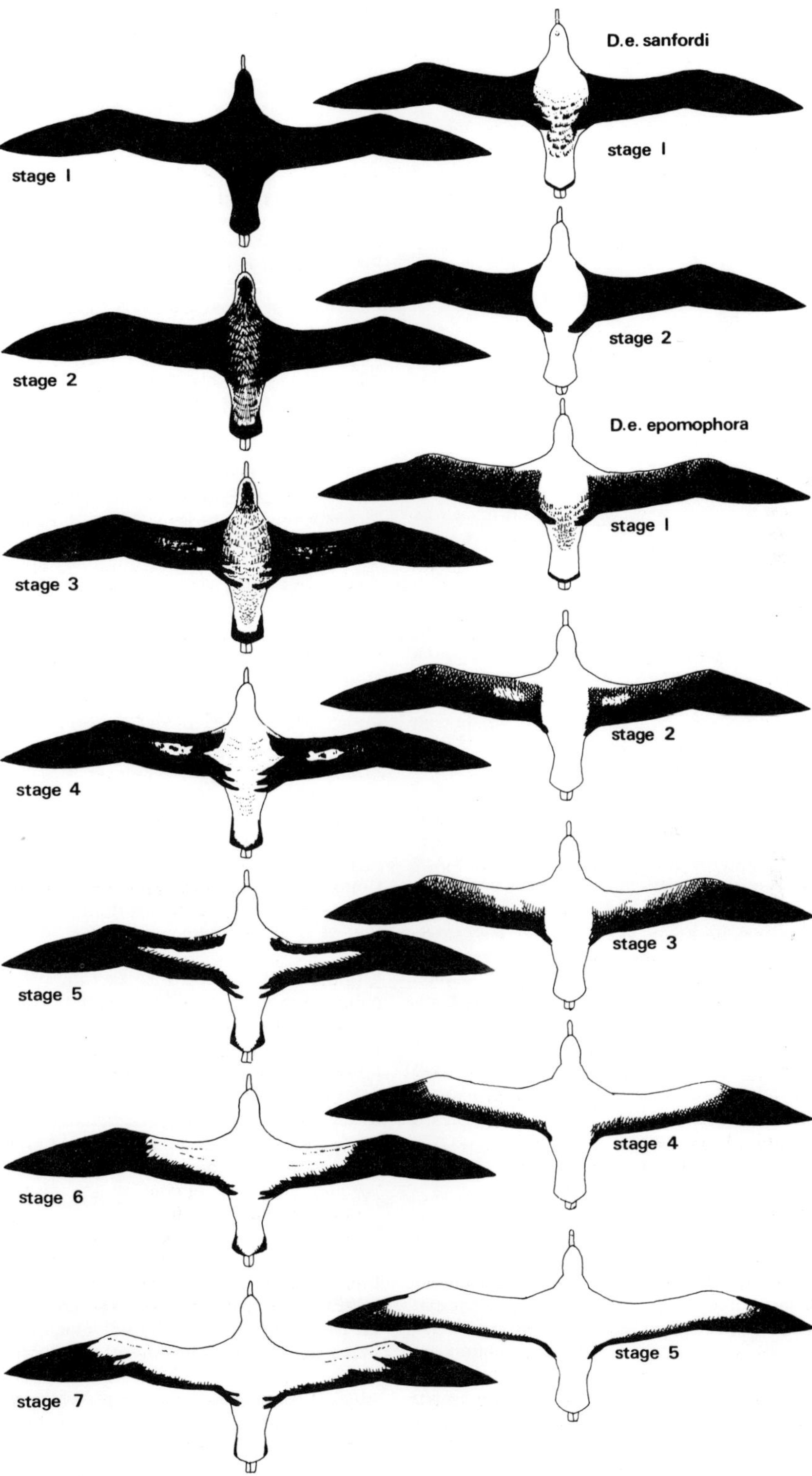

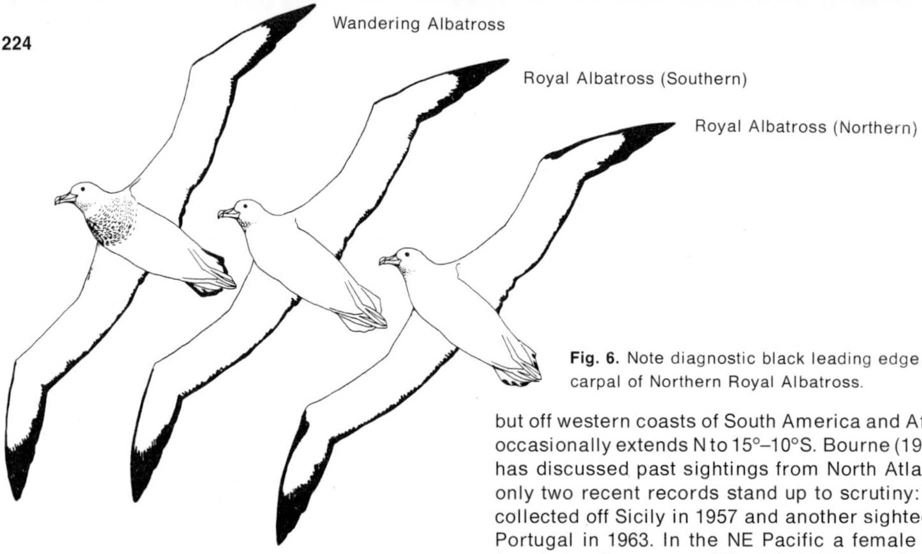

Wandering Albatross

Royal Albatross (Southern)

Royal Albatross (Northern)

Fig. 6. Note diagnostic black leading edge near carpal of Northern Royal Albatross.

and narrow trailing edge. **Tail** White, but some retain dark outer feathers.

FHJ: Magnificent and masterly, an accomplished exponent of dynamic soaring with long sweeping glides on stiff, outstretched wings. In storms wings held bowed and flexed; during calmer weather glides shorter, interspersed with short periods of flapping, but in these conditions most Wanderers loaf on sea. A long run-off is then required to become airborne. Habitually follows ships. Compared with the smaller dark-backed albatrosses (known as mollymawks to southern birders), present species much larger with proportionately larger bill and longer wings, and feet project well beyond tail in flight. Normally silent at sea but often 'bleats' when competing for offal.

DM: *D.e. exulans* breeds at Inaccessible and Gough (formerly at Tristan da Cunha), Amsterdam, Auckland, Campbell and Antipodes Is; *D.e. chionoptera* breeds South Georgia, Marion, Prince Edward, Heard (?), Crozet, Kerguelen and Macquarie Is (has bred Falklands). Biennial breeding cycle: returns to loose colonies Nov/Dec; egg-dates Dec/Jan; fledging and departure Dec–Feb, of following year. Non-breeders of all age groups wander widely at sea; work by Tickell & Gibson (1968) has shown that many ringed at South Georgia, Crozet, Kerguelen, Antipodes, etc. visit Australian coasts. Normal pelagic range extends from about 60°S northwards to the Tropic of Capricorn, but off western coasts of South America and Africa occasionally extends N to 15°–10°S. Bourne (1967b) has discussed past sightings from North Atlantic; only two recent records stand up to scrutiny: one collected off Sicily in 1957 and another sighted off Portugal in 1963. In the NE Pacific a female was found standing on sea cliffs, July 1967, in California (Roberson 1980).

SS: The underwing pattern and white face mask with pink bill separate juveniles and immatures of this species from both species of giant petrels and of sooty albatrosses (p. 233, p. 234, p. 231, p. 232). The smaller dark-backed albatrosses (mollymawks) have dark tails and generally broader margins to the underwing (but see Shy Albatross, p. 229). Most confusion arises with equallylarge white-backed Royal Albatross (p. 224); neither race of that species undergoes complex transitionary stages of young Wanderer, so that any large albatross with pronounced brown or black on crown, breast, back or tail will be a Wanderer. In most later stages Wanderers can be safely separated from Royal due to difference in progressive whitening sequence of upperwing: in Wanderer wing whitens from a central white patch which further whitens to include leading edge of wing; in Royal wing whitens from leading edge backwards. Unfortunately upperwing pattern of old male Wanderers of race *chionoptera* is little different from that of *epomophora* race of Royal. Separation of most white-winged birds at sea therefore still problematical except at close range, when black cutting edges of mandible would indicate a Royal and black in the tail a Wanderer. Northern race of Royal Albatross *D.e. sanfordi* has mostly black upperwings and diagnostic underwing pattern (Fig. 6).

---

41 ROYAL ALBATROSS
Diomedea epomophora

PLATE 12 Figs 41a-41g
MAP 41

Length 107–122cm (42–48in.). Wingspan 305–351cm (120–138in.). Iris dark brown, orbital ring black. Bill pinkish-yellow, cutting edge of upper mandible black. Legs/feet pinkish or bluish-white.

Circumpolar in Southern Oceans although far less common away from breeding islands than similar Wandering Albatross (p. 222). See under that species for discussion on separation of two species. Males average larger and whiter; no seasonal variation. Juveniles separable from adults. Two subspecies listed; they are separable at sea and thus described separately below. Robertson (1980) has recorded cross-breeding of the two subspecies at Taiaroa Head, New Zealand.

D.e. sanfordi

JUVENILE: Much as adult except for indistinct brownish mottling on crown, blackish vermiculation across lower back, and narrow black tip to tail.

ADULT: Head and Body Wholly white. **Wings** Upperwing mainly brownish-black except for small white area at base of leading edge. Underwing mostly white except for black primary tips, narrow trailing edge and diagnostic margin extending outward from carpal joint towards tip (Fig. 6, p. 224).

D.e. epomophora

STAGE 1 (JUVENILE): Head and Body Mostly white except for indistinct blackish vermiculation across lower back. **Wings** Upperwing mostly blackish except for small white area at base of leading edge and an indistinct whitish patch in centre of inner wing. Underwing as in Wandering Albatross. **Tail** White; tips occasionally black (never outer sides of tail).

STAGE 2: As stage 1 except upperwing shows more pronounced white patch in centre of inner wing and narrow white leading edge to wing. See Wandering Albatross (p. 222).

STAGES 3 and 4: As second stage but upperwing becomes progressively whiter from the *leading edge backwards* (see Wandering Albatross, p. 222). **Tail** White.

ADULT: Head and Body Wholly white. **Wings** Upperwing mostly white, with black primaries and narrow trailing edge (compared with Wanderer, white forewing merges more evenly into dark trailing edge due to finer vermiculation across greater secondary-coverts). Underwing as Wandering Albatross. **Tail** White.

FHJ: As described for Wandering Albatross (p. 222) but less inclined to follow vessels, though attends trawlers. In flight appears slightly more hump-backed than Wanderer, but this character of little use for separation purposes.

DM: Breeds only in New Zealand sector, although presence off South America has raised speculation (Murphy 1936, Humphrey *et al.* 1970). *D.e. sanfordi* breeds Chatham Is and on mainland of South Island, New Zealand, at Taiaroa Head, near Dunedin. *D.e. epomophora* breeds Auckland and Campbell Is. Breeds biennially; returns to colonies Oct; egg-dates Nov/Dec; fledging and departure Dec/Jan of following year. Non-breeders of both races and of all age groups appear to wander widely. Many occur along both coasts of South America and may be the commoner white-backed albatross of the region (Murphy 1936; Hughes, pers. comm.). Occurs N to about 10°S off western South America and to about 23°S off Brazil on the eastern littoral; due to increased observers/ability a few have now been recorded off southern Africa (Sinclair, pers. comm.), and Australia, thus indicating a circumpolar route across Atlantic and Indian Oceans back to natal islands. Interestingly, all sightings off Africa have been of *sanfordi*.

SS: The combination of white head, body and tail with mostly black upperwings diagnostic for *D.e. sanfordi*; it also has diagnostic underwing pattern (Fig. 6, p. 224). A Wandering Albatross with upperwing as dark would show brown or black on crown, breast and back with a mostly black tail. Separation of southern race of Royal (*D.e. epomophora*) from Wandering Albatross is discussed under latter species (p. 222).

42 WAVED ALBATROSS
other: Galapagos Albatross
Diomedea irrorata

PLATE 17 Fig. 42

MAP 42

Length 85–93cm ($33\frac{1}{2}$–$36\frac{1}{2}$in.). Wingspan 230–240cm ($90\frac{1}{2}$–$94\frac{1}{2}$in.). Iris dark brown. Bill dull yellow. Legs/feet pale lead-blue.

The only exclusively tropical albatross, confined to Galapagos and seas off Ecuador and Peru. Unlikely to be confused with other seabirds of area, but off northern Peru Royal/Wandering Albatrosses and Southern Giant Petrel (p. 224, p. 222, p. 234) could occasionally occur. Sexes alike, males average larger; no seasonal variation. Juveniles barely distinguishable. No subspecies.

JUVENILE: As adult except bill duller, head whiter.

ADULT: Head Wholly white tinged buffish-yellow on crown and nape; hindneck similar but becoming barred with narrow, wavy vermiculations. **Body** Upperparts mostly pale chestnut-brown finely barred grey and white in narrow, but variable, wavy lines. Barring becomes coarser over rump and uppertail-coverts which, at distance, can appear as whitish horseshoe over base of tail. Underparts: upper breast whitish, remainder as upperparts with heaviest vermiculation on sides of breast, flanks and belly. **Wings** Upperwing: pale chestnut-brown, primary shafts white. Underwing: coverts and axillaries whitish, finely vermiculated with brown and grey; primary tips and wing margins brown. **Tail** Brown, base whitish.

FHJ: Jizz resembles larger Wandering Albatross (p. 222), with massive bill and feet projecting beyond tail in flight. In light winds flight laboured with much purposeful flapping; even in stiff breezes flight lacks the dynamic soaring found in congeners. Often seen sitting in loose rafts of 20–200 but very timid, rarely allows approach (pers. obs.); does not follow boats.

DM: Until recently known to breed only at Hood I., Galapagos, where about 12,000 pairs breed each year (Harris 1973); a few pairs now also known to breed at Las Platas Is, off Ecuador (Owre 1976). At Galapagos birds return late Mar onwards; egg-dates Apr–Jul; fledging and departure begins Jan with most absent from Galapagos until Mar (Harris 1973). Post-breeding dispersal eastwards to coasts of Ecuador and Peru, mainly between 4°N and 12°S but occasionally S to Mollendo (R Hughes, pers. comm.). Main concentrations in Gulf of Guayaquil and near Lobos de Tierra Is off northern Peru, where rafts of several hundred regularly encountered. Juveniles probably remain in these areas until their third year before returning to natal islands.

SS: The only albatross of the area, although Fleming (1950) recorded a Wandering/Royal type at Galapagos and both these species and Southern Giant Petrel (p. 234) may be expected to occur from time to time N to about 10°S off Peru in the cold Humboldt Current. If well seen, however, confusion should not arise.

43 SHORT-TAILED ALBATROSS
other: Steller's Albatross
Diomedea albatrus

PLATE 16 Figs 43a-43f

MAP 43

Length 84–94cm (33–37in.). Wingspan 213–229cm (84–90in.). Iris blackish. Bill pink, blue at tip, with narrow black line at base extending along gape. Legs/feet bluish-white, can appear dark grey at sea.

N Pacific; formerly widespread, now rarest of all albatrosses. Range overlaps with Black-footed Albatross (p. 227); care needed to separate from juveniles and old/aberrant birds of that species. Morphology resembles that of Wandering Albatross (p. 222). Sexes alike, no seasonal variation. Juveniles and immatures separable but Tickell (1973) has shown that some breed in so-called immature plumage, birds becoming progressively whiter with age. For convenience, the terms 'immature' and 'sub-adult' have been retained in the following entry, much of which is based on Hasegawa (pers. comm.) and Yanagisawa (1973).

JUVENILE (FIRST STAGE): Bill and legs pale flesh, often appearing whitish at long range. **Head, Body, Wings and Tail** Wholly blackish-brown except for paler chin and narrow line below eye.

JUVENILE (SECOND STAGE): As first stage except: **Head** Forehead, base of bill and chin whitish, extending under and behind eye as narrow streak; ear-coverts and lores paler and greyer. Throat remains dark, forming noticeable collar. **Body** Underparts dark buff-brown wearing to off-white on centre of breast and belly; flanks, thighs and ventral area remaining dark. **Wings** Upperwing shows first signs of diagnostic whitish patch on inner greater coverts, an excellent in-flight character.

IMMATURE (FIRST STAGE): Bill and legs as adult. **Head** White except for sepia-brown hindcrown, nape, hindneck and sides of neck. **Body** Upperparts mainly sepia-brown, scaled buff and white; rump and uppertail-coverts whitish. Underparts off-white except for brownish sides of breast and mottling along flanks, thighs and ventral area. **Wings** Upperwing mostly sepia-brown with two diagnostic whitish patches, one on innermost greater coverts, the other adjoining scapulars. Underwing mostly brown, primary-coverts whitish, remainder of coverts variably tipped with white. **Tail** Blackish, base white.

IMMATURE (SECOND STAGE): Head Mostly white, crown and sides of face washed yellow; nape browner, forming partial cap and collar. **Body** Upperparts whitish, lightly scaled buff. Underparts mostly white, flanks, thighs and ventral area faintly brown. **Wings** Upperwing: whitish patches larger. Underwing becoming progressively whiter. **Tail** As adult.

SUB-ADULT: Head Resembles adult except for brownish cervical collar. **Body and Wings** As adult but rather dingy with variable buffish feather tips.

ADULT: Head Mostly white with yellow cast on crown extending, in some, from nape across throat to form continuous collar. **Body** Wholly white. **Wings** Upperwings: mostly white; primaries, their coverts, secondaries and tertials black (extent of black varies individually). Underwing mostly white with narrow black margins; inner coverts and axillaries variably streaked greyish-brown. **Tail** Black, base white.

FHJ: Largest N Pacific albatross; jizz recalls Wandering Albatross (p. 222) but smaller, proportionately shorter wings. Larger size and massive pink bill enable separation between juveniles of this and of Black-footed Albatross (p. 227). Not normally attracted to ships, apparently timid at sea.

DM: Formerly abundant in N Pacific, where bred within Bonin, Izu, Senkaku, Pescadores and Daito groups. Pelagic range extended from Japan and coasts of China E to Bering Sea and western coasts of N America. Brought to verge of extinction by Japanese plume-hunters in late 19th and 20th centuries; reduced to about ten pairs by 1953, has since increased slowly. Tickell estimated about 57 pairs in 1973 but Hasegawa (pers. comm.) estimated 1982 population at 250 birds. Only definite breeding site now at Tori Shima, a volcanic island some 580km S of Tokyo. Recently suspected of breeding at Minami Kojima in the Senkatu Retto (25°45′N, 123°36′E), but reports yet to be confirmed. Returns to colonies Oct; egg-dates Oct–Nov; fledging May onwards. Now only rarely reported away from natal island but formerly dispersed into Pacific following tradewinds N to Bering Sea, E and S past California and then westwards back to natal islands. Stragglers occasionally occur at Hawaiian group in Leeward Is; one has been at Midway for about six years (Warham, pers. comm.). Recent status off western N America summarised by Roberson (1980), who listed six records off Alaska; one record each from British Columbia and Oregon; two records from California. Most occurred Jun–Nov.

SS: Juveniles closely resemble juvenile Black-footed Albatrosses (p. 227) but differ in massive pink bill, pinkish legs, lack of white at base of bill and in larger size. All subsequent stages would differ from aberrant Black-footed or Black-footed × Laysan hybrids by distinctive white patches on upperwings which become progressively larger with age. See notes under old/atypical Black-footed Albatross (p. 227). Morphology similar to Wandering Albatross, which has occurred in N Pacific but has underwing white with black margins at all ages (juvenile and immature Short-tailed have dark underwings). Adults of the two species differ in head colour, upperwing and tail patterns.

44 BLACK-FOOTED ALBATROSS
Diomedea nigripes

PLATE 16 Figs 44a-44c
MAP 44

Length 68–74cm (27–29in.). Wingspan 193–213cm (76–84in.). Iris blackish-brown. Bill colour varies: dark chestnut with blackish base and nail to (more usually) wholly glossy, blackish-grey. Legs/feet black.

N Pacific Ocean; easily separated from Laysan Albatross (p. 227) but confusion always possible with juvenile or immature Short-tailed (p. 226). Latter differs mainly in size, bill and leg colour and, in subsequent stages, upperwing pattern. Sexes alike, males average slightly larger; no seasonal variation although old or perhaps aberrant birds show almost white head and paler plumage. Juveniles separable but complicated by incomplete knowledge of plumage stages and by some variance in colour of uppertail-coverts and ventral areas of many adults. Black-footed × Laysan hybrids recorded; Warham (pers. comm.) reported at least five at Midway in 1980/81 season.

JUVENILE: Bill and legs blackish. Plumage wholly sooty-brown except for whitish area at base of bill.

IMMATURE: As juvenile except: **Body** Uppertail-coverts tipped whitish, sometimes forming indistinct horseshoe over tail; undertail-coverts vary from grey to white.

ADULT (typical): **Head** Mostly blackish-brown or greyish-brown, except for narrow whitish area around base of bill and under eye (some lack this). **Body** Upperparts mainly blackish-brown, often with mauve cast, indistinctly fringed buff-grey but soon wearing to even colour; rump and uppertail-coverts usually white. Underparts slightly paler, some showing white undertail-coverts and ventral area. **Wings** As upperparts, outer primary shafts white. **Tail** Blackish-brown.

ADULT (aberrant or aged): Often mistaken for immature Short-tailed Albatross (p. 226); differs from typical Black-footed Albatross in dull yellowish or dusky-pink bill and legs. **Head** Mostly pale brownish-white. **Body** Upperparts pale sandy-brown, lower back scaled darker; rump and uppertail-coverts whiter. Underparts variable, occasionally almost wholly dirty-white except for indistinct band across upper breast. **Wings** Upperwings as upperparts, distal third blackish (lacks white patches of Short-tailed Albatross). Underwing variable, sometimes whitish. **Tail** Blackish above, occasionally white below.

FHJ: Typical albatross jizz, with large hooked bill and long sabre-like wings. Rarely seen from land, except at colonies; regularly follows ships, attends trawlers.

DM: Formerly more widespread; breeds on islands in central and western Pacific, chiefly Leeward chain of islands and atolls of Hawaiian archipelago, Marshall Is and Johnston I.; also at Tori Shima where breeds alongside Short-tailed Albatross (p. 226). Returns to colonies Oct/Nov: egg-dates Nov/Dec; fledging and departure mainly Jul, dispersing over much of N Pacific from Taiwan to Bering Sea and E to Baja California. The only albatross seen regularly off Pacific coast of N America. Young birds probably remain in these areas for first 3–4 years before returning to natal colonies.

SS: See notes under Short-tailed Albatross.

45 LAYSAN ALBATROSS
Diomedea immutabilis

PLATE 15 Fig. 45
MAP 45

Length 79–81cm (31–32in.). Wingspan 195–203cm (77–80in.). Iris dark, white lower lid. Bill varies, light grey with darker tip and base or yellowish with grey tip. Legs/feet flesh-pink.

Northern Pacific Ocean; the only dark-backed albatross of the region with white head and underparts. Sexes alike; no seasonal variation. Juveniles barely separable (hence *immutabilis*), although bare parts probably greyer. Albinism and hybrid Laysan × Black-footed Albatrosses reported (Palmer 1962, Fisher 1972, Warham, pers. comm.).

PLUMAGE: Head Mainly white, lores dark grey or black, sides of face often grey (at close range). **Body** Upperparts: mantle, scapulars and back blackish, rump white. Underparts white or yellowish-white. **Wings** Upperwing blackish above, primary shafts white; browner in worn plumage. Underwing mainly white with narrow, irregular margins broadest at carpal and primary tips; white coverts show irregular blackish streaks (varies individually). **Tail** Greyish.

FHJ: The only dark-backed albatross regularly occurring in N Pacific with white head and underparts. Occasionally follows ships. Appearance resembles Southern Oceans mollymawks but, unlike that group, feet project slightly beyond tail in flight.

DM: Although formerly widespread throughout N Pacific, numbers decimated in early part of 20th century and during Second World War when some colonies exterminated. Until recently known to breed only in central Pacific on northwest Hawaiian chain, mainly at Laysan, Midway, Lisianski Is, Pearl and Hermes Reef. See Palmer (1962) for minor breeding stations. Has recently nested at Kilauea Point, Kauai I., Hawaii. Kurata (in Hasegawa 1978) recently reported breeding south of Japan at Bonin Is, the only modern record of breeding away from Hawaiian chain. Returns natal islands Oct onwards; egg-dates Nov/Dec; fledging May. Rarely seen off breeding stations during summer. Post-breeding range E to North America, where regular but scarce off California and Washington; occurs N to Aleutians and W to Japan. Southern limits of pelagic distribution poorly known. Non-breeders scattered over N Pacific throughout year.

SS: Although most abundant N Pacific albatross, scarcer off western N America than wholly dark Black-footed Albatross. Adult Short-tailed has white back; see under that species (p. 226) for differences at other plumage stages.

46 BLACK-BROWED ALBATROSS
other: Black-browed Mollywawk
Diomedea melanophris

PLATE 13 Figs 46a-46e

MAP 46

Length 83–93cm (32½–36½in.). Wingspan averages 240cm (94½in.). Iris brown. Bill bright waxy or orange-yellow, redder at tip, narrow black line at base. Legs/feet bluish-white.

Circumpolar in Southern Oceans; range overlaps with Grey-headed, Bullers and Yellow-nosed Albatrosses (p. 230, p. 228, p. 230); beware especially of confusing juvenile and immature *D.m. impavida* with corresponding stages of Grey-headed Albatross. Sexes alike; no seasonal variation. Juveniles separable from adults. Two subspecies listed; *D.m. impavida* is separable at sea and thus described separately below.

JUVENILE: Bill horny or dusky-grey with culmen and nails blackish; often appears black-tipped at sea (Warham & Sinclair, pers. comm.). **Head** Mainly white, dark mark before and passing through eye; nape grey. **Body** Upperparts: mantle dark grey merging into blackish-grey scapulars and back; rump white. Underparts mostly white; partial or complete greyish breast band extending from mantle. **Wings** Upperwing brownish-black, outer primary shafts white. Underwing variable, most show ghost-image of adult's pattern. **Tail** Grey.

SUB-ADULT: As juvenile except: bill dull yellow with dark tip, an excellent diagnostic character. **Head** Paler on nape. **Body** Underparts: breast band, if present, weakly pigmented. **Wings** Underwing: variable, resembles adult, greater and primary-coverts mostly white.

ADULT: Head White, dark eyebrow before and passing through eye. **Body** Upperparts as juvenile. Underparts white. **Wings** Upperwing as juvenile. Underwing: dark primaries, leading and trailing edges enclose white coverts. Black leading edge broadest of any albatross and forms dark wedge midway along inner wing. **Tail** Grey.

ADULT (*D.m. impavida*): As nominate except: iris pale yellow. **Head** Eyebrow more extensive. **Wings** Underwing: variable but many show dusky-grey (not white) axillaries and inner greater coverts and, possibly, a wider black leading edge to underwing (at sea underwing may thus appear dark with a central rectangle of white: see photo in Terres 1980 p. 39 and compare with photo in Serventy *et al.* 1971 p. 72). Using bill colour as a guide to age, most immature *impavida* show darker underwings than found in corresponding nominate (pers. obs.).

FHJ: Readily follows ships, attends trawlers. Typical flight of genus (p. 221), occasionally submerges to retrieve offal.

DM: Possibly commonest and most widespread albatross. *D.m. melanophris* breeds Staten, Falklands, South Georgia, Kerguelen, Heard, Antipodes and Macquarie Is and a few at Campbell I.; *D.m. impavida* at Campbell Is. Normal circumpolar range extends from about 65°S to 23°S, but to about 10°S off Peru and 20°S off West Africa in cold-water zones of Humboldt and Benguela Currents. Ringing recoveries have shown that this species has a strong northwards migratory tendency, with different populations going to different areas (Tickell, in Bourne 1967b); this migratory urge helps explain the now almost annual sightings in the North Atlantic (although assisted passage cannot be ruled out).

SS: See notes under Grey-headed Albatross (p. 231).

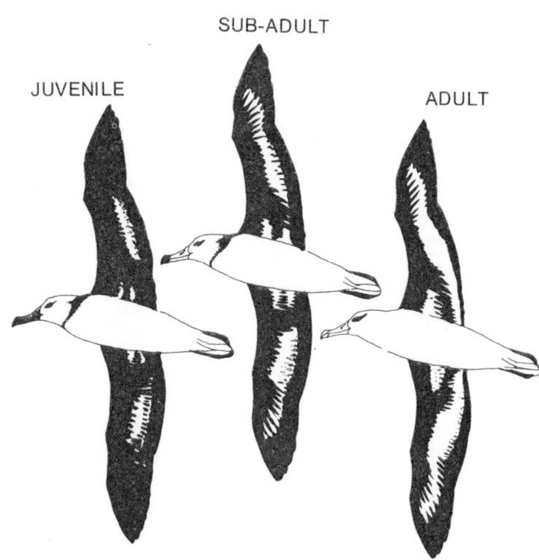

Fig. 7. *D.m. impavida* underwing patterns. Compared with nominate *D.m. melanophris* underwing usually darker, particularly axillaries and innermost underwing-coverts

47 BULLER'S ALBATROSS
other: Buller's Mollymawk
Diomedea bulleri

PLATE 14 Figs 47a-47c

MAP 47

Length 76–81cm (30–32in.). Wingspan 205–213cm (81–84in.). Iris brown. Bill mostly black with lemon-yellow culminicorn and ramicorn. Legs/feet pink, bluish at joints.

Breeds in New Zealand sector, migrating to coasts of South America; range thus overlaps with all southern albatrosses. See especially White-capped *D.c. salvini* and Grey-headed Albatrosses (p. 229, p. 231). Sexes alike, no seasonal variation. Juveniles separable from adults. Two subspecies.

JUVENILE: Much as adult except bill brownish-horn, tip darker, head darker brownish-grey.

IMMATURE: As juvenile but culminicorn and ramicorn gradually turn horn-colour; head greyer in tone.

ADULT: Head Mostly grey or greyish-brown contrasting with whitish forehead and dusky eyebrow. **Body** Upperparts: saddle brownish-black; rump white. Underparts white. **Wings** Upperwing brownish-black; shafts of outer primaries whitish. Underwing mostly white with moderately broad leading margin and narrow trailing margin (pattern thus resembles that of Yellow-nosed Albatross, p. 230). **Tail** Greyish-black.

FHJ: Intermediate in size between Yellow-nosed and Grey-headed Albatrosses (p. 230, p. 231). Compared with larger Salvin's Albatross (p. 229), head and body proportionately smaller with shorter wings and, at long range, bill appears wholly black. Attends trawlers, follows ships.

DM: Restricted as breeding species to New Zealand. *D.b. bulleri* breeds Solander and Snares Is. Returns to colonies Dec–Feb; egg-dates Jan/Feb; fledging and dispersal Jul/Aug. Thought to disperse only to adjacent Australasian seas, including coasts of S and SE Australia where formerly regarded as rare (Serventy *et al.* 1971). Recent 'observer-activity' has shown that small numbers occur regularly off Tasmania, where Barton (1978b) saw about 20 attending a trawler. See also Brothers (1978). *D.b. platei* breeds at Chatham Is; season normally 2–3 months earlier than nominate. Appears to be highly migratory, ranging from New Zealand across southern Pacific to Chile and Peru, although numbers and frequency little known. It seems likely in absence of sightings off South Africa, that they wander N in Humboldt Current before returning to natal islands.

SS: All ages can be safely distinguished from Grey-headed Albatross (p. 231) by narrower leading margin on underwing and bold white forehead. Confusion more likely with larger and longer-winged *D.c. salvini* (p. 229), which also has whitish forehead with remainder of head dark; differs from that species in greyer head, darker saddle and distinctly different underwing pattern; at long range, bill appears black in present species, grey in *D.c. salvini*.

48 WHITE-CAPPED ALBATROSS

PLATE 14 Figs 48a-48b

other: Shy Albatross/Mollymawk (includes Salvin's and Chatham Island Albatrosses, 48X and 48Y)

Diomedea cauta

MAP 48

Length 99cm (39in.). Wingspan 198–256cm (78–101in.). Iris dark brown. Bill yellowish-grey shading to yellowish at tips. Legs/feet pinkish, bluish at joints.

Breeds Australasian area, dispersing throughout Southern Oceans. All races probably the easiest of albatrosses to identify due to diagnostic black 'thumbmark' on leading edge of underwing. Sexes alike; no seasonal variation. Juveniles separable from adults. Three subspecies, separable at sea and thus described separately below beginning with nominate.

JUVENILE: Differs from adult in dull blue-grey bill with black tip to both mandibles. Head, including nape and hindneck, is grey and merges evenly into mantle. (Diagnostic underwing identical to that of adult.)

SUB-ADULT: Bill as adult but some retain blackish tip to lower mandible. Head also variable: some have white hindnecks separating greyish head from darker mantle, others much as adult but with more pronounced grey sides to face.

ADULT: Head Mostly white with dusky eyebrow shading into light grey cheeks, imparting white-capped appearance. **Body** Upperparts: mantle pale ashy-brown merging into darker brown scapulars and back; rump white. Underparts white. **Wings** Upperwing blackish-brown, darker than saddle; outer primary shafts whitish, often forming patch on outer wing. Underwing white with very narrow margins and dark thumbmark at base of leading edge, an excellent flight character, visible at considerable range. **Tail** Dark grey.

48X SALVIN'S ALBATROSS

PLATE 14 Figs 48Xa-48Xb

other: Grey-backed Albatross/Mollymawk

Diomedea cauta salvini

MAP 48X

JUVENILE: As nominate with wholly grey head merging into mantle; differs in larger, greyer, tip to underwing.

SUB-ADULT: Much as adult but bill greyer with black tip to both mandibles. (Lacks white hindneck found in nominate.)

ADULT: Slightly smaller than *D.c. cauta*; bill differs in ivory-horn to yellowish culminicorn, slightly tipped yellow, lower nail with dark mark. Plumage as nominate, except head mostly brownish-grey with whitish forehead merging evenly into paler ashy-brown mantle. Underwing bears same narrow margins and diagnostic thumbmark as nominate, but has larger, though greyer, wingtip (this character useful for subspecific separation of juveniles).

48Y CHATHAM ISLAND ALBATROSS

PLATE 14 Fig. 48Y

other: Chatham Island Mollymawk

Diomedea cauta eremita

MAP 48Y

JUVENILE: As adult except bill dark olive-brown with black tip to both mandibles. Plumage similar to adult but a grey wash sometimes extends over upper breast.

ADULT: Smallest of the *cauta* group; bill yellow with dark tip to lower mandible. Plumage resembles *D.c. salvini* but darker; lacks white cap.

FHJ: All forms larger and proportionately longer-winged than other Southern Oceans mollymawks, flight recalling grace and effortlessness of Wanderer. Follows ships; attends trawlers.

DM: *D.c. cauta* breeds Albatross Rock, Bass Strait, the Mewstone and Pedra Branca off Tasmania, and at Auckland Is, S of New Zealand; *D.c. salvini* at Snares and Bounty Is; *D.c. eremita* at Chatham Is (Pyramid Rock). Returns to colonies Aug/Sep; egg-dates Sep/Oct; fledging and dispersal Mar/Apr. As far as is known, *D.c. eremita* differs from other two members of group in dispersing only to adjacent seas. The pelagic range and movements of both *salvini* and *cauta* have often been misrepresented in past literature; *salvini* usually credited with a circumpolar range, and supposed to occur commonly off southern Africa. Personal observations in Southern Oceans support neither of these assumptions, which appear to be based on belief that any grey-headed *cauta* is *D.c. salvini*. In reality juveniles of the two races can be separated only by greater amount of dark on tip of *salvini*'s underwing. During my three years of research off Cape Town the several hundreds of sightings were all referable to *D.c. cauta* (see also Bourne 1977). It seems more likely that, whilst adults of both races disperse to Australasian seas after breeding, juveniles migrate to separate regions: *D.c. salvini* occurs commonly off western South America in Humboldt Current N to about 5°S and, in absence of acceptable records from southern Africa, probably returns via lower latitudes of the Pacific; *D.c. cauta* occurs commonly off South Africa but its route to and from this area as yet remains a mystery. I have recorded them in mid Indian Ocean off Amsterdam and also near Marion I. See also Paulian (1953). Vagrants have occurred N to Washington, western USA, and to Elat, northern Red Sea.

SS: The black thumbmark at base of leading edge on underwing diagnostic and found in all three *cauta* albatrosses. In juvenile and immature *salvini* and *cauta*, the head may become almost white with partial grey collar extending to sides of breast (pers. obs. off South Africa); beware of immature Black-browed and Grey-headed Albatrosses (p. 228, p. 231).

---

49 YELLOW-NOSED ALBATROSS
other: Yellow-nosed Mollymawk
Diomedea chlororhynchos

PLATE 14 Figs 49a-49c

MAP 49

Length 71–81cm (28–32in.). Wingspan 178–205cm (70–81in.). Iris brown. Bill mostly black with yellow culminicorn and pinkish tip. Legs/feet pinkish-blue.

South Atlantic and Indian Oceans; range overlaps with Grey-headed, Black-browed and White-capped Albatrosses (p. 231, p. 228, p. 229). Sexes alike; no seasonal variation. Juveniles separable from adults. Two subspecies listed: *D.c. bassi* differs from nominate in having very pale grey to white head with grey wash confined to cheeks (this soon abrades and, at sea, most appear white-headed, see Brooke *et al.* 1980). Nominate is described below.

JUVENILE: Much as adult except head wholly white, bill black. Sinclair (pers. comm.) reports immatures with wider black leading edge to underwing, approaching, in some, width of adult Black-browed.

ADULT: Head Mostly grey, nape and hindneck white (wears paler but usually retains grey-headed appearance at sea: Sinclair, pers. comm.). **Body** Upperparts: saddle blackish-grey; rump white. Underparts mostly white, sides of breast faintly grey. **Wings** Upperwing blackish, outer primary shafts whitish. Underwing mainly white except for black primaries and narrow margins, broadest along leading edge. **Tail** Grey.

FHJ: Smallest and most slender of the smaller southern albatrosses (mollymawks) with proportionately longer bill, neck and tail. At sea upperwings and saddle of both races appear black (rather than brown) with narrowly margined white underwings. Occasionally follows ships, but rather shyer than the more robust bull-necked Black-browed Albatross, with a preference for more temperate seas.

DM: *D.c. chlororhynchos* breeds Tristan da Cunha group and Gough I. in southern Atlantic. *D.c. bassi* breeds southern Indian Ocean at St Paul, Amsterdam, Prince Edward Is and Crozets. Returns to colonies Aug/Sep; egg-dates Sep/Oct; fledging and departure Mar–May. Movements and dispersal not fully known but generally to warmer subantarctic and subtropical waters of Atlantic and Indian Oceans from about 45°S to 15°S. In southern Atlantic particularly numerous off Rio de la Plata, Argentina, and off western coasts of southern Africa where flocks of several hundreds not uncommon around trawlers. Recent sightings in Gulf of Mexico and off Atlantic seaboard of North America suggest that a few regularly penetrate N to lower latitudes of western N Atlantic. As yet no acceptable records from NE Atlantic (Bourne 1967b). The most plentiful albatross off southern Western Australia, extending N to Point Cloates with occasional sightings N to Cocos Keeling Is (Serventy *et al.* 1971). Range extends E to Tasman Sea, where common off eastern North Island, New Zealand, and SE Australia; rarer further E in Pacific.

SS: Combination of whitish head, blackish bill and narrow underwing margins diagnostic in Indian Ocean race *D.c. bassi*. Juvenile Black-browed and Grey-headed Albatrosses (p. 228, p. 231) also have blackish bills, but markings on head and underwing distinctly different; adults of last two species differ in bill coloration and in much wider black leading margins to underwing. Nominate Yellow-nosed in S Atlantic difficult to separate from adult Grey-headed as both have grey heads, but latter has different bill pattern, wider black margins to underwing and different jizz. See also Buller's and White-capped Albatrosses (p. 228, p. 229).

50 GREY-HEADED ALBATROSS

other: Grey-headed Mollymawk

Diomedea chrysostoma

PLATE 13 Figs 50a-50d

MAP 50

Length 81cm (32in.). Wingspan 220cm (87in.). Iris brown. Bill black, chrome-yellow upper and lower ridges shading to red or orange at tip. Legs/feet whitish-flesh.

Circumpolar in Southern Oceans; range overlaps with Black-browed, Yellow-nosed and Buller's Albatrosses (p. 228, p. 230, p. 228). See also *D. cauta salvini* (p. 229). Sexes alike; no seasonal variation. Juveniles separable from adults. No subspecies.

JUVENILE: Bill blackish-grey. **Head** Including nape mostly grey, usually darker than adult's, with barely discernible dark eyebrow before, and passing through, eye; ear-coverts paler. **Body** Upperparts: mantle dark grey (extension from nape) merging into blackish-grey scapulars and back; rump white. Underparts mostly white, greyish band across upper breast. **Wings** Blackish-brown above, primary shafts paler. Underwing at this stage averages darkest of any southern *Diomedea* albatross. **Tail** Dark grey.

IMMATURE: Bill black, tip of upper mandible yellowish. **Head** As juvenile, but during first year at sea feather tips may abrade revealing whiter bases, particularly on ear-coverts, forehead and crown, imparting white-headed appearance. **Body** Underparts: breast band retained though faded or incomplete. **Wings** Underwing shows ghost-image of adult's pattern.

SUB-ADULT: As adult except: bill duller. **Head** Paler. **Wings** Underwing as adult but scattered grey tips across coverts.

ADULT: Head Mostly blue-grey, paler on forehead and crown, dark mark before and passing through eye. In worn plumage or at long range can appear white-headed, though blackish bill separates it from Black-browed Albatross (see Yellow-nosed Albatross, p. 230). **Body** Upperparts as juvenile. Underparts white. **Wings** Upperwing brownish-black, outer primary shafts whitish. Underwing mainly white with irregular black margins, broadest on leading edge midway along inner wing but not forming conspicuous black wedge as in Black-browed and, by comparison, demarcation sharp (fuzzy in Black-browed: Warham, pers. comm.). **Tail** Grey.

FHJ: Much as Black-browed but flight often higher; nearly always holds head angled with bill pointing at 45° or more downwards (Sinclair, pers. comm.). Differs from latter in more southerly distribution, preferring colder surface waters, and in less migratory tendencies.

DM: Circumpolar in Southern Oceans, breeding on Diego Ramirez off Cape Horn, South Georgia, Marion, Prince Edward, Crozet and Kerguelen Is; in New Zealand area at Macquarie and Campbell Is. Normal circumpolar range extends from about 65°S to 35°S, but to about 15°S off Peru in Humboldt Current. No records from North Atlantic stand up to scrutiny (Bourne 1967b) whereas sightings of Black-browed and Yellow-nosed Albatrosses now almost annual.

SS: Adults readily separated from adult Black-browed (p. 228) by head, bill and underwing patterns. Juveniles more difficult to separate: on average Grey-headed juveniles show darker head, breast band and underwing but there is some overlap (especially in *D.m. impavida* underwing). Most reliable character at this age is bill colour: Grey-headed fledge with wholly blackish bills, Black-browed with greyish or horn-coloured bills, tipped black (Sinclair & Warham, pers. comm.). Immatures and sub-adults of these two species are more easily separable by differences in head, bill and underwing patterns. Observers in S Atlantic should beware adult nominate Yellow-nosed which in fresh plumage, has head as dark and as grey as Grey-headed. Experienced birders should notice different jizz, underwing and bill pattern of Yellow-nosed (see Brooke *et al*. 1980). Both Buller's and Salvin's Albatrosses (p. 228, p. 229) also have grey heads, but with contrasting white foreheads; their underwing patterns differ from that of present species.

Genus *PHOEBETRIA*

Two species; moderately large. Adults separable given reasonable views. Juveniles and immatures more difficult and, in some cases, may be impossible. To facilitate identification, record degree of contrast between mantle, back and upperwings. Bill colour (sulcus), if visible, should be accurately recorded.

51 SOOTY ALBATROSS

other: Dark-mantled Sooty Albatross

Phoebetria fusca

PLATE 15 Figs 51a-51c

MAP 51

Length 84–89cm (33–35in.). Wingspan averages 203cm (80in.). Iris brown, with incomplete white crescents. Bill black, sulcus yellow or orange (see p. 12) Legs/feet mauve or greyish-flesh.

Southern Atlantic and Indian Oceans; range overlaps with Light-mantled Sooty Albatross (p. 232). Beware also pink-billed juvenile Wandering Albatross and both species of giant petrel (p. 222, p. 233, p. 234). Sexes alike; no seasonal variation but mantle and upper back subject to extreme bleaching. Juvenile separable from adult. No subspecies.

JUVENILE: As adult except: Bill blackish, flesh-grey sulcus, and crescents above and below eye (some authors report yellow, grey or bluish sulcus). **Head** Paler, particularly nape, sometimes forming buffy collar. **Body** Upperparts: indistinct paler fringes to mantle (but not extending to lower back and rump as in Light-mantled). **Wings and Tail** Quill shafts dark.

IMMATURE/WORN ADULT: Much as juvenile but plumage highly variable. **Head** Some show buffy or white collar over nape. **Body** Upperparts: mantle and upper back scaled buff or grey (but not usually extending to lower back and rump as in Light-mantled).

ADULT: Head Sooty-brown, sides of face darker. **Body** Wholly brown, slightly paler in tone than head. **Wings and Tail** Mostly dark brown, primaries and tail blackish with white or yellowish shafts.

FHJ: Both sooty albatrosses are easily separated from the bulky, all-dark pale-billed giant petrels (p. 233, p. 234) by slender jizz, long, narrow wings, and pointed tail imparting a 'pointed' appearance at both ends. Their pliable, slender wings and more lightly built jizz may suggest graceful quality of flight not normally seen in other albatrosses; this quality best seen in gales. Highly inquisitive, readily follows ships, attends trawlers.

DM: Breeds in S Atlantic at Tristan Da Cunha and Gough Is. Also in S Indian Ocean at Amsterdam, St Paul, Marion, Prince Edward, Crozet and Kerguelen Is. Returns to colonies Jul/Aug; egg-dates Sep–Nov; fledging and departure Apr/May. Prefers warmer surface water than Light-mantled Sooty, although the two are sympatric at Marion, Prince Edward, Crozet and Kerguelen Is. Pelagic range extends E to Australian Bight and Tasmania, occasionally to New South Wales but apparently not across Tasman Sea to New Zealand. In the W does not normally extend beyond 50°W in southern Atlantic, although there is a record in eastern Pacific at 61°S, 90°W (Watson 1975). Birds occasionally range S to 60°S and N to about 30°S.

SS: Differs from giant petrels (p. 233, p. 234) in dark bill and slender streamlined jizz. Most problems lie in separation from Light-mantled Sooty Albatross (p. 232). Typical adults readily separated, given reasonable views, by differences in sulcus and upperparts coloration. At end of breeding season (Apr/May) adults in worn plumage often show heavy wear and bleaching to mantle and upper back feathers. Immatures at sea can also show similar plumage characters. Superficially these types resemble Light-mantled Sooty Albatross, but can usually be told by darker brown lower back and rump (buffy-grey and brown in Light-mantled). There are, however, individuals which defy identification, both at sea and in museum collections.

---

52 LIGHT-MANTLED SOOTY ALBATROSS
Phoebetria palpebrata

PLATE 15 Figs 52a-52c
MAP 52

Length 79–89cm (31–35in.). Wingspan 183–218cm (72–86in.). Iris brown, eye-crescents white. Bill black, sulcus violet or blue (see p. 12). Legs/feet mauve or greyish-flesh.

Southern Oceans; range overlaps with similar Sooty Albatross (p. 231). Beware especially worn adults and immatures of latter, which have buffy or white collars and pale mantles. See also pale-billed juvenile Wandering Albatross and giant petrels (p. 222, p. 233, p. 234). Sexes alike, males average larger; no seasonal variation but subject to wear and bleaching. Juveniles separable. No subspecies.

JUVENILE: Sulcus pale yellow or grey. In fresh plumage differs from adult only in dark primary and tail shafts; mantle and breast may show buff tips.

IMMATURE: Feathers subjected to extreme wear during first year at sea, resulting in buffish tips to mantle and upper breast, otherwise as adult (except sulcus and eye-crescents).

ADULT: Head Vinaceous dark brown, becoming greyer in worn plumage. **Body** Upperparts pale ash-grey, lower back and rump lightly edged brown. Underparts pale greyish-brown. **Wings and Tail** Dark brown; blackish primaries and tail show white or yellow shafts.

FHJ: Notes under Sooty Albatross (p. 232) also apply to this species.

DM: Circumpolar, breeds S Atlantic Ocean at South Georgia and in S Indian Ocean at Marion, Prince Edward, Crozet, Kerguelen, Heard and Macquarie Is; also off New Zealand at Auckland, Campbell and Antipodes Is. Returns to colonies Sep/Oct; egg-dates Oct/Nov; fledging and departure Apr/May. Pelagic range generally more southerly than Sooty Albatross, extending S to pack ice and N to about 33°S. Off western South America however occurs N to 20°S off Peru (R Hughes, pers. comm.). Further south often seen in large numbers in the Beagle Channel; peak counts up to 3,000 Feb/Mar (Humphrey *et al.* 1970).

SS: See notes under Sooty Albatross (p. 231).

Family *PROCELLARIIDAE*

fulmars, prions, petrels, shearwaters

The most diverse group of *Procellariiformes*: twelve genera comprising about 55 species, ranging in size from huge giant petrels to the diminutive prions. Bill structure differs from *Diomedeidae* in nostrils united in single tube placed on top of culminicorn.

The various forms can be divided into four natural groups. (1) Fulmars: *Macronectes*, *Daption*, *Fulmarus*, *Thalassoica* and *Pagodroma*. (2) Prions: *Pachyptila* and monotypic *Halobaena*. (3) Gadfly-petrels: *Pterodroma* and *Bulweria*. (4) Larger petrels and shearwaters: *Procellaria*, *Calonectris* and *Puffinus*. Identification at sea can be problematical, *Pterodroma* in particular posing perhaps the greatest challenge. The all-dark forms of petrels and shearwaters are equally difficult. With comparative experience, however, after jizz and flight committed to memory, positive identification usually possible given reasonable conditions. Much of following based on Fullagar, van Tets and Warham (pers. comm.) and photographs and sketches supplied by Piet and Kathy Meeth.

Genus *MACRONECTES*

Related to *Daption*, *Fulmarus* and *Thalassoica*. Genus comprised of two sibling species (Bourne & Warham 1966): a polymorphic southern form, *M. giganteus*, and monomorphic northern form, *M. halli*. The two forms have breeding seasons 6–8 weeks apart. Northern form normally breeds alone, or in loose colonies, in more sheltered situations. By comparison, southern form nests socially in more open situations and at later date. The two forms are sympatric at several islands. Populations with intermediate characters occur at Staten, Falkland and Gough Is (Johnstone *et al.* 1976). They are the largest of petrels, equal in size to a small albatross, but jizz distinctly different, flight less graceful, with laboured, stiff-winged beats and short glides. Males are, on average, larger and heavier-billed than females. They are the only petrels to feed on land, where they are ungainly and uncouth scavengers.

Confusion with albatrosses, particularly juvenile Wandering and both sooty albatrosses (p. 222, p. 231, p. 232), could occur by observers new to southern latitudes. In reality all three are distinctly different. Specific separation of the two giant petrels at sea, however, less straightforward, particularly in all-dark juvenile stages. Bill colour at this stage seems most reliable character, although further fieldwork seems necessary before all juveniles with dark tips to bill can be safely regarded as Northern Giant Petrels. Position further complicated by intermediate populations in southern Atlantic. The white morph found in Southern Giant Petrel is unique to that species (never occurs in Northern Giant Petrel): it appears to be a genetic variation, as white and dark phase birds form mixed pairs producing either a dark or white fledgling, whilst pairs of dark phase are also capable of producing a white fledgling.

53 NORTHERN GIANT PETREL
other: Northern Giant Fulmar
Macronectes halli

PLATE 17 Figs 53a-53d
MAP 53

Length 81–94cm (32–37in.). Wingspan 180–200cm (71–79in.). Iris pale grey. Bill horn-coloured often with reddish tinge and dark marks at tip. Legs/feet blackish or grey.

Southern Oceans; size equals that of Black-browed Albatross but jizz distinctly different from that and all other albatrosses. Range overlaps with Southern Giant Petrel (p. 234). Sexes similar, males average larger; no seasonal variation. Juveniles and immatures separable, but exact ageing, over perhaps seven years to maturity, impossible due to individual variation. Adults with intermediate characters of both Northern and Southern Giant Petrels have been described by Johnstone *et al.* (1976) from Gough, Staten and Falkland Is. (Not plotted on maps 53 or 54.)

JUVENILE (FIRST STAGE): Iris brown; bill as adult. Plumage wholly sooty-black but quickly fades to warm brownish-black, often with scattered rusty feather tips.

JUVENILE (SECOND STAGE): As first stage except has whitish feather tips over base of bill, and on lores, sides of face and chin.

IMMATURE: Head Medium or dark grey freckled black and white, except for whitish forehead extending narrowly over eye, lores, sides of face, chin and throat. **Body** Upperparts variably freckled black, white and grey. Underparts similar but paler; border of throat and upper breast usually darker, forming narrow collar (from nape). **Wings** Upperwing freckled as upperparts, primaries with whitish bases. Underwing dusky-grey, streaked darker, bases of primaries and some secondaries paler, trailing edge and leading edge of inner wing darker. **Tail** Blackish-grey.

ADULT: Head and Body Similar in all respects to immature but much paler and greyer particularly on head and underparts, though former always retains capped effect to greater or lesser extent, never wholly white. (See Southern Giant Petrel, p. 234.) **Wings** Underwing: coverts paler, less marked; bases of inner primaries and some secondaries pale silvery-grey, often appearing white at sea.

FHJ: Size suggests small albatross but proportionately shorter, narrower wings and bulkier body, often appearing hump-backed, impart distinctive jizz. Flight somewhat laboured, rarely matching grace and dynamic soaring of albatrosses: normally four or five flaps followed by stiff-winged glide. An aggressive and pugnacious scavenger, gathering in large numbers at dead cetaceans, seals, coastal meatworks etc. Submerges to retrieve offal; regularly follows ships.

DM: Southern Oceans, generally N of Antarctic Convergence, breeding at Prince Edward, Marion, Crozet, Kerguelen, Macquarie, Chatham, Stewart, Auckland, Antipodes and Campbell Is. Egg-dates Aug; fledging Feb. Juveniles disperse widely reaching coasts of Africa and Australia but extent of dispersal unknown; probably less migratory than Southern Giant Petrel. Adults present at colonies and adjacent seas throughout winter (Warham, pers. comm.).

SS: Inexperienced observers could confuse White-chinned Petrel, juvenile Wandering Albatross and both sooty albatrosses (p. 255, p. 222, p. 231, p. 232) with either species of giant petrel. Specific identification of giant petrels at sea can be problematic; only white morph of Southern Giant Petrel is distinctive. Juveniles and those forms with intermediate characters breeding at Gough, Staten and Falkland Is pose biggest problems. For notes on intermediate forms refer to Johnstone *et al.* (1976). Juveniles of both species fledge with identical blackish plumage, which later fades to brown; at this stage juveniles of the two species (which are sympatric on Marion, Kerguelen, Crozet, South Georgia and Macquarie Is) had bill colour as in adults, and were thus readily separable (pers. obs.). Sinclair (pers. comm.) has also failed to find juveniles with atypical bill colours. He reports that when adult and 'immature' Southern Giant Petrels are warm, especially if they have been resting with bills tucked into scapulars, their bills become suffused with blood, hence darkening whole appearance and giving appearance of a darker-tipped bill. This factor may have given rise to reports of atypical bill colour in some juveniles. Immature Northern Giant Petrels have whitish sides of face extending to throat and contrasting with darker crown, giving capped effect. By comparison, immature Southern Giant Petrels are paler-headed, lacking pronounced capped effect; and underparts, unlike Northern, are not noticeably paler than upperparts. Adults are more easily separable. Southern Giant Petrel has an almost white head and upper breast contrasting with brownish-grey body and wings. Northern Giant Petrel always shows a darker crown and upperparts contrasting with paler underparts. Warham (pers. comm.) confirms observations by Johnstone (1974) that leading edge of Northern Giant Petrel's inner wing, viewed from below, is very dark, whilst in Southern Giant Petrel it is very pale.

---

54 SOUTHERN GIANT PETREL
other: Southern Giant Fulmar
Macronectes giganteus

PLATE 17 Figs 54a-54e

MAP 54

Length 86–99cm (34–39in.). Wingspan 185–205cm (73–81in.). Iris pale grey or brown. Bill pale horn, tip greenish. Legs/feet blackish or grey, sometimes fleshy.

Southern Oceans; size suggests small albatross, but proportionately shorter wings and heavier body impart distinctive jizz. White phase diagnostic but all stages of dark morph require careful treatment to separate from Northern Giant Petrel (p. 233). Bill colour diagnostic. Sexes alike, males average larger; no seasonal variation, but polymorphic. Only juvenile and immature dark morphs separable from adults, but exact ageing impossible due to individual variation over perhaps seven years to maturity. Adults with intermediate characters of both Northern and Southern Giant Petrels have been described by Johnstone *et al.* (1976) from Gough, Staten and Falkland Is. (Not plotted on maps 53 or 54.)

JUVENILE (FIRST STAGE): Iris brown; bill as adult. Plumage wholly sooty-black but quickly fades to warm brownish-black.

JUVENILE (SECOND STAGE): As first stage except has whitish feather tips over base of bill, on lores, sides of face and chin.

IMMATURE: Closely resembles adult Northern Giant Petrel (p. 233); differs in paler freckling on crown giving only slight capped effect, though difference small and some overlap probably occurs. Underparts normally as upperparts and not paler as in Northern Giant Petrel, the white throat merging evenly into breast without dark collar effect.

ADULT (DARK MORPH): Head Mostly white, crown and nape faintly mottled with fawn-white. **Body** Upperparts greyish-brown. Underparts similar but slightly paler, with whitish upper breast. **Wings** Upperwing as upperparts. Underwing paler than in immature, less marked; leading edge of inner wing white (dark in Northern Giant Petrel), bases of inner primaries and some secondaries pale silvery-grey, often appearing white or silvery at sea. **Tail** Brownish-grey.

ADULT (WHITE MORPH): Juveniles and adults alike; wholly white except for asymmetrical black spots or patches, creating 'spotted-dog' effect. About 10% of population show these characters.

FHJ: As for Northern Giant Petrel (p. 233), although Johnstone (1974) suggested they were less attracted to vessels.

DM: Southern Oceans S to pack ice, breeding at South Georgia, South Sandwich, South Orkney, South Shetland, Antarctic Peninsula and scattered sites on continent; also Bouvet, Prince Edward, Marion, Crozet, Kerguelen, Heard and Macquarie Is. Egg-dates Oct onwards; fledging Mar. Most adults probably disperse only to adjacent seas, but juveniles disperse rapidly downwind under influence of the 'Roaring Forties'. Some ringed South Georgia recovered in Western Australia and New Zealand within 5 weeks, distances of over 16,000km (Alexander 1955). See also Serventy *et al.* (1971). First 2–3 years are spent at sea, ranging N to about 10°S in cool-water zones off western America and Africa and regularly reaching N to tropics elsewhere. Only one valid record for northern hemisphere, off Ushant, France (Meeth 1969). A giant petrel sp. was reported at Midway Atoll, Hawaii, Dec 1959, 1961 and 1962 (Fisher 1965).

SS: See notes under Northern Giant Petrel (p. 233).

Genus *FULMARUS*

Two species, geographically isolated. Sexes outwardly alike; males usually with larger bills. No seasonal variation but polymorphic. Identification reasonably straightforward but poor or distant views can suggest either gull (pale morph) or shearwater (dark morph). Structure, jizz and flight should prevent confusion, unless observer inexperienced.

55 NORTHERN FULMAR

PLATE 19 Figs 55a-55b

other: Fulmar, Arctic Fulmar

Fulmarus glacialis

MAP 55

Length 45–51cm (18–20in.). Wingspan 102–112cm (40–44in.). Iris dark brown. Bill variable; typically bluish-grey with yellow tips to both mandibles. Legs/feet greenish to livid-flesh.

Northern Pacific and Atlantic Oceans; polymorphic, pale morphs suggest gull spp., whilst dark morphs can suggest shearwater spp. Sexes outwardly alike although males have larger bills; no seasonal variation. Juveniles and adults alike. Three subspecies listed: in North Pacific *F.g. rodgersii* has more slender bill, with lightest colour morph lighter and darkest darker than in Atlantic forms. Double light and double dark morphs are described below; intermediate forms grade imperceptibly between the two extremes. Albinism occasionally reported.

DOUBLE LIGHT MORPH: Head Mostly white; lores dusky. **Body** Upperparts pale grey mottled silvery, becoming browner with wear. Underparts pure white. **Wings** Upperwing mostly pale grey, darker on carpal area and primaries, these with pale whitish bases and inner webs forming conspicuous pale wing patch. Underwing mostly white except for greyish primary tips, carpal area and narrow trailing edge. **Tail** Pale grey, fringed white.

DOUBLE DARK MORPH: Uniform smoky-grey with carpal area and primaries correspondingly darker than in light morph; pale bases to primaries reduced or even absent. Plumage wears to deep plumbeous-brown.

FHJ: A stocky, bull-necked petrel with stout bill. Larger and more heavily built than most shearwaters, superficially resembling gull, but flap-and-glide flight on bowed wings distinctly different, with bursts of stiff wingbeats between periods of effortless banking and gliding, bounding in high arcs, sliding down troughs and soaring over wave crests. Usually gregarious, a noisy participant at trawlers throughout year.

DM: North Pacific and Atlantic Oceans, where recent remarkable increase in range and numbers (see Cramp *et al.* 1974). *F.g. rodgersii* breeds Kurile, Commander, Kamchatka, Wrangel, Pribiloff, St Lawrence Is and coasts of eastern Siberia and Alaskan Peninsula. *F.g. glacialis* breeds high Arctic regions of N Atlantic including Baffin I., NE Greenland, Spitsbergen, Bear I., Franz Josef Land and probably Novaya Zemlya. *F.g. auduboni* breeds mainly low Arctic and boreal N Atlantic region including NW Greenland, Newfoundland, Jan Mayen, Iceland, Faeroes, British Isles, France (Brittany and Normandy), western Norway. Returns to inspect colonies from Nov/Dec before short pre-breeding dispersal prior to egg-laying May/Jun; fledging and dispersal begins Aug/Sep. Young Fulmars apparently spend several years at sea before returning to inspect colonies. In winter wanders widely, occurring from Beaufort Sea S to Japan and Baja California, but extent of southward movement largely dependent on presence of cold waters with high salinity. In Atlantic they regularly range S to 43°N in west but to only about 55°N in east; recent records off NE America show that it is regular but scarce S to about 34°N.

SS: At close or moderate range stubby bill and bull-necked jizz should prevent confusion with shearwaters and gulls. At longer distance, flight suggests large shearwater; pale morphs easier to separate due to whiteness of head, grey upperparts and white 'window' on outer primaries. Double dark morph *F.g. rodgersii* in worn plumage can be problematical and, at distance, could be confused with Flesh- and Pink-footed Shearwaters (p. 258, p. 257). Beware also partial albinos or mottled individuals, which can suggest Cape Petrel (p. 236).

56 ANTARCTIC FULMAR

PLATE 19 Figs 56a-56b

other: Silver-grey/Southern Fulmar

Fulmarus glaciafoides

MAP 56

Length 46–50cm (18–19½in.). Wingspan 114–120cm (45–47in.). Iris brown. Bill pink, black at tip with blue nasal tube and yellowish subterminal band. Legs/feet pinkish-blue.

Southern Oceans counterpart of Northern Fulmar (p. 235). Sexes alike; no seasonal variation. Juveniles apparently resemble adults except for weaker and more slender bill. Monomorphic, although some show marked variation in amount of black and white on wingtip.

PLUMAGE: Head Mostly whitish, shading to pale grey on nape; lores dusky. **Body** Upperparts light bluish-grey. Underparts white, lightly washed with grey on sides of breast and flanks. **Wings** Upperwing variable; typically mostly light bluish-grey, with blackish outer primaries and trailing edge of inner wing contrasting with white 'window' on inner primaries. Atypical shows similar blue-grey inner wing but black on wingtip extends to include alula, primary-coverts, primaries and secondaries with white inner webs restricted to primaries 4–8. Underwing mostly white; alula dark grey, trailing edge of wing dusky-grey, axillaries pale grey. **Tail** Blue-grey above, white below.

FHJ: Superficially resembles northern counterpart but with longer, more delicate bill, lighter jizz, proportionately longer wings, and more strongly patterned upperwings. Feeding habits may be primarily nocturnal. A quarrelsome, pugnacious scavenger; gregarious, often feeding and resting together. Distinctive in Southern Oceans, with typical bowed, stiff-winged gliding flight of genus. Rarely follows ships, attends trawlers.

DM: Breeds at South Sandwich, South Orkney, South Shetland, South Georgia, Bouvet and Peter Is and at several localities on Antarctic Peninsula

and continent. Returns to colonies Oct; egg-dates Nov/Dec; fledging and dispersal Mar/Apr. Moves N from pack ice during austral winter to about 45°S, but regularly to about 10°S off western South America in Humboldt Current region. Casual off South Africa and Australia, but numbers subject to great fluctuation with many appearing during 'wreck' years; in 1978 an unprecedented wreck occurred throughout much of Southern Oceans area, with large numbers of beached derelicts from South Africa, Australia and New Zealand.
SS: Distinctive in Southern Oceans, where most other petrels are black or brown.

Genus *THALASSOICA*

Monotypic genus restricted to Antarctic region. Confusion possible only with Cape Petrel, but critical examination of upperparts pattern should enable straightforward separation.

57 ANTARCTIC PETREL

Thalassoica antarctica

PLATE 18 Figs 57a-57b
MAP 57

Length 40–46cm (16–18in.). Wingspan 101–104cm (40–41in.). Iris brown. Bill brownish, sides faintly olive. Legs/feet flesh or greyish-flesh.

Circumpolar in higher latitudes of Southern Oceans; distinctive. Sexes alike; no seasonal variation, although in worn plumage (Oct–Jan) dark brown upperparts often much paler. Juveniles resemble adults in fresh plumage but have black bills. No subspecies.
PLUMAGE (fresh): **Head** Mostly dark chocolate-brown; throat and sides of neck often mottled with white. **Body** Upperparts mainly dark chocolate-brown; lower rump and uppertail-coverts white. Underparts white. **Wings** Upperwing: forewing, including outer 3–5 primaries, mostly dark chocolate-brown; inner primaries and all secondaries white, narrowly tipped brown, forming conspicuous white subterminal edge to wing. Underwing white with narrow, dark brown margins. **Tail** White, narrowly tipped black.
FHJ: Typically fulmarine; flight consists of series of stiff-winged glides interspersed with rigid wingbeats; usually flies high over waves. Hovers above water before plunging, often hitting water with wings outspread. Gregarious, some colonies exceeding 1 million; during winter normally encountered in small flocks, seldom far from icefloes, upon which they rest. Occasionally follows ships.
DM: Breeds in huge colonies on a few islands close to Antarctic continent and along Antarctic coast. Returns to colonies Oct; egg-dates Nov/Dec; fledging and departure Feb/Mar, with limited dispersal to adjacent seas bordering pack ice. Small numbers occasionally wander N, particularly in 'wreck' years of Antarctic Fulmars, with sightings and beached derelicts from South America, South Africa and Australia N to about 33°N.
SS: Smaller Cape Petrel has distinctly different upperparts pattern, broader dark margins to underwing and blackish tail.

Genus *DAPTION*

One species; medium-sized fulmarine petrel restricted mainly to Southern Oceans, but N to Equator off western South America. Confusion possible with Antarctic Petrel and symmetrically albinistic Sooty Shearwaters and dark morph Northern Fulmars.

58 CAPE PETREL

other: Pintado Petrel, Cape Pigeon
Daption capense

PLATE 18 Figs 58a-58b
MAP 58

Length 38–40cm (15–16in.). Wingspan 81–91cm (32–36in.). Iris brown. Bill, legs/feet black.

Southern Oceans; unmistakable, but in northern hemisphere beware mottled Northern Fulmars (p. 235) and symmetrically partial albinistic Sooty Shearwaters (p. 260). Sexes alike; no seasonal variation, although upper surfaces may show more white when worn. Juveniles and adults alike. Two subspecies listed; *D.c. australe* differs from nominate in smaller size and less white on upperparts. In fresh plumage races can be separated at sea, but in worn plumage differences less distinct and many birds show characters intermediate between the two forms.
PLUMAGE: Head Sooty-black. **Body** Upperparts: black mantle merges into white back and rump, both of which are boldly marked with black chevrons forming distinctive chequerboard pattern. Underparts white; undertail-coverts faintly spotted black. **Wings** Upperwing mostly black except for conspicuous white patch on bases of innermost 5–6 primaries, their coverts and inner webs of outer primaries, and another on innermost greater and median coverts. Underwing mostly white except for narrow black margins and tip; coverts often faintly spotted with black. **Tail** Mostly black, base white.
FHJ: Medium-sized, chunky petrel with chequered black and white plumage. Flight typically fulmarine, with bursts of five to eight quick, stiff-winged flaps interspersed with periods of gliding. In strong winds flight high, bounding and buoyant, often towering several hundred feet above waves.

Characteristically feeds from surface in erect and buoyant manner, facing into wind or surface current, pecking in pigeon-like fashion at small organisms. Also treads water storm-petrel fashion and, on occasions, executes shallow surface-dives from both air and water. Gregarious throughout year; often attends trawlers in huge flocks, where noisy and quarrelsome; in New Zealand sector often enters harbours. Habitually follows ships.
DM: Circumpolar in Southern Oceans. *D.c. capense* breeds South Georgia, South Sandwich, South Orkney, South Shetland, Bouvet, Crozet, Kerguelen, Heard, Macquarie, Balleny Is, and at Peter First I. and several sites on Antarctic Peninsula and continent. *D.c. australe* breeds at Snares, Antipodes, Bounty and Campbell Is off New Zealand. Returns to colonies Aug–Oct; egg-dates Nov/Dec. Fledging and widespread circumpolar dispersal begins Feb/Mar, with birds ranging N to about 25°S but commonly to Equator in the cool Humboldt Current off Peru and Ecuador. Several sight records off California, some questionable (see Stallcup 1976, Roberson 1980); it seems likely, however, that individuals could stray from Humboldt region N to California. See Bourne (1967b) for other northern hemisphere records.
SS: Unmistakable if seen well, but beware partially albinistic Sooty Shearwaters and mottled Northern Fulmars (p. 260, p. 235).

Genus *PAGODROMA*

One species; medium-sized petrel restricted to Antarctic seas. Thought to be related to fulmars and may be a connecting form between *Fulmarus* and *Pterodroma*. Wholly white plumage unique in southern petrels, but beware albino shearwater and petrel spp.

59 SNOW PETREL
Pagodroma nivea

PLATE 18 Fig. 59
MAP 59

Length 30–35cm (12–14in.). Wingspan 76–79cm (30–31in.). Iris and bill black. Legs/feet bluish-grey.

Confined to pack ice and adjacent Antarctic seas; distinctive. The world's only small all-white petrel. Sexes alike, no seasonal variation. Juveniles and adults alike. Two subspecies listed; *P.n. confusa* averages larger with stouter bill, may be a distinct species.
PLUMAGE: Wholly white (in poor light and at distance may appear pale grey).
FHJ: A characteristic bird of the pack ice. Appears long-winged in flight, with nearly square tail when folded but distinctly wedge-shaped when fanned. Normal flight erratic, with shallow bat-like wingbeats and infrequent gliding, fluttering and jinking between icefloes and icebergs; occasionally hovers low over water but rarely seen swimming. Groups often loaf on icebergs; does not normally follow ships.
DM: Antarctic continent. *P.n. nivea* breeds South Georgia, South Shetland, South Sandwich, South Orkney, Bouvet and Scott Is, and several localities on Antarctic Peninsula and continent; *P.n. confusa* breeds Balleny Is and at Géologie Archipelago on Adélie coast (see Prevost 1969). Birds return to inspect nest-sites Sep–Nov; egg-dates Nov/Dec; fledging and departure Mar–May, with dispersal to pack ice and adjacent Antarctic seas S of 55°S. Many remain near colonies throughout year.
SS: Unmistakable.

Genus *PTERODROMA*

Widely distributed genus confined mainly to tropical and subtropical seas, particularly in Pacific Ocean; some species, e.g. Kerguelen Petrel, range S to 50°S. Taxonomic classification complex, comprising some of the world's rarest and least-known species in diverse assortment of small to medium-sized, hook-billed petrels. Few groups engender such fierce arguments as to number of distinct species, even among experts; 27 forms normally reduced to about 26 species. Sexes alike, males of some species perhaps averaging larger. No seasonal variation, but several species polymorphic with closely similar sibling species compounding identification process.

Few groups pose such a challenge, and identification criteria for many still evolving. The following texts and distribution maps should be read with this in mind. Accurate identification often impossible at sea, but in all cases facilitated by accurately recording head markings, upperwing patterns and exact distribution of underwing margins. Flight characters also important.

60 GREAT-WINGED PETREL
other: Grey-faced Petrel
Pterodroma macroptera

PLATE 21 Figs 60a-60b
MAP 60

Length 41cm (16in.). Wingspan 97cm (38in.). Bill, legs/feet black.

Almost circumpolar in Southern Oceans; range overlaps with Kerguelen and Parkinson's Petrels (p. 242, p. 255). See also Flesh-footed and Short-tailed Shearwaters (p. 258, p. 261). Sexes alike; no seasonal variation. Juveniles of nominate race differ only in greyer face. Two subspecies listed; *P.m. gouldi* (Grey-faced Petrel) differs from nominate in distinctive grey face, but subspecific separation at sea usually impossible due to similar coloration of these areas on immature *P.m. macroptera*.

ADULT (*P.m. macroptera*): Mostly blackish-brown except for indistinct greyish area at base of bill. In strong sunlight underwing shows paler bases to primaries and irregular silvery flash across coverts. (Beware Sooty and Short-tailed Shearwaters, p. 260, p. 261).

ADULT (*P.m. gouldi*): As nominate; differs in more pronounced grey at base of bill which, in New Zealand population, extends to include sides of face, chin and throat.

FHJ: Smaller and browner than White-chinned Petrel (p. 255), with swift-like proportions and characteristic switchback flight; habitually towers high into sky in wild pendulum-motion progression. (See also Kerguelen Petrel, p. 242.) In a light breeze flight less bounding, resembling that of larger Flesh-footed Shearwater (p. 258) but with less flapping and higher flight peaks. At close range stubby black bill separates it from all shearwater spp. Occasionally follows ships.

DM: *P.m. macroptera* breeds at Tristan da Cunha, Gough, Crozet, Marion, Prince Edward and Kerguelen Is, possibly also at Ile Amsterdam; and on islands off south coast of Western Australia from Albany to Cape Arid. *P.m. gouldi* at offshore islands and certain mainland cliffs of North Island, New Zealand. A winter breeder: returns to colonies Feb onwards; egg-dates May–Jul; fledging and departure Nov/Dec. Adults probably sedentary; juveniles of all populations disperse more widely. Tristan population disperses mainly E towards African coast, but several observed between 56°W and 72°W near Cape Horn (Brown *et al.* 1975) suggests that some may wander westwards. New Zealand juveniles disperse towards SE Australian coast and E into Pacific but extent of dispersal unknown. Normal pelagic range in Atlantic and Indian Oceans between 25°S and 50°S.

SS: Differs from all dark shearwaters in stocky, bull-necked jizz, short stubby bill and swift towering flight. Kerguelen Petrel (p. 242) smaller and greyer, with stockier jizz and even wilder flight.

61 MASCARENE PETREL
other: Reunion Petrel
Pterodroma aterrima

PLATE 27 Fig. 61
MAP 61

Length about 36cm (14in.). Wingspan unknown. Iris brown. Bill black. Legs pink, inner third of centre toe pink, outer toes and web black.

Recently collected on Reunion I. The status and distribution of this previously 'lost' species remain unknown. Range probably overlaps with Wedge-tailed and Flesh-footed Shearwaters (p. 259, p. 258) and with Herald petrel (dark morph, p. 244). Juveniles and adults probably alike. No subspecies; some authorities consider it conspecific with *P. rostrata*.

PLUMAGE: Wholly blackish-brown; reports of probable sightings off Reunion suggest that underwing may be grey-black (Bourne & Dixon 1972).

FHJ: Until recently known only from four skins collected over 100 years ago. Measurements from these show it to be a gadfly of medium build and size, with large bill, long wings and moderately long, slightly wedge-shaped tail. At sea flight probably swift, bounding in high arcs with rather heavy, powerful jizz.

DM: Jouanin (1969) has recently reviewed this species but its status remains obscure. Possible sight records off Reunion and rumours of petrels nesting on inland cliffs indicate presence of a small colony. It may also occur at Mascarene Is. Lack of possible sightings by Bailey (1968) suggests that it may be a cool-water bird breeding in N and dispersing S in winter.

SS: Dark morph Herald Petrel (p. 244), which also occurs in Mascarene waters, would closely resemble present species in form but has white at base of primaries extending narrowly across underwing-coverts. Dark shearwaters have slender bills and different flight.

62 WHITE-HEADED PETREL
Pterodroma lessonii

PLATE 24 Fig. 62
MAP 62

Length 40–46cm (16–18in.). Wingspan 109cm (43in.). Iris dark brown. Bill black. Feet pinkish with black joints of toes, outer toes and distal halves of webs.

Southern Oceans; range overlaps with Soft-Plumaged and Grey Petrels (p. 245, p. 254). Sexes alike; no seasonal variation. Fledglings probably indistinguishable from adults. No subspecies.

PLUMAGE: Head Appears white at sea with dark eye patch. **Body** Upperparts: mantle and upper back blue-grey, tipped darker, heaviest across lower back; rump and uppertail-coverts white, faintly spotted grey. Underparts white; under optimum conditions partial grey collar sometimes visible. **Wings** Upperwing brownish-black with indistinct M mark joining across lower back. Underwing dark dusky-grey, darkest on coverts, with silvery-grey cast to primaries. **Tail** Wedge-shaped; mostly white above, finely peppered with grey. Undertail white.

FHJ: Large gadfly-petrel. Flight strong and swift, with wings held bowed and angled forward, rising and falling in great arcs. Strength of flight best judged in raging storms, during which I have seen them hanging motionless against the wind some 50m above the water, strangely gull-like, only to slip into the maelstrom and allow the wind to carry them in a wild and towering flight—a truly remarkable sight. Does not normally follow ships.

DM: Southern Oceans, breeds on Kerguelen and Crozet Is, and off New Zealand at Auckland, Antipodes and Macquarie Is. May breed Prince

Edward and Marion Is in Indian Ocean, where comes ashore at nightfall (pers. obs.); perhaps also at Campbell I. off New Zealand (see Bailey and Sorensen 1962). Returns to colonies Aug–Oct; egg-dates Nov–Jan; fledging and departure Apr/May. Pelagic dispersal not precisely known, although adults at Macquarie I. absent from area for only about 11 weeks (Warham 1967). Those breeding S of New Zealand presumably move rapidly N to Australian Bight and off Tasmania, where peak figures of 200 recorded around trawlers during May (Carter 1981). Elsewhere records suggest that immatures or non-breeders have a more or less circumpolar range from about 30°S to Antarctic continent. Holgersen (1957) reported 'great numbers' at west end of Straits of Magellan during Dec, whilst it appears scarcer in S Atlantic with only occasional sightings off Tristan da Cunha and just two records from South Africa (Brooke & Sinclair 1978).

SS: Distinctive; combination of white head and tail contrasting with dark underwing enables identification at considerable distance. Within its normal range only the smaller Soft-Plumaged Petrel (p. 245) and the larger Grey Petrel (p. 254) have predominantly white underparts and dark underwings, but neither has white head and tail.

63 BLACK-CAPPED PETREL
other: Diablotin (includes Jamaica Petrel)
Pterodroma hasitata

PLATE 23 Figs 63a-63c

MAP 63

Length 35–46cm (14–18in.). Wingspan 89–102cm (35–40in.). Iris blackish-brown. Bill black. Legs/feet whitish-flesh, webs distally black.

Western North Atlantic from seas off Brazil N to about 36°N; range overlaps with Bermuda Petrel and Great Shearwater (p. 239, p. 258). Sexes alike; no seasonal variation but much variation in extent of white on hindneck and rump; some examples have plumage characters intermediate between present species and Bermuda Petrel (p. 239), which strengthens argument for considering them conspecific. Juveniles and adults alike. Jamaica Petrel, now thought to be extinct, is generally regarded as melanistic race of present species.

PLUMAGE (typical): **Head** Brownish-black cap extending to eye and nape; remainder, including hindneck, white. **Body** Upperparts mostly brownish, shading to blackish on lower back; rump and uppertail-coverts white, forming conspicuous broad band over base of tail. Underparts mostly white except for narrow dark collar on sides of breast (extension from mantle) and blackish feather tips on thighs. **Wings** Upperwing brownish-black, primaries and secondaries slightly darker. Underwing mainly white, with irregular blackish margins, tip and short diagonal bar of variable width and length extending inwards across coverts. **Tail** Blackish-brown.

PLUMAGE (atypical): Slightly smaller than typical, differing in reduced or complete absence of white hindcollar and/or rump; darkest individuals would probably be indistinguishable from Bermuda Petrel (p. 239) at sea. (Atypical birds reported off Maryland and North Carolina, thus confusing issue of Bermuda Petrel's distribution: Naveen, pers. comm.)

FHJ: Medium to large petrel with distinct black cap, broad white band over hindneck and conspicuous white rump. Compared with Bermuda Petrel (p. 239), which may be conspecific, present species slightly larger with heavier bill, browner cap and darker brown upperparts. Flight typical of medium/large gadfly-petrels (see under Hawaiian Petrel, p. 246). Springs clear of water when flushed.

DM: Formerly widespread in West Indies, breeding in mountains of Jamaica, Guadeloupe and Dominica but now restricted to highlands of Hispaniola, breeding on steep cliffs of Massif de la Seele, Haiti (see Wingate 1964). Breeding biology little known; returns to colonies about Nov; departs about May, dispersing to adjacent seas along western edge of Gulf Stream N to Cape Hatteras (see Lee & Booth 1979), Virginia and Maryland (Naveen, pers. comm.) and S to NE Brazil. Formerly regarded as rare, the recent 'pelagic-push' by ardent seabirders has shown this species to be a regular, if uncommon, visitor to offshore waters of eastern USA with peaks off Cape Hatteras of up to about 40 per day.

SS: Typical examples easily separated from Bermuda Petrel (p. 239) by white hindcollar and broad white band over rump. Atypical examples often lack white collar and/or rump, resembling a large Bermuda Petrel with rather darker upperparts and faint suggestion of a paler hindcollar. Great Shearwater (p. 258) bears superficial resemblance to present species but differs in distinctly different flight and jizz, less white on hindneck and rump, longer, more slender bill, upperparts coloration and, if present, diagnostic dark smudge on belly (Naveen, pers. comm.).

64 BERMUDA PETREL
other: Cahow
Pterodroma cahow

PLATE 23 Fig. 64

MAP 64

Length 38cm (15in.). Wingspan 89cm (35in.). Iris blackish-brown. Bill black. Legs/feet whitish-flesh, webs distally black.

Restricted to Bermuda, western Atlantic, pelagic movements unknown; range overlaps with Black-capped Petrel and Great Shearwater (p. 239, p. 258). Sexes alike; no seasonal variation. Juveniles and adults alike. Sometimes treated as conspecific with Black-capped Petrel; see notes under that species (p. 239) for details of birds with intermediate plumage characters.

PLUMAGE: Head Blackish-brown cap extends to eye-level, nape and hindneck; remainder, includ-

ing forehead, white. **Body** Upperparts mostly greyish-brown, shading to blackish on rump; pale bases of longer uppertail-coverts form obscure band over base of tail (but never as broad and white as in typical Black-capped Petrel). Underparts mostly white except for dusky sides of upper breast (extension from mantle). **Wings** Upperwing blackish-grey, coverts fringed paler. Underwing white with blackish margins and tip; some may show short diagonal bar. **Tail** Blackish.
FHJ: Resembles Black-capped Petrel (p. 239) but differs in darker cap and more uniform upperparts; lacks both white hindcollar and conspicuous white band over base of tail.
DM: Thought to have been exterminated, and considered 'lost' for 300 years before its rediscovery in 1935. Probably fewer than 100 birds remaining, breeding on Nonsuch I., Bermuda, and now vigorously protected. Returns to colonies Oct/Nov, departing about May. Pelagic dispersal unknown; Pocklington (1971) has suggested that they probably disperse N or NW towards axis of Gulf Stream, remaining on warm side of Current.
SS: See notes under Black-capped Petrel (p. 239).

65 ATLANTIC PETREL
other: Schlegel's Petrel
Pterodroma incerta

PLATE 22 Figs 65a-65b
MAP 65

Length 43cm (17in.). Wingspan 104cm (41in.). Iris brown. Bill black. Legs/feet flesh-pink, outer toe mostly brown, other two brown at joints.

S Atlantic Ocean, rarely W Indian Ocean. Distinctive, unlikely to be confused with other petrels, but both White-headed and Soft-plumaged Petrels have white underparts contrasting with dark underwings (p. 238, p. 245). See also Grey Petrel (p. 254). Sexes alike; no seasonal variation, although many birds differ in worn plumage. Juveniles in fresh plumage show greyish tips on mantle (Sinclair, pers. comm.). No subspecies.
FRESH PLUMAGE: Head Rich brown; nape and chin greyer. **Body** Upperparts uniform rich dark brown. Underparts white except for dark upper breast, flanks, lower belly and undertail-coverts. **Wings** Upperwing rich dark brown, primaries and secondaries darker. Underwing brown. **Tail** Brown.
WORN PLUMAGE: Similar except: **Head** Nape and hindneck pale grey, sometimes white, forming pale collar. Sides of face greyer, chin and throat almost white, occasionally extending to unite with white breast. **Body** Upperparts: Greyish edges enhanced by wear. **Wings** Upperwing: coverts as upperparts with paler edges to inner primaries.
FHJ: Stocky jizz; long wings bowed at carpal, with proportionately long, wedge-shaped tail, impart typical gadfly jizz. Readily follows ships. Flight swift and careening.
DM: S Atlantic Ocean, rarely E to W Indian Ocean. Breeds Tristan da Cunha group and Gough I. Returns to colonies Feb/Mar; egg-dates Jun/Jul; departure date unrecorded. Pelagic range in S Atlantic extends from about 20°S to 50°S, and from 60°W east to Cape of Good Hope, South Africa, where rare. Large numbers occur in central southern Atlantic, particularly along subtropical convergence where it is one of the most abundant petrels. Status in western Indian Ocean requires clarification. Claims of sightings by RNBWS members E to 20°S, 78°E, may refer to Soft-plumaged Petrel (p. 245).
SS: Distinctive, unlikely to be confused; lacks white flashes in wings of other congeners. See White-headed and Soft-plumaged Petrels (p. 238, p. 245).

66 TAHITI PETREL
(Includes Beck's Petrel)
Pterodroma rostrata

PLATE 24 Fig. 66
MAP 66

Length 38–40cm (15–16in.). Wingspan 84cm (33in.). Iris dark brown. Bill black. Legs flesh-coloured, webs blackish.

Tropical Pacific Ocean; range overlaps with slightly smaller Phoenix Petrel (p. 241). Sexes alike; no seasonal variation. Juveniles probably inseparable from adults. Two subspecies listed, one of which, Beck's Petrel *P.r. becki*, differs in its much smaller size (29cm, 11½in.). The Mascarene Petrel *P. aterrima* is considered conspecific by some authorities.
PLUMAGE: Head Sooty-brown. **Body** Upperparts blackish-brown. Underparts: upper breast sooty-brown extending narrowly along flanks and thighs; remainder white. **Wings** Upperwing dark sooty-brown; primary shafts black. Underwing sooty-brown; at sea generally appears dusky-grey, reflected light often giving impression of a narrow, pale line along centre of underwing. **Tail** Wedge-shaped; blackish (but base somewhat paler in museum skins).
FHJ: A small to medium white-bellied gadfly-petrel with an entirely dark head and upper breast. Jizz somewhat heavier than similar Phoenix Petrel (p. 241). Flight in winds typical of genus, with much swooping and soaring. In calm weather flight more leisurely, with alternating sequences of languid flaps and glides.
DM: Confined to Tropical Pacific Ocean. *P.r. rostrata* breeds New Caledonia, Marquesas and Society Is. Egg-dates Oct (Alexander 1955). *P.r. becki* still known only from two specimens collected at sea near the Solomon Is in 1920s, although Bourne & Dixon (1971) suggested that a flock of ten birds seen by D M Simpson off Wuvula Is on NE coast of New Guinea on 12 Apr 1969 may have been this species, as they were rather far from the recognised ranges of anything else. Formerly thought to disperse only to seas adjacent to natal islands, but recent records suggest wider dispersal through equatorial western Pacific

Ocean ranging W to outer fringes of Australian Great Barrier Reef and seas off eastern New Guinea. Status in NW Pacific unknown, but one collected NE of Formosa during May 1937 (Bourne 1967b).
SS: See notes under Phoenix Petrel (p. 241).

67 PHOENIX PETREL
Pterodroma alba

PLATE 24 Fig. 67
MAP 67

Length 35cm (14in.). Wingspan 83cm (32½in.). Iris dark brown. Bill black. Legs flesh-coloured, distal half of toes and webs black.

Tropical Pacific Ocean; range overlaps with similar Tahiti Petrel (p. 240). Sexes alike; no seasonal variation though blackish-brown plumage probably wears/bleaches lighter. Juveniles probably inseparable from adults. No subspecies, but see notes under Magenta Petrel (p. 244).
PLUMAGE: Head Mostly sooty-brown; chin and throat white with variable amount of scattered, brownish feather tips. **Body** Upperparts sooty-brown. Underparts mainly white except for sooty-brown breast band extending back along flanks and thighs. **Wings** Upperwing sooty-brown, shafts black (see intermediate phase Kermadec Petrel, p. 243, which has white shafts). Underwing entirely sooty-brown; at sea reflected light often gives impression of narrow, pale line along centre of underwing. **Tail** Wedge-shaped, blackish-brown.
FHJ: A medium-sized, white-bellied gadfly-petrel with typical pendulum-motion flight of genus. Jizz slightly lighter, less robust, than that of Tahiti Petrel (p. 240).
DM: Confined to Tropical Pacific Ocean, breeding Phoenix, Marquesas, Tonga, Line (including Christmas) and Pitcairn Is, perhaps also Raoul I., Kermadec Is. Egg-dates Jan; Jun/Jul (Alexander 1955). Extent of pelagic range largely unknown, due mainly to confusion with other gadfly-petrels. Gould (pers. comm.) observed them N of Hawaiian chain to 24°N, whilst they have occurred SW to Kermadec Is.
SS: Gadfly-petrels pose many identification problems at sea, particularly if observer has little or no previous experience with the genus. Present species could be confused with one of the intermediate phases of Kermadec and Herald Petrels (p. 243, p. 244) and also the similar Tahiti Petrel (p. 240). It differs from all colour phases of Kermadec Petrel in having a uniformly dark underwing and black primary shafts. All phases of Herald Petrel have white bases to primaries. Most confusion occurs with the slightly larger, more robust, Tahiti Petrel, which, however, lacks the white throat patch of the Phoenix; at sea, this difference not always easy to discern. See also Magenta Petrel (p. 244).

68 MOTTLED PETREL
other: Scaled/Peale's Petrel
Pterodroma inexpectata

PLATE 26 Figs 68a-68b
MAP 68

Length 33–35cm (13–14in.). Wingspan 74–75cm (29–29½in.). Iris brown. Bill black. Legs/feet flesh, distal webs and toes black.

Breeds New Zealand offshore islands, migrating NE across Pacific to Gulf of Alaska and western coasts of North America S, rarely to California. Range overlaps with many *Pterodroma* spp. but none has combination of broad, black diagonal bar on underwing, dark grey belly and white undertail-coverts. See especially Bonin, Black-winged and Chatham Island Petrels (p. 248, p. 249, p. 249). Sexes alike; no seasonal variation but some, perhaps in fresh plumage, show frosty-grey heads with conspicuous dark eye patches. Juveniles as adults except upperparts more prominently scaled. No subspecies.
PLUMAGE: Head Forehead, narrow streak above eye, chin and throat white; forecrown white scaled greyish-black, merging into greyish-black crown and blackish eye patch. **Body** Upperparts: mantle and back frosty-grey merging into darker blackish-brown rump and uppertail-coverts, all narrowly fringed whitish imparting scaled appearance at close range. Underparts variable, usually: upper breast and undertail-coverts white; lower breast, belly and flanks dark grey. **Wings** Upperwing brownish-grey with darker primaries and greater coverts forming open M mark linked across lower back. Underwing white except for conspicuous broad, black diagonal stripe; tips of primaries and secondaries greyish. **Tail** Blackish-brown, outermost feathers whitish.
FHJ: Medium-sized gadfly-petrel with conspicuous black bar on underwing and dark grey belly patch of variable extent; these features, even in less well-marked examples, visible at considerable distances and excellent, diagnostic, flight characters (see also darkest forms of smaller Collared Petrel, p. 248). Some authors mention that the white inner webs of outer primaries are partially revealed during banking flight but, of several hundred sightings off their natal islands, I did not record this character. Flight wild and impetuous, swinging high over ocean in vigorous, bounding arcs. Does not usually attend trawlers or follow ships.
DM: Breeds only at islands in Foveaux Strait, islands off Stewart I. and at Snares Is, New Zealand. Returns to colonies Oct/Nov; egg-dates Dec; fledging and departure begins Mar/Apr. During breeding season ranges from New Zealand waters S to Antarctic pack ice. Undertakes rapid post-breeding transequatorial migration during Mar–May on broad northerly front, often with other migratory species: see, for instance, Mobberley (1974), who recorded about 1,500 in a constant stream progressing northwards with 6,000 Sooty Shearwaters and smaller numbers of Short-tailed

and Pale-footed Shearwaters at 36°N 179°E on 27 Apr 1973. Winters N to Aleutians and Gulf of Alaska, occasionally N towards Bering Strait. Regarded as rare further E off western coast of North America from British Columbia S to California, but numbers well offshore in this region possibly greater than currently realised. (See Bourne & Dixon 1975 for RNBWS reports, including sightings of up to 540 at 48°N 126°W on 28 Apr 1972.) Before Europeans caused its decline on natal islands, specimens were taken off Tierra del Fuego during Cook's first expedition in 1769, and by Peale in 1848 at 68°S 95°W. It seems likely that itinerant non-breeding individuals may occasionally still occur in these areas.

SS: Has occurred off N. Carolina, USA. Combination of black diagonal bar on underwing, grey belly patch and white undertail-coverts diagnostic. See also Cook's, Black-winged, Bonin, Chatham Island and dark morph Collared Petrels (p. 247, p. 249, p. 248, p. 249, p. 248).

69 PROVIDENCE PETREL
other: Solander's Petrel
Pterodroma solandri

PLATE 22 Figs 69a-69b
MAP 69

Length 40cm (16in.). Wingspan 94cm (37in.). Iris brown. Bill black. Legs/feet dark grey, sometimes particoloured.

Pacific Ocean; range overlaps with similar dark phases of Kermadec and Herald Petrels (p. 243, p. 244). See also Great-winged Petrel (p. 237). Sexes alike; no seasonal variation. Juveniles not separable from adults. No subspecies.

FRESH PLUMAGE: Head Mainly blackish-brown, darker before eye; forehead strongly scaled; chin paler. **Body** Upperparts mainly greyish-brown, appearing frosty-grey at close range. Underparts similar but paler and slightly browner. **Wings** Upperwing as mantle but with brownish cast, primaries blacker. Underwing mainly dark except for conspicuous whitish base to primaries, tips of which are grey.

WORN PLUMAGE: Similar, but much browner in tone; underparts may show white tips to belly.

FHJ: Typical gadfly jizz. Kuroda (1955) reported slow, unhurried wingbeats, flying effortlessly over calm seas. Typical dashing gadfly flight at higher wind speeds. At long range appears largely brown, but greyer when close.

DM: Pacific Ocean; formerly bred Norfolk I., breeding now confined to Lord Howe I. Estimated population 20,000 pairs. Returns to colonies Mar; egg-dates May; fledging Oct–Nov (all based on Fullagar 1976, Fullagar *et al.* 1974). Formerly thought to be only casual off Australia, where previously recorded mostly as a beach derelict. Past RNBWS records, however, show several sightings of small groups of this species S to 35°S and W to 152°E. More recently, Cheshire & Jenkins (1981) have published reports of small but regular sightings during the breeding period S of Lord Howe I. and E to seas off Sydney, Australia. A further record off SE Tasmania (Carter 1981) appears to confirm that this species ranges S and W to seas off Australia and SE Tasmania during Mar–Nov. Pelagic dispersal and migration practically unknown. Some appear to move N into central Pacific, where Kuroda quoted 'many' 320km NE of Japan in Jul. There are tentative sight records in mid Pacific off Hawaii in Apr, Oct and Nov (King 1970).

SS: Murphy's and Great-winged Petrels (p. 243, p. 237) are darker overall and lack prominent white areas on underwing. See notes under dark and intermediate Kermadec Petrels (p. 243). Dark and intermediate Herald Petrels have different underwing pattern.

70 KERGUELEN PETREL
Pterodroma brevirostris

PLATE 21 Fig. 70
MAP 70

Length 36cm (14in.). Wingspan 81cm (32in.). Iris brown. Bill, legs/feet black.

Probably circumpolar in higher latitudes of Southern Oceans; range overlaps with Soft-plumaged and Great-winged Petrels (p. 245, p. 237). Sexes alike; no seasonal variation. Juveniles and adults alike. No subspecies.

PLUMAGE: Wholly slate-grey except for narrow whitish tips along leading edge of wing and underwing-coverts. In sunlight, plumage highly reflective appearing silvery-grey, especially on underwing, an excellent flight character.

FHJ: Head shape imparts big, blunt-headed jizz at sea, with short, squat body and long wings held bowed and slightly forward; head often appears darker than rest of body, giving hooded appearance at sea (Sinclair, pers. comm.). Usually solitary. Flight extremely fast, swooping and weaving in switchback progression with long, sweeping glides broken by short bursts of frantic wingbeats; habitually towers high above waves, floating aloft on outstretched wings for long periods. Also has a curious, fast wing-flicking action, either in a wave trough or at peak of its arc (Sinclair, pers. comm.). Does not usually follow ships.

DM: Breeds at Tristan da Cunha group, Gough, Marion, Prince Edward, Crozets and Kerguelen Is. Returns to colonies Aug/Sep; egg-dates Sep/Oct; fledging and dispersal Jan–Mar. Little is known of its pelagic dispersal but penetrates to very high latitudes; often seen among pack ice. Records at sea off Cape Horn (Watson 1975) plus storm derelicts from South Africa, Australia and New Zealand suggest a circumpolar range from pack ice N to about 30°S.

SS: Smaller and greyer than Great-winged Petrel with characteristic silvery underwing. The rare dark morph Soft-plumaged Petrel (p. 245) differs in lack of silvery highlights, browner plumage, broader and darker bases to underside of primaries and in retaining a ghost-image of typical form's breast band; it also occupies a lower air space, seldom if ever soaring high above waves over open sea.

71 MURPHY'S PETREL
Pterodroma ultima

PLATE 25 Fig. 71
MAP 71

Length 38–41cm (15–16in.). Wingspan 97cm (38in.). Iris dark brown. Bill black. Legs/feet flesh with distal webs and toes black.

Central South Pacific Ocean; range overlaps with Herald Petrel (p. 244; beware dark morph). See also Providence and Great-winged Petrels (p. 242, p. 237). Sexes alike; no seasonal variation but some may show partial albinism (see photo in Harper & Kinsky 1978). Juveniles and adults alike. No subspecies.

PLUMAGE: Head Mostly blackish-brown except for whitish mottling at base of upper and lower mandibles, chin, throat and variably on sides of face (beware Grey-faced Petrel, p. 237). **Body, Wings and Tail** Wholly blackish-brown.

FHJ: Little known. Recalls Great-winged Petrel (p. 237) but with entirely dark underwing and pale legs. Compared with dark phase Herald Petrel (p. 244) is larger and stockier with heavier stubby bill and wedge-shaped tail. Flight typical of genus; does not follow ships.

DM: Central South Pacific Ocean, where discovered during the Whitney Expedition off the Bass Rocks, at Rapa and Oeno Is and in the Austral group; also at Tuamotu and Pitcairn groups. Breeding dates not known but birds taken in mid Apr during Whitney Expedition were in breeding condition (Murphy & Pennoyer 1952). Pelagic distribution not precisely known; probably only to adjacent seas but one at Kure Atoll, in Hawaiian Leeward Islands, on 7 Oct 1963 (Gould *in litt.*) and a beached derelict in N. California may indicate a northwards post-breeding dispersal.

SS: Providence Petrel is greyer in tone with conspicuous whitish bases to underwing primaries (p. 242). Dark morph Herald Petrel (p. 244) also has pale area on underwing, whilst Great-winged Petrel (p. 237) has a more southerly distribution and blackish feet.

72 KERMADEC PETREL
Pterodroma neglecta

PLATE 22 Figs 72a-72b
MAP 72

Length 38cm (15in.). Wingspan 92cm (36in.). Iris brown. Bill black. Legs/feet flesh-pink with blackish webs and toes. Some dark morphs have blackish legs/feet.

Pacific Ocean. Polymorphic, occurring in three main colour phases (which interbreed) although much individual variation. Variety of plumages complicates separation from other Pacific gadfly-petrels, especially Providence and Herald Petrels (p. 242, p. 244). Identification criteria still evolving and the following notes should be read with this in mind. (Observers in Pacific would do well to record accurate at-sea descriptions of all gadfly-petrels.) The wings of all morphs show diagnostic white primary shafts at close range. Sexes alike; no seasonal variation. Juveniles not separable. Two subspecies.

PALE MORPH: Head Mainly white; forehead, crown and nape variably mottled grey and brown. Some show darker eye patch. **Body** Upperparts brown, with darker and lighter tips enhanced by wear. Underparts white. **Wings** All morphs show dark primaries with inner web of each and its shaft white. Remainder of upperwing as upperparts. Underwing shows conspicuous white base to primaries, tips of which are black. Coverts and secondaries largely brownish-grey with paler feather tips. Basal portion of leading edge normally shows some white feather tips. **Tail** Blackish-brown.

INTERMEDIATE MORPHS: Retain upper and lower wing patterns of pale morph but vary considerably on underparts. Typical variation includes: a) Dark head, white underparts crossed by greyish breast band; b) Similar but with brownish-grey cast to white underparts; c) Mainly dark greyish-brown on underparts, with variable white freckling on breast and belly.

DARK MORPH: Wholly blackish-brown except for varying amounts of white on forehead, face and chin. Primaries as pale morph.

FHJ: Shorter, squarer tail than most similarly-plumaged gadfly-petrels. In light or moderate winds flight also differs, being more leisurely with deep wingbeats followed by a long, unhurried glide, banking in broad arcs. No information available for higher wind speeds.

DM: Pacific Ocean. *P.n. neglecta* breeds Lord Howe, Kermadec, Austral, Pitcairn, and Easter groups; perhaps also Tuamotu. *P.n. juana* breeds Juan Fernandez and on San Ambrosio and San Felix Is off Chile. Previously regarded as mainly sedentary but recent sightings suggest northerly dispersal across tropics, some to about 40°N in central Pacific (Gould, pers. comm.). In eastern Pacific, birds regularly occur N to 15°N off western America and should be looked for off southern California. There is a disputed occurrence of a vagrant in Pennsylvania, N America, 1959 (Palmer 1962).

SS: Variation in plumage of this and other gadfly-petrels complicates identification. Pale morphs differ from White-headed Petrel (p. 238) in distribution and wing pattern. Providence Petrel (p. 242) very similar to dark and intermediate morphs but upperparts much greyer, webs of primaries whitish, shafts dark. From Great-winged Petrel (p. 237) by different wing pattern and more northerly distribution, although the two do overlap in Tasman Sea area. Dark and intermediate morphs of Herald Petrel (p. 244) very similar to present species and, even in the hand, often difficult to separate. At sea the whiter bases of primaries on underwing of Kermadec Petrel should be apparent. By contrast underwing of Herald Petrel shows less white at base of primaries, but this then extends back across coverts as a narrow pale line.

73 MAGENTA PETREL
Pterodroma magentae

PLATE 25 Fig. 73
MAP 73

Exact dimensions unknown. Iris brown. Bill black. Legs/feet flesh, webs and toes mostly black.

Thought extinct until 1978, when David Crockett rediscovered a few pairs on Chatham Is E of New Zealand; but status unknown. Fullagar and van Tets (pers. comm.) have suggested that the Magenta Petrel specimen (type) may only be a form of Phoenix Petrel (p. 241) from SW Pacific, Range overlaps with Soft-plumaged Petrel (p. 245); see also more tropical Phoenix and Tahiti Petrels (p. 241, p. 240). Sexes alike, no seasonal variation. Juveniles probably indistinguishable from adults.
PLUMAGE: Head Mostly dark brownish- or slate-grey; forehead buffish-grey, chin and throat greyish-white. **Body** Upperparts brownish- or slate-grey. Underparts mainly white, upper breast brownish-grey extending narrowly along flanks. **Wings** Upperwing slate- or brownish-grey. Underwing dusky-grey except for faintly paler midwing stripe (as in Soft-plumaged Petrel, p. 245). **Tail** Blackish-grey.
FHJ: Slightly larger and heavier in jizz than Soft-plumaged Petrel (p. 245) with characteristic, impetuous flight of genus. Appears mostly grey or slate-brown at sea with white underparts contrasting with dusky breast and underwings.
DM: Until its recent rediscovery on the Chatham Is in 1978 known only from a single specimen taken at 39°S 126°W south of Pitcairn Is in Jul 1867. Nothing known of its biology or movements; only a few pairs are thought to remain in existence. Judging from where type specimen was obtained, it seems likely that post-breeding dispersal is towards central southern Pacific, perhaps even to Humboldt region.
SS: Superficially resembles geographically isolated Atlantic Petrel (p. 240) but undertail-coverts white. The more tropical Phoenix Petrel (p. 241), of which present species may only be a form, is similarly patterned but smaller with dark brown upperparts. The smaller Soft-plumaged Petrel (p. 245), which occurs off SE New Zealand, has distinctive eye patch and white underparts broken by diffuse breast band.

74 HERALD PETREL
other: Trinidade Petrel, Trinidad Petrel (error)
Pterodroma arminjoniana

PLATE 22 Figs 74a-74c
MAP 74

Length 35–39cm (14–15½in.). Wingspan 88–102cm (34½–40in.). Iris brown. Bill black. Legs/feet vary according to morph, see below.

Wide-ranging, occurs in Pacific, Atlantic and Indian Oceans. Polymorphic, three main colour phases although much individual variation. This complicates separation from other gadfly-petrels, particularly Kermadec and Providence Petrels (p. 243, p. 242) and to lesser extent Tahiti and Phoenix Petrels. Sexes alike; no seasonal variation. Two subspecies listed.
LIGHT MORPH: Legs/feet white, webs black. **Head** Largely ashy-brown, merging into whitish forehead, cheeks, chin and throat. **Body** Upperparts ashy-brown; paler feather edges show at close range. Underparts mainly white except for dusky, ill-defined breast band extending from nape across breast and narrowly along flanks. Undertail-coverts blackish tipped white. **Wings** Upperwing as back; primaries, secondaries and tertials darker producing faint M mark in good light. Underwing variable; most show white base to primaries extending back across secondaries and coverts as a narrow whitish line. **Tail** Blackish-brown.
INTERMEDIATE MORPH: Legs/feet pink with blackish webs. Resembles dark morph but variable amounts of white tips on chin, lower breast and belly.
DARK MORPH: Legs/feet black. Resembles pale morph but head and body including whole of underparts slaty-brown. NOTE: See Murphy (1936) for details of birds showing partial albinism. Most intermediate and dark morph birds show typical underwings, but a few may show dark underwing with paler bases to primaries visible only when wing is flexed. (See Tahiti and Phoenix Petrels, (p. 240, p. 241, which have dark bases to primaries but which would otherwise be similar at sea.)
FHJ: Typical gadfly jizz and flight. In low wind speeds flight can recall Sooty Shearwater (p. 260). Occasionally follows ships.
DM: *P.a. arminjoniana* breeds S Atlantic at Trinidade and Martin Vaz. Pelagic range largely unknown but thought to be mainly sedentary. Three records from N Atlantic, the most recent 20 Aug 1978 (Lee 1979) off North Carolina. A record at 21°51′N, 43°35′W (Murphy 1936), may indicate wider pelagic range than is supposed. In Indian Ocean recently found breeding at Round I., Mauritius, and may also breed at Reunion I. Pelagic range in Indian Ocean less known than for Atlantic population and complicated by presence of sympatric Mascarene Petrel (p. 238), Jouanin's Petrel (p. 254) to north and Great-winged Petrel (p. 237) to south. A bird with intermediate plumage seen S of Cape Agulhas, South Africa (pers. obs.), plus sightings which may have been this species off eastern South America N of subtropical convergence (Rumboll & Jehl 1977), could indicate unknown colonies or wide pelagic dispersal. *P.a. heraldica* breeds Chesterfield Is, Tonga, Marquesas, Tuamotu group, Gambier Is, Pitcairn group, and Easter I.; may breed Raine off NE Australia, where one found in a burrow (Serventy *et al.* 1971) and three more recently handled and banded (Fullagar and van Tets, pers. comm.). Some birds apparently visit their nesting stations throughout year, others disperse northwards through tropics and central Pacific to about 40°N (Gould, pers. comm.). Southern limits of pelagic range poorly known.

SS: To inexperienced birders dark morphs may suggest either Sooty Shearwater or dark morph skua (p. 260, p. 323). From the former by chunky jizz, short bill, different underwing pattern and, in wind speeds over F4, 'gadfly' flight. From skuas by jizz, flight and feeding methods. Intermediates in N Atlantic would differ from Soft-plumaged Petrel (p. 245) in much darker upperparts, lack of eye patch, and darker underwing with conspicuous flash. See also Mascarene and Great-winged Petrels (p. 238, p. 237), Kermadec and Providence Petrels (p. 243, p. 242).

75 SOFT-PLUMAGED PETREL
Pterodroma mollis

PLATE 21 Figs 75a-75d
MAP 75

Length 32–37cm (12½–14½in.). Wingspan 83–95cm (32½–37½in.). Iris dark brown. Bill black. Legs/feet pinkish, distal two-thirds of webs blackish.

Discontinuous distribution in Atlantic and Indian Oceans; range overlaps with Herald and Kerguelen Petrels (p. 244, p. 242). Sexes alike; no seasonal variation. Juveniles and adults probably alike. Four subspecies listed. The northern populations lack a pronounced breast band and there is some variation in head, upperparts and outer tail feather colours (see Clancey *et al.* 1981). It is not yet clear whether wholly dark forms are a result of polymorphism, melanism or *P. mollis* × *P. brevirostris* crossing. *P.m. mollis* is described below; see Plate 21 for subspecific variation.

PLUMAGE: Head Forehead and crown greyish-brown, narrowly scaled with white on forehead and over eye; sides of face, chin and throat white with blackish mask before and below eye. **Body** Upperparts mostly neutral grey fringed paler; long scapulars brownish-black. Underparts mostly white, variably complete greyish breast band; sides and flanks lightly streaked grey. **Wings** Upperwing mostly brownish-grey, darker primaries and some median and lesser coverts forming variable M mark across upperwing. Underwing mainly grey with faintly paler stripe down centre of coverts. **Tail** Grey.

DARK MORPH: Varies in colour from wholly sooty-grey with ghost-image of typical form's breast band, (pers. obs.) to individuals with broad dark chest bands and heavily streaked underparts (Elliot 1954, see also Schramm 1982).

FHJ: Medium-sized grey and white gadfly-petrel with partial or complete breast band and grey underwing. Typical rapid, impetuous flight of all gadfly-petrels interspersing glides with rapid wingbeats and zigzag progression. Compared with Kerguelen Petrel (p. 242), flight less impetuous with shallower flight peaks. Less gregarious in North Atlantic, but in southern hemisphere highly gregarious with loose flocks of up to a thousand. Occasionally follows ships.

DM: Small population in N Atlantic: *P.m. feae* breeds Cape Verde Is and Bugio, Desertas Is, off Madeira; *P.m. madeira* in highlands of Madeira. Staggered breeding season results in some birds present off islands for much of year. Movements little known; has been recorded S at 9°N along western African coast. In southern hemisphere, where far more numerous, *P.m. mollis* breeds Gough and Tristan da Cunha; *P.m. dubia* Prince Edward, Marion, Crozet and Antipodes Is, S of New Zealand. Returns to colonies Sep/Oct; egg-dates Nov/Dec; fledging and dispersal begins May. Movements imperfectly understood; occurs commonly off South America and South Africa during austral winter (though rarely seen from shore) and then eastwards across Indian Ocean to Australia between 25°S and 60°S. Scarcer off New Zealand and in SW Pacific Ocean.

SS: Readily identified by combination of grey underwing, breast band and white underparts. See also White-headed and Grey Petrels (p. 238, p. 254). The rare dark morph resembles Kerguelen Petrel (p. 242) but is browner in tone with different jizz and flight.

76 BARAU'S PETREL
Pterodroma baraui

PLATE 24 Fig. 76
MAP 76

Length 38cm (15in.). Wingspan not recorded. Iris dark brown. Bill black. Legs pink, distal half of webs and toes black.

Tropical Indian Ocean; pelagic range overlaps with Herald and Atlantic Petrels (p. 244, p. 240). Sexes alike; no seasonal variation. Juveniles probably inseparable from adults. No subspecies.

PLUMAGE: Head Forehead and lores mostly white, merging into blackish cap; chin and throat white. **Body** Upperparts: mantle and upper back brownish, each feather fringed grey giving frosted-grey appearance at sea; lower back and rump blackish-grey. Underparts mostly white; sides of breast and flanks mottled grey. **Wings** Upperwing: primaries, their coverts, alula and secondaries blackish-grey; coverts greyer forming slight M across opened wings. Underwing-coverts mostly white, primaries and secondaries blackish with short, narrow black line running diagonally inwards from carpal (from museum specimen, in which exact extent and pattern of black difficult to ascertain on set wing). **Tail** Wedge-shaped; blackish.

FHJ: A medium-sized, white-bellied gadfly-petrel with mostly white underwing. Only recently discovered; flight and habits little known, presumably as for other medium-sized gadfly-petrels.

DM: Breeds on inland cliffs of Reunion I. in tropical western Indian Ocean; one nest recently found on Rodrigues I. Egg-dates about Nov; fledging in Apr (Jouanin & Gill 1965). Pelagic dispersal unknown but not recorded in NW Indian Ocean by Bailey (1968), which may indicate pelagic dispersal in subtropical convergence zone S of about 20°S.

SS: Unlike any other medium-sized gadfly-petrel of Indian Ocean. See Herald and Atlantic Petrels (p. 244, p. 240), which have dark undertail-coverts and mostly dark underwings.

77 HAWAIIAN PETREL
other: Dark-rumped Petrel
Pterodroma phaeopygia

PLATE 23 Fig. 77

MAP 77

Length 43cm (17in.). Wingspan 91cm (36in.). Iris brown. Bill black. Legs/feet bluish-flesh, webs distally black.

Tropical Pacific Ocean; range overlaps with White-necked Petrel and Buller's Shearwater (p. 246, p. 260). Sexes alike; no seasonal variation but individual variance in rump colour. Juveniles and adults alike. Two subspecies listed, not separable at sea.

PLUMAGE: Head Dark blackish-brown cap extending below eye and to sides of neck forming partial collar; remainder, including forehead, white. **Body** Upperparts mostly dark velvet-brown, a little paler than cap. Many, but not all, show varying degrees of white on sides of rump, normally as two oval-shaped patches. Underparts white. **Wings** Upperwing dark velvet-brown, primaries and secondaries slightly darker, but lacks obvious M mark. Underwing mostly white, with blackish margins, tip and distinct diagonal bar extending across coverts; axillaries white with small blackish patch (diagnostic). **Tail** Blackish-brown.

FHJ: A large, long-winged gadfly with characteristic pendulum-motion flight of three or four quick wingbeats to gain height followed by long downwards glide on bowed and angled wings, producing distinctive bounding, rising and falling, progression. In high winds flaps less, gliding in spectacular sweeping arcs up to 30m over ocean. In flight dark sides of neck impart darker overall aspect than in White-necked Petrel (p. 246) and differs further in darker upperparts lacking distinctive 'M' mark. A blackish axillary mark usually visible when tilting into wind at apex of flight plan. General impression is of a dark-backed gadfly-petrel with dark sides of face and neck and a distinctive underwing pattern.

DM: Tropical Pacific. *P.p. sandwichensis* formerly bred throughout Hawaiian chain but now extirpated from many areas; largest remaining colony is on Maui in walls of Haleakala Crater; recently rediscovered nesting on Lanai and, more recently, possibly also on Kauai. *P.p. phaeopygia* breeds in Galapagos Is on Santa Cruz, James, San Cristobal, Floreana and Isabela, where numbers have also decreased due to depredations by introduced animals and clearance of nesting areas for agriculture. Returns to colonies from Apr onwards; egg-dates May–Aug; adults desert colonies before juveniles, which fledge Nov/Dec. Pelagic dispersal poorly known but both populations usually absent from seas adjacent to breeding islands during Dec–Mar. Hawaiian population probably moves N and W; those from Galapagos appear to disperse E towards South American littoral, extending N to seas off western Mexico and Panama and S to Gulf of Guayaquil and northern Peru.

SS: See notes above and under White-necked Petrel (p. 246 below).

78 WHITE-NECKED PETREL
(Includes Juan Fernandez Petrel)
Pterodroma externa

PLATE 23 Figs 78a-78b

MAP 78

Length 43cm (17in.). Wingspan 95cm (37in.). Iris brown. Bill black. Legs/feet flesh, marked black.

Tropical Pacific Ocean; range overlaps with Hawaiian Petrel and Buller's Shearwater (p. 246, p. 260). Sexes alike; no seasonal variation. Juveniles and adults alike. The two subspecies, separable at sea, are described separately below beginning with nominate.

PLUMAGE: Head Dark brownish-grey cap extending to eye-level and hindneck; forehead, sides of face, chin and throat white. **Body** Upperparts brownish-grey narrowly fringed white, forming scaly pattern at close range; lower back blackish. Underparts mostly white except for narrow brownish-grey collar on sides of upper breast (extension from mantle). **Wings** Upperwing mainly brownish-grey; outer primaries and greater coverts blackish, linking across back to form open M mark. Underwing white; tip and trailing edge blackish with short, indistinct diagonal bar extending across coverts. **Tail** Brownish-grey. NOTE: In worn plumage hindneck becomes faintly paler.

P.e. cervicalis: Differs from nominate in blackish cap, white cervical collar, greyer tail, and more pronounced diagonal bar on underwing.

FHJ: Large, powerful gadfly-petrel with dark head and obvious open M mark across upper surfaces. White hindcollar of Kermadec race is conspicuous and diagnostic field character within its range. Flight strong, wheeling in broad arcs high over ocean; compared with smaller gadfly-petrels, e.g. Cook's Petrel (p. 247), flight less vigorous and darting, not so fast and swooping; tail appears rather long and wedge-shaped in flight, wings bowed and angled. Does not usually follow ships but is not diverted by them, often soars high over rigging.

DM: The two races breed at opposite sides of southern Pacific: *P.e. externa* at Mas Afuera, Juan Fernandez Is, off Chile; *P.e. cervicalis* at Sunday I. (Raoul), Kermadec Is, N of New Zealand. Returns to colonies Oct/Nov; egg-dates Dec/Jan; fledging and dispersal begins Jun. During breeding period Kermadec population extends W into Tasman Sea to within 400km of Australian coast (see Harrison P. 1978c, Barton 1980). Both populations migrate high into northern Pacific but movements poorly known. Kermadec population appears to move N past Fiji towards Japan; Juan Fernandez breeders move N during Jun/Jul to seas N of Hawaii and are present Jul–Oct off western Mexico, where Beck (in Murphy 1936) collected 15 NW of Clipperton I. Could wander to Californian waters and should be looked for over areas such as the Davidson Seamount, Jul–Oct.

SS: Hawaiian Petrel (p. 246) differs in more extensive cap extending on sides of neck as partial collar, darker brown upperparts and more pronounced diagonal bar on underwing. Many Hawaiian Petrels also show conspicuous white sides to rump. Buller's Shearwater (p. 260) bears superficial resemblance to present species but flight and jizz obviously different.

79 COOK'S PETREL
Pterodroma cooki

PLATE 26 Fig. 79
MAP 79

Length 26cm (10½in.). Wingspan 66cm (25in.). Iris brown. Bill black. Legs/feet bluish-purple, variably black on webs and toes.

Transequatorial migrant in Pacific Ocean; range overlaps with Pycroft's, Stejneger's and Gould's Petrels (p. 250, p. 249, p. 247). Sexes alike; no seasonal variation although in worn plumage upperparts and upperwings become darker. Juveniles resemble adults but with paler feather tips on upper surfaces. Taxonomy of this (and other) small *Pterodroma* remains to be fully agreed upon. Recent (1979) edition of Peters's *Birds of the World* lists apparently sedentary Chilean population as separate species *P. defilippiana*. Many sources regard those birds taken at sea off Chile as probably immatures of *P. cooki*, on migration from their SW Pacific natal islands. As no firm evidence of breeding has apparently yet been found, I have not included '*P. defilippiana*' in this guide. (The 'two' forms are not separable at sea.)

PLUMAGE: Head Forehead, chin and throat white; forecrown white mottled with grey and merging into frosty-grey crown, nape and hindneck. A darker dusky-grey patch passes through and below eye. **Body** Upperparts mostly frosty-grey (little or no contrast with hindneck and crown). Underparts white. **Wings** Upperwing frosty-grey; darker outer primaries and greater coverts form distinct broad open M linked across lower back (appears more contrasting than in Pycroft's or Stejneger's Petrels). Underwing often appears wholly white at sea; at close range shows narrow blackish borders and tip with indistinct short diagonal bar. **Tail** Slightly darker grey than back with faintly browner tip and noticeable white outer tail feathers.

FHJ: Small gadfly-petrel appearing rather pale above, including head, with white underwings lacking prominent dark diagonal bar found in most of its congeners. Flight rapid and erratic, rather bat-like with fast jerky wingbeats and much weaving and banking interrupted by high arcs. Does not usually follow ships. At distance appears generally pale greyish above with darker wings; white outer tail feathers are more apparent during banking manoeuvres; upperparts thus lack contrast between head and mantle found in similar Stejneger's Petrel (p. 249).

DM: Breeds at Little and Great Barrier Is, New Zealand, with small colony on Codfish I., near Stewart I. Status at San Felix, San Ambrosio and Juan Fernandez in eastern South Pacific requires clarification. Returns to colonies Oct; egg-dates Nov/Dec; fledging and dispersal Mar/Apr. During breeding season extends W into Tasman Sea, where relatively abundant in offshore Australian waters (Harrison 1978c, Barton 1980) though rarely seen from land (Serventy *et al.* 1971). Pelagic range and movements not fully understood. From the little evidence available it seems likely that this species moves NE through central Pacific to winter in contra-nuptial quarters in NE Pacific. Several sighted in Jun and Aug off Aleutian Is and also N of Hawaiian Is at 34°N (Gould, pers. comm.). Recent reports indicate that it occurs regularly off Baja California during northern summer with some occurring in Californian offshore waters (see especially account in Roberson 1980). Occurs in some numbers off Chile and Peru but status in this area requires clarification.

SS: Pycroft's and Stejneger's Petrels (p. 250, p. 249) are only other small gadfly-petrels which appear to have a mostly white underwing at sea. They differ from present species in distinctly darker crown and nape and lack white outer tail feathers. The upperwings of both appear browner in tone than Cook's, and the M mark is less defined. The underwing of Cook's also shows a paler tip. Gould's Petrel (p. 247) has broader diagonal stripe and more noticeably dark margins and tip on underwing than present species, and differs further in sooty-black crown and hindneck extending to sides of breast as partial collar. Black-winged Petrel (p. 249) has partial grey collar on sides of breast and distinctive broad diagonal stripe, margins and tip to underwing. Bonin Petrel (p. 243) has darker head, wider diagonal stripe and margins on underwing, and lacks white outer tail feathers. See also palest examples of Collared Petrel (p. 248).

80 GOULD'S PETREL
other: White-winged Petrel
Pterodroma leucoptera

PLATE 26 Fig. 80
MAP 80

Length 30cm (12in.). Wingspan 71cm (28in.). Iris brown. Bill black. Legs/feet flesh, faintly greyish-blue, webs and toes distally blackish.

Breeds off Australia, perhaps dispersing towards central Pacific, but precise movements unknown; range overlaps with several gadfly spp. (see especially Black-winged, Cook's and Pycroft's Petrels, p. 249, p. 247, p. 250). Sexes alike; no seasonal variation, but in worn plumage upperparts darker with less pronounced 'M' mark. Juveniles and adults alike. Collared Petrel *P.l. brevipes* is usually regarded as a melanistic central Pacific race of Gould's Petrel. It is described separately below (80X).

PLUMAGE: Head Area at base of bill, chin and throat white; forehead white, scaled blackish, merging into sooty-brown crown, hindneck and sides of face. **Body** Upperparts dark grey. Underparts mostly white except for blackish smudges on sides of breast forming partial collar (extension from hindneck). **Wings** Upperwing dark brownish-grey with blackish primaries and greater coverts forming M mark linked across lower back. Underwing mostly white except for narrow blackish margins, tip and diagonal stripe extending inwards across coverts (more pronounced than in Cook's Petrel). **Tail** Blackish-brown.

FHJ: The darkest of all the 'cookilarias' petrels with blackish head and dark upperparts imparting distinctive appearance at sea. Underwing pattern intermediate between Cook's and Black-winged Petrels. Compared with Cook's Petrel (p. 247) has much slower and lower-profiled flight more akin to that of a small shearwater, with bursts of quick wingbeats followed by low glides with stiff wings held parallel to waves. This slow, atypical gadfly progression sometimes broken by a sudden turn of speed, sprinting off, banking and twisting in steep arcs with great agility, before returning to rather pedestrian flight. Does not normally follow ships.

DM: Breeds only at Cabbage Tree I. off Port Stephens, New South Wales, eastern Australia. Returns to colony Oct; egg-dates Nov; fledging and departure begins Mar/Apr. During breeding season disperses into adjacent sea areas extending to Tasman Sea, often joining with shearwaters and Sooty Terns to form large flocks over profitable feeding areas. Post-breeding dispersal unknown; thought to be mainly sedentary, dispersing only to Tasman Sea and tropical SW Pacific. Stragglers have reached New Zealand and Galapagos Is.

SS: Differs from all congeners in sooty-brown crown and hindneck, and dark upperparts which, with comparative experience, enables ready separation from other Tasman Sea cookilarias. Experienced observers will note that present species has broader leading margin, darker tip and diagonal stripe than either Cook's or Pycroft's Petrels (p. 247, p. 250). Black-winged Petrel (p. 249) has much paler grey head and upperparts extending to breast as a noticeable collar, and distinctive underwing pattern.

80X COLLARED PETREL *Pterodroma (leucoptera) brevipes*

PLATE 26 Fig. 80
MAP 80

Length 30cm (12in.). Wingspan 71cm (28in.). Iris brown. Bill black. Legs/feet greyish-blue, webs and toes distally black.

Tropical western Pacific Ocean, where range overlaps with several gadfly spp. (see especially Cook's, Stejneger's and Gould's Petrels, p. 247, p. 249, p. 247). Sexes alike; no seasonal variation but in worn plumage upperparts darker with less pronounced M mark. Juveniles and adults alike. Usually regarded as a melanistic race of Gould's Petrel (p. 247).

PLUMAGE: As for nominate *P.l. leucoptera* except: **Body** Upperparts paler grey. Underparts highly variable; typically with diffuse grey breast band separating white throat from white lower breast and belly. Palest forms lack complete breast band whilst darkest forms have completely grey underparts (except chin and throat).

FHJ: As nominate.

DM: Breeds tropical western Pacific at Fiji Is and possibly on the Samoa Is. Birds with characters intermediate between *leucoptera* and *brevipes* or forming undescribed races occur on the Solomons, New Caledonia and New Hebrides. Range at sea poorly known, thought to move towards central Pacific; has been recorded Phoenix Is. Meeth (pers. comm.) has photographed them 800km W of Galapagos.

SS: See notes under nominate (p. 247). Beware especially Black-winged Petrel (p. 249), which has partial grey breast band but differs in distinctive underwing pattern, greyer upperparts, and much paler head.

81 BONIN PETREL *Pterodroma hypoleuca*

PLATE 25 Fig. 81
MAP 81

Length 30cm (12in.). Wingspan 63–71cm (25–28in.). Iris dark brown. Bill black. Legs/feet flesh with blackish toes.

Tropical North Pacific from Bonins E to Hawaii; range overlaps with several gadfly spp. but see especially Hawaiian, Black-winged, Cook's and Stejneger's Petrels (p. 246, p. 249, p. 247, p. 249). Sexes alike; no seasonal variation. Juveniles and adults alike.

PLUMAGE: Head Forehead, chin and throat white; forecrown white, scaled black, merging into blackish-grey crown, nape, hindneck and sides of face. **Body** Upperparts dull blue-grey narrowly fringed white, giving faint scaly effect. Underparts mostly white except for greyish sides of breast forming partial collar (extension from hindneck). **Wings** Upperwing: coverts as upperparts but browner in tone with blackish primaries and secondaries forming M mark linked across lower back. Underwing white with blackish margins and diagonal bar extending from carpal inwards across coverts. **Tail** Blackish-grey.

FHJ: Typical pendulum-motion progression of genus, fast and swooping on bowed, angled wings. Does not follow ships.

DM: Tropical northern Pacific breeding at Volcano and Bonin Is S of Japan, and on NW Hawaiian chain where Midway I. colony, formerly third largest in world, in very real danger of extinction due to rats. Returns to colonies Aug/Sep; egg-dates Nov–Feb; fledging and dispersal from about Jun. Migratory, ranging in central Pacific to about 30°N (Gould, pers. comm.) and to Taiwan, Ryukyu and Izu Is and Sakhalin.

SS: Hawaiian Petrel (p. 246) is much larger with browner back and different underwing pattern. Transient Cook's and Stejneger's Petrels (p. 247, p. 249) have different head and underwing patterns.

82 BLACK-WINGED PETREL
Pterodroma nigripennis

PLATE 25 Fig. 82
MAP 82

Length 30cm (12in.). Wingspan 63–71cm (25–28in.). Iris dark brown. Bill black. Legs/feet usually flesh, occasionally blue; toes and webs distally black.

Breeds extreme SW Pacific, migrating NE into North Pacific. Range overlaps with several gadfly spp. but see especially Bonin, Cook's and Gould's Petrels (p. 248, p. 247, p. 247). Sexes alike; no seasonal variation although upperparts probably wear browner. Juveniles and adults alike.

PLUMAGE: Head Forehead, chin and throat white with dark patch passing through and below eye; forecrown white, mottled with grey, merging into frosty-grey crown, nape, hindneck and sides of face. **Body** Upperparts mostly frosty-grey merging into blackish-brown across rump. Underparts white except for grey sides of upper breast forming partial but conspicuous collar (excellent flight character). **Wings** Upperwing brownish with darker outer primaries and greater coverts forming distinct open M mark linked across rump. Underwing white with broad blackish margins, tip and diagonal bar extending from carpal inwards across coverts. **Tail** Blackish-grey.

FHJ: One of easiest of all gadfly-petrels to identify due to combination of greyer upperparts than congeners, partial grey collar and conspicuously patterned underwings. Flight rapid and strong, bounding and wheeling in great arcs; occasionally soaring high over ocean and hanging motionless into wind. During Oct–Feb often indulges in spectacular mid-ocean courtship flights, pairs or groups engaging in close-contact pursuit-chases towering high into air whilst uttering shrill 'weet-weet-weet' or 'reep-wee-weet' (see Harrison P. 1978c). Does not usually follow ships.

DM: Breeding restricted to SW Pacific, where numbers apparently increasing with possible range extension in progress. Breeds at New Caledonia, Lord Howe I., Norfolk I., Three Kings, Kermadec, Chatham and Austral groups. Recently reported ashore at Poor Knight's I., New Zealand, and off Australia from Heron I., and several islands of E Australia S to Muttonbird I., NSW (Fullager & van Tets, pers. comm.). Returns to colonies Oct/Nov; egg-dates Dec/Jan; fledging and dispersal Apr/May. Pelagic movements not fully known; during breeding season ranges W into Tasman Sea. Dispersal extends into tropical and subtropical Pacific with sight records extending N of Hawaii to at least 30°N (Gould, pers. comm.).

SS: Separated from other SW Pacific gadfly-petrels by partial grey collar and conspicuous underwing pattern (but see Chatham Island Petrel, p. 249). From Bonin Petrel (p. 248) by greyer upperparts and less pronounced underwing pattern.

83 CHATHAM ISLAND PETREL
Pterodroma axillaris

PLATE 25 Fig. 83
MAP 83

Length 30cm (12in.). Wingspan 63–71cm (25–28in). Iris dark brown. Bill black. Legs/feet flesh, distal webs and toes blackish.

Confined to Chatham Is off New Zealand and adjacent seas; range overlaps with Black-winged and Cook's Petrel (p. 249, p. 247). Sexes alike; no seasonal variation although upperparts probably wear browner. Juveniles and adults alike. No subspecies.

PLUMAGE: Head Forehead, chin and throat white, forecrown white, scaled greyish, merging into frosty-grey crown, nape, hindneck and sides of face. **Body** Upperparts mostly grey, narrowly edged white, forming indistinct scaly pattern. Underparts white; sides of breast frosty-grey forming partial but distinctive collar (extension from hindneck). **Wings** Upperwing brownish-black. Underwing white with conspicuous broad black margins, tip and diagonal bar extending from carpal to black axillaries. **Tail** Blackish-brown.

FHJ: Differs from Black-winged Petrel in diagnostic black axillaries. Flight typical of genus.

DM: Breeds only at South-east Island, Chatham Is, E of New Zealand; thought to disperse to adjacent seas only. Egg-dates Dec/Jan.

SS: Diagnostic underwing pattern separates from Black-winged Petrel (p. 249).

84 STEJNEGER'S PETREL
Pterodroma longirostris

PLATE 26 Fig. 84
MAP 84

Length 26cm (10in.). Wingspan 66cm (26in.). Iris brown. Bill black. Legs/feet bluish, webs brown.

Transequatorial migrant in Pacific Ocean, where range overlaps with Cook's Petrel (p. 247); see also Gould's and Bonin Petrels (p. 247, p. 248). Sexes alike; no seasonal variation, although in worn plumage contrast between hindneck and mantle less pronounced (increasing possible confusion with Cook's or Gould's Petrels). Juveniles much as adults but upperparts greyer, contrasting more with dark cap and hindneck. Taxonomy not fully agreed upon but most authors treat Pycroft's Petrel *P.(l.) pycrofti* (described separately below, 84X) as an allopatric form breeding in SW Pacific and which probably also migrates N in austral winter.

PLUMAGE: Head Forehead white, scaled blackish-brown and merging into dark cap; remainder white. **Body** Upperparts deep brownish-grey (darker than Cook's Petrel, p. 247). Underparts white. **Wings** Upperwing deep brownish-grey, with blackish outer primaries and greater coverts forming indistinct open M mark linked across lower back (less pronounced than in Cook's). Underwing often appears wholly white at sea; at close range shows

narrow blackish borders and tip with indistinct short diagonal stripe. **Tail** Uniformly deep brownish-grey (unlike Cook's Petrel).
FHJ: Much as Cook's Petrel (p. 247) but flight possibly less vigorous.
DM: Breeds Mas Afuera, Juan Fernandez, off Chile. Returns to colonies from late Oct; egg-dates Nov; fledging and dispersal begins Mar with broad movement N through subtropical and tropical Pacific during Mar–May to reach main wintering area near Japan Jun–Aug. Return movement begins Sep/Oct. Recently recorded off California and may regularly occur there offshore during austral winter (see Roberson 1980). Several beach derelicts recovered from New Zealand (Falla *et al.* 1975).
SS: Post-breeding dispersal overlaps that of Cook's Petrel (p. 247), which also has an apparently white underwing at sea. Present species differs in darker upperparts, usually with dark cap clearly demarcated from grey mantle, and uniformly dark tail. (Cook's Petrel has whitish outer tail feathers.) In worn plumage mantle and back darken, lessening contrast between cap, but upperparts always comparatively darker than in Cook's Petrel. Gould's Petrel (p. 247) has wider margins, tip and diagonal stripe on underwing than present species, with blackish hindneck extending to form partial collar.

84X PYCROFT'S PETREL
Pterodroma (longirostris) pycrofti

PLATE 26 Fig. 84X
MAP 84X

Length 26cm (10in.). Wingspan 66cm (26in.). Iris brown. Bill black. Legs/feet bluish, webs brown.

Breeds New Zealand offshore islands; unconfirmed transequatorial migrant. Range overlaps with Cook's and Gould's Petrels (p. 247, p. 247). Sexes alike, no seasonal variation though upperparts wear browner. Juveniles differ only in more pronounced whitish fringes to upperparts but these soon abrade. Usually considered conspecific with eastern Pacific Stejneger's Petrel (see under that species for notes on taxonomy, p. 249).
PLUMAGE: Differs from nominate *longirostris* in: **Head** Forehead, chin and throat white; forecrown white, scaled grey, and merging into medium-grey crown, nape and hindneck. A darker, dusky-grey patch extends through and below eye. **Tail** Outermost feathers paler but not white as in Cook's Petrel (p. 247).
FHJ: As nominate.
DM: Breeds Hen, Chicken, Poor Knights, Mercury, Stanley and Stephenson Is off New Zealand; breeding cycle as nominate, departing from natal islands Mar/Apr, probably into northern Pacific (unconfirmed).
SS: Differs from nominate *P.l. longirostris* (p. 249) in paler cap and upperparts. At sea appears very like Cook's Petrel (beware). Differs in darker head and browner upperwings which lack the pronounced M mark of Cook's; outer tail feathers darker.

85 MACGILLIVRAY'S PETREL
Pterodroma macgillivrayi

PLATE 27 Fig. 85
MAP 85

Length 30cm (12in.). Wingspan unknown. Iris brown. Bill black. Legs/feet pink.

Seas off Fiji, SW Pacific. Movements and habits unknown.
PLUMAGE: Known only from one fledgling found Ngua Is, Fiji group, which in fresh plumage was wholly blackish-brown.
FHJ: Unknown; probably as closely related Bulwer's Petrel, but stouter bill, slightly larger size and heavier build.
DM: Fledgling found Oct. Reports of small wholly dark petrels in Fiji area in Nov and Dec 1964, Jan and May 1965, could possibly refer to this lost species (Bourne 1967a).
SS: Would closely resemble Bulwer's Petrel at sea.

Genus *HALOBAENA*

Monotypic genus; small, blue-grey petrel of Southern Oceans. Sexes alike; no seasonal variation. Bears superficial resemblance to a miniature *Pterodroma* but more closely resembles *Pachyptila* group. Distinguished from all other petrels by unique, white-tipped tail. Separation from *Pachyptila* group at sea straightforward given reasonable views and comparative experience, but accurate notes of bill colour, head pattern and tail colour essential.

86 BLUE PETREL
Halobaena caerulea

PLATE 18 Fig. 86
MAP 86

Length 28–30cm (11–12in.). Wingspan 58–66cm (23–26in.). Iris brown. Bill blackish. Legs/feet blue-grey, webs pale flesh.

Circumpolar in Southern Oceans N to about 30°S during austral winter, but occasionally to about 20°S off Peru (Meeth & Meeth 1977). Range overlaps with similar prion spp., from which difficult to separate without comparative experience; present species differs in darker head and unique white-tipped tail. Sexes alike; no seasonal variation. Juveniles differ from adults only in ash-grey forehead and browner cast to upperparts. No subspecies.

PLUMAGE: Head Forehead and forecrown white mottled with grey and merging into dark blackish-grey crown, nape, hindneck and sides of neck; remainder, except dusky eye patch, white. **Body** Upperparts mostly steel-grey, lower back darker. Underparts white except for incomplete but obvious dark grey collar (extension from hindneck). **Wings** Upperwing mostly steel-grey; outer primaries and tips of greater coverts darker, linking across lower back to form open M mark. Underwing white, narrowly margined with grey. **Tail** Square; steel-grey with narrow black subterminal band and white tip (unique among petrels).

FHJ: Small, cold-water petrel with prion-like jizz. Differs from that genus in slightly larger size, and less erratic flight with more frequent glides on stiff, bowed wings low to surface. Even at long range greyer upperparts and darker head impart more contrasting pattern than prions, which is perhaps best field character to look for. Occasionally follows ships (unlike prions). Gregarious throughout year; usually encountered at sea in small, loose flocks of up to 100 or so or in loose association with dense multitudes of prions, particularly along edges of upwellings etc.

DM: Known to breed for certain only at South Georgia, Prince Edward, Marion, Crozet and Kerguelen Is; recently rediscovered nesting on offshore stacks of Macquarie I. (see Johnstone 1980); may also breed on Diego Ramirez, off Cape Horn, where numbers congregate offshore during breeding season. Returns to colonies Sep; egg-dates Oct/Nov; fledging and departure begins Feb/Mar. Adults probably disperse only to adjacent waters as they occasionally return to nesting chambers during winter. Non-breeders undertake dispersal from pack ice N in all three oceans to about 40°S, but to about 20°S off Peru (Meeth 1977). Regular but uncommon visitors to seas off South America, South Africa and Australia, normally during May–Oct.

SS: At extreme range or under poor conditions difficult to separate from prion spp., but with comparative experience separation possible by less erratic flight and more contrasting upperparts. At close or moderate range differs from all prion spp. in white forehead, black bill and much darker crown and nape extending in partial but obvious collar and imparting distinctive dark-headed appearance (but see also *P.v. vittata*, p. 251). White-tipped tail, if seen, diagnostic.

Genus *PACHYPTILA*

Taxonomy not fully agreed upon. Formerly treated as five or six species, but Cox (1980) convincingly argues case for reducing to three species. His taxon is followed in this guide (in anticipation of wider acceptance by progressive birders) and his paper is strongly recommended for further reading. If, as he states, *P. vittata* and *P. belcheri* do hybridise wherever their ranges overlap, it would, however, seem better to regard them as forms of one species, irrespective of their apparent dissimilarity. Not wishing to anticipate this revision, Cox's taxon is, as stated, followed here. An alternative treatment is that of Harper (1980).

Prions are small, Southern Ocean blue-grey petrels with distinctive open M mark and black-tipped tail; often regarded as impossible to separate at sea but, given reasonable conditions and comparative experience, no more difficult than some other pelagic groups.

At sea prions can be divided into two basic groups: (1) Broad-billed and Thin-billed Prions, with distinct head patterns and narrow dark upper-tail bands; (2) Fairy Prions, with indistinct head patterns but with broader, more extensive upper-tail bands. The undertail pattern in both groups also differs and is particularly important to record. Whilst the difficulty of identifying prions at sea should not be underestimated, the problems should not be overestimated.

87 BROAD-BILLED PRION (Includes Salvin's and Antarctic Prions)

Pachyptila vittata

PLATE 20 Figs 87a-87b

MAP 87

Length 25–30cm (10–12in.). Wingspan 57–66cm ($22\frac{1}{2}$–26in.). Iris brown. Bill blackish. Legs/feet blue.

Circumpolar in Southern Oceans; range overlaps with smaller Fairy and Thin-billed Prions (p. 252, p. 253); see also Blue Petrel (p. 250). Sexes alike; no seasonal variation. Juveniles indistinguishable from adults at sea. Three subspecies listed; formerly treated as two or three separate species but Cox (1980) convincingly argues that *desolata* and *vittata*, whilst allopatric in southern Atlantic and New Zealand regions, are connected by intermediate *salvini* in southern Indian Ocean. *P.(v.) salvini* indistinguishable at sea from *P.v. vittata* (pers. obs.); *P.(v.) desolata* can be separated from nominate *vittata* and is described separately below. *P.(v.) desolata* × *P. belcheri* hybrids apparently occur at Ile de L'Est, Crozets, and Iles Kerguelen (Cox 1980).

PLUMAGE: Head Mostly dark blue-grey with short, white superciliary highlighted by blackish stripe passing below eye from lores to ear-coverts; lower sides of face, chin and throat white. **Body** Upperparts pale blue-grey except for blackish bar across lower back. Underparts white. **Wings** Upperwing: Mainly pale blue-grey; blackish outer primaries, their coverts and tips of some median and secondary-coverts form conspicuous broad open M mark linked across lower back. Underwing mostly white. **Tail** Blue-grey, tip black; sides pale grey.

ANTARCTIC PRION (*P.(v.) desolata*): As nominate *vittata* except: bill blue, smaller and narrower.

Head Similar but dark blue-grey nape and hindneck extend downwards to form incomplete but obvious collar (excellent field character). NOTE: some *P.(v.) salvini* may also show this character.
FHJ: Largest of the prions, differing from smaller Fairy Prion (p. 252) in dark-headed appearance with distinctive facial pattern and narrower, less extensive black tip to tail. Flight slower, less erratic than that species, often feeding in dense flocks. Murphy (1936) aptly described feeding method as 'hydroplaning', the birds moving slowly over the water with wings outstretched, creeping into wind with bodies resting lightly upon surface, 'peddling' continually with feet, disappearing and reappearing whilst scooping up small organisms. Broad bill and large head impart thickset, chunky jizz, giving heavier, larger appearance at sea than Fairy Prion. Does not normally follow ships.
DM: Circumpolar. *P.(v.) desolata* breeds South Shetlands, South Orkney, South Sandwich, South Georgia, Kerguelen, Heard, Macquarie, Auckland, Scott I. and at Cape Denison, Antarctica. *P.(v.) salvini* breeds Marion, Prince Edward and Crozet Is. *P.v. vittata* breeds Tristan da Cunha, Gough I., St Paul, Amsterdam, Snares, Chatham and Stewart Is, also on certain mainland coasts bordering Foveaux Strait and southwestern fiords of Southland, South Island, New Zealand. Northern *P.v. vittata* returns to colonies Jul–Sep; egg-dates Aug/Sep; fledging and dispersal Dec–Mar. Southern *P.(v.) desolata* returns to colonies late Oct/Nov; egg-dates Nov/Dec, sometimes Jan if burrows have been blocked by snow; fledging and dispersal begins mid Mar. Adult *P.v. vittata* appear to remain in seas adjacent to breeding islands as they occasionally return to nesting burrows throughout winter (Serventy *et al.* 1971); but southern *P.(v.) desolata* and *P.(v.) salvini* and perhaps juveniles of nominate race may undertake more extensive wanderings. Records at sea and beached derelicts indicate northwards dispersal to coasts of Australasia, Africa and South America extending to about 10°S in tropical Indian Ocean and to about 15°S off coast of Peru (*P. belcheri*, p. 253, is commonest prion of western South American littoral). Rare in higher latitudes of Central Pacific.
SS: See notes under Fairy Prion (p. 252). Differs from that species in distinctive head pattern and less extensive, narrower band on uppertail. From below undertail pattern of Broad-billed and Thin-billed Prions shows long, dark central streak extending from blackish terminal band towards undertail-coverts. By comparison Fairy Prions show only a broad blackish terminal band. Thin-billed Prion (p. 253) lacks dark crown and has a prominent white superciliary (although some atypical *desolata* apparently have similar plumage characters and are indistinguishable, see details in Cox 1980). Blue Petrel (p. 250) has conspicuous black crown, nape and hindneck extending as partial but conspicuous collar, and a white-tipped tail.

---

88 FAIRY PRION (Includes Fulmar Prion)
Pachyptila turtur

PLATE 20 Figs 88a-88b

MAP 88

Length 25–28cm (10–11in.). Wingspan 56–60cm (22–23½in.). Iris brown. Bill, legs/feet blue.

Circumpolar in Southern Oceans; range overlaps with Broad-billed and Thin-billed Prions (p. 251, p. 253); see also Blue Petrel (p. 250). Sexes alike; no seasonal variation. Juveniles not distinguishable from adults at sea. Three subspecies listed; two formerly treated as separate species but Cox (1980) has shown that characteristics of *turtur* and *crassirostris* intergrade over a wide area, indicating conspecificity. Typical examples of both forms separable at sea (given optimum conditions and comparative experience). They are described separately below beginning with nominate *P.t. turtur*.
PLUMAGE: Head Mostly pale blue-grey with small, diffuse white superciliary often shaded behind eye with blue-grey; chin, throat and sides of face white. **Body** Upperparts mostly pale blue-grey; lower back and tips of longer uppertail-coverts blackish. Underparts white. **Wings** Upperwing mainly pale blue-grey; blackish outer primaries, their coverts and tips of some median and secondary-coverts form conspicuous broad open M mark linked across lower back. Underwing white. **Tail** Base mostly blue-grey; broad blackish terminal band, outer feathers pale grey. Undertail white, broadly tipped black.
FULMAR PRION (*P.(t.) crassirostris*): Differs from nominate in: stouter bill. **Head** Slightly paler, less distinct superciliary. **Body and Wings** Bluer in tone with more apparent, clearly defined open M mark across upperwings and lower back.
FHJ: Small; both *turtur* and *crassirostris* differ from other forms of prion in lack of noticeable head pattern and broader, more apparent blackish tail band. These characters readily seen at sea, given reasonable conditions. In flight *P.t. turtur* has a buoyant, erratic flight, usually feeding in large flocks, picking from surface with fluttering wingbeats and trailing legs. *P.(t.) crassirostris* similar, but differs in more erratic flight, during which it habitually executes a remarkable 'loop the loop' manoeuvre high into air before rejoining original course (Harper 1980; pers. obs.).
DM: Circumpolar. *P.t. turtur* breeds at Beauchene I., Falkland Is, southern Atlantic; Marion and Prince Edward Is, southern Indian Ocean. Main breeding colonies situated Australasian region on islands in Bass Strait and off Tasmania, and on islands off New Zealand from Poor Knights Is S to Snares Is, also at Big and Little Mangere Is, Chatham Is. *P.t. eatoni* breeds Heard and Auckland Is. *P.(t.) crassirostris* breeds near New Zealand at Bounty Is, and at Pyramid Rock, Chatham Is. Returns to colonies from Aug onwards (although Serventy *et al.* 1971 record Heard Is population as roosting at colonies during winter); egg-dates mid Oct–mid Nov; fledging and dispersal begins Dec through to Feb.

Thought to disperse mainly to adjacent seas during winter, with limited northwards dispersal in some populations; others may range along subtropical convergence.
SS: Both *P.t. turtur* and *P.(t.) crassirostris* differ from larger Broad-billed Prion group and Thin-billed Prion (p. 251, p. 253) in lack of distinctive head pattern or noticeable darkening on crown and nape; this character, combined with broader and more extensive tail band, enables at-sea identification given reasonable views. Subspecific separation of *turtur* and *crassirostris* more difficult; compared with former, *crassirostris* has brighter blue upperparts, more distinctive M mark and the broadest tail band of any prion; looping flight also distinctive. Blue Petrel (p. 250) differs from both forms in conspicuous head pattern and black bill.

89 THIN-BILLED PRION
other: Slender-billed Prion
Pachyptila belcheri

PLATE 20 Fig. 89
MAP 89

Length 26cm (10in.). Wingspan 56cm (22in.). Iris brown. Bill, legs/feet blue.

Restricted breeding range; pelagic range overlaps with Broad-billed and Fairy Prions (p. 251, p. 252): see also Blue Petrel (p. 250). Sexes alike; no seasonal variation. Juveniles indistinguishable from adults at sea. Retention as a full species follows work of Cox (1980) although his argumentation, including notes on hybridisation with *P.(v.) desolata*, inevitably leads to conclusion that *belcheri* and *P.(v.) desolata* are conspecific (see notes on p. 251).
PLUMAGE: Head Mostly pale blue-grey; lores and long superciliary conspicuously white with dark grey stripe passing below and behind eye; lower sides of face, chin and throat white. **Body** Upperparts pale blue-grey except for narrow, greyish-black bar across lower back. Underparts white. **Wings:** Upperwing mostly blue-grey; greyish-black outer primaries, their coverts and tips of some median and secondary-coverts form narrow, ill-defined open M mark linked across lower back. Underwing white. **Tail** Blue-grey, tip narrowly black, sides pale grey or whitish.
FHJ: Small; differs from all other prions in long, white superciliary backed by dark grey eye-stripe and white lores. At sea appears white-faced with paler blue upperparts, poorly defined open M mark and narrow tail band; during flight manoeuvres whiter outer tail feathers a useful character. Flight fast, buoyant and erratic; often forms large feeding flocks at sea, not normally attracted to ships.
DM: Restricted breeding distribution; breeds Falkland Is, southern Atlantic, where probably one of the commoner breeding petrels (Woods 1975). In southern Indian Ocean breeds Crozet, and Kerguelen Is where it apparently hybridises with *P.(v.) desolata* (Cox 1980). Falkland population returns to colonies Aug/Sep; egg-dates Oct/Nov; fledging and departure begins late Feb/Mar, dispersing along coasts of Chile and Peru as far N as about 15°S, occurring in thousands during Jul/Aug. The few South African records, compared with numerous beach recoveries in Australia and New Zealand, suggest that most Indian Ocean breeders move E after breeding.
SS: See notes under Broad-billed and Fairy Prions (p. 251, p. 252). Some atypical *P.(v.) desolata* on Kerguelen and Crozet Is indistinguishable from present species (Cox 1980); the two forms apparently interbreed on those islands.

Genus *BULWERIA*

Two species; almost wholly dark brown small gadfly-like petrels intermediate in size between storm-petrels and true gadfly-petrels. Bulwer's Petrel (p. 253) occurs in Atlantic, Pacific and Indian Oceans whilst Jouanin's is restricted to NW Indian Ocean; separation best based on size, flight and jizz.

90 BULWER'S PETREL
Bulweria bulwerii

PLATE 27 Figs 90a-90c
MAP 90

Length 26–27cm (10–10½in.). Wingspan 65–70cm (25½–27½in.). Iris brown. Bill black. Legs/feet mainly pink, darker webs.

Breeds Atlantic and Pacific Oceans with recent evidence of westwards dispersal from Pacific to Indian Ocean area; range may thus overlap with larger Jouanin's Petrel (p. 254). Sexes alike; no seasonal variation. Juveniles and adults alike. No subspecies.
PLUMAGE: Almost wholly sooty-brown except for paler diagonal wing bar formed by buff tips to upperwing-coverts. In good light these bars usually visible to about 100m range, thereafter plumage usually appears wholly dark. Chin and face sometimes paler, rarely seen at sea.
FHJ: Size intermediate between storm-petrels and gadfly-petrels. Appears long-winged with rather long *pointed* tail (wedge-shape apparent only briefly during flight manoeuvres). Flight buoyant, erratic and twisting with wings held forward and slightly bowed. Normally weaves and twists close to surface rather prion-like, two to five rapid wingbeats followed by short twisting glide. Rarely flies higher than 2m above waves (see Jouanin's Petrel, p. 254). Whilst feeding, circles low over waves zigzagging loosely, occasionally fanning tail to change direction. Does not normally follow ships.
DM: In Atlantic Ocean breeds on Azores, Desertas Is off Madeira, Salvage, Canary and Cape Verde Is. Returns to colonies Apr/May; egg-dates May–Jul; fledging and dispersal begins Sep/Oct, most moving SW to winter in tropical seas between 20°W

and 50°W. Sightings off western Cape, South Africa (Brooke & Sinclair 1978), during austral summer suggest wider dispersal than at present realised. Non-breeders probably remain in wintering areas throughout year. Vagrants have occurred N to Ireland, Britain and Portugal. In North Pacific main breeding areas are off China and Taiwan, Bonin, Marquesas, Johnston, Volcano, Hawaiian and Phoenix Is; breeding season as in Atlantic population. Dispersal from East China Sea colonies poorly understood; recent sightings and collection of specimens in Indian Ocean, including 37 individuals seen between Fremantle and Java in Nov (Harrison, P 1979), suggest a regular dispersal into Indian Ocean. (This movement would parallel the east–west migration of such species as Swinhoe's and Matsudaira's Storm-petrels, which migrate on longitudinal tract from NW Pacific to Indian Ocean.) Extent of penetration into Indian Ocean unknown but certainly W to Maldives.

SS: Range probably overlaps with Jouanin's Petrel (p. 254); see notes under that species.

91 JOUANIN'S PETREL

Bulweria fallax

PLATE 27 Figs 91a-91b
MAP 91

Length 30–32cm (12–12½in.). Wingspan 76–83cm (30–32½in.). Iris brown. Bill black, plates occasionally pale horn. Legs/feet pink with dark outer edge and nails. (Measurements based on only three birds measured by RNBWS members.)

Endemic in NW Indian Ocean; range overlaps with Wedge-tailed and Flesh-footed Shearwaters (p. 259, p. 258). Sexes alike; no seasonal variation. Juveniles and adults alike. No subspecies.

PLUMAGE: Wholly blackish-brown; under optimum conditions some may show greyer feather tips to chin and forehead. In worn plumage a few may have pale upperwing diagonal as found in smaller Bulwer's Petrel (p. 253).

FHJ: Heavy bill and fast swooping flight suggest small gadfly-petrel. Jizz resembles Bulwer's Petrel but heavier, larger; flight quicker, more powerful, careening in high broad arcs with long slender wings bowed and held slightly forward.

DM: Endemic in NW Indian Ocean (Jouanin 1957). Recorded from southern Red Sea, Gulf of Aden, coasts of SE Arabia and throughout Arabian Sea S to Kenya. Extent of dispersal unknown but Bailey (1968) records them E to 58°E and S to the Equator. See also Sinclair (1979). Breeding areas unknown but large concentrations occur off Arabia, especially Kuria Muria Is during Mar–Aug where breeding is suspected. Three off Italy (Giol 1957, in Cramp & Simmons 1977) suggests assisted passage, whilst one collected Hawaiian Is (Clapp 1973) defies logical explanation.

SS: Likely to be confused with Bulwer's Petrel (p. 253) where range possibly overlaps in central Indian Ocean. Present species larger with proportionately larger bill and head and usually lacks pale diagonal bar on upperwing-coverts. Flight also different, Jouanin's Petrel normally towering 15–20m above waves in typical *Pterodroma* manner. Recently discovered Mascarene Petrel (p. 238) is larger overall with shorter, squarer tail. Wedge-tailed Shearwater (p. 259) is larger with different flight, loose-winged jizz, and long slender bill.

Genus *PROCELLARIA*

Four species; large shearwater-like petrels with pale bills, restricted mainly to Southern Oceans; Black Petrel is known to winter off western Mexico (Jehl 1974).

At sea identification can be problematical in New Zealand region, where mainly dark-plumaged White-chinned, Westland and Black Petrels all likely to be encountered. In all sightings bill colour and relative, overall body size and proportions useful characters, but specific identification often impossible. In southern Atlantic and Indian Oceans both White-chinned and Grey Petrels are well-known wake-dwellers and, in absence of confusing species, should provide few difficulties to the careful birder. In all sectors beware of confusing *Procellaria* types with dark-plumaged shearwaters, particularly Pale-footed Shearwater, which also has a pale dark-tipped bill.

92 GREY PETREL

other: Brown Petrel, Pediunker, Great Grey Shearwater

Procellaria cinerea

PLATE 28 Fig. 92
MAP 92

Length 48cm (19in.). Wingspan 117–127cm (46–50in.). Iris brown. Bill grey-green with yellow tip, blackish culmen and groove along lower mandible. Legs/feet greyish-flesh; webs yellowish, blackish toes.

Circumpolar in Southern Oceans; range overlaps with Cory's Shearwater (p. 257); see also White-headed Petrel (p. 238). Sexes alike; no seasonal variation. Juveniles and adults alike. No subspecies.

PLUMAGE: Head Mostly ash-grey merging without contrast into whitish chin. **Body** Upperparts ash- or brownish-grey. Underparts mostly white except for brownish-grey undertail-coverts. **Wings** Upperwing as upperparts but faintly darker. Underwing uniform grey. **Tail** Dark grey.

FHJ: A large ash-grey petrel with grey underwings and undertail-coverts contrasting with white belly. Resembles Cory's Shearwater in jizz but with rather jerky, duck-like wingbeats between long glides; flight often high and wheeling. Readily plunges from heights of up to 10m, swims underwater using wings. Regularly follows ships, attends trawlers and cetaceans.

DM: Sub-antarctic species with circumpolar distribution. Breeds Tristan da Cunha group, Gough, Marion, Prince Edward, Crozet, Kerguelen, Campbell and Antipodes Is; status on Ile Saint-Paul unclear (birds present in adjacent waters during breeding season). Returns to colonies Feb/Mar; egg-dates Mar/Apr; fledging and departure Aug/Sep, with circumpolar dispersal between 60°S and 25°S but further N in cold-water zones off western South America and Africa; uncommon off Australia (see Serventy *et al.* 1971).

SS: The smaller White-headed Petrel (p. 238) also has grey underwing but with white head and lacks dark undertail-coverts. Cory's Shearwater (p. 257) has different flight and mostly white underwings. See also Atlantic Petrel (p. 240).

93 WHITE-CHINNED PETREL
other: Shoemaker/Cape Hen
Procellaria aequinoctialis

PLATE 28 Figs 93a-93b

MAP 93

Length 51–58cm (20–23in.). Wingspan 134–147cm (53–58in.). Iris brown. Bill ivory-white to greenish-white; culmen and mandibular groove blackish. Legs/feet black.

Circumpolar in Southern Oceans; range overlaps with Westland and Parkinsons Petrels in Australasian sector; separation difficult, perhaps impossible, unless bill colour precisely determined. Sexes alike; no seasonal variation. Juveniles and adults alike. Two subspecies listed; *P.a. conspicillata* differs from nominate in more extensive, but highly variable, amount of white on sides of head (usually asymmetrical). Nicholls (1978) lists several partial albinos and a complete albino, all apparently otherwise referable to nominate race.

PLUMAGE: Wholly blackish-brown with variable amounts of white on chin and sides of face (see above) and greyish bases to undersides of primaries.

FHJ: Large heavily-built petrel with wedge-shaped tail and broad wings; intermediate in size between the larger all-dark shearwaters and giant petrels. The white chin, when present, discernible only at close range. Flight measured and powerful, with slow wingbeats interspersed with sustained glides; frequently soars high over waves. A common and aggressive scavenger around trawlers, habitually follows ships.

DM: Circumpolar. *P.a. aequinoctialis* breeds Falklands, South Georgia, Prince Edward, Marion, Crozet, Kerguelen, Auckland, Campbell and Antipodes; perhaps also Gough and Macquarie Is. *P.a. conspicillata* breeds Inaccessible I. Tristan da Cunha group. A summer breeder with some variation in egg-laying between populations. Generally returns to colonies Oct/Nov; egg-dates Nov to Jan; fledging and departure begins Apr/May. Adults probably remain in adjacent seas (Rowan *et al.* 1951). Non-breeders disperse widely, showing preference for offshore shelf waters rather than deep pelagic habitat. Normal range extends from about 55°S to 30°S but N to 6°S in Humboldt Current, and perhaps casually to the Equator elsewhere (see Bourne 1967b).

SS: In sub-antarctic waters large size, plumage and pale bill diagnostic. Problems occur in Australasia, where range overlaps with that of Westland Petrel (p. 256): the two are so similar that unless unmarked pale bill of present species can be seen separation would appear to be impossible.

94 PARKINSON'S PETREL
other: Black Petrel
Procellaria parkinsoni

PLATE 21 Fig. 94

MAP 94

Length 46cm (18in.). Wingspan 115cm (45in.). Iris brown. Bill bluish-white with black culmen, edge of nasal tubes, tips, and grooves. Legs/feet black.

Breeds New Zealand, dispersing E towards central Pacific during northern summer. Range overlaps with Westland and Great-winged Petrels (p. 256, p. 237) and with Flesh-footed Shearwater (p. 258). Sexes alike; no seasonal variation although plumage wears browner. Juveniles as adults except for indistinct paler edges to feathers of mantle and back (fresh plumage).

PLUMAGE: Wholly blackish-brown except for silvery bases to underwing primaries.

FHJ: Subtropical, blackish medium-sized petrel with a black-tipped, ivory-coloured bill. At sea has a less laboured flight than the larger Westland or White-chinned Petrels (p. 256, p. 255), but without comparative experience it would probably be impossible to separate from either. Does not usually follow ships; occasionally attends trawlers.

DM: Unlike Westland Petrel, breeds in austral summer at Little and Great Barrier Is, Hauraki Gulf, New Zealand. Returns to colonies Nov; egg-dates Nov/Dec; fledging and dispersal begins May/Jun. Pelagic dispersal not fully understood but appears to move eastwards into central Pacific, dispersing widely over subtropical waters during southern winter. Specimens have been collected off Galapagos (see Murphy 1936). More recently they have been observed wintering N of Equator off western Mexico (see Jehl 1974). During temperature and salinity fluctuations could occur off southern California and should be looked for Jun–Oct. Has occurred once Australia (Serventy *et al.* 1971).

SS: Probably impossible to separate at sea from larger Westland Petrel (p. 256) unless seen together but bill smaller, more delicate. Differs from larger White-chinned Petrel (p. 255) in black chin, black-tipped bill, more buoyant flight and subtropical habitat. Great-winged Petrel (*P.m. gouldi*, p. 237) is smaller with greyish-white chin, black bill and faster, more swooping flight.

95 WESTLAND PETREL
other: Westland Black Petrel
Procellaria westlandica

PLATE 28 Fig. 95

MAP 95

Length 51cm (20in.). Wingspan 137cm (54in.). Iris dark brown. Bill ivory coloured with dusky areas on bases of nasal tubes and culmen; nasal groove and gonys black. Legs/feet black.

New Zealand sector; extremely rare elsewhere. Range overlaps with similar White-chinned and Parkinson's Petrels (p. 255, p. 255); separation difficult, if not impossible, at sea unless bill colours precisely seen. Sexes alike; no seasonal variation. Juveniles and adults alike. No subspecies although Oliver (1955) considered this species conspecific with White-chinned Petrel.

PLUMAGE: Wholly blackish-brown except for greyish bases to underside of primaries.

FHJ: Large, heavily-built petrel closely resembling in all respects the more widespread sub-antarctic White-chinned Petrel (p. 255). Differs in black-tipped, ivory-coloured bill and more subtropical distribution.

DM: Breeds New Zealand mainland during austral winter (unlike White-chinned Petrel) in densely forested hills between Barrytown and Punakaiki, South Island. Returns to colonies Mar/Apr; egg-dates May/Jun; fledging and dispersal Dec (see Best & Owen 1976, Jackson 1958). Large rafts occur offshore during breeding period, providing best opportunity to view this rare petrel (population 3,000–6,000). Pelagic range not precisely known, probably mainly to New Zealand subtropical waters. Beached derelicts have occurred near Sydney, Australia (Serventy *et al*. 1971), during Dec/Jan and recent observations have shown that small numbers occur off SE Tasmania (see Carter 1981) during Apr/May.

SS: See notes under White-chinned Petrel (p. 255). Parkinson's Petrel (p. 255) is a smaller version of present species but a summer breeder at Hauraki Gulf, New Zealand. All three are closely related, and where ranges overlap in New Zealand sector field identification should be treated with caution. See also Flesh-footed Shearwater and Great-winged Petrel (p. 258, p. 237).

Genus *CALONECTRIS*

Two species geographically isolated. Cory's Shearwater breeds in North Atlantic, Streaked Shearwater in North Pacific; both migrate S during northern winter. Intermediate in structure between *Procellaria* and *Puffinus*, both *Calonectris* species have characteristic soaring flight often likened to that of a mollymawk.

At sea identification is normally straightforward. Degree of contrast between head and mantle, colour of uppertail-coverts and underwing pattern are essential criteria to record. At close range bill colour a useful confirmatory character. Beware especially those larger *Puffinus* spp. with white underparts.

96 STREAKED SHEARWATER
other: White-faced Shearwater
Calonectris leucomelas

PLATE 29 Fig. 96

MAP 96

Length 48cm (19in.). Wingspan 122cm (48in.). Iris brown. Bill horn-coloured, tip greyish. Legs/feet flesh pink.

NW Pacific Ocean; occasionally wanders with more migratory species. Sexes alike; no seasonal variation although during moult white tips over tail sometimes form conspicuous white horseshoe. Juveniles and adults alike. No subspecies.

PLUMAGE: Head Forehead, lores and crown mostly white, imparting white-faced aspect, remainder mainly white with blackish streaks, heaviest on nape; chin and throat white. **Body** Upperparts brownish-grey with greyish-buff fringes; white tips to long tail-coverts may form indistinct band over tail. Underparts white. **Wings** Upperwing as upperparts but darker and browner in tone. Underwing white, with narrow brown margins and tip. **Tail** Blackish-grey; wedge-shaped.

FHJ: A large shearwater; at distance appears grey-brown above, white below, with whitish face and dark nape. Flight recalls Cory's Shearwater, languid but purposeful with loose, rather angled wings. Gregarious; flocks numbering many thousands congregate off natal islands and in winter quarters; migrates in small flocks.

DM: Breeds Japanese coastal islands from Hokkaido S to Kyushu; also off northern China and Korea, from Izu Is to Bonins and on the Pescadores. Returns to colonies Feb/Mar; egg-dates May/Jun; departure and fledging Oct/Nov with very few N of 20°S in NW Pacific by Dec. Some winter off northern Borneo but most pass from S China Sea through Sula Sea to reach main wintering area off New Guinea, where flocks of many thousands occur Nov–Feb. Often associates with other, more migratory species, thus increasing potential for long-distance vagrancy. Recent sightings of individuals suggest that small numbers probably occur regularly off eastern Australia S to Gabo I., Victoria (38°S), in association with Flesh-footed Shearwaters (see Barton 1978a). More intriguing are three recent records off California, USA, during Oct (see Roberson 1980). These Australian and American records plus RNBWS reports suggest that this species wanders further S and E than at present realised. Occasionally strays through Malacca Straits W to Maldives, with specimens collected Sri Lanka, but extent of westwards penetration into Indian Ocean unknown.

SS: White face combined with streaked hindcrown and nape diagnostic. See Pink-footed, Wedge-tailed and Buller's Shearwaters (p. 257, p. 259, p. 260).

97 CORY'S SHEARWATER
other: Mediterranean Shearwater
Calonectris diomedea

PLATE 29 Fig. 97
MAP 97

Length 46–53cm (18–21in.). Wingspan 111cm (44in.). Iris brown. Bill horn-yellow, tip dusky. Legs/feet flesh-pink.

Mediterranean Sea and Atlantic Ocean, dispersing into western Indian Ocean during austral summer. Range overlaps with Great Shearwater and Grey Petrel (p. 258, p. 254). Sexes alike; no seasonal variation but off South Africa, in late summer, many show incredible abrasion and bleaching, appearing pale, creamy-brown (Sinclair, pers. comm.). Juveniles and adults alike. Three subspecies listed; *C.d. edwardsii* averages smaller with blackish bill, darker head and upperparts. Albinism occasionally reported.

PLUMAGE: Head Mostly greyish-brown merging into white chin and throat without obvious demarcation. **Body** Upperparts greyish-brown; long uppertail-coverts occasionally tipped white, forming indistinct horseshoe over tail. Underparts white. **Wings** Upperwing greyish-brown; primaries and secondaries darker. Underwing mostly white with narrow brownish margins and dark wingtip. **Tail** Blackish-grey.

FHJ: Resembles Great Shearwater (p. 258) in size but flight more languid with broad wings held looser, more flexed, with characteristic bow from carpal to wingtip particularly noticeable when seen flying head on. During feeding, several deep wingbeats are usually followed by low, long glide, with an occasional upwards loop or circle, before returning to previous course. This seemingly lazy flight can, in fact, be very fast. Feeds more from the wing than Great Shearwater, skimming along over surface and dipping or executing shallow surface-dives from up to about 10m. Unlike that species appears rather featureless at sea, lacking distinct capped effect and broad white band over tail. Follows ships; attends trawlers.

DM: *C.d. diomedea* breeds at many Mediterranean Is; *C.d. borealis* at Azores, Madeira, Canary and Berlenga Is; *C.d. edwardsii* at Cape Verde Is. Nominate race returns to colonies from late Feb with peak figure passing Gibraltar during Mar, 3,600 per hour (Garcia 1971); egg-dates May/Jun; fledging and dispersal Aug/Sep with main exodus through Straits of Gibraltar during Oct/Nov peaking at 26,272 per day (Telleria 1980). During northern summer and autumn occurs regularly W to Atlantic coast of North America from New England N to about 50°N, with flocks peaking at 2,000 plus in Nov; scarcer in NE Atlantic but occasionally occurs in thousands in southern Irish Sea during summer and autumn. Most move S in late autumn to winter off Namibia and South Africa, where regular E to Natal. Contrary to popular belief many disperse into western Indian Ocean with a few progressing E to at least 73°34′E, 39°01′S (Harrison 1978a), and S to Marion I. 46°50′S, 37°45′E (Williams & Burger 1978). More intriguing is their recent appearance in northern Red Sea, where small flocks off Elat (including several flying inland at nightfall) could indicate circuitous route back to Mediterranean after migrating N in wrong ocean (Norman & Raynor, pers. comm.). Small numbers extend westwards across southern Atlantic to seas off Brazil and Uruguay. Non-breeders may remain in southern latitudes throughout year. Vagrant E to New Zealand.

SS: See notes under Great Shearwater and Grey Petrel (p. 258, p. 254).

Genus *PUFFINUS*

About 17 species comprising small to medium-large shearwaters occurring in both hemispheres and all oceans. As with genus *Pterodroma*, few groups engender such fierce arguments, even among experts, as to number of recognisable species. In anticipation of future taxonomic revisions each recognisable form is treated separately in this guide. Sexes alike; no seasonal variation but feather wear and active moult may cause temporary instability in plumage patterns. Some species polymorphic.

Shearwaters nest in vast colonies from sea-level cliffs to snow-covered mountain tops and forests; they normally return to land under cover of darkness. Many species undertake long migrations and are highly social, often forming dense feeding rafts on sea. They feed from surface or by underwater pursuit, entering water from air or surface, normally to no great depth but I have recovered several Sooty Shearwater corpses from crayfish pots set at over 20 fathoms off New Zealand.

At sea identification can be problematical, particularly in the all-dark forms when jizz and flight characters often the only criteria on which to base specific identity (these characters fully appreciated only with comparative experience). In all sightings colour of head, and rump or uppertail-coverts, plus acurate details of underwing margins essential if specific identification to be made. Bill and leg colour are additional confirmatory characters to record.

98 PINK-FOOTED SHEARWATER
Puffinus creatopus

PLATE 29 Fig. 98
MAP 98

Length 48cm (19in.). Wingspan 109cm (43in.). Iris brown. Bill pinkish to pinkish-yellow, tip dusky. Legs/feet pink.

Breeds off Chile, migrating N to western North America. Range overlaps with Buller's and Wedge-tailed Shearwaters (p. 260, p. 259). Sexes alike; no seasonal variation. Juveniles and adults alike. No subspecies, although some authors consider *creatopus* a southern form of Flesh-footed Shearwater (p. 258).

PLUMAGE: Head Mostly greyish-brown, merging into whitish chin and throat. **Body** Upperparts uniform grey-brown. Underparts mainly white; flanks and undertail-coverts mottled brownish. **Wings** Upperwing mostly uniform grey-brown; primaries and secondaries darker. Underwing: coverts mottled grey and white, with broad, ill-defined dark margins and tip. **Tail** Blackish-brown. NOTE: Extent of mottling on underwing and flanks variable.

FHJ: Large, variably plumaged species. Flight languid and unhurried with slow wingbeats interspersed with low glides; in high winds swifter and stronger, banking in high broad arcs. Solitary or gregarious, often with other migratory species; prefers shallow shelf water.

DM: Eastern Pacific; breeds Mocha and Juan Fernandez Is off Chile. Returns to colonies Nov/Dec; egg-dates Dec/Jan; fledging and dispersal begins Mar/Apr, birds moving N along western coasts of South America towards North America. Present off California and Oregon Apr–Nov, some moving N to Gulf of Alaska; peak figures occur from late Jul to late Oct, only a few remaining during winter months. Stragglers W to Hawaiian and Line Is.

SS: Beware double dark morph Northern Fulmar (p. 235) off NW America. On migration present species' range overlaps with Wedge-tailed Shearwater (p. 259): beware especially pale morph of Western Mexico, very similar in appearance including variable mottling on underwing-coverts and flanks; present species much heavier and broader-winged with more lumbering flight (Stallcup, pers. comm.). See also Black-vented Shearwater (p. 264).

---

99 FLESH-FOOTED SHEARWATER
other: Pale-footed Shearwater
Puffinus carneipes

PLATE 30 Fig. 99

MAP 99

Length 41–45cm (16–18in.). Wingspan 99–106cm (39–42in.). Iris brown. Bill pale horn, culmen and tip black. Legs/feet flesh-pink.

Indian and Pacific Oceans; range overlaps with Wedge-tailed Shearwater and Parkinson's Petrel (p. 259, p. 255). Sexes alike; no seasonal variation. Adults and juveniles alike. No subspecies. Considered con-specific with Pink-footed Shearwater (p. 257) by some authors.

PLUMAGE: Head and Body Wholly brownish-black. **Wings** Similar, but blackish primaries on upperwing form dark 'triangles' at wingtips in good light. Underwing mostly very dark brown; in good light bases of primaries silvery (see Fig. 8, p. 259).

FHJ: Large broad-winged species resembling Pink-footed Shearwater in jizz. Flight progression slow, unhurried, long glides on stiff wings broken by slow effortless flaps, wings rising and falling well above and below body. In higher winds flight assumes typical shearwater careening. Dives well; also feeds by skimming surface with pink feet extended to tread water between shallow belly-flops; often gregarious at sea.

DM: Transequatorial migrant with populations in two main localities, migrating to separate regions. In SW Pacific Ocean breeds Lord Howe I., and offshore islands of New Zealand from Hen and Chicken Is S to Cook Strait. Returns to colonies late Sep; egg-dates Nov/Dec; fledging and departure Apr/May moving N into Pacific past Japan to winter N of subtropical convergence. Some move E to western North America, where a few recorded annually Jul–Dec from British Columbia S to California. Status off Baja California requires clarification; past records may refer to Parkinson's Petrel (see Jehl 1974). In Indian Ocean breeds St Paul I. and islands off southern coast of Western Australia from Cape Leeuwin to Recherche Archipelago; breeding and departure as for Pacific breeders but moves W across Indian Ocean to Mascarenes and Seychelles to winter in Arabian Sea; some occur S to Agulhas Current off South Africa, more rarely to Benguela Current. Some non-breeders of both groups remain in wintering quarters throughout year.

SS: Larger than Short-tailed and Sooty Shearwaters (p. 261, p. 260) with darker underwing and diagnostic bill. From slightly smaller but broad winged dark phase. Wedge-tailed Shearwater p. 259) by bill and underwing colour and by wings held straighter, not bowed and well forward. White-chinned Petrel (p. 255) larger, heavier-billed, and feet project slightly beyond tail. See also juvenile Heermann's Gull (p. 331) if off California.

---

100 GREAT SHEARWATER
other: Greater Shearwater
Puffinus gravis

PLATE 29 Figs 100a-100b

MAP 100

Length 46–53cm (18–21in.). Wingspan 100–111cm ($39\frac{1}{2}$–44in.). Iris brown. Bill black. Legs flesh, outer webs brown.

Atlantic Ocean; range overlaps with Cory's Shearwater and Black-capped Petrel (p. 257, p. 239). Sexes alike; no seasonal variation, but during moult (Jul/Aug) most show white across upperwing-coverts. Juveniles as adults although somewhat greyer with paler feather edgings; photographs supplied by Kellow (pers. comm.) showed some (juveniles?) off Bermuda with wholly brown hindnecks. No subspecies.

PLUMAGE: Head Cap brown (appears black at sea); remainder, including hindneck, mostly white. **Body** Upperparts: mantle, back, scapulars and short uppertail-coverts dark greyish-brown faintly edged grey-buff; long uppertail-coverts white, forming conspicuous horseshoe over tail. Underparts mostly white except for brownish sides of breast, blackish-brown belly patch and undertail-coverts. **Wings** Upperwing: primaries, their coverts, and secondaries blackish; remainder as upperparts. Underwing mostly white; coverts marked with brown, forming broken diagonal across coverts. **Tail** Blackish.

FHJ: A large, powerful species. Flight strong and purposeful with quick beats, wings held more stiffly than Cory's Shearwater (p. 257) and usually straighter, not bowed; in high winds rapid and bounding. Attends trawlers, where noisy and aggressive sounding like fighting cats. Often plunge-dives from the air, 6–10m above surface; also pursuit-dives from surface.

DM: Breeds in southern Atlantic Ocean at Nightingale and Inaccessible Is, Tristan da Cunha; and at Gough I. Numbers apparently increasing, some estimates of numbers on Nightingale I. having risen from 2 to 4 million. A pair found breeding at Kidney I., Falklands, may represent a hitherto unknown small colony (Woods 1975) or, equally, the beginning of a range expansion. Returns to colonies Sep onwards; egg-dates Nov; fledging and dispersal of juveniles begins May. Adults begin transequatorial migration in Apr, moving NW to eastern littoral of South America, and then N passing Bermuda May–Jul (Pellow, pers. comm.) to reach Grand Banks area off Newfoundland Jul/Aug. Many penetrate N to about 66°N before moving eastwards past Greenland to NE Atlantic sector, where relatively abundant off SW Ireland Sep/Oct; casual off Scandinavia and in North Sea. Most have departed from North Atlantic by Nov, but there appears to be a non-breeder staging area in western North Atlantic during late autumn with flocks of up to 200,000 off Cape Cod, Massachusetts (Powers and van Os 1979). Only Pacific record is of single bird in Monterey Bay, California, Feb 1979 (see Roberson 1980). Has been recorded W of Strait of Magellan.

SS: Separated from Cory's Shearwater (p. 257) by distinctly capped appearance, white nape, band over tail and different underwing pattern; dark belly patch difficult to observe at sea but, if seen, diagnostic. Off eastern North America Black-capped Petrel (p. 239) has broad white rump patch, different underwing pattern and fast, swooping flight. Beware distant views of Northern Fulmar (p. 235), see notes under that species.

101 WEDGE-TAILED SHEARWATER
Puffinus pacificus

PLATE 30 Figs 101a-101b
MAP 101

Length 41–46cm (16–18in.). Wingspan 97–104cm (38–41in.). Iris brown. Bill dark grey. Legs/feet flesh-white.

Tropical Pacific and Indian Oceans; range overlaps with Flesh-footed and Pink-footed Shearwaters (p. 258, p. 257). Sexes alike; no seasonal variation but upperwing-coverts sometimes wear paler. Juveniles and adults alike. No subspecies; polymorphic, occurs in two colour morphs with individual variation (beware!).

DARK MORPH: Wholly blackish-brown, primaries and tail darker.

PALE-MORPH: Head Crown, nape and sides of face brown, chin and throat white. **Body** Upperparts paler brown than in dark morph. Underparts mostly white, sides of breast, flanks and undertail-coverts mottled with brown. **Wings** Upperwing as dark morph. Underwings mostly white; axillaries and margins brown. **Tail** Brown.

FHJ: Fairly large shearwater; experienced observers will notice bowed wings held slightly above body and well forward to impart characteristic jizz. Wings broad, particularly secondaries, primaries short, rounded at tip. Tail shape not reliable character though imparting more slender appearance to body. Flight in ±F5 or below drifting, unhurried, with slow flaps followed by short upward glide before banking down to water; often circles at low speed; in higher winds swifter, bounding, wings remaining bowed and well forward.

DM: Tropical Pacific and Indian Oceans, breeding in former from Pescadores (near Taiwan) and Bonin and Volcano Is throughout most of tropical and subtropical Pacific from Barrier Reef islands of Australia E to Revilla Gigedo Is off Mexico and SW to Pitcairn group. In Indian Ocean sector breeds off Madagascar, Seychelles, Amirante, Mascarene, Cargados Carajos Shoals, Chagos Archipelago, Cocos (Keeling) Is and on islands off Western Australia. Egg-dates vary with locality. Tropical populations probably non-migratory. Some subtropical populations range widely throughout tropical parts of Indian and Pacific Oceans. Distribution probably linked with preference for warm water. Now recorded annually off South Africa (Sinclair, pers. comm.).

SS: Differs from Flesh-footed Shearwater (p. 258) in bill colour, darker underwing shafts, broad bases to wings and characteristic buoyant, drifting flight with wings held bowed and well forward. From Jouanin's Petrel (p. 254) by flight, jizz and much larger size, longer grey bill and pale legs. Pale phase differs from Buller's Shearwater (p. 260) by lack of cap, uniform upperparts and underwing markings. Range overlaps with larger, broader-winged Pink-footed Shearwater (p. 257) off W Mexico.

Fig. 8. *P. carneipes* has whitish bases to underside of primaries, and in flight wings normally held straighter. By comparison *P. pacificus* has wholly dark underwing and holds wings bowed and well forward. If seen, bill colour of *P. carneipes* diagnostic

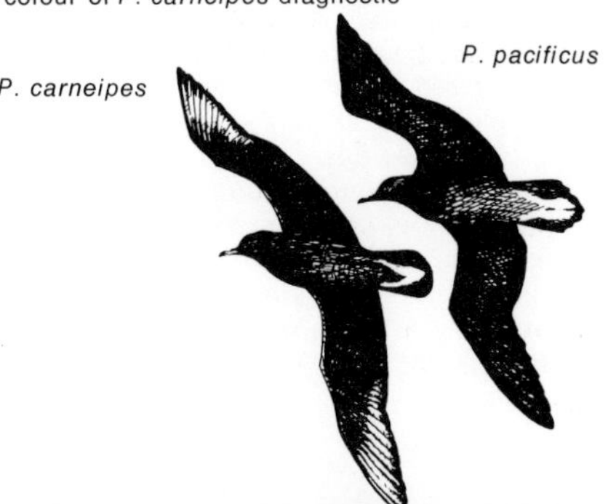

102 BULLER'S SHEARWATER **PLATE 28 Fig. 102**
other: New Zealand/Grey-backed Shearwater
Puffinus bulleri MAP 102

Length 46cm (18in.). Wingspan 97cm (38in.). Iris brown. Bill blue-black, darker at tip. Legs/feet pinkish, black at extremities.

Breeds New Zealand sector, migrating E across Pacific to the Americas. Range overlaps with Pink-footed and Wedge-tailed Shearwaters (p. 257, p. 259). Sexes alike; no seasonal variation. Juveniles and adults alike. No subspecies.

PLUMAGE: Head Blackish-brown cap; remainder white. **Body** Upperparts mostly brownish-grey, edged buff-grey, imparting frosted appearance shading to blackish-brown across rump. Underparts white. **Wings** Upperwing greyish-brown with conspicuously pale greater coverts, and striking, blackish W pattern linked across rump (an excellent character found in no other shearwater). Underwing white with narrow blackish margins. **Tail** Blackish.

FHJ: Large, slender-bodied shearwater with strikingly patterned underparts and graceful, measured flight. Jizz recalls Wedge-tailed Shearwater. In low winds flight recalls that of smaller albatrosses, with slow, measured wingbeats and long glides close to surface; in higher winds arcs in graceful, effortless progression with little flapping (a stunning species). Feeds by briefly alighting to pick off the surface or submerge head. Gregarious, often forms small flocks at sea.

DM: Transpacific migrant breeding at Poor Knights Is, New Zealand, where population has undergone massive expansion in recent years. Returns to colonies Aug/Sep; egg-dates Nov/Dec; fledging and dispersal begins Apr, birds moving to Tasman Sea and then E across Pacific. Little known of movements and routes but it occurs from Valparaíso, Chile, N to American Pacific coast, where regular off California from late Jun through Nov. Range extends N to Oregon, Washington and British Columbia; occasionally Alaska. Numbers vary year to year, apparently governed by water temperature and salinity; peak count off Oregon up to about 1,000 per day. Small numbers remain in NE Pacific throughout northern winter. Not recorded in Australia until 1954; since then several found in burrows on islands off New South Wales but breeding not yet proved (see Serventy *et al.* 1971). Some remain S during austral winter (Fullagar and van Tets, pers. comm.)

SS: Boldly patterned upper surfaces contrasting with white underparts separate this species from all other Pacific shearwaters. Beware *Pterodroma externa* group (p. 246).

103 SOOTY SHEARWATER **PLATE 30 Fig. 103**
Puffinus griseus MAP 103

Length 40–46cm (16–18in.). Wingspan 94–104cm (37–41in.). Iris brown. Bill dark grey. Legs/feet blackish-grey.

Wide-ranging in Pacific and Atlantic Oceans; range overlaps with Short-tailed Shearwater and Great-winged Petrel (p. 261, p. 237). See also Kerguelen Petrel (p. 242) and, in North Atlantic, Balearic Shearwater (p. 263). Sexes alike; no seasonal variation. Juveniles and adults alike. Partial albinism occasionally reported; beware especially symmetrically partial albinistic Sooty Shearwaters, which can suggest Cape Petrel (p. 236) (Stallcup 1976).

PLUMAGE: Head and Body Mostly sooty-brown; chin and throat greyer, underparts slightly paler. **Wings** Upperwing mostly sooty-brown, primaries and secondaries darker. Underwing brownish-black with silvery coverts, variable in extent, normally showing as white wing-flash; atypical shows mostly grey underwing (see Short-tailed Shearwater, p. 261). **Tail** Blackish-brown.

FHJ: Wings long, narrow, with back-swept posture and rather heavy body imparting characteristic jizz. Flight normally strong and direct, two to eight quick, stiff-winged flaps on ascending tack followed by long glide; in higher winds fast and careening. A gregarious species often seen in huge, loose flocks during migration in Pacific, less so N Atlantic. Plunges head first from about 1 m with wings open, submerging for short periods. Does not normally follow ships; attends trawlers.

DM: Transequatorial migrant in Pacific and Atlantic Oceans. Breeds off South America at Staten, Wollaston and Deceit Is near Cape Horn; perhaps also on islands off southern Chile. In Australasian region small numbers breed on islands off New South Wales and SE Tasmania. Principal colonies situated off New Zealand at Snares, Auckland, Campbell, Chatham, Antipodes and Stewart Is, and islets in Foveaux Strait; smaller numbers at Macquarie I. Returns to colonies Sep–Nov; egg-dates Nov/Dec; fledging and departure Mar–May. Most South American breeders depart N into Pacific reaching Monterey Bay, California, where commonest shearwater Jul–Nov when flocks of several million often seen from shore. Many continue N to Alaska. Return migration begins Aug, peak numbers off Ecuador and Peru Oct/Nov. Proportionately fewer migrate northwards along eastern South America to reach Atlantic coasts of USA and Canada in Jun. Disperses eastwards across N Atlantic Jul; present European waters Aug–Nov, with peak daily figures off NW Spain (Estacia de Bares) around 3,000 (Huyskens & Maes 1971). Small numbers recently recorded E Mediterranean Aug–Dec (H Shirihai, pers. comm.). Australasian breeders move rapidly N and E past Japan to reach Alaska Jul/Aug. Non-breeders occasionally remain N of Equator in both oceans. Common inshore migrant off western South Africa but origins unclear; most likely from South America but may also be non-breeders observed moving W along Australian Antarctic coast in late summer

(see Serventy *et al.* 1971). Now recorded almost annually Elat, northern Red Sea (Krabbe 1979), suggesting hitherto unknown movements of small numbers into northern Indian Ocean. Some may remain S during austral winter (see Fullagar & van Tets 1976).
SS: See notes under Short-tailed Shearwater (p. 261). Does not bound in such high broad arcs as Great-winged Petrel (p. 237), which has stubby bill, broader wings, darker underwing. See also Flesh-footed and dark phase Wedge-tailed Shearwaters (p. 258, p. 259). In North Atlantic dark race of Manx Shearwater *P. puffinus mauretanicus* (p. 263) as large, sometimes as dark, as *P. griseus* but underparts show some white with dark undertail-coverts; wings appear shorter, less swept back. See also notes under skuas/jaegers (p. 323).

104 SHORT-TAILED SHEARWATER
other: Slender-billed Shearwater
Puffinus tenuirostris

PLATE 30 Fig. 104
MAP 104

Length 41–43cm (16–17in.). Wingspan 97–100cm (38–39½in.). Iris brown. Bill, legs/feet blackish-grey.

Breeds off southern Australia, migrating N to Alaska and western coasts of North America. Range overlaps with Sooty Shearwater and Great-winged Petrel (p. 260, p. 237). Sexes alike; no seasonal variation but plumage may wear rather grey with faint capped appearance on crown. No subspecies. Partial albinism recorded.
PLUMAGE: Head and Body Mostly sooty-brown, underparts slightly paler. **Wings** Upperwing: sooty-brown, primaries and secondaries darker. Underwing normally brownish-black with dull grey coverts but variable, some with whiter coverts (beware Sooty Shearwater, p. 260). **Tail** Blackish-brown.
FHJ: Gregarious, resembling Sooty Shearwater in habits and jizz. At close range bill shorter than that species. Sometimes follows boats.
DM: Pacific transequatorial migrant; breeds in huge numbers Bass Strait, and off Tasmania, New South Wales, Victoria and S Australia; perhaps also in W Australia in Recherche Archipelago (Fullagar & van Tets, pers. comm.). Returns to colonies late Sep; egg-dates Nov/Dec; fledging and departure Apr/May, moving rapidly NE into Pacific past Japan to reach main wintering area off Aleutian Is mid May/Jun. Some move N to Bering and Chukchi Seas; common Bering Strait Jul, occurring off Barrow till late Sep. Small numbers move E to western coasts of North America, where uncommon from Washington S to California, most occurring Nov–Feb (Stallcup 1976). A few non-breeders remain in Alaskan waters throughout winter to 30°N. Rapid return movement mainly through central Pacific, beginning Sep and completing vast figure-of-8 movement to reach Australian coast Oct/Nov, where peak counts 60,000 per hour off New South Wales (Carter & Barton, in Fullagar 1978). Stragglers have reached India, Macquarie I. and west coast of New Zealand. Status off W Thailand, where known from two birds captured live at sea off Phuket I., requires clarification; fishermen report that this (or dark shearwater of some species) occurs off W Thailand in reasonable numbers (P Round, pers. comm.; see also Frith 1978).
SS: Difficult to separate from Sooty Shearwater (p. 260) at any range. Main diagnostic feature is shorter bill and, usually, greyer underwing-coverts (Fullagar & van Tets, pers. comm.). In winter quarters Short-tailed appear darker, more evenly coloured than Sooty, some with indistinct caps and whitish chins. See also Wedge-tailed, Flesh-footed Shearwaters and Great-winged Petrel (p. 259, p. 258, p. 237).

105 HEINROTH'S SHEARWATER
Puffinus (lherminieri) heinrothi

PLATE 31 Fig. 105
MAP 105

Length 27cm (10½in.). Wingspan not recorded. Iris brown. Bill blackish. Legs/feet flesh-pink.

Known only from seas off Rabaul, New Britain, tropical western Pacific Ocean; range probably overlaps with migrating Short-tailed Shearwaters (p. 261). Sexes probably alike; no seasonal variation but marked individual variation in amount of white on underparts. Juveniles and adults alike. A little-known species; the following descriptions are based on notes supplied by Dr G Mauersberger (pers. comm.) after examination of six skins in the Berlin Museum (including the type specimen). No subspecies but considered conspecific with Audubon's Shearwater by some authors.
PLUMAGE: Head Sooty-brown; chin and throat sometimes greyer. **Body** Upperparts sooty-brown. Underparts variable; either wholly sooty-brown (a little paler than upperparts), or with small white tips across lower breast forming distinct patch, which, in one specimen, extended to lower belly. Undertail-coverts in all types sooty-brown. **Wings** Upperwing sooty-brown. Underwing white with variable dark margins and tip.
FHJ: Unknown.
DM: Known only from seas near Rabaul, New Britain. Breeding islands as yet undiscovered but Dr Mayr (pers. comm.) reports that 'one recently flew into a light in a mountain village on Bougainville, Solomon Islands, and there seems little doubt that it breeds there'. Breeding dates and pelagic distribution unknown.
SS: Combination of small size, white on underwing and (if present) on belly should impart appearance distinct from transient Short-tailed Shearwater (p. 261).

106 CHRISTMAS SHEARWATER *Puffinus nativitatis*

PLATE 31 Fig. 106
MAP 106

Length 35–38cm (14–15in.). Wingspan 71–81cm (28–32in.). Iris brown. Bill, legs/feet black.

North and central Pacific Ocean, where range overlaps with transient Sooty and Short-tailed Shearwaters (p. 260, p. 261). See also larger Wedge-tailed Shearwater (p. 259). Sexes alike; no seasonal variation. Juveniles and adults alike. No subspecies.

PLUMAGE: Wholly sooty-brown.

FHJ: Slender-bodied shearwater, with short, rounded tail; relatively shorter and less pointed wings than Short-tailed Shearwater, and comparatively long slender bill (Naveen, pers. comm.). Flight light and buoyant with rather fast, stiff wingbeats followed by long glides close to surface.

DM: Pacific Ocean, breeding at Hawaiian Is and North West Chain including Laysan and Wake Is, and at Marcus, Christmas, Phoenix, Marquesas, Tuamotu, Austral, Pitcairn and Easter Is. Egg-dates Apr–Jul; period of fledging unknown. Pelagic dispersal poorly understood; probably only to adjacent seas but known to be absent from breeding area during contra-nuptial season. Thus sightings of small, wholly dark shearwaters off Mollendo, southern Peru (RA Hughes, pers. comm.), could be of this species from Easter Is (27°S 109°W), some 3,200km W of South American littoral.

SS: Resembles Sooty and Short-tailed Shearwaters (p. 260, p. 261) but smaller with dark brown underwing, more rounded wingtip and lower, less careening flight. Separated from dark phase Wedge-tailed Shearwater (p. 259) by much smaller size, shorter tail and stiffer, faster wingbeats.

107 MANX SHEARWATER *Puffinus puffinus puffinus*

PLATE 32 Fig. 107
MAP 107

Length 30–38cm (12–15in.). Wingspan 76–89cm (30–35in.). Iris brown. Bill blackish. Legs/feet pink with black markings.

North Atlantic, migrating S in winter; range overlaps with Sooty, Little and Audubon's Shearwaters (p. 260, p. 265, p. 266). Sexes alike; no seasonal variation. Juveniles and adults alike. Taxonomy highly complex and not fully agreed upon. There are six 'forms', all distinguishable at sea, and which were first united as a single ('allopatric') species by Murphy (1952). There is growing opinion, based on differences in breeding biology (e.g. *opisthomelas* is a winter breeder whilst nearby *auricularis* is a spring breeder), in favour of splitting the group into two or more species. See Jehl (1974). In anticipation of future revision on status, each form is described separately below beginning with nominate *P.p. puffinus*. Partial albinism recorded (Harris, in Cramp & Simmons 1977).

PLUMAGE: Head Mostly blackish, extending to include lores and ear-coverts; chin and throat white, extending upwards on sides of neck behind ear-coverts. **Body** Upperparts blackish. Underparts mostly white; sides of breast mottled grey-black, thighs black, undertail-coverts sometimes lightly spotted black. **Wings** Upperwing blackish. Underwing mostly white; wingtip and trailing edge blackish with small dusky mark on carpal and variable mottling on axillaries. **Tail** Black above, white below. NOTE: Black upperparts wear to brownish-black.

FHJ: Commonest West Palearctic shearwater. In low or moderate winds flight consists of rapid, stiff-winged shallow strokes followed by shearing glide low over wave contours, rising and falling, banking from side to side, alternately showing black upperside then white underside. In high winds capable of fast sustained banking and gliding, rising up to 10m above waves with only occasional bursts of wing action. Gregarious; swims buoyantly and dives freely. Forages at some distance from breeding islands, returning to congregate offshore late afternoon/evening. Does not normally follow ships; attends trawlers.

DM: North Atlantic: breeds Westmann Is, southern Iceland; Faeroes; off Scotland at Shetland, Orkney and Inner Hebrides; off Wales at Skokholm and Skomer (smaller British colonies at Anglesey, Caernarvonshire, and Scilly Isles); off SW Ireland at Blaskets, and Puffin Is, Co Kerry, with smaller colonies off W and NE Ireland; also off France at Molène archipelago, Brittany, and in eastern Atlantic at Azores and Madeira. Formerly bred Bermuda, western Atlantic; new colony recently discovered off Cape Cod, USA (Finch 1973). Returns to colonies Feb/Mar; egg-dates Apr/May; adults desert juveniles Jul/Aug; juveniles fledge Aug/Sep. Both age groups move S and W to complete rapid southwards migration to main wintering area off eastern South America from about 10°S to 50°S; small numbers move E to Cape seas, South Africa, where a scarce summer visitor off Namibia and Cape Province E to Algoa Bay (Brooke & Sinclair 1978). White-vented *P. puffinus* ssp. have recently been observed off western USA (see Roberson 1980), and it has been suggested that these might be nominate *P.p. puffinus* which have wandered W of Cape Horn and subsequently migrated N in wrong ocean; most southerly records from eastern South America however are at 49°S (Cooke & Mills 1972) and it seems equally, or perhaps more, likely that 'white-vented' types observed off Alaska and California were *P.(p.) newelli* which breeds on Hawaii. Juveniles probably remain in southern hemisphere until their second year. Return migration begins Dec/Jan, passing Bermuda Feb/Mar; 'winter records' during Dec off eastern coasts of N America may refer to early migrants. Small numbers occur regularly off eastern England (Wallace & Bourne 1981), but casual in southern and eastern sectors of North Sea. Vagrant to Australia, New Zealand, West Indies.

SS: See notes under Little and Audubon's Shearwaters (p. 265, p. 266).

107X MANX SHEARWATER (Balearic race)
Puffinus p. mauretanicus

PLATE 32 Fig. 107X
MAP 107X

Length 35–40cm (14–16in.). Wingspan 80–93cm (31½–36½in.). Bare parts as nominate.

Western Mediterranean, moving W and N up coasts of Europe after breeding; range overlaps with transient Sooty Shearwater (p. 260). Sexes alike; no seasonal variation but marked individual variation. Juveniles and adults alike. For taxonomy see notes under Manx Shearwater (p. 262).

PLUMAGE: Head Mostly dusky-brown, merging without demarcation into dusky-white chin and throat. Lacks whitish crescent on side of neck. **Body** Upperparts dusky-brown. Underparts variable, some dusky-white with variable brownish mottling on sides of breast, flanks and undertail-coverts; darkest examples have underparts almost wholly brown but usually show scattered white tips on belly. **Wings** Upperwing dusky-brown. Underwing very variable, usually dusky-white with brownish tip, trailing edge and axillaries; some almost as dark as Sooty Shearwater (p. 260). **Tail** Brown.

FHJ: Slightly larger and heavier than nominate; lacks sharp contrast between brown upperparts and variably white underparts. Pattern often suggests larger Sooty Shearwater (p. 260), but latter has proportionately heavier body and longer, narrow or scythe-like wings, and stronger flight.

DM: Breeds Balearic Is, western Mediterranean Sea. Egg-dates Mar onwards. After breeding disperses into greater part of Mediterranean before entering Atlantic; some move N reaching Irish Sea and English Channel Jul–Oct, with a few N to Scotland, Denmark and Norway. Darker forms appear to predominate in late autumn although significance not understood (pers. obs.).

SS: Darker forms can appear almost identical to Sooty Shearwater (p. 260). See notes above on jizz difference; most individuals of present species, however, retain some white tips on underparts. See also Manx Shearwater (Levantine race, p. 263).

107Y MANX SHEARWATER (Levantine race)
P.p. yelkouan

PLATE 32 Fig. 107Y
MAP 107Y

Size and bare parts as nominate.

Mediterranean; range overlaps with breeding *P.p. mauretanicus* and Cory's Shearwaters (p. 263, p. 257). Sexes alike; no seasonal variation although upperparts wear browner. Juveniles and adults alike. For taxonomy see notes under Manx Shearwater (p. 262).

PLUMAGE: Pattern as nominate *P.p. puffinus* (p. 262); differs in browner upperparts; brown wash to flanks, undertail- and underwing-coverts.

FHJ: As nominate but appears brown and white, not black and white.

DM: Breeds central and eastern Mediterranean at islets off Elba, Sardinia, Malta, Sicily, Yugoslavia, Crete, and off Greece in Aegean Sea. May breed Marmara (Cramp & Simmons 1977). Dispersal not fully known; generally throughout Mediterranean W to Gibraltar, where many moult Aug/Sep; few, if any, emerge into Atlantic. Thought to move eastwards back into Mediterranean from Sep onwards; regular in varying numbers off Libya Dec–Mar (Bundy 1950).

SS: See notes under Sooty, Little and Audubon's Shearwaters (p. 260, p. 265, p. 266). See also Manx Shearwater (Balearic race, p. 263).

---

108 FLUTTERING SHEARWATER
Puffinus gavia

PLATE 32 Fig. 108
MAP 108

Length 31–36cm (12–14in.). Wingspan 76cm (30in.). Iris blackish. Bill greyish-black. Legs/feet brown, marked flesh-white.

Breeds New Zealand, dispersing W to Australia; range overlaps with Hutton's and Little Shearwaters (p. 264, p. 265). Sexes alike; no seasonal variation but upperparts usually fade to rich rusty-brown (see Hutton's Shearwater, p. 264). Juveniles and adults alike. No subspecies.

PLUMAGE: Head Mostly dark greyish-brown, extending well below eye and merging without demarcation into dusky-white chin and throat. **Body** Upperparts mostly dark brown; white flanks extend upwards to sides of rump, imparting narrow, brown-backed appearance. Underparts mainly white except for conspicuous brown thigh patch and brownish wash on sides of body. **Wings** Upperwing dark brown. Underwing mostly greyish-white; tip and trailing edge brown, axillaries dusky-grey. **Tail** Dark brown. NOTE: In worn plumage (Nov–Jan) upperparts rusty-brown.

FHJ: Averages smaller than Manx Shearwater. Differs from Hutton's Shearwater (p. 264) in browner upperparts and whiter underparts which, at distance, appear to have definite demarcation below eye. At close range sides of face, neck and axillaries mottled grey. Often difficult to separate from Little Shearwater (p. 265) at sea, but appears brown and white with broader wings, less 'aukish' jizz, dark sides of face, and longer bill. Flight also higher with more typical banking and shearing and deeper, slower, less jerky wing strokes. Often enters small sounds and creeks, where spends much time sitting on water.

DM: Breeds in New Zealand at many islands from Three Kings S to Cook Strait. Returns to colonies Aug/Sep; egg-dates Sep/Oct. Adults probably disperse only to adjacent waters; juveniles fledge Feb/Mar and appear to disperse W and N across Tasman Sea to coasts of Australia from Tasmania E and N to Queensland; some non-breeders remain throughout summer.

SS: Little Shearwater (p. 265) smaller, with proportionately shorter wings, faster wingbeats, and is black and white with definite demarcation at or above eye (but see *P.a. elegans* p. 265). See under that species for flight. Hutton's Shearwater (p. 264) remains consistently blackish-brown throughout year and has darker head, sides of breast and underwing than present species.

109 HUTTON'S SHEARWATER

Puffinus huttoni

PLATE 32 Fig. 109
MAP 109

Length 38cm (15in.). Wingspan 90cm (35½in.). Iris blackish. Bill greyish-black. Legs/feet blackish, marked pink.

Breeds on high mountains of South Island, New Zealand, dispersing W to Australia; range overlaps with Fluttering and Little Shearwaters (p. 263, p. 265). Sexes alike; no seasonal variation (upperparts remain consistently blackish-brown throughout year; see Fluttering Shearwater, p. 263). Juveniles apparently differ from adults in white chin and throat (Harper & Kinsky 1978). No subspecies.

PLUMAGE: Head Mostly blackish-brown, extending well below eye and merging without demarcation into dusky chin and throat. **Body** Upperparts blackish-brown; white flanks extend upwards to sides of rump, imparting narrow, brown-backed appearance. Underparts mainly dull off-white; sides of breast and body brownish with conspicuous dark brown thigh patch. **Wings** Upperwing blackish-brown. Underwing mostly dull greyish; tip and trailing edge brown with brownish axillaries extending to carpal area. **Tail** Blackish-brown.

FHJ: Differs from Fluttering Shearwater (p. 263) in generally darker upperparts, with duller, browner underparts and noticeably dusky underwing. At distance head often appears wholly dark merging gradually into brownish-white throat and upper breast.

DM: Recently discovered breeding above 1,300m on Seaward Kaikoura Range, South Island, New Zealand (see Harrow 1965). Returns to colonies late Aug; egg-dates Nov; fledging and dispersal Feb–Apr. Some probably sedentary, ranging S to Banks Peninsula, occasionally to Foveaux Strait, South Island (pers. obs.). Others appear to move W and N across Tasman Sea to coasts of southern Australia, ranging W to NW Australia and E to New South Wales; some non-breeders may remain there throughout year. May occur Torres Strait.

SS: Fluttering Shearwater (p. 263) has browner upperparts which, in worn plumage, fade to rusty-brown, and whiter underparts and underwing. Little Shearwater (p. 265) smaller, with 'aukish' jizz, pure white underparts and underwing-coverts, whiter face, and shorter bill.

110 NEWELL'S SHEARWATER
other: Manx Shearwater (Hawaiian race)

Puffinus (p.) newelli

PLATE 32 Fig. 110
MAP 110

Length 30–35cm (12–14in.). Wingspan 76–89cm (30–35in.). Iris and bill blackish. Legs/feet blackish, webs pinkish.

Hawaii and adjacent seas, Pacific Ocean; thought to be sedentary; distinctive within range but see Audubon's Shearwater (p. 266). Sexes alike; no seasonal variation. Juveniles and adults alike. For taxonomy see notes under nominate Manx Shearwater (p. 262).

PLUMAGE: Head Mostly black extending to below eye and sides of neck; chin and throat white extending upwards on sides of neck behind ear-coverts. **Body** Upperparts almost black, sides of rump conspicuously white (extension from flanks). Underparts mostly white; sides of breast mottled blackish, thighs black. Some may show mixed black and white on undertail-coverts (Jehl, pers. comm.). **Wings** Upperwing blackish. Underwing mostly pure white, tip and trailing edge black. **Tail** Blackish.

FHJ: Typical low, fast flight of smaller shearwaters. White flanks extend round sides of rump, so that in flight it appears to have a narrow white patch on each side of uppertail; this forms conspicuous field character. Wingbeats slower than Audubon's or Little.

DM (based on Shallenberger 1978): Known to breed only on forested slopes on Kauai and Hawaii. Status and breeding biology largely unknown but thought to breed mainly Apr–Oct, when frequently seen offshore. Dispersal unknown. 'White-vented' *P. puffinus* ssp. seen off Alaska and California (see Roberson 1980) generally suspected as being itinerant *P.p. puffinus* migrating N in wrong ocean, but could also be this 'form' (see notes on p. 262).

SS: Distinctive within known range; Audubon's Shearwater (p. 266) smaller with different jizz, browner upperparts, different underwing and dark undertail-coverts. See also Townsend's and Black-vented Shearwaters (p. 265, p. 264). Present 'form' differs from Manx Shearwater (p. 262) in conspicuous white sides of rump.

111 BLACK-VENTED SHEARWATER

Puffinus opisthomelas

PLATE 32 Fig. 111
MAP 111

Length 30–38cm (12–15in.). Wingspan 76–89cm (30–35in.). Iris and bill blackish. Legs/feet black, webs purplish.

Breeds islands off Baja California, dispersing N and S after breeding; range overlaps with Townsend's, Pink-footed and perhaps Audubon's Shearwaters (p. 265, p. 257, p. 266). Sexes alike; no seasonal differences although marked individual variation. Juveniles and adults alike. For taxonomy see notes under Manx Shearwater (p. 262). The new ABA and AOU checklists now consider this form to be a separate species.

PLUMAGE: Head Dark brown extending well below

eye and merging into dusky chin, throat and foreneck. **Body** Upperparts dark brown. Underparts variable; mostly dull white, with dusky flanks and brownish undertail-coverts merging into white belly without obvious demarcation. In some examples dusky sides of breast extend completely across breast; more rarely underparts uniform greyish with scattered white tips. **Wings** Upperwing brownish. Underwing mostly dull white; tip, trailing edge and axillaries smudgy-brown. **Tail** Brown.

FHJ: Larger and distinctly browner than Townsend's Shearwater (p. 265) without obvious demarcation between brown upperparts and whitish underparts. Underwing pattern can suggest Pink-footed Shearwater (p. 257) but much smaller and slimmer than that species with typical, fast, flutter-and-glide flight low over wave contours and, usually, with whiter underwing.

DM: A winter breeder on islands off Baja California, including San Benito, Natividad and Guadelupe Is. Returns to colonies from Jan onwards; egg-dates Feb/Mar; fledging and dispersal begins Jun/Jul. Most disperse to adjacent Mexican waters although RNBWS sightings (Bourne & Dixon 1975) during Jun and Jan suggest some move S to seas just N of Galapagos Is, where 288 recorded at 13°N 90°W; main dispersal, however, is northwards following the warm Davidson Current along coasts of California N to Monterey Bay, usually from mid Oct to late Nov but numbers and timing irregular and fluctuate with water temperature; during years of high water temperature extends N to Mendicino County, California.

SS: See notes under Townsend's Shearwater (p. 265). Pink-footed Shearwater (p. 257) larger, more heavily built and usually occupies a higher air space, typically banking and soaring in slow leisurely flight—quite unlike fast, contour-hugging flight of present species.

112 TOWNSEND'S SHEARWATER
Puffinus auricularis

PLATE 32 Fig. 112
MAP 112

Length 31–35cm (12–14in.). Wingspan 76cm (30in.). Iris and bill blackish. Legs/feet blackish, webs slightly purple.

Seas off western Mexico; range overlaps with Black-vented and possibly with Audubon's Shearwaters (p. 264, p. 266). Sexes alike; no seasonal variation. Juveniles and adults alike. For taxonomy see notes under Manx Shearwater (p. 262). Following notes are based on material supplied by Jehl (pers. comm.).

PLUMAGE: Head Mostly brownish-black extending below eye and contrasting sharply with white chin, throat and foreneck. **Body** Upperparts mostly brownish-black, sides of rump conspicuously white (extension from flanks). Underparts mainly white; sides of upper breast mottled blackish, thighs and entire undertail-coverts uniform blackish. **Wings** Upperwing blackish-brown. Underwing mostly pure white; wingtip and trailing edge blackish with dusky patch on carpal area.

FHJ: Flight low and fast, with very little gliding. Appears dark-necked at sea, but best field mark is a white patch on flanks extending onto sides of rump and which contrasts strongly with blackish thighs and undertail-coverts.

DM: Restricted to eastern Pacific, breeding off western Mexico at Revilla Gigedo S of Baja California. Egg-dates Apr/May. Thought to be mainly sedentary but reports by RNBWS members (see Bourne & Dixon 1975) indicate a probable dispersal S to 8°N and W to 100°W (seas just north of Galapagos Is).

SS: Black-vented Shearwater (p. 264) slightly larger and always distinctly brownish without clear-cut demarcation between dark upperparts and white underparts; neck often dusky and may extend across entire breast, and underwing has smudgy-brown margins and brownish axillaries. Audubon's Shearwater (p. 266) much browner with different underwing pattern and distinctly different jizz. Present species would differ from nominate *P.p. puffinus* (p. 262) in white sides of rump and wholly black undertail-coverts. Newell's Shearwater (p. 264) differs in less black on sides of breast, white undertail-coverts and even more pronounced white sides to rump.

113 LITTLE SHEARWATER
other: Dusky Shearwater
Puffinus assimilis

PLATE 31 Figs 113a-113c
MAP 113

Length 25–30cm (10–12in.). Wingspan 58–67cm (23–26½in.). Iris brown. Bill black. Legs/feet blue, outer toe and sole black.

Fragmented distribution in all three major oceans, most occurring in southern hemisphere; range overlaps with Audubon's and Manx Shearwaters (p. 266, p. 262). Sexes alike, no seasonal variation. Juveniles and adults alike. Seven or eight subspecies listed, differing mainly in relative blackness or brownness of upperparts and colour of undertail-coverts. *P.a. elegans* has dark cap extending well below level of eye (Plate 31, 113b). Some authors (e.g. Vaurie 1965) have united both Little and Audubon's Shearwaters into a single, worldwide species of small shearwater. At sea, however, the two distinctly different both in appearance and jizz and are thus retained here as separate species. Unless stated, the following notes refer to nominate *assimilis*. Status of *P.(a.) boydi* open to question: formerly treated as a race of Little Shearwater (Cramp & Simmons 1977) but placed with Audubon's Shearwater in Mayr & Cottrell (1979).

PLUMAGE: Head Forehead, crown and hindneck slate or blue-black, remainder mostly white, usually with faint mottling on upper cheeks; division between white and black occurs above eye and imparts white-faced aspect. **Body** Upperparts slate or blue-black. Underparts white. **Wings** Upperwing slate or blue-black. Underwing mostly white with black margins and tip. **Tail** Black.

FHJ: Recalls miniature Manx Shearwater (p. 262) but whiter face and shorter wings impart distinctive 'aukish' jizz. Normal flight in winds below F5 consists of four to six shallow, whirring wingbeats followed by short, low glide, usually with both wingtips parallel to water's surface. This flutter-and-glide flight low over waves markedly different from that of Manx Shearwater, which has slower wingbeats and much longer, banking and twisting glides. In winds above F5 flight can assume more typical shearwater progression with more extensive gliding, banking and sideslipping over wave crests, but characteristically executes low, parallel flutter-and-glide flights down centres of deep troughs. Feeds, usually in small rafts, by pattering across surface with wings raised above back, hanging into wind like a large storm-petrel, and executing shallow surface-dives. Often follows ships.

DM: All three oceans. In North Atlantic *P.a. baroli* breeds Azores, Desertas, Salvage and Canary Is. *P.(a.) boydi* (perhaps better placed with Audubon's Shearwater, p. 266) breeds Cape Verde Is. *P.a. elegans* breeds Tristan da Cunha group and Gough, and on Auckland, Chatham and Antipodes near New Zealand. *P.a. tunneyi* breeds offshore islands of W Australia from Abrolhos group S to Recherche Archipelago; birds breeding St Paul I., Indian Ocean, are doubtfully assigned to this subspecies. *P.a. assimilis* breeds Norfolk and Lord Howe Is. *P.a. kermadecensis* Kermadec Is. *P.a. haurakiensis* breeds islets off E coast North Island, New Zealand. *P.a. myrtae* breeds Rapa I., Austral group. Egg-dates in North Atlantic Feb/Mar; Jun/Jul in Australasian region. Pelagic dispersal not fully known. Formerly thought to disperse only to adjacent waters, with consequent lack of genetic interchange resulting in the high degree of subspeciation (Warham 1958). However, Australian *P.a. tunneyi* occurs nearly as frequently off South Africa as *P.a. elegans* from Tristan da Cunha and Gough I. (Brooke & Sinclair, in prep.), and these (or other) forms relatively common from offshore waters of South Africa S to Marion I. (pers. obs.), where small numbers congregate offshore at dusk although breeding not yet confirmed (Williams & Burger 1978). Distribution and status of this species off South America even more confused. Three collected from a small flock off Chiloe I., Chile, by Dr Jehl, Jun 1970 were first South American Pacific records and may suggest a breeding station in area. Others, including those seen off eastern South America 39°20′S, 56°25′W (Brown *et al.* 1975), may have been Tristan da Cunha breeders. The foregoing thus suggests certain populations, or age classes of populations, may undertake regular movements; this further supported by recent sightings in NW Atlantic off southern Carolina N to Nova Scotia and in North Sea, off Flamborough Head, England (see Wallace & Bourne 1981, who suggest that small numbers of this species may wander within flocks of more migratory Cory's Shearwater).

SS: Audubon's Shearwater larger and longer-billed than present species with proportionately broader wings and thickset body imparting distinctive chunky jizz; differs further in darker face, browner upperparts and dark undertail-coverts (but see *P.(a.) boydi*, Fig. 113c, Plate 31), and in broadly margined underwings. Manx Shearwater (p. 262) differs in flight progression, larger size, darker face, broader trailing edge and darker tip to underwing. With comparative experience, under reasonable conditions, the three species readily separable at sea. *P.a. elegans* (Fig 113b, Plate 31) has dark cap exending well below eye.

114 AUDUBON'S SHEARWATER (Includes Persian and Baillon's Shearwater)

PLATE 31 Figs 114a-114b

Puffinus lherminieri

MAP 114

Length 30cm (12in.). Wingspan 69cm (27in.). Iris brown. Bill black. Legs/feet flesh with outer side blackish.

Tropical oceans; range overlaps with Little and Manx Shearwaters (p. 265, p. 262). Sexes alike; no seasonal variation. Juveniles and adults alike. Taxonomy complex and not fully agreed upon; Audubon's and Little Shearwaters often treated as conspecific. Nine or ten subspecies listed (*P.(a.) boydi* recently placed with this species by Mayr & Cottrell 1979). Birds with intermediate characters are known (see Bourne & Loveridge 1978); melanism reported. Some authors regard Heinroth's Shearwater (p. 261) as conspecific with Audubon's Shearwater.

PLUMAGE: Head Forehead, crown and hindneck brown, remainder mostly white, the division between white and brown occurring at or just below eye and spreading to sides of face and neck. **Body** Upperparts brown. Underparts mostly white except for brownish sides of breast (extension from hindneck) and brownish undertail-coverts. **Wings** Upperwing brown. Underwing mostly white with conspicuous broad smudgy-brown margins and tip (distinctly different from both Little and Manx Shearwaters (p. 265, p. 262). In some populations underwings often completely fuscous, e.g. Galapagos Is (Warham, pers. comm.). **Tail** Brown.

PERSIAN SHEARWATER (*P.l. persicus*): Differs from nominate in slightly larger size, longer bill, darker underwing and variable brown streaking to flanks and axillaries.

FHJ: Distinctive small, stocky shearwater with broad wings and thickset body; appears shorter-winged and longer-tailed than Manx. Normal flight a rapid flutter (faster than Newell's, Black-vented and Manx but not as fast as Little), followed by a short glide. At times gregarious, small flocks sitting on water with wings held half raised, pattering across surface with head held low; frequently submerging and swimming with use of wings, for up to 20 seconds. At Galapagos Is, flocks feeding in this manner can number several thousands. Feeds inshore at some locations, offshore at others; does not usually follow ships.

DM: Widespread in tropical oceans. *P.l. subalaris* breeds Galapagos Is; in Atlantic *P.l. lherminieri* West Indies and Bahama Is, formerly Bermuda but now extirpated (Pellow, pers. comm.). *P.l. loyemilleri* islets off Caribbean coast of Panama; birds from Venezuelan offshore islands doubtfully assigned to this subspecies. *P.l. persicus* found throughout year in Arabian Sea; breeding grounds unknown, perhaps islets off Iranian Baluchistan and Mekran coast of Pakistan. *P.l. bailloni* breeds Mascarene Is. *P.l. nicolae* breeds Aldabra, Seychelles, Amirante and Maldive Is; perhaps also this race on Chagos Is. *P.l. bannermani* breeds Bonin and Volcano Is (Pacific Ocean). *P.l. gunax* probably breeds Banks group, New Hebrides. *P.l. dichrous* breeds throughout central Pacific including Samoan, Society, Tuamotu, Marquesas, Phoenix and Christmas Is. Egg-dates throughout year. The number of races suggests restricted gene pool indicative of a mainly sedentary species, precise pelagic dispersal however unknown. Found in Gulf Stream along Atlantic coast of North America, with late summer influx reaching to about 40°N in Sep with peak figures in excess of 1,500 off Virginia, where a few remain till Nov. Casual all year round in northern Gulf of Mexico. Occasionally strays to Mozambique Channel and Natal off South Africa and to coast of Ecuador in Pacific. Should be looked for off NW Queensland, Australia (may breed Fiji).).
SS: See notes under Little Shearwater (p. 265).

Family *OCEANITIDAE* (formerly *Hydrobatidae*) storm-petrels

Smallest of *Procellariiformes*; eight genera comprising about 20 species. Generally arranged into two main groups, one in each of the hemispheres with some overlap in tropics. The southern genera (*Oceanites*, *Garrodia*, *Pelagodroma*, *Fregetta* and *Nesofregetta*) characterised by long legs and short, rounded wings. The northern genera (*Hydrobates*, *Halocyptena* and *Oceanodroma*) have short legs and, usually, longer, more pointed wings. Plumage in both groups usually black, some with white on rump or underparts and paler wing bars. Storm-petrels provide one of the greatest identification challenges.

Some storm-petrels abundant and distributed in several oceans; others confined to one area, where may be locally abundant. Many are migratory: Wilson's Storm-petrel for instance migrates from Antarctic breeding grounds to subarctic oceans of northern hemisphere on a north–south latitudinal axis; Matsudaira's Storm-petrel appears to migrate from Pacific to Indian Ocean in a west–east longitudinal axis. All except the Galapagos Storm-petrel nocturnal at colonies.

At sea identification of storm-petrels is fraught with difficulties, due mainly to small size and generally similar coloration.

Flight and feeding action are important identification criteria to note down at the time of observation. The degree and extent of white on rump and lateral undertail-coverts, wing markings and wing and tail shape will also facilitate positive identification. With comparative experience most can be distinguished at sea but the basis of identification is often a subjective impression rather than detail. The excellent 4-part series on storm-petrel identification by Naveen (1981) is recommended for further reading.

Genus *OCEANITES*

Two species; small to medium-sized storm-petrels with short, rounded wings and long legs projecting beyond tail in flight. Both show paler upperwing bar and white rump. Elliot's Storm-petrel restricted to coasts of western South America and differs from abundant, migratory Wilson's Storm-petrel in whitish belly. Both species have yellow webs to feet but these rarely seen at sea; they are habitual wake-dwellers, skipping across water with wings raised and feet pattering surface.

At sea separation from *Oceanodroma* spp. problematical even with comparative experience. Best based on amount of white on rump and undertail-coverts; relative conspicuousness of paler upperwing bar; tail shape; and, perhaps most importantly, wing shape, overall jizz and flight.

115 WILSON'S STORM-PETREL *Oceanites oceanicus*

PLATE 33 Figs 115a-115d
MAP 115

Length 15–19cm (6–7½in.). Wingspan 38–42cm (15–16½in.). Iris brown. Bill black. Legs/feet black with yellow or greenish-yellow webs (latter rarely seen at sea).

Wide-ranging; range overlaps with many other storm-petrel spp. but see especially Leach's, British and Madeiran Storm-petrels (p. 274, p. 272, p. 273). Sexes alike; no seasonal difference although in worn plumage diagonal upperwing bar more prominent. Juveniles not safely separable from adults. Two subspecies listed, not separable at sea although *exasperatus* about 10% larger in wing and tail measurements than nominate. Cape Horn birds may have pale vents (Naveen, pers. comm.). Another form, *O.o. maorianus*, now possibly extinct, known only from three specimens collected New Zealand sub-antarctic zone, differed in having a partly white breast (see Murphy & Snyder 1952). Leucistic individuals noted in western N Atlantic (Naveen, pers. comm.).

PLUMAGE (fresh): **Head** Sooty-brown. **Body** Upperparts mostly sooty-brown except for conspicuous white rump. Underparts mainly sooty-brown; thighs and lateral undertail-coverts white. (This lateral extension of the white on the rump much more extensive than in Madeiran or British; minimal in Leach's.) **Wings** Upperwing sooty-brown except for narrow greyish band across greater coverts. Underwing normally dark but may show considerable paleness extending from axillaries across coverts. **Tail** Blackish-brown.

PLUMAGE (worn, May–Oct): Much browner in tone with wider and more prominent grey band across greater coverts, tips of which often show whiter. (In very worn examples upperwing bar sometimes as extensive as in larger Leach's Storm-petrel.)

FHJ: Size intermediate between British and Leach's Storm-petrels (p. 272, p. 274). At sea wing shape appears rather short with little or no bend at carpal, broad, rounded tip and nearly straight trailing edge (see Leach's Storm-petrel, p. 274). Tail short, and rounded or square; long legs usually, but not invariably, carried projecting just beyond tail. Overall jizz thus suggests British Storm-petrel rather than larger, longer-winged, fork-tailed Leach's. Flight purposeful, generally without Leach's bounding and veering, higher above waves than its congeners (up to 3m). Wilson's flies with shallower, faster wingbeats and fewer glides than Leach's, producing flight pattern suggesting small tern or swallow. During feeding, patters feet, bounding or skipping along low over surface, or pausing, wings held vertically over back, legs trailing. Gregarious at sea, some flocks reaching several thousands at staging points during migration. Normally avoids deep oceanic water, preferring to feed over shallow shelf water. Readily follows ships; attends trawlers and cetaceans, attracted to 'chum'.

DM: Transequatorial migrant in all oceans although uncommon in North Pacific. *O.o. oceanicus* breeds South Georgia, Crozets, Kerguelen, Falklands, Tierra del Fuego and islands off Cape Horn; perhaps also at Peter, Balleny and Bouvet Is; *O.o. exasperatus* breeds South Shetlands. South Sandwich and most if not all suitable sections of Antarctic coastline. Returns to colonies Nov/Dec; egg-dates Dec/Jan; fledging and dispersal begins Apr/May with proportionately fewer birds migrating N into eastern Pacific, where regular in good numbers Apr–Nov off Mollendo, Peru (Hughes, pers. comm.). Extent of northwards penetration in NE Pacific poorly understood but a few recently seen off California, USA, Aug–Oct (see Roberson 1980 for details). In Atlantic main movement N occurs in western sector, with many reaching seas off New England coasts Apr/May; smaller movement occurs in eastern sector, reaching NW Africa late Apr. Range in North Atlantic extends to about 47°N in both sectors and occasionally N to about 53°N. Virtual absence of beached derelicts and authentic sight records from Britain (see Tucker 1981) suggests they are well adapted to survive strong winds. Return movement southwards in Atlantic begins Aug. In Indian Ocean birds progress in a clockwise route through western sector, reaching Gulf of Aden and southern Red Sea by May, where flocks of several thousands not uncommon before main departure in Jul to reach India Jul/Aug, NW Australia Oct/Nov. Proportionately few move N past Australia in Apr to winter off Malaysian coasts, with stragglers N to Japan and greater Pacific area generally. Non-breeders may remain N throughout year.

SS: At sea jizz suggests a large British Storm-petrel (p. 272) but lacks bat-like flight and underwing bar of that species; legs project beyond tail and upperwing bar usually much more prominent. Compared to Wilson's, flight of British shows weaker (but continuous) flapping and shorter glides. Leach's (p. 274) has longer, more slender wings with definite angle on leading edge at carpal, and usually a more pronounced upperwing bar (but beware worn Wilson's during moult, May–Oct). At close range tail of Leach's forked, and divided rump never so white as in Wilson's with little side extension to lateral undertail-coverts. See main text for flight differences.

---

116 ELLIOT'S STORM-PETREL
other: White-vented Storm-petrel
Oceanites gracilis

PLATE 36 Fig. 116

MAP 116

Length 15–16cm (6–6½in.). Wingspan not recorded. Iris brownish. Bill black. Legs/feet mostly black, webs yellow.

NE Pacific Ocean; range overlaps with migrating Wilson's Storm-petrels (p. 267). Sexes alike; no seasonal variation. Juveniles presumably as adults. Two subspecies; nominate averages smaller than *galapagoensis* with less white on belly.

PLUMAGE: Head Brownish-black. **Body** Upperparts mostly brownish-black; rump and uppertail-coverts white. Underparts variable: most show brown upper breast, flanks and undertail-coverts with white belly extending (usually) to upper ventral area; darker examples show brown underparts with small white belly patch separated from white rump and lateral undertail-coverts by brown flanks and thighs. **Wings** Upperwing mostly brownish-black; primaries and secondaries darker, paler greater coverts form prominent diagonal bar. Underwing mostly dark brown except for obvious whitish suffusion across coverts. **Tail** Blackish-brown.

FHJ: Resembles miniature Wilson's Storm-petrel but with smudgy-white belly and diffuse pale stripe on underwing. Wings short, broad at base, rounded at tip, giving compact jizz; legs project beyond tail. Flight normally buoyant, direct and low over water, circling occasionally with intervals of rapid, shallow wingbeats. When feeding habitually 'walks on water' with wings raised in shallow V over back, inclining forwards slowly and dipping downwards, occasionally submerging head and breast or bounding and hopping across surface, springing clear with long legs. At Galapagos often forms large diurnal feeding rafts, particularly in shel-

tered bays. Habitually follows ships (unlike sympatric Wedge-rumped and Madeiran Storm-petrels). **DM:** Confined to eastern Pacific Ocean. *O.g. galapagoensis* almost certainly breeds Galapagos Is but no nests have ever been found (Harris 1974). Similarly, breeding grounds of Humboldt Current race *O.g. gracilis*, which occurs from Ecuador S to Valparaiso, Chile, also remain undiscovered. Pelagic dispersal unknown but should be looked for off Colombia and Panama.
SS: Differs from Antarctic race of Wilson's (p. 267) in smaller size, white belly and pale suffusion on underwing. Cape Horn race of Wilson's may show white on vent (beware!). Sympatric Wedge-rumped and Madeiran Storm-petrels (p. 273, p. 273) differ in flight and colour patterns, and latter is larger than Elliot's.

Genus *GARRODIA*

Monotypic genus; small grey-backed storm-petrel restricted to Southern Oceans. Distinctive at sea, lacking white rump of some storm-petrels but with mainly white underparts.

Separation from other storm-petrel spp. straightforward.

117 GREY-BACKED STORM-PETREL — *Garrodia nereis*

PLATE 34 Fig. 117
MAP 117

Length 16–19cm (6½–7½in.). Wingspan 39cm (15½in.). Iris dark brown. Bill/legs black.

Southern Oceans; distinctive at sea. Sexes alike; no seasonal variation but adults in fresh plumage, and juveniles, have upperparts scaled whitish. No subspecies.
PLUMAGE: Head Blackish-grey. **Body** Upperparts ash-grey, rump paler grey. Underparts white. **Wings** Upperwing: primaries, their coverts, and secondaries black, remaining coverts mostly dark grey; greater coverts paler grey, forming midwing bar at close range. Underwing: coverts white, margins blackish, widest on leading edge. **Tail** Grey, broadly tipped black.
FHJ: Small, compact grey and white species lacking white rump; feet project beyond square, rather short tail in flight. Normal flight fairly direct, resembling Wilson's. When feeding adopts one of several techniques: 1) In high winds hovers into wind walking on water, wings raised, occasionally side-slipping to retrace original path; 2) In lower wind speeds hovers less, dipping and skipping across waves (can suggest *Fregetta* spp., see Klapste 1981); 3) Has fast, darting flight, low to water, splashing down momentarily before springing clear. Occasionally follows ships, attends trawlers.
DM: Circumpolar. Breeds Falklands, South Georgia, Gough, Crozet, Kerguelen, Chatham, Auckland and Antipodes, perhaps also Macquarie Is. May also breed Prince Edward I., where comes ashore at nightfall (pers. obs.) Status on other sub-antarctic islands not clear; suspected breeding Snares Is

Pelagodroma marina

FIG. 9. Underwings of three southern storm-petrels

(New Zealand), possibly also islets off Cape Horn. Returns to colonies Oct/Nov; egg-dates Nov/Dec; fledging Apr/May. Pelagic dispersal poorly understood; appears to reach seas only close or adjacent to breeding stations. Non-breeding visitor to Tierra del Fuego (Humphrey *et al.* 1970); not recorded from South African inshore waters (Brooke & Sinclair 1978). Occurs regularly off western Tasmania and Victoria (pers. obs.). Movements in southern Indian Ocean not clear.
SS: Combination of small size, short tail, long legs, mainly ashy-grey plumage lacking white rump but with white underparts and darker head, wings and tail should prevent confusion with other species.

Genus *PELAGODROMA*

Monotypic genus; medium-sized greyish-brown and white storm-petrel with broad, rounded wings, distinctive flight and long legs projecting beyond tail in flight. Migratory and dispersive in all three major oceans, tending to feed in true pelagic habitat where loosely social, sometimes roosting in rafts.

118 WHITE-FACED STORM-PETREL — other: Frigate Petrel — *Pelagodroma marina*

PLATE 34 Figs 118a-118d
MAP 118

Length 20cm (8in.). Wingspan 42cm (16½in.). Iris pale brown. Bill black. Legs black, yellow webs not normally visible at sea.

Widespread; range overlaps with Grey-backed Storm-petrel (p. 269) and phalarope spp. (p. 317). Sexes alike; no seasonal variation but in worn plumage pale upperwing bar more pronounced.

Juveniles differ from adults in paler head, whiter rump and more pronounced upperwing bar. Six subspecies. *P.m. eadesi* has whiter forehead and hindneck, latter forming whitish cervical collar. High-latitude breeders generally smaller, darker and more heavily marked, with proportionately longer and more forked tail; some New Zealand breeders may show complete breast bands (Naveen 1981). Following description refers to nominate.

ADULT: Head Dark grey-brown cap and ear-coverts contrast with white forehead, superciliary, chin and throat. **Body** Upperparts brownish-grey; rump pale grey. Underparts white, sides of breast greyish. **Wings** Upperwing: mostly brownish-grey, secondaries and primaries blackish; tips of coverts paler. Underwing white; broad dusky trailing margin. **Tail** Blackish-brown.

FHJ: At long range appears brown above, white below; closer views reveal distinctive patterned face, dark upperwing arcs and pale rump. Non-feeding flight weaving, rather prion-like with much banking and erratic progression; wing strokes often jerky and rhythmic, suggesting Common Sandpiper *Actitis hypoleucos*. Feeding flight strong and direct, dancing along with short glides between splashdowns, body swinging wildly from side to side. Legs normally carried projecting well beyond tail, dropping only on point of impact and retracted almost immediately. Occasionally walks on water, normally into strong headwind. Rarely follows ships. Prefers pelagic waters, often seen in small rafts of five to 15 birds; beware phalaropes (p. 317).

DM: In N Atlantic *P.m. hypoleuca* breeds Salvage Is; status on Tenerife requires clarification. *P.m. eadesi* Cape Verde Is. In southern Atlantic *P.m. marina* breeds Tristan da Cunha and Gough; status on St Helena and Amsterdam Is (where formerly bred) requires clarification. *P.m. dulciae* breeds off Western and southern Australia. *P.m. maoriana* breeds islets off New Zealand and at Stewart, Auckland and Chatham Is. *P.m. albiclunis* reputed to breed Kermadec I. probably invalid (Fullagar & van Tets, pers. comm.). Egg-dates variable, Jan–Mar in North Atlantic, Oct/Nov in Australian region. Pelagic and dispersive movements imperfectly understood. North Atlantic breeders probably move W towards central Atlantic, as vagrants have occurred eastern USA; recent sightings may indicate small numbers regularly reach Maryland and North Carolina waters late summer/fall. Nominate *P.m. marina* disperses greater part of tropical S Atlantic, occurring off eastern South America N almost to Equator; not yet recorded off South Africa or Namibia (Brooke & Sinclair 1978). Southwest Australian breeders more strongly migratory, moving northwest on broad front into Indian Ocean passing India, Laccadives and Mombassa during May en route for Arabian Sea upwellings, where moult occurs. Return movement begins Aug. In southern Pacific records from near Galapagos and between there and Peru during Jul (Bourne 1967) plus numerous sightings in central Pacific probably due to itinerant New Zealand breeders which appear to move E towards South American littoral.

SS: The only North Atlantic storm-petrel with white underparts. Patterned face and broad, dark arcs on upperwing should prevent confusion with other storm-petrels. Beware of confusing rafts of this species with phalaropes (p. 317). In Pacific see also Hornby's, White-throated and *Fregetta* storm-petrels (p. 277, p. 271, p. 270).

Genus *FREGETTA*

Two sibling species; medium-sized storm-petrels, mostly black above, generally white below. Taxonomy complex. Each species usually credited with two colour phases plus intermediates, but validity of these forms remains uncertain and requires further investigation. Bourne (1960) described some light morph Black-bellied with belly stripe reduced or even lacking, whereas Serventy *et al.* (1971) mention a dark phase White-bellied population at Lord Howe I. as entirely sooty-black, only rump and bases of belly feathers showing white. In southern Indian and Atlantic Oceans, however, intermediates extremely rare and both species separable at sea given reasonable views (Sinclair, pers. comm.). Only typical forms are described in following account.

119 BLACK-BELLIED STORM-PETREL *Fregetta tropica*

PLATE 34 Fig. 119
MAP 119

120 WHITE-BELLIED STORM-PETREL *Fregetta grallaria*

PLATE 34 Fig. 120
MAP 120

Length 20cm (8in.). Wingspan 46cm (18in.). Iris brown. Bill, legs/feet black.

Southern Oceans, migrating N to tropics; ranges overlap with several storm-petrels, see especially Wilson's. Sexes alike; no marked seasonal variation but in fresh plumage upperparts fringed paler. Several subspecies as listed below.

BLACK-BELLIED FORM: Head Mostly black; chin usually white. **Body** Upperparts blackish (darker and without paler fringes of White-bellied); rump and uppertail-coverts white. Underparts: upper breast blackish, extending thickly down centre of white belly; flanks and undertail-coverts mottled blackish. **Wings** Upperwing blackish. Underwing: smudgy blackish margins enclose white, almost triangular-shaped coverts (a conspicuous field mark). **Tail** Blackish.

WHITE-BELLIED FORM: Typical examples differ from corresponding Black-bellied in: **Head** Chin usually dark. **Body** Upperparts: broader pale frin-

ges of back feathers impart greyer appearance. Underparts: white belly lacks central black division; 'demarcation' line is located on lower breast.
FHJ: Slightly larger and stockier than Wilson's Storm-petrel (p. 267). *Fregetta* spp. usually adopt characteristic contour-hugging, direct flight with legs dangling and body swinging wildly from side to side, splashing breast first into water every few seconds, springing clear with long legs. Often foot-patters. Occasionally follows in wake; more often seen ahead of, or accompanying, vessels.
DM: Both forms breed in southern hemisphere. White-bellied Storm-petrel more northerly: *F.g. leucogaster* breeds Tristan da Cunha and Gough, also St Paul, Amsterdam (?) in Indian Ocean; *F.g. grallaria* breeds Lord Howe and Kermadec Is; *F.g. titan* breeds Rapa I., Austral group (south-central Pacific Ocean); *F.g. segethi* breeds Juan Fernandez Is off Chile. Egg-dates vary between populations. Pelagic dispersal poorly understood; in southern Atlantic ranges W to Brazil and Argentina and E to western Africa, where scarce off Namibia and South Africa. Range in Indian Ocean requires clarification. In Pacific Lord Howe breeders disperse N to Tasman and Coral Seas, some reaching central Pacific. Juan Fernandez breeders occasionally occur E to Valparaiso and N to Lima; casual Galapagos area (Harris 1974). Black-bellied Storm-petrel more southerly in breeding distribution. *F.t. tropica* breeds South Georgia, South Orkney, South Shetland, Bouvet (?), Crozets, Kerguelen, Auckland, Bounty and Antipodes Is. Almost certainly on Prince Edward I., where seen ashore at nightfall (pers. obs.). Claims of a white-bellied form, *F.t. melanoleuca*, breeding on Gough I. requires clarification. Egg-dates Dec/Jan; fledging mid Apr onwards. Indian Ocean birds disperse northwards to tropics, passing Mombassa in May, N to central Arabian Sea where common Aug/Sep (Bailey 1971). New Zealand breeders disperse N to Tasman Sea and Australian Bight. South Atlantic birds move N along both coasts of South America reaching even Peru in cold Humboldt Current, and W to Namibia, South Africa; and Gulf of Guinea.
SS: Typical forms of both *Fregetta* spp. differ from Wilson's Storm-petrel in characteristic flight, paler underparts and underwing pattern. Much confusion persists in separation of the two *Fregetta* due to claims of wide variation in underparts coloration, frequency of which has probably been overestimated. Most variation appears to occur in Lord Howe I. breeders. Typical examples are safely separable at sea given reasonable views. Compared with White-bellied, Black-bellied appear darker on upperparts with blackish breast extending further down breast, uniting, in most cases, with more extensive black undertail-coverts. Problematical morphs can be identified, in the hand, by combination of wing, middle toe and tarsus lengths: **WHITE-BELLIED:** Wing length 146–163mm; Middle Toe 20–23mm; Tarsus 33–37mm; **BLACK-BELLIED:** Wing length 154–167mm; Middle toe 26–30mm; Tarsus 39–44mm.

Genus *NESOFREGETTA*

Monotypic genus; large-sized storm-petrel with broad, rather rounded wing and long, deeply forked tail. Restricted to tropical western Pacific Ocean. Sexes alike; no seasonal variation but polymorphic.

Distinctive at sea; confusion with *Fregetta* and *Oceanites* spp. should not occur if seen well. Note particularly jizz, narrow white uppertail-coverts and, in pale morph, whiter underparts.

121 WHITE-THROATED STORM-PETREL *Nesofregetta fuliginosa*

PLATE 37 Figs 121a-121c
MAP 121

Length 24–26cm (9½–10in.). Wingspan not recorded. Bare parts blackish.

Western tropical Pacific; range overlaps with Tristram's and perhaps also with migrant *Fregetta* spp. (p. 270). Sexes alike; polymorphic, ranging from typical pale morphs to wholly dark forms. No subspecies.
TYPICAL MORPH: Head Blackish-brown, chin white. **Body** Upperparts blackish-brown, rump and uppertail-coverts narrowly white. Underparts mostly white except for brownish breast band and undertail-coverts. **Wings** Upperwing blackish-brown with short, paler bar across inner greater coverts. Underwing: coverts white, margins blackish, widest on trailing edge. **Tail** Blackish-brown; deeply forked.
INTERMEDIATE MORPHS: On Christmas I. 50% of population show some dark flecking or streaks on white underparts. (Phoenix and McKean Is populations show continuous gradation between typical pale morph and dark morph.)
DARK MORPH: Samoan form wholly sooty-brown except for short, pale upperwing bar on inner greater coverts (beware Tristram's Storm-petrel).
FHJ: Largest storm-petrel; wing shape broad with rounded tip and no apparent angle on either leading or trailing edges. Tail appears relatively long and deeply forked. Flight distinctive, using long legs and spatulate feet to spring clear of water, sailing on broad wings for up to 30 seconds before splashing down and kicking off again from wave with change of direction and sudden increase of speed (see Crossin 1974).
DM: Tropical western Pacific, breeding New Hebrides, Fiji, Phoenix, Line, Austral, Marquesas and Gambier Is; perhaps also Samoa, where collected offshore. Egg-dates protracted; see Schreiber & Ashmole (1970). Pelagic dispersal not fully known; thought to remain in adjacent waters with limited dispersal eastwards along S Equatorial Current.
SS: At distance typical morphs could be confused with *Fregetta* spp. (although ranges not known to overlap); distinctive flight, jizz and breast band best characters to look for. Wholly dark morphs could be confused with Tristram's Storm-petrel (p. 276) but that species has typical *Oceanodroma* wing shape (long, rather narrow, with distinct angle on leading edge) and different flight.

Genus *HYDROBATES*

Monotypic genus; small, short-winged storm-petrel with white rump and short legs. Restricted mainly to NE Atlantic, migrating S to southern Atlantic during northern winter. One of the smallest seabirds.

Separation from *Oceanodroma* and *Oceanites* spp. problematic under poor conditions or without comparative experience. Best based on size, virtual absence (at sea) of paler upperwing bar, darker overall plumage and tail shape. Jizz and flight characters additional important characters to note during observation.

122 BRITISH STORM-PETREL
other: Storm-petrel, European Storm-petrel
Hydrobates pelagicus

PLATE 33 Fig. 122
MAP 122

Length 14–17cm (5½–6½in.). Wingspan 36–39cm (14–15½in.). Iris brown. Bill, legs/feet black.

Breeds eastern North Atlantic and Mediterranean, migrating S to seas off west Africa; range thus overlaps with several storm-petrel spp. but see especially Wilson's, Leach's and Madeiran (p. 267, p. 274, p. 273). Sexes alike; no seasonal variation. Juveniles in fresh plumage show more pronounced diagonal bar on upperwing but this soon abrades. No subspecies.

PLUMAGE: Head Sooty-black. **Body** Upperparts mostly sooty-black except for conspicuous white rump and uppertail-coverts (longer of which tipped black but rarely seen at sea). Underparts mostly sooty-black except for white lower flanks and lateral undertail-coverts. Extension of white from rump greater than Leach's but less than Wilson's. **Wings** Upperwing usually appears sooty-black; at close range and in fresh plumage greater coverts narrowly tipped white, forming barely discernible diagonal bar. Underwing mainly black, with whitish tips and edges of axillaries and greater coverts forming irregular stripe. **Tail** Blackish.

FHJ: Smallest and darkest Atlantic storm-petrel. At sea wing shape appears short and broad, with little or no bend at carpal and rounded, slightly tapering tip. Tail short, square-ended with rounded corners. In flight feet do not project beyond tail. Flight weak and fluttering, recalling that of a bat, with almost continuous wing action interspersed with short glides. During feeding wings are raised midway over back with legs pattering surface. Progression normally direct but in strong winds erratic, often being blown backwards or sideways many metres due to buffeting. Follows ships, attends trawlers.

DM: Transequatorial migrant, breeding eastern North Atlantic and Mediterranean with small colonies Iceland, Faeroes and Lofoten Is, Norway. Main colonies are off SW Ireland, particularly Co Kerry, where over 50,000 pairs estimated, 25,000 of which nest on Inishtearaght (Evans 1970). Other colonies at Shetlands, Orkneys, islands off Welsh coast, Isles of Scilly, and up to 10,000 pairs at Little Burhou, Channel Is; also at Brittany and Biarritz. Status in western Mediterranean not precisely known: breeds off Sardinia, Sicily, Balearics, Malta and a few islets in Adriatic; formerly off Tunisia but status now uncertain. Returns to colonies Apr/May; egg-dates usually Jun/Jul; fledging and dispersal S begins Sep, with most absent from British waters by late Oct though stragglers occur till Nov/Dec. Birds pass NW Africa from mid Nov and may occur there in small numbers throughout year but most move S to seas off Namibia and South Africa E to Natal. Mediterranean population may remain in adjacent waters throughout winter. Return migration begins Mar/Apr. Vagrant North American Atlantic coast.

SS: Smaller than most other storm-petrels, with weaker bat-like flight and narrow, irregular underwing bar. Differs from Wilson's (p. 267) in more obscure upperwing bar and lack of projecting feet. Leach's (p. 274) has longer, more angular wings, duller rump, usually a more prominent upperwing bar, and characteristic erratic, bounding flight. See also Madeiran Storm-petrel (p. 273).

Genus *HALOCYPTENA*

Monotypic genus; small, wholly dark storm-petrel with short, wedge-shaped tail and relatively short wings. Restricted to eastern Pacific.

Separation from sympatric *Oceanodroma* spp. best based on size, tail shape and flight. (The new AOU checklist is expected to place *Halocyptena* into *Oceanodroma*.)

123 LEAST STORM-PETREL
Halocyptena microsoma

PLATE 35 Fig. 123
MAP 123

Length 13–15cm (5–6in.). Wingspan 32cm (12½in.). Bare parts blackish.

NE Pacific Ocean; range overlaps with several storm-petrels, see especially Black and Ashy plus dark-rumped forms of Leach's (p. 276, p. 277, p. 274). Sexes alike; no seasonal variation. Juveniles as adults. No subspecies.

PLUMAGE: Wholly blackish-brown except for slightly paler upperwing-coverts forming diagonal bar.

FHJ: Smallest Pacific coast storm-petrel with proportionately short, rounded wings and short wedge-shaped tail (may appear rounded at sea). Flight usually swift and direct with rather deep wingbeats, similar to Black Storm-petrel (p. 276) but more rapid (Stallcup 1976). When feeding wings held in V over back, sometimes whilst sitting on surface before fluttering short distance and splashing down (Crossin 1974).

DM: Restricted to islands off western Baja California and on northern islands in Gulf of California. Breeding biology little known; egg-dates Jul. Disperses S after breeding, reaching seas off Central America, extending S to Colombia and Ecuador although status in these areas requires clarification.

SS: See notes under Ashy Storm-petrel (p. 277). Black Storm-petrel (p. 276) considerably larger with longer wings, forked tail and slower, more deliberate wingbeats. Dark-rumped Leach's Storm-petrels (p. 274) larger with longer wings, forked tail and erratic, bounding flight.

Genus *OCEANODROMA*

Nine or ten species; medium-sized, rather narrow-, long-winged storm-petrels with moderately forked tail and short legs. Plumage usually wholly dark with or without white rump and pale upperwing bar. Some species grey and black above, white below. Centre of distribution mainly in northern hemisphere, many migrating southwards during winter.

Separation of darker forms from *Oceanites*, *Halocyptena* and *Hydrobates* spp. problematical under poor conditions or without comparative experience. Identification best based on size, and paler upperwing bars or patches (if present). Perhaps of more importance are flight and jizz characters, although some experience usually required to appreciate differences fully under given conditions.

124 WEDGE-RUMPED STORM-PETREL
other: Galapagos Storm-petrel
Oceanodroma tethys

PLATE 36 Fig. 124
MAP 124

Length 18–20cm (7–8in.). Wingspan not recorded. Bare parts blackish.

Restricted to seas off western South America, moving N after breeding; range overlaps with several storm-petrel spp., see especially Madeiran, Leach's, Wilson's and Elliot's (p. 273, p. 274, p. 267, p. 268). Sexes alike; no seasonal variation but upperwing-coverts wear rapidly to reveal paler diagonal bar. Juveniles as adults. Two subspecies, *O.t. kelsalli* averages smaller.

PLUMAGE: Head and Body Mostly blackish except for large, triangular-shaped white rump which reaches almost to notch of tail and extends to upper flanks and lateral undertail-coverts (a conspicuous and diagnostic character). **Wings** Upperwing blackish; greater coverts usually paler, forming distinct diagonal bar. Underwing blackish, some with paler suffusion across coverts. **Tail** Black; appears short and notched.

FHJ: At sea plumage appears mostly black with large white rump (largest of any storm-petrel), imparting distinctive white-ended or white-tailed appearance at certain angles. Pale upperwing bars visible only at close range. Wing shape proportionately long, narrow and pointed with distinct angle at carpal; wings usually held bowed and slightly forward. Flight fast, direct and forceful, often quite high above waves, even in calm conditions, with deep wingbeats and much banking and twisting. When feeding has a skipping, bounding flight, dipping down to water with legs trailing on surface, though does not habitually 'walk on water' as does sympatric Elliot's Storm-petrel (p. 268). Occasionally follows ships; the only storm-petrel to visit colonies during daylight (at Galapagos Is).

DM: Eastern Pacific Ocean. *O.t. tethys* breeds Galapagos Is on Isla Pitt, Tower and probably Roca Redonda (Harris 1974). *O.t. kelsalli* breeds at several Peruvian guano islands, including Pescadores and San Gallan. At Galapagos some birds present all year; egg-dates chiefly May/Jun. Both forms appear to move N after breeding, reaching seas off Ecuador and Colombia N to Panama, more rarely to seas off west Mexico. Two have reached N to Monterey, California (Aug–Jan, see account in Roberson 1980).

SS: White rump so large that it gives present species a distinctive and characteristic appearance which, coupled with unusually forceful flight, should prevent confusion with most other species. Separated from Elliot's Storm-petrel (p. 268) by blacker coloration, long wings, flight and rump pattern. Madeiran Storm-petrel (p. 273) browner with wider-based wings, different flight and rump pattern. See also Wilson's and Leach's Storm-petrels (p. 267, p. 274).

125 MADEIRAN STORM-PETREL
other: Harcourt's/Band-rumped Storm-petrel
Oceanodroma castro

PLATE 33 Fig. 125
MAP 125

Length 19–21cm (7½–8½in.). Wingspan 42–45cm (16½–18in.). Iris brown. Bill, legs/feet black.

Pacific and Atlantic warm-water species; range overlaps with several similar storm-petrel spp. but see especially Wilson's, Leach's, British and Wedge-rumped (p. 267, p. 274, p. 272, p. 273). Sexes alike; no seasonal variation. In fresh plumage juveniles show greyer greater coverts but these soon abrade. No described subspecies, but four collected Gulf of Guinea, of unknown breeding population, averaged larger with little white in rump; possibly a distinct subspecies (Harris 1969).

PLUMAGE: Head Blackish-brown. **Body** Upperparts mostly blackish-brown except for conspicuous narrow and evenly-cut white rump band and uppertail-coverts (longer of which tipped black but this rarely seen at sea). Underparts blackish-brown. **Wings** Upperwing mainly blackish-brown; greater coverts brownish-grey forming paler diagonal band (not as pronounced as in Leach's or in worn Wilson's but much more obvious than in British Storm-petrel). Underwing dark; coverts of some tipped paler. **Tail** Blackish.

FHJ: Size equals that of Leach's Storm-petrel. At sea wing shape intermediate between Wilson's, which shows little or no bend to a moderately broad, rounded wing, and Leach's, which has longer, narrower, somewhat angular wing. Tail moderately long with very shallow fork, though this not usually seen at sea; in flight legs do not project beyond tail. Flight usually buoyant, working a steady zigzag progression between quick wingbeats and low shearing glides with wings held flat or bowed below the horizontal, producing flight pattern recalling a small shearwater (much more pronounced than in Leach's shearing flight). At times, however, steady flight becomes erratic, doubling back on previous course, banking and twisting in tight circles close to surface. Appears shy at sea. Off Galapagos Is, where most birds are easily approached, small rafts of this species could not be approached in either large or small boats (pers. obs.). Does not normally follow ships.

DM: Tropical Pacific and Atlantic Oceans. In NW Pacific breeds on islets off Japan, with colony of some 25,000 pairs at Hide Is, off Honshu (Cheke 1967). Further E breeds at Hawaiian and Galapagos Is. In Atlantic breeds at Cape Verde, Ascension, St Helena and Madeira; possibly also at Azores. Egg-dates throughout year at tropical localities, with some islands (e.g. Galapagos) having two populations, each breeding annually but six months out of phase. Japanese population probably returns to colonies May; egg-dates Jun; fledging and dispersal begin about Oct. Post-breeding dispersal of all populations poorly understood due to difficulty of identification. Sightings and reports of beached derelicts from western Atlantic (Brazil N through Gulf of Mexico to mid Atlantic States of USA) may indicate that it has a fairly wide pelagic dispersal into mid Atlantic and even west Atlantic sectors.

SS: Differs from Wilson's and British Storm-petrels (p. 267, p. 272) in wing shape, flight and overall jizz. At sea differs from Leach's Storm-petrel in rather shorter, broader wings (which make it look noticeably smaller) with brighter white rump and duller diagonal bars. Flight also smoother, with quicker, less rhythmic wingbeats interspersed with much more pronounced shearwater-like gliding and zigzagging. Wedge-rumped Storm-petrel (p. 273) smaller, with diagnostic large white rump reaching almost to notch of distinctly forked tail.

126 SWINHOE'S STORM-PETREL
Oceanodroma monorhis

PLATE 37 Fig. 126
MAP 126

Length 20cm (8in.). Wingspan 45cm (18in.). Bare parts blackish.

Breeds NW Pacific, migrating W to Indian Ocean; range overlaps with several storm-petrel spp., see especially Matsudaira's and Tristram's (p. 276, p. 276). Sexes alike; no seasonal variation. Juveniles as adults. Taxonomy complex; possibly conspecific with Leach's Storm-petrel.

PLUMAGE: Mostly dark brown except for inconspicuous bar on upperwing and greyish suffusion on underwing-coverts.

FHJ: Resembles dark-rumped form of Leach's Storm-petrel. Compared with Matsudaira's Storm-petrel present species smaller with narrower, more angled wings and faster, swooping flight, which sometimes includes erratic bounding and vertical leaping of Leach's Storm-petrel. Forked tail difficult to observe at sea.

DM: NW Pacific Ocean; breeds on islands off northern and northeastern Honshu and northern Kyushu (Japan), southern and western Korea and China (Yellow Sea). Egg-dates May/Jun; fledging date not known. Migrates westwards on longitudinal axis to northern Indian Ocean although precise route unknown, possibly through Straits of Malacca. Range in Red Sea not fully known but has reached N to Gulf of Aqaba in Red Sea and W to seas off Cape Guardafui, Somalia. Bailey *et al.* (1968) found them less common in northern Indian Ocean than Matsudaira's Storm-petrel, mostly in Arabian Sea.

SS: Larger Tristram's Storm-petrel (p. 276) differs in more obvious diagonal upperwing bar, deeper fork to tail, and, usually, bluer or greyer cast to plumage. NOTE In the hand Swinhoe's does show white at base of primaries but not normally visible at sea (see Matsudaira's Storm-petrel).

127 LEACH'S STORM-PETREL
Oceanodroma leucorhoa

PLATE 33 Figs 127a-127c
MAP 127

Length 19–22cm ($7\frac{1}{2}$–$8\frac{1}{2}$in.). Wingspan 45–48cm (18–19in.). Iris brown. Bill, legs/feet black.

Widespread; various forms occur in all three oceans, range thus overlaps with many storm-petrel spp., see especially British, Madeiran, and Wilson's (p. 272, p. 273, p. 267). Sexes alike; no seasonal variation. Juveniles and adults alike although juveniles in fresh plumage may show more pronounced wing bars. Taxonomy complex; three subspecies listed (see Ainley 1980). Nominate form breeding in eastern North Pacific best treated as a single polychromatic population in which proportion of dark-rumped individuals increases with decreasing latitude (Loomis 1918); in this area birds range from those with wholly white rumps and uppertail-coverts (northern) to individuals with rump and uppertail-coverts concolorous with dark back (southern). These plumages not described below; refer to Ainley (1980) and to Plate 33 for illustrations. Following description refers to nominate North Atlantic form.

PLUMAGE: Head Brownish-black. **Body** Upperparts mostly brownish-black except for whitish rump usually divided down centre by grey stripe (division rarely seen at sea but grey centre can have effect of visibly dulling whiteness of rump when compared with Wilson's or Madeiran Storm-petrels). Underparts brownish-black, upper flanks white; little extension of white from rump to lateral undertail-coverts. **Wings** Upperwing mostly brownish-black; greater coverts grey, tipped white forming conspicuous diagonal band. Underwing dark brown. **Tail** Blackish-brown.

FHJ: Larger than British or Wilson's Storm-petrels (p. 272, p. 267), often appearing dark brown rather than black. At sea wing shape appears long and rather narrow with obvious angle at carpal, and more pointed tip than either Wilson's or British Storm-petrels. As wings usually bowed and held slightly forward, trailing edge also has definite angle. Tail 'long' and, under reasonable conditions, obviously forked; feet do not project beyond tail. Overall jizz thus of a slender, long-winged species and, with comparative experience, quite distinct from either Wilson's or British Storm-petrels. Flight usually buoyant and graceful, weaving an irregular course between deep, tern-like wingbeats and short shearwater-like glides on bowed wings with sudden, swift changes of speed and direction. In strong winds, or when feeding, often hangs motionless on still wings raised slightly above body, moving slowly forward into wind with feet pattering surface. Does not normally follow ships; occasionally attends trawlers.

DM: Northern Pacific and Atlantic Oceans, migrating S towards and through tropics during northern winter. In North Pacific *O.l. leucorhoa* breeds from Hokkaido, Japan, NE to Aleutian Is and Alaska and then S on offshore islands of western North America to Islas San Benitos, Mexico. This form also found in North Atlantic with major colonies at Nova Scotia, Massachusetts, Maine and Newfoundland where numbers estimated in millions. Smaller colonies occur Westmann Is, southern Greenland, and in eastern Atlantic at Faeroes, Lofoten and off Scotland at St Kilda, Flannan, North Rona and Sula Sgeir. In eastern Pacific *O.l socorrensis* breeds only at Guadelupe I., off western Mexico, during summer (May–Sep), with *O.l. cheimomnestes* breeding there during winter (Oct–Apr) (Ainley 1980). All, except last form, undertake protracted return to colonies, most arriving about May; egg-dates May/Jun. Failed breeders disperse to adjacent seas late Aug followed by breeding adults in Sep, after chick-desertion, before undertaking slow dispersal S towards wintering quarters. In Pacific most white-rumped populations apparently winter S in equatorial Pacific, whilst dark-rumped birds winter at eastern portion of this region (Crossin 1974, Ainley 1980). Limits of southwards dispersal not known but probably S to Peru (beware Madeiran Storm-petrels off Galapagos Is). In Atlantic main wintering area thought to be in Gulf of Guinea and off Brazil, but also S to Namibia and South Africa. A few evidently pass E of Cape of Good Hope, as beach derelicts reported from Port Alfred, Eastern Cape. Of more interest are records from NW Indian Ocean, presumably due to birds migrating N in wrong ocean; Lapthorn *et al.* (1970) cite two records from this area, one from Kenya, the other from the Persian Gulf. These occurrences may be more commonplace than realised, however, as Krabbe (pers. comm.) has forwarded convincing descriptions of four possible Leach's observed at close range from a fishing boat at 20°N in southern Red Sea on 10 Jun 1971. Beach derelicts have occurred E to Australia and New Zealand.

SS: See notes under Wilson's, Madeiran and British Storm-petrels (p. 267, p. 273, p. 272). Dark-rumped forms in NE Pacific resemble both Ashy and Black Storm-petrels (p. 277, p. 276) but differ in bounding, erratic flight and lighter jizz. See further notes under those species.

128 MARKHAM'S STORM-PETREL
other: Sooty Storm-petrel
Oceanodroma markhami

PLATE 36 Fig. 128

MAP 128

Length 23cm (9in.). Wingspan not recorded. Bare parts blackish.

Seas off NW South America; range overlaps with several wholly dark storm-petrels, see especially Black Storm-petrel (p. 276). Sexes alike; no seasonal variation but in fresh plumage distinct bluish cast. Juveniles as adults. No subspecies.

PLUMAGE: Wholly blackish-brown except for indistinct paler bar across upperwing-coverts (unlike Black Storm-petrel, upperwing bar extends almost to carpal joint). In fresh plumage shows bluish or lead-grey cast (Austin 1952).

FHJ: Size and jizz recall Black Storm-petrel but with deeper fork to tail. Flight differs from that species in shallower wingbeats (only 20–30° above and below horizontal) and rather more gliding (but separation difficult). Perhaps better clue to identity is water temperature, present species preferring cooler water whereas Black Storm-petrel is a warm-water species which extends further S in years of 'El Niño' occurence (warm-water current). Does not normally follow ships.

DM: Breeding thought to occur in coastal deserts of Peru but no conclusive evidence to date. Some may move N to about 15°N from Nov onwards, but movements obscured by confusion with closely similar Black Storm-petrel which moves S from California during autumn. Observations by RNBWS members indicate that some, at least, remain in seas off Peru S to about 26°S throughout year.

SS: Tristram's and Matsudaira's Storm-petrels (p. 276, p. 276) not known to occur within present species' range. Black Storm-petrel very similar in appearance to Markham's and separation extremely difficult. Present species differs in longer upperwing bar, slower and shallower wingbeats with more prolonged gliding, and preference for cooler water. See also smaller Least Storm-petrel (p. 272). Dark-rumped Leach's Storm-petrel smaller with different flight.

129 TRISTRAM'S STORM-PETREL
other: Sooty Storm-petrel
Oceanodroma tristrami

PLATE 37 Fig. 129
MAP 129

Length 24–25cm (9½–10in.). Wingspan 56cm (22in.). Bare parts blackish.

Central Pacific W to Japan; range overlaps with several storm-petrel spp., see especially Matsudaira's and Swinhoe's Storm-petrels (p. 276, p. 274). Sexes alike. No seasonal variation but blue or greyish cast to plumage wears browner; some may show paler patches on sides of rump. No subspecies.

PLUMAGE: Mostly sooty-brown with distinct bluish or greyish cast in fresh plumage; upperwing-coverts paler forming prominent diagonal bar.

FHJ: Slightly larger than Black and Markham's Storm-petrels, appreciably larger than Leach's or Swinhoe's with deeper fork to tail. Flight characters not well known. King (1967) described flight as fairly strong with steep-banked arcs and glides interspersed with fluttery wingbeats. Sometimes patters on water.

DM: Breeds in central tropical Pacific Ocean on Leeward Hawaiian Is and in western tropical Pacific S of Japan on Volcano and southern Izu Is. Breeding biology and pelagic dispersal little known. Thought to disperse only to adjacent seas with limited northwards dispersal to coasts of Honshu (Japan).

SS: Pelagic range not known to overlap with Markham's Storm-petrel (p. 275), the other large, wholly dark storm-petrel with bluish cast. Matsudaira's Storm-petrel generally browner in cast with white on outer primaries of upperwing and less pronounced upperwing bar than present species. Dark-rumped Leach's and Swinhoe's Storm-petrels appreciably smaller with shallower-notched tails.

130 BLACK STORM-PETREL
Oceanodroma melania

PLATE 35 Fig. 130
MAP 130

Length 23cm (9in.). Wingspan 46–51cm (18–20in.). Bare parts blackish.

NE Pacific, migrating south in winter; range overlaps with several storm-petrel spp., see especially Markham's, Least, Leach's and Ashy (p. 275, p. 272, p. 274, p. 277). Sexes alike; no seasonal variation. Juveniles as adults. No subspecies.

PLUMAGE: Mostly brownish-black, with paler greater coverts forming noticeable bar on upperwing.

FHJ: Larger than Leach's Storm-petrel with long, rather angular wings and notched tail. Flight buoyant and deliberate, recalling Black Tern, with steady wingbeats raised high and then deep, to 60° above and below the horizontal (see Ashy Storm-petrel, p. 277). This steady flight rhythm of leisurely high and deep wingbeats sometimes interrupted by shallower beats and occasional glides. Markham's generally has shallower wingbeats (only 20–30° above and below the horizontal) and glides more often. Occasionally follows ships.

DM: NE Pacific Ocean, breeding on islands off coast of southern California on Santa Barbara and Sutil Is (Sowls *et al.* 1980); off Pacific coast of Baja California at Coronados and San Benito Is and in northern Gulf of California on San Luis and Partida Is. Returns to colonies Apr/May; egg-dates May/Jun; fledging Sep/Oct. In warm-water years occurs in large numbers in autumn N to Monterey Bay and Point Reyes, where almost as abundant as smaller Ashy Storm-petrel, but uncommon in cold-water years (Stallcup 1976). Migrates southwards to seas off Ecuador and Peru but status there, and at sea between mainland and Galapagos Is, confused due to presence of similar Markham's Storm-petrel (p. 275).

SS: Dark-rumped examples of Leach's Storm-petrel (p. 274) similar but smaller with erratic bounding flight. Markham's Storm-petrel presents greatest identification challenge: very similar to present species in all respects but has deeper-notched tail, shallower wingbeats and generally more persistent gliding. Pelagic ranges of Matsudaira's and Tristram's not known to overlap with present species. See notes under Ashy and Least Storm-petrels (p. 277, p. 272).

131 MATSUDAIRA'S STORM-PETREL
Oceanodroma matsudairae

PLATE 37 Fig. 131
MAP 131

Length 24–25cm (9½–10in.). Wingspan 56cm (22in.). Bare parts blackish.

Breeds Volcano Is S of Japan, migrating to Indian Ocean; range overlaps with several storm-petrel spp., see especially Swinhoe's and Tristram's (p. 274, p. 276). Sexes alike; no seasonal variation. Juveniles presumably as adults. No subspecies. Notes under DM are based largely on the excellent paper by Bailey *et al.* (1968).

PLUMAGE: Mostly dark brown except for paler diagonal bar on upperwing-coverts. During flight white shafts of outer primaries (1–7) show as small white forewing patch as birds turn or spread wings.

FHJ: Considerably larger than Swinhoe's Storm-petrel with broader bases to wings and distinctive white patch on distal portion of upperwing. Forked tail not always apparent at sea. Flight slower than that of Swinhoe's; flaps then glides for short

distance, but at no great speed, imparting somewhat lethargic progression. Occasionally, however, sprints off, twisting, corkscrewing, low over waves. When feeding raises wings over back in shallow V and dips down to surface. Follows ships.
DM: Known to breed only on Volcano Is, S of Japan (25°N), in subtropical western Pacific Ocean. Present at colonies from Jan to early Jun. Bailey *et al.* (1968) have shown species to be highly migratory, moving westwards to winter over upwellings of equatorial western Indian Ocean in seas off Seychelles Is and off coasts of Somalia and Kenya. Still not known where they gain entry into Indian Ocean. Records within and S of Indonesian Chain suggest an access point N of Australia rather than through South China Sea and Malacca Strait.
SS: Black and Markham's Storm-petrels not known to occur within present species' range. Tristram's Storm-petrel (p. 276) as large as Matsudaira's, but greyer in tone with more prominent upperwing bar, but lacks white in primaries. Dark-rumped forms of Leach's and Swinhoe's Storm-petrels (p. 274, p. 274) much smaller and, although latter have obscure white bases to primaries, they do not show prominent white forewing patch. Broader-based wings of Matsudaira's, plus its slower flight, enhance size disparity. NOTE Separation of Black, Markham's, Tristram's and Matsudaira's Storm-petrels (not to mention melanistic Leach's) is no easy matter: differences subtle and depend as much on probability factors (location and water temperature) as on plumage details and flight characters (which are normally subjective).

132 ASHY STORM-PETREL
Oceanodroma homochroa

PLATE 35 Fig. 132
MAP 132

Length 18–21cm (7–8¼in.). Wingspan not recorded. Bare parts blackish.

Restricted range in NE Pacific Ocean; range overlaps with several storm-petrel spp., see especially Black and Least (p. 276, p. 272). Sexes alike; no seasonal variation. Juveniles as adults. No subspecies.
PLUMAGE: Mostly blackish-grey except for paler coverts on *both* upper- and underwings forming paler bars.
FHJ: Noticeably smaller with proportionately shorter wings than Black Storm-petrel. Legs do not project beyond forked tail. Flight rather fluttering with wingbeat rhythm between that of Black and Least Storm-petrels but more shallow (wings raised only to and not above horizontal before downstroke, Stallcup 1976); but, when accelerating to gain flight, wings are raised as high as Black's for 10–15 strokes before settling down to style described above (Stallcup, pers. comm.).
DM (based on Sowls *et al.* 1980): Restricted to NE Pacific Ocean, most breeding off coast of California. Largest colony (4,000 individuals) at Farallon Is, with smaller colonies at Bird Rock and Channel Is. Jehl (in Sowls *et al.* 1980) reported up to six breeding at Los Coronados Is off Mexico. Egg-dates prolonged: Jan–Jun Channel Is; May–Aug Farallon Is, with fledging peaking Sep. Pelagic movements not well known but probably only to adjacent waters with limited southwards dispersal, as some seen offshore during winter months; completely absent from Farallons only Nov and Dec (Stallcup, pers. comm.).
SS: Differs from larger, longer-winged Black Storm-petrel (p. 276) in paler underwing-coverts and flight. Least Storm-petrel (p. 272) smaller with shorter, wedge-shaped tail, and more fluttery flight with deeper wingbeats. See also dark-rumped Leach's Storm-petrel, which has erratic, bounding flight.

133 HORNBY'S STORM-PETREL
other: Ringed Storm-petrel
Oceanodroma hornbyi

PLATE 36 Fig. 133
MAP 133

Length 21–23cm (8¼–9in.). Wingspan not recorded. Bare parts blackish.

Seas off western South America; distinctive. Sexes alike; no seasonal variation. Juveniles probably resemble adults but an individual seen 13 Oct (Chapman, in *Sea Swallow* 22: 49) 'with a darker back and a sub terminal tail band was thought to be an immature'. Notes under FHJ and DM based on material supplied by RA Hughes (pers. comm.).
PLUMAGE: Head Forehead broadly white contrasting with blackish cap and sides of face; chin, throat and narrow cervical collar white. **Body** Upperparts dark grey; uppertail-coverts tipped paler. Underparts mostly white except for conspicuous grey breast band. **Wings** Upperwing: primaries and secondaries blackish; coverts mostly dark grey, tips of greater coverts edged paler forming conspicuous diagonal bar. Underwing dark grey. **Tail** Blackish; forked.
FHJ: Distinctive grey-backed storm-petrel with dark cap, grey breast band and deeply forked tail. Flight erratic and unpredictable; slow, rather deep wingbeats followed by sailing glide interrupted by periods of skipping and bouncing with legs dangling, darting over wave contours. Sometimes gathers in flocks of several thousands.
DM: Thought to nest in coastal deserts of southern Peru and northern Chile between about 25°S and 35°S, where common offshore Jul–Nov. Non-breeding pelagic range not certainly known, but occurs commonly Aug–Dec N to Equator off Ecuador.
SS: Distinctive within range under normal viewing conditions.

134 FORK-TAILED STORM-PETREL *Oceanodroma furcata*

PLATE 35 Fig. 134
MAP 134

Length 20–23cm (8–9in.). Wingspan 46cm (18in.). Iris bluish. Bill, legs/feet blackish.

NE Pacific Ocean; distinctive at sea, most likely to be confused with phalarope spp. (p. 317). Sexes alike; no seasonal variation but individual variation in amount of marking on outer tail feathers, shoulder, chin and vent (Palmer 1962). Juvenile similar to adult. Two subspecies; *O.f. plumbea* averages smaller and darker.

PLUMAGE: Mostly pale blue-grey; forehead darker with distinctive blackish patch passing through and below eye to ear-coverts. **Body** Upperparts medium bluish-grey. Underparts pale bluish-grey fading to whitish at vent. **Wings** Upperwing mostly medium bluish-grey; primaries, secondaries and lesser coverts darker. Underwing blue-grey with blackish axillaries and underwing-coverts. **Tail** Blue-grey, edged and tipped white.

FHJ: Between Wilson's and Leach's Storm-petrels in size; distinctive owing to colour (congeners mostly blackish). Contour-hugging flight recalls Leach's, but not as buoyant or erratic with shallower wingbeats and rather stiff-winged glides. In bright sunlight can appear whitish at distance. Frequently settles on water, often in groups. Follows ships.

DM: NE Pacific. *O.f. furcata* breeds from Kurile and Commander Is through Aleutian chain E to Sanak Is; perhaps also on SE coasts of Kamchatka Peninsula. Largest known Alaskan colony (540,000) at Buldir I. (Sowls *et al.* 1978, who estimated nominate Alaskan population at some 5 million). *O.f. plumbea* breeds islands off southern Alaska, Washington, Oregon and northern California. Returns to colonies about May; egg-dates Jun/Jul; fledging period not recorded. During winter nominate form ranges from Bering Sea ice front S to Hokkaido, Japan, more rarely Honshu. *O.l. plumbea* appears to disperse mainly to adjacent seas; a few move S to southern California (see Stallcup 1976).

SS: None; see phalarope spp. (p. 317).

Family *PELECANOIDIDAE* diving-petrels

One genus comprising four species; all with characteristics of family as noted below in genus treatment.

Genus *PELECANOIDES*

Four species bearing close resemblance to each other. Restricted to southern hemisphere mostly between 35°S and 60°S, though they do occur further north off western South America in Humboldt Current. Size, jizz and habits recall Little Auk (p. 392) of Arctic Oceans (an excellent example of convergent evolution). All are generally black and white with stocky jizz, short neck and small wings. Short legs are placed well back on body. Bill shape diagnostic in the hand (Fig. 10), all being broad at base, hooked at tip, and differ from other petrels in that paired tubular nostrils open upwards rather than forwards, presumably an adaptation for diving. Except in case of *P. magellani* (p. 280), which has distinct colouring, identification at sea at best optimistic as the diagnostic characters of

Fig. 10. Bill shapes of Diving-petrels

Following sketches and notes based on Murphy & Harper (1921)

135 *P. georgicus* Bill proportionately broad at base, septal process in middle of nostril opening. Nostrils shorter in relation to bill length than in *P. urinatrix*. When viewed from underside broad at base, converging gradually in pointed 'Gothic' arch to tip. Wing length 104–122mm

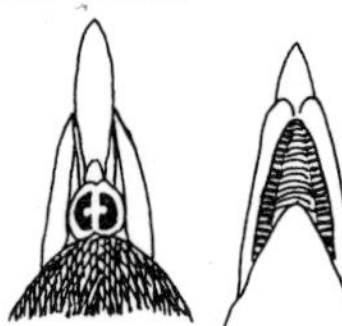

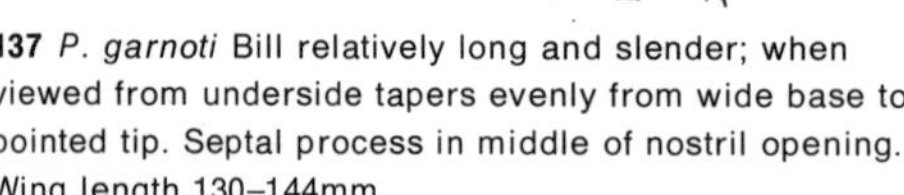

137 *P. garnoti* Bill relatively long and slender; when viewed from underside tapers evenly from wide base to pointed tip. Septal process in middle of nostril opening. Wing length 130–144mm

136 *P. urinatrix* Bill proportionately stout and blunt, septal process towards rear of nostril opening. Nostrils longer in relation to bill length than in *P. georgicus*. When viewed from underside sides nearly parallel, converging only at tip. Wing length 106–125mm

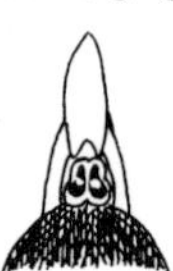

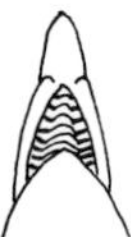

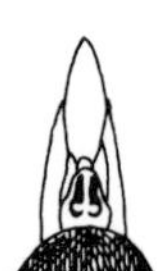

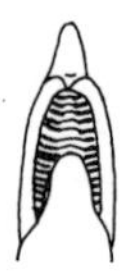

138 *P. magellani* Bill relatively slender, septal process in middle of nostril opening, nostrils widely divergent posteriorly. When viewed from underside broad at base, converging gradually in pointed 'Gothic' arch to tip. Wing length 120–135mm

scapular bars, distribution of markings on throat and flanks, underwing pattern and bill shape are seen only in the hand or at close range. In the past breeding and oceanic ranges of the four species were thought not to overlap, thus locality of sighting was considered sufficient clue to identity. Recent work, however, has shown that *P. georgicus* and various forms of *P. urinatrix* are sympatric at South Georgia, Marion, Crozet, Kerguelen, Heard, Auckland and possibly Macquarie Is.

Flight and habits of the four species similar. They are normally encountered in offshore waters close to breeding grounds, although mid-ocean sightings, usually ascribed to examples of *P. urinatrix*, indicate some, at least, undertake a wider dispersal. Flight swift and low, wings in constant motion, buzzing and whirring over waves; in rough weather even observed to 'fly' through crests of waves without so much as a pause. Usually enter water in full flight, simply flying into waves and disappearing; emerge in same manner, suddenly appearing from depths; use wings for propulsion underwater and appear to 'fly' through both air and water with equal ease. Rest on water singly or in small rafts, when hard to detect at sea unless they take flight, due to small size and colouring. Do not follow ships though occasionally attracted to their lights at night; visit land only at night, probably due to predation by skuas. During moult some species, perhaps all, are flightless for short periods.

135 GEORGIAN DIVING-PETREL
Pelecanoides georgicus

PLATE 38 Fig. 135
MAP 135

Length 18–21cm (7–8¼in.). Wingspan 30–33cm (12–13in.). Iris brown. Bill black. Legs/feet blue, webs black.

Southern Atlantic and Indian Oceans, where range overlaps with Common Diving-petrel (p. 279). The two probably inseparable at sea. Sexes alike; no seasonal variation although white tips to scapulars and secondaries probably wear fainter. Juveniles not separable at sea from adults. No subspecies.

PLUMAGE: Head Forehead and lores brownish, crown and nape blackish shading to blue-grey on sides of face and neck, each feather narrowly tipped with white. Chin and throat mainly white but variable, some with grey chins extending as faint collar from sides of neck, others with indistinct mottling on sides of neck and throat forming only partial collar (Murphy & Harper 1921). **Body** Upperparts glossy-black; scapulars greyish-white, variably tipped grey forming, in most specimens, a diagonal stripe. Underparts mostly white, sides of breast and flanks variably barred with grey. **Wings** Upperwing glossy-black, primaries faintly browner, inner webs greyer; secondaries narrowly edged with white. Underwing-coverts white, axillaries grey, primaries and secondaries deep grey. **Tail** Glossy black above, greyer below.

FHJ: See family introduction (p. 278) for flight and habits.

DM: Confined to sub-antarctic zone, breeding at South Georgia, Marion, Prince Edward, Crozet, Kerguelen, Heard and Auckland Is (where probably extinct), and Codfish I. (near Stewart I.); perhaps also on Macquarie I. but status there unclear. Egg-dates Nov–Jan; fledging begins Mar. Probably sedentary although a beach derelict recovered south of Sydney, Australia (Serventy *et al.* 1971).

SS: See notes under Common Diving-petrel (p. 279).

136 COMMON DIVING-PETREL
other: Sub-antarctic Diving-petrel
Pelecanoides urinatrix

PLATE 38 Figs 136a-136b
MAP 136

Length 20–25cm (8–10in.). Wingspan 33–38cm (13–15in.). Iris brown. Bill black. Legs/feet blue or lavender, webs black.

Southern Oceans, the most widespread of all diving-petrels. Range overlaps with Georgian, perhaps also Magellan, Diving-petrels (p. 279, p. 280). At close range separable from latter, but separation at sea from former probably impossible. Sexes alike; no seasonal variation. Juveniles differ from adults only in weaker, smaller bills. Six subspecies listed varying from each other in size, bill dimensions and amount of grey on throat and sides of breast, although some individual variation within each population. Following descriptions refer to *P.u. urinatrix*.

PLUMAGE: Head Forehead, crown and nape black; ear-coverts and sides of neck mottled grey, usually extending across white throat as indistinct collar, but in some chin and throat wholly white. **Body** Upperparts black. Underparts mostly white except for grey barring on sides of breast, flanks and undertail-coverts. **Wings** Upperwing: browner in hue than back, particularly primaries, inner webs of which noticeably brown. Underwing: coverts and axillaries grey, primaries and secondaries blackish. **Tail** Black above, greyer below.

FHJ: See family introduction (p. 278); perhaps the most pelagic of the diving-petrels and probably partially migratory in some parts of range.

DM: Southern Oceans, generally between 35°S and 55°S. *P.u. berard* breeds Falklands; *P.u. dacunhae* Tristan da Cunha group and Gough I.; *P.u. exsul* South Georgia, Marion, Prince Edward, Crozets, Heard, Kerguelen, Auckland and Antipodes, possibly also Macquarie and Campbell. *P.u. urinatrix* islands of Bass Strait, coasts of Victoria, Tasmania and New Zealand. *P.u. chathamensis* Chatham and Snares Is. Status of *P.u. copperingeri*, collected southern Chile (Murphy 1936), remains unclear. Breeding season varies between populations but all in southern summer. In Australia returns to colonies Jul, on Tristan and Falklands in Sep, whilst on Heard I. not until Nov or Dec. Falkland population disperses N in winter to coasts of Argentina, reaching N to at least 40°S.

SS: Due to small size and low, whirring flight the four diving-petrels are unlikely to be confused with other seabirds in Southern Oceans. Specific identification usually impossible at sea. The following notes are based on examination of museum skins and should be regarded as tentative. See Fig. 10 for identification in the hand. *P. urinatrix* differs from *P. georgicus* in browner upperwings contrasting with black back (although when wet difference probably negligible), lack of diagonal white bar across scapulars, and in usually more pronounced collar across throat and grey underwing-coverts (white in *P. georgicus*). Last character extremely hard to see at sea when wings constantly whirring, especially from the high, unstable vantage of a ship. *P. garnoti* differs from *P. urinatrix* in distribution, larger size, blacker upperwing with conspicuous diagonal stripe across scapulars, and secondaries narrowly edged with white. These characters should impart a more contrasting black and white effect at sea. *P. magellani* differs from all other diving-petrels in whitish fringes to upperpart feathers (in fresh plumage) and clearly defined facial pattern.

137 PERUVIAN DIVING-PETREL *Pelecanoides garnoti*

PLATE 38 Fig. 137
MAP 137

Length 20–24cm (8–9½in.). Wingspan not recorded. Iris brown, bill black. Legs/feet blue, webs black.

Confined to western coasts of South America. Range normally diagnostic, although in far south overlaps with Magellan Diving-petrel (p. 280). If seen closely the two can be separated at sea. Sexes alike; no seasonal variation though white tips to scapulars probably wear fainter. Juveniles differ from adults only in weaker, smaller bill. No subspecies.

PLUMAGE: Head Mostly blackish, anterior forehead and lores browner, chin and throat white. **Body** Upperparts black, scapulars variably ash-white forming distinct diagonal stripe. Underparts mostly white, sides of breast mottled with dark grey, extending in some to form indistinct breast band; sides and flanks deep grey. **Wings** Upperwing glossy black, primaries washed with brown, secondaries narrowly tipped with white. Underwing: coverts ash-white, axillaries dark grey or black, primaries and secondaries dark grey; in some underwing mostly dark grey with lighter flecks along leading edge (Warham, pers. comm.). **Tail** Black above, white below.

FHJ: See family introduction (p. 278).

DM: Restricted to coasts of Peru and northern Chile from Lobos de Tierra at 6°S to Corral 37°S (de Schauensee 1966). Egg-dates throughout year. Movements not known, probably sporadic, linked with fluctuations of Humboldt Current; ranges S to 42°S. Formerly much more numerous, now in serious decline due to destruction of nesting habitat by the guano industry.

SS: See notes under Common Diving-petrel (p. 279). Off Peru locality is sufficient clue to identity. Range overlaps with Magellan Diving-petrel (p. 280) further S off Ancud, Chile, but that species has distinctive plumage and at close range separation should be possible.

138 MAGELLAN DIVING-PETREL *Pelecanoides magellani*

PLATE 38 Figs 138a-138c
MAP 138

Length 19–20cm (7½–8in.). Wingspan not recorded. Iris brown. Bill black. Legs/feet blue, webs black.

Confined to extreme southern South America, where range overlaps with Peruvian and perhaps also Common Diving-petrels (p. 280, p. 279). At close range separable from both by distinctive plumage. Sexes alike; no seasonal variation but in worn plumage whitish tips to upperparts reduced or absent. Unlike other members of family, juveniles distinguishable from adults. No subspecies.

JUVENILE: As adult except for weaker bill, dark scapulars, back and rump.

ADULT: Head Lores and anterior part of forehead blackish-brown, remainder mostly glossy black, cheeks and ear-coverts slightly greyer and sharply demarcated from white chin and throat. A conspicuous white crescent extends upwards behind ear-coverts towards hindcrown. **Body** Upperparts mostly glossy black, narrowly fringed with grey on middle back and upper rump; scapulars variably grey, tipped with white forming, in most individuals, distinct diagonal stripe. Underparts white except for dark grey barring on sides of breast and flanks. **Wings** Upperwing: primaries blackish-brown, inner webs paler; secondaries blackish edged with white, coverts black, fringed greyish-white. Underwing mostly white, axillaries grey or blackish-grey, outer primaries dusky. **Tail** Blackish above, greyer below. NOTE White fringes to wing-coverts, back and rump most noticeable in fresh plumage (Aug); in worn plumage (Mar) reduced or absent (Murphy 1936).

FHJ: See family introduction (p. 278). Apparently wings proportionately longer than in Common Diving-petrel (Alexander 1955).

DM: Coasts and fiords of southern Chile, Patagonia and Tierra del Fuego, from Cape Horn and Staten Is, N to Chiloé Is; egg-dates Dec (Alexander 1954). The only diving-petrel collected in Straits of Magellan (Humphrey *et al.* 1970). Occurs in Fuegian waters throughout year although some disperse N to Puerto Deseado, perhaps even further, during austral winter. Recorded up to 128km from landfall off Tierra del Fuego (Humphrey *et al.* 1970).

SS: Separated from other diving-petrels by distinctive plumage, particularly white fringes to upperparts and diagnostic white half-collar extending from throat upwards towards hindcrown.

Order *PELECANIFORMES* pelicans, boobies, cormorants, frigatebirds, tropicbirds, anhingas

Six families, one of which, *Anhingidae*, is not covered in this guide; the remaining five comprise five genera and 48–55 species. Medium-sized to huge aquatic birds frequenting both marine and fresh water.

Appearance of five families diverse. *Phaethontidae* and *Fregatidae* most aberrant of order, which contains many colourful species. Widely distributed but mainly in tropical and temperate seas. Some members enjoy a circumtropical or almost cosmopolitan distribution whilst others, e.g. Abbott's Booby, breed only on one island. Generally less pelagic than many seabird orders, although tropicbirds, frigatebirds and some boobies are often encountered in mid ocean, but others, notably some pelicans and cormorants, are found on inland waters. Many species breed in colonies, often densely, and may number over 1 million birds (Guanay Cormorant and Peruvian Booby). *Pelecaniformes* generally have more arboreal nesting habits than any other seabird order.

The five genera comprising the *Pelecaniformes* order are easily separable from each other but specific identification within each genus often difficult and in some cases, e.g. juvenile/immature frigatebirds, may be impossible.

Family *PHAETHONTIDAE* tropicbirds

Three species in single genus; smallest of the *Pelecaniformes*. Characteristics of family discussed below under genus heading.

Genus *PHAETHON*

Three species; medium-sized, highly aerial seabirds, all closely related and resembling each other in appearance. Plumage mainly white in adults, variously marked with black on head and wings; central tail feathers elongated to wispy streamers as long as or longer than rest of body. Distributed throughout tropical and subtropical latitudes of all three major oceans. Mainly pelagic outside breeding areas, ranging far from land where mostly solitary, but several may attend large flocks of feeding terns and shearwaters.

Normally occupies air space 10–17m above water's surface with graceful, pigeon-like flight, fluttering wing strokes alternated with soaring glides producing 'butterfly-progression'. Feed by first hovering and then plunging on half-closed wings in manner of a gannet and, like that group and diving pelicans, all tropicbirds have a cushion of air-cells under skin in front of body. On surfacing they float lightly with tails cocked. Often attracted to ships, circling with loud screams.

Specific identification of tropicbirds complicated by their soaring habits, during which the various distinguishing characters on head, mantle, scapulars, back and upperwings difficult to see. With comparative experience differences in jizz and flight, particularly relative width of wings and 'weight' of body, useful characters in these circumstances. Colour of bill and tail streamers also important and should be accurately recorded.

139 RED-BILLED TROPICBIRD *Phaethon aethereus*

PLATE 39 Figs 139a-139b
MAP 139

Length 46–50cm (18–19½in.) without 46–56cm tail streamers. Wingspan 99–106cm (39–42in.). Iris blackish-brown. Bill red. Legs yellowish, webs distally black.

Tropical eastern Pacific, Caribbean, Atlantic and northern Indian Ocean; in some areas range overlaps with Red- and White-tailed Tropicbirds (p. 282, p. 282). Sexes similar, streamers of males average longer; no seasonal variation. Juveniles separable from adults. Three subspecies listed; Atlantic *P.a. mesonauta* differs in rosy cast (fresh plumage) and paler barring on upperparts. Indian Ocean *P.a. indicus* has reddish-orange bill with black cutting edges and reduced black eye-stripe. Following descriptions refer to nominate.

JUVENILE: Bill yellowish, tip often black. Much as adult except: **Head** Black eye-stripes usually joined across nape; crown, nape and hindneck faintly barred dark grey. **Body** Upperparts: broader and coarser barring. **Tail** Lacks streamers, tips black.

ADULT: Head Mostly white except for conspicuous black eye-stripe and faint grey mottling on nape and hindneck. **Body** Upperparts white with narrow greyish-black barring and vermiculation. Underparts white; lower flanks mottled grey. **Wings** Upperwing: outer four primaries and their coverts greyish-black, remainder mostly white with blackish barring on innermost lesser and median coverts and secondaries. Underwing white; inner secondaries edged dusky-grey. **Tail** White; long streamers.

FHJ: See notes under genus. Equal in size to Red-tailed Tropicbird (p. 282) but with lighter jizz. At close range broad eye-stripe, barred upperparts and long white tail streamers diagnostic, at sea, however, in strong sunlight at even moderate range upperparts (except wingtips) can appear wholly white or dusky-grey. Compared with White-tailed Tropicbird (p. 282) larger, with broader wings and slower, more purposeful wingbeats. Occasionally follows ships.

DM: *P.a. mesonauta* breeds eastern Pacific from Gulf of California S to Galapagos Is, islands off Ecuador and San Lorenzo (Peru); in Atlantic from Virgin Is in Caribbean S to Panama and Venezuela and at Cape Verde Is and islands off Senegal. *P.a. aethereus* breeds tropical Atlantic at Fernando Noronha, Ascension and St Helena Is. *P.a. indicus* Red Sea, Persian Gulf and Arabian Sea. Egg-dates throughout year (see Palmer 1962 for details). No regular migration, disperses to adjacent seas; immatures probably wander further than adults. Off southern California, USA, singles regularly occur in summer, peaking during Sep, with vagrants N to Washington. Off eastern USA occasionally occurs N to Florida and North Carolina but Lee *et al.* (1981) suggest that it may occur off eastern USA more than is generally realised. Unconfirmed reports of this species from Philippines and Micronesia.

SS: No other adult tropicbird has combination of red bill, long white tail streamers and barred upperparts. Juveniles of present species differ from those of White-tailed Tropicbird (p. 282) in finer, denser barring on upperparts and distinct blackish nuchal collar joined across nape. See also Red-tailed Tropicbird juvenile (p. 282). When soaring present species usually shows distinct barring on inner secondaries and tertials of underwing; White-tailed shows dusky 'shadow' of black inner secondaries and tertials of upperwing, whilst Red-tailed shows little or no marks on underwing. See above for structure and flight differences.

140 RED-TAILED TROPICBIRD *Phaethon rubricauda*

PLATE 39 Figs 140a-140b
MAP 140

Length 46cm (18in.) without 30–35cm tail streamers. Wingspan 104cm (41in.). Iris brown. Bill red. Legs/feet blue-grey, webs distally black.

Tropical Indian and Pacific Oceans; range overlaps with smaller White-tailed (p. 282) and perhaps with Red-billed Tropicbird (p. 281) in Indian Ocean. Sexes similar; no seasonal variation but pink flush (fresh plumage) often wears white. Juveniles separable from adults. Four subspecies listed; none separable at sea.

JUVENILE: Bill usually blackish (unlike other juvenile tropicbirds). Plumage much as adult's except: **Head** Crown, nape and hindneck faintly barred grey. **Body** Upperparts white barred blackish-grey. **Wings** Upperwing: coverts as upperparts. **Tail** Lacks streamers, tips black.

ADULT: Head Mostly white; black stripe from gape, curving upwards and passing through eye. **Body** Mostly white (flushed pink in fresh plumage); scapulars tipped black. **Wings** Upperwing mostly white; shafts of outer primaries black. Underwing wholly white; occasionally shows dusky edgings to a few inner secondaries (see Red-billed Tropicbird, p. 281). **Tail** White, streamers red.

FHJ: See notes on p. 281. Intermediate in size between Red-billed and White-tailed Tropicbirds with proportionately shorter tail and heavier jizz. Flight less graceful than those species, rather ponderous and laboured. Rarely shows interest in ships (see 'White-tailed Tropicbird).

DM: Tropical Pacific and Indian Oceans. *P.r. melanorhynchos* breeds in Pacific Ocean on many islands including Bonin, Hawaiian, Volcano and New Caledonia S to Pitcairn. *P.r. roseotincta* in SW Pacific at Rain, Herald, Coringa, Lord Howe, Norfolk and Kermadec Is. In Indian Ocean *P.r. rubricauda* breeds Aldabra, Comoro, Mauritius and Seychelles. *P.r. westralis* off NW Australia, including Christmas and Cocos (Keeling) Is and perhaps islands in Banda Sea. Races may also breed at Paracel Reefs, South China Sea, and at Easter I., SE Pacific Ocean. Egg-dates throughout year. Dispersal poorly understood but appears to wander more widely than other tropicbirds; frequently encountered in mid ocean, many hundreds of miles from nearest landfall, often in association with Sooty Terns and feeding shearwaters. Recent sightings in Pacific have shown that some range N of Hawaii to 36°N (Gould, pers. comm.) and to within 160km of south California coast (see Roberson 1980). Stragglers have reached Japan, Bay of Bengal, and Kommetjie, South Africa (the only Atlantic record) (Brooke & Sinclair 1978).

SS: Adults with mostly white upperparts and red tail (visible at range of 1.6km (1 mile) at sea) readily identified. Immatures recall Red-billed Tropicbird (p. 281) but lack extensive black eye-stripes and dusky secondaries on underwing of that species. Immature White-tailed Tropicbirds (p. 282) similarly barred above but have yellowish bills and feet. NOTE Juveniles of present species fledge with blackish bills but these quickly change to yellow, then orange and finally red in adults (Shallenberger 1978).

141 WHITE-TAILED TROPICBIRD *Phaethon lepturus*

PLATE 39 Figs 141a-141c
MAP 141

Length 38–40cm (15–16in.) without 33–40cm tail streamers. Wingspan 89–96cm (35–38in.). Iris brownish. Bill yellowish to orange. Legs/feet yellowish, webs blackish.

Tropical oceans; range overlaps with Red-billed and Red-tailed Tropicbirds (p. 281, p. 282). Sexes similar, streamers of males average longer; no seasonal variation. Juveniles separable from adults. Four or five subspecies; *P.l. fulvus* differs in rich, golden-apricot wash over white plumage.

JUVENILE: Bill dull yellowish, tip often black. Plumage much as adult except: **Head** Crown, nape

and hindneck faintly barred grey. **Body** Upperparts barred greyish-black. **Wings** Upperwing: coverts as upperparts. **Tail** Lacks streamers; tips black.
ADULT: Head Mostly white; black stripe from gape curving upwards and passing through eye. **Body** Upperparts mostly white, scapulars tipped black. Underparts white; longer flank feathers tipped black. **Wings** Upperwing: outer webs of outer 4–5 primaries mostly black, with black median coverts, inner secondaries and their coverts forming conspicuous diagonal stripe on otherwise white wing. Underwing translucent white, innermost tertials sometimes edged dusky. **Tail** White; streamered.
FHJ: See notes on p. 281. Smallest, most delicate and graceful of the tropicbirds with diagnostic upperwing pattern and orange or yellow bill. Compared with larger Red-billed Tropicbird wings proportionately narrower; wingbeats faster. Habitually attracted to ships, hovering over rigging before attempting to perch.
DM: Tropical oceans. *P.l. catesbyi* breeds from Bermuda and Bahamas S through Caribbean islands; those breeding Fernando de Noronha, Ascension and islands in Gulf of Guinea sometimes treated as *P.l. ascensionis* although doubtfully distinct from nominate. In Indian Ocean *P.l. lepturus* breeds Comoro, Aldabra, Seychelles, Mauritius, Reunion, Chagos, Maldives, Andaman (?), and Cocos (Keeling) Is; *P.l. fulvus* at Christmas I. *P.l. dorothea* at numerous islands in tropical Pacific from Hawaiian and Christmas I. to Tuamotu Is and New Caledonia. Egg-dates throughout year. Migratory in some parts of range, e.g. Bermuda, arriving Feb/Mar; egg-dates Mar–Jun; final departure Sep/Oct. Occurs casually along Gulf coast to Florida, N to South Carolina; vagrant N to Nova Scotia. See Roberson (1980) for only North American Pacific record.
SS: When upperparts seen adults with yellowish or orange bill, diagnostic upperwing pattern and white streamers readily identifiable. See notes under Red-billed Tropicbird for separation of juveniles.

Family *PELECANIDAE* pelicans

One genus containing seven species (or eight if *P.o. thagus* considered a distinct species, see p. 286). Characteristics of family discussed under genus heading.

Genus *PELECANUS*

Seven or eight species; distinctive owing to size, broad wings, large bill and distensible pouch. Plumage in five species mainly black and white in adults, grey in one species, and brown in the marine species which differs further in executing spectacular plunge-dives in manner of a gannet. Juveniles generally duller than adults with varying amounts of brown in plumage. Maturity reached in 3–4 years. At all stages wings often appear ragged due to absence of one or more flight feathers, most birds thus appearing somewhat scruffy.

Social, breeding, feeding and flying together. Flight consists of heavy flaps followed by long glide, frequently low to surface of water, in extended skeins; sometimes at considerable height during movements, gaining height by soaring on outstretched wings in thermals. Requires ungainly run across surface to become airborne. Most species fish together in small flocks, gathering in horseshoe-shaped lines and driving fish from deeper water into shallows, where birds submerge their opened pouches to scoop up fish. Whilst discussing habits some readers may be unaware that all pelican species are extremely sensitive to human disturbance and freely desert eggs; breeding colonies should not, therefore, be visited without care and consideration. Numbers in America and Europe are declining and although at present plentiful in Third World countries pressure wrought on all life forms by industrial development will, presumably, eventually reduce numbers globally.

Distributed throughout most tropical and temperate regions of both hemispheres. Dispersive and migratory with such species as *P. erythrorhynchos* forming large flocks before migrating, mainly overland and normally at considerable heights, even to 3,050m.

Identification where sympatric black-and-white-plumaged forms occur should be based on extent of black on wings and bare parts coloration.

142 EASTERN WHITE PELICAN
other: White Pelican
Pelecanus onocrotalus

PLATE 40 Figs 142a-142c

MAP 142

Length 140–175cm (55–69in.). Wingspan 270–360cm (106½–142in.). Iris red with pinkish-yellow facial skin (sometimes bright orange in females). Bill blue-grey and yellow with reddish cutting edges and tip. Pouch yellow to orange. Legs/feet red.

Confined to Old World, where range overlaps with Dalmatian and Pink-backed Pelicans (p. 285, p. 284). Distinguished at all ages by diagnostic wing pattern and, in adults, by bare parts colours. Sexes alike; seasonal variation in plumage and bare parts colours. Juveniles separable from adults. No subspecies.
JUVENILE: Iris brown. Bill yellow, greyer at base

with yellowish pouch. Legs/feet grey. **Head** Mainly greyish-brown, whiter on forehead, crown and foreneck. **Body** Upperparts: mantle, scapulars and back brown, tipped white; rump and uppertail-coverts white. Underparts greyish-white. **Wings** Upperwing: dark brown, blacker on primaries and outer secondaries; coverts edged white. Underwing appears largely brown with white central stripe.

ADULT NON-BREEDING: Legs/feet pink. Plumage as breeding adult except: **Head** Lacks crest and yellow at base of foreneck. **Body and Wings** White areas often show buffish cast, appearing dirty and unkempt.

ADULT BREEDING: Head Wholly white except for yellow patch at base of foreneck; short ragged crest on hindcrown. **Body** Wholly white with variable pinkish cast. **Wings** Upperwings: largely white with black primaries and primary-coverts; outer secondaries black shading to grey on inner secondaries. Underwing white; black primaries and secondaries diagnostic within range.

FHJ: Huge, the second largest pelican. Typical gregarious habits of genus (p. 283).

DM: Now rare in southern Europe, breeding only Romania, Danube Delta; Greece, Lake Mikra Prespa. African colonies widely distributed from Ethiopia southwards through Rift Valley Lakes; also Mauritania, Namibia and South Africa. In Asia at Black, Caspian and Aral Seas, also Lakes Rezaiyeh and Balkash. Breeding status Indo-China and Indus Delta uncertain. Northern populations migratory; less so in tropics but precise movements largely unknown. Many winter Nile Delta, Suez and Red Sea. Occasionally occurs Cyprus, and Libya W to Malta and Algeria; stragglers recorded N to Finland and France may have been escapes. Asiatic birds largely absent from wintering populations of Dalmatian Pelicans on Caspian Sea but direction of dispersal unknown. Many reach Indian subcontinent, occasionally Malay Peninsula.

SS: Likely to be confused with storks *Ciconiidae* when seen high overhead. Differs from Dalmatian Pelican (p. 285) at all ages in diagnostic underwing pattern. Adult also differs in bare parts coloration. Pink-backed Pelican (p. 284) smaller, and has greyer primaries and secondaries on underwing with pinkish coverts; bare parts coloration also different.

---

143 PINK-BACKED PELICAN
Pelecanus rufescens

PLATE 40 Figs 143a-143d
MAP 143

Length 125–132cm (49–52in.). Wingspan 265–290cm (104½–114in.). Iris dark, orbital ring pink with black spot before eye. Bill pale pinkish-yellow. Legs/feet dull apricot.

African; range overlaps with Eastern White Pelican (p. 283). Distinguished by smaller size, wing pattern and bare parts colours. Sexes alike; seasonal variation in plumage and bare parts colours. Juveniles separable from adults. No subspecies.

JUVENILE: Resembles adult except bare parts greyer. **Head** Brown cast to nape and hindneck. **Body** Upper and lower parts dirty-white with brown and white feather tips. Rump and uppertail-coverts white. **Wings** Upperwing: primaries and secondaries blackish-grey, forewing brownish with white tips. **Tail** Pale brown.

IMMATURE: As juvenile except mantle, scapulars, back and upperwing-coverts paler.

ADULT NON-BREEDING: Orbital ring grey. As breeding adult except mantle, back, scapulars and upperwing-coverts sullied with brown.

ADULT BREEDING: Head Mostly white, short grey crest on nape. **Body** Upperparts white with pinkish cast. Underparts grey with paler lanceolate streaks and pinkish cast. **Wings** Upperwing: primaries and secondaries dull greyish-brown; forewing as upperparts. Underwing shows greyish primaries and secondaries, pale greater coverts, pinkish lesser and median coverts. **Tail** Pinkish-grey.

FHJ: Smaller than Eastern White and Dalmatian Pelicans (p. 283, p. 285). Normally roosts in trees (unlike Eastern White Pelican).

DM: Occurs throughout Africa S of Sahara including Madagascar and N to 25°N in Red Sea. Movements probably linked to local rains and food supply. Stragglers N to Egypt, Israel and SW Arabia.

SS: From Eastern White Pelican (p. 283) by smaller size, pinker cast to plumage in breeding adults and grey primaries and secondaries. Non-breeders greyer. Juveniles resemble more closely Dalmatian Pelican (p. 285); best told by size, bill coloration and pinkish-white or yellow legs.

---

144 SPOT-BILLED PELICAN
other: Grey Pelican
Pelecanus philippensis

PLATE 40 Figs 144a-144c
MAP 144

Length 127–152cm (50–60in.). Wingspan unrecorded. Iris white or yellow, orbital ring yellowish. Bill pinkish-yellow with blue or blackish spots along sides, orange-yellow tip. Pouch dull purple with blackish markings. Legs/feet dark brown.

Asiatic; range overlaps with Eastern White and Dalmatian Pelicans (p. 283, p. 285). Distinguished by smaller size, wing pattern and bare parts colours. Sexes alike; seasonal variation in plumage and bare parts colours. Juveniles separable from adults. No subspecies (treated as conspecific with Dalmatian Pelican by some authors).

JUVENILE: Legs/feet grey. Resembles non-breeding adult but: **Head** Browner, particularly on nape and hindneck. **Body** Upperparts: browner on mantle, scapulars and back; rump and uppertail-coverts white. **Wings** Upperwing: primaries and trailing edge of secondaries dark brown. Forewing mainly white, greater coverts sullied with brown. Underwing largely white, primaries brown. **Tail** Pale brown.

ADULT NON-BREEDING: Orbital ring whiter. Plumage as breeding adult except: **Head** Browner cast to nape. **Body and Wings** Browner cast to mantle, scapulars and wing-coverts.

ADULT BREEDING: Head Mainly white; ragged crest and nape brown, tipped white. **Body** Mainly white, lower back, rump, flanks and undertail-coverts washed pink (beware Pink-backed Pelican, p. 284). Underparts greyer. **Wings** Upperwing: primaries, primary-coverts and outer secondaries blackish, paling to white at tertials. Remainder white tinged pink. Underwing mostly white, primaries dark brown. **Tail** White with brownish feather edges.

FHJ: Typical of genus, preferring freshwater localities throughout much of range. Smaller than most other pelicans and rather dirty in appearance, the back and coverts having a brownish cast.

DM: Asiatic; breeds India, Sri Lanka, Burma, Malay Peninsula, southern China and the Philippines. Migratory and dispersive, birds ranging widely over Indian subcontinent; stragglers E to Japan.

SS: Larger Eastern White Pelican (p. 283) has diagnostic underwing pattern. Range overlaps that of Dalmatian Pelican during winter months on Indian subcontinent. Best told by smaller size, pink base to bill (grey in Dalmatian) and dingy appearance. (Some Spot-billed Pelicans show grey legs.)

145 DALMATIAN PELICAN *Pelecanus crispus*

PLATE 40 Figs 145a-145c
MAP 145

Length 160–180cm (63–71in.). Wingspan 310–345cm (122–136in.). Iris pale yellow, facial skin purple. Bill grey at base with yellower culmen shading to red distally. Pouch bright orange. Legs/feet dark grey.

Eurasian; range overlaps with Eastern White and Pink-backed Pelicans (p. 283, p. 284). Distinguished by size, wing pattern and bare parts colours. Sexes alike; seasonal variation in plumage and bare parts colours. Juveniles separable from adults. No subspecies (treated as conspecific with Spot-billed Pelican by some authors).

JUVENILE: Bill and pouch lead-grey. **Head** Mainly greyish-brown, whiter on forehead and over eyes. **Body** Upperparts: mantle, scapulars and back greyish-brown, scapulars tipped brown; rump and uppertail-coverts white. Underparts greyish-white. **Wings** Upperwing: as mantle with darker primaries and outer secondaries, coverts tipped darker brown. Underwing as adult. **Tail** White.

IMMATURE: Similar except: **Body and Wings** Whiter.

ADULT NON-BREEDING: Facial skin and pouch yellow. Plumage as breeding adult except: **Head** Crest reduced, lacks yellow base to foreneck. **Body and Wings** Dirtier in appearance, plumage somewhat dingy.

ADULT BREEDING: Head and Body Mainly silvery-white; untidy crest on nape. Underparts show blue/grey cast. **Wings** Upperwing: largely white except for dark grey primaries and a few outer secondaries. Underwing white with grey primaries (see Eastern White Pelican, p. 283).

FHJ: Largest pelican but more slender than Eastern White Pelican. Typical habits of genus (p. 283).

DM: Marked decline throughout range. Now breeds Romania: Danube Delta; Yugoslavia: Lake Skadar; Greece: Lake Mikra Prespa and near Prewesa; Albania: Lake Malik; Turkey: near Eregli, Kizil Irmak Delta and Lake Manyas; USSR: Sea of Azov, north Caspian Sea, Aral Sea, Lake Balkash and several other scattered sites, E to Chinese border. Colonies also in northern China, Mongolia and southern Iran but present status in these areas unknown. Migratory in N, Iranian birds probably only dispersive. Most European breeders winter eastern Mediterranean S to Egypt. Asiatic stock winters southern Caspian and across Indian subcontinent, particularly Indus and Ganges rivers. Immatures normally remain in wintering areas throughout year.

SS: See notes under Eastern White Pelican (p. 283).

146 AUSTRALIAN PELICAN *Pelecanus conspicillatus*

PLATE 41 Figs 146a-146c
MAP 146

Length 152–183cm (60–72in.). Wingspan 244–260cm (96–102½in.). Iris brown with yellowish orbital ring. Bill pink, yellow at tip with pink or pink and red pouch bordered with blue-black line on each side.

Breeds Australia; only pelican of the region. Sexes alike; slight seasonal variation. Juveniles separable from adults. No subspecies.

JUVENILE: Orbital ring, pouch and bill mostly pink, latter tipped orange; legs brownish-grey. Plumage resembles non-breeding adult except: **Head** Lacks crest; crown and nape washed with brown. **Body and Wings** Brown where adults black.

ADULT NON-BREEDING: As breeding adult except pouch mostly pink. **Head** Nape darker grey, sometimes tipped with black; foreneck white.

ADULT BREEDING: Head Mostly white except for short grey nuptial crest on nape and hindneck. Base of foreneck yellowish or pinkish. **Body** Upperparts and underparts white except for broad black V across rump. **Wings** Upperwing mainly black except for broad white patch extending from leading edge across coverts. Underwing: coverts white, primaries and secondaries black. **Tail** White broadly tipped with black.

FHJ: Typical pelican jizz, found mainly on fresh water, but also at marine locations. Nests colonially and to some extent feeds co-operatively, several birds forming loose circle or line and sifting water in unison. Flight typical of genus, with laboured flaps and soaring on outstretched wings.

DM: Breeds throughout Australia. Egg-dates Jul–Nov. Status in New Guinea uncertain, probably only a casual visitor. In Australia subject to irregular movements when local rains fail and inland

waters dry up. Disperses widely, some reaching New Zealand, Lesser Sunda Is, Java, and even N of Equator to Palau Is.
SS: The only pelican of the region. At distance or extreme height could be confused with Black-necked Stork or White-breasted Sea Eagle (consult local bird guide).

147 AMERICAN WHITE PELICAN
Pelecanus erythrorhynchos

PLATE 41 Figs 147a-147c
MAP 147

Length 127–178cm (50–70in.). Wingspan 244–299cm (96–118in.). Males average larger. Iris orange-yellow with orange orbital ring. Facial skin and pouch yellowish. Bill pink or yellow with paler upper ridge; in breeding season, prominent horny knob on upper mandible. Legs/feet orange-red.

Confined to North America, the only black and white pelican of the region. Sexes alike; slight seasonal variation. Juveniles separable from adults. No subspecies.
JUVENILE: Pouch and facial skin grey. Resembles non-breeding adult except: **Head** Crown, nape and hindneck brownish. **Wings** Brown where adults black.
ADULT NON-BREEDING: As breeding adult except: Upper mandible lacks horny knob (shed Jun/Jul). **Head** Crown and nape grey, varies in extent between individuals.
ADULT BREEDING: Head Including neck mostly white except for yellowish cast to upper breast. **Wings** Upperwing white except for black primaries and outer secondaries. Underwing similar. **Tail** White.
FHJ: Differs from Brown Pelican (p. 286) in preferring mainly freshwater habitat. Feeding habits also differ; present species feeds in small groups, assembling in line and driving fish into shallows before dipping bills and scooping fish (Brown Pelican usually executes plunge-dives). Flight typical of genus, slow flaps followed by long glide, neck hunched back to body. Migrates almost exclusively overland, often at considerable heights in extended skeins or V formations. During fall and winter some frequent shallow coastal bays.
DM: Confined to North America where breeds on islands of inland lakes. Formerly more widespread, ranging from British Columbia and Prairie Provinces of Canada S to Texas where a small colony S of Corpus Christi. Main breeding areas now in Prairie Provinces and in scattered colonies in E Washington, S and N California, W Nevada, S Idaho, N Utah, Montana, Wyoming, the Dakotas, W Minnesota and coastal Texas. Egg-dates Apr–Jun. Thousands congregate in southern Great Plains during fall before moving S to winter mainly Gulf of Mexico, Florida and coasts of Central America S to West Indies and Guatemala. In the W flocks numbering hundreds winter coast of central California S through Gulf of California. Stragglers reach N to eastern Alaska; scarce in eastern States N to Nova Scotia.
SS: More likely to be confused with Wood Stork, Whooping Crane or Snow Goose, which are also large and have black and white plumages but fly with necks extended; refer to N American field guides (p. 406).

148 BROWN PELICAN
Pelecanus occidentalis

PLATE 41 Figs 148a-148d
MAP 148

Length averages 114cm (45in.). Wingspan 203cm (80in.). Iris pale yellow, pupil dark with pink orbital ring and blue-grey facial skin. Bill grey or yellowish with scarlet cast on distal portion and yellow tip. Pouch varies from red to blackish. Legs/feet blue-grey to black.

Confined to North and South America. Sexes outwardly alike, males average larger; slight seasonal variation. Juveniles separable from adults. Six subspecies listed but specific status of *P.o. thagus*, which may be separate species (Wetmore 1945), remains uncertain. See also Marchant (1958). Many authors treat *thagus* as conspecific with *occidentalis*. In the field and by comparing living specimens in zoos there is a very marked size difference between the two forms, the larger *thagus* showing greyer underparts with irregular whitish streaks on belly. Non-breeding plumage may also be different (pers. obs.). However, separation in the field complicated by size variation within each subspecies and also by plumage variation of the several subspecies of *occidentalis*. Type form has darkest brown cast to belly whereas *urinator* on Galapagos shows greyer underparts as found in *thagus*, but lacks the white streaks on belly. *Thagus* is treated separately below.
JUVENILE: Facial skin, bill and legs grey. **Head** Including neck, pale sepia-brown. **Body** Upperparts brown, extending to upper breast and merging evenly into white underparts. **Wings** Upperwing: primaries and secondaries blackish, coverts brown. Underwing dark with irregular whitish band across coverts. **Tail** Blackish.
FIRST-SUMMER: Similar to juvenile but crown and neck show whitish tips.
ADULT NON-BREEDING: Resembles breeding adult but head and neck mostly white, yellowish cast to crown (wholly white in some birds).
ADULT BREEDING: Head Forehead, crown and ear-coverts white with variable yellow cast; nape and hindneck dark chestnut, sides of neck white, base of foreneck black and yellow. **Body** Upperparts silvery-grey with warm brownish cast. Underparts blackish-brown with greyer lanceolate feathers on sides of breast and flanks. **Wings** Upperwing: primaries blackish, outer shafts white, secondaries black, coverts as upperparts. Underwing as juvenile. **Tail** Dark grey.
FHJ: Unusual in genus due to marine location and plunge-diving habits, although juveniles particularly will dip bills from surface to retrieve food. Mainly coastal, rarely seen inland or far out at sea.

DM: North and South America. *P.o. occidentalis* breeds West Indies. *P.o. carolinensis* Atlantic coasts of tropical America from southern Carolina S to Orinoco. *P.o. californicus* on American Pacific coast from California S to Mexico. *P.o. murphy* Colombia to northern Peru. *P.o. urinator* at Galapagos Is. Egg-dates throughout year in scattered populations in North America; most Mar/Apr. Partial migrant particularly in northern populations, but timing of movements erratic, depending on local conditions. Occasionally winters in northern breeding areas. Stragglers have reached British Columbia, Nova Scotia and Bermuda. Recently declined in USA due to pesticides causing calcification failure of egg-shells, but more recent work suggests position now stabilising.
SS: From American White Pelican (p. 286) by invariably darker plumage, and feeding habits. From Peruvian Pelican (which may only be race of present species) by size and darker underparts.

148X PERUVIAN PELICAN
other: Chilean Pelican
Pelecanus (occidentalis) thagus

PLATE 41 Figs 148Xa-148Xb

MAP 148X

Resembles Brown Pelican (p. 286) in bare parts coloration but generally brighter in hue with caruncles between base of culmen and eye. Size much larger, averaging: Length 152cm (60in.). Wingspan 228cm (90in.).

ADULT NON-BREEDING: Closely resembles Brown Pelican but birds observed in Peru during Aug (pers. obs.) differed mainly in: **Head** Including neck, white. **Body** Upperparts: mantle, scapulars and back mostly white with blackish feather tips. **Wings** Upperwing: innermost coverts as back. Thus appears very much whiter on upperparts than corresponding Brown Pelican. I have been unable to locate birds with similar plumages in zoo specimens; whiter appearance may therefore be due to effect of bleaching and wear.
ADULT BREEDING: As Brown Pelican (p. 286) except: Bill pinker. **Head** Straw-coloured, crest more developed. **Body** Underparts generally greyer with white streaks on belly.
FHJ: As Brown Pelican but larger. An abundant and characteristic bird of Humboldt Current, forming mixed feeding flocks with boobies and cormorants.
DM: *P.(o.) thagus* breeds from central Peru S to 33½°S in Chile, where a small colony on Pupuya Islet, southwest Santiago Province. Occasionally strays S even to Tierra del Fuego.
SS: See Brown Pelican (p. 286).

Family *SULIDAE* boobies, gannets

One genus containing six or nine species. Characteristics of family discussed below under genus heading.

Genus *SULA*

Six or nine species comprising six boobies, and three gannets which sometimes considered conspecific. *Sula* spp. are large seabirds with long wings, wedge-shaped tails and stout, conical bills. At sea conspicuous due to size and contrasting plumage. Often fly higher than most other seabirds, appearing above horizon either singly or in ragged lines. Food obtained by plunge-diving from as high as 30m in case of gannets, but boobies dive from lesser heights and tend to plunge-dive at an angle rather than the perpendicular dives of the more robust gannets. All have a direct flight with alternating periods of flapping and gliding to produce steady, slightly undulating progression. Large flocks form over profitable feeding areas, but birds also met with singly. During post-breeding dispersal gannets roost on the water, but boobies normally return to land to roost at nightfall. Whereas gannets only occasionally show interest in ships (though readily attend trawling operations), boobies are attracted to ships and perch on masts etc.

Both types nest in colonies, often congregating in thousands on their islands and rock stacks. Boobies have tropical and subtropical distribution. Brown Booby *S. leucogaster*, Masked Booby *S. dactylatra*, and Red-footed Booby *S. sula* are sympatric pantropical species, the three remaining species of group having restricted ranges. The three gannets more temperate in breeding distribution, but range into tropics during non-breeding season; indeed they are inclined to undertake lengthy dispersals, thus differing from boobies, which appear more sedentary.

Identification at sea can be problematic, especially in juvenile and immature stages of certain boobies. The allopatric gannets can also cause identification problems, particularly off equatorial West Africa where a nursery and post-breeding dispersal area exists for two of gannet species (see main text). Adults of the nine species can be separated by comparing head, body, primary and tail coloration. Leg and bill colour, whilst useful for separating brighter coloured boobies from gannets, has only limited use in specific identification of the boobies. Bare parts coloration varies considerably in this group and only Red-footed and Blue-footed Boobies (p. 291, p. 289) have diagnostic coloration; the remaining four species can show marked geographical, sex, age and seasonal differences in leg and bill coloration.

Refer to Nelson (1978), Cramp *et al.* (1974) and Serventy *et al.* (1971) for further information on genus.

149 NORTHERN GANNET
other: North Atlantic Gannet, Gannet
Sula bassana

PLATE 42 Figs 149a-149e

MAP 149

Length 87–100cm (34–39½in.) (males average larger). Wingspan 165–180cm (65–71in.). Iris pale grey with blue ring; dark grey facial skin and gular stripe appear black. Bill pale blue-grey with blackish horizontal lines to plates and cutting ridges. Legs/feet dark grey, females with greenish lines along tops of toes but yellower in males.

North Atlantic Ocean; range overlaps with Masked Booby (p. 291) and perhaps Cape Gannet (p. 289). See also Brown Booby (p. 292). Sexes outwardly alike; no marked seasonal variation although yellowish crown and nape often spotted white or paler. Juveniles separable from adults. No subspecies, but both Cape and Australian Gannets treated as subspecies by some authors; they are described separately below (150 and 151).

JUVENILE: Head Including neck, dark brownish-grey. **Body** Upperparts dark brown to almost black (varies) with small white spots concentrated to form white V over base of tail. Underparts paler, sometimes whitish with darker breast band. **Wings** Upperwing: primaries and secondaries blackish, coverts as back. Underwing white with brownish streaks. **Tail** Blackish.

IMMATURE: During first 3 years at sea plumage becomes progressively whiter. Head, rump and underparts first to whiten, former showing golden hue on crown and nape. By end of second year most show broad white tips to mantle, scapulars and back. Upperwing has blackish primaries and primary-coverts, remainder mostly white, with irregular blackish streaks to greater coverts and along secondaries. Tail mainly white. By end of third year most differ from adults only in irregular blackish streaks along secondaries and dark central tail feathers.

ADULT: Head Mostly white except for golden cast to crown and nape (more intense in breeding males). **Body** Wholly white. **Wings** Upperwing: primaries and primary-coverts black except for small white mark on alula; remainder white. Underwing similar but primary-coverts white. **Tail** White.

FHJ: Flight steady and purposeful, a series of shallow flaps between glides. In higher wind speeds flight often like a large shearwater with undulating progression, banking and sidestepping but with higher flight peaks. Plunge-dives from about 10m to secure prey in spectacular vertical descent with wings folded. Shallower, raking dives also executed. After feeding often roosts in loose rafts on water, where also sits out severe gales. Occurs singly or in variably sized flocks, ranging mainly over continental shelf waters, rarely wandering to true pelagic habitat. Appears large at sea, long neck and wedge-shaped tail imparting distinctive 'pointed at both ends' jizz. Small flocks often fly in single file.

DM: Breeding stations in Gulf of St Lawrence, coasts of Newfoundland, Labrador and Iceland. Main Atlantic colonies situated off western and northern British Isles and Ireland, of which St Kilda (±50,000 pairs) the largest (Cramp *et al.* 1974). Recent expansion in range and numbers; breeding first recorded in Norway 1946, now occupies three sites although numbers probably below 1,000 pairs in total. First bred Channel Is 1940, now about 3,000 pairs plus colony off Britany, France, of some 2,500 pairs first established in 1939 (Cramp *et al.* 1974). Egg-dates Apr/May. Non-breeders disperse first in all colonies. North American breeders move S to winter off New England States and E Florida, with smaller numbers to Gulf of Mexico where regular off Alabama but scarce further W off Texas. Eastern Atlantic birds disperse widely but some adults appear to make only limited dispersal to adjacent continental shelf waters. Most birds move S, some reaching equatorial waters off Western Africa where some first-year birds probably remain until second or third year before returning N. Although rare in Mediterranean before 1940, now regular along North African coast in small numbers Oct–Apr with stragglers E to Cyprus (Stewart, pers. comm.).

SS: Largest indigenous seabird of North Atlantic, adults unlikely to be confused with any other species if seen properly. At long range or under poor conditions could be mistaken for one of the larger shearwaters. Range overlaps Masked Booby (p. 291) in Gulf of Mexico, and care needed as sub-adult Northern Gannets show ragged dark secondaries and some dark feathers in tail; head however has yellowish cast, whereas Masked Boobies have white heads with all-black secondary and tail feathers. Inexperienced observers could confuse first- or second-year Northern Gannet with smaller Brown Booby, but it differs in having speckled appearance and by end of first year head mainly white (sometimes with a dark cap) with a pronounced white V over rump. Greatest identification problems, however, off equatorial Western Africa, where range of *S. capensis* and *S. bassana* may overlap. Adults easily separated, latter having all-white secondaries and tail. I know of no way to separate first-year birds of the two species (considered sub-specific by some authors). Examination of skins suggests that second-year and subsequent immature *S. bassana* should be separable by white feathering in secondaries and white outer tail feathers.

Fig. 11. 1st year Northern Gannet

150 CAPE GANNET *Sula capensis*

PLATE 42 Figs 150a-150b
MAP 150

Resembles Northern Gannet (p. 288) in all respects but size; averages smaller with longer black gular stripe.

Ranges of Cape and Northern Gannets may overlap off equatorial western Africa. Sexes alike; no marked seasonal variation. Juveniles separable from adults. Cape × Australian Gannet hybrid recorded.

JUVENILE and IMMATURE: Resembles those of Northern Gannet (p. 288). By second and third years only wing-coverts show white; primaries, secondaries and tail remain wholly dark blackish-brown. Adult plumage acquired in third or fourth year.

ADULT: As for Northern Gannet (p. 288) but with diagnostic black secondaries and tail. (Some show tail pattern of Australian Gannet; Sinclair, pers. comm.)

FHJ: As for Northern Gannet.

DM: Breeds in Southern Africa on offshore islands off Namibia and Cape Province; largest colony at Ichaboe where about 100,000 pairs. Egg-dates Sep/Oct. Unlike juvenile Northern Gannets begins post-breeding dispersal by flying and not swimming (Nelson 1978). Disperses N to Mozambique, more rarely to Tanzania, on eastern littoral and N to Gulf of Guinea on west where range may overlap that of Gannet. Nelson (1978) has recently published a record of a Cape Gannet apparently collected in 1831 on the Bass Rock, but its authenticity remains uncertain. More recently a Cape Gannet has successfully interbred with Australian Gannet at a colony near Northern Melbourne (van Tets, pers. comm.).

SS: See Northern Gannet (p. 288), where notes on confusion between sub-adult Northern Gannet and adult Masked Booby also apply to present species. Old records of latter in Cape seas no longer considered valid and probably refer to present species which, because of greater amount of black on secondaries, may suggest Masked Booby to the unwary.

151 AUSTRALASIAN GANNET *Sula serrator*

PLATE 42 Figs 151a-151b
MAP 151

Resembles Cape Gannet but averages smaller.

Confined to Australasian region. Sexes alike; no marked seasonal variation. Juveniles separable from adults.

JUVENILE and IMMATURE: Paler underparts than Cape Gannet but probably indistinguishable; ranges do not normally overlap.

ADULT: Resembles Cape Gannet in having dark secondaries but only the four central tail feathers are black. (Some birds however show wholly dark tails as in Cape Gannet.)

FHJ: As Cape Gannet.

DM: Breeds in the Australasian region on islands off Tasmania and Victoria. There are also about twelve colonies in the New Zealand region, mainly on islands off North Island from the Three Kings group S to Hawkes Bay but also two small colonies in South Island, at Otago and at Little Solander, Foveaux Straits. Largest New Zealand colony is at White Island which has about 5,000 pairs. Egg-dates Oct/Nov; fledging and departure Apr/May. Most adults probably remain in adjacent seas but juveniles move quickly W across Tasman Sea to southern and eastern coasts of Australia, where many remain until adulthood. In west birds occur N to Sharks Bay and in east N to Tropic of Capricorn. Vagrant W to Crozets, Marion I. and South Africa (Sinclair, pers. comm.).

SS: See notes under Cape Gannet and Northern Gannet (p. 289, p. 288).

152 BLUE-FOOTED BOOBY *Sula nebouxii*

PLATE 43 Figs 152a-152b
MAP 152

Length 76–84cm (30–33in.). Wingspan averages 152cm (60in.). Iris pale yellow, pupil larger in female; orbital ring and facial skin bluish-grey. Legs/feet bright blue.

Western coasts of tropical America; range overlaps with Peruvian, Masked, Brown and Red-footed Boobies (p. 290, p. 291, p. 292, p. 291). Sexes outwardly alike, females average larger; no seasonal variation. Juveniles separable from adults. Two subspecies listed; *S.n. excisa* slightly larger with brighter plumage.

JUVENILE: Head Mostly dark brown with broad white patch at junction of hindneck and mantle. **Body** Upperparts: mainly brown with broad white tips forming scaly pattern; uppertail-coverts white forming narrow horseshoe over rump. Underparts mostly white with greyish-brown throat terminating in clearly defined line across upper breast. **Wings** Upperwing as adult but duller and darker brown. Underwing pattern as adult but sullied, less defined. **Tail** Blackish-brown with white shafts.

IMMATURE: As adult but head dull greyish-brown with faint whitish streaks merging into whitish-grey chin and throat. Underwing pattern less defined.

ADULT: Head Mostly pale cinnamon-brown with dense white streaks and broad white patch at junction of hindneck and mantle; chin and throat less streaked merging into white foreneck. **Body** Upperparts mostly pale cinnamon-brown with white tips forming scaly lines across back and scapulars; upper rump and lower uppertail-coverts white, mid rump as back. Underparts white. **Wings** Upperwing dark brown. Underwing: broad white, rectangular axillary patch extends narrowly across underwing as two white stripes; remainder brown. (NOTE Rectangular axillary patch diagnostic at all ages; particularly useful for separating juveniles from those of Masked and Peruvian Boobies, p. 291, p. 290.) **Tail** Dark brown, longest central feathers whitish.

FHJ: Medium-sized booby; feeds mainly inshore, even along tideline of sandy beaches with water less than 1m deep. Small flocks fish communally; flying up to 25m above water, the first to sight fish dives at raking angle and is immediately followed by remainder of group, flock striking the water in compact formation almost simultaneously.

DM: Confined to tropical and subtropical waters off western coasts of South and Central America. *S.n. nebouxii* breeds at islands off Mexico, Ecuador and northern Peru. *S.n. excisa* at the Galapagos Is. Egg-dates throughout year, subject to local conditions. Post-breeding dispersal seems dependent on oceanic fluctuations and in years of poor productivity birds wander widely, moderate numbers occurring well to N and S of normal range. During these 'invasion years' occurs N to California (see Roberson 1980). Status in N Chilean waters unknown but probably occurs in years of wide post-breeding dispersal.

SS: Most problems occur in separation of juvenile and immature Blue-footed Boobies from those of Brown and Masked Boobies (p. 292, p. 291). Present species differs from all stages of Brown Booby in white patch at base of hindneck and white rump; underwing pattern also different. Juvenile Masked Booby (p. 291) has brown head divided from mantle by white collar, and lacks narrow white horseshoe over base of tail; underwing pattern also lacks rectangular white axillary patch found in all stages of Blue-footed Booby. Adult Peruvian Booby (p. 290) differs in white head and upper and lower wing patterns; juveniles differ from those of present species in white-tipped upperwing-coverts, underwing pattern and brownish mottling to white underparts.

---

153 PERUVIAN BOOBY *Sula variegata*

PLATE 43 Figs 153a-153b
MAP 153

Length 74cm (29in.). Wingspan not recorded. Iris pale yellow. Bill greyish-black with blackish facial skin. Legs/feet blackish-blue.

Endemic to Humboldt Current off western South America; range overlaps with Blue-footed and Masked Boobies (p. 289, p. 291). Sexes alike; no seasonal variation. Juveniles separable from adults. No subspecies.

JUVENILE: Generally as adult but with narrower white tips to upperparts imparting darker appearance; head and underparts with diffuse brownish or yellowish-grey streaks imparting dingy cast.

ADULT: Head White. **Body** Upperparts: mostly brown with white tips imparting scaly pattern; uppertail-coverts white forming narrow horseshoe over rump. Underparts white; upper thigh mottled brown (extension from back). **Wings** Upperwing: primaries and secondaries blackish-brown, coverts browner tipped white. Underwing resembles Blue-footed Booby (p. 289) but lacks rectangular white axillary patch. **Tail** Brownish, longer central feathers white.

FHJ: One of the characteristic birds of Humboldt Current, joining with cormorants and pelicans to form impressive feeding flocks of many thousands. Jizz resembles that of Blue-footed Booby.

DM: Confined to Humboldt Current region, breeding islands off Peru and Chile from Point Parinas, Peru, S to Concepcion, Chile. Egg-dates throughout year. Relatively sedentary but subject to mass irruptions at irregular intervals, normally every 10–12 years when warm, nutritively poor 'El Niño' current pushes too far S, forcing the anchovies to desert Peruvian waters. Mass mortality ensues with irruptions S to Chiloe I., Chile, and N to coasts of Ecuador. In stable years small numbers found off SW Ecuador throughout year. Population now in decline due to reduction of anchovies through commercial overfishing.

SS: Blue-footed Boobies show darker heads at all ages with different underwing pattern and white patch at junction of hindneck and mantle.

---

154 ABBOTT'S BOOBY *Sula abbotti*

PLATE 43 Figs 154a-154d
MAP 154

Length 71cm (28in.). Wingspan unrecorded. Iris brown, orbital ring and facial skin blue-black, gular pale yellowish. Bill in males blue-grey with pinkish cast; in females pinkish; both sexes with black tip. Legs/feet grey, distally black.

Endemic to Christmas I., NE Indian Ocean; range overlaps with Brown, Masked and Red-footed Boobies (p. 292, p. 291, p. 291). Sexes alike (except bill colour); no seasonal variation but upperparts wear browner. Juveniles resemble bleached/worn adult but have grey bills. No subspecies. (See Nelson 1971 for excellent account on which much of following is based.)

PLUMAGE: Head White. **Body** Upperparts: mantle and upper back blackish with narrow white line extending from hindneck to lower back; remainder white with large black spots. Underparts mostly white, thigh spotted black. **Wings** Upperwing mostly blackish; inner webs of primaries whitish, carpal area and some coverts with small white spots. Underwing mostly white with black tip. **Tail** Black (small white tips are not usually visible at sea).

FHJ: Large, tree-nesting sulid with biennial breeding season. Flight more leisurely than other boobies with slow flaps and languid glides; heavy head, long neck and narrow, rakish wings impart distinctive jizz. Undertakes long foraging journeys.

DM: Confined to Christmas I., Indian Ocean, where 2,000–3,000 pairs breed in tall trees on central plateau. Egg-dates Apr–Jul; dispersal at sea poorly understood but certainly occurs off coast of Java where there are rich upwellings. The recent phosphate-mining and subsequent destruction of nesting habitat could prove a serious threat to this species' survival.

SS: Distinctive at all ages.

155 MASKED BOOBY
other: Blue-faced Booby/White Booby
Sula dactylatra

PLATE 42 Figs 155a-155c
MAP 155

Length 81–92cm (32–36in.). Wingspan 152cm (60in.). Iris yellow. Blue-grey facial skin and gular pouch appear black at sea. Bare parts vary geographically; generally males have bright yellow bills, duller and greener in females. Legs/feet yellow.

Widespread; adults superficially resemble gannet. Beware of confusing juveniles, which are mostly brown above, white below, with adult Brown Booby (p. 292). Off western South America care needed to separate juveniles and immatures from similarly-aged Blue-footed Boobies (p. 289). Sexes alike; no marked seasonal variation. Juveniles and immatures separable. Four subspecies listed, none separable at sea. Masked × Brown Booby hybrids have occurred (Palmer 1962).

JUVENILE: Head Including neck, chin and throat brown; narrow white hindcollar extending to foreneck. **Body** Upperparts: mantle, scapulars and back greyish-brown, tips whiter; rump shows narrow white cross-bar. Underparts white. **Wings** Upperwing: primaries and secondaries blackish-brown, coverts sandy-brown. Underwing-coverts mostly white except for dark band running from carpal towards axillaries. **Tail** Blackish.

IMMATURE: Similar to juvenile. **Head** Remains dark, white nape more extensive. **Body** Upperparts: whiten first from rump, spreading to include back and scapulars then mantle. **Wings** Upperwing: secondary-coverts edged white, later extending to include median and lesser coverts.

ADULT: Head Including neck white. **Body** Wholly white except for black tips to longer scapulars. **Wings** Upper and lower wings mostly white, contrasting with black primaries and secondaries. **Tail** Black.

FHJ: Largest and heaviest booby; prefers deep water for fishing, executes near vertical plunge-dives.

DM: Pantropical. *S.d. personata* breeds islands of central and western Pacific W to Coral Sea, the Banda Sea and islands off western Australia, including Cocos (Keeling). *S.d. granti* breeds islands off western Mexico S to Galapagos Is and San Felix and San Ambrosio Is, off Chile. *S.d. dactylatra* breeds Caribbean and Atlantic islands including Greater and Lesser Antilles, Ascension I. and Fernando de Noronha. *S.d. melanops* breeds western Indian Ocean, including Kuria Muria Is, Seychelles, Assumption, Reunion and Mauritius. Egg-dates throughout year in scattered populations. Pelagic range not well documented, probably mainly sedentary although ringing recoveries have shown fairly extensive dispersal tendencies in adults and juveniles (Serventy *et al.* 1971). Occasionally occurs Gulf coast of Texas, N to Carolina in USA; single record off southern California, USA.

SS: Juvenile bears superficial resemblance to adult Brown Booby and juvenile Blue-footed Booby (p. 292, p. 289). Differs from former in brown extending only to throat and divided from brown back by a white collar extending from white underparts across nape, an excellent flight character. Blue-footed Booby has grey bill, and white patch at junction of neck and back; underwing pattern also different. White morph of smaller Red-footed Booby (p. 291) has white tail and red feet (beware Galapagos Is black-tailed form) and a diagnostic black carpal patch on underwing. See notes under Northern Gannet (p. 288).

156 RED-FOOTED BOOBY
Sula sula

PLATE 43 Figs 156a-156h
MAP 156

Length 66–77cm (26–30in.). Wingspan 91–101cm (36–40in.). Iris brown, orbital ring blue. Bill pale blue, pinkish at base with blackish gular (in breeding males base of bill orange to bluish-green). Legs/feet red.

Tropical oceans; range overlaps with Masked, Blue-footed and Brown Boobies (p. 291, p. 289, p. 292). Sexes alike; no seasonal variation. Juveniles separable from adults. Three subspecies listed but taxonomy complex (see Murphy 1936, Palmer 1962). Polymorphic; few seabirds display such a variety of seemingly arbitrary colour phases; different morphs form mixed pairs. Due to variability of plumages and because some adults breed in what is outwardly an 'immature plumage', following descriptions refer to morphs and types, *not* ages. Juveniles of all morphs streaked brownish at fledging and can be separated from adult brown morphs by their blackish-brown bills, purplish facial skin and yellowish-grey legs. Immatures in transitional plumage differ from adult intermediate morphs in their dull blue bills and brownish-red legs.

WHITE MORPH: Head and Body White with variable golden or apricot cast. **Wings** Upperwing: coverts as body; primaries and secondaries black. Underwing similar in pattern but with diagnostic black patch on carpal. **Tail** White (Galapagos population has blackish tail, beware Masked Booby, p. 291).

BROWN MORPH: Wholly brownish to brownish-grey with variable yellowish cast on crown and hindneck.

WHITE-TAILED BROWN MORPH: As brown morph but with lower back, rump, lower belly, tail-coverts and tail white or yellowish-white.

WHITE-TAILED and WHITE-HEADED BROWN MORPH: As white-tailed brown morph but head and neck white.

FHJ: Small, tree-nesting booby with marked plumage variation. Has largest eye of any booby, which may be linked to its partially nocturnal habits. Gregarious, both at sea and on land; attracted to ships, freely perches on rigging etc. Undertakes long foraging trips, often seen several hundred miles from land (pers. obs.).

DM: Pantropical. *S.s. sula* breeds Caribbean islands and off Brazil at Trinidad and Fernando de

Noronha. *S.s. rubripes* islands of tropical Pacific and Indian Oceans. *S.s. websteri* islands off western coasts of Mexico and Central America and at Galapagos Is. Egg-dates throughout year, subject to local conditions. Adults probably sedentary but lack of sub-adult birds at some colonies (see Schreiber & Ashmole 1970) suggests that juveniles disperse from natal islands. Extent of pelagic dispersal poorly known, however, due to diversity of plumage phases, which, without comparative experience, appear confusing and may suggest other species.

SS: White morphs differ from adult Masked Boobies (p. 291) in smaller size, bare parts coloration, white scapulars and black carpal patch on underwing. Despite diversity of intermediate plumages adult Red-footed Boobies identified by diagnostic red feet and, if present, white tails (all other boobies have dark tails). Underwing pattern, though variable between white and brown morphs, unlike any other booby and, combined with head and tail colour, should enable accurate specific identification. See also Northern Gannet (p. 288).

157 BROWN BOOBY *Sula leucogaster*

PLATE 42 Figs 157a-157c
MAP 157

Length 64–74cm (25–29in.). Wingspan 132–150cm (52–59in.). Bare parts vary geographically. Nominate leucogaster*: Iris silver, orbital ring blue (males); yellow with dark spot before eye (females). Bill yellowish, facial skin yellowish to yellowish-green. Legs/feet yellowish-green.*

Pantropical; range overlaps with most booby spp. but beware especially juvenile Masked and Blue-footed Boobies (p. 291, p. 289). Sexes usually similar; no seasonal variation. Juveniles similar in pattern to adults (thus lacking complex transitional stages found in most other sulids). Four subspecies listed; *S.l. brewsteri* separable at sea. Brown × Masked Booby hybrids recorded (Palmer 1962). Total albinism recorded (pers. obs.).

JUVENILE and IMMATURE: Resembles adult but bill and facial skin grey. White underparts and underwing sullied with brown, markedly so in juveniles, less so in immatures.

ADULT (typical): **Head** Including neck dark brown. **Body** Upperparts dark brown. Underparts white except for brown upper breast. **Wings** Upperwing: blackish-brown. Underwing white with brown margins. **Tail** Brown.

ADULT (*S.l. brewsteri*): Males differ from nominate in having forehead, forecrown and chin white merging into greyish-brown hindneck and breast. In females these areas greyer than in nominate. (Juveniles differ in smooth, mouse-brown crissum and more uniform mouse-brown lower breast and belly: Stallcup, pers. comm.)

FHJ: Smaller than gannets (p. 288) with lighter jizz, quicker wing action and proportionately longer tail. Gregarious, occurring in small groups, but also forms large flocks particularly when predatory fish drive smaller prey towards surface. Groups fly in extended skeins, usually close to water, and execute low-level, raking plunge-dives. Inshore feeder, preferring to perch on rocks, buoys etc. rather than settle on water. Also perches in trees but nests only on ground.

DM: Possibly commonest and most widespread booby. In E Pacific *S.l. brewsteri* breeds in Gulf of California S along Mexican mainland and at Revilla Gigedos, and at Clipperton, Tres Marias and Isabel Is. *S.l. etesiaca* off Central America and Colombia. *S.l. leucogaster* breeds Gulf of Mexico, Caribbean and in tropical Atlantic including Ascension, Cape Verde and islands off Brazil. *S.l. plotus* breeds islands in Red Sea and tropical Indian Ocean, northern shores of Australia, Great Barrier Reef Is and on many Pacific islands from Gulf of Siam and Bonin I. E to Gambier I. Egg-dates throughout year in the scattered populations. Although habitat primarily shallow inshore waters, there is evidence to support small-scale dispersal. In W Atlantic stragglers from Caribbean and Gulf of Mexico colonies are casual visitors to Gulf and New England states N even to Nova Scotia. In eastern Atlantic stragglers occur N to Azores. No evidence to support widely held but erroneous view that this species occasionally occurs off South Africa; only southern African record was of a beached bird at Beira, Mozambique, in 1954. Status in Red Sea unclear; regular but small numbers off Elat, Israel, in N Red Sea indicate continuous distribution from southern portion where common off Aden. Pacific breeders occur N to Japan, and in east occur as stragglers off SE California and Galapagos Is. Stragglers have also reached southern Australia and New Zealand.

SS: Inexperienced observers in eastern Atlantic could confuse this species with immature Northern Gannet (p. 288). Latter differs in size and jizz and has distinctly spotted or spangled upperparts. See also notes under immature Masked, Red-footed and Blue-footed Boobies (p. 291, p. 291, p. 289).

Family *PHALACROCORACIDAE* cormorants, shags

Most successful and diverse family of *Pelecaniformes* order. One genus containing about 27–28 species, although flightless Galapagos Cormorant sometimes retained in separate genus of *Nannopterum*.

Genus *PHALACROCORAX*

Contains 27–28 medium to large-sized aquatic species distributed mainly along temperate and tropical marine coasts and inland waters; some species extend to Arctic and Antarctic regions. Sexes outwardly alike, males usually average larger. Plumage generally dark with metallic sheen; most species show seasonal variation. Maturity reached in third to fourth calendar year. Albinism rare.

All cormorants are underwater-pursuit swimmers, some reaching depths of 30m. Characterised by hooked bills, long necks, elongated bodies, short rather rounded wings and long, normally wedge-shaped tails. Unlike some aquatic species, e.g. ducks, their feathers are not completely waterproof and they are thus frequently seen drying wings in typical spreadeagled posture. Gregarious, nesting in small to large colonies; some species social outside breeding, loafing and fishing together. Migratory and dispersive, particularly in higher latitudes of both hemispheres or in areas of infrequent but heavy rains causing temporary flood plains.

Identification of all cormorants complicated by seasonal variation in plumage and several transitional plumage stages before juveniles reach full maturity. Whilst plumage details, particularly distribution of white on head, neck and body, position of crests etc., should be accurately recorded, it is often size and jizz which secure a positive identification. In particular, relative proportions of bill, size of head, thickness of neck and length of tail important characters to note. In flight rhythm and depth of wingbeats, size of head, position of neck (straight, crooked) and length of tail important identification criteria. At close range coloration of bare parts often diagnostic.

158 DOUBLE-CRESTED CORMORANT *Phalacrocorax auritus*

PLATE 49 Figs 158a-158c
MAP 158

Length 74–91cm (29–36in.). Wingspan 122–137cm (48–54in.). Iris pale green; facial skin and gular orange or yellow. Bill blackish or grey, tip of lower mandible faintly yellow. Legs/feet blackish.

North America from Alaska and Newfoundland S to California and Florida; range overlaps with Olivaceous, Brandt's, Pelagic and Great Cormorants (p. 294, p. 298, p. 299, p. 295). Sexes outwardly alike, males average larger. Juveniles separable from adults. Four subspecies listed differing mainly in size, darkness of upperparts, and amount of white in prenuptial crest. *P.a. cincinatus* is the largest form with most white in crest.

JUVENILE: Bill yellowish, culmen brown. **Head** Mostly dark brownish-grey shading to greyish-white on chin, throat and foreneck with brownish feather tips imparting scaled or mottled appearance. **Body** Upperparts dark brownish or greyish-black with darker feather edges imparting scaled appearance (appears blackish-grey at distance). Underparts: upper breast as foreneck, extending in some to lower belly; remainder blackish-brown. **Wings** Upperwing mostly dark greyish-black; coverts as upperparts. Underwing blackish. **Tail** Blackish-grey.

IMMATURE: Much as juvenile except throat, foreneck and underparts mostly dull brown or whitish.

ADULT NON-BREEDING: Head Including neck, blackish with variable greenish gloss; lacks crest. **Body** Upperparts dark coppery-brown, scaled black, shading to blackish on rump. Underparts blackish-green. **Wings** Upperwing: coverts as upperparts, remainder blackish-green. Underwing blackish. **Tail** Blackish-green. NOTE Becomes browner and duller with wear.

ADULT BREEDING: Much as non-breeding adult except: **Head** Mostly black with greenish gloss, occasionally with white flecks in superciliary area, on neck, and in the short blackish recurved crest springing from behind eyes on sides of crown (shed May onwards, after pair-formation). **Body** Upperparts glossier green.

FHJ: Medium to large species generally appearing blackish with conspicuous, orange-yellow facial skin and gular pouch; pre-nuptial crests rarely seen. Occurs at both marine and inland habitats, nesting on cliffs, islands and trees; the only North American cormorant likely to be seen at freshwater locations. Compared with larger Great Cormorant (p. 295), where range overlaps in NE North America, present species appreciably smaller, with lighter jizz, proportionately slenderer bill and smaller, less angular head. In flight present species separated from Brandt's and Pelagic Cormorants (p. 298, p. 299) by its comparatively large bill and head carried on crooked neck above level of body. Compared with Brandt's has long-tailed appearance and back and scapular feathers are blunter in shape and more prominently scaled at any age (Stallcup, pers. comm.). Gregarious throughout year; commonly seen in small groups standing on piers, etc. in typical spreadeagled posture.

DM: North America. *P.a. cincinatus* breeds from Four Mountain Is in Aleutians E across Gulf of Alaska to Alexander Archipelago; *P.a. albociliatus* from Vancouver I. S to Gulf of California; *P.a. auritus* from Gulf of St Lawrence S to Cape Cod and locally W to Utah; *P.a. floridanus* from North Carolina S through Florida to Cuba. Egg-dates mostly Apr–Jul; fledging and dispersal Jul–Sep. *Auritus* the most migratory, moving S Sep/Oct with impressive coastal and inland movements to winter S to Florida and Gulf coast; numbers at staging points may exceed 10,000. Some *cincinatus* may move E towards coasts of British Columbia. Marine population of *albociliatus* non-migratory. Recent increase in numbers, see Scharf & Shugart (1981).

SS: Breeding adults differ from larger Great Cormorant (p. 295) in bright orange-yellow facial skin and gular and dark thighs; see also structural differences above. Juveniles of present species differ further in bright yellowish bill, orange facial skin and scaled upper breast. In southern USA range overlaps with rare Olivaceous Cormorant (p. 294). That species smaller and proportionately slimmer. Adults differ from present species in narrow, white triangular-shaped border to yellowish gular. Immature Olivaceous have less pronounced white borders to gular but differ from those of present species in generally darker appearance, especially head, with brownish cap and hindneck extending to below eye; the brownish-white upper breast merges into belly and suffuses with brownish ventral area. See also notes under Brandt's and Pelagic Cormorants (p. 298, p. 299).

159 OLIVACEOUS CORMORANT
other: Neotropic Cormorant, Bigua Cormorant
Phalacrocorax olivaceus

PLATE 50 Figs 159a-159d
MAP 159

Length 58–73cm (23–29in.). Males average larger but also geographical variation. Wingspan averages 101cm (40in.). Iris green with brownish yellow or orange facial skin and gular pouch. Bill brownish-yellow with darker ridge. Legs/feet black.

Occurs from southern North America S to Cape Horn. Breeding adults show diagnostic white border to gular pouch but at long range confusion likely with Double-crested Cormorant (p. 293) in North America and juvenile Rock Shags (p. 300) in southern South America. Sexes outwardly alike, slight seasonal variation. Juveniles and immatures separable from adults. Two subspecies listed but not separable in the field.

JUVENILE: Bare parts duller. Plumage mostly dull brown; wings and tail darker.

IMMATURE: As juvenile but differs in underparts showing whitish cast to chin, foreneck and breast.

ADULT NON-BREEDING: Head Blackish with diagnostic white border to gular pouch. **Body** Including underparts blackish. Mantle and scapulars browner with darker feather edges giving scaly appearance. **Wings** Blackish primaries with olive-brown coverts edged black. Underwing blackish. **Tail** Blackish. NOTE Appears wholly black at long range.

ADULT BREEDING: As adult non-breeding except: **Head** Blue-green lustre with conspicuous white tufts to sides of face and scattered white filoplumes to neck. **Body** Differs only in richer blue-green lustre; breast and mantle with scattered white filoplumes.

FHJ: Frequents marine and freshwater locations. Habitually perches on branches, slender twigs etc. Rather slender in jizz but head and neck thicker than sympatric Rock Shag (p. 300) occurring in southern part of range, but thinner than that of Double-crested Cormorant (p. 293) in north. Gregarious, often fishes in loose flocks. Flies in extended skeins, head slightly hunched back.

DM: *P.o. olivaceus* breeds from Panama S to Cape Horn; habitat ranges from high mountain lakes in Andes to offshore islands. *P.o. mexicanus* breeds NW Mexico, and Bahamas, Cuba, parts of Central America, and southern USA where numbers apparently increasing. Stragglers N to Nevada, Colorado and Kansas, and W to California (absent Baja). Most appear sedentary, dispersing to adjacent coasts, but high-altitude populations presumably move lower during winter.

SS: See notes under Double-crested Cormorant (p. 293). In particular note difference in shape of gular pouch, white border of Olivaceous and differences in overall structure and jizz. Present species is only wholly dark adult cormorant in South America; immatures resemble juvenile Rock Shag (p. 300), separation can be problematical.

160 LITTLE BLACK CORMORANT
Phalacrocorax sulcirostris

PLATE 46 Figs 160a-160c
MAP 160

Length 61cm (24in.). Wingspan 81cm (32in.). Iris green; facial skin purple-grey. Bill blackish-grey. Legs/feet black.

Malay Archipelago S to Australia and New Zealand; range overlaps with Javanese and Little Pied Cormorants (p. 306, p. 305). Sexes outwardly alike; slight seasonal variation. Juveniles separable from adults. No subspecies.

JUVENILE: Iris brown. Plumage mostly silky dark or rusty brown.

ADULT NON-BREEDING: As breeding adult but duller and browner; lacks white filoplumes.

ADULT BREEDING: Wholly blackish-brown with green or purple iridescence to head, mantle and scapulars; wing-coverts greyer with black borders giving scaly appearance. At close range small white filoplumes over head, neck and upperparts, densest over and behind eye normally forming small white tuft.

FHJ: Small, wholly blackish cormorant preferring freshwater locations but also found on tidal creeks and coasts. Compared with much larger, all-dark Great Cormorant (p. 295), present species conspicuously gregarious with flocks of anything from ten to several hundred birds indulging in co-operative fishing. Normally flock forms line or semicircle shepherding a fish shoal before it, birds at rear of flock flying over main body and diving on impact so that there is continuous, often frantic activity. Small numbers of other cormorant spp. and Australian Pelicans often attend these feeding flocks.

DM: Breeds from Borneo and Java through Moluccas to New Guinea, Australia, Tasmania and North Island, New Zealand. Egg-dates May–Dec. Sedentary throughout much of range.

SS: Dark morph Little Pied Cormorant (p. 305) differs in shorter, yellowish bill. Great Cormorant (p. 295) is much larger, usually with yellow throat-pouch. Non-breeding Javanese Cormorant (p. 306) has shorter yellowish bill, whitish chin and throat.

161 GREAT CORMORANT

other: Common Cormorant (includes White-breasted Cormorant)

Phalacrocorax carbo

PLATE 44 Figs 161a-161g

MAP 161

Length 80–101cm (31½–40in.). Wingspan 130–160cm (51–63in.). Iris green. Bill grey, yellower at base with black culmen; facial skin variable, usually yellowish or orange. Legs/feet black.

Almost cosmopolitan in temperate regions of Old World, absent from most of North America; range overlaps with many cormorant spp; see especially Double-crested and Japanese Cormorants (p. 293, p. 297), and Shag (p. 298). Sexes outwardly alike, males average larger; seasonal variation. Juveniles separable from adults; six subspecies listed some safely distinguishable in the field and thus described separately below. Unless stated following notes refer to North Atlantic *P.c. carbo*.

JUVENILE: Iris grey-brown; facial skin dull yellow. **Head** Mostly dull brown; sides of face, throat and foreneck mottled fawn-white. **Body** Upperparts dull brown edged darker imparting scaly appearance. Underparts vary from mostly silky brown to dull white with brownish flanks and thighs and mottling on sides of breast and lateral undertail-coverts. Some show more extensive and brighter white underparts. **Wings** Upperwing: coverts as upperparts, primaries and secondaries brownish-black. **Tail** Brownish-black.

IMMATURE: Much as juvenile but iris green, plumage becomes progressively darker; white on underparts usually disappears by second autumn.

ADULT NON-BREEDING: As breeding adult except plumage generally duller without white filoplumes on head; thigh patch also absent.

ADULT BREEDING: Head Including neck, mostly black with blue or greenish gloss; except for whitish plumes on sides of head and white or grey throat and forecheeks. **Body** Wholly black with blue or greenish gloss and white oval thigh patch. **Wings** Upperwing-coverts bronze-brown edged black, forming scaly pattern; primaries and secondaries blackish-brown. Underwing blackish-brown. **Tail** Black, glossed green or blue.

ADULT BREEDING (*P.c. sinensis*)**:** Eurasian. Differs from nominate in greener gloss to plumage, more extensive white on throat and forecheeks and conspicuous white plumes in solid stripe on sides of nape (some old *P.c. carbo* also show as much white on sides of nape during breeding and are therefore indistinguishable).

ADULT BREEDING (*P.c. maroccanus*)**:** NW Africa. As *sinensis* but with greener gloss and whole of throat and upper neck white.

ADULT BREEDING (*P.c. lucidus*)**:** Africa. Treated as full species by some authors under name 'White-breasted Cormorant'. Resembles *sinensis* but with blackish or purple gloss and white chin, throat and foreneck extending to include upper breast, occasionally belly.

ADULT BREEDING (*P.c. novaehollandiae*)**:** Australia and New Zealand; as *sinensis* but white nuptial plumes restricted to small patch on side of upper neck.

FHJ: Large, long-necked species found at inland as well as marine locations. Compared with smaller and almost exclusively marine Shag (p. 298), present species longer and thicker-necked with proportionately heavier jizz, more angular head and larger bill. In flight wings broader with more purposeful and slower beats than Shag; longer neck supports a heavier, more apparent head. During feeding and dispersive movements often flies in long ragged skeins close to sea, but much higher when over land. When perched posture usually more upright than Shag, and differs further in freely perching, and even building nests, in trees. Unlike Shags, which rarely stray even to estuaries, can be found at any freshwater location from reservoirs to smaller, slow-flowing rivers and streams. On water swims low with tail submerged and bill tilted slightly upwards (beware diver spp., p. 208, along sea coasts).

DM: Almost cosmopolitan in Old World with discontinuous distribution from NW Europe through Asia and Africa to Australasia. *P.c. carbo* breeds southern Greenland, Iceland, Labrador, Nova Scotia, Newfoundland and Gulf of St Lawrence: in NW Europe Faeroes, Norway, Ireland and British Isles. Generally non-migratory although American population undertakes regular movements, extending S to New Jersey, occasionally Florida, in winter with small coastal movements southwards off NE Atlantic States Aug–Oct and northwards during Mar/Apr. *P.c. sinensis* breeds Netherlands, southern and central Europe E to central Asia, India and China. More migratory than nominate, some moving S to Egypt and Persian Gulf, but movements largely dependent on severity of winter. *P.c. maroccanus* breeds NW Africa, dispersal not known. *P.c. lucidus* NE Africa, eastern and southern Africa. *P.c. hanedae* Japan. *P.c. novaehollandiae* Australia, Tasmania, New Zealand and Chatham Is. Egg-dates Apr–Jul (north temperate regions), Aug–Dec (south temperate regions), throughout year in tropics.

SS: Differs from smaller, almost exclusively marine Eurasian Shag (p. 298) in heavier jizz, white chin and sides of face, lack of prominent crest during breeding, thicker neck, slower wingbeats and heavier bill. Thigh patch if present diagnostic (but see Japanese Cormorant, p. 297). See also Double-crested Cormorant (p. 293) in USA and diver spp. (p. 208) in northern hemisphere.

162 INDIAN CORMORANT

other: Indian Shag

Phalacrocorax fuscicollis

PLATE 45 Figs 162a-162c

MAP 162

Length 61–68cm (24–27in.). Wingspan unrecorded. Iris green, facial skin varies from greenish or black to purple or red; pouch yellow. Bill brown. Legs/feet black.

Asiatic, range overlaps with Javanese and Great Cormorants (p. 306, p. 295). Sexes alike; slight seasonal variation. Juveniles separable from adults. No subspecies.

JUVENILE: Iris brown. Much as non-breeding adult but upperparts duller and browner; underparts mostly whitish, flanks and thighs mottled with brown.
ADULT NON-BREEDING: As breeding adult except upperparts duller brown, lacking bronze lustre; lower cheeks, chin and throat speckled white, variable in extent.
ADULT BREEDING: Mostly blackish-bronze with darker feather edges producing scaly pattern on mantle, scapulars and wing-coverts. Small white tuft usually present behind eye.
FHJ: Frequents marine and freshwater locations. Compared with smaller Javanese Cormorant (p. 306), present species slimmer with longer, more slender bill and tail.
DM: Asiatic; breeds India, Sri Lanka, Burma, Thailand, Kampuchea and Cochin-China. Egg-dates Jul–Nov.
SS: Great Cormorant (p. 295) much larger with stouter bill and yellowish facial skin. Javanese Cormorant (p. 306) much smaller with less scaly upperparts.

163 CAPE CORMORANT *Phalacrocorax capensis*

PLATE 45 Figs 163a-163c
MAP 163

Length 61–64cm (24–25in.). Wingspan 109cm (43in.). Iris green. Bill black, facial skin and pouch bright yellow. Legs/feet black.

Endemic to Namibia and South Africa; range overlaps with White-breasted, Bank and Crowned Cormorants (p. 295, p. 297, p. 306). Sexes alike; slight seasonal variation. Juveniles separable from adults. No subspecies.
JUVENILE: Iris grey, facial skin dull brown. Legs brownish. Much as non-breeding adult but duller and browner above with whiter chin, foreneck and upper breast.
ADULT NON-BREEDING: Facial skin dull brown. Plumage mostly dull blackish-brown with greyish-brown chin, foreneck and upper breast.
ADULT BREEDING: Whole plumage blackish with strong, metallic green iridescence; darker feather edges impart scaled appearance on mantle, scapulars and wing-coverts.
FHJ: Rather small and short-tailed; breeding adults appear wholly black with bright yellow facial skin. Almost exclusively marine, the most abundant cormorant of Cape seas. Their long, extended skeins a characteristic sight off coasts of Namibia and South Africa, often number many thousands. During 'sardine runs' along Cape coast this species and Cape Gannet predominate in huge concentrations that recall the more spectacular seabird flocks in Humboldt Current off South America.
DM: Endemic to southern Africa, breeding at mainland cliffs and offshore islands of Namibia and Cape Province. Egg-dates Sep/Oct; fledging and dispersal begins Jan/Feb. Non-breeders range N to Congo River mouth and E to southern Mozambique.
SS: At close range combination of wholly blackish plumage and bright yellow facial skin diagnostic within its limited range. Sympatric Bank and White-breasted Cormorants (p. 297, p. 295) larger and do not normally fly in such huge, concentrated skeins as present species. See also Crowned Cormorant (p. 306).

164 SOCOTRA CORMORANT *Phalacrocorax nigrogularis*

PLATE 45 Figs 164a-164d
MAP 164

Length 76–84cm (30–33in.). Wingspan 102–110cm (40–43½in.). Iris green. Bill blackish-grey; base of lower mandible greenish. Bare facial skin and pouch blackish. Legs/feet black.

Endemic in NW Indian Ocean; range overlaps with Pygmy and Great Cormorants (p. 306, p. 295). Sexes outwardly alike, males average larger. Slight seasonal variation; juveniles separable from adults. No subspecies.
JUVENILE: Iris grey; bill dark grey with yellowish or pink facial skin; legs brownish. **Head** Dull greyish-brown, chin, throat and foreneck whiter. **Body** Upperparts mostly greyish-brown with indistinct paler edges and darker centres. Underparts dirty-white, washed and speckled brownish. **Wings** Upperwing as upperparts. Underwing brown. **Tail** Brown.
IMMATURE: Much as juvenile except mantle and scapulars more spotted; underparts browner with darker spotting on throat and breast.
ADULT NON-BREEDING: As adult breeding except generally duller with fewer white filoplumes on neck and body; usually lacks white streak behind eye.
ADULT BREEDING: Head Blackish with purple sheen and scattered white filoplumes of variable extent but usually concentrated in dense white streak behind eye. **Body** Upperparts blackish with greyish-green sheen and darker feather centres imparting spotted appearance. Underparts blackish with purple sheen. **Wings** Upperwing: coverts as upperparts, primaries and secondaries blackish-green. Underwing black. **Tail** Blackish-green.
FHJ: Resembles Eurasian Shag (p. 298) in size and jizz. Highly gregarious, often gathering in vast flocks of several thousands. Flies in close V-shaped skeins, sometimes at wave height but also up to 150m (Meinertzhagen 1954). Compared with much larger Great Cormorant, present species has slim, snaky head and neck, longer, more slender bill, lighter jizz and shorter wings. Exclusively marine.
DM: Breeds on a few islands in Persian Gulf; may also nest on islets off Dhufar, Aden, and Socotra (Bailey 1966). Returns to vast colonies Dec/Jan; egg-dates Jan–Mar; fledging and dispersal dates unknown. Movements little known; disperses

throughout Persian Gulf and beyond Straits of Hormuz S to Gulf of Aden, where may also breed. **SS:** Larger than Pygmy Cormorant (p. 306), which has much shorter bill and prefers freshwater locations. Great Cormorant (p. 295), the only other cormorant of region, differs in head shape, much larger size, proportionately shorter more robust bill, white chin and does not feed in large, dense flocks.

165 BANK CORMORANT
Phalacrocorax neglectus

PLATE 45 Figs 165a-165c
MAP 165

Length 76cm (30in.). Wingspan 132cm (52in.). Iris (unique) brown above, green below. Bill and facial skin black. Legs/feet black.

Endemic to Namibia and South Africa; range overlaps with White-breasted form of Great Cormorant and Cape Cormorant (p. 295, p. 296). See also Crowned Cormorant *P.a. coronatus* (p. 306). Sexes alike; slight seasonal variation. Juveniles and non-breeding adults alike. No subspecies.

JUVENILE/NON-BREEDING ADULT: Wholly dull blackish-brown; rather woolly in appearance.

ADULT BREEDING: Mostly dull brownish-black except: **Head** White flecking concentrated behind eyes and on nape. **Body** Upperparts: white band across rump (as with white flecking on head, soon wears off).

ATYPICAL: Leucistic individuals (frequently encountered) have varying degrees of white on face and neck.

FHJ: A large woolly-brown species intermediate in size between sympatric White-breasted Cormorant and smaller Cape Cormorant with rotund, pot-bellied jizz. Differs from all-black Cape Cormorant in blackish facial skin and less gregarious habits. Usually met with singly or in small parties hunting among inshore kelp-beds. Entirely marine.

DM: Endemic to cold-water zone off Namibia and South Africa. A few thousand breed in small groups and scattered colonies from Namibia S to Agulhas. Breeding recorded for all months except Apr, Aug and Nov (Liversidge & McLachlan 1978). Sedentary.

SS: Differs from smaller, abundant Cape Cormorant (p. 296) in larger size, jizz and lack of yellow skin on face; white rump, if present, diagnostic. White-breasted Cormorant (p. 295) larger with conspicuous white face and upper breast. See also Crowned Cormorant (p. 306).

166 JAPANESE CORMORANT
other: Temminck's Cormorant
Phalacrocorax capillatus (=P. filamentosus)

PLATE 48 Figs 166a-166c
MAP 166

Length 92cm (36in.). Wingspan 152cm (60in.). Iris green. Facial skin yellowish-orange. Bill greyish-horn. Legs/feet black.

Confined to Japan and adjacent Asiatic coasts; range overlaps with Great, Red-faced and Pelagic Cormorants (p. 295, p. 299, p. 299). Sexes alike; marked seasonal variation. Juveniles separable from adults. No subspecies. Following based on notes and research by Dr M. Brazil (pers. comm.).

JUVENILE: Almost wholly dull blackish-brown paling to brownish-white on underparts; chin, throat and foreneck whitish.

IMMATURE: Resembles juvenile except underparts show scattered darker tips on breast and belly.

ADULT NON-BREEDING: As breeding adult except duller, lacks white filoplumes on sides of head and neck; white thigh patch also absent.

ADULT BREEDING: Head Mainly blackish-green except for white cheeks and chin extending under lower mandible and narrow white filoplumes on sides of head and neck. **Body** Upperparts: mantle, scapulars and back greenish, each feather fringed black (slightly broader than in *P. carbo*). Underparts blackish-green, thigh patch white. **Wings** Upperwing: primaries and secondaries blackish; coverts as upperparts. Underwing black. **Tail** Blackish.

FHJ: Frequents steep, rocky cliffs; apparently never perches in trees. Differs from local race of Great Cormorant in green (not bronze) mantle, scapulars and upperwing-coverts; habits apparently more marine, rarely visiting freshwater locations.

DM: Asiatic, breeding along rocky cliffs on Sakhalin Is, Japan (Honshu Is) and Korea. Extent of dispersal poorly known but Japanese birds disperse in winter throughout rocky coasts of Japan, some reaching coasts of China.

SS: Separated from Great Cormorant by more marine habits, greener plumage, narrower, longer white filoplumes, and white extending forwards below lower mandible (separated from base of lower mandible by yellowish facial skin in *P. carbo*).

Fig. 12. *P. carbo* (left) differs from *P. capillatus* in less white on sides of face and more extensive yellow skin. By comparison the white sides of face in *P. capillatus* extend under lower mandible and the white filoplumes are narrower. Notes and sketches based on research by Dr Mark Brazil from skins at Yamashina Institute, Japan.

167 BRANDT'S CORMORANT *Phalacrocorax penicillatus*

PLATE 49 Figs 167a-167c
MAP 167

Length 81–89cm (32–35in.). Wingspan 112–124cm (44–49in.). Iris blue; facial skin dull grey, border around pouch pale or brownish-yellow, pouch brilliant sky-blue. Bill slate-grey.

Coasts of western North America; range overlaps with Double-crested and Pelagic Cormorants (p. 293, p. 299). Sexes outwardly alike, males average larger; seasonal variation. Juveniles separable from adults. No subspecies.

JUVENILE: Head Mostly dull brownish; darkest on crown, slightly paler on foreneck with pale greyish-brown border along gular. **Body** Upperparts mainly brownish-black, tips slightly paler with darker fringes. Underparts: mostly dull ochreous-brown with paler area at junction of foreneck and upper breast forming indistinct V across upper breast. **Wings** Upperwing brownish-black; coverts as upperparts. Underwing blackish-brown. **Tail** Blackish-brown.

ADULT NON-BREEDING: Whole plumage generally dull blackish or oily-grey with faint greenish gloss on head and rump; border of gular brownish or yellowish-tan.

ADULT BREEDING: Whole plumage blackish with variably oily, purplish-green gloss except for hair-like, whitish plumes on sides of head, neck, over scapulars and rump.

FHJ: Almost as large and bulky as Double-crested Cormorant; jizz differs in more upright stance, legs seemingly placed further back causing upright, rather sentry-like posture with tail almost touching ground. In flight head and neck usually carried straight, not crooked and raised as in Double-crested Cormorant (see also Pelagic Cormorant, p. 299). Compared with Double-crested appears shorter-tailed; back and scapular feathers more pointed at any age (Stallcup, pers. comm.). Swims very low, usually only head, neck and upper back visible. Habits exclusively marine, restricted to rocky coasts; gregarious throughout year, flocks flying in extending skeins, feeding and roosting together.

DM: Commonest cormorant from Oregon S to California. Has bred Seal Rocks, Alaska, but status there and in SE Alaska generally sporadic, subject to fluctuation, although occurs with some regularity in Prince William Sound (see Sowls *et al.* 1978). Breeds mainly from Washington S to Natividad I. and Gulf Rocks, Baja California; also Gulf of California at San Pedro Martir Is and Roca Blanca near Isla Partida. Egg-dates Mar–Jul; period to fledging apparently unknown. Resident, dispersing to adjacent seas and S to Mazatlán, Sinaloa, Mexico (Alden, pers. comm.).

SS: Breeding adults with sky-blue gular pouch and hair-like plumes distinctive. Non-breeding adults differ from Double-crested Cormorant (p. 293) in flight profile, brownish or yellowish-tan border to gular, lack of bright orange facial skin and less scaly upperparts. Juveniles differ from those of Double-crested in greyish-brown border to gular and lack of pronounced white on underparts.

168 SHAG *Phalacrocorax aristotelis*

PLATE 44 Figs 168a-168d
MAP 168

Length 65–80cm ($25\frac{1}{2}$–$31\frac{1}{2}$in.). Wingspan 90–105cm ($35\frac{1}{2}$–$41\frac{1}{2}$in.). Iris green. Bill black with yellow gape and cutting edges. Legs/feet black (brown with yellow webs in desmarestii*).*

Confined to NW Europe and Mediterranean Basin; range overlaps with larger Great Cormorant (p. 295). See also Pygmy Cormorant (p. 306). Sexes outwardly alike, males average larger; seasonal variation. Juveniles separable from adults. Three subspecies listed but not safely separable at sea.

JUVENILE: Iris yellowish-white; facial skin yellowish; bill pinkish-yellow. **Head** Mostly dull brown; chin, throat and foreneck variably white. **Body** Upperparts dull brown, with darker feather edges imparting slight scaly effect. Underparts usually brown with dull white upper breast and variable amount of white mottling on belly (heaviest in Mediterranean race *P.a. desmarestii*). **Wings** Upperwing: coverts as upperparts, primaries and secondaries slightly darker. Underwing blackish-brown. **Tail** Blackish-brown.

IMMATURE: As non-breeding adult but chin, throat, foreneck and belly variably speckled off-white; upperparts duller and browner in tone.

ADULT NON-BREEDING: Much as breeding adult but lacks crest; plumage generally duller and browner with paler brown chin and throat.

ADULT BREEDING: Wholly blackish with strong green iridescence. Both sexes have long, wispy recurved crest on crown at start of breeding season.

FHJ: Smaller than Great Cormorant, differing from that species in finer bill, smaller, less apparent head and thinner neck. Unlike Great Cormorant, habits almost exclusively marine, rarely strays to estuaries and does not usually perch in trees; much prefers rocky coasts and deeper oceanic water. In flight wingbeats quicker than Great Cormorant with head held lower. When swimming sits low in water, bill tilted slightly upwards and, when diving, often springs forwards higher than Great Cormorant. See further notes under latter species (p. 295).

DM: Mainly European with outposts on coasts of Morocco, Tunisia, Cyprus and Turkey. *P.a. aristotelis* breeds western Iceland, Faeroes, Britain, Ireland, Channel Is, and on mainland Europe from Kola Peninsula, USSR, S to Stavanger, Norway, with other groups off coasts of Brittany, France, and Iberia (Spain). *P.a. riggenbachi* breeds coasts of Morocco from about Casablanca S to Tarfaya. *P.a. desmarestii* breeds Mediterranean Basin from Balearics eastwards to Aegean Sea, Cyprus and Crimea with outposts at scattered sites along North

African coast. Egg-dates variable, usually Apr–Jun but occasionally from Feb. Adults mainly resident, juveniles undertake short dispersive movements, but both age classes more strongly migratory in some northern populations dispersing S and W from Jul onwards, returning Feb/Mar. Rare along flat sandy coasts of North Sea, i.e. Holland, Denmark and eastern England.

SS: Adults separated from Great Cormorant (p. 295) by smaller size, glossier, greener plumage without pronounced scaling on wing-coverts, and yellow gape; in nuptial plumage recurved, wispy crest and absence of white on flanks. Juveniles of the two species harder to separate; structure and jizz (see above and under Great Cormorant) best characters, coupled with flight differences and, usually, whiter underparts of Cormorant. In winter beware diver spp. (p. 208), which have pointed not hooked bills, white underparts and do not normally spring clear when pursuit-diving from surface. See also smaller Pygmy Cormorant (p. 306).

169 PELAGIC CORMORANT *Phalacrocorax pelagicus*

PLATE 49 Figs 169a-169c
MAP 169

Length 63–73cm (25–29in.). Wingspan 91–102cm (36–40in.). Iris green, facial skin and gular reddish. Bill dark greyish-yellow. Legs/feet black.

North Pacific from Wrangel I. and Bering Strait S to Japan and California; range overlaps with Double-crested, Brandt's and Red-faced Cormorants (p. 293, p. 298, p. 299). Sexes outwardly alike, males average larger; seasonal variation. Juveniles separable from adults. Two subspecies listed but not separable at sea.

JUVENILE: Iris brownish, facial skin ashy-flesh; bill and legs brown. Plumage wholly dark brown; underparts slightly paler (but never shows contrast found in larger Brandt's or Double-crested Cormorants).

ADULT NON-BREEDING: Facial skin and gular pouch dull brownish-orange. Plumage wholly black with variable greenish or violet gloss, becoming browner with wear; head lacks crest.

ADULT BREEDING: Head Two short crests springing from forehead and nape; mostly black with rich green iridescence and scattered long white filoplumes on sides of neck. **Body** Mostly rich greenish-black except for conspicuous white oval patch on flanks. **Wings and Tail** Blackish-green.

FHJ: Smallest west coast cormorant, distinguished from all others within its range (except Red-faced, p. 299) by consistently blackish-green plumage and more slender bill. In flight head and neck held straight and, unlike both Double-crested and Brandt's, there is very little apparent head (Stallcup 1976); wingbeats faster. Compared with these two species, Pelagic Cormorant much smaller and more delicate in jizz; most of body submerged when swimming, appearing about same size as Western Grebe (p. 220). Back and scapular feathers pointed in shape but, unlike Double-crested and Brandt's, centre so dark as not to contrast with blackish edges (Stallcup, pers. comm.). Exclusively marine, usually breeding on sheer cliffs, but much less gregarious than other two West Coast cormorants. Feeds both along rocky shores, hunting in kelp beds, and in deeper oceanic water.

DM: North Pacific. *P.p. pelagicus* breeds from Wrangel I. and Arctic coasts of Siberia S through Bering Strait to Sea of Okhotsk, Kurile Is and Hokkaido, Japan; also in North America from Cape Lisburne S through Bering Strait to Aleutian Is and E to British Columbia. *P.p. resplendens* breeds from British Columbia S to Los Coronados Is, Baja California. Eggs usually May/Jun; fledging Aug onwards. Mainly sedentary and dispersive throughout range, but more northern population departs from NE Siberia from mid Oct onwards, returning mid May. Elsewhere undertakes limited dispersal S but extent of winter range in Asia unknown; vagrants have reached Hawaii.

SS: Breeding adults with white flank patches and crested heads distinctive. Non-breeders can be separated from Double-crested and Brandt's Cormorants (p. 293, p. 298) by smaller size, flight profile, finer bill and lack of either yellow or brownish-tan in gular region; reddish facial skin difficult to observe at any season, of only limited use in identification. Immatures wholly brown, underparts lacking white upper breast of Double-crested Cormorant. In Alaska range overlaps with very similar Red-faced Cormorant (p. 299); see notes under that species.

170 RED-FACED CORMORANT *Phalacrocorax urile*

PLATE 49 Figs 170a-170c
MAP 170

Length 79–89cm (31–35in.). Wingspan 110–122cm (43–48in.). Iris tawny; facial skin bright red extending continuously over base of upper mandible, pouch dark grey narrowly bordered red. Bill yellowish, culmen and tip darker, gape and base bluish.

Range restricted to coasts of southern Alaska W to Aleutian and Commander Is; overlaps with Double-crested, Brandt's and Pelagic Cormorants (p. 293, p. 298, p. 299). Sexes outwardly alike, males average larger; seasonal variation. Juveniles separable from adults. No subspecies.

JUVENILE: Iris and facial skin brownish, bill dull grey. Plumage wholly dark brown, underparts slightly paler.

ADULT NON-BREEDING: Facial skin dull reddish. Plumage mostly blackish with dull violet or greenish gloss, becoming browner with wear; upperwings browner; head lacks crest.

ADULT BREEDING: Head Two crests springing from forehead and nape; mostly black with rich violet or greenish gloss and scattered pre-nuptial white filoplumes on sides of neck. **Body** Mostly blackish with rich greenish or violet gloss except for conspicuous white oval patch on flanks (absent or reduced from Jun onwards); some show a few white filoplumes on breast. **Wings and Tail** Browner in tone than body (unlike Pelagic Cormorant, p. 299).

FHJ: Closely resembles Pelagic Cormorant but larger with bigger head, proportionately longer bill, thicker neck and brighter, more extensive red facial skin uniting over bill. In flight flat-brown upperwings sharply contrast with iridescent body (Stallcup, pers. comm.). Exclusively marine, preferring wild, rocky coastlines.

DM: Moyururi I., Japan, and at Commander and Aleutian Is E along coasts of S Alaska. Sowls *et al.* (1978) put main centre of abundance from Shumagin Is and Sandman Reefs W to end of Aleutian Chain. Other colonies extend N to Nunivak I. and E to Cordova. Population in Alaska thought to be about 130,000 (Sowls *et al.* 1978). Status in Siberia not fully known. (See account in Palmer 1962.) Formerly bred Kurile Is and Kamchatka Peninsula. Egg-dates May/Jun; fledging date not precisely known. Mainly resident, dispersing to adjacent seas and S to Kurile Is and to St Michael, Alaska; stragglers S to Japan.

SS: Breeding adults, with white flank patches, crested heads and red facial skin distinctive. Non-breeders separated from Brandt's and Double-crested Cormorants (p. 298, p. 293) by smaller size, flight profile (as in Pelagic), finer, proportionately longer bill and reddish facial skin. Juveniles have reddish-brown facial skin and uniform brown underparts. Separation from smaller Pelagic Cormorant (p. 299) more difficult and, at distance, perhaps impossible. Adult of present species differs in larger head, proportionately longer bill, more apparent crest, thicker neck and brighter red facial skin extending broadly across forehead; at close range base of bill bluish. Juveniles of the two species very similar, differing only in size and extent of brownish-red (or greyish) facial skin at base of bill.

---

171 ROCK SHAG
other: Magellan Shag
Phalacrocorax magellanicus

PLATE 50 Figs 171a-171d
MAP 171

Length 66cm (26in.). Wingspan 92cm (36in.). Iris red during breeding, otherwise brown. Facial skin red, bordered with black. Bill black. Legs/feet pink with darker webs.

Confined to southern South America, where range overlaps with Imperial and Olivaceous Cormorants and (occasionally) Guanay Cormorant (p. 303, p. 294, p. 300). See also Red-legged Shag (p. 304). Breeding adults distinctive; confusion most likely in separating juveniles from Olivaceous Cormorants. Sexes alike; seasonal variation. Juveniles separable from adults. No subspecies.

JUVENILE: Legs black. **Head** Including neck, dull brown. **Body** Upperparts dull brown. Underparts: breast, flanks and thighs brown, belly and ventral area white. **Wings and Tail** Brown.

IMMATURE: Similar to juvenile except white belly and ventral area shows increasing amounts of brown to produce mainly dark underparts.

SUB-ADULT: Similar to immature except: **Head** White chin and throat. **Body** Upperparts: dull greenish cast to mantle and back. Underparts become increasingly whiter as brown feather tips abrade to reveal their white bases. (White underparts now retained throughout all subsequent stages.)

ADULT NON-BREEDING: Dull brown above, mostly white below except for brownish flanks and thighs.

ADULT BREEDING: Head Including neck, mostly bluish-black with nuptial crest on forehead, whitish tufts to sides of head and scattered filoplumes on crown and neck. NOTE White auricular patch grows larger later in breeding season and chin and throat develop white feather tips. **Body** Upperparts blue-black to greenish-black. Underparts: mostly white, thighs and undertail-coverts blackish. **Wings** Upperwing as upperparts but primaries blackish. Underwing black. **Tail** Brownish-black.

FHJ: Medium-sized, small-billed species with red facial skin. Flight usually low, with rapid wingbeats, very litle gliding or soaring, neck well extended. Nests colonially, normally on exposed sea cliffs. (See Guanay Cormorant, p. 300.)

DM: Breeds southern Chile from about 37°S S to Cape Horn and N to 50°S in Patagonia; also Falklands. Egg-dates Oct–Dec. Disperses after breeding, some N to 35°S in Uruguay and to about 33°S in Chile.

SS: Dark-bellied immatures smaller with slenderer jizz, thinner neck and smaller head than sympatric Olivaceous Cormorant (p. 294). In flight neck lacks slight 'hunched' appearance of latter.

---

172 GUANAY CORMORANT
Phalacrocorax bougainvillii

PLATE 50 Figs 172a-172c
MAP 172

Length 76cm (30in.). Wingspan unrecorded. Iris brown, orbital ring green. Facial skin red. Bill horn-yellow. Legs/feet pink.

Confined to coasts of Peru and Chile. Range overlaps with Olivaceous Cormorant and Red-legged Shag and (occasionally) Rock Shag (p. 294, p. 304, p. 300). Breeding adults distinctive. Sexes alike; seasonal variation. Juveniles separable from adults. No subspecies.

JUVENILE: Resembles non-breeding adult but generally duller brown above. White underparts sullied with brown.

ADULT NON-BREEDING: Head Mainly brown, extending from hindneck to form continuous band below white chin. **Body** Upperparts: brown. Underparts mostly white; flanks, thighs and undertail-coverts brownish. **Wings and Tail** Brown.

ADULT BREEDING: As non-breeding adult except: **Head** Mostly blackish-blue with short white tufts over eye and scattered filoplumes to neck; crown has short crest. **Body** Upperparts blue-black;

underparts as non-breeding adult. **Wings and Tail** Blue-black.

FHJ: A large, black and white species frequenting western coasts of South America, where often forms flocks of many thousands. Freely associates with boobies, forming mixed skeins flying at considerable height, from where descends rapidly once fish sighted. Sits lower in water than Red-legged Shag (p. 304), appearing completely dark except for tip of white upper breast showing above water line. Crest normally flattened when wet. Unlike Rock Shag (p. 300), nests in huge colonies, some up to 6 million strong, on mainly flat or gently sloping areas.

DM: West coast of South America, breeding on islands and coastal promontories of Peru S to Mocha I., Chile. Egg-dates throughout year. A characteristic bird of Humboldt Current. At irregular intervals of low oceanic productivity, subject to mass movements, some reaching N to Colombia and even Panama and S to southern Chile, where range thus overlaps with Rock Shag (p. 300). Normal range extends N to Ecuador, where a few occur throughout year, and S to Valdivia, Chile. Appears to be declining due to fishmeal industry.

SS: Separated from Rock Shag by yellow, thicker bill and greater amount of white on throat. Immatures resemble pale-breasted immature Olivaceous Cormorants (p. 294) but are larger with white chins and reddish-brown legs and feet.

---

173 PIED CORMORANT *Phalacrocorax varius*

PLATE 46 Figs 173a-173b
MAP 173

Length 66–84cm (26–33in.). Wingspan 106–137cm (42–54in.). Iris green; orbital ring and skin below greenish-blue; facial skin yellow or orange, pouch pinkish. Bill grey with dark ridge. Legs/feet black.

Australia and New Zealand; range overlaps with Great, Little Black, Little Pied, Black-faced and King Cormorants (p. 295, p. 294, p. 305, p. 301, p. 302). Sexes outwardly alike, males average larger. Slight seasonal variation. Juveniles separable. Two subspecies; *P.v. hypoleucos* differs mainly in bright orange facial skin and bluer sheen on upperparts. *P.v. varius* described below.

JUVENILE: Iris brown, facial skin dull yellow. **Head and Body** Upperparts brown, extending across foreneck to divide whitish chin and throat from streaked white and grey underparts. During first few weeks brownish tips on foreneck wear to reveal white bases leaving indistinct brownish wash at base of foreneck, remainder of underparts and foreneck white. **Wings and Tail** Brown.

IMMATURE: Iris green. Mostly brown above and mottled white below; some in New Zealand virtually all brown below.

ADULT NON-BREEDING: Much as breeding adult except bare parts and plumage duller.

ADULT BREEDING: Head Crown and hindneck narrowly marked black, remainder white, demarcation occurring above eye. **Body** Upperparts black. Underparts mostly white, thighs black. **Wings** Upper and lower black. **Tail** Black.

FHJ: Large black and white cormorant with striking white face and brilliant yellow or orange facial skin. Commonest Australian cormorant, normally seen in flocks or loafing on piers, buoys etc.; mainly marine, frequenting coasts and estuaries, but also occurs inland at larger lakes etc. Highly gregarious; at favoured localities some colonies numbered in thousands.

DM: In Australia *P.v. hypoleucos* breeds coasts of W Australia from about Wyndham S to Albany; and at more inland locations from Northern Territory S through Queensland, New South Wales and Victoria, although less common in these localities; absent Tasmania (see Black-faced Cormorant, p. 301). *P.v. varius* breeds New Zealand: more plentiful on North Island with discontinuous distribution on South Island, where colonies situated mainly at Marlborough Sounds, Nelson, Canterbury and at Stewart I. Double breeding season throughout range, although autumn more favoured in marine locations (Serventy *et al.* 1971). Adults appear mostly sedentary; juveniles wander more extensively.

SS: See polymorphic Little Pied Cormorant and notes under Black-faced Cormorant (p. 305, p. 301). In New Zealand occurs alongside King Cormorant group (p. 302), from which differs mainly in absence of white wing bars, greater extent of white on face and black legs.

---

174 BLACK-FACED CORMORANT *Phalacrocorax fuscescens*

PLATE 46 Figs 174a-174c
MAP 174

Length 61–69cm (24–27in.). Wingspan 107cm (42in.). Iris blue-green. Bill, facial skin and pouch black. Legs/feet black.

Endemic to southern Australia; range overlaps with Great, Little Black, Pied and Little Pied Cormorants (p. 295, p. 294, p. 301, p. 305). Sexes alike; slight seasonal variation. Juveniles separable from adults. No subspecies.

JUVENILE: Iris brown, facial skin pale buff, pouch pinkish, legs brown. Plumage much as non-breeding adult except for greyish cheeks and brownish wash across foreneck and upper breast; upperparts browner.

ADULT NON-BREEDING: Head Crown, nape and hindneck black; remainder white, demarcation occurring behind eye. **Body** Upperparts blackish-blue. Underparts white; thighs black. **Wings** Upper and lower black. **Tail** Black.

ADULT BREEDING: As non-breeding adult except for dense mat of white filoplumes on hindneck, rump and thighs.

FHJ: Differs from Pied Cormorant (p. 301) in blacker-faced appearance, exclusively marine habits and, in flight, head and neck held lower creating hump-backed jizz.

DM: Endemic to southern Australia: breeds Recherche Archipelago, Western Australia; Bay of Islands, Victoria; Spencer and St Vincent Gulfs, South Australia; coasts and islands of Tasmania.

Egg-dates usually Sep–Jan. Sedentary.
SS: Little Pied Cormorant (p. 305) differs in much smaller size, compressed yellow bill, longer tail and, in adults, white thighs. Adult Pied Cormorant (p. 301) differs in bill colour, yellow or orange facial skin and demarcation between black and white occurring well above eye. Juveniles of the two species similar but differ in bare parts colours.

175 NEW ZEALAND KING CORMORANT

PLATE 47 Figs 175a-175b

(Includes Stewart and Chatham Island Cormorants, Figs 175X and 175Y)

Phalacrocorax carunculatus

MAP 175

Length 76cm (30in.). Wingspan not recorded. Iris hazel; orbital ring blue, caruncles yellow or orange; facial skin and gular greyish-red. Bill horn-yellow. Legs/feet pink.

Endemic to New Zealand; range overlaps with Pied Cormorant (p. 301). Sexes alike; seasonal variation. Juveniles separable from adults. Three subspecies listed, separable in the field and thus described separately below beginning with nominate. (Further work may show these to be distinct species.)
JUVENILE: Bill and facial skin grey; legs pink. Pattern much as adult but upperparts mouse-brown with indistinct alar bar and dorsal patch; underparts dirty-white.
IMMATURE: As juvenile except facial skin pink; upperparts darker with green sheen.
ADULT NON-BREEDING: As breeding adult except bare parts duller, lacks crest on forehead and nape. White alar bar and dorsal patch reduced or lacking.
ADULT BREEDING: Head mostly blue-black with crest on forehead and shorter crest on nape; chin, throat and foreneck white. **Body** Upperparts blue-black with white dorsal patch of variable extent. Underparts white, thighs black. **Wings** Upperwing: mainly black except for white alar bar and white tips on scapulars forming a second, smaller bar. Underwing black with narrow white leading edge on inner wing. **Tail** Blue-black to blackish-brown, base of shafts white.
FHJ: Large black and white cormorant. Prefers sheltered marine inlets and bays for fishing; nests in small colonies on rocky islets where shy and timid. Does not spread wings for drying.
DM: Restricted to Cook Strait, New Zealand. Principal colony Duffer's Reef with scattered groups on nearby islands within area bounded by White Rocks in E to Trios in W (Falla *et al.* 1975). Total population probably less than a few hundred. Egg-dates normally Jun/Jul; fledging Aug/Sep, but juveniles about to fledge occur until late Dec, suggesting staggered season (pers. obs.). Sedentary, returns to nesting islets to roost.
SS: Pied Cormorant (p. 301) has much whiter face and normally lacks white bars on upperwings and white dorsal patch; bare parts also different. Stewart Island Cormorant (175X) usually treated as southern race of *P. carunculatus* (but which may be a good species) is smaller and dimorphic; their ranges do not normally overlap.

175X STEWART ISLAND CORMORANT

Phalacrocorax carunculatus chalconotus

PLATE 47 Figs 175Xa-175Xc

MAP 175X

Length 66–71cm (26–28in.). Wingspan unrecorded. Iris brown, orbital ring blue or lavender, caruncles orange; facial skin and gular brownish-red. Bill horn-yellow to grey. Legs/feet pink.

Dimorphic subspecies of *P.c. carunculatus*, intermediate plumage types also occur; range overlaps with Pied Cormorant (p. 301). Only breeding adults described below.
PALE MORPH: As nominate except only one bar on upperwing and a small, barely distinguishable white dorsal spot. Upperparts generally with greener lustre.
DARK MORPH: Wholly blackish with rich bronze-green lustre and crested head.
INTERMEDIATE MORPH: Generally as dark morph but has irregular white spotting on lower breast and belly; palest examples have white bellies and undertail-coverts.
DM: South Island, New Zealand, from Otago Peninsula S to Foveaux Strait and Stewart I.; northern birds average larger with more pronounced orange-yellow caruncles.
SS: See notes under *P.c. carunculatus* above. A small population of Pied Cormorant (p. 301) occurs in Stewart I. area.

175Y CHATHAM ISLAND CORMORANT

Phalacrocorax carunculatus onslowi

PLATE 47 Fig. 175Y

MAP 175Y

Length 63cm (25in.). Wingspan unrecorded. Iris dark brown, orbital ring blue, caruncles bright orange, gular and facial skin crimson. Bill horn-yellow. Legs/feet pink.

PLUMAGE: As nominate but stronger, metallic lustre and smaller dorsal spot.
DM: Occurs only at Chatham Is, E of New Zealand.
SS: Great Cormorant and Pitt Island Shag also occur at the Chatham Is. *P.c. onslowi* differs from both in white underparts and pink feet.

176 CAMPBELL ISLAND CORMORANT (Includes Auckland and Bounty Islands Cormorants, 176X and 176Y)

PLATE 47 Figs 176a-176c

Phalacrocorax campbelli

MAP 176

Length 63cm (25in.). Wingspan 105cm (41in.). Iris brown, pouch and facial skin purple. Bill greyish-horn. Legs/feet pink, soles blackish.

New Zealand sub-antarctic islands. Range overlaps with Little Pied and vagrant Great Cormorants (p. 305, p. 295). Sexes alike; seasonal variation. Juveniles separable from adults. Three subspecies listed, geographically divided and separable in the field; they are described separately below beginning with nominate (further work may show them to be separate species).

JUVENILE: Pattern much as non-breeding adult except chin and upperparts dark brown.

ADULT NON-BREEDING: As breeding adult but lacks crest.

ADULT BREEDING: Head Including whole of neck, mostly blue-black with wispy crest; chin and throat white with scattered white filoplumes on side of head. **Body** Upperparts blue-black. Underparts white; thighs black. **Wings** Upperwing black with white alar bar of variable extent. Underwing black. **Tail** Blue-black; base of shafts white.

FHJ: Breeds in small colonies. Congregates in large rafts offshore and in sheltered inlets, numbers varying from 20–2,000 birds. Rafts densely packed, normally diving together, regrouping on surface. Flight rather laboured.

DM: Occurs only at Campbell I. S of New Zealand Returns to colonies Sep/Oct; egg-dates Nov/Dec; fledging Jan–Mar. Sedentary, dispersing to adjacent seas only.

SS: Differs from Little Pied Cormorant (p. 305), which also breeds at Campbell I., by pink feet and plumage pattern. Vagrant Great Cormorants (p. 295) also occur.

176X AUCKLAND ISLAND CORMORANT

Phalacrocorax campbelli colensoi

PLATE 47 Fig. 176X

MAP 176X

Length 63cm (25in.). Wingspan 105cm (41in.). Iris brown, orbital ring pinkish-blue, facial skin brownish-red, pouch red. Bill greyish or brown. Legs/feet pink.

ADULT BREEDING: Generally as nominate but chin, throat and foreneck narrowly white; some may show narrow black necklace or complete band at base of foreneck and small white dorsal spot.

DM: Found only at Auckland Is, S of New Zealand.

SS: The only resident cormorant at Auckland Is. Little Pied and Great Cormorants occur as vagrants.

176Y BOUNTY ISLAND CORMORANT

Phalacrocorax campbelli ranfurlyi

PLATE 47 Fig. 176Y

MAP 176Y

Length 71cm (28in.). Wingspan unrecorded. Iris brown, orbital ring red or brown, pouch and facial skin bright red. Bill greyish-horn. Legs/feet pink.

ADULT BREEDING: Resembles *P.c. colensoi* but chin, throat and foreneck more extensively white with larger alar bar, and a white dorsal patch variable in extent.

DM: Confined to Bounty Is, SE of New Zealand; straggler Antipodes Is.

SS: No other cormorants recorded within range.

177 IMPERIAL SHAG (Formerly Blue-eyed and King Cormorants)

PLATE 47 Figs 177a-177d, 177X-177Z

Phalacrocorax atriceps

MAP 177

Length 72cm (28in.). Wingspan 124cm (49in.). Iris brown, orbital ring blue; caruncles bright orange to greenish-yellow, facial skin blue-grey, sometimes reddish; pouch black. Legs/feet pink.

Coasts of southern South America, Antarctic Peninsula and sub-antarctic islands. Sexes alike; seasonal variation. Juveniles separable from adults. Devillers & Terschuren (1978) have shown that Blue-eyed ('*P. atriceps*') and King Cormorants ('*P. albiventor*'), originally treated as separate species, are conspecific in southern South America. Intermediates occur in all colonies where the two 'types' co-exist; South American population is therefore probably better treated as polymorphic population of *P.a. atriceps*, with *P.a. albiventor* restricted to the unvarying dark-cheeked, orange-caruncled population isolated in Falkland Is. *P.a. verrucosus* often treated as separate species; I have followed Watson (1975) and included it with *atriceps/albiventor* group after Derenne *et al.* (1974) observed cormorants with field characters of '*P. albiventor*' interbreeding successfully with *P.(a.) verrucosus* on Iles Kerguélen. Unless stated, following notes refer to nominate *P.a. atriceps*; eight subspecies listed, those separable at sea described separately below.

IMMATURE: Pattern as non-breeding adult but upperparts duller and browner.

ADULT NON-BREEDING: As breeding adult except caruncles smaller and duller, lacks wispy crest, white alar bar reduced or absent.

ADULT BREEDING: Head Crown, nape and hindneck blue-black with wispy recurved crest; lower cheeks, chin, throat and foreneck white, demarcation occurring on a line level with eye. **Body** Upperparts: mostly blue-black; white dorsal patch usually present from about Dec to May. Underparts white, thighs black. **Wings** Upperwing blue-black; white alar bar. Underwing black. **Tail** Blue-black, shafts white. NOTE Dark individuals resemble *P.a.*

albiventor; intermediates show continuous gradation between the two.

ADULT BREEDING (*P.a. nivalis*): Differs from nominate *atriceps* in slightly lower cheek line and larger size.

ADULT BREEDING (*P.a. albiventor*): Differs from nominate in: **Head** Demarcation between black and white occurs on a line level with gape which, with broader black hindneck, imparts distinctly blacker-faced aspect. **Body** Upperparts: lacks white dorsal bar.

ADULT BREEDING (*P.a. verrucosus*): Typical examples resemble *P.a. albiventor* but lack white alar bar. Some on Kerguelen Is apparently do have white alar bars (Derenne *et al.* 1974); not known whether these are mutants occurring naturally or birds from *P.a. melanogenis* group on Crozets and Marion Is (juveniles occasionally have brownish underparts). May be a good species.

FHJ: Large black and white cormorant; gregarious throughout year, sometimes gathering in large flocks, particularly in austral winter when thousands often form dense rafts. In flight neck usually held fully extended with fast, shallow wingbeats.

DM: Southern hemisphere. *P.a. atriceps* breeds southern South America from Mocha I., Chile, S to Cape Horn and then N to Punta Tombo, Argentina. *P.a. albiventor* breeds Falkland Is. *P.a. georgianus* breeds South Georgia. *P.a. bransfieldensis* South Orkney, South Shetland, South Sandwich and islands of Antarctic Peninsula S to about 65°S. *P.a. nivalis* breeds Heard I. *P.a. melanogenis* Crozet and Prince Edward Is. *P.a. verrucosus* Kerguelen Is. *P.a. purpurascens* breeds Macquarie I. Colony sites often used throughout year as roosts; courtship activities begin late Aug–Oct; egg-dates Oct–Jan; fledging Feb–Apr, dispersing to adjacent waters. Antarctic Peninsula population moves N to open leads.

SS: Distinctive within range.

---

178 RED-LEGGED SHAG
Phalacrocorax gaimardi

PLATE 50 Figs 178a-178c
MAP 178

Length 76cm (30in.). Wingspan 83cm (32½in.). Iris green, facial skin orange. Bill yellow, orange blush at base. Legs/feet bright red.

Confined to southern South America; a distinctive species unlikely to be confused with other cormorants. Sexes alike, slight seasonal variation. Juveniles separable from adults; no subspecies.

JUVENILES: As non-breeding adult but with pale brownish cast to upperparts. Belly and vent white.

ADULT NON-BREEDING: As breeding adult but lacks white filoplumes on crown.

ADULT BREEDING: Head Mainly dark lead-grey except for conspicuous white patches on sides of neck and scattered white filoplumes on crown. **Body** Upperparts: mostly dark lead-grey except for conspicuous silver-grey edges on mantle and back. Underparts grey, paler on upper breast and belly with mauve cast. **Wings** Upperwing: primaries and secondaries blackish, coverts as upperparts.

FHJ: A large, mainly grey species with paler wing-coverts, white patches to sides of neck, and red at base of bill. Freely associates with boobies and other cormorants to form large mixed flocks but less gregarious in habits than other South American cormorants. When swimming wet plumage can look completely black except for white neck patch. Red legs visible when springing clear of water during diving. Nests singly or in small groups, usually in caves.

DM: Breeds along coast of Peru from about 6°S to Estero Elefantes, Chile, at 46°S; also on eastern littoral at Puerto Deseado near Cape Blanco. Egg-dates throughout year. Occasionally wanders S to Straits of Magellan and N to SW Ecuador.

SS: Differs from other cormorants of Humboldt region in grey plumage and red feet.

---

179 SPOTTED SHAG
other: Blue Shag/Pitt Island Shag
Phalacrocorax punctatus (includes *P.p. featherstoni*)

PLATE 48 Figs 179a-179d
MAP 179

Length 64–74cm (25–29in.) (includes geographic variation). Wingspan not recorded. Iris hazel, orbital ring and facial skin blue-green. Bill pale greyish-horn. Legs/feet orange-yellow.

Confined to New Zealand; distinctive in all plumages and unlikely to be confused with sympatric 'black and white' members of genus. Sexes alike; marked seasonal difference. Juveniles separable. Three subspecies; *P.p. featherstoni* is separable (though ranges do not overlap) and may prove to be a distinct species.

JUVENILE: (*P.p. punctatus*) **Head** Mostly mouse-brown, chin and throat paler. **Body** Upperparts mouse-brown, darker tips giving spotted appearance at close range. Underparts mainly off-white except for brownish upper breast and flanks; thighs and ventral area black. **Wings** Upperwing: primaries and secondaries brown, coverts similar, spotted black. Underwing brown. **Tail** Brown.

ADULT NON-BREEDING: (*P.p. punctatus*). As adult breeding but head lacks crest and white stripe and filoplumes on sides of face and neck.

ADULT BREEDING: (*P.p. punctatus*). **Head** Mostly blackish-green except for white filoplumes and stripe extending from base of bill, over eye to sides of lower neck. **Body** Upperparts greyish-green, darker tips on mantle, scapulars and back giving spotted appearance. Underparts mostly grey; sides of breast white, flanks, thighs, ventral area and undertail-coverts black. NOTE On west coast of South Island, Foveaux Strait and Stewart I. area *P.p. oliveri* generally darker with narrower white stripe on sides of face and neck (originally described as Blue Shag *P. steadi*).

PITT ISLAND SHAG *P.p. featherstoni*: As nominate except in nuptial dress head lacks white stripe on sides of face and neck; remainder of plumage generally darker throughout.
FHJ: Distinctive in breeding dress, though for much of year lacks crests and white stripe to sides of face and neck. Feeds offshore, up to 15km from land, occasionally forming dense rafts of several thousands, particularly off the large Otago Peninsula colonies.
DM: Confined to New Zealand. *P.p. punctatus* breeds North Island in Hauraki Gulf and along Auckland west coast, and on South Island in Marlborough Sounds S to Otago Peninsula. *P.p. oliveri* breeds west coast and Stewart I. area of South Island. *P.p. featherstoni* confined to Chatham Is. Egg-dates Jul–Oct (Alexander 1955).
SS: Unlikely to be confused with other New Zealand shags.

180 LITTLE PIED CORMORANT
other: Little/White-throated Shag
Phalacrocorax melanoleucos

PLATE 46 Figs 180a-180e

MAP 180

Length 58–63cm (23–25in.). Wingspan 84–91cm (33–36in.). Iris brown; facial skin and gular yellow. Bill yellowish, culmen black. Legs/feet black.

New Zealand and Australia N to Malay Archipelago; range overlaps with Pied, Little Black and Black-faced Cormorants (p. 301, p. 294, p. 301). Sexes outwardly alike, males average larger; no appreciable seasonal variation. Juveniles separable from adults. Three subspecies listed; *P.m. brevirostris* (New Zealand) differs in polymorphic plumages and is described separately.
JUVENILE: Much as breeding adult except demarcation between black crown and white cheeks occurs below eye; thighs black.
ADULT: Head Crown and hindneck narrowly marked black; remainder white (during breeding season a short white crest develops on either side of crown). **Body** Upperparts black. Underparts white. **Wings** Upper and lower black. **Tail** Black.

P.m. brevirostris: Polymorphic, palest forms as nominate above but three other morphs occur more frequently:
WHITE-THROATED SHAG: Commonest morph. Head as in nominate but upper breast and whole of underparts blackish.
INTERMEDIATE MORPH: As White-throated morph but white extends to include upper breast; remainder of underparts blackish.
DARK MORPH: Wholly blackish except for variable amount of whitish tips on chin and throat. (Beware Little Black Shag, p. 294, which also occurs in New Zealand.)
FHJ: Typical morphs resemble larger Pied and Black-faced Cormorants in pattern but with compressed yellowish bill, upright perching posture and longish tail. Mainly a freshwater species but also along coasts.
DM: Australasian region. *P.m. melvillensis* breeds eastern Java S through New Guinea and Solomon Is to Australia and Tasmania. *P.m. brevicauda* breeds Rennel Is (Solomon Is). *P.m. brevirostris* breeds New Zealand. Egg-dates throughout year according to local conditions, usually at freshwater locations. Mainly sedentary but subject to local movements following flooding of inland localities, or to coasts in droughts.
SS: Differs from larger Pied and Black-faced Cormorants (p. 301, p. 301) in stubby yellowish bill, brown iris and (in adults) white thighs. Dark morphs of *P.m. brevirostris* differ from sympatric Little Black Cormorant (p. 294) in yellowish bill, brown eye, and, usually, white flecking on chin and throat.

181 LONG-TAILED CORMORANT
other: Reed Cormorant
Phalacrocorax africanus

PLATE 44 Figs 181a-181c

MAP 181

Length 50–55cm ($19\frac{1}{2}$–$21\frac{1}{2}$in.). Wingspan 80–90cm ($31\frac{1}{2}$–$35\frac{1}{2}$in.). Iris red, facial skin yellowish. Bill orange to reddish, culmen black. Legs/feet black.

Confined to Africa S of Sahara, mainly on freshwater locations. Sexes outwardly alike, males average larger; seasonal variation. Juveniles separable from adults. Three subspecies listed, one of which, *P.(a.) coronatus* (Crowned Cormorant), is treated as separate species by some authors and it seems likely that further work will endorse this view. It is described separately below (181X).
JUVENILE: Iris brown or dull red; bill yellowish. Plumage resembles non-breeding adult except browner above without noticeable black blotches on scapulars and wing-coverts; foreneck, breast and belly whiter.
ADULT NON-BREEDING: As breeding adult except: **Head** Lacks crest; mostly dull brown, chin white, foreneck brownish-white. **Body** Upperparts browner with buffish feather edges. Underparts: upper breast pale brown, belly white, flanks and undertail-coverts blackish. **Wings** Upperwing-coverts as upperparts.
ADULT BREEDING: Head Short crest on forehead; mostly blackish with green gloss and white flecking on sides of head. **Body** Upperparts blackish with silvery gloss. Underparts black. **Wings** Upperwing: coverts and scapulars silvery-grey with black tips and edges imparting scaly blotched appearance, primaries and secondaries blackish. Underwing blackish. **Tail** Blackish.
FHJ: At inland locations small size, long-tailed jizz and more upright perching posture separate it from African races of much larger Great Cormorant. Frequents mainly freshwater locations, also lagoons and tidal estuaries and quiet coastal bays; less gregarious away from colonies than many

cormorant spp., usually seen singly or in small groups.

DM: Africa S of Sahara including Madagascar. *P.a. africanus* breeds from Mauritania in the west and Ethiopia in the east S to South Africa. *P.a. pictilis* Madagascar. Egg-dates throughout year. Movements not fully understood; dispersive tendencies appear to be governed by rains and ability to quickly establish colonies at temporary flood plains.

SS: Great Cormorant (*P.c. lucidus*) is almost twice present species size and many have pronounced white on throat, sides of face, foreneck, breast and sometimes belly. See also Bank and Cape Cormorants (p. 297, p. 296).

181X CROWNED CORMORANT *Phalacrocorax (africanus) coronatus*

PLATE 44 Fig. 181X
MAP 181X

Length 50–55cm ($19\frac{1}{2}$–$21\frac{1}{2}$in.). Wingspan 80–90cm ($31\frac{1}{2}$–$35\frac{1}{2}$in.). Iris red, facial skin yellowish. Bill orange to reddish, culmen black. Legs/feet black.

Confined to coasts of Namibia and parts of South Africa. Sexes outwardly alike, males average larger; seasonal variation. Juveniles separable from adults. Previously regarded as race of Long-tailed Cormorant (181) but now considered by some authors to be distinct species.

JUVENILE: Much as Long-tailed (Reed) Cormorant (p. 305) but with all-dark breast and belly (Sinclair, pers. comm.).

ADULT NON-BREEDING: Much as breeding adult but duller; crest retained throughout year.

ADULT BREEDING: As breeding Long-tailed Cormorant but upperparts usually darker with narrower black margins.

FHJ: Differs from Long-tailed Cormorant in shorter tail and longer legs. Habits almost exclusively marine.

DM: Breeds on offshore islands and mainland cliffs of western southern Africa from Namibia (see Shaughnessy 1979) S and E to Cape Agulhas. Egg-dates Jul–Apr. Sedentary.

SS: See notes in this section under 181.

182 JAVANESE CORMORANT other: Little Cormorant *Phalacrocorax niger*

PLATE 48 Figs 182a-182c
MAP 182

Length 56cm (22in.). Wingspan 90cm ($35\frac{1}{2}$in.). Iris dark, facial skin blackish. Bill brownish–yellow, gular yellowish. Legs/feet black.

Asiatic freshwater species; range overlaps with Indian Cormorant and Little Black Shag (p. 295, p. 294). Sexes alike; seasonal variation. Juveniles separable from adults. No subspecies.

JUVENILE: As non-breeding adult, except whole of plumage generally duller and browner; chin, throat and upper breast dirty-white.

ADULT NON-BREEDING: As breeding adult except whole of plumage duller and browner; chin and throat whitish.

ADULT BREEDING: Plumage wholly blackish-green with scattered white filoplumes on head and neck; mantle, scapulars and upperwing-coverts edged darker.

FHJ: A small freshwater species, common on Asiatic inland waters, paddyfields, jheels etc. Closely allied to Pygmy Cormorant (p. 306), with short compressed bill and long tail. Occasionally hunts in small groups.

DM: Asiatic, distributed throughout lower-altitude regions of India, Pakistan, Sri Lanka, Burma, Thailand, Malay Peninsula, Borneo and Java.

SS: From sympatric Indian Cormorant (p. 295) by smaller size, compressed bill, and lack of distinctly scaled appearance on wing-coverts, scapulars and mantle.

183 PYGMY CORMORANT *Phalacrocorax pygmeus*

PLATE 44 Figs 183a-183d
MAP 183

Length 45–55cm (18–$21\frac{1}{2}$in.). Wingspan 80–91cm ($31\frac{1}{2}$–36in.). Iris brown, facial skin black. Bill, legs/feet black.

Eurasian inland species; range overlaps with much larger, shorter-tailed Great Cormorant (p. 295). Sexes alike; seasonal variation. Juveniles separable from adults. No subspecies.

JUVENILE: Bill dull yellowish with brownish culmen; legs brownish. **Head** Mostly dull brown paling to white on chin; foreneck brownish-white. **Body** Upperparts dull brown with blackish subterminal fringes and buffish edges imparting scaly appearance. Underparts: upper breast, flanks and undertail-coverts brownish to brownish-white; belly white.

ADULT NON-BREEDING: As breeding adult except: Bill brown, yellowish at gape. **Head** Mostly dull brown; chin white, throat and foreneck brownish-white. **Body** Upperparts duller and browner with paler feather edges. Underparts dark brown variably mottled buff.

ADULT BREEDING: Head Mostly blackish with short, tufted crest on forehead and speckled with dense white filoplumes on crown and sides of head. As season progresses head becomes rich velvety-brown with fewer filoplumes. **Body** Upperparts greyish-black with green sheen and darker feather edges imparting scaled appearance. Underparts blackish with scattered white filoplumes. **Wings** Upperwing: coverts as upperparts, primaries and secondaries blackish. Underwing blackish. **Tail** Blackish.

FHJ: Small, long-tailed species normally frequenting freshwater lakes, marshes and reed-beds. Compared with Great Cormorant (only other cor-

morant of region) much smaller, about half size, with short neck, rounded crown and long tail imparting distinctly different jizz; when perched usually sits upright with neck hunched. In flight small size, with rather short neck and long tail, at once apparent. Flight buoyant with rapid, shallow wingbeats interspersed with short glides.
DM: Eurasian, status in serious decline due to drainage of habitat throughout much of range. Breeds Yugoslavia, Romania, Greece, Turkey, Crimea, Iran, Caspian and Aral Seas. Returns to colonies Mar/Apr; egg-dates Apr–Jul. European breeders disperse generally southwards from Aug onwards but some (or others) present in breeding areas throughout year. North Caspian population appears more migratory, wintering S to southern Caspian. Iraq population probably resident though dispersive during floods. Vagrants have wandered N to Sweden, W to France, S to Tunisia and E to Pakistan.
SS: Size and structure should ensure ready separation from sympatric Great Cormorant (p. 295).

184 GALAPAGOS CORMORANT
Nannopterum (=Phalacrocorax) harrisi

PLATE 48 Figs 184a-184b
MAP 184

Length 91–99cm (36–39in.). Males average larger with more robust bills. Iris turquoise, lead-grey facial skin and pinkish gular pouch. Bill blackish, paler at tip. Legs/feet black.

Only at Galapagos; no other cormorants within area. Sexes outwardly alike; no seasonal variation. Juveniles separable from adults.
JUVENILE: Iris brown. Resembles adult, plumage blacker; primaries and secondaries neater, lacking ragged appearance of older birds in worn plumage.
ADULT: Mostly blackish-brown except: **Head** Whitish base to lower mandible and scattered white filoplumes to sides of face and neck. **Body** Underparts browner, often showing yellowish-ochre hue.
FHJ: Only cormorant of region. Swims low in water (beware Galapagos Penguin, p. 207). Does not wander, rarely venturing even a kilometre from natal shoreline, returns evenings to roost on rocks.
DM: Endemic to Galapagos Is, where less than 1,000 pairs on Fernandina and Isabela. Sedentary, has never been recorded at any other islands within Galapagos Archipelago.
SS: None.

Family *FREGATIDAE* frigatebirds

Five species in single genus. Family characteristics discussed under genus heading below.

Genus *FREGATA*

Five species; large, spectacular, highly aerial seabirds; neither walk nor swim. Sexually dimorphic; adult males tend to be almost wholly black with, at most, a white abdominal patch (Christmas Frigatebird) or white 'spurs' across axillaries (Lesser Frigatebird). Females of group (except Ascension Frigatebird) have large white areas on breast extending in Magnificent, Christmas and Lesser Frigatebirds as white 'spurs' of variable extent onto otherwise dark underwing. Several species show dimorphism of bare parts colours between different populations and even within a particular island population. All adult males have a scarlet throat pouch which is inflated to balloon-like proportions during courtship rituals.

All juvenile frigatebirds, except Magnificent and Ascension and some races of Great, have rufous on either head or underparts. Distribution of black and white differs from that of their respective adults. In later stages, as they near full maturity, immatures possess, in part at least, adults' distributional pattern of black and white. Period to maturity unknown, probably 4–6 years.

Pantropical; parasitic to some extent on boobies and tropicbirds although this may be overstated in literature; many obtain food by honest endeavour. Characterised by long, slender, hooked bill, short neck, slender body, disproportionately long, narrow wings and deeply forked tail. Excellently adapted for dynamic soaring flight with only occasional, deep wingbeats, using tail as rudder to achieve remarkable aerial manoeuvres; plummets vertically to surface of water to snatch at flying fish or engage in pursuit of booby. Also picks up stranded fish and hatching sea-turtles on wing from beach or steals eggs and chicks from seabird colonies. Readily attracted to offal during fish-gutting operations (keep camera handy), sometimes congregating in hundreds; more usually solitary at sea. Strictly diurnal, normally returning to soar over islands during evening prior to overnight roosting, usually in trees. Colonial, usually in small groups; unusual in biennial breeding and long juvenile-dependency period. (See excellent account by Nelson 1976.)

At sea identification of frigatebirds notoriously complex and represents, perhaps, the most difficult identification challenge in any seabird group. This particularly true of seemingly arbitrary variety of juvenile and immature plumage stages which, when initially encountered, is certainly daunting. In all observations failure accurately to record distribution of white on underparts and underwing (if present) will prevent any possibility of even tentative identification. In particular check how far white extends towards vent and whether it encroaches in narrow spurs onto underwing. Width, shape and position of partial or complete breast bands and colour of head in juveniles also important identification criteria. In mostly all-black male frigatebirds leg colour should be noted and upperwings checked for pale bar across coverts.

The accompanying line drawings are based on several hundred photographs taken over many years at colonies known to contain only one species. They represent the first serious attempt (except for Nelson 1976) to portray the diverse plumages between fledging and adult; they do not represent particular ages. Some plumage stages have been assumed or deduced following examination of museum skins; these have been marked with an asterisk. It should be appreciated that identification criteria are still evolving for this long-neglected genus.

---

185 ASCENSION FRIGATEBIRD
Fregata aquila

PLATE 52 Figs 185a-185d
MAP 185

Length 89–96cm (35–38in.). Wingspan 196–201cm (77–79in.). Females average larger. Iris brown; orbital ring black (males), pale blue (females). Bill greyish-horn (in skins). Legs/feet black (males), reddish (females).

Confined to Ascension I. and adjacent seas in tropical Atlantic Ocean; pelagic range could overlap with Lesser, Great and Magnificent Frigatebirds (p. 315, p. 313, p. 310). At sea all-black adult males would probably be indistinguishable from those of Magnificent Frigatebird. All other stages bear diagnostic markings. Marked sexual variation. Some birds apparently breed in what would appear to be 'immature' plumage; status of these pale-breasted 'morphs' remains obscure. They are shown below as transitional stages of the gradual darkening process. Juveniles separable from adults. No subspecies.

JUVENILE (FIRST STAGE): Bill, orbital ring and legs pale blue. **Head** Mostly biscuit-white; nape spotted brown. **Body** Upperparts brown, merging to blackish on rump. Underparts mainly white; partial brown breast band more or less obscured by white down on upper breast; lower flanks and ventral area black. **Wings** Brownish-black above except for whitish-fawn alar bar across coverts. Underwing mostly blackish except for random white patches on coverts (this character consistently appears in juvenile stages of this species), and large white spur on axillaries. **Tail** Black.

JUVENILE (SECOND STAGE): As first-stage juvenile except: **Head** White. **Body** Underparts: mostly white except for broad, dark brown patches on sides of upper breast; flanks and ventral area blackish-brown.

JUVENILE (THIRD STAGE): As second-stage juvenile except: **Body** Underparts: mostly white except for broad, dark brown or tawny-brown band across upper breast; flanks and ventral area blackish.

JUVENILE (FOURTH STAGE): As third-stage juvenile except: **Head** Crown and sides of face white, chin and throat mottled tawny-brown (linking with breast band).

IMMATURE MALE: As fourth-stage juvenile except: **Head** Crown and sides of face dusky, spotted black. **Body** Breast band darker, almost black.

ADULT MALE (PALE MORPH): **Head** Black. **Body** Upperparts black, lanceolate feathers glossed green. Underparts: mostly white except for black upper breast, flanks and ventral area. **Wings** Blackish above, glossed green. Underwing mostly blackish, except for rectangular white spur on axillaries.

SUB-ADULT MALE (DARK MORPH): As adult male pale-morph except: **Body** Underparts: white lower breast and belly spotted/streaked black. **Wings** Underwing: spur on axillaries reduced.

ADULT MALE (DARK MORPH): Wholly black, lanceolate feathers of head, upperparts and upperwing-coverts strongly glossed green.

ADULT FEMALE (PALE MORPH): **Head** Mostly dull black, nape and hindneck dull brown. **Body** Upperparts mostly blackish-brown, occasionally with scattered tawny feather tips. Underparts as adult male pale morph except black throat bordered by broad brownish breast band (extension from nape and hindneck) ending on upper breast in sharp V. **Wings** Upperwing blackish-brown, usually with pale alar bar across coverts. Underwing mostly black; white rectangular spur on axillaries.

SUB-ADULT FEMALE (DARK MORPH): As adult female pale morph except: **Body** Underparts: white breast and belly spotted/streaked black. **Wings** Underwing: white rectangular spur reduced.

ADULT FEMALE (DARK MORPH): Unique in female frigatebirds. Mostly blackish with brownish nape and hindneck extending in continuous band across upper breast. (This is the typical morph. Breeding females with white breasts may represent polymorphism, rare mutant or simply a stage in the slow and gradual darkening of plumage from juvenile to adult.)

FHJ: See notes on p. 307.

DM: Restricted to Boswainbird Islet, Ascension I., tropical Atlantic Ocean, where Stonehouse & Stonehouse (1963) estimated 8,000–10,000 breeding birds. Breeding activity apparently begins from May, egg-laying peak Oct, most fledging Mar/Apr (Stonehouse 1963). Restricted to adjacent waters. Vagrant E to coast of West Africa.

SS: Murphy (1936) wrongly concluded juveniles were 'at first nearly indistinguishable from those of *F. magnificens*'. They are unique in absence of breast band, and differ further from juvenile *F. magnificens* in broad white spur on axillaries and in subsequent plumages by retention of broad band across upper breast. These characters shown to some degree in all stages of plumage except in wholly black adult male which, presumably, would be indistinguishable at sea from adult male *F. magnificens*. See Murphy (1936) for diagnostic bill characters of *F. aquila* in the hand. Most ages of *F. magnificens* have narrow, wavy, white tips across axillaries (diagnostic). Lesser Frigatebird, only other species with white axillaries likely to occur in Atlantic, differs at all ages in black belly and breast markings.

Fig. 13. Ascension Frigatebird

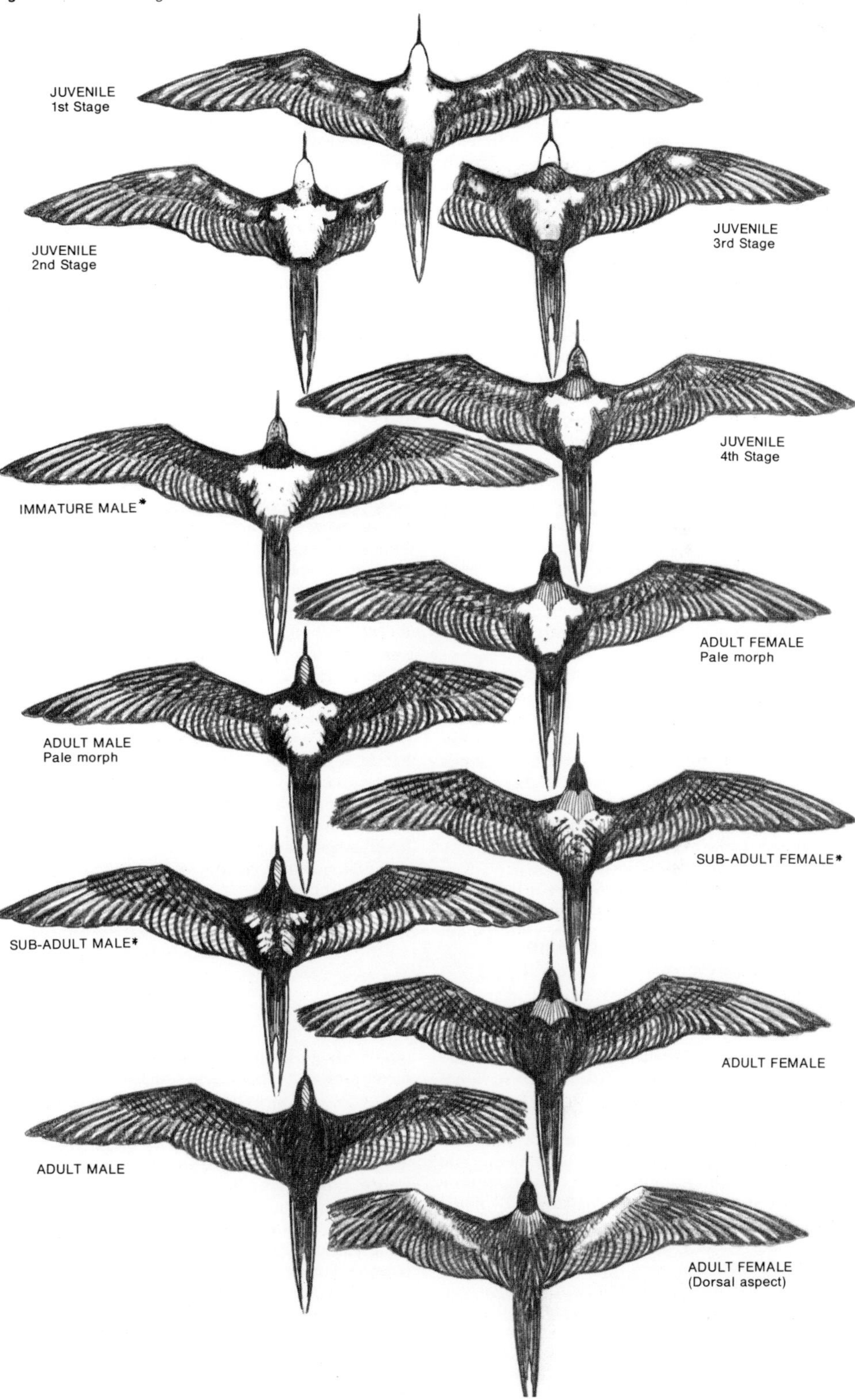

186 CHRISTMAS FRIGATEBIRD
other: Andrews's Frigatebird
Fregata andrewsi

PLATE 52 Figs 186a-186d

MAP 186

Length 89–100cm (35–39½in.). Wingspan 206–230cm (81–90in.). Females average larger. Iris brown. In males orbital ring, bill and legs blackish. In females orbital ring and bill pink, legs flesh-white.

Restricted to Christmas I., NE Indian Ocean, regularly wandering N to coasts of Java. Range overlaps with Great and Lesser Frigatebirds (p. 313, p. 315). Adult male unique. Other stages most closely resemble corresponding stages of Lesser Frigatebird, present species differs in longer white spur on underwing and mostly white breast and belly. Marked individual variation; no seasonal variation. Juveniles separable from adults. No subspecies.

JUVENILE: Bill blue, legs flesh-white. **Head** Pale tawny-yellow, darkest on crown, chin and throat; nape whitish, extending as short collar to sides of neck. **Body** Upperparts dark brown, feathers of lower back and scapulars fringed buff. Underparts: upper breast mottled white, tinged tawny-yellow; sides of breast blackish extending broadly across lower breast; flanks and ventral area blackish; belly white. **Wings** Upperwing brownish except for whitish alar bar across marginal and median coverts. Underwing mostly blackish-brown; indistinct white spur on axillaries. **Tail** Blackish.

IMMATURE MALE: As juvenile except: **Head** Mostly brown, perhaps with some scattered blackish streaks. **Body** Underparts: upper breast white spotted with black, merging into partial blackish breast band.

SUB-ADULT MALE (museum skin): As adult male except lower breast scaled black and white.

ADULT MALE: Mostly black except: lanceolate feathers of upperparts glossed green. **Body** Underparts: diagnostic white patch on lower belly. **Wings** Upperwing: pale alar bar across coverts.

IMMATURE FEMALE (FIRST STAGE): As juvenile except: **Body** Underparts: white upper breast divided from white belly by narrow brownish band; flanks and ventral area blackish.

IMMATURE FEMALE (SECOND STAGE): As first stage except: **Head** Mostly brown with whitish nape collar. **Body** Underparts mostly white except for narrow broken band across upper breast; sides of breast, flanks and ventral area blackish.

SUB-ADULT FEMALE: As immature second stage except head blackish-brown.

ADULT FEMALE: Head Blackish-brown, nape and hindneck narrowly white. **Body** Upperparts blackish-brown. Underparts mostly white except for blackish sides of breast extending as short dark spurs on upper breast; flanks and ventral area blackish. **Wings** Upperwing as juvenile, wing bar browner. Underwing blackish except for conspicuous whitish spur on axillaries. **Tail** Blackish.

FHJ: See notes on p. 307.

DM: Only known breeding colony at Christmas I., NE Indian Ocean, where fewer than 2,000 pairs (Nelson 1980). Egg-dates Apr–Jun (Alexander 1955). Pelagic dispersal largely unknown but regularly occurs off coasts of Java and Sumatra N to Andaman Sea, where specimens collected off Phuket, Thailand (Muller 1882). Extent of dispersal through Sunda Straits to coasts of Borneo and Gulf of Siam not known, but Boonsong & Cronin (1974) include Gulf of Siam within its range. Also occurs off NW Borneo (ex photographs supplied by Simpson, RNBWS), which suggests that it regularly wanders N to at least southern South China Sea, perhaps also E to Banda Sea. An adult male recently photographed near Darwin, Australia (Fullagar & van Tets, pers. comm.).

SS: Males unique. Females and all other stages separable from all plumages of Lesser Frigatebirds by mostly white underparts and conspicuous black spurs on sides of upper breast. Separation from juvenile stages of Great Frigatebird (p. 313) more difficult but that species lacks indistinct white spur on underwing.

187 MAGNIFICENT FRIGATEBIRD
Fregata magnificens

PLATE 51 Figs 187a-187f

MAP 187

Length 89–114cm (35–45in.). Wingspan 217–244cm (85½–96in.). Females average larger. Iris brown; orbital ring black (males), blue (females). Bill dull horn-pink, leaden-blue or blackish. Legs/feet black or brown (males), reddish (females).

Atlantic and Pacific coasts of the Americas. Range overlaps with Great Frigatebird (p. 313) at Galapagos Is, off Mexico and perhaps NE South America, where may also overlap with Lesser Frigatebird. All three species can probably be distinguished, at most ages, if axillary colour and distribution of white on underparts seen. Marked sexual variation; no seasonal variation. Juveniles separable from adults. Several subspecies described, but validity doubtful and therefore not listed here.

JUVENILE (FIRST STAGE): Bill pale grey, tip yellowish; legs/feet flesh-white. **Head** Wholly white. **Body** Upperparts dark sepia-brown, lower back and scapulars faintly edged buff. Underparts: ventral area and flanks blackish-brown, latter extending in wedge-shaped spurs on sides of breast to form partial breast band enclosing triangular-shaped white lower belly patch. **Wings** Upperwing dark sepia-brown except for pronounced whitish fringes forming alar bar from marginal coverts, across median coverts towards inner secondaries (more pronounced in females, Diamond 1972). Underwing wholly blackish-brown. **Tail** Blackish.

JUVENILE (SECOND STAGE): As first-stage juvenile except: **Body** Underparts: dark wedge-shaped spurs on sides of breast moult or wear to white, producing mostly white breast much like white-headed *F. minor* juveniles at this stage, although at Galapagos (where ranges overlap) juvenile *F. minor* have rusty head and upper breast.

Fig. 14. Christmas Frigatebird

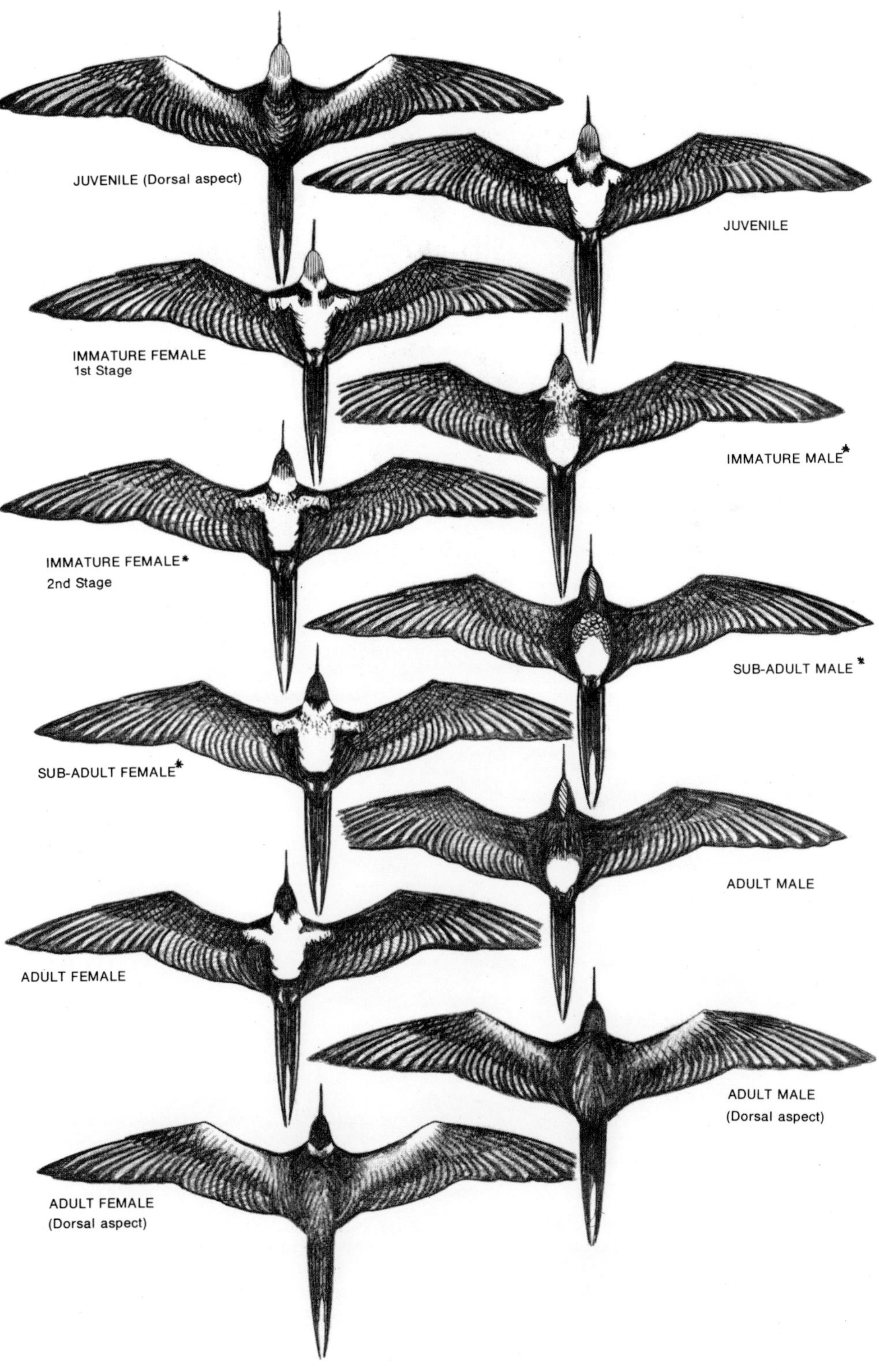

Fig. 15. Magnificent Frigatebird

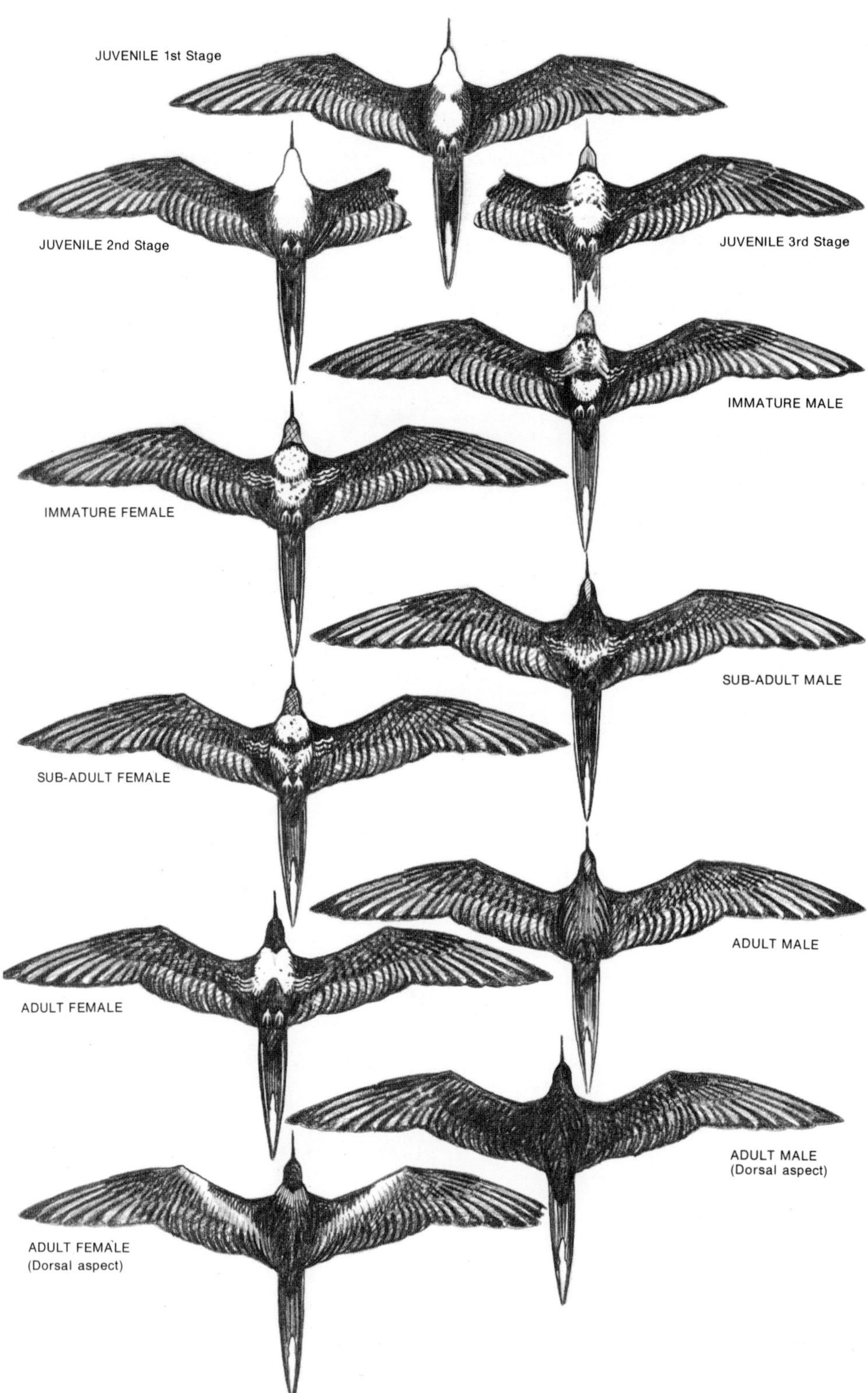

JUVENILE (THIRD STAGE): **Head** Mostly dusky-white, variably tipped brown, heaviest on nape and extending across chin and throat as narrow collar (possibly heaviest in males as some, females?, retain whitish heads). **Body** Upperparts as first-stage juvenile. Underparts: mostly white; upper breast sparsely spotted brown, faint brownish spurs on sides of breast often forming partial band across lower breast. Flanks and ventral area blackish. **Wings** Underwing mostly blackish-brown but axillaries narrowly edged white forming indistinct spur on underwing. (Spur is retained in all subsequent female plumages and up to male sub-adult stage; at close range a useful and diagnostic means of separating present species from all stages of male and female Great Frigatebirds.)

IMMATURE MALE: As third-stage juvenile except: **Head** Mostly dull blackish-brown. **Body** Underparts mostly dusky-white broken by indistinct blackish band across lower breast; white upper breast and belly spotted black, more so on former. (Immature females generally show heavier spotting on belly patch.) Flanks and ventral area blackish. **Wings** Upperwing bar less pronounced than in juveniles or immature females.

SUB-ADULT MALE: Bill pale blue; legs dull red. As immature male except: **Head** Glossy black, occasionally mottled with brown. **Body** Upperparts blackish glossed purple and green. Underparts mostly black, brownish on lower breast merging into mottled white triangular belly patch which links with whitish spurs on axillaries (distinctly different from sub-adult male Great Frigatebird). **Wings** Upperwing shows last traces of brownish wingbar.

ADULT MALE: Wholly black; lanceolate feathers on head and upperparts glossed purple and green. NOTE Some adults observed off Peru and Ecuador retained faint brownish upperwing bars; whether last traces of immaturity or due to wear could not be ascertained (pers. obs.). Stallcup (pers. comm.) also reports 'adult' males off W Mexico with brown carpal bars Feb/Mar.

IMMATURE FEMALE: As third-stage juvenile except: **Head** Variable, mostly dull blackish-brown or mottled with white. **Body** Underparts: mostly dusky-white, broken by narrow, indistinct brownish band across lower breast; upper breast and belly sparsely spotted brown; flanks and ventral area blackish-brown.

SUB-ADULT FEMALE: As third-stage juvenile except: **Body** Underparts: mostly dusky-white broken by blackish band across lower breast; white upper breast and belly spotted black, more so on latter (see immature male). Flanks and ventral area black.

ADULT FEMALE: Head Including chin and throat blackish-brown terminating in sharp V at white upper breast. Nape and hindneck greyish-brown forming indistinct greyish collar. **Body** Upperparts blackish-brown, slightly glossed green. Underparts: breast and upper flanks white terminating in inverted V at black lower breast; remainder black. **Wings** Upperwing as first-stage juvenile, except wing bar browner. Underwing as third-stage juvenile but white axillary tips unite with white lower breast. **Tail** Black.

FHJ: See notes on p. 307.

DM: Tropical Atlantic and Pacific Oceans. Breeding stations at Galapagos, and along American Pacific coast from Baja California S to Ecuador; also American Atlantic coast from Marquesas Keys, Florida, and Bahamas S and W along coasts of Central America and Caribbean Sea, also off Brazil from Fernando de Noronha S to São Paulo. (See Palmer 1962 for detailed account of American breeding stations.) In east Atlantic breeds Cape Verde Is (Boa Vista) and perhaps at Bissagos Is. Egg-dates throughout year. Pre-breeders and non-breeders disperse widely in Atlantic, reaching N to Gulf coast regions during Jun–Sep. Hurricanes cause displacement N to Newfoundland and E Canada with several E to Europe; the northernmost, an immature female, was taken at Inner Hebrides, Scotland, July 1953 (see account in *Brit. Birds* 47: 58–59). On Pacific coast of North America occurs N to Oregon, and more rarely Vancouver I., British Columbia and even Gulf of Alaska (Roberson 1980). In South America occasionally wanders to Peru (though common on beaches from Tumbes to Cabo Blanco, pers. obs.). On Atlantic coast occurs regularly in summer S to Uruguay, occasionally S to Argentina.

SS: Most stages of Magnificent Frigatebird have white tips on axillaries forming three or four diagnostic narrow wavy lines on underwing, which enables ready separation (given reasonable views) from corresponding Great Frigatebirds. Exceptions are found in adult male, and first- and second-stage juveniles. First-stage juveniles differ from most populations of Great Frigatebird in white head, and from all populations in narrow, partial breast band enclosing triangular-shaped belly patch. Second-stage juveniles probably indistinguishable from white-headed populations of Great Frigatebird until white tips of axillaries appear (but any tawny-headed frigatebird with similar breast and belly markings would be Great, as Magnificent have whitish heads). Male Great Frigatebirds usually show pronounced brownish upperwing bars, but wings in some populations are wholly black (Diamond 1975). Separation of adult male Magnificent and Great Frigatebirds further complicated by retention of pale upperwing bar in some individuals of present species. Field identification of adult males on basis of present knowledge thus appears impossible, although legs/feet of Great Frigatebird usually brighter, more red.

---

188 GREAT FRIGATEBIRD
Fregata minor

PLATE 51 Figs 188a-188f
MAP 188

Length 86–100cm (34–39½in.). Wingspan 206–230cm (81–90½in.). Females average larger. Iris brown or black; orbital ring black (males), red or pink (females). Bill pale blue-grey to blackish, often with rosy tinge. Legs/feet red or reddish-brown (males), pink or reddish-pink (females).

Mainly Indo-Pacific distribution with two outposts in Atlantic. Sympatric with Lesser Frigatebird throughout much of range but both sexes at all ages distinguishable. Also occurs with Magnificent

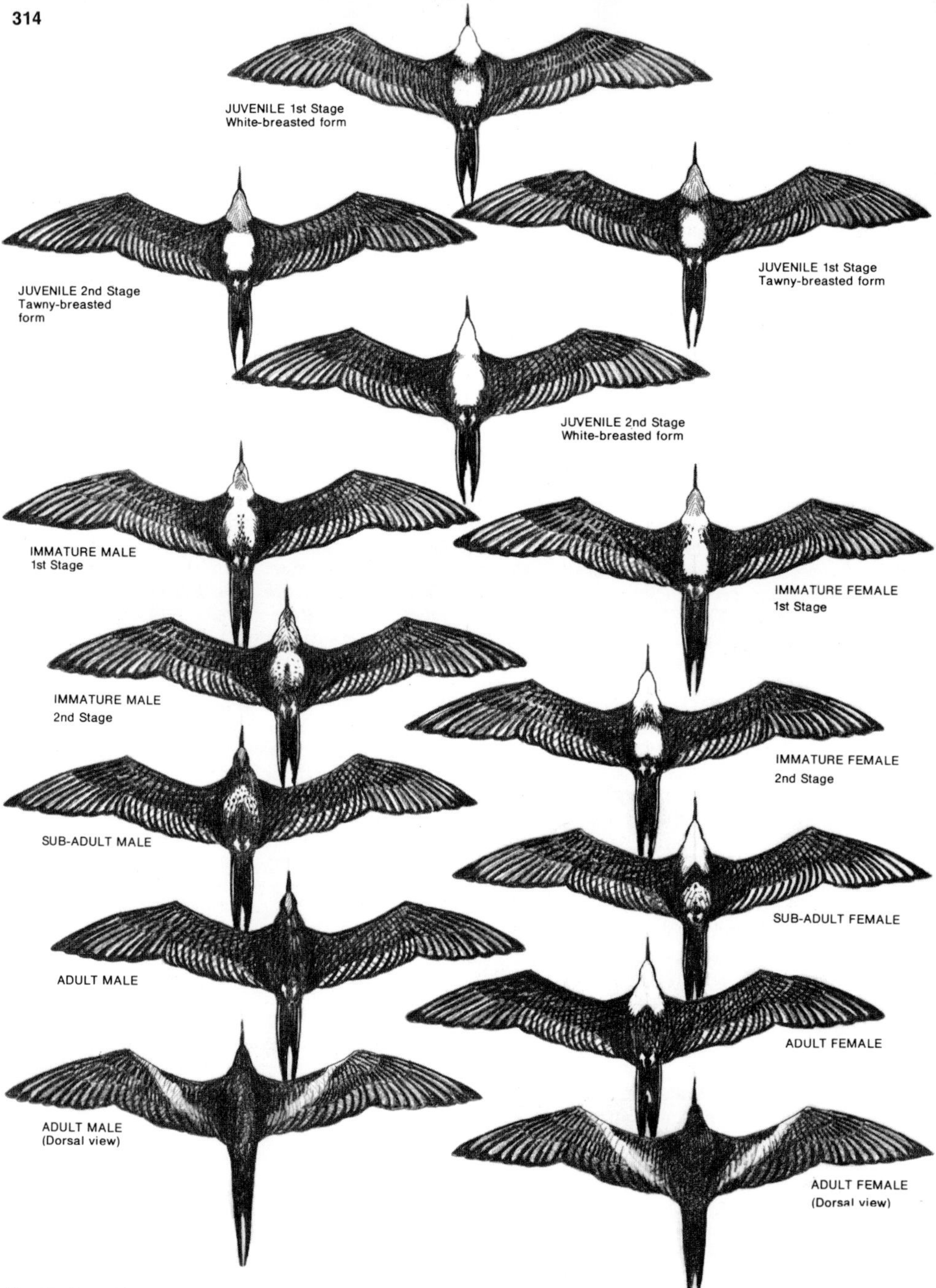

Fig. 16. Great Frigatebird

Frigatebird off Galapagos and coasts of western Mexico, and with Christmas Frigatebird in NE Indian Ocean. Separation of adult male Great and Magnificent Frigatebirds probably impossible on present knowledge, but most other classes separable given reasonable views. Marked sexual variation; no seasonal variation. Juveniles, which are separable from adults, occur in tawny-headed forms, and more rarely white-headed forms (beware Magnificent Frigatebird, p. 310). Five subspecies.

JUVENILE (FIRST STAGE): Bill pinkish or bluish. **Head** Mostly yellowish-white in some populations (Aldabra, Diamond 1975); in others (Galapagos) forehead white, crown, nape and sides of face faintly tawny, chin and throat markedly so. **Body** Upperparts as adult female except paler tips to scapulars. Underparts in some populations mainly white, extending almost to position of feet; flanks and ventral area black, former extending across breast as wide diffuse band. In tawny-headed populations underparts similar except tawny upper breast divided from white belly by dark breast band. **Wings** Upperwings mostly blackish-brown with whitish-brown alar bar across coverts. (NOTE This bar present to some extent in all subsequent male and female plumages, although some populations of adult males wholly black—beware male Magnificent Frigatebird, p. 310.) Underwing wholly black. **Tail** As adult.

JUVENILE (SECOND STAGE): As first stage except: **Body** Underparts: black breast band fades to produce white-breasted and tawny-breasted forms.

IMMATURE MALE (FIRST STAGE): As second-stage juvenile except: **Head** Wholly white or small tawny patch on chin and throat. **Body** Underparts: blackish mottling extends down centre of belly to unite with black ventral area.

IMMATURE MALE (SECOND STAGE): As first stage except: **Head** White with scattered dusky feather tips. **Body** Underparts: white upper breast spotted black, forming partial breast band; blackish centre to lower belly larger and blacker.

SUB-ADULT MALE: Head Mostly black, a few scattered white feather tips. **Body** Underparts mainly black except for mottled white horseshoe across belly. **Wings** Underwing, including axillaries, wholly blackish (see corresponding Magnificent Frigatebird).

ADULT MALE: Mostly black; head and lanceolate feathers of upperparts glossed green. Upperwing in most populations shows pronounced sandy-brown bar, as in all adult females.

IMMATURE FEMALE (FIRST STAGE): As second-stage juvenile except: **Head** Wholly white or small tawny patch on chin and throat. **Body** Upperparts as juvenile male except for brown hindneck. Underparts: white upper breast divided from white belly by narrow spotted band across lower breast.

IMMATURE FEMALE (SECOND STAGE): As first stage except: **Head** Mostly white. **Body** Underparts: white upper breast divided from white belly patch by continuous black breast band.

SUB-ADULT FEMALE: Head Mostly black except for scattered white feather tips and whitish-grey chin and throat. **Body** Underparts as adult female except for mottled white belly patch.

ADULT FEMALE: Head Mainly blackish-brown, some populations faintly browner on nape and hindneck; chin and throat greyish-white. **Body** Mantle dark brown, shading to almost black on lower back with faint greenish gloss. Underparts mostly black, upper breast white (does not extend onto underwing as in female Christmas and Lesser Frigatebirds). **Wings** Upperwing mostly blackish-brown with sandy-brown alar bar across coverts. Underwing wholly blackish. **Tail** Black.

FHJ: See notes on p. 307.

DM: Mainly Indo-Pacific distribution. *F.m. palmerstoni* breeds islands of western and central Pacific including Hawaiian, Phoenix and Coral Sea Is, E to Pitcairn and Sala-y-Gomez Is (NW of Easter Is). Disperses through Polynesia W to coasts of Australia; vagrant New Zealand. *F.m. ridgwayi* breeds eastern Pacific on Revilla Gigedo, Cocos and some Galapagos Is. In Atlantic Ocean *F.m. nicolli* breeds Trinidade and Martin Vaz Is; strays to coast of Brazil and (perhaps this race) coast of South Africa. *F.m. aldabrensis* breeds western Indian Ocean on Aldabra, Tromelin and at Cargados Carajos Shoals. *F.m. minor* breeds Cocos (Keeling) and Christmas Is in Indian Ocean, but not, apparently, at Chagos or Maldives (see Bailey 1968); also Paracel Is in South China Sea and Gunung Api in Banda Sea.

SS: Adult males closely resemble those of Magnificent and Ascension Frigatebirds. They usually vary in pronounced alar bar and brighter red legs, although some Magnificent may also show these characters. Females and juveniles are separable from those of Lesser Frigatebirds by wholly black axillaries and differences in breast, belly and chin markings. See notes under Christmas Frigatebird juveniles (p. 310) for differences in underparts and underwing markings. White-breasted 'second-stage' juveniles of present species probably indistinguishable from those of 'second-stage' juvenile Magnificent Frigatebird. (See p. 310 for further treatment.)

189 LESSER FRIGATEBIRD
Fregata ariel

PLATE 52 Figs 189a-189f
MAP 189

Length 71–81cm (28–32in.). Wingspan 175–193cm (69–76in.). Iris brown; orbital ring black (males), pink, red or blue (females). Bill greyish or black (males), pink, blue or mauve-grey (females). Legs/feet reddish-brown or black (males), pinkish or red (females).

Widespread in tropical Pacific and Indian Oceans with two outposts in Atlantic; range overlaps with Great, Christmas and perhaps Magnificent Frigatebirds (p. 313, p. 310, p. 310). All-black males with diagnostic white spurs and axillaries are easiest of the frigatebirds to identify. Adult females and all other intermediate plumage stages require more careful treatment to separate from Great and Christmas Frigatebirds, but axillary pattern, combined with extent and pattern of white on underparts, diagnostic at all ages, in both sexes, but distance/height can negate usefulness. Marked sexual variation; no seasonal variation. Juveniles separable from adults. Three subspecies.

JUVENILE (FIRST STAGE): Bill blue; legs flesh-white. **Head** Dark russet. **Body** Upperparts sepia-brown, mantle, scapulars and lower back edged buff. Underparts: upper breast white with partial or complete blackish-brown breast band; sides of breast, flanks, belly and ventral area blackish-brown. **Wings** Upperwings mostly blackish-brown except for greyish-white wing bar from marginal coverts across median coverts to inner secondaries. Underwing mainly blackish-brown except for white spur across axillaries. **Tail** Blackish.

JUVENILE (SECOND STAGE): As first stage except: **Head** Dull greyish-white on crown and sides, variably washed pale russet; chin and throat deeper russet (extending narrowly to upper breast). **Body** Breast band absent, belly mottled black and white.

IMMATURE MALE (FIRST STAGE): **Head** Mostly

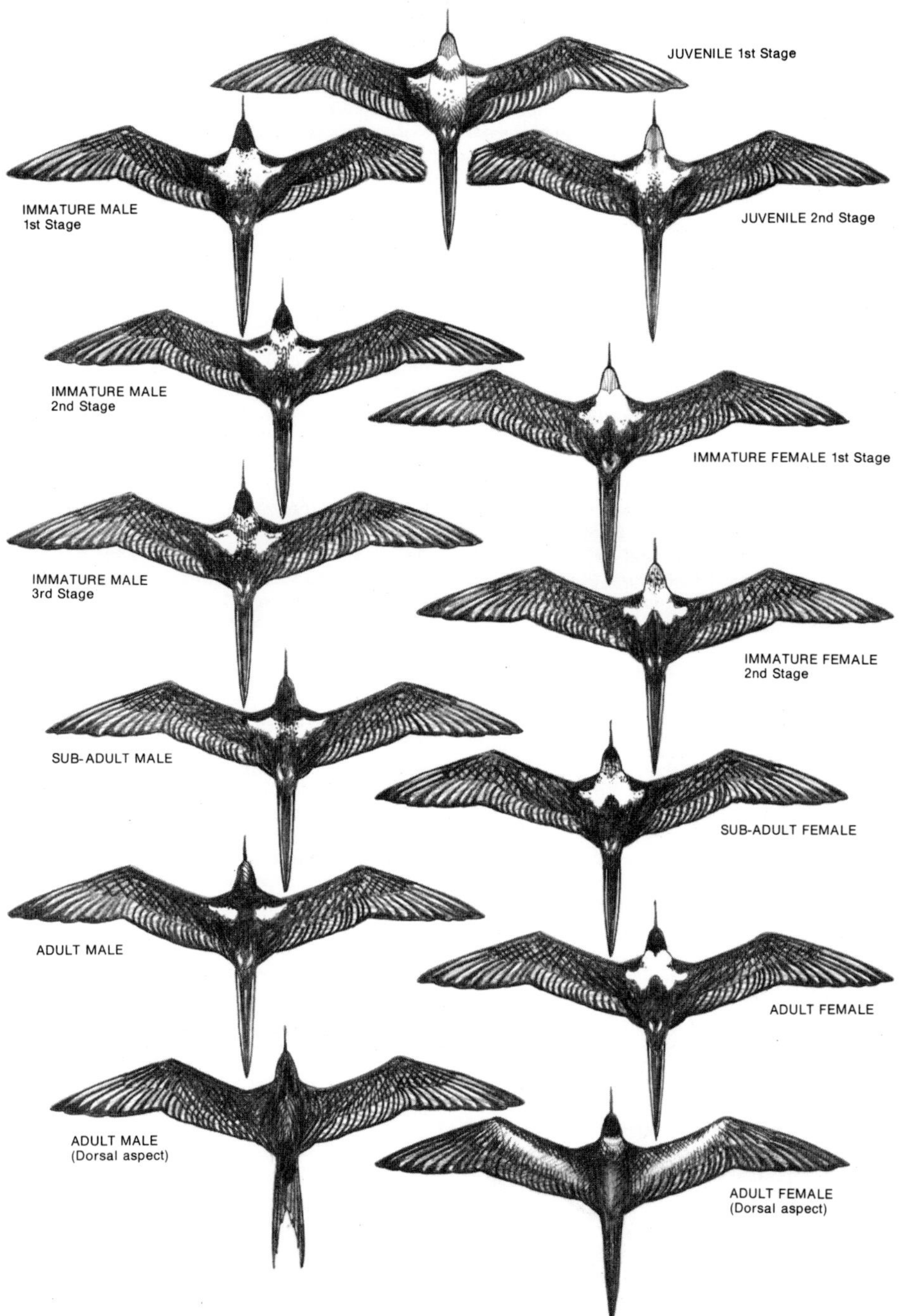

Fig. 17. Lesser Frigatebird

dull black, otherwise as second-stage juvenile.

IMMATURE MALE (SECOND STAGE): **Head** Dull black. **Body** Upperparts dull blackish-brown. Underparts: ventral area, flanks and lower belly mostly black extending upwards over centre of belly to lower breast and then to underwing, dividing white triangular flank patches from white upper breast. **Wings and Tail** As first-stage juvenile.

IMMATURE MALE (THIRD STAGE): As second-stage immature male except narrow breast band more pronounced, upper breast clouded/spotted black.

SUB-ADULT MALE: Mostly glossy black except:

Body Underparts: white flank patches wider than in adult male and linked by mottled black and white band across centre of lower breast/upper belly (the last area to become black in males).
ADULT MALE: Mostly glossy black except for white flank patches and spurs on underwings; lanceolate feathers of upperparts glossed blue, purple or green.
IMMATURE FEMALE (FIRST STAGE): As second-stage juvenile except: **Body** Upperparts: breast whiter, belly more or less black terminating in inverted V at lower breast.
IMMATURE FEMALE (SECOND STAGE): As adult female except: **Head** Spotted/streaked brown.
SUB-ADULT FEMALE: As adult female except head dark brownish-grey. (Head appears to be last area to attain adult plumage in females, unlike males in which lower breast/belly between white flanks is last to become dark.)
ADULT FEMALE: Head Blackish-brown; nape and hindneck browner, edged white, forming narrow collar. **Body** Upperparts blackish-brown. Underparts: upper breast white; flanks, belly and ventral area black terminating in inverted V at white breast. **Wings** Upperwing blackish-brown except for whitish fringes along marginal and median coverts forming conspicuous upperwing bar. Underwing mostly blackish-brown except for white spur across axillaries. **Tail** Black.
FHJ: Smallest frigatebird; see p. 307 for habits etc.
DM: Largely Indo-Pacific distribution. *F.a. ariel* breeds islands in central and eastern Indian Ocean including Cocos (Keeling) and islands off NW Australia, and many islands in central Pacific S of Johnston Atoll including Phoenix and Line groups, Fiji, Marquesas and Tuamotu Is. Sibley & Clapp (1967) have shown that central Pacific juveniles disperse on broad WSW front, first to Solomon Is, Bismarck Archipelago and New Guinea, and then N to Philippines, with some N to Japan, even Siberia. Vagrant Hawaiian Is. In S Atlantic *F.a. trinitatis* breeds Trinidade and Martin Vaz; may wander to coasts of Brazil. Vagrant N to NE USA (Snyder, in Palmer 1962). In western Indian Ocean *F.a. iredalei* breeds Aldabra, Tromelin, Agalega, Chagos and Maldive Is (based on Bailey 1968); disperses N to coasts of India and Somalia.
SS: Adult males distinctive; adult females safely separable from female Great Frigatebirds by black chin and throat and white spur on axillaries. All other plumages of both sexes differ from corresponding Great Frigatebirds in axillary colour and distribution of white on underparts. Female Christmas Frigatebirds have more extensive white spur on axillaries and differ further in more black on head and sides of breast and also in greater extent of white on lower belly. Juveniles of the two species separable by extent of white on lower belly.

Order *CHARADRIIFORMES* shorebirds, skuas, gulls, terns, auks

Diverse order of cosmopolitan distribution comprising about 16 families and some 314 species. Members of the order spend much time in or near water but, because of the diversity within the order, taxonomists have divided it into three sub-orders: *Charadrii* (shorebirds); *Lari* (gulls, terns, skuas and skimmers); *Alcae* (auks).

Family *PHALAROPODIDAE* phalaropes

Three species; small swimming waders breeding in northern hemisphere.

Genus *PHALAROPUS*

Two of the three species are circumpolar, breeding in Arctic and sub-arctic tundra; the third, Wilson's Phalarope (p. 319), nests around freshwater sloughs and ponds of central plains of N America. All strongly migratory; the two Arctic species spend much of their time at sea and, as in most pelagic species, have developed salt glands and are thus able to dispense with fresh water indefinitely. Another adaptation is their lobed, semi-palmated toes. Their dense plumage provides a platform of trapped air on which they float, high and cork-like, bobbing their heads as they swim jerkily about. Occasionally spin on water. Tame and confiding, particularly on breeding grounds. The flight of all three species rather weak and nervous; during migration severe gales often 'wreck' large numbers.

Unusual in that the sexual role is reversed, females in all species being larger and more brightly coloured than males who incubate and tend the young. In winter, plumage of both sexes similar.

Separation of the three species straightforward if seen closely, or during breeding season when nuptial plumage distinctly different. In autumn and winter care needed to separate the two Arctic species.

190 RED PHALAROPE
other: Grey Phalarope
Phalaropus fulicarius

PLATE 53 Figs 190a-190c

MAP 190

Length 18–23cm (7–9in.). Wingspan 35–38cm (14–15in.). Iris brown. Bill yellow with black tip. Legs/feet grey.

Circumpolar in Arctic regions, migrating S to winter at sea; range overlaps with both Wilson's and Red-necked (Northern) Phalaropes (p. 319, p. 318). Distinctive in breeding plumage but care required to separate from latter in autumn/winter. Sexes differ in breeding plumage; similar in non-breeding plumage. Juveniles separable from adults. No subspecies.

JUVENILE: Bill black, resembles adult non-breeding except: **Body** Upperparts mostly dull blackish-grey edged tawny-buff, sides of rump tawny-red. Underparts mostly white, sides of breast tawny-buff.

ADULT NON-BREEDING: Bill blackish, base of lower mandible sometimes yellowish. **Head** Mostly white; crown, eye-stripe and hindneck blackish. **Body** Mostly pale grey faintly edged white (in autumn some retain irregular dark streaks); rump slate-grey, sides white. Underparts mainly white, sides of breast grey. **Wings** Upperwing: primaries, their coverts and secondaries blackish, base of inner primaries and tips of greater coverts white, forming conspicuous wing bar; coverts grey faintly edged white. Underwing white, margins black. **Tail** Black, sides and tip white.

ADULT FEMALE BREEDING: Head Forehead, crown, lores, short stripe through eye, chin and hindneck blackish; sides of face and nape white, remainder of throat and neck brick-red. **Body** Upperparts mostly blackish edged tawny-buff, rump blackish, sides brick-red. Underparts brick-red. **Wings and Tail** As non-breeding adult.

ADULT MALE BREEDING: Similar to adult female breeding but duller and slightly smaller. Tawny-red underparts broken with white on belly.

FHJ: A little larger, more robust than Red-necked (Northern) Phalarope, with shorter, thicker bill. Generally nests further N than that species and migrates further S. Pelagic outside breeding season, forms large flocks at sea, readily alights on water, floats buoyantly. Call: A sharp metallic 'beek' and Ruddy Turnstone-like rattle.

DM: Circumpolar in Arctic regions; breeds Alaska, Canada, Greenland, Iceland, Novaya Zemlya and northern Siberia. Most return late May/early Jun; egg-dates Jun/Jul; fledging and departure begins late Jul/Aug. Unlike spring migration, autumn movements protracted, large numbers lingering off both coasts of North America until early Dec. Peak count in NW Atlantic off Nova Scotia, 20,000 (Finch 1973). Some may winter in these latitudes as small numbers reported throughout winter period in N Pacific off Aleutian Is S to California, and in NW Atlantic off N Carolina S to Gulf of Mexico. Large numbers evidently migrate further S; available evidence suggests that most N American breeders move SE to winter mainly off West Africa from Canary Is S to Gulf of Guinea, smaller numbers reaching S to Cape of Good Hope; occurs also in SW Atlantic off Argentina. Asiatic breeders move SE across N Pacific to winter off western South America S to Chile.

SS: Most confusion arises in winter with Red-necked (Northern) Phalarope (p. 318). Present species larger with heavier, pot-bellied jizz, paler grey upperparts and thicker, shorter bill. Caution required during autumn, however, as juveniles and some adults show darker mantle and back; adults may also retain some tawny-red on underparts. Although both species have been noted together during winter months, most Red (Grey) Phalaropes appear to winter mainly off western coasts of Africa and South America whilst majority of Red-necked (Northern) winter off Arabia and in South China Sea. Wilson's Phalarope (p. 319) lacks white wing bar, has whitish rump, and legs project beyond tail in flight. Sanderling (consult local field guide) similar during winter months but wrist of wing distinctly black and head lacks black eye patch found in both 'Arctic' phalaropes.

191 RED-NECKED PHALAROPE
other: Northern Phalarope
Phalaropus lobatus

PLATE 53 Figs 191a-191d

MAP 191

Length 15–20cm (6–8in.). Wingspan 33–35cm (13–14in.). Iris brown. Bill black. Legs/feet dark grey.

Breeds low Arctic and sub-arctic zones, migrating S to winter at sea; range overlaps with both Wilson's and Red (Grey) Phalaropes (p. 319, p. 318). Distinctive in breeding plumage but separation from latter in autumn/winter requires care. Sexes differ in breeding plumage; similar in non-breeding plumage. Juveniles separable from adults. No subspecies.

JUVENILE (AUTUMN): Legs pale pink. resembles non-breeding adult but upperparts darker, back and scapulars broadly striped rich golden-brown.

ADULT NON-BREEDING: Sexes alike. **Head** Mainly white except for blackish streak through eye; crown, nape and hindneck dusky. **Body** Upperparts mostly dark grey, whitish edges on back and scapulars; sides of rump white. Underparts mostly white, sides of breast grey. **Wings** Upperwing mostly dark grey; white bases of inner primaries and tips of greater coverts form conspicuous white wing bar. Underwing: primaries, secondaries and most lesser coverts dark grey, axillaries and greater coverts white forming paler centre. **Tail** Blackish, sides and tip white.

ADULT FEMALE BREEDING: Head Including hindneck mostly blackish-slate, small tuft above eye and chin white; sides of neck and throat chestnut. **Body** Upperparts: mostly blackish-slate, back and scapulars striped buff and ochre, sides of rump white. Underparts: sides of breast chestnut, greyer on flanks, remainder white. **Wings and Tail** As non-breeding adult.

ADULT MALE BREEDING: Resembles adult female but smaller and duller, chestnut confined mainly to sides of neck; breast and flanks greyer.

FHJ: Somewhat smaller than other phalaropes, more slender neck, smaller head and finer bill, particularly at tip. Pelagic when not breeding, forms flocks at sea, readily alights on water, occasionally submerges when feeding. Call: in flight an explosive 'chip-chip'; 'chowk-chowk' when spinning or feeding on water.

DM: Circumpolar in low Arctic and sub-arctic zones, breeding Alaska, Canada, southern Greenland, Iceland, Spitsbergen, Scandinavia, British Isles (Shetland Is), Russia, Siberia, Sakhalin, Commander and Aleutian Is. Northernmost populations arrive late May/early Jun; egg-dates May/Jun; fledging and departure begins mid Jul, most Aug, occurring on both coasts of USA, western and southern Europe, Japan, China and Philippine Is. In NW Atlantic Ocean during Aug/Sep huge annual aggregation of up to 3 million occurs off Maine, USA, in Bay of Fundy (Finch 1978), where small numbers linger till late Oct before dispersing S. Likely to be encountered in oceanic habitat anywhere throughout lower latitudes of southern hemisphere during austral summer with large concentrations in favoured areas, namely SE Pacific off coasts of Peru, SE Atlantic off equatorial W Africa, NW Indian Ocean in Arabian Sea, and in South China Sea.

SS: In non-breeding plumage most likely to be confused with Red (Grey) Phalarope (p. 318). Sanderlings (refer to local field guide) similar but present species has finer bill, darker back and shorter wing bar.

---

192 WILSON'S PHALAROPE *Phalaropus tricolor*

PLATE 53 Figs 192a-192d
MAP 192

Length 20–25cm (8–10in.). Wingspan 35–38cm (14–15in.). Iris brown. Bill, legs/feet black.

Breeds mainly freshwater locations in temperate North America, migrating S to South America in winter; small numbers occur annually during autumn in western Europe. Sexes differ during breeding season; similar in non-breeding plumage. Juveniles separable from adults. No subspecies.

JUVENILE: Legs yellowish. Resembles non-breeding adult but upperparts, including wing-coverts, buffish-brown in tone with broader, paler feather margins.

ADULT NON-BREEDING: Legs yellowish-grey. **Head** Including neck, mostly white tinged grey-buff; crown, eye-stripe and hindneck greyer. **Body** Upperparts mostly grey with faint white edges giving scaled appearance; rump and uppertail-coverts white. Underparts mostly white, sides of breast often dusky. **Wings** Upperwing: primaries, their coverts and secondaries dark grey, scapulars similar, edged white. Greater coverts brownish-grey, faintly tipped white forming barely noticeable wing bar; remainder of coverts grey. Underwing mostly white. **Tail** Pale grey, sides and tip white.

ADULT FEMALE BREEDING: Head Forehead, crown and lower hindneck blue-grey, supercilium, nape, chin, throat and foreneck white. Eye-stripe black, continuing across ear-coverts and down sides of neck where it becomes chestnut. **Body** Upperparts mostly grey except for irregular chestnut stripe on mantle and along edge of scapulars. Rump and uppertail-coverts white. Underparts mostly white, breast buffy-cinnamon. **Wings** Mostly brownish-grey, primaries and secondaries darker, coverts and tertials margined paler; underwing mostly white. **Tail** Pale grey with white sides and tip.

ADULT MALE BREEDING: Resembles female but smaller, upperparts duller and browner.

FHJ: Rarely occurs at sea. Wades much more frequently than other phalaropes, spins when swimming. Longer, more needle-like bill and longer legs than other phalaropes, latter projecting beyond tail in flight. Call: soft 'coit-coit-coit'.

DM: Breeding confined to southwestern and south central Canada (see Godfrey 1966), then S to south central California, northern Utah, central Kansas and northern Indiana. Northernmost breeding area interior British Columbia; summer stragglers have reached southern Alaska and N to Point Barrow. Returns to sites early May; egg-dates May/Jun; fledging and departure begins late Jul, most birds moving S along Pacific coast, reaching Ecuador and Peru from late Jul (some still in nuptial dress). Evidence suggests that from southwest Peru migration is across Andes, large concentrations reported moving S at 2,400–4,770m in Aug/Sep (Hughes, pers. comm.); at Lake Titicaca hundreds seen during Aug (pers. obs.). Main wintering area Patagonia, some S to Tierra del Fuego. A few remain in winter quarters throughout year. In autumn small numbers regularly reach western Europe; regular Galapagos Is, straggler to Hawaii. Has occurred in Antarctic Peninsula (see Conroy, JWH, 1971).

SS: In non-breeding plumage likely to be confused with any wader of similar size and coloration by inexperienced birders. From other phalaropes by white rump, long bill and lack of wing bar; legs project beyond tail in flight.

Family *CHIONIDIDAE* sheathbills

Two species, geographically isolated. Family characters discussed under genus.

Genus *CHIONIS*

Two species; jizz and behaviour resemble domestic fowl. Plumage mainly white; the two species separated by differences in bare parts colours although ranges not known to overlap. In both, face has fleshy wattles at base of bill and below eyes; a large horny sheath covers nasal openings of the stout bill. Legs sturdy with only rudimentary webs between the three front toes; hindtoe well developed.

Often referred to as paddies, these are the only birds without webbed feet found on the shores of the Antarctic continent. Inquisitive, freely approaching humans, they depend on their speed, running with great agility, to escape possible danger. Habitually attend penguin rookeries, cormorant colonies and seals during summer months. Base rubbish dumps and shorelines are frequented during austral winter. Scavengers and opportunistic feeders, quarrelling over corpses and placentae; adept egg-stealers. Flight pigeon-like, strong over open water but over land appear awkward; legs often dangled.

193 AMERICAN SHEATHBILL
other: Snowy Sheathbill/Paddy
Chionis alba

PLATE 19 Fig. 193

MAP 193

Length 40cm (16in.). Wingspan 79cm (31in.). Iris brown; facial wattles white or pinkish-white. Bill brownish or yellow at tip shading to pinkish-yellow at base. Legs/feet bluish-grey.

Antarctic Peninsula and Scotia Arc; unmistakable within range. Sexes outwardly alike; no seasonal variation. Juveniles differ from adults only in their less developed sheaths and caruncles. No subspecies.

PLUMAGE: Entirely white.

FHJ: Terrestrial scavenger normally seen with bobbing, rather pigeon-like gait, padding along between ranks of penguins and seals eating anything remotely suggestive of food. Inquisitive and tame, entering human camps etc. During short flights legs often dangled; in mid ocean, however, flight appears much stronger, though readily pitches onto ships' decks.

DM: Breeds South Georgia, South Orkney, South Shetlands, and Antarctic Peninsula S to about 65°S. Returns to territories Oct/Nov; egg-dates Dec/Jan; fledging and departure begins Feb/Mar. Adults appear more sedentary and probably undertake only limited dispersal during winter. Juveniles appear more migratory and disperse N over open ocean to reach shores of Falklands, Tierra del Fuego and Patagonia, occasionally Uruguay. At Falklands some wintering groups number 200–300 (Woods 1975). Small numbers of non-breeders remain in wintering quarters throughout year. Ship-assisted vagrants have occurred N to England (Tucker, pers. comm.).

SS: Lesser Sheathbill sedentary, occurs only on sub-antarctic islands of Indian Ocean.

194 LESSER SHEATHBILL
other: Black-faced Sheathbill/Paddy
Chionis minor

PLATE 19 Fig. 194

MAP 194

Length 38–41cm (15–16in.). Wingspan 74–79cm (29–31in.). Iris brown; facial wattles pinkish to mauve. Bill wholly black. Leg colour varies between races, pinkish-white to black.

Sub-antarctic islands of Indian Ocean; unmistakable within range. Sexes alike; no seasonal variation. Juveniles differ only in less developed sheath and caruncles. Four subspecies listed, differing mainly in shape of sheath and colour of facial wattles and legs/feet.

PLUMAGE: Entirely white.

FHJ: As American Sheathbill (p. 320).

DM: *C.m. minor* breeds Kerguelen I.; *C.m. nasicornis* Heard I.; *C.m. crozettensis* Crozet Is; *C.m. marionensis* Marion and Prince Edward Is. Egg-dates Dec/late Jan; fledging begins Mar. Sedentary.

SS: Unmistakable, although Cattle Egrets sometimes occur S to Prince Edward I. (pers. obs.).

Family *STERCORARIIDAE* skuas/jaegers

Six or seven species in two genera. Medium to large, piratical seabirds breeding in higher latitudes of both hemispheres, normally on tundra or islands; migrating towards, or to, opposite hemisphere in their respective winters. Robust, gull-like birds with mostly brown plumage. Bill structure, unlike that of gulls, is divided into four separate plates, one a fleshy, hawk-like cere across base of upper mandible. Sexes outwardly alike, females usually slightly larger.

Genus *CATHARACTA*

Taxonomy complex and not fully agreed upon, see especially Devillers (1977) who proposed three species. Brooke (1978) on present knowledge considered there to be four species in *Catharacta*: *skua* monotypic; *chilensis* monotypic; *maccormicki* monotypic; and *antarctica* with three races. Brooke's treatment is followed in this guide.

Catharacta are rather large, thickset, mostly brown piratical seabirds with conspicuous white area at base of primaries. Characteristically, bill strongly hooked at tip; head large; neck short; wings broad but pointed at tip; tail wedge-shaped, two central feathers only slightly elongated.

Identification problematical, particularly at long range or without comparative experience; complicated by individual variation of overall body hue (beware) and, in *maccormicki*, by polymorphism. Only recently has latter species been shown to migrate into northern hemisphere in all three major oceans. In western N Atlantic all *Catharacta* sightings should be checked carefully. South Polar Skuas of any age are colder in hue than Great Skuas, rather grey in cast as opposed to tawny, and lack the paler U-shaped marks on upperparts of that species. Any *Catharacta* sp. with a uniformly pale nape and underparts contrasting with darker, uniform upperparts and wings will be a South Polar Skua (pale and intermediate morphs). Off coasts of Chile and southern Argentina three *Catharacta* spp. occur together during austral winter, two of which hybridise to limited extent; they require careful treatment. Refer to main text for further details.

195 GREAT SKUA
other: Bonxie
Catharacta skua

PLATE 54 Figs 195a-195b
MAP 195

Length 51–66cm (20–26in.). Wingspan 145–155cm (57–61in.). Iris brown. Bill usually blackish-grey but in some medium or pale grey with darker tip. Legs/feet blackish-grey.

Northern hemisphere; range overlaps with South Polar and Pomarine Skuas (p. 322, p. 324). Sexes alike; no seasonal variation but marked individual variation, some with white areas on inner coverts of upperwing (see Norman & Tucker 1979). Juveniles separable from adults. No subspecies.

JUVENILE: Much as adult except: **Head** Lacks noticeable golden shaft-streaks; cap less distinct. **Body** Upperparts more uniform brown with paler rufous edges or barring. Underparts similar but more uniform and tawny in tone. **Wings** Upperwing: coverts as upperparts, many show slightly less white at bases of primaries (but perhaps never as little as in upperwing of some South Polar Skuas).

ADULT: Head Mostly brown with gold and rufous shaft-streaks; indistinct blackish cap. **Body** Upperparts vary in tone from dark sepia-brown to cinnamon with dense streaks, spots and U-shaped marks of gold and/or rufous-brown (never uniform brown or cold grey-brown as in South Polar Skua). Underparts similar but more uniform, warmer brown, mottled cinnamon and buff. **Wings** Upperwing: primaries and secondaries blackish-brown, former with white bases and shafts forming conspicuous wing flash; coverts as upperparts. Underwing mostly dark brown; white at base of primaries larger, more conspicuous than on upperwing. **Tail** Blackish-brown.

FHJ: The largest, most powerful and predatory of the northern skuas, with conspicuous white wing patches in upper- and underwing. Tail short and slightly rounded, lacking noticeable tail projections of the smaller adult skuas. Differs from smaller Pomarine Skua (p. 324) in much heavier body, more powerful and menacing jizz which, to the unwary, may suggest a very large deep-chested, thickset, immature gull but with rather broad wings, pointed at tips. Flight direct and purposeful, hugging wave contours or up to 50m with shallow constant wingbeats. Usually initiates pursuit-chases with low-level sneak attack, harrying birds up to size of Gannet, forcing them to disgorge, often grabbing a wing or tail and pulling them down into sea. Follows ships, attends trawlers, eats carrion.

DM: North Atlantic; breeds Iceland, Faeroes, Shetland and Orkney Is, as well as scattered sites on mainland of northern Scotland. Pairs recently bred Spitsbergen and Finnmark. Returns to colonies from late Mar to Apr; egg-dates Apr–Jun; fledging and protracted dispersal S begins Aug onwards. Most have left NW European waters by Nov though a few occur through winter months. Main wintering area thought to be from Bay of Biscay S to NW Africa, with limited dispersal into western Mediterranean. Rare off east and west coasts of North America (see South Polar Skua, p. 322).

SS: Refer to notes under South Polar and Pomarine Skuas (p. 322, p. 324).

196 CHILEAN SKUA
Catharacta chilensis

PLATE 54 Fig. 196
MAP 196

Length 55–61cm (21½–24in.). Wingspan not recorded. Iris brown. Bill, legs/feet blackish.

Confined to coasts of Chile and southern Argentina; extent of northwards migration unknown; range overlaps with Antarctic and South Polar Skuas (p. 323, p. 322). Sexes alike; no seasonal variation. Juveniles not readily separable from adults at sea. Chilean and Antarctic Skuas co-exist with limited hybridisation on Argentinian coast (Devillers 1977). No subspecies.

JUVENILE: Much as adult except: **Head** Cap less pronounced. **Body** Upperparts varyingly marked with cinnamon bars, heaviest over rump. Underparts usually brighter cinnamon. **Wings** Underwing: coverts more extensively tawny-cinnamon.
ADULT: Head Greyish-brown cap merges into cinnamon sides of face, chin and throat; cheeks often greyer. Nape and sides of neck indistinctly streaked and spotted yellow or white. **Body** Upperparts mostly blackish-brown, mantle and scapulars indistinctly spotted dull rufous. Underparts mostly uniform reddish-cinnamon, upper breast lightly streaked yellow or white. **Wings** Upperwing mostly blackish-brown; shafts and bases of primaries white, forming conspicuous wing flash. Underwing: coverts bright cinnamon (diagnostic), otherwise as upperwing. **Tail** Blackish-brown.
FHJ: Slightly smaller than Great Skua (p. 321), weaker bill; habits and jizz otherwise resemble that species.
DM: Confined mainly to western South America, breeding from about 37°S in Chile southwards to Tierra del Fuego; also breeds along coasts of Argentina where limited hybridisation occurs with Antarctic Skua (Devillers 1977). Returns to breeding areas mid Oct/Nov, some may form large loose colonies (see Moynihan, in Humphrey *et al.* 1970); egg-dates Dec; fledging and dispersal begin Mar/Apr. Many, perhaps mostly juveniles, move N but extent of dispersal on both littorals of South America poorly known. Formerly thought to migrate N into Pacific to winter off North America (Grinnell & Miller 1944) but Devillers (1977) has shown specimens taken in those latitudes to be South Polar Skua (p. 322). Certainly occurs to northern Peru (pers. obs.) and perhaps even N to Panama.
SS: Combination of dark cap and cinnamon underparts and underwing-coverts diagnostic at all ages. See Antarctic and South Polar Skuas (p. 323, p. 322).

197 SOUTH POLAR SKUA
other: McCormick's Skua
Catharacta maccormicki

PLATE 54 Figs 197a-197d

MAP 197

Length 53cm (21in.). Wingspan 127cm (50in.). Iris dark brown. Bill, legs/feet blackish-grey.

Breeds Antarctic continent migrating to northern parts of Atlantic, Indian and Pacific Oceans; range overlaps with other species of skua. Sexes alike, no seasonal variation although head and underparts often wear buffer or greyer. Juveniles separable at sea. No subspecies; polymorphic, occurring in light and dark morphs with intermediates.
JUVENILE (LIGHT MORPH): Bill pale blue, tip black; legs/feet blue. (Beware – some Great Skuas show grey bills with dark tips.) Plumage as adult except: **Head** Pale to medium grey or dusky greyish-brown, chin and throat paler (darker examples appear slightly hooded). Hindnape uniformly pale greyish-buff encircling neck to form diagnostic, unmarked paler collar. **Body and Wings** Greyer, less brown some with light grey or buffish edges to scapulars, upper-back and upperwing coverts (enhanced by wear but usually finer and perhaps never as pronounced as in Great Skua). Upperwing: often shows much less white in upperwing but this character variable, some with white bases to all ten primaries.
ADULT (LIGHT MORPH): **Head** Mostly pale pinkish-brown to greyish-white, usually with diagnostic uniformly paler area on hindnape extending as partial collar; forenape and sides of neck with variable amount of golden streaks (but not usually as pronounced as in Great Skua). **Body** Upperparts: uniform brownish-black with only a few, scattered pale tips. Underparts pale pinkish-brown to greyish-white. **Wings** Upper and lower uniform brownish-black; shafts and bases of all primaries white, forming noticeable wing flash. **Tail** Blackish.
ADULT (INTERMEDIATE MORPH): As light morph except head, hindneck and underparts uniform straw or buff-brown. (NOTE There is continuous gradation between light and dark morphs.)
JUVENILE (DARK MORPH): Much as adult except for blue base to bill and blue legs.
ADULT (DARK MORPH): **Head** Most dark brown to blackish, some with faintly paler nape. A paler grizzled area at base of bill, particularly base of upper mandible, appears as a pale line around bill and is a good field character, particularly when seen head on, flying low over water (Sinclair, pers. comm.). **Body** Upperparts uniform blackish-brown. Underparts dark brown, slightly paler than upperparts. **Wings and Tail** As light morph.
FHJ: Resembles Great Skua (p. 321) in jizz, but averages smaller with rather variable polymorphic plumages ranging from almost white-bodied to blackish. At sea appears smaller-headed with comparatively short, slender bill and, in pale morphs, a striking contrast between blackish upperparts and pale head and underparts. Habits and flight much as Great Skua; attends trawlers.
DM: Breeds Antarctica; geographically orientated polymorphism occurs, dark morphs predominating on northern part of Antarctic Peninsula, light morph more prevalent elsewhere on continent (see Devillers 1977). Returns to colonies Sep/Oct; egg-dates Nov/Dec; fledging and dispersal begins Feb–Apr. Adults may undertake only limited movements, whereas juveniles appear to undertake a regular migration into N Pacific and Atlantic Oceans and perhaps also into N Indian Ocean; some may remain throughout year. In Pacific occurs in some numbers off Japan and North America; movements suggest a clockwise loop passing Japan May–Jul, arriving off British Columbia and Washington Jul/Aug and California Sep/Oct. In western North Atlantic, where Great Skua (p. 321) also occurs, it has become clear that many sightings of skua spp. are referable to South Polar Skua (see Veit 1978). They occur mainly Jun–Sep; a specimen has been taken from Greenland with sight records of two (1982) at St Ives, England (pers. obs.), the first records for NW Europe where they may occur regularly on passage. In N Indian Ocean records of skua spp. seem more

likely to be of South Polar Skua (see Devillers 1977).

SS: Light morphs of present species virtually unmistakable, showing uniform blackish upperparts contrasting strongly with pale head and underparts and prominent paler hindnape; in flight, when wings are raised, contrast between pale body and dark underwings particularly conspicuous and easily seen. Intermediate morphs also show contrast between uniform pale or straw-brown head and underparts and blackish upperparts. By comparison adult Great and Antarctic Skuas have head, nape, body and scapulars heavily marked with whitish or yellow and rufous streaks and spots; their general tone is warm brown, rufous or cinnamon, thus lacking obvious contrast between cold, blackish or brown, upperparts and pale head and underparts. Juvenile dark morphs difficult to separate from juvenile Great Skua; criteria to enable separation still evolving and complicated by some Great Skuas (of all ages) showing two-tone bill. Some juvenile *maccormicki* have pale tips on upperparts but with diagnostic paler hindcollar. See Chilean Skua (p. 321).

198 ANTARCTIC SKUA *Catharacta antarctica*

PLATE 54 Fig. 198
MAP 198

Length 61–66cm (24–26in.). Wingspan not recorded. Iris pale brown. Bill, legs/feet blackish-grey.

Southern Oceans S to Antarctic Peninsula; range overlaps with Chilean and South Polar Skuas (p. 321, p. 322). Sexes alike; no seasonal variation. Juveniles not readily separable at sea. Three subspecies listed (Brooke 1978), each described separately below. Chilean and *C.a. antarctica* coexist on Argentinian coast with limited hybridisation (Devillers 1977).

C.a. antarctica

JUVENILE: Legs and feet sometimes mottled black and white (Woods 1975). Plumage variable; uniformly dark brown to reddish-brown or cinnamon, with paler buff and cinnamon bars on mantle, back scapulars and wing-coverts. Wing flash as adult.

ADULT: Head Brownish, most with darker cap and fine yellow streaks on nape. **Body** Upperparts dark brown, flecked with buff or pale yellow and rufous. Underparts similar but greyer in tone; upper breast sometimes mottled yellowish. **Wings** Upperwing: primaries blackish-brown with white bases and shafts forming conspicuous wing flash, secondaries uniform blackish-brown; coverts as upperparts. Underwing mostly dark brown, some with reddish tinge on coverts (beware Chilean Skua, p. 321). Underwing flash more prominent than on upperwing. **Tail** Blackish-brown.

C.a.lonnbergi

JUVENILE: As adult except warmer brown above with fewer paler spots and streaks, most with reddish-brown cast on underparts.

ADULT: Averages larger than nominate, with more powerful bill. Plumage differs in: **Head** Lacks darker cap. **Body** Fairly uniform brown above and below, most with varying amounts of pale yellowish streaks and tawny blotches.

C.a. hamiltoni

JUVENILE: Much as nominate; upperparts perhaps more heavily streaked, underparts more reddish-brown.

ADULT: Resembles *lonnbergi* but averages smaller.

FHJ: Much as for northern counterpart Great Skua (p. 321). See Sinclair (1980) for hunting techniques over land (including forcing Wandering Albatrosses to regurgitate).

DM: Southern hemisphere. *C.a. antarctica* breeds Falkland Is and coasts of southern Argentina; *C.a. hamiltoni* at Gough and Tristan da Cunha; *C.a. lonnbergi*, the most widespread, circumpolar breeds Antarctic Peninsula and sub-antarctic islands including Australasian region (see Watson 1975 for details). Returns to colonies Sep/Oct; egg-dates Oct/Nov; fledging and departure begin Jan/Feb. Disperses to coasts of South America, South Africa and Australia N to about 30°S. Status in northern Indian Ocean remains to be determined; see notes under South Polar Skua (p. 322).

SS: Juveniles with tawny underwing-coverts could be confused with Chilean Skua (p. 321). See notes under South Polar Skua (p. 322).

Genus *STERCORARIUS*

Three species; medium-sized, piratical seabirds, differing from larger, more robust *Catharacta* in polymorphic and seasonal variations in plumage, and elongated central tail feathers. All three species breed in Arctic tundra during northern summer, returning to pelagic habitat during winter, penetrating as far S as about 55°S.

Stercorarius skuas are strong, agile fliers, assuming same roles over ocean as hawks and falcons perform over land. They live largely by chasing smaller seabirds and forcing them to disgorge. On their breeding grounds they live on lemmings and other rodents, also carrion and small birds.

Many observers are unaware that there is a definite winter or non-breeding plumage, which generally resembles corresponding immatures but lacks barring on underwing-coverts. In winter plumage (when tail streamers may be absent) and in juvenile and immature plumages identification more difficult and may even be impossible. In all observations record as accurately as possible degree of contrast between forewing and secondaries on upperwing (see Long-tailed Skua, p. 326); number and extent of white primary shafts; degree of 'warmth' or 'coldness' in overall plumage; details of any barring on upper- and undertail-coverts, also underwing; and, at close range, exact shape of tail projections. Additionally size, jizz and flight should be gauged, perhaps compared with a nearby, better-known species (Kittiwake, Sandwich Tern).

199 POMARINE SKUA
other: Pomarine Jaeger
Stercorarius pomarinus

PLATE 54 Figs 199a-199d

MAP 199

Length 65–78cm ($25\frac{1}{2}$–31in.). Includes 17–20cm ($6\frac{1}{2}$–8in.) tail streamers. Wingspan 122–127cm (48–50in.). Iris brown. Bill greyish, tipped darker. Legs/feet blackish-grey.

Circumpolar in Arctic tundra regions migrating S to pelagic habitat in winter; range overlaps with other skuas, see especially Arctic, Great and South Polar Skuas (p. 325, p. 321, p. 322). Sexes alike; seasonal variation. Juveniles separable from adults although precise plumage stages to maturity not fully known. No subspecies. Polymorphic; light morph outnumbers dark by about 20:1 (Serventy *et al.* 1971).

JUVENILE (LIGHT MORPH): Bill grey, blue or yellowish-brown, tip black; legs bluish, webs distally black. **Head** Dull brownish white, indistinct darker cap. **Body** Upperparts: mantle and back brownish (often grey or slaty in tone) with narrow paler edges forming indistinct transverse bars; rump and uppertail coverts more broadly and distinctly barred. Underparts mostly dusky or brownish-white with grey-brown breast band and paler barring on flanks and undertail coverts. (Some show uniform dusky, grey-brown underparts with barred undertail coverts.) **Wings** Upperwing: coverts as saddle; primaries and secondaries blackish-brown, outermost primary shafts white. Underwing as adult except for broadly barred brown and white coverts and axillaries. **Tail** Blackish; short, blunt central projections.

JUVENILE (DARK MORPH): Mostly blackish-brown except for barred tail-coverts, axillaries and underwing-coverts; primary flash as for adult.

IMMATURE (LIGHT MORPH): Generally as adult except: **Head** Indistinct blackish-brown cap (heavier than in juvenile); remainder including hindneck whitish. **Body** Upperparts faintly tipped buff; rump and uppertail-coverts conspicuously barred brown and white. Underparts: breast band less distinct, more scaled; undertail-coverts and flanks barred as in juvenile. **Wings** Underwing-coverts and axillaries barred brown and white. **Tail** Short, blunt, central feathers extend 3–5cm (not twisted).

ADULT NON-BREEDING (LIGHT MORPH): Not well known but sightings off Australia (pers. obs.) suggest that head becomes dark brownish-grey, extending as dusky hood to chin and throat, uniting (in some) with breast band. Upper- and undertail-coverts barred as in juvenile. Tail streamers short (perhaps replaced by shorter new pair).

ADULT BREEDING (LIGHT MORPH): **Head** Sooty-black cap; remainder including hindneck yellowish-white. **Body** Upperparts brownish-black. Underparts mostly yellowish-white; breast band and undertail-coverts dark brown. **Wings** Upperwing blackish-brown; bases and shafts of outer 5–8 primaries white. Underwing similar but with more extensive white crescent on outer primaries. **Tail** Blackish; from below basal two-thirds and outer feathers paler. Diagnostic spoon-shaped central feathers can project as much as 17–20cm.

ADULT BREEDING (DARK MORPH): Mostly blackish-brown except for brownish-yellow cheeks and hindcollar of variable extent; white wing crescents as in light morph.

FHJ: Between Great and Arctic Skuas in size, although some overlap with latter. Appears much more thickset, menacing and powerful than Arctic Skua, with broader bases of wings giving buzzard-like jizz; head larger and bill proportionately longer, more distinctly hook-tipped than that species. At distance bulk and sheer power often suggest Great Skua, a comparative error rarely made when viewing long-range Arctic Skuas. Pursues birds up to size of Glaucous Gull, more rarely Gannet (see Great Skua). Normal flight differs from Arctic Skua in slower, more purposeful, steady, flapping beats which, with broader wings and deep, barrel-chest, often emphasised by heavier, more distinct breast band, allows reasonably quick and accurate identification (with comparative experience). Follows ships; attends trawlers; feeds off carrion.

DM: Circumpolar in tundra N of Arctic Circle; returns to loose colonies May; egg-dates Jun; fledging begins mid Aug onwards. Does not nest consistently year to year, breeding success dependent on lemming abundance. In years of low lemming numbers many adults simply disperse throughout breeding latitudes before early migration S during late Jul/Aug. In good breeding years adults begin southwards movements during late Aug/Sep, followed by juveniles Sep/Oct. Passage off E and W coasts of America and western Europe mid Sep/late Oct. Main wintering areas in Atlantic in Gulf of Mexico and West Indies from about 10°N to 27°N and 60°W to 90°W; also off tropical West Africa from 17°N southwards to Namibia and South Africa; a few may remain in N Atlantic throughout winter. In Indian Ocean regular off Arabia during northern winter, with smaller numbers occurring throughout year (see Bailey 1966). In Pacific main wintering area appears to be off SE Australia; smaller numbers off western coasts of Central and South America and also Hawaii. Non-breeders may remain in winter quarters throughout year.

SS: Unless diagnostic 'spoon' or blunted tail projections seen, light morphs have no single character enabling instant separation from corresponding Arctic Skuas (p. 325). With comparative experience, however, sheer bulk and power, broader wings, differing flight, barrel-chest, heavier breast band and often greater amount of white in wings enable separation. Dark morphs resemble more closely larger Great Skua (p. 321) but lack the nape hackles and more obvious white wing patches of latter; Great Skuas show no apparent tail projections at any age. Immature and juvenile pale morphs of present species best separated from corresponding Arctic Skuas by jizz and more conspicuous barring on upper- and undertail-coverts. Beware larger species of immature gulls if inexperienced.

200 ARCTIC SKUA
other: Parasitic Jaeger
Stercorarius parasiticus

PLATE 55 Figs 200a-200g

MAP 200

Length 46–67cm (18–26½in.), includes 8–14cm (3–5½in.) tail streamers. Wingspan 96–114cm (38–45in.). Iris brown. Bill greyish-black, cere whitish. Legs/feet blackish-grey.

Circumpolar in Arctic tundra regions, migrating S to pelagic habitat in winter. Most likely to be confused with smaller Long-tailed Skua (p. 326) and, to lesser extent, with larger, more powerful Pomarine Skua (p. 324). Sexes alike; slight seasonal variation. Juveniles and immatures separable from adults but precise plumage stages to maturity not fully known. No subspecies. Polymorphic, occurring in light and dark forms with intermediates; dark form the more typical with light forms more frequent in northern parts of breeding range.

JUVENILE (DARK MORPH): Much as adult dark morph except: Base of bill pale blue-grey to pinkish-grey, tip blackish. **Head** Cap less defined; chin, throat and sides of face tipped tawny and buff. **Body** Upperparts brown, indistinctly barred rufous and buff, more apparent on uppertail-coverts (but usually never so pronounced as in either Pomarine or Long-tailed Skuas, p. 324, p. 326). Underparts vary from mostly uniform blackish or tawny-brown to brown with rufous and buff barring; undertail-coverts as uppertail-coverts. **Wings** Underwing-coverts and axillaries barred dark brown, rufous and white.

JUVENILE (INTERMEDIATE MORPH): As dark morph but underparts paler, more rufous-brown, with more apparent barring.

JUVENILE (PALE MORPH): As dark morph except: **Head** Brownish-grey cap; chin, throat, sides of face, nape and hindneck greyer. **Body** Underparts greyish-white, barred brownish or rufous, heaviest on undertail-coverts.

FIRST-SUMMER TYPES: Generally as juveniles, some with uniform upperparts. Light and intermediate morphs with whiter, more barred underparts and indistinct breast band. All morphs retain barred underwing-coverts, axillaries and upper and lower tail-coverts.

SECOND-SUMMER TYPES: Much as corresponding adult morphs but with barring on underwing-coverts, axillaries and upper and lower tail-coverts.

ADULT NON-BREEDING (DARK MORPH): As breeding adult; some show indistinct barring on upper- and undertail-coverts.

ADULT NON-BREEDING (LIGHT AND INTERMEDIATE MORPHS): As breeding adults except: **Head** Indistinct cap and duskier sides of face and neck. **Body** Upperparts: mantle, back and scapulars edged buff or white; upper- and undertail-coverts barred brown and white.

ADULT BREEDING (LIGHT MORPH): Diffuse brownish cap; hindneck, sides of face, chin and throat white, usually with yellowish cast. **Body** Upperparts mostly warm fulvous-brown shading darker or richer on lower back and rump. Underparts highly variable, most with mainly white underparts and dusky ventral area (although sometimes wholly white) and complete or imperfect breast band of variable width and extent. **Wings** Upperwing generally as upperparts, with little or no contrast between trailing edge and forewing. Unlike Long-tailed Skua (p. 326), outer four primary shafts and bases white forming noticeable but variable crescent on outer wing. Underwing dusky-grey to blackish-grey with white crescent as on upperwing. **Tail** Blackish-brown above with indistinct blackish terminal band in good light. From below base and shafts of outer feathers whitish-buff. See under FHJ for tail streamers.

ADULT BREEDING (DARK MORPH): Generally dark fulvous-brown; cap and flight feathers slightly darker, usually with yellowish or olive-brown cheeks and hindcollar. White primary shafts and bases of primaries as light morph.

INTERMEDIATE MORPH: Very variable; essentially warm brown with whitish chin, throat, cheeks and hindcollar grading arbitrarily into light morphs.

FHJ: Some variation in length of tail streamers, which can project 8–14cm; thus with tail compressed and 'pointed' outline can suggest Long-tailed Skua. See under that species and Pomarine for comparisons (p. 326, p. 324). Arctic Skua seems less dependent on rodent populations during breeding season than those species and more inclined to robbing terns and kittiwakes of their catch (kleptoparasitism). These piratical habits are practised during non-breeding cycle and at all ages. Flight usually purposeful, dashing and rather falcon-like, with jerky wingbeats interspersed with low glides—in any wind conditions. Often approaches gulls/terns in low-level, sneak attack and selects one individual, harrying in close pursuit until victim disgorges.

DM: Circumpolar in Arctic regions, breeding generally further S than Long-tailed or Pomarine Skuas. From western Alaska and Aleutian Chain E along coasts and archipelagos of northern Canada to Hudson Bay and North Labrador and S to Great Slave and Landing Lakes; also on W and E coasts of Greenland and in Europe at Iceland, Faeroes, Orkneys and Shetland Is off Scotland, as well as certain scattered mainland localities and western islands; also Sweden, Norway, Finland, Bear I. and Spitsbergen. Also from Murmansk area along Arctic coasts of USSR to Kamchatka Peninsula. Returns to breeding areas Apr/May, non-breeders and a few immatures arriving after main influx; egg-dates May/Jun; departure of non-breeders begins Jul, fledging and main departure Aug/Sep, most accompanying migrating flocks of terns S. Exact wintering areas unknown, but probably Pacific and Atlantic Oceans at 30°–50°S. Perhaps greatest concentrations occur along littorals of South America and western Africa, especially off Namibia and Angola where mixed flocks of skuas around trawlers frequently exceed 500. Many immatures remain in wintering areas during first and second summers. Records from northern Indian and tropical latitudes of Atlantic and Pacific Oceans during midwinter may be due to confusion with Pomarine Skua.

SS: See discussions under Long-tailed and Pomarine Skuas (p. 326, p. 324). Beware distant Heermann's Gulls (p. 331) off western coasts of North America, and immature gulls generally if inexperienced.

201 LONG-TAILED SKUA
other: Long-tailed Jaeger
Stercorarius longicaudus

PLATE 55 Figs 201a-201f

MAP 201

Length 50–58cm (19½–23in.), includes 15–25cm (6–10in.) tail streamers. Wingspan 76–84cm (30–33in.). Iris dark brown. Bill blackish-grey, cere blue or horn. Legs bluish, webs and toes distally black.

Circumpolar in Arctic tundra regions, migrating S to pelagic habitat in winter; range overlaps with other skuas, see especially larger, more robust Arctic Skua (p. 325). Sexes alike; marked seasonal variation. Juveniles separable from adults although exact plumage stages to maturity not precisely known. No subspecies. Adults polymorphic but dark phase very rare, intermediate morphs almost unheard of; juveniles, however, occur in three basic colour variations but most presumably moult into typical (pale morph) adults.

JUVENILE INTERMEDIATE MORPH (the more usual type): Base of bill pink, tip black; legs pale blue-white to pink, webs distally black. **Head** Mostly buffish-grey indistinctly streaked brown on forehead, crown and ear-coverts, giving indistinct capped effect with paler hindcollar (appears uniform buff-grey at distance). **Body** Upperparts mostly cold greyish- to blackish-brown (never gingery-brown as Arctic Skua) neatly scaled buff-white forming thin transverse bars. Uppertail-coverts usually more heavily barred, forming paler horseshoe over base of tail. Underparts variable, most show whitish belly enclosed by brownish-grey breast band and obvious barring on flanks: undertail-coverts more strongly barred in equal divisions of black and pale buff (a conspicuous field character). Paler examples similar but lack complete breast band. **Wings** Upperwing: coverts as upperparts; primaries, primary-coverts, alula and secondaries blackish-brown. Unlike Arctic Skua, only outer one or two primary shafts are white forming thin white edge to outer wing (at sea upperwing may appear to lack white). Underwing: coverts and axillaries coarsely barred ashy-brown and buff; primaries and secondaries blackish, former with white bases forming extensive white crescent. **Tail** Blackish, paler base often visible from below. Unlike juvenile Arctic Skua, two central feathers project 1–4cm with blunt or rounded (not pointed) tips.

JUVENILE (PALE MORPH): As intermediate type except: **Head** Strikingly yellowish-white, crown faintly streaked grey. **Body** Upperparts greyer in tone; more pronounced transverse barring. Underparts paler, base colour creamy-white, some without breast band but all with barred flanks and conspicuously barred undertail-coverts. **Wings** Underwing-coverts more conspicuously barred.

JUVENILE DARK MORPH (rarely encountered, probably overlooked): Mostly blackish-brown or sepia-brown except: **Head** Chin, throat, sides of neck and hindneck paler yellowish-brown. **Body** Upperparts faintly barred buff, heaviest on uppertail-coverts. Underparts variable; darkest examples mostly dark brown with conspicuously barred brown and white undertail-coverts, others with more apparent barring on flanks and lower belly. **Wings** Underwing-coverts and axillaries less distinctly barred than in paler morphs.

IMMATURE (probably second-summer but plumage stages poorly understood): As breeding adult except: **Body** Upperparts: uppertail-coverts narrowly barred with white forming pale horseshoe over tail. Underparts usually show partial breast band with ill-defined barring on undertail-coverts. **Wings** Underwing: coverts and axillaries retain coarse barring of juvenile but less apparent, often appearing patchy; white crescent across base of primaries reduced or lacking. **Tail** Central feathers project 4–10cm.

ADULT NON-BREEDING (Acquired late Aug/Sep, may be retained in part until Mar/Apr): As breeding adult except: **Head** Cap flecked white and grey, sometimes heavily with only a faint suggestion of darker cap; chin, throat and sides of face spotted and tipped dusky-grey or brown. **Body** Upperparts scaled white or buff as in juvenile but with darker grey feather centres; uppertail-coverts broadly barred black and white. Underparts variably barred brown and white, some heavily, usually with pronounced, more or less solid, breast band; undertail-coverts as uppertail-coverts. **Tail** Streamers replaced by shorter pair. (?)

ADULT BREEDING: Head Neat blackish-brown cap, remainder white, usually with yellowish cast. **Body** Upperparts cold greyish-brown; uppertail-coverts often paler forming indistinct horseshoe over base of tail. Underparts variable, two main types: darkest (more usual example) has whitish breast merging into grey-brown lower breast and belly, becoming darker, almost black, on undertail-coverts; pale examples have white breast extending to include belly and, exceptionally, undertail-coverts (originally described as *S.l. pallescens* by Loppenthin 1934, now known to occur in all populations, particularly Greenland). **Wings** Upperwing: unlike Arctic Skua, distinct contrast between cold brownish-grey forewing and narrow blackish trailing edge; only outer one or two primary shafts (sometimes base of third) white (upperwing thus lacks noticeable wing flash). Underwing dusky-grey (appears blackish at sea); white shafts to outer 2 primaries only. **Tail** Blackish-brown, paler at base, two central streamers project 15–25cm. NOTE Very rare adult melanistic or dark morphs also occur (see for instance *American Birds* 34(2): 193): mostly dark smoky-brown with indistinct blackish cap, primaries, secondaries and tail. Such types should be separable from dark phase Arctic Skua by less white on wing, overall structure and, if present, longer tail streamers.

FHJ: Size usually about that of Kittiwake but with proportionately thinner body and more slender, shearwater-like wings; larger examples may be larger than smallest Arctic Skua (p. 325) whilst smallest are comparable to Sandwich Tern. Compared with former, Long-tailed Skuas, whatever size or age, have proportionately slimmer bodies with smaller heads and weaker bills; wings also proportionately longer and narrower throughout their entire length, particularly at base, which accentuates attenuated rear end. In breeding adults floppy tail streamers can appear as long as rest of body, although at sea, against a dark background, streamers often invisible. Even when streamers broken, invisible, or lacking as in juveniles, tail appears proportionately longer and narrower at base than in Arctic Skua. When perched or resting on sea wings extend at least 4cm past outer tail feathers, whereas wing and tail points are more or less equal in Arctic Skua. Normal flight usually light and floating with distinct tern-like buoyancy, thus lacking direct falcon-like wingbeats and purposeful directness of Arctic Skua; flight often appears rather weak and, during strong gales, may hug water closely, tilting from side to side, slinking into and over wave troughs. Flight path occasionally interrupted by upward swoops or dips down to surface, where may hover into wind, picking from water. Probably less piratical than other skuas; on migration regularly attracted to carrion. Attends trawlers.

DM: Circumpolar in high Arctic; from islands and coasts of Arctic Ocean S to tundra regions of North America and Eurasia, generally N of Arctic Circle. Return to breeding areas dependent on snow conditions, usually late May with many non-breeders, including birds in 'immature' plumage, arriving after main influx. Egg-dates Jun/Jul but in years of rodent scarcity many fail to breed and may depart as early as mid Jun (see Anderson 1976). In successful years departure and fledging late Aug onwards, birds moving S both overland and far out to sea. Precise wintering areas unknown; available evidence suggests wide pelagic dispersal in both Pacific and Atlantic Oceans S to about 50°S, with main wintering areas probably off Atlantic and Pacific coasts of South America and off coasts of Namibia and South Africa. There is evidence to support theory that, during both N and S migrations, may form small flocks, occasionally gathering in hundreds, stretching for several miles (see Wynne-Edwards 1935). Status in Australasian region, where rare vagrant, requires clarification.

SS: Difficult to separate from Arctic Skua (p. 325) without comparative experience, but adults generally smaller and neater with proportionately smaller head, slimmer body, longer narrower wings, and obvious tail streamers more or less equal in length to rest of body. Distinctive dark trailing edge to upperwing coupled with lack of breast band (breeding adults) and little or no white in wings most reliable plumage features. Juveniles and immatures require more careful treatment: best separated from corresponding Arctic Skua by structure, 'colder' grey-brown plumage with crisp whitish transverse bars on upperparts, and conspicuous black and white barring on undertail-coverts and axillaries (see also Pomarine Skua, p. 324); if seen, short, blunt tail projections and only two white outer primary shafts diagnostic. By comparison Arctic Skuas have heavier structure, 'warmer' or richer plumage barred tawny-buff, and three or four white primary shafts which, with white bases, form noticeable crescent across base of primaries on both surfaces of wing.

Family *LARIDAE* gulls, terns and noddies

About 87 species in ten genera; number of genera not fully agreed upon. Present opinion is towards reducing numbers of previously recognised genera, i.e. placing *Leucophaeus*, *Xema*, *Gabianus*, *Rissa* and *Creagrus* in *Larus*. In this guide only *Pagophila* and *Rhodostethia* have been retained, as they are atypical and their closest relatives unknown. Similarly, within the tern assemblage *Gelochelidon*, *Hydroprogne* and *Thalasseus* have been placed in *Sterna*.

Gulls and terns are small to medium or large birds, usually with grey and white plumage, some with black on head and wings. Horny covering of bill undivided. Tail variously shaped, from wedge through square to deeply forked.

Gulls are predominantly a northern hemisphere group which have made limited attempts at colonising the southern hemisphere. Highly adaptable, with breeding-habitat tolerance ranging from bleak pack ice, sea cliffs and buildings to torrid inland deserts. Many forms increasing due to reliance on man's waste (factory ships, garbage dumps etc.). Most are coastal, only a few can be classed as truly pelagic. Whilst many species undertake regular post-breeding dispersals (some lengthy), only a few undertake long-range migations.

Terns differ from gulls in generally smaller size, forked tail, more slender and graceful proportions. Generally more marine, and a mainly tropical group with different flight and feeding habits. Wide nesting-habitat tolerance, from bare branches of trees without a nest (White Tern), through sand dunes and rocks, to floating vegetation (marsh terns). Many undertake long migrations: best illustrated by wanderings of Arctic Tern, which breeds in Arctic and winters S to Antarctica, thus enjoying more daylight hours than any other bird but at expense of an annual round trip of about, in some cases, 35,200km (22,000 miles).

Genus *LARUS*

About 45 species; generally white and grey, ranging in size from the large and menacing Great Black-backed Gull to the diminutive Little Gull. Sexes outwardly alike; seasonal variation in some species. Maturity reached second to fourth winter after fledging.

Field identification of gulls represents one of the greatest challenges to be found in any sphere of birding. Specific identification complicated by the several plumage stages between fledging and maturity and, ultimately, may be thwarted by albinos or hybrids. Even experts cannot always assign every individual to species. Readers are cautioned that such terms as first-winter, first-summer etc. used in this guide do not imply a known and definite age, merely types: see especially Monaghan & Duncan (1979) in reference to plumage variability in known ages of Herring Gull. By necessity gull descriptions contain terms and references not used in the majority of species accounts found in this guide. Fig. 18 below shows a diagrammatic topographical representation of a *Larus* sp. See also further explanation of terms in glossary (p. 11).

The treatment of gulls in this guide is necessarily limited. Progressive birders are urged to consult Dwight (1925), and especially the excellent five-part series published on west Palearctic Gulls in *British Birds* by Grant (1978, 1979, 1980, 1981a, 1981b). This series, now published with updated revisions in book form (Grant 1982), is an absolute necessity—no progressive birder should be without a copy.

Identification of any adult gull is reasonably straightforward given adequate views. Note in particular colour of all bare parts; saddle and upperwing colour; wingtip pattern. Obvious features, e.g. full or partial hood, tail band etc., should of course also be noted. Juveniles and immatures pose more serious threats to identification capabilities, but familiarisation with locally abundant gulls should enable rarer transients to be located more quickly. The same features as noted above for adults should also be recorded for juveniles and immatures. Additionally pay particular attention to upperwing patterns: dark bar along secondaries; number of 'mirrors' on primaries; extent of black at wingtip; colour of coverts; paler 'windows' on inner primaries; relative width and extent of tail bands should also be scrutinised. As in all difficult identifications, relative size and jizz are further points to note down.

202 PACIFIC GULL
other: Large-billed Gull
Larus pacificus

PLATE 56 Figs 202a-202c

MAP 202

Length 58–66cm (23–26in.). Wingspan 137–157cm (54–62in.). Males average larger. Iris white, pupil dark, orbital ring red. Bill massive, bright chrome-yellow broadly tipped on both mandibles with red. Legs/feet yellow.

Restricted to Australia, where range overlaps with smaller Kelp Gull (p. 343). Sexes outwardly alike; slight seasonal variation. Juveniles separable from adults. No subspecies.

JUVENILE: Iris dark. Bill pink, tip dark; legs flesh-brown. **Head** Mainly dull brown with some whitish tips; forehead, lores and chin white. **Body** Upperparts: saddle brown with obscure buffish tips and darker mottling; rump similar but paler. Underparts mostly dull brown with variable whitish tips. **Wings** Upperwing: primaries and their coverts dull black, secondaries blackish tipped white; coverts much like saddle. Underwing white with brown streaks. **Tail** Mostly brownish-black, tip buffish-grey.

FIRST-WINTER: Similar to juvenile but greyer on upperparts, paler below.

FIRST-SUMMER: As first-winter except head, rump and underparts whiter. Wings and tail unmoulted, faded through wear.

SECOND-WINTER: As first-winter except head paler; mantle and back with slate grey tips. Wings and tail further faded.

SECOND-SUMMER: As second-winter except head and rump whiter; mantle and back becoming increasingly slatey; underparts white.

THIRD-WINTER: Bill yellowish, dusky tip. **Head** White, with dusky streaks. **Body** Upperparts: mantle and back blackish with brown tips; rump whitish. Underparts white with dusky markings on breast. **Wings** Upperwing: outer primaries black, paler from fourth inwards with white tips. Remainder slate-black, trailing edge white. Underwing: as adult except coverts streaked dusky. **Tail** White; ill-defined subterminal band.

THIRD-SUMMER: As third-winter except bare parts resemble adults; head white.

FOURTH-WINTER/ADULT NON-BREEDING: As breeding adult except bare parts duller.

ADULT BREEDING: Head White. **Body** Upperparts: saddle slate-black; rump white. Underparts white. **Wings** Upperwing mainly black, broad white trailing edge. Underwing: primaries black, secondaries grey, tipped white; coverts white. **Tail** White, black subterminal band.

FHJ: Has the most robust bill of any gull in the world. Occasionally dives to catch food. Takes young birds up to size of Short-tailed Shearwater. Call a harsh 'kiaw' and variants of 'ow-ow' and 'yow-yow'.

DM: Endemic to southern and southwestern Australia. Adults sedentary but immatures tend to disperse widely throughout southern coasts of Australia. Egg-dates Sep–Jan.

SS: Differs from Kelp Gull (p. 343) at all ages in larger size and massive bill. Adults have diagnostic tail pattern; juveniles diagnostic bill.

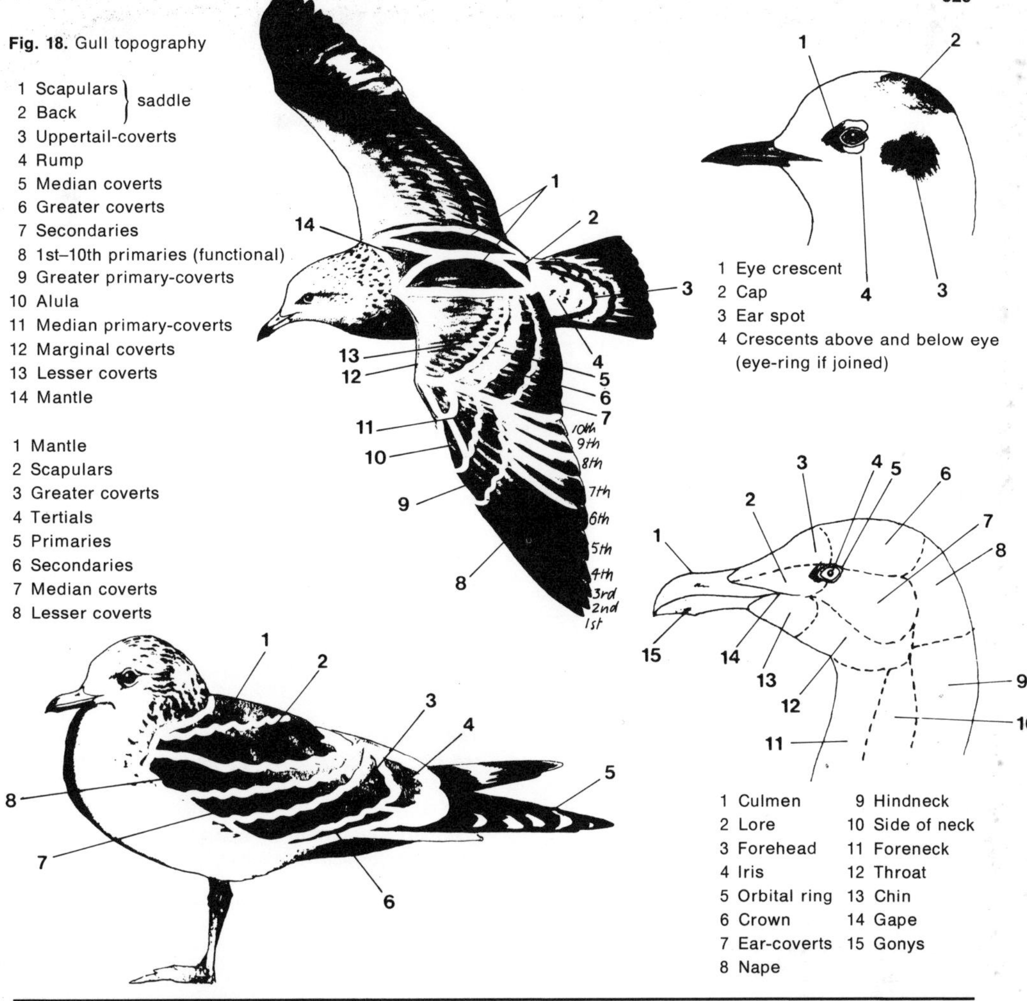

203 DOLPHIN GULL

other: Magellan/Scoresby's Gull

Larus scoresbii

PLATE 67 Figs 203a-203d

MAP 203

Length 43–46cm (17–18in.). Wingspan 104cm (41in.). Iris pale yellow, pupil dark, orbital ring crimson. Bill, legs/feet crimson.

Southern South America, where range overlaps with Kelp and Band-tailed Gulls (p. 343, p. 333). Sexes alike; seasonal variation. Juveniles separable from adults. No subspecies.

JUVENILE: Iris dark, bill blackish, legs brown or grey. **Head** Mostly slaty-brown, chin and throat whiter. **Body** Upperparts: saddle dark sepia, rump similar paling to white on uppertail-coverts. Underparts: upper breast brownish paling to white on remainder. **Wings** Upperwing blackish-brown; primaries darker, inner 4 primaries, secondaries and tertials tipped white. Underwing mostly greyish-brown, primaries and secondaries blackish-brown, most tipped white. **Tail** White, black subterminal band.

FIRST-WINTER: As juvenile except pink base to bill; sooty-grey hood, paler on forehead, lores and chin. Underparts whiter, indistinct mottling on sides of breast.

FIRST-SUMMER: As first-winter except dark grey head mottled with brown.

SECOND-WINTER: Bill pink, red at base, black subterminal bar; legs brownish-red. **Head** Almost uniform sooty-grey. **Body** Upperparts: saddle deep grey, rump white. Underparts pale grey. **Wings** Upperwing slate-brown; inner 7 primaries and all secondaries tipped white. **Tail** White, some with blackish shaft streaks.

SECOND-SUMMER: As second-winter except iris pale straw; bill reddish, dusky at tip. Sooty-grey hood degrades to clear grey.

THIRD-WINTER/ADULT NON-BREEDING: Head Dusky-grey hood. **Body** Upperparts: saddle slaty-black, rump white. Underparts pale grey. **Wings** Upperwing: slaty-black; tertials, secondaries and all primaries except outer 2 tipped white, forming trailing edge to wing. Underwing mostly grey, primaries blackish, trailing edge white. **Tail** White.

ADULT BREEDING: As non-breeding adult except head whitish-grey.
FHJ: Medium-sized 'black-backed' gull with stout red bill. Opportunistic scavenger attending tideline, and seal, penguin, and cormorant colonies. Regularly visits urban areas, particularly during winter. Call: in flight a short 'kyik'; when excited a screaming 'keear-keear-keear'.
DM: Restricted to southern South America, breeding Falklands, Tierra del Fuego and N to about 42°S in both Chile and Argentina. Egg-dates Dec/Jan. In winter some disperse N to about 35°S.
SS: Kelp Gull (p. 343) differs in larger size, bare parts colours and, in adults, white head throughout year. Range may overlap with Band-tailed Gull (p. 333) in Patagonia, but latter has different coloured bare parts and banded tail at all ages.

204 LAVA GULL
other: Dusky Gull
Larus fuliginosus

PLATE 66 Figs 204a-204d

MAP 204

Length 53cm (21in.). Wingspan not recorded. Iris lemon yellow. Bill black, reddish towards tip. Legs/feet purplish-black.

Endemic to Galapagos Is, unlikely to be mistaken. Sexes alike; slight seasonal variation. Juveniles separable from adults. No subspecies.
JUVENILE: Iris brown, bare parts black. Plumage mostly dull sooty-brown; mantle, scapulars, back and upperwing-coverts edged paler; uppertail-coverts whitish, lower belly and ventral area greyer.
FIRST-WINTER: Much as juvenile but with emergent grey feathers on mantle, scapulars, back and underparts; wings and tail unmoulted though some grey coverts often evident.
FIRST-SUMMER: As first-winter except for sooty-grey head with thin whitish crescents; saddle mostly slate-grey.
SECOND-WINTER: As non-breeding adult but rather browner in tone on head and body; wings and tail as first-summer but with narrow trailing edge.
SECOND-SUMMER: As second-winter but greyer.
THIRD-WINTER / ADULT NON-BREEDING: As breeding adult but bare parts duller, crescents around eye greyer.
ADULT BREEDING: Head Sooty-brown hood, thin white crescents. **Body** Upperparts: saddle dusky-grey, rump and uppertail-coverts greyish-white. Underparts: breast dusky-grey paling to almost white at ventral area. **Wings** Upperwing mostly dusky-grey; outer primaries, their coverts and alula blackish, trailing edge greyish-white. **Tail** Dark grey centre paling to whitish on outer tail feathers.
FHJ: Coastal scavenger attending fishing operations, settlements and camps. Does not wander far from shoreline, rarely alights on water.
DM: Endemic to Galapagos Is, Pacific Ocean, where estimated 300–400 pairs breed (Snow & Snow 1969).
SS: Only dusky gull found at Galapagos Is. See Laughing and Franklin's Gulls (p. 349, p. 352), which occasionally occur.

205 GREY GULL
other: Gray Gull
Larus modestus

PLATE 67 Figs 205a-205d

MAP 205

Length 46cm (18in.). Wingspan unrecorded. Iris brown. Bill, legs/feet black.

Western coasts of South America; distinctive species with remarkable nesting habits, unlikely to be confused within range. Sexes alike; seasonal variation. Juveniles separable from adults. No subspecies.
JUVENILE: Head Greyish-brown; forehead, chin and sides of face paler, darker streaks on nape. **Body** Upperparts brownish-grey, broadly edged buffish-grey. Underparts similar but narrower buffish edges. **Wings** Primaries, their coverts and secondaries blackish brown, latter tipped white; tertials and secondary-coverts as mantle but median and lesser coverts with broader, buffish edges forming distinct paler area on closed wing (enhanced by wear). Underwing mainly greyish-brown, primaries blackish. **Tail** Brownish-black, tipped buff.
FIRST-WINTER: As juvenile except nape darker, upperparts greyish-brown without buff edges. Juvenile wings and tail unmoulted, edges of coverts sometimes faded to off-white.
FIRST-SUMMER: Similar but forehead and sides of face whiter, upperparts greyer.
SECOND-WINTER: Head Dark brownish hood; forehead and chin paler, nape streaked darker extending to throat. **Body** Upperparts: saddle grey with brownish cast; rump and underparts similar but slightly paler. **Wings** Upperwing much as juvenile except for grey coverts. **Tail** As adult but with wider subterminal band.
SECOND-SUMMER: As second-winter except for whitish-grey hood, absence of streaks on throat, greyer saddle.
THIRD-WINTER / ADULT NON-BREEDING: As second-winter but hood paler, saddle clearer grey.
ADULT BREEDING: As non-breeding adult except for whitish-grey hood.
FHJ: A remarkable species, nesting some 50km from coast in harsh desert. Flies through the night, visiting coast daily to forage off Chile and Peru, congregates in thousands around trawlers; also forms huge flocks along tideline, running swiftly behind retreating breakers picking up shrimps and sand fleas, sandpiper-fashion. Has cat-like call.
DM: Breeds coastal deserts of northern Chile (Antofagasta province). Egg-dates Nov/Dec; fledging and dispersal begin Apr/May, some N to Colombia (vagrant) but regular SW Ecuador where

occurs throughout year, although more numerous May–Nov. Ranges S to at least Valparaiso, Chile, but southern limit of dispersal not known. Impressive coastal movements occur involving thousands converging towards breeding areas Sept–Nov (Hughes, pers. comm.).

SS: Distinctive species, unlikely to be confused with other gulls.

206 HEERMANN'S GULL
Larus heermanni

PLATE 60 Figs 206a-206d
MAP 206

Length 46–53cm (18–21in.). Wingspan 117–124cm (46–49in.). Iris black, orbital ring red. Bill bright red, tip black. Legs/feet blue-grey.

Islands in Gulf of California, and coast of Mexico, dispersing N to British Columbia; distinctive at all seasons. Sexes alike; seasonal variation. Juveniles separable from adults. No subspecies.

JUVENILE: Bill black; legs/feet blackish-grey. Plumage wholly sooty-brown except: **Body** Upperparts: indistinct tawny-brown tips on mantle, scapulars and back. Underparts faintly paler and greyer. **Wings** Upperwing: primaries and secondaries dull blackish-brown; coverts broadly edged pale tawny-brown, usually with some whitish edges, forming noticeably pale area when perched. **Tail** Dull blackish, usually with narrow buff tip. NOTE In worn plumage browner overall.

FIRST-WINTER: Much as juvenile except: Bill yellow, distal third black; head and body greyer in tone.

FIRST-SUMMER: Base of bill pink, subterminal tip black, tip white. Legs/feet blackish. Plumage as juvenile except: **Head** Whitish tips on forehead and chin extending on some to form partial whitish hood. **Body** Saddle and underparts greyer. **Wings and Tail** Unmoulted; faded and worn, more tawny.

SECOND-WINTER: Bill orange-red, black tip reduced. Plumage resembles non-breeding adult except: **Head** Darker, more heavily streaked hood. **Body** Upperparts browner; underparts with scattered brownish tips. **Wings** Upperwing-coverts browner (some show white primary-coverts forming noticeable wing flash, perhaps linked with moult sequence). **Tail** Narrow white tip.

SECOND-SUMMER: As second-winter except for imperfect whitish hood.

THIRD-WINTER / ADULT NON-BREEDING: As breeding adult except: **Head** Dusky grey-brown hood; forehead and chin tipped whiter, nape white.

ADULT BREEDING: Head White. **Body** Upperparts: saddle deep velvet-grey; rump and uppertail-coverts pale french-grey. Underparts pale neutral grey, darkest on upper breast, paling to white on ventral area. **Wings** Upperwing mostly deep velvet-grey shading to blackish on primaries and secondaries; all secondaries and innermost 5–6 primaries tipped white forming noticeable trailing edge to wing. Underwing dusky-grey, primaries and secondaries tipped white as upperwing. **Tail** Black, tipped white.

FHJ: Distinctive, the only North American dusky gull. Adults generally grey with conspicuous white head, black tail and bright red bill. Habits almost exclusively marine, spending less time on beaches than congeners, feeding more over open water where attend flocks of cormorants and pelicans, following them diligently, swooping down to retrieve or steal. They likewise attend sea-otters and seals. Flight buoyant, with rather long, angled wings and rhythmic, flicking wingbeats (brown juveniles flying head on or at distance can thus appear skua-like). When perched wings project well beyond tail, almost trailing ground when 'upright' stance assumed. Call note 'aow-aow' normally delivered with upwards toss of head; also a laughing 'ah-ah-ah-ah'.

DM: Breeds almost entirely on Raza I., Gulf of California (600,000 pairs), with smaller outposts on islands along middle of peninsula off west coast of Baja California; has bred once Alcatraz I. (Stallcup, pers. comm.). Returns to colonies about Mar; egg-dates mostly Apr/May. Dispersal begins Jun, moving N and S; most appear to move N reaching Monterey Jun/Jul, Vancouver I., British Columbia, Jul. Return passage begins about Aug with coastal movements southwards passing Farallon Is Aug–Dec. A few non-breeders and immatures remain in northern sectors throughout year. Vagrants have occurred E to Arizona and western Great Lakes region.

SS: Distinctive at all ages but distant views of immatures can suggest skua spp. (p. 323).

207 WHITE-EYED GULL
other: Red Sea Black-headed Gull
Larus leucophthalmus

PLATE 70 Figs 207a-207c
MAP 207

Length 39cm ($15\frac{1}{2}$in.). Wingspan not recorded. Iris dark brown (never white), orbital ring red. Bill bright red, tip black. Legs/feet bright yellow.

Endemic to Red Sea and adjacent coasts of Arabia and Somalia, where range overlaps with similar but larger and browner Sooty Gull (p. 332). Sexes alike; marked seasonal variation. Juveniles and subsequent stages separable from adults. No subspecies.

JUVENILE: Bill blackish, base of lower mandible brown; legs greenish-grey. **Head** Mostly brown, white on forehead, lores, chin and throat with thin white crescents above and below eye. **Body** Upperparts: mantle, scapulars and back grey-brown without obvious paler edges (see juvenile Sooty Gull, p. 332). Rump and uppertail-coverts greyish-white. Underparts mainly white; brownish breast band extends back along flanks. **Wings** Upperwing mostly dark grey-brown with inconspicuous paler fringes; primaries and secondaries almost black with narrow white trailing edge on secondaries and innermost primaries. Underwing dark grey-brown. **Tail** Mainly greyish-black; often shows white at base of outer feathers.

FIRST-WINTER: Much as juvenile except: **Head** More pronounced white crescents above and below eye, more defined blackish mask through eye to nape. **Body** Upper- and underparts greyer, more diffuse. **Wings and Tail** Unmoulted, faded through wear.

FIRST-SUMMER: As first-winter except for imperfect black hood and bib; wings and tail unmoulted, becoming worn and faded.

SECOND-WINTER: As non-breeding adult except: Bare parts duller. **Head** Grizzled brownish hood with imperfect white hindcollar. **Body** Upperparts mostly greyish-brown; rump greyish-white. **Wings** Upperwing mostly greyish-brown; outer primaries, their coverts, alula and secondaries blackish with narrow white trailing edge on secondaries and innermost primaries; marginal and lesser coverts often browner. **Tail** White; blackish subterminal band variable in extent.

SECOND-SUMMER: Much as second-winter but with imperfect blackish hood and grizzled bib; wings and tail unmoulted, faded through wear.

THIRD-WINTER / ADULT NON-BREEDING: As breeding adult except: Bare parts duller. **Head** Hood and bib grizzled with white merging into whitish hindcollar. **Wings** Upperwing: primaries, outer primary-coverts, alula, secondaries and tertials black, with white tips from 3rd–5th primary inwards forming broad trailing edge to wing; coverts deep grey, inner marginal white. Underwing greyish-brown, coverts and axillaries blackish, trailing edge white. **Tail** White.

ADULT BREEDING: Head Mostly glossy black (extending as bib to upper breast), with prominent white crescents above and below eye and white hindneck. **Body** Upperparts deep grey, rump and uppertail-coverts white. Underparts mostly white; breast band and flanks pale grey. **Wings and Tail** Much as non-breeding adult.

FHJ: Slightly smaller than similar Sooty Gull (p. 332) with correspondingly slimmer jizz, thinner, more pointed wings and noticeably more slender bill. These differences in structure useful field characters at all ages. Sociable, occurring in large flocks about harbours etc., where an accomplished scavenger. Call unrecorded.

DM: Confined to Red Sea, breeding as far N as Gulf of Suez on islands near Hurghada S to Somalia and Yemen. Egg-dates not certainly known, perhaps Jun–Sep. Most winter Gulf of Aden and adjacent Somalia coast. Only one record from Kenya (Britton 1980); claimed records from Eastern Cape and Southern Mozambique seem unlikely. Some, however, stray N to SE Mediterranean, occurring Port Said and even Haifa, Israel.

SS: The following notes compare White-eyed Gull with Sooty Gull (p. 332). All stages show more slender, darker bill with white crescents above and below eye (Sooty has only a prominent upper crescent, the lower, if present, faint). Juveniles generally darker-headed and the upperparts and upperwing-coverts lack the promiment pale fringes of Sooty. First- and second-calendar-year White-eyed have blackish bills and generally more uniform greyish plumage, although head less uniform; show either a partial hood (summer) or a blackish eye patch extending to meet on nape with grizzled white chin and throat; legs greenish. In adults leg and bill colour distinctly different, with blacker hood and greyer upperparts in present species.

208 SOOTY GULL
other: Aden/Hemprich's Gull
Larus hemprichi

PLATE 70 Figs 208a-208e

MAP 208

Length 44–47cm (17½–18½in.). Wingspan not recorded. Iris dark brown, orbital ring red. Bill yellowish with black subterminal band and red tip. Legs/feet yellow or greenish-yellow.

Endemic to NW Indian Ocean and Red Sea; range overlaps with smaller, more slender-billed White-eyed Gull (p. 331). At any age bill colour and proportions, coupled with jizz, are best specific differences. Sexes alike; marked seasonal variation. Juveniles and subsequent stages separable. No subspecies.

JUVENILE: Bill blue-grey, tip black; legs dull grey. **Head** Mostly pale brownish-grey; sides of face and chin whiter; nape browner. Indistinct white crescent above eye. **Body** Upperparts: mantle, scapulars and back brown, fringed buff forming scaly pattern (unlike White-eyed Gull, p. 331); rump and uppertail-coverts greyish-white. Underparts mostly white, brownish breast band extends to flanks. **Wings** Upperwing: primaries, their coverts, alula and secondaries blackish with narrow white trailing edge extending to inner 3 or 4 primaries. Greater and median coverts dark brown tipped whitish; remaining coverts paler, sandy-brown with whitish fringes. Underwing grey-brown, coverts darker, trailing edge white. **Tail** Mostly black, white at base and sides, with narrow terminal fringe.

FIRST-WINTER: Much as juvenile except generally greyer in tone with whiter rump; wings and tail unmoulted, faded through wear.

FIRST-SUMMER: As first-winter except plumage further worn and faded; wing-coverts and tertials with fewer pale fringes.

SECOND-WINTER: As non-breeding adult except bill dull yellowish-grey with blackish subterminal band and reddish tip. **Head** As first-winter. **Body** Upperparts: mantle, scapulars and back patchy grey-brown. Underparts: breast band and flanks less uniform brownish-grey. **Wings** Upperwing: broader blackish subterminal bar along secondaries, narrower white trailing edge. **Tail** White; blackish subterminal band highly variable in extent.

SECOND-SUMMER: As second-winter except for imperfect brownish or brownish-grey hood.

THIRD-WINTER / ADULT NON-BREEDING: As breeding adult except: Bare parts duller. **Head**

Paler and browner, white hindneck reduced or lacking. **Wings** White tips more prominent.

ADULT BREEDING: Head Mostly sooty-brown (extending as bib to upper breast) with white crescent above, and occasionally smaller, fainter crescent below, eye; hindneck white. **Body** Upperparts: mantle, scapulars and back brownish-grey; rump and uppertail-coverts white. Underparts mostly white, grey-brown breast band bordering bib extends to flanks. **Wings** Upperwing: primaries, their coverts, alula and secondaries blackish with whitish trailing edge extending to 3rd or 4th primary; remainder uniform brownish-grey. Underwing dull brown, coverts and axillaries blackish, trailing edge white. **Tail** White.

FHJ: Unlike any other gull of west Palearctic or Middle East except for White-eyed (p. 331). Compared with latter is larger, with heavier build and broader, more rounded wingtips in flight. When seen together thicker bill and larger gonys of present species easily seen and, coupled with difference in bill colour (at all ages), perhaps best way of separating the two species. Call unrecorded.

DM: Breeds southern Red Sea from about Jeddah S to Gulf of Aden, off Mekran coast, and then locally along E Somalia coast to Kiunga, Kenya; also Persian Gulf. Egg-dates Jul/Aug (Meinertzhagen 1954). Although present off Arabian coast throughout year, many migrate S to Kenya and Tanzania with peak figures during Oct–May; also to W coasts of India. Bailey (1966) found it abundant off SE Arabia, with large flocks of several thousands in Kuria Muria Bay, off Oman, during Jun–Aug. Further N in Red Sea Krabbe (1979) records it as vagrant to Elat, only five records over three years.

SS: See notes under White-eyed Gull (p. 331).

---

209 BAND-TAILED GULL

other: Belcher's/Simeon Gull

Larus belcheri

PLATE 67 Figs 209a-209d

MAP 209

Length 51cm (20in.). Wingspan 124cm (49in.). Iris brown, orbital ring yellow. Bill yellow with black subterminal band and red tip. Legs/feet bright yellow.

Coasts of South America, where range overlaps with Kelp and Dolphin Gulls (p. 343, p. 329). Sexes alike; marked seasonal variation. Juveniles separable from adults. Two subspecies.

JUVENILE: Bill pink or yellow, tip black; legs greyish. **Head** Dark brown, paler on forehead, nape browner. **Body** Upperparts: mantle and scapulars greyish-brown merging into brown back, scaled with buff; uppertail-coverts white. Underparts: breast brownish, tipped white, paling to white at ventral area. **Wings** Upperwing: primaries and secondaries blackish-brown, latter fringed white; coverts as back. Underwing brownish-buff, primaries darker. **Tail** Dull black, fringed buff-white, with whitish base.

FIRST-WINTER: As juvenile except head darker, saddle much faded, breast and belly greyer.

FIRST-SUMMER: As first-winter but head mainly white.

SECOND-WINTER: Much as non-breeding adult except bare parts duller; head rather grizzled, this extending to sides of neck and upper breast. Saddle and upperwings browner in tone; tail as juvenile but with whiter base.

SECOND-SUMMER: As second-winter but head white.

THIRD-WINTER / ADULT NON-BREEDING: Head Brownish-black hood; forehead and crescents above and below eye often whiter; nape and sides of neck pale grey. **Body** Upperparts: saddle slaty-black, rump white. **Wings** Upperwing slaty-black with prominent white trailing edge. Underwing pale grey, outer primaries blackish. **Tail** White, black subterminal band.

ADULT BREEDING: As non-breeding adult but head white.

FHJ: Medium-sized 'black-backed' gull, primaries lacking white spots or mirrors. Often associates with cormorants, harrying them to regurgitate food and plundering unguarded eggs and chicks. Rarely follows ships, though competes for galley waste.

DM: Confined to South America. *L.b. belcheri* breeds Pacific coast from northern Peru S to Coquimbo, Chile, occasionally wanders N to Panama. *L.b. atlanticus* breeds Atlantic coast near Bahia Blanca at San Blas Is, Argentina, perhaps also at other nearby localities. In winter some range S to Patagonia but status on this littoral not fully known. Recent record from Florida, USA.

SS: Kelp Gull (p. 343) much larger differs in bill and plumage colours at all ages. Confusion more likely with juvenile and adult winter Dolphin Gulls (p. 329), but range overlaps only in Patagonia.

---

210 BLACK-TAILED GULL

other: Japanese/Temminck's Gull

Larus crassirostris

PLATE 56 Figs 210a-210c

MAP 210

Length 46–48cm (18–19in.). Wingspan not recorded. Iris pale straw, pupil dark, orbital ring red. Bill mainly yellow with black and red bands, tip white. Legs/feet yellowish-green.

Asiatic; range overlaps with larger, white-tailed Slaty-backed Gull (p. 343). Sexes alike; slight seasonal variation. Juveniles separable from adults. No subspecies.

JUVENILE: Iris dark, bill pink, tip black; legs pinkish. **Head** Mainly brown with tawny cast to nape and sides of neck; forehead and chin whitish. **Body** Upperparts: saddle dull brown edged buff or grey; rump paler with greyish-white uppertail-coverts showing brown spots and streaks. Underparts mainly white, faintly mottled with brown. **Wings** Upperwing: primaries and secondaries brownish-

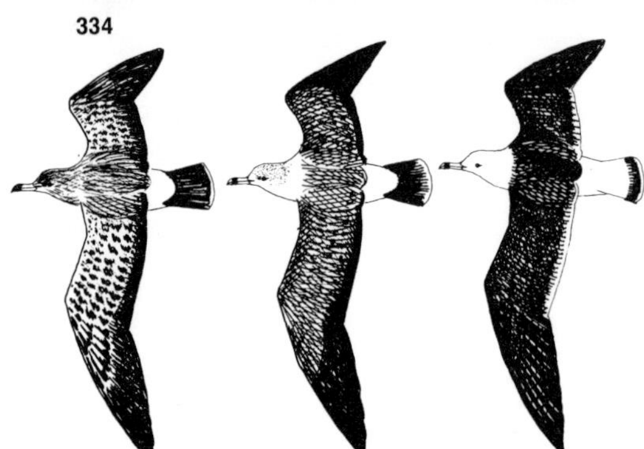

Fig. 19. Black-tailed Gull. *Based on notes and sketches supplied by Dr. Mark Brazil*

black, latter tipped white; remainder as saddle. **Tail** Brownish-black with buff tip.
FIRST-WINTER: As juvenile except head white with grey streaks concentrated in narrow band over crown; saddle and uppertail-coverts greyer, underparts whitish with dusky streaks on throat.
FIRST-SUMMER: As first-winter but head and underparts whiter, saddle showing grey or slaty tips.
SECOND-WINTER: Head Mostly white, greyish streaks over crown. **Body** Upperparts: saddle as breeding adult but usually with scattered brown tips. Underparts white. **Wings** Upperwing mostly brownish-black with broad white trailing edge; coverts with scattered brownish tips. **Tail** Generally as adult but band extends to outer feathers.
SECOND-SUMMER: As second-winter except head white; little or no brown in saddle.
THIRD-WINTER/ADULT NON-BREEDING: Resembles breeding adult but bare parts duller; head white, grey streaks on crown.
ADULT BREEDING: Head White. **Body** Upperparts: saddle slate-grey, rump white. Underparts white. **Wings** Upperwing: primaries all-black, except outer 2 or 3 faintly tipped white. Remainder of upperwing slate-grey, secondaries broadly tipped white forming trailing edge. Underwing: outer primaries black, inner and all secondaries grey tipped white, coverts white. **Tail** Mostly white, subterminal band black, outer tail feathers and tip white.
FHJ: About size of California Gull (p. 341) but wings proportionately longer; bill rather heavy with black and red bands and white tip. Habits little known. Call a plaintive mewing.
DM: Asiatic; breeds northern coasts and islands of Sea of Japan bordering eastern Siberia, China and both islands of Japan. In winter disperses N to Sakhalin and S regularly to Hong Kong; some may wander further S. One record from Attu I., Aleutians, May 1980 (Gibson *et al.*, pers. comm.).
SS: Adults easily separated by combination of banded bill and tail, and slate-grey upperparts. Criteria to enable separation of juveniles from those of other species still evolving; heavy, banded bill and almost wholly black tail should prove reliable characters. Second-calendar-year types generally resemble adults but have some brownish motting on wing-coverts, and tail band (unlike adult's) extends wholly across width of tail. Much larger, white-tailed Slaty-backed Gull (p. 343) is only other dark-backed gull of region.

211 AUDOUIN'S GULL

Larus audouinii

PLATE 69 Figs 211a-211c
see also Fig. 20, p. 335
MAP 211

Length 51cm (20in.). Wingspan unrecorded. Iris brown, orbital ring red. Bill dark red, black subterminal band, yellow tip. Legs/feet olive-grey.

Confined to Mediterranean Basin, migrating W and S to coasts of NW Africa; range overlaps with several gull spp. but see especially Herring (p. 337) and, in juvenile or immature plumages, Lesser Black-backed Gull (p. 340). Sexes alike; slight seasonal variation. Juveniles separable from adults. No subspecies.
JUVENILE: Bill black; legs/feet dark grey. **Head** Grey-brown; ear-coverts darker, forehead and crown whiter imparting white-capped appearance. **Body** Upperparts: mantle grey-brown, darker on scapulars and back, fringed buff; rump pale grey-brown. Underparts mostly grey-brown, whiter on belly and undertail-coverts, latter with dark chevrons at sides. **Wings** Upperwing: primaries and their coverts blackish, secondaries and their coverts blackish with narrow white fringes. Median, lesser coverts, and tertials much as scapulars. **Tail** Mostly black, greyish at base, whitish tips.
FIRST-WINTER: As juvenile except: Base and tip of bill yellowish-grey. **Head** Whiter. **Body** Upperparts: mantle, scapulars and back grey with brownish spotting on scapulars and back; rump white, spotted grey-brown. Underparts white; brown mottling chiefly on sides of breast. **Wings and Tail** Unmoulted; faded through wear.
FIRST-SUMMER: As first-winter except head whiter; mantle, scapulars and back with some clear-grey; greyish inner wing panel across greater and median coverts.
SECOND-WINTER: Base of bill reddish. **Head** White; lores and ear-coverts dusky with faint streaking on hindcrown and nape. **Body** Upperparts: mantle, scapulars and back mostly clear grey; rump white. Underparts mostly white. **Wings** Upperwing: outer primaries dull black, all except outer 1 or 2 tipped white; inner primaries greyish. Secondaries subterminally marked blackish-brown, forming subterminal trailing edge to wing; coverts mainly grey, carpal, lesser and median faintly tipped brown. **Tail** White; black subterminal band, outer feathers white.
SECOND-SUMMER: As second-winter except head white; upperwing and tail faded through wear.
THIRD-SUMMER: As breeding adult except white primary tips reduced or lacking, outer primary-coverts edged black.
FOURTH-WINTER/ADULT NON-BREEDING: Head Mostly white, faint streaks on crown and nape; hindneck greyer. **Body** Upperparts: mantle, scapu-

lars and back pale grey merging into white rump (without obvious contrast). Underparts white; sides of breast grey. **Wings** Upperwing: outer primaries black, decreasing in extent inwards to black subterminal spots on 5th and 6th, all tipped white with white mirror on inner web of first. Remainder of upperwing pale grey with narrow white leading and trailing edges. **Tail** White.

ADULT BREEDING: As non-breeding adult except head white; white primary tips reduced or lacking through wear.

FHJ: Compared with slightly larger Herring Gull (p. 337), has smaller head, more sloping crown with shorter, deeper bill. Flight buoyant and graceful, long wings and shorter, squarer tail imparting elegant jizz. More maritime in habits than Herring Gull, less aggressive.

DM: One of world's rarest gulls; breeding range restricted to scattered localities in Mediterranean, mainly Cyprus, Aegean Sea, Sardinia, Corsica, Balearic Is and islets off western Italy, Libya, Tunisia and Morocco. Egg-dates Apr/May. Disperses mainly W after breeding; autumn passage past Gibraltar into Atlantic Jul–Sep, with most wintering Atlantic coast of Morocco and Spanish Sahara. Some, however, remain in Mediterranean; peak counts for Libya (Misurata) in Jan of up to 72 (Bundy 1950). Return passage begins Mar/Apr. Vagrant N to Portugal, SE to Elat (Krabbe 1979).

SS: Likely to be confused at all ages with local race of Herring Gull *L.a. michahellis* (p. 337). Juveniles differ from that species in: lack of pronounced darker ear-coverts; darker scapulars and back with crisp, pale feather edges imparting distinct scaly appearance and contrasting with white horseshoe-shaped uppertail-coverts and mostly black tail. Additionally, darker secondary-coverts merge with secondaries to form double-width trailing edge along rear of upperwing, and inner primaries lack pale window found in juvenile Herring Gulls (first-calendar-year Lesser Black-backed Gull, p. 340, has similar upperwing pattern but darker head and upperparts and neater tail pattern). At rest other confirmatory characters are bill size, structure, and grey (not pink) legs. In subsequent immature plumages, primaries, secondaries and their coverts remain darker than corresponding stages of Herring Gull; tail and bare parts colours also differ. Adults at distance difficult to separate from Herring Gulls; best told by smaller size and slenderer jizz with sloping crown, and dark bill and eye imparting distinctly different facial aspect even at ranges when bare parts coloration cannot be precisely determined.

Fig. 20. JUVENILE GULLS (note width of dark trailing edges on wing, colour of inner primaries, and tail patterns)

212 RING-BILLED GULL *Larus delawarensis*

PLATE 61 Figs 212a-212e
MAP 212

Length 45–53cm (18–21in.). Wingspan 121–127cm ($47\frac{1}{2}$–50in.). Iris pale yellow, pupil black, orbital ring red. Bill yellow, subterminal band black, tip white or yellow. Legs/feet yellow.

North America; range overlaps with Herring, California and Common (Mew) Gulls (p. 337, p. 341, p. 336). Separation possible at all ages but more difficult during first calendar-year; see Grant (1979, 1982) and Lauro & Spencer (1980) for further details. Sexes alike; seasonal variation. Juveniles and all subsequent stages to adult plumage separable. No subspecies. Terres (1980) and Atherton & Atherton (1981) note both partial and complete albinos, latter with pink eyes, legs and feet and white bill.

JUVENILE: Iris brown. Bill pink, subterminally black, tip white. Legs/feet flesh-pink. **Head** Mostly dull white crown streaked dull brown, becoming spotted on nape and hindneck; eye-crescent dusky. **Body** Upperparts: mostly clove-brown with broad buff edges imparting variegated pattern; rump and uppertail-coverts white, spotted with brown. Underparts mostly dull white; throat and breast spotted with brown (from hindneck), crescentic bars on sides of breast, flanks and undertail-coverts. **Wings** Upperwing: outer 4–5 primaries, alula, and most primary-coverts blackish-brown; innermost primaries pale grey, subterminally black, decreasing in extent inwards; secondaries blackish-brown, fringes buff-white. Coverts mostly pale grey except for brownish carpal and diagonal bar; tertials blackish-brown, narrowly edged buff. Underwing off-white, streaked brown on coverts and axillaries, outer primaries and secondaries blackish. **Tail** Mostly white; blackish subterminal band has mottled edges, particularly on outer feathers above band.

FIRST-WINTER: Bill pinkish or yellowish-pink, subterminally black, tip white. As juvenile except: **Head** Whiter, less defined spots and streaks. **Body** Upperparts pale grey, irregular brown tips; rump and uppertail-coverts white, lightly spotted with brown, varying in extent. **Wings and Tail** Unmoulted, but faded, paler fringes reduced.

FIRST-SUMMER: Bill yellowish, subterminal band black; legs yellowish. As first-winter except: **Head** Whiter, crown mostly white, faint spots on nape. **Body** Upperparts: mantle, scapulars and back pale grey, rump white. Underparts mostly white. **Wings and Tail** Unmoulted; buffish edges to tertials much faded and ragged.
SECOND-WINTER: Bare parts resemble adults. Plumage as first-summer except: **Head** Faintly streaked with brown on crown, becoming heavier and spotted on nape and hindneck; eye-crescent dusky. **Wings** Upperwing: outer 4–5 primaries blackish, white mirror on outer primary. Primary-coverts and alula edged black. Remainder mostly pale grey, trailing edge of secondaries white; some retain indistinct darker secondary bar. **Tail** Most have partial band on outer feathers.
SECOND-SUMMER: As second-winter except head whiter; wing and tail pattern faded.
THIRD-WINTER/ADULT NON-BREEDING: Bill and legs dull yellow, former with black subterminal band. **Head** Mostly white, dark spots on nape and hindneck. **Body** Upperparts pale grey, rump white. Underparts white. **Wings** Upperwing: outer 4 primaries mostly black, 5th–6th subterminally black, all tipped white with white mirror on outer 2. Remainder pale grey, secondaries and tertials tipped with white. Underwing mostly white, primaries as upperwing. **Tail** White.
ADULT BREEDING: As non-breeding adult except head wholly white; white tips to primaries reduced or lacking.
FHJ: Resembles small, lightly-built Herring Gull (p. 337) but with banded bill. In Europe most concern is with separation from Common (Mew) Gull (p. 336). Compared with latter, is larger, heavier-bodied and with longer bill which appears expanded at tip (quite unlike tapered tip of Common Gull); heavier bill and less rounded crown of Ring-billed also impart fiercer facial expression. When perched, larger size, paler mantle and longer legs usually obvious. Call a shrill 'ky-ow'.
DM: Breeds North America from prairies and lakes of Canada, mid-western states and northern Great Basin S to NE California. Returns to colonies Mar/Apr; egg-dates May/Jun. Winters from southern Ontario and Washington S to California, southern Mexico, Bermuda and Cuba. Stragglers have reached Hawaii, Trinidad and Panama; may also occur Venezuela. Due probably to increased observer ability, now recorded annually in Europe during winter months. Numbers vary year to year but in 1980 no fewer than 13 different individuals occurred during Dec–Mar in Penzance area, England (Williams & Hirst, pers. comm.).
SS: In western USA adult California Gull larger with darker mantle, dark iris and red-spotted bill. In Europe separation from Common Gull (p. 336) more difficult but, with practice, straightforward.

---

213 COMMON GULL
other: Mew Gull
Larus canus

PLATE 61 Figs 213a-213f

MAP 213

Length 40–46cm (16–18in.). Wingspan 119–122cm (47–48in.). Iris brown, orbital ring red. Bill, legs/feet yellowish-green.

Almost circumpolar in northern hemisphere where range overlaps with Herring and Ring-billed Gulls (p. 337, p. 335). Separation from these species possible at all ages but more difficult during first calendar-year. See Grant (1979) and Lauro & Spencer (1980) for further details. Sexes alike; seasonal variation. Juveniles separable from adults. Three subspecies, one of which, *L.c. brachyrhynchus* recognisable in the field and thus described separately below.
JUVENILE: Bill pink, tip black, legs flesh-pink. **Head** Dense grey-brown streaks form partial hood; forehead, chin and throat white. **Body** Upperparts: mantle and back buff, fringed paler; rump and uppertail coverts white with dark chevrons. Underparts white; breast, flanks and undertail coverts mottled or barred brownish-grey. **Wings** Upperwing: outer 3–5 primaries, most of primary-coverts and alula blackish-brown, inner primaries grey-brown on outer webs with subterminal blackish tips; secondaries blackish-brown, tipped white. Greater coverts grey-brown, remainder light brown. Underwing whitish, streaked brown. **Tail** White with broad, blackish, sharply defined subterminal band.
FIRST-WINTER: As juvenile except for paler head, clear grey mantle, scapulars and back, whiter rump and underparts. Wings and tail unmoulted, faded through wear.
FIRST-SUMMER: As first-winter except head whiter, less streaked. Wings and tail further faded; darker areas bleached to light brown.
SECOND-WINTER: As first-winter except dark tip to yellowish or grey bill. **Head** Whiter, less streaked. **Wings** As non-breeding adult but white mirrors on outer 2 primaries smaller, outer primary-coverts and alula blackish. **Tail** White.
SECOND-SUMMER: As second-winter except head and sides of breast mostly white. Blackish areas on upperwing bleached browner.
THIRD-WINTER/ADULT NON-BREEDING: Bill yellowish with indistinct darker subterminal band. **Head** Mostly white, streaked and mottled grey-brown, heaviest on lower nape. **Body** Upperparts blue-grey, rump white. Underparts mainly white except greyish-brown streaks on sides of breast. **Wings** Upperwing: outer 4 primaries mostly black, 5th and 6th subterminally black, most tipped white with large white mirror on outer 2. Remainder of wing blue-grey, except thin white leading edge and broader trailing edge. Underwing mostly white, primaries as upperwing. **Tail** White.
ADULT BREEDING: As non-breeding adult except head and sides of breast white.

L.c. brachyrhynchus
Differs from nominate race in generally darker, more uniform plumage:
FIRST-WINTER: As for *L.c. canus* except: **Head** Browner, more even in tone. **Body** Upperparts: mantle, scapulars and back darker, rump and uppertail-coverts whitish, heavily marked with

brown. Underparts much browner, especially breast and flanks, with darker chevrons on vent and undertail-coverts. **Wings** Tertials lack noticeable pale fringes. **Tail** Subterminal band diffused, merging into dusky tail (as in Herring Gull).

SECOND-WINTER: Mantle, scapulars and back darker than nominate; unlike nominate, retains partial tail band. (Beware second-year Ring-billed Gull if birding on W coast of North America.)

FHJ: See notes under Ring-billed Gull (p. 335) for comparison with that species. Differs from Black-headed Gull (p. 356) in larger size, bare parts colours and deeper grey upperparts and upperwings. In flight, more rounded and broader wings of present species usually obvious. Many observers find difficulty in separating Common from Herring Gull (p. 337), particularly in flight when bare parts colours less easily seen. Present species much smaller, with neater more elegant proportions and more graceful, buoyant unlaboured flight; smaller bill, proportionately longer, thinner wings and more prominent mirror on outer 2 primaries usually obvious. Common Gulls breed mainly inland. Even in winter they rarely wander to true pelagic habitat, preferring to forage mostly on beaches, mudflats, refuse tips and pastures. Call a mewing 'kee-er'. All other notes similar to those of Herring Gull but higher-pitched and thinner.

DM: Almost circumpolar in northern hemisphere. *L.c. brachyrhynchus* breeds Alaska S along coast to British Columbia and NW Canada; *L.c. canus* Iceland, and NW Europe S to Switzerland; *L.c. kamtschatschensis* breeds eastern Siberia, USSR. Returns to colonies Mar/Apr; egg-dates May–Jul. Resident in many parts of range. *L.c. brachyrhynchus* winters eastern Pacific from SE Alaska S to southern California; *L.c. canus* in Europe S to Mediterranean Basin and coast of North Africa in west to northern Red Sea, Egypt, Iraq and Persian Gulf in east; *L.c. kamtschatschensis* winters S to Japan and Formosa.

SS: Most likely to be confused with Herring or Ring-billed Gulls (p. 337, p. 335). See notes above for former; refer to notes opposite Plate 61 for plumage differences with latter, plus notes under that species in main text.

---

214 HERRING GULL

Larus argentatus

PLATE 58 Figs 214a-214h
see also Plate 62 Fig. 214a
MAP 214

Length 56–66cm (22–26in.). Wingspan 137–142cm (54–56in.). Iris pale yellow, orbital ring red. Bill yellow, gonys-spot red. Legs/feet pinkish.

Cosmopolitan in northern hemisphere; range overlaps with many gull spp., see especially Lesser Black-backed, Great Black-backed, Audouin's and Western Gulls (p. 340, p. 344, p. 334, p. 342). Sexes outwardly alike; slight seasonal variation. Juveniles separable from adults. Taxonomy complex and not fully agreed upon: I have followed Barth (1975a, 1975b) in including *L.a. argenteus* and excluding *L.a. omissus*; there are thus ten subspecies, typical forms of which could probably be separated in the field. Identification however not always possible due to extensive intergradation between subspecies where ranges overlap, and complicated even further by hybridisation with Glaucous-winged, Glaucous, Lesser Black-backed and Great Black-backed Gulls (p. 345, p. 346, p. 340, p. 344). Interbreeding for instance occurs in at least 50% of Icelandic population of Glaucous Gulls, and in some parts of that country pure Glaucous are virtually absent (see Ingolfsson 1970). Offspring from mixed pairs bear some characters of each parent. See Grant (1981b, 1982) for identification pitfalls when dealing with hybrids, and also under Glaucous Gull (p. 346). Total albinism has been recorded (see Plate 62, Fig. 214a). *L.a. argenteus* is described below, followed by notes on other subspecies and their ranges.

JUVENILE: Iris brown; bill blackish, base of lower mandible pinkish; legs dull flesh or greyish. **Head** Streaked grey-brown, darkest on ear-coverts, with paler face and nape. **Body** Upperparts: mantle, scapulars and back grey-brown, narrowly fringed paler; rump and uppertail-coverts slightly paler. Underparts heavily mottled and barred grey-brown. **Wings** Upperwing: primaries and secondaries mostly dark brown; inner primaries distinctly paler forming conspicuous pale window (Fig. 20), an excellent flight character for separation from juvenile Lesser Black-backed Gull (p. 340). Coverts much as upperparts. **Tail** Base whitish, barred brown, merging into blackish-brown subterminal band.

FIRST-WINTER: As juvenile except head and underparts whiter, upperparts pattern less scaly.

FIRST-SUMMER: As first-winter except head and underparts generally whitish with pale brown tips. Wings and tail unmoulted, much faded and worn.

SECOND-WINTER: Iris paler; bill pink, distally black. **Head** Whitish, variably streaked brown. **Body** Upperparts: mantle, scapulars and back clearer grey; rump mostly white. Underparts mainly white. **Wings** Upperwing: pale window on inner primaries more apparent; wing-coverts greyer, fewer brown tips. Underwing whiter. **Tail** White, merging into broad, blackish subterminal band.

SECOND-SUMMER: As second-winter except head and underparts whiter; mantle and back clearer grey. Wings and tail faded and worn.

THIRD-WINTER: As non-breeding adult except bill yellowish with dusky subterminal mark. Upperwing shows less well-defined black on wingtip, extending to include outermost primary-coverts and alula, without obvious mirrors; some brownish mottling usually present on innermost wing-coverts. Faint tail band.

THIRD-SUMMER: As third-winter except head whiter; wings and tail faded through wear.

FOURTH-WINTER/ADULT NON-BREEDING: Head White, clouded and streaked grey-brown, heaviest

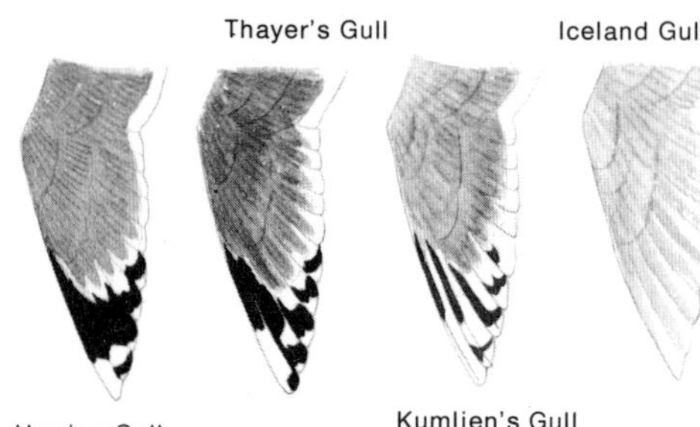

Fig. 21. Upperwing patterns of some adult gulls

on nape. **Body** Upperparts: mantle, scapulars and back grey, rump white. Underparts mainly white, sides of breast as nape. **Wings** Upperwing mostly grey with white trailing edge; outermost primaries black, decreasing in extent inwards to subterminal black bar on 6th, all tipped white with mirror on outer 2 primaries. Underwing white; primaries as upperwing. **Tail** White.

BREEDING ADULT: As non-breeding adult except head and sides of breast white.

FHJ: Most familiar and widespread gull of northern hemisphere. Compared with Lesser Black-backed Gull (p. 340), is larger with proportionately shorter legs; in flight wings appear proportionately shorter and broader. An opportunistic scavenger, follows inshore shipping, attends refuse tips, follows plough. Call a strident 'kyow'.

DM: *L.a. argenteus* Breeds southern Iceland, Faeroes, British Isles, NW France, Holland and Belgium. Egg-dates Apr–Jun. Winters within breeding range S to N Iberia (Spain).

SS: Juveniles differ from juvenile Lesser Black-backed Gull in pale window on inner primaries, narrower subterminal bar on trailing edge of upperwing (Fig. 20), less contrast in tail pattern. Upperparts and wing-coverts lack distinctive chequered pattern of larger, more robust first-year Great Black-backed (p. 344). In subsequent stages upperparts colour of the three species allows more instant separation. See also Great Black-headed and Audouin's Gulls (p. 348, p. 334).

SUBSPECIFIC VARIATION (All compared with *L.a. argenteus*)

L.a. smithsonianus: Size averages larger, bare parts and grey upperparts and upperwings similar. First-calendar-year birds much darker and browner with mostly blackish-brown tail (see photo in Terres 1980, p. 423). Confined to North America: breeds SE Alaska E to NW Greenland and S to North Carolina; winters S to Mexico, Panama, Bermuda and Barbados. Recently recorded Venezuela, S America. NOTE Interbreeds with Glaucous-winged Gulls in Gulf of Alaska. In Canada hybrid Herring × Great Black-backed Gulls are becoming commoner, especially Ottawa region; resultant hybrids suggest Lesser Black-backed or Western Gulls (p. 340, p. 342) (see Foxall 1979). On W coast of North America separation of juvenile Herring and Western Gulls problematical, but Herring generally paler tan and buff, Western darker, more sooty-grey.

L.a. argentatus: Size averages larger. Adult: Bill larger, duller yellow; legs pink or greyish but yellow-legged types occur in NE of range (treated as *L.a. omissus* by some authors). Grey upperparts and upperwings darker, with less black on wingtip and larger white mirrors. Breeds Scandinavia E to White Sea, USSR; winters S to N Iberia (Spain).

L.a. heuglini: Size averages larger. Adult: Legs yellowish. In winter nape heavily streaked grey-brown. Grey upperparts and upperwings darkest of any race, approaching palest examples of Lesser Black-backed Gull (*L.f. graellsii*). Breeds USSR from White Sea E to Kara Sea; winters S through Black and Aral Seas, NW India and Gulf of Aden, perhaps also to Kenya (see Britton 1980).

L.a. taimyrensis: Size averages larger. Adult: Legs pink or yellow. In winter head only faintly streaked. Grey upperparts and upperwings darker, intermediate between *heuglini* and *vagae*. Breeds Siberia, USSR; winter range not known, may reach Kenya (Britton 1980).

L.a. vagae: Legs pink or yellow. Grey upperparts and upperwings considerably darker than *argenteus*, paler than *taimyrensis*. Breeds USSR along coasts of Laptev Sea E to Bering Strait; winters S to Japan and China.

L.a. atlantis: Size equal or slightly larger. Adult: Red gonys-spot larger; legs bright yellow. Grey upperparts and upperwings darker in tone, intermediate between *argentatus* and *L. fuscus graellsii*, with only one mirror on outer primary. In winter head often heavily streaked. First-calendar-year birds darker and browner with darker tail. Breeds Azores, Madeira and Canaries in NE Atlantic; may wander to NW African coast.

L.a. michahellis: Size averages larger. Adult: Bare parts as in *atlantis*. Grey upperparts and upperwings darker than *argenteus* but with similar extensive black on outer primaries and two white mirrors. Paler-headed than *argenteus* during winter. First-calendar-year birds darker and browner than *argenteus*, with distinctive tawny cast and more contrasting tail pattern. Breeds Mediterranean Basin N to Iberia (Spain), with recent northwards range expansion into southern France; winters from Holland (de Heer 1981) S throughout breeding range; extent of dispersal along NW African coast unknown.

L.a. cachinnans: Size averages larger. Adult: Bare parts as *atlantis*. Plumage as *michahellis* but grey upperparts and upperwings slightly paler with less black, more white, on wingtip. Breeds from Black Sea E through southern USSR, including southern shores of Caspian Sea to about Lake Balkash; winters eastern Mediterranean, Red Sea, Persian Gulf and NW India.

L.a. mongolicus: Size averages larger, legs bluish, grey or pink. Plumage recalls *michahellis*. Breeds from approximately Lake Balkash, southern USSR, east to Mongolia; winter range not precisely known, probably coasts of China straying S to Bangkok.

215 THAYER'S GULL *Larus thayeri*

PLATE 60 Figs 215a-215c
MAP 215

Length 56–63cm (22–25in.). Wingspan unrecorded. Iris greyish, speckled brown, appearing wholly dark in some; orbital ring purplish-pink. Bill yellow, gonys-spot red. Legs/feet deep flesh-pink.

Arctic coasts of Canada, N to Baffin I., migrates SW to winter on Pacific coast of North America; range overlaps with many gull spp., but see especially Herring, Kumlien's and Glaucous-winged (p. 337, p. 348, p. 345). Sexes outwardly alike, males average larger; slight seasonal variation. Juveniles separable from adults. Previously considered a subspecies of Herring Gull but presently considered separate species (AOU 1973). References to Herring Gull in following refer to *L.a. smithsonianus*.

JUVENILE: Bill black; legs/feet deep flesh-pink; iris dark brown. **Head** Streaked grey-brown with paler face and nape; ear-coverts and eye-crescent dusky. (Generally paler overall than Herring Gull.) **Body** Upperparts: mantle, scapulars and back greyish-brown or brown, edged and barred buff or greyish (producing more even, less chequered pattern than either Herring or Kumlien's Gulls, p. 337, p. 348). Rump whiter. Underparts streaked grey-brown; undertail-coverts barred brownish. **Wings** Upperwing: coverts as upperparts; secondaries and tertials grey-brown as mantle but tipped and barred whitish-grey. Primaries uniform greyish-brown or chocolate-brown, only slightly darker in tone than mantle and back (averaging lighter than Herring, darker than Kumlien's, and lacking any suggestion of darker subterminal spots). Underwing mostly uniform pale grey-brown shading to whitish on outer (unmarked) primaries. **Tail** Pale brownish, irregular white barring towards base.

FIRST-WINTER: Much as juvenile except generally greyer, less contrasting; head and underparts sometimes whiter.

FIRST-SUMMER: As first-winter except: **Head** Whitish. **Body** Mantle, scapulars and back greyer, more watered. Underparts whitish. **Wings and Tail** Unmoulted, becoming worn and faded.

SECOND-WINTER: Base of bill pinkish, extreme tip sometimes white. **Head** Greyish-white streaked grey-brown, heaviest on ear-coverts, nape and hindneck. **Body** Upperparts: mantle, scapulars and back as first-winter but usually with much clearer grey; rump whitish. Underparts white, mottled grey-brown; undertail-coverts barred grey-brown. **Wings** Upperwing: coverts as upperparts; secondaries and inner primaries grey-brown, outer 4–6 primaries slightly darker grey-brown. (Upperwing lacks prominent blackish-brown secondary bar of Herring Gull.) Underwing generally whitish. **Tail** Whiter at base than first-winter type.

SECOND-SUMMER: As second-winter except: **Head** Mainly white. **Body** Mantle, scapulars and back mostly uniform grey. **Wings and Tail** Unmoulted, becoming much worn and faded.

THIRD-WINTER: As non-breeding adult except: Bill duller and greyer. **Wings** Upperwing: brownish edges to primary-coverts, alula and some greater and median coverts; blackish-grey on wingtip less clear cut, and lacks prominent white mirror on tips. **Tail** Faint brownish mottling.

ADULT NON-BREEDING: As breeding adult except: **Head** Brownish-grey streaks heaviest on nape and hindneck (averaging somewhat paler than Herring but darker than Kumlien's Gulls, p. 337, p. 348). **Body** Underparts: upper breast variably streaked greyish-brown (extension from head).

ADULT BREEDING: Head White. **Body** Upperparts: mantle, scapulars and back grey (averaging darker than either Herring or Kumlien's Gulls); rump white. **Wings** Upperwing resembles that of Herring Gull, usually differing in black areas less extensive and often decidedly paler or greyer, the white tongue in outermost primary often joining a long white tip, and on the next primary reaching to, or nearly to, the white apical spot (Godfrey 1966). Underwing whitish, including underside of primaries (Jehl & Smith 1970). **Tail** White.

FHJ: Midway between Kumlien's (Iceland) and Herring Gull in jizz. Compared with Herring, averages slightly smaller with more streamlined jizz, more rounded crown and proportionately shorter, finer bill. When perched most give impression of less black on closed wing than Herring, with undersides of rear primaries white (Herring shows black subterminal tip and greyish underside to rear primaries). Wings project well past tail, an important character for separation from larger, more robust Glaucous-winged Gull (p. 345) on North American west coast (at any age).

DM: Breeds in Arctic Canada and locally in NW Canada, where reproductive isolation from Herring Gull apparently maintained by dark eye and difference in choice of breeding habitat: Herring Gulls nest on low, flat islands and Thayer's in cliff colonies (Smith 1966). Egg-dates May/Jun. Dispersal begins about Aug, most moving SW to winter mainly NW Washington and SW British Columbia with smaller numbers S to California; few winter central and eastern N America from middle western prairie and Great Lakes regions to Nova Scotia, and then S to Florida and Texas (see *Amer. Birds* 1976–82).

SS: Experienced birders will know that it is not possible positively to identify all gulls specifically. Separation of present species from Herring and Kumlien's (p. 337, p. 348) must be considered very difficult at all ages, and should be based on a combination of certain characters, as there is no one clinching characteristic. Adult Thayer's Gulls can be separated from Herring by white underside to outer primaries and, usually, by dark eye and less extensive, blackish-grey wingtip. Kumlien's Gull also has whitish underside to primaries and a proportionately smaller bill than Herring Gull, but differs from Thayer's in yellow iris, paler mantle and more silvery primaries usually with inconspicuous dark grey or blackish outer webs and subterminal bars confined to outer 3–4 primaries; moreover, tips of outer 2 primaries are extensively white (see Fig. 21 opposite). First-winter Herring

Gull (p. 337) has dark brown or blackish primaries and secondary bar, contrasting with lighter saddle and wing-coverts. By comparision Thayer's Gull has uniform grey-brown or chocolate-brown primaries and shows very little contrast in the barring and tips of upperparts, giving less contrasting chequered pattern; the underside of the outer primaries are white. In subsequent stages Herring should show a more pronounced darker wingtip, a secondary bar on upperwing and blackish undersides to outer primaries. Atypical first-winter Kumlien's can appear quite dark in the field, with primaries almost as dark as in Thayer's; mantle, scapulars and back, however, are more chequered (see Gosselin & David 1975). Hybrids further complicate identification and should always be considered: Herring × Glaucous, Herring × Glaucous-winged and Glaucous-winged × Western could produce offspring with characters similar to Thayer's Gull. Consideration of these types is, unfortunately, outside the scope of this guide; refer to Godfrey (1966), Wahl & Paulson (1974), Gosselin & David (1975), Kautesk (1976) and Mark (1981).

216 LESSER BLACK-BACKED GULL

Larus fuscus

PLATE 59 Figs 216b-216f
see also Plate 58 Fig. 216a
MAP 216

Length 51–61cm (20–24in.). Wingspan 124–127cm (49–50in.). Iris pale yellow, orbital ring red. Bill deep yellow, gonys-spot red. Legs/feet pale yellow.

NW Europe, S to central Africa in northern winter. Range overlaps with Great Black-backed, Audouin's, Herring and (possibly) Kelp Gulls (p. 344, p. 334, p. 337, p. 343). Sexes alike; slight seasonal variation. Juveniles separable from adults. Taxonomy complex. I have followed Barth's (1975) treatment in recognising three subspecies, all of which can be distinguished in the field. Hybrid Lesser Black-backed × Herring Gulls occur. *L.f. graellsii* is described below, followed by subspecific differences and ranges of other forms.

JUVENILE: Iris brown; bill black, legs dull flesh. **Head** Brownish-white; distinctly darker ear-coverts, whiter forehead, chin and throat. **Body** Upperparts: mantle, scapulars and back dark sepia-brown edged white, producing darker, more scaly pattern than in juvenile Herring Gull (p. 337), contrasting with whiter rump. Underparts greyish-white; sides of breast, flanks and undertail-coverts distinctly barred brown. **Wings** Upperwing: primaries, secondaries and their coverts blackish-brown forming broad dark margin to trailing edge (Fig. 20); coverts as scapulars but less scaly. **Tail** Whiter at base than in juvenile Herring Gull; broader, more defined blackish band.

FIRST-WINTER: As juvenile except ear patch and scaly pattern on saddle more diffuse.

FIRST-SUMMER: As first-winter except head and underparts whiter; mantle, scapulars, back and upperwings more uniform brown (thus darker and more uniform than corresponding Herring Gull).

SECOND-WINTER: Bill pale, tip blackish. **Head** White with heavy dark streaking around eye, crown, nape and hindneck. **Body** Upperparts: mantle, scapulars and back as first-summer but with dark grey tips; rump mostly white. Underparts white; sides of breast, flanks and undertail-coverts barred brown. **Wings** As first-summer but coverts more uniform. **Tail** Subterminal band reduced.

SECOND-SUMMER: As second-winter except head and underparts whiter; saddle clearer slate-grey. Wings and tail unmoulted; wing-coverts browner often fading to rich sepia-brown.

THIRD-WINTER: Bare parts duller than adult, bill with dusky subterminal mark. **Head** As second-winter. **Body** Mantle, scapulars and back dark slate-grey; rump white. Underparts white; sides of breast streaked brown. **Wings** As adult winter except browner in tone with more extensive, less defined black on outer primaries and only one mirror. **Tail** White; faint subterminal band.

THIRD-SUMMER: As third-winter except head and underparts whiter. Upperwing fades to patchy brown and slate-grey.

FOURTH-WINTER/ADULT NON-BREEDING: Head and Body As third-winter. **Wings** Upperwing mostly dark slate-grey shading to black on outermost primaries, with broad white trailing edge to secondaries and inner primaries; two white mirrors. Underwing white; outer primaries black (except mirrors) merging into dusky-grey inner primaries and subterminal band along secondaries. **Tail** White.

ADULT BREEDING: As non-breeding adult except head and underparts white; white primary tips reduced or lacking.

FHJ: Much smaller than Great Black-backed Gull (p. 344), the only other European gull with dark saddle and upperwings. Compared with Herring Gull (p. 337), *L.f. graellsii* darker above and smaller, with lighter jizz and proportionately longer, slimmer wings which, when perched, give rear end more attenuated appearance. Head and bill proportionately smaller with more rounded crown, imparting gentler facial expression. These structural differences also apparent in juveniles and first-summer types, which differ further from those of Herring Gull in generally darker upperparts contrasting with much whiter rump and underparts. Call as Herring Gull but deeper-toned.

DM: *L.f. graellsii* breeds southern Iceland, Faeroes, British Isles, Netherlands and Brittany. Egg-dates Apr–Jun; fledging Jul/Aug. Disperses S and SW to wintering areas in western Europe and western Africa; many now winter S and SW England but extent of southern dispersal not precisely known; Wallace (1973) recorded *L.f. fuscus* as more plentiful than *graellsii* at Lagos, Nigeria. A westwards drift of a few individuals from southwards-migrating Icelandic population probably accounts for the regular, but small wintering population which now passes through Newfoundland, N America, wintering S to Florida. Many first- and second-year birds remain S in wintering quarters throughout year. Return migration begins Jan, with impressive coastal movements and flocks of several thousands at staging points in S and SW England Feb/Mar.

SS: See notes under Herring and Great Black-backed Gulls (p. 337, p. 344). In North America problems presented by Great Black-backed × Herring Gull hybrids, which resemble present species, have been discussed by Foxall (1979). In Europe see immature Audouin's Gull (p. 334).

SUBSPECIES (All compared with *L.f. graellsii*; only adults described).

L.f. fuscus: Mantle, scapulars, back and upperwings almost black (as in Great Black-backed Gull, p. 344). In winter head remains more or less white (unlike other two subspecies). Breeds Baltic and northern Norway; disperses on broad southerly front, reaching S to Nigeria and throughout Red Sea S to Kenya. Listed as scarce summer visitor to coasts of Natal and Mozambique (Brooke & Sinclair 1978); beware local Kelp Gull (p. 343), which is larger with darker iris, duller legs and a wider white trailing edge to wing.

L.f. intermedius: Resembles *graellsii* but slightly darker on mantle, back and upperwings. Breeds southern Norway, west Sweden and Denmark. Migration also similar tending to head S and W, rather than SE to eastern Mediterranean and Red Sea areas.

---

217 CALIFORNIA GULL
Larus californicus

PLATE 60 Figs 217a-217c
MAP 217

Length 51–58cm (20–23in.). Wingspan 122–140cm (48–55in.). Iris brownish, orbital ring red. Bill yellow, gonys-spot red, edged black. Legs/feet yellowish.

Inland North American species wintering mainly on coasts of western North America S to Baja California; range overlaps with several gull spp. but see especially Herring, Western and Ring-billed Gulls (p. 337, p. 342, p. 335). Sexes alike; slight seasonal variation. Juveniles separable from adults; no subspecies. Hybrids: a probable California × Ring-billed or Mew Gull (Stallcup & Harrison, pers. obs.).

JUVENILE: Iris dark brown; bill pink with clearly defined black tip; legs pinkish. **Head** Mostly greyish-brown, streaked and blurred silvery-white. **Body** Upperparts; saddle greyish-brown edged and barred golden and silvery; rump and uppertail-coverts whiter. Underparts mottled and barred greyish-brown; whitest on chin, throat and upper breast; undertail coverts more distinctly barred. **Wings** Upperwing: primary coverts and primaries dull brownish black, innermost 4–5 primaries paler forming indistinct 'window'; secondaries and tertials dark brown fringed buff-white, coverts as saddle except for darker tips to greater coverts. Underwing dusky greyish-brown; primaries and secondaries darker. **Tail** Variable; mostly dark brown or blackish, some barred whitish across base.

FIRST-WINTER: Much as juvenile except plumage wears generally greyer; silvery and golden tints on upperparts lacking; chin, throat and upper breast whiter.

FIRST-SUMMER: Little change from first-winter: **Head** Whiter. **Body** Saddle with some grey tips. Underparts white.

SECOND-WINTER: Bill greyish-pink with black subterminal band and small white tip; legs/feet greyish-pink. **Head** Generally greyish-white, faint brownish streaks becoming broader and forming necklace of dusky spots on nape and hindneck. Chin and throat whiter. **Body** Upperparts: saddle mostly grey; rump whitish. Underparts off-white mottled and clouded brown, heaviest across breast. **Wings** Upperwing much as juvenile except paler inner window more pronounced, some grey in coverts; outermost primary sometimes with small white mirror. **Tail** Base whiter than juvenile.

SECOND-SUMMER: Much as second-winter except head and breast whiter.

THIRD-WINTER: Resembles non-breeding adult except: Bill and legs duller, dusky band on tip of former more extensive. **Wings** Upperwing: primary-coverts, alula, and some greater coverts faintly edged brown. Underwing: scattered brownish tips across coverts. **Tail** Partial band retained across central feathers.

THIRD-SUMMER: As third-winter except head, hindneck and upper breast white.

ADULT NON-BREEDING: As breeding adult except: Blackish subterminal band bordering red gonys-spot more extensive. **Head** As for second-winter.

ADULT BREEDING: Head White. **Body** Upperparts white. **Wings** Upperwing: mostly deep neutral grey, with broad white tips to secondaries and innermost primaries forming conspicuous trailing edge; outermost primaries black, decreasing in extent inwards to subterminal bar on 5th or 6th, all with white apical spots; outer 2 primaries with white mirror, usually elongated on 1st primary and extending to tip. Underwing: white, with similar wingtip pattern. **Tail** White.

FHJ: Primarily an inland species during summer months; much venerated, feeding on a host of agricultural pests from locusts to mice. Between Ring-billed and Herring Gulls in size, bearing some characters of both. When perched has rather upright posture with wings almost trailing ground. Compared with Herring Gull (p. 337), head proportionately smaller, with more rounded crown, larger eye and longer, more slender bill giving distinctly different facial expression. Call a soft 'kow-kow-kow' or 'kuk-kuk-kuk'.

DM: Breeds interior N America near, or on islands of, large lakes from northern prairie provinces of Canada E to N Dakota, S to Wyoming and Utah, and W to NE California where status of about 50,000 pairs at Mono Lake now seriously threatened. Returns to colonies from Apr; egg-dates May/Jun; fledging and dispersal begins Aug, moving SW towards coasts of western North America to winter

from British Columbia S to Baja California. Stragglers occasionally wander to eastern USA, occurring S to Florida and Texas; vagrants have reached Hawaii and, apparently, Japan (Bent 1921).
SS: Most juveniles and first-winter types separated from those of Herring Gull (p. 337) by clear-cut, black tip to bill; about 15% of Herring may also share this character, see structure in FHJ (Stallcup, pers. comm.). In second calendar-year present species has greyish-yellow bill and legs (pink in Herring Gull) and plumage generally neater and greyer, less brown. Adults separable by leg colour and structural differences (see FHJ). Juvenile Ring-billed Gulls (which also have black-tipped bills) are smaller, with black subterminal band across white tail and different upperwing pattern; subsequent stages separable by difference in saddle and upperwing colour, bill and iris colour and jizz/structure.

218 WESTERN GULL (Includes Yellow-footed Gull *L.o. livens*)

Larus occidentalis

PLATE 57 Figs 218a-218e

MAP 218

Length 61–68cm (24–27in.). Wingspan 132–142cm (52–56in.). Iris yellowish-grey, orbital ring yellowish-pink. Bill chrome-yellow, gonys-spot red. Legs/feet pink.

Western coasts of North America; range overlaps with Herring, California and Glaucous-winged Gulls (p. 337, p. 341, p. 345). Sexes alike; no appreciable seasonal variation (adults of *L.o. occidentalis* with heavy grey mottling on head and nape, and larger eye, may be Western × Glaucous-winged hybrids: Stallcup, pers. comm.). Juveniles separable from adults. Three subspecies listed, adults of which can probably be separated in the field. Nominate *occidentalis* has a lighter saddle and upperwings than *wymani*, whilst *livens*, which has yellow legs, is sometimes considered a distinct species. Interbreeds with Glaucous-winged Gulls (p. 345), producing fertile offspring. Following notes refer to nominate race.

JUVENILE: Iris and bill black; legs pink. **Head** Mostly dark greyish-brown, nape often paler. (Averages darker, more sooty-grey than Herring Gull, p. 337.) **Body** Upperparts dark greyish-brown, narrowly edged paler; rump and uppertail-coverts barred whiter. Underparts mostly mottled and clouded dark grey-brown; undertail-coverts more distinctly barred. **Wings** Upperwing: outer 5–6 primaries and their coverts blackish-brown, innermost 4–5 primaries with slightly paler inner webs forming faint inner window (but perhaps never to same extent as in Herring Gull); secondaries blackish-brown tipped white; remainder much as saddle. Underwing mottled brown and white; primaries and secondaries darker. **Tail** Mostly blackish-brown.

FIRST-WINTER: Much as juvenile except: **Head** Paler, especially on crown, nape and chin. **Body** Upperparts: paler feather edges and dark centres create 'spotted' effect; rump whiter. Underparts paler, less clouded. **Wings and Tail** Unmoulted, faded through wear.

FIRST-SUMMER: Base of bill pinkish. As first-winter but head and body paler, wings and tail further faded.

SECOND-WINTER: Much as first-winter except: **Head** Whiter, especially forehead, crown and sides of neck. **Body** Upperparts greyer, less spotted; rump and tail whiter. Underparts whiter, less clouded. **Wings** Upperwing: paler and greyer with less contrast; secondaries more broadly tipped white. **Tail** Base whitish.

SECOND-SUMMER: As second-winter except head whiter; saddle with some grey; underparts whiter.

THIRD-WINTER: Bill: tip blackish, base pink. **Head** White, lightly streaked grey-brown, heaviest on nape and sides of neck. **Body** Upperparts: saddle mostly grey, tinged brown; rump white. Underparts white, variably streaked grey-brown. **Wings** Upperwing: much as second-winter except primaries and secondaries paler, coverts with some grey. **Tail** Variable; in some mostly black except for whitish base; in others white with broad, blackish tail band.

THIRD-SUMMER: Base of bill yellowish merging to black at tip, extreme tip white. Plumage much as third-winter except head and underparts white.

FOURTH-WINTER/ADULT WINTER: As breeding adult except nape and hindneck very faintly streaked grey-brown (appears white-headed). NOTE Backward types show dusky subterminal marks on bill and incomplete tail band.

ADULT BREEDING: Head White. **Body** Upperparts: saddle slate-grey, rump white. Underparts white. **Wings** Upperwing mostly slate-grey; outer 4–5 primaries blackish, decreasing in extent inwards to small blackish subterminal bar on 5th; outermost primary with one mirror, and all with broad apical spots uniting with white-tipped secondaries to form conspicuous white trailing edge. Underwing mostly white, primaries and secondaries dusky-grey (unlike Herring and California Gulls, p. 337, p. 341).

FHJ: The darkest-backed white-bellied gull of N American Pacific coast. Compared with Herring Gull (p. 337), averages larger, fiercer, more powerful with thicker-set jizz. Saddle and upperwing colour varies considerably: southern *wymani* very much darker, showing little contrast with black wingtips, but nominate usually paler, some not that much darker than Herring Gull. Almost exclusively marine, common on beaches, wharves etc. Call a deep 'kuk-kuk-kuk'.

DM: Pacific coast of North America. *L.o. occidentalis* breeds from British Columbia and Washington S along coasts of Oregon, and northern California; see Hoffman *et al.* (1978) for notes on interbreeding with Glaucous-winged Gulls; largest colony (32,000) Farallon Is (Sowls *et al.* 1980). *L.o. wymani* breeds lower and southern California. *L.o. livens* islands in Gulf of California. Egg-dates May–Jul. Winters mostly within breeding range.

SS: Adults differ from those of Herring and California Gulls (p. 337, p. 341) in darker saddle and upperwings, different wingtip pattern and dusky trailing edge to underwing; California Gull differs further in smaller size, dark eye and yellowish legs. Juveniles difficult to separate from those of Herring Gull; differ mainly in sheer bulk, heavier jizz and rather darker, sooty-grey cast to plumage without such defined barring on mantle. In flight inner primaries not usually so conspicuously pale as in Herring. In first-winter plumage saddle of present species more spotted, less barred; subsequent stages differ in greyness of saddle and upperwings, and underwing pattern. See also Slaty-backed Gull (p. 343).

219 KELP GULL
other: Dominican/Southern Black-backed Gull
Larus dominicanus

PLATE 56 Figs 219a-219c
MAP 219

Length 58cm (23in.). Wingspan 128–142cm (50–56in.). Iris straw-yellow, pupil blackish, orbital ring red. Bill yellow with red gonys-spot. Legs/feet greenish-yellow.

Southern hemisphere; range overlaps with Dolphin, Band-tailed and Pacific Gulls (p. 329, p. 333, p. 328). Sexes alike; slight seasonal variation. Juveniles separable from adults. Two subspecies; *L.d. vetula* (see Brooke & Cooper 1979) has a darker eye. Sometimes considered as a subspecies of Lesser Black-backed Gull (p. 340).

JUVENILE: Iris and bill blackish; legs pinkish-brown. **Head** Dull brown tipped white, palest on forehead; nape and ear-coverts darker. **Body** Upperparts: saddle dull brown with obscure buff edges and darker barring; rump and uppertail-coverts similar but barred white and brown. Underparts mottled brown and white, darkest on belly; undertail-coverts as rump. **Wings** Upperwing: primaries, their coverts, alula and secondaries dull black, latter tipped white; coverts much as saddle. Underwing dirty-white profusely streaked with brown; secondaries show white trailing edge. **Tail** Blackish-brown, narrowly tipped with buff.

FIRST-WINTER: As juvenile except head whiter with coarse brownish streaks; upperparts greyer, underparts whiter, particularly chin and throat. Wings and tail unmoulted, faded and worn.

FIRST-SUMMER: As first-winter except head whiter; saddle may show scattered slaty tips.

SECOND-WINTER: Iris brown. Legs greyish-brown. **Head** White with faint brown streaking. **Body** Upperparts: saddle brown, tips slaty. Underparts white with brownish streaks. **Wings** As first-winter but upperwing darker. **Tail** White at base.

SECOND-SUMMER: Resembles second-winter but saddle darker, underparts whiter. Bill and legs dull yellowish.

THIRD-WINTER: As non-breeding adult except: **Head** Faint brown streaks to crown, nape and sides of neck. **Body** Underparts: mostly white faintly tipped with brown. **Wings** Upperwing blackish-brown with irregular buff margins to coverts and white trailing edge. **Tail** White.

THIRD-SUMMER: As third-winter except head and underparts whiter.

FOURTH-WINTER/ADULT NON-BREEDING: As breeding adult but bare parts duller.

ADULT BREEDING: Head White. **Body** Upperparts: saddle blackish, rump white. Underparts white. **Wings** Upperwing mostly black, outermost primary with white mirror variable in extent; remaining primaries with white apical spots uniting with white-tipped secondaries to form noticeable trailing edge to wing. Underwing: outer primaries black with white mirror on outermost; inner primaries and most secondaries grey with white tips; remainder white.

FHJ: Generalistic coastal forager throughout most of range, but wanders far inland throughout New Zealand, and some parts of Patagonia. Voice a strident 'ki-och', often repeated rapidly.

DM: Circumpolar in southern hemisphere. *L.d. vetula* breeds coasts of southern Africa. *L.d. dominicanus* breeds southern South America from southern Brazil (23°S) and Peru (6°S) through Chile, Uruguay and Argentina S to Tierra del Fuego; also on South Shetlands, South Georgia and Antarctic Peninsula to about 65°S; at Prince Edward, Crozet, Kerguelen and Heard Is in Indian Ocean, and in Australasian region along coasts of New South Wales, Victoria, Tasmania and New Zealand.

SS: See Dolphin Gull (p. 329), Lesser Black-backed Gull (p. 340), Band-tailed Gull (p. 333) and Pacific Gull (p. 328).

220 SLATY-BACKED GULL
Larus schistisagus

PLATE 57 Figs 220a-220d
MAP 220

Length 61–68cm (24–27in.). Wingspan 132–137cm (52–54in.). Iris yellowish, orbital ring pink to red-purple. Bill yellow, gonys red. Legs/feet dark pink.

NE Asiatic species, wintering coasts of NE Asia S to China; range overlaps with Herring and Black-tailed Gulls (p. 337, p. 333). See also Western Gull (p. 342). Sexes alike; slight seasonal variation. Juvenile separable from adult. No subspecies.

JUVENILE: Iris and bill blackish. **Head** Mostly dull white densely streaked brownish-grey; chin whiter. **Body** Upperparts: mantle, scapulars and back mostly greyish-brown with darker centres edged pale grey; rump and uppertail-coverts whitish, barred brown. Underparts uniform dark greyish-brown, with rather abrupt change on lower belly and ventral area to whitish barred with brown. **Wings** Upperwing: primaries dark brown, innermost paler forming window (as in Herring Gull); alula, primary-coverts, secondary-coverts and secondaries dark brown, latter tipped greyish-white; remainder as saddle. Underwing mostly white with brownish streaks, heaviest on axillaries. **Tail** Brownish; base marbled with white, tip narrowly buff.

FIRST-WINTER: As juvenile except: **Head** Paler and

greyer. **Body** Upperparts much paler; grey feather edges rapidly fading to whitish. Underparts paler, more mottled grey-brown and white. **Wings and Tail** Unmoulted, faded through wear.

FIRST-SUMMER: Bill pink at base. Plumage as first-winter but bleached and faded: **Head** Mostly white, faintly streaked grey-brown. **Body** Upperparts: saddle pale greyish-white, streaked and spotted brown; rump white. Underparts white, spotted brown. **Wings and Tail** Further faded and worn.

SECOND-WINTER: Base of bill pink merging to black at tip, extreme tip white. **Head** White, streaked and spotted brown. **Body** Upperparts: saddle slate-grey mixed with brown and variably edged white; rump white. Underparts as first-summer. **Wings** Upperwing: pattern much as first-winter but primaries and secondaries blacker, latter with broad white tips; coverts as saddle. **Tail** Usually whiter at base and on outer feathers.

SECOND-SUMMER: Much as second-winter except: **Head** Mostly white. **Body** Upperparts clearer grey. Underparts whiter, less spotted and streaked. **Wings and Tail** Unmoulted, much faded, with more pronounced whitish edges to coverts, secondaries and tertials.

THIRD-WINTER: Bill pinkish-yellow with dusky subterminal band. Plumage much as non-breeding adult except: **Body** Upperparts: saddle browner in tone, less uniform grey, with scattered white tips. Underparts faintly streaked brown. **Wings** Upperwing: primary-coverts, alula and some secondary-coverts edged browner. **Tail** White, broad subterminal band.

THIRD-SUMMER: As third-winter except head whiter, saddle and wing-coverts clearer slate-grey.

FOURTH-WINTER / ADULT NON-BREEDING: As breeding adult except head lightly streaked grey-brown, heaviest on nape and hindneck.

ADULT BREEDING: Head White. **Body** Upperparts: saddle deep slate-grey; rump white. Underparts white. **Wings** Upperwing mostly deep slate-grey merging to blackish on outermost primaries, outer 2 of which have one white mirror; remaining primaries and all of secondaries broadly tipped white, forming conspicuous trailing edge. Underwing mostly white, primaries and secondaries greyer, edged white. **Tail** White.

FHJ: Resembles darkest race of Western Gull (*wymani*) but saddle and upperwings slightly darker; jizz heavier, more powerful, with proportionately larger head and bill. Overall appearance thus suggests diminutive Great Black-backed Gull (ranges do not normally overlap).

DM: Asiatic coasts of North Pacific and Bering Sea from Chukotskiy and Kamchatka Peninsulas S through Kurile Is and Sea of Okhotsk to Hokkaido, Japan. Returns to northern parts of range late Apr; egg-dates May/Jun; fledging and dispersal begins Aug. Winters from Kurile Is S to Honshu (southern Japan). Stragglers occur E to Aleutian and Pribilof Is, Alaskan mainland and (once) to British Columbia, mainly May–Aug; see Roberson (1980) for details.

SS: Adult has much darker saddle and upperwings than nominate Western Gull (p. 342), with proportionately larger bill and head; differs further in blackish tips to outer 4–5 primaries usually separated from dark, slate-grey upperwing by a narrow indistinct whitish band. Siberian Herring Gull *L.a. vagae* (p. 338) has paler saddle and upperwings, different wingtip pattern and lacks dusky trailing edge on underwing. First-calendar-year birds of present species usually appear more 'bleached out' on mantle, scapulars and back than corresponding *L.a. vagae*, with whitish fringes to upperwing-coverts and mainly dark tail; in subsequent plumages darker saddle and underwing pattern useful characters.

221 GREAT BLACK-BACKED GULL
other: Greater Black-backed Gull
Larus marinus

PLATE 59 Figs 221a-221d

MAP 221

Length 71–79cm (28–31in.). Wingspan 152–167cm (60–66in.). Iris pale yellow, pupil black, orbital ring red. Bill yellow, gonys-spot red. Legs/feet pale flesh.

N Atlantic. Largest black-backed gull of region; adults could be confused with Scandinavian race of Lesser Black-backed Gull *L.f. fuscus* (p. 340) but size, wing pattern and leg colour differ. Separation of juveniles and immatures from both Herring and Lesser Black-backed Gulls (p. 337, p. 340) requires care. Sexes alike; slight seasonal variation. Juveniles separable from adults. No subspecies. Great Black-backed × Herring Gull hybrids reported (Foxall 1979).

JUVENILE: Iris brown, bill black, legs dull flesh. **Head** White; indistinct grey-brown streaks. **Body** Upperparts: mantle, scapulars and back blackish-brown with wide and angular whitish edges forming chequered pattern; rump white, streaked darker. Underparts whitish; sides of breast, belly and undertail-coverts barred brown. **Wings** Upperwing: primaries and secondaries mostly blackish-brown except for paler window on inner primaries; coverts much as saddle. Underwing: outer 4 primaries blackish-brown, paling to greyish-white on innermost primaries and all secondaries; coverts tipped blackish-brown. **Tail** White at base with diffuse subterminal band.

FIRST-WINTER: As juvenile except head and underparts whiter, chequered pattern less defined.

FIRST-SUMMER: As first-winter except head and underparts whiter, saddle more uniformly dark.

SECOND-WINTER: Bill pale at base. **Head** As first-winter. **Body** Upperparts: mantle, scapulars and back dark grey with scattered brown and white bars; rump mostly white. **Wings** Upperwing: primaries and secondaries blackish-brown with greyer window on inner primaries; coverts mostly brownish except for greyer greater coverts. **Tail** White, broad blackish subterminal band.

SECOND-SUMMER: As second-winter except bill yellowish, distally black; head and underparts whiter, saddle more uniform blackish.

THIRD-WINTER: As non-breeding adult except saddle and upperwing browner with less white on wingtip; faint tail band.

THIRD-SUMMER: As third-winter except head and body white; saddle and upperwing wear browner; somewhat patchy.

FOURTH-WINTER/ADULT NON-BREEDING: Head White with dark eye-crescent and a few dark streaks on nape (looks white-headed at distance). **Body** Upperparts: saddle black, rump white. Underparts white. **Wings** Upperwing mostly blackish, with broad, white trailing edge and large mirrors on 1st and 2nd primaries combining to form diagnostic pattern. Underwing white; outer primaries black (except mirrors) merging into dusky-grey inner primaries and subterminal band along secondaries. **Tail** White.

ADULT BREEDING: As non-breeding adult except head white, saddle and upperwing browner in tone, white tips reduced through wear.

FHJ: Largest gull of region; at all ages pugnacious, predatory and domineering. Combination of overall size, bulk, heavy bill, fierce expression and barrel-chest imparts more menacing jizz than congeners. Flight heavy and powerful; slow, deep wingbeats; broad-based wings and sheer bulk impart distinctive appearance. Call a deep 'owk'.

DM: Breeds North America from Labrador and Quebec S along maritime provinces almost to New York; further E breeds Greenland, Iceland, Spitsbergen, Faeroes, also western Europe from Murmansk coast of USSR S along shores of Finland, Norway and Sweden to Baltic Sea, British Isles and NW France. Egg-dates Apr–Jun; fledging Jul–Sep. American population joined by those from Greenland, wintering from E Labrador S to Florida. In Europe some populations (i.e. British) mainly sedentary, but Russian and Scandinavian populations move S to Britain, France and Mediterranean Sea.

SS: Adults differ from Lesser Black-backed Gull (p. 340) in larger size, pinkish (not yellow) legs and diagnostic mirror pattern; in winter head much whiter than that of western *L.f. graellsii*. Juveniles differ from those of both Herring and Lesser Black-backed Gulls in whiter head and more contrasting chequered pattern on saddle; upperwing pattern recalls that of juvenile Herring Gull with narrower subterminal bar along trailing edge and pale window on inner primaries. In subsequent stages colour of saddle enables more ready separation of the three species. See also juvenile Great Black-headed Gull (p. 348).

---

222 GLAUCOUS-WINGED GULL
Larus glaucescens

PLATE 64 Figs 222a-222c
MAP 222

Length 61–68cm (24–27in.). Wingspan 132–137cm (52–54in.). Iris blackish, orbital ring dull red. Bill yellow, gonys red. Legs/feet pink.

North Pacific, in winter S to Kurile Is and California; range overlaps with several gull spp., see especially Glaucous and Thayer's (p. 346, p. 339). Sexes alike; seasonal variation. Juveniles separable from adults. No subspecies. Hybridises freely with Western Gull (p. 342) where ranges overlap in Washington and British Columbia; also with Herring Gull in parts of Alaska. Resulting hybrids show continuous gradation from one form to the other in primary feather pigmentation (see Patten 1976).

JUVENILE: Bill black. **Head** Mostly pinkish- or buffish-grey; lores and ear-coverts grey, hindneck and sides of neck streaked whiter. **Body** Upperparts: mantle, scapulars and back pinkish- to greyish-buff, mottled and tipped paler; rump and uppertail-coverts whiter, more distinctly barred. Underparts clouded buff-grey, undertail-coverts barred grey and white. **Wings** Upperwing: primaries and secondaries uniform pinkish- or buffish-grey with faintly darker subterminal tips and narrow pale fringes; coverts much as upperparts. Underwing pinkish-grey, streaked darker on coverts and axillaries. **Tail** Uniform pinkish-grey, base of outermost feathers faintly mottled.

FIRST-WINTER: As juvenile but generally paler, becoming bleached and worn; nape and upper breast whiter, saddle and wing-coverts edged white.

FIRST-SUMMER: Base of bill pinkish, tip dusky-black. Plumage as first-winter but further degraded, appearing generally silvery-grey or buff with heavier brownish mottling on coverts; primaries almost white. (Extremely variable.)

SECOND-WINTER: Head Whitish, streaked grey-brown heaviest on nape. **Body** Upperparts mostly pale grey; rump and uppertail-coverts indistinctly barred grey-brown. Underparts as first-winter but whiter on upper breast. **Wings** As first-winter but paler, coverts more finely barred, with more prominent white edging to secondaries and tertials. **Tail** Whiter at base and sides.

SECOND-SUMMER: As second-winter except: Black on bill reduced, tip pink or white. **Head** Whiter, less streaked. **Body** Underparts whiter. **Wings and Tail** Unmoulted, further faded.

THIRD-WINTER: Bill yellowish with dusky subterminal marks. **Head** White, heavily clouded or streaked particularly on nape. **Body** Upperparts pale grey; rump white. Underparts white; breast, and sometimes belly, clouded with grey. **Wings** Upperwing resembles adult but primaries faintly browner with smaller white apical spots (mirror often lacking on outer primary); inner secondaries perhaps faintly browner. **Tail** Mostly white, innermost feathers freckled greyish.

THIRD-SUMMER: As third-winter except bill brighter yellow, dusky subterminal marks reduced; head and underparts white.

FOURTH-WINTER/ADULT NON-BREEDING: As breeding adult except head as third-winter.

ADULT BREEDING: Head White. **Body** Upperparts pale grey; rump white. Underparts white. **Wings** Upperwing mostly pale grey; outer 4–5 primaries with slightly darker subterminal tips, outermost primary with white mirror, all with white apical spots increasing in extent inwards and uniting with white-tipped secondaries to form broad trailing edge. Underwing white. **Tail** White.

FHJ: Most abundant and widely distributed gull of NE Pacific; intermediate between Herring and Glaucous Gulls in appearance. Compared with Herring, jizz more powerful, fiercer, thicker-set; when perched wings project only 3–4cm giving rear end decidedly blunt appearance, enhancing robust, rather squat and chunky jizz. Flight direct and powerful with slow, measured wingbeats. Almost exclusively marine; opportunistic coastal scavenger, common about harbours and garbage dumps. Within their range the principle predators on eggs and chicks at most seabird colonies. Call usually 'kow-kow' or a screaming 'ka-ka-ako'.

DM: North Pacific, breeding coasts and islands of southern Bering Sea from Commander and Aleutian Is E through Gulf of Alaska to NW Washington. Egg-dates May–Jul; fledging and dispersal begins Aug. Winters from northern parts of breeding range, where one of commonest surface-feeders at the ice front, S to Baja California and northern Japan. Vagrant to Hawaii.

SS: Adults differ from both Western and Herring Gulls (p. 342, p. 337) in upperparts colour, grey wingtips and whitish undersides of primaries. Viewed from behind, when perched, primary tips can appear slate-grey suggesting Thayer's Gull (p. 339), a conclusion reinforced by pale underside of primaries. Present species however much bulkier, heavier, with wings projecting only a short distance past tail. Glaucous and Iceland Gulls (p. 346, p. 347) have silvery-white primaries. Immatures of present species separated from those of Glaucous Gull by bill colour and uniform brown tail. Separation from juvenile and first-winter Thayer's more difficult, but that species has more fragile jizz and chocolate-coloured primaries (Stallcup, pers. comm.).

---

223 GLAUCOUS GULL *Larus hyperboreus*

PLATE 62 Figs 223a-223d
MAP 223

Length 66–77cm (26–30in.). Wingspan 132–142cm (52–56in.). Iris pale lemon, pupil black, orbital ring yellow. Bill yellow, gonys-spot red. Legs/feet pinkish.

Circumpolar in northern hemisphere; range overlaps with smaller Iceland Gull (p. 347) in North Atlantic and with Glaucous-winged Gull (p. 345) in North Pacific. Sexes alike; seasonal variation. Juveniles separable from adults. No subspecies. Hybridises with several gull spp. throughout range; Ingolfsson (1970) records 50% of population hybridising with Herring Gulls (p. 337) in Iceland. There are also records of Glaucous × Lesser Black-backed, × Iceland, and × Great Black-backed Gulls.

JUVENILE: Iris brown. Bill pinkish, tip black. Legs/feet flesh-white. **Head** Mostly biscuit-white streaked grey-brown, more so on nape, ear-coverts and eye-crescent. **Body** Upperparts biscuit-white barred and clouded grey-brown, heaviest on rump. Underparts similar but normally darker; undertail-coverts distinctly barred. **Wings** Upperwing: primaries and secondaries mostly greyish-white fringed biscuit-white; remainder as upperparts but barring heavier on tertials. Underwing: coverts generally as underparts, primaries and secondaries often appearing translucent. **Tail** Biscuit-white, marbled grey-brown, with indistinct whitish, terminal band.

FIRST-WINTER: As juvenile except whiter on head, chin, throat and breast.

FIRST-SUMMER: Resembles first-winter but generally paler; bases and fringes of most primaries and secondaries wear to white, appearing silvery on closed wing.

SECOND-WINTER: Black on bill less distinct, with extreme tip white and base often yellowish. **Head** Mostly white; crown, nape and ear-coverts indistinctly streaked grey-brown. **Body** Upperparts buffish-white or creamy-white, indistinctly mottled grey-brown. Underparts mainly white; creamy-buff clouding on lower breast and belly, undertail-coverts variably barred grey-brown. **Wings** Upperwing: primaries mostly pale buff or whitish; remainder as back but quickly fades to whitish. **Tail** White, indistinctly mottled grey-brown. NOTE Although some popular field guides show second-year Glaucous and Iceland Gulls (p. 347) as mainly white, such individuals are very rare; most are generally pale fawn or buff-white.

SECOND-SUMMER: Bill pinkish-yellow, tip dusky. As second-winter except mantle and back mostly grey; wings and tail unmoulted, much faded.

THIRD-WINTER: Bare parts as adult but bill usually with blackish marks and lacking red on gonys. **Head** Mostly white with dense pinkish-grey streaking on nape and neck; eye-crescent dusky. **Body** Upperparts: saddle pale grey, rump white. Underparts mainly white; belly greyish-buff, undertail-coverts faintly barred. **Wings** Upperwing: as non-breeding adult but less uniform, with faint brownish mottling, heaviest on inner greater coverts and tertials. Underwing whitish. **Tail** Mostly white, with faint greyish marbling towards tip.

THIRD-SUMMER: Bare parts brighter. Head, neck and underparts whiter, otherwise as third-winter.

FOURTH-WINTER/ADULT WINTER: Head White with dense brownish streaks on crown, nape and neck. **Body** Upperparts: saddle pale grey, rump white. Underparts white. **Wings** Upperwing: primaries and secondaries broadly tipped with white, merging evenly into pale-grey upperwing; tertials tipped white. **Tail** White.

FOURTH-SUMMER/ADULT BREEDING: As non-breeding adult except bare parts brighter, head and neck white.

FHJ: Compared with smaller and more elegantly proportioned Iceland Gull (p. 347), present species has longer, heavy, often massive bill which, combined with flatter crown, imparts fiercer facial expression. General appearance of a large, thick-set gull with distinctive barrel-chested jizz and lumbering flight. Size usually between that of Herring and Great Black-backed Gulls. Aggressive, attacks smaller shorebirds, particularly if weak or injured; more marine in habits than most gulls. Call: usually silent, occasionally utters hoarse, deep Herring Gull-like scream.

DM: Circumpolar. Breeds mainly N of Arctic Circle from Alaska, USA, E across Arctic Canada to Greenland, Iceland, Spitsbergen; and in northern Europe from Murmansk, USSR, along shores and islands of USSR bordering Arctic Ocean to Wrangel I. and Bering Strait. Returns to 'colonies' May; egg-dates May–Jul. Dispersal begins mid Sep; occasionally forms flocks during migration. American population winters along Pacific coast from Aleutian Is S to California, and along Atlantic coast from Labrador and Greenland S to Florida, Bermuda and Cuba. In Europe S to Baltic, southern England and northern France, occasionally to Biscay, Spain and Portugal; vagrant Mediterranean Basin E to Egypt and Black Sea. Asiatic population winters S to China, Japan; vagrant Hawaii.

SS: White wingtips distinguish it from all other gulls except Iceland (p. 347) and very different Ivory Gull (p. 363). Glaucous-winged Gull (p. 345) has grey primaries with white mirrors. Very small females can occur and may be smaller than some male Herring Gulls. Size alone not, therefore, wholly reliable for separating it from similar but usually smaller Iceland Gull, from which differs in heavier, pot-bellied jizz, and wings projecting only a little past tail when perched; this varies according to moult but wings always proportionately shorter in appearance than in Iceland Gull, both when perched and in flight. Perhaps best distinction is heavier bill and fiercer facial expression of Glaucous, which has a bill length of at least half width of the head, whereas in Iceland Gull bill length is less than half width of head. Given reasonable views the two species are readily separable, typical Glaucous being somewhat larger and more powerful in jizz than Herring Gull, whereas Iceland is generally smaller with smaller bill and lacks barrel-chested aspect. Further problems are caused by albino or leucistic Herring Gulls, and still further by hybrids. Any one of the resulting anomalous plumages can suggest either Glaucous or Iceland Gull. Any wholly white bird is almost certainly an albino; hybrids show one or a combination of following characters: darker primaries, a secondary bar, blackish ear-coverts, indistinct tail band. Examples of both these anomalous plumages are illustrated on Plate 62. For fuller treatment see Grant (1981b, 1982).

---

224 ICELAND GULL (Includes Kumlien's Gull, 224X)

Larus glaucoides

PLATE 62 Figs 224a-224d

MAP 224

Length 58–64cm (23–25in.). Wingspan 125–130cm (49–51in.). Iris lemon-yellow, pupil dark, orbital ring red. Bill yellow, gonys red. Legs/feet pink.

Confined to North Atlantic, where range overlaps with similar but larger, more robust and heavier-billed Glaucous Gull (p. 346). See under latter for differences. Sexes alike; seasonal variation. Juveniles and all subsequent stages to adult plumage separable. Taxonomy complex; Kumlien's Gull is variously considered a subspecies of Iceland Gull, a hybrid population of Iceland × Thayer's Gull or even a separate species. It is separable in the field from Iceland Gull and described separately under 224X below. Hybrid Iceland × Glaucous and × Lesser Black-backed Gulls have been recorded (Gray 1958).

JUVENILE: Bill appears blackish but at close range base dull flesh or greyish. **Head** Mostly biscuit-white, indistinctly streaked grey-brown heaviest on nape, eye-crescent and ear-coverts. **Body** Upperparts biscuit-white finely barred and clouded grey-brown, more so on rump. Underparts similar, undertail-coverts noticeably barred. **Wings** Upperwing: primaries mainly greyish-white, outermost whitish with innermost subterminally tipped biscuit-white; secondaries biscuit-white, edged white; remainder as upperparts, tertials more distinctly barred. Underwing as underparts but primaries and outer secondaries often appear translucent. **Tail** Biscuit-white marbled grey-brown at base, with variable though obvious whitish terminal band.

FIRST-WINTER: Bill variable, usually pinkish-horn at base with darker tip. Plumage as juvenile except chin, throat and breast whiter, less streaked (varies individually).

FIRST-SUMMER: Resembles first-winter but paler.

SECOND-WINTER: Bill pinkish-grey, tip black (extreme tip often white). **Head** Mostly white; faint grey-brown streaks on crown, nape, neck and ear-coverts. **Body** Upperparts buffish or pinkish-white, finely mottled grey-brown heaviest on scapulars. Underparts mainly white; pinkish-buff clouding on lower breast and belly, undertail-coverts barred grey-brown. **Wings and Tail** As first-winter but paler, barring less distinct.

SECOND-SUMMER: As second-winter except saddle greyer; wings and tail unmoulted, much faded.

THIRD-WINTER: Bill yellowish-grey, tip dusky. **Head** Mostly white, streaked grey-brown on crown, nape, neck and ear-coverts. **Body** Upperparts: saddle pale grey; rump and uppertail-coverts white. Underparts mainly white, washed pinkish-brown on breast. **Wings** Creamy-fawn except for whitish outer primaries and grey median coverts. **Tail** White.

THIRD-SUMMER: As third-winter except head and sides of breast whiter; wings and tail unmoulted, much faded.

FOURTH-WINTER/ADULT NON-BREEDING: As breeding adult except head and neck streaked grey-brown.

ADULT BREEDING: Head White. **Body** Upperparts: saddle very pale silvery-grey; rump and uppertail-coverts white. Underparts white. **Wings** Mostly pale silvery-grey above; tertials, secondaries and primaries edged white, broadly so on outer primaries. **FHJ:** Usually smaller than similarly-plumaged Glaucous Gull (p. 346), with more elegant, less robust jizz and longer wings. Compared with that species, bill smaller, head shape more rounded, giving gentler facial expression. In flight much-quoted quicker wing action and more buoyant flight difficult to ascertain and dependent on prevailing conditions and stage of moult. At distance usually appears whiter (at all ages) than Glaucous Gull, latter in immature plumages appearing 'creamy' (Tucker, pers. comm.). Less predatory, more of a scavenger. Mostly silent outside breeding season; call resembles that of Herring Gull.

DM: Restricted to North Atlantic; breeds North America from Ellesmere I. and Greenland S to Baffin I., Canada; occasionally Iceland. Returns to breeding sites May; egg-dates May–Jul. Winters along North American coast from Newfoundland S to Virginia, occasionally Florida. Smaller numbers occur inland and on Great Lakes. In Europe winters Iceland to Faeroes, Norway and occasionally S to Sweden, Baltic, N France, N Belgium, N Netherlands and British Isles. Small but regular spring passage off SW Britain may indicate some regularly winter S to Bay of Biscay.

SS: See notes under Glaucous and Thayer's Gulls (p. 346, p. 339); also hybrids (Plate 62).

224X KUMLIEN'S GULL
Larus glaucoides kumlieni

PLATE 62 Fig. 224X
MAP 224

Plumage as for Iceland Gull (p. 347) except:

FIRST-WINTER: Primaries greyer, tail almost uniform pale grey.

SECOND-WINTER: As first-winter; outer primary may show indistinct white mirror, mantle pale grey.

THIRD-WINTER: As second-winter but some grey in upperwing-coverts.

ADULT: Differs from Iceland Gull (p. 347) in variable slate or brown outer web and subterminal bar on outer 5 primaries.

DM: Breeds southern Baffin I., Canada; winters eastern shores of Canada and in USA from New England S to Long Island.

SS: See notes under Thayer's and Iceland Gulls (p. 339, p. 347).

225 GREAT BLACK-HEADED GULL
Larus ichthyaetus

PLATE 70 Figs 225a-225e
MAP 225

Length 69cm (27in.). Wingspan not recorded. Iris dark brown, orbital ring red. Bill orange-yellow with broad, black subterminal band and red tip. Legs/feet greenish-yellow.

Asiatic; vagrant to W Europe. Breeding adult unmistakable; other stages most likely to be confused with Herring and Great Black-backed Gulls (p. 337, p. 344), although direct comparison of plumage and especially structural features ensures straightforward separation. Sexes alike; marked seasonal variation. Juveniles and all subsequent stages separable from adults. No subspecies.

JUVENILE: Bill blackish with grey base; thin white crescents above and below eye. Legs grey, brown or flesh. **Head** White; eye-crescent dusky, with variable brownish streaks behind eye. Nape and hindneck spotted brown. **Body** Upperparts warm sepia-brown strongly scaled with buff; rump whitish. Underparts mainly white; sides of breast mottled brown (from hindneck), often forming well-defined pectoral band and extending back to flanks. **Wings** Upperwing: outer primaries, their coverts, alula, carpal bar and secondaries brownish-black, with prominent pale midwing panel across all but inner greater and median coverts (an excellent flight character). Underwing white, tips of outer primaries and subterminal band along secondaries blackish; coverts tipped darker forming lines. **Tail** White, broad black subterminal band.

FIRST-WINTER: As juvenile except: Bill paler, sometimes with broad subterminal band. **Head** Mostly white; dusky eye patch usually extends diffusely over crown; nape and hindneck spotted brown, heaviest at junction with grey mantle. **Body** Upperarts: mostly clear grey, occasionally with brownish tips. Underparts white, sides of breast spotted brown (from hindneck). **Wings and Tail** Unmoulted, dark areas faded browner.

FIRST-SUMMER: Much as first-winter except for more extensive hood; wings and tail further faded; carpal bar reduced; midwing panel paler, often conspicuously white.

SECOND-WINTER: Bill yellowish with clear-cut black subterminal band; legs dusky yellowish-green. **Head** As first-winter. **Body** Upperparts mostly grey; rump white. Underparts white. **Wings** Upperwing mostly grey; outer webs and tips of outer primaries and their coverts blackish, decreasing in extent inwards to small subterminal marks on 7th or 9th primaries. Outer median and median primary-coverts spotted brown, sometimes with indistinct subterminal bar along secondaries. **Tail** White, subterminal band black.

SECOND-SUMMER: Much as second-winter except for imperfect blackish hood; tail band reduced.

THIRD-WINTER: As non-breeding adult except for blacker wingtips and faint tail band.

THIRD-SUMMER: As third-winter except for full black hood and white eye-crescents.

FOURTH-WINTER/ADULT NON-BREEDING: Head As first-winter. **Body** Upperparts: mantle and back grey, rather dark in tone; rump white. Underparts white. **Wings** Upperwing mainly grey (paler than mantle), with prominent white leading edge from carpal to primary tip broken by a subterminal black crescent across outer 6 primaries (at long range upperwing can appear to lack black, Harvey 1981); broad white trailing edge along secondaries. Underwing mostly white; subterminal black crescent across outer primaries; dusky edges to some inner coverts. **Tail** White.

ADULT BREEDING: As non-breeding adult except for full black hood and white crescents above and below eye; white primary tips reduced through wear.

FHJ: Between Herring and Great Black-backed Gulls (p. 337, p. 344) in size but jizz and structure distinctly different. Present species combines the bulk of the larger gulls with the narrow long-winged jizz of some of the smaller species. When perched head shape distinctive, characteristically showing long sloping forecrown which peaks well behind eye and accentuates length and heaviness of bill. Primaries project well past tail, giving rear end attenuated appearance; legs noticeably long. These structural features important at all ages. In flight appears deep-chested with longer, thinner, more bowed wings than other large gulls; steady purposeful flight.

DM: Breeds Black and Caspian Seas E to Aral Sea, Sea of Azov and freshwater lakes of SE USSR and central Asia E to Mongolia. Winter range extends from E Mediterranean, where rare (Meinertzhagen noted up to 50 together in Egypt but there are few recent records), S through Red Sea to Yemen and then E to W India, where relatively numerous; less so Bay of Bengal but further E in Sea of Japan reported as common Nakhodka harbour, USSR. Vagrants have occurred NW to Britain, W to Madeira and S to Kenya.

SS: Breeding adults unmistakable. Non-breeders may be overlooked as Herring Gulls (p. 337) when perched, but can be told by structural features (see above), especially bill proportions and colour, head pattern and, in flight, wingtip pattern. It is a common misconception that 'immatures' of present species most closely resemble those of Great Black-backed Gull. In reality confusion possible only with juveniles as by first-winter plumage (acquired Aug onwards) present species has more or less grey saddle. By comparison it is not until the second winter that Great Black-backed Gulls lose their brown saddle. Thus any large gull with brown mantle and back from Oct onwards is most unlikely to be present species. Juveniles certainly similar but close examination of individual feathers of Great Black-backed will reveal distinct chevron/chequerboard pattern on upperparts and covert feathers, whereas present species has more uniform brown feathers with distinct buffish fringes producing scaly pattern; rump and tail patterns and bill proportions also differ. From first winter onwards present species thus more likely to be confused with Herring Gull (p. 337).

226 LAUGHING GULL *Larus atricilla*

PLATE 64 Figs 226a-226c
MAP 226

Length 38–43cm (15–17in.). Wingspan 99–107cm (39–42in.). Iris black, orbital ring dull red. Bill, legs/feet dull red.

Eastern North America, wintering S to Peru and Brazil; range overlaps with several gull spp., see especially Franklin's (p. 352). Sexes alike; marked seasonal variation. Juveniles separable from adults. No subspecies. Albinism, complete and partial, recorded with anomalous bare parts colours (see Atherton & Atherton 1981); see also Weston (1934) for melanistic record.

JUVENILE: Bill/legs blackish. **Head** Brownish-white, darkest on lores, ear-coverts and hindcrown; forehead, throat and crescents above and below eye whitish. **Body** Upperparts mostly dull brown fringed paler, imparting scaly appearance; rump white. Underparts: upper breast and flanks greyish-brown; remainder white. **Wings** Upperwing: primaries, their coverts, and alula mostly dull blackish-brown; secondaries blackish, fringed and tipped white; remaining coverts similar to upperparts. Underwing whitish with smudgy blackish tip and subterminal trailing edge; coverts and axillaries tipped and streaked brown (thus much darker than in smaller Franklin's Gull, p. 352, appearing predominantly dark in field). **Tail** Whitish with complete blackish terminal band; fringe white.

FIRST-WINTER: As juvenile except: **Head** Partial, ill-defined, greyish-brown hood restricted mainly to ear-coverts, nape and hindneck; forehead, forecrown, chin and crescents dull white. **Body** Upperparts: saddle dark grey, perhaps a few brown tips and whitish fringes remaining. Underparts: breast band and flanks more mottled. **Wings and Tail** Unmoulted, faded through wear.

FIRST-SUMMER: Little change from first-winter, usually with less grey on head, nape and breast; wings and tail further faded.

SECOND-WINTER: Head Dull white with partial grey hood extending from ear-coverts to nape and hindneck (varies individually). **Body** Upperparts: saddle uniform dark grey, rump white. Underparts white except breast and flanks pale grey. **Wings** Upperwing: outer primaries and their coverts blackish, remainder mostly dark grey; secondaries and inner 5–6 primaries tipped white forming trailing edge. **Tail** White; partial broken band.

SECOND-SUMMER: Bill/legs dusky-red. As second-winter except: **Head** Partial blackish hood; white crescents. **Body** Underparts: breast and flanks whiter.

THIRD-WINTER / ADULT NON-BREEDING: Bill blackish-brown, tip often red; legs blackish-grey. Plumage as second-winter except: **Body** Underparts: grey confined to sides of breast. **Wings** Upperwing mostly dark grey; outer primaries black decreasing in extent inwards to small subterminal bar on 5th and 6th, all except outer 2 primaries with small white apical spots increasing in size inwards and uniting with white tips of secondaries to form trailing edge. Underwing mostly grey, tip smudgy-black; white trailing edge along secondaries and inner primaries. **Tail** White.

ADULT BREEDING: As non-breeding adult except: **Head** Smooth-black hood extending to hindneck and throat; thin white crescents above and below eye.

FHJ: Compared with smaller Franklin's Gull (p.

352) has distinctly flatter, longer crown and heavy (particularly at tip) drooping bill. In flight appears much larger due to longer, narrower wings, which taper to thin points. When perched wings project well beyond tail, accentuating attenuated jizz; thin legs longer than in Franklin's Gull, and in flight reach almost to tip of tail. Capable scavenger along tidelines and harbours, often competing with larger gulls. Call 'ha-ha-ha-ha'.
DM: Eastern North America, breeding from Nova Scotia, Maine and Massachusetts S through Caribbean and Gulf coasts to Venezuela. Returns to North American colonies Apr/May; egg-dates Apr–Jul; fledging begins Jul/Aug. Winters from southern parts of breeding range (N Carolina) S through Caribbean to NE Brazil; also Pacific coast of South America S to Peru and northern Chile. Vagrants have occurred W to Hawaii, N to Greenland and E to western Europe.
SS: See notes under Franklin's Gull (p. 352). At long range dark first-year birds, with powerful, jerky flight, can suggest Arctic Skua (p. 325).

---

227 INDIAN BLACK-HEADED GULL
other: Brown-headed Gull
Larus brunnicephalus

PLATE 68 Figs 227a-227c
MAP 227

Length 41–43cm (16–17in.). Wingspan not recorded. Iris pale yellow or grey, orbital ring red. Bill mostly bright red, tip dusky. Legs/feet bright vermilion.

Breeds central Asia, dispersing to coasts during winter; range overlaps with smaller Eurasian Black-headed Gull (p. 356) in some parts of Asia. Sexes alike; seasonal variation. Juveniles separable from adults. No subspecies.
JUVENILE: Head Mostly white; crown, nape and ear-coverts clouded brownish-grey. **Body** Upperparts: mostly greyish-brown with paler brown edgings; rump white. Underparts white. **Wings** Upperwing resembles adult's but all primaries and secondaries tipped blackish-brown, forming wide, dark subterminal trailing edge; brownish carpal and diagonal bar across median coverts. **Tail** White, brownish subterminal band.
FIRST-WINTER: As juvenile except head whiter, saddle mostly clear grey. Wings and tail unmoulted, faded through wear.
FIRST-SUMMER: As first-winter except bare parts redder; partial brown hood. Wings and tail further faded.
SECOND-WINTER/ADULT NON-BREEDING: Head As first-winter. **Body** Upperparts: saddle pale grey; rump white. Underparts white. **Wings** Upperwing: outer 2 primaries mostly black with prominent white mirror; remaining primaries white at base, becoming greyer inwards, except for black tips and narrow margins along edge of inner webs decreasing in extent inwards (produces wingtip pattern recalling more widespread Grey-headed Gull, p. 351); remainder of upperwing mostly grey with paler secondaries and whitish marginal coverts. Underwing mostly grey, outer primaries as upperwing. **Tail** White.
ADULT BREEDING: As non-breeding adult except for brown hood.
FHJ: Recalls more widespread Grey-headed Gull (p. 350). Larger and somewhat heavier in appearance than Eurasian Black-headed Gull (p. 356), which often winters alongside present species in some parts of Asia.
DM: Breeds lakes, marshes etc. of central Asia, including Turkestan, Tibet, northern India and southern Mongolia. Returns to colonies May; egg-dates May–Jul; fledging and departure Aug/Sep. Disperses S to coasts and harbours of southern Asia from Persian Gulf E to coasts of India, Burma and Thailand, where can often be seen in harbours etc.; extent of dispersal E of Hong Kong not known.
SS: Separated from Eurasian Black-headed Gull (p. 356) at all ages by larger size, more robust bill and distinctive wingtip pattern. Much smaller Chinese Black-headed Gull (p. 358) has upperwing pattern recalling Bonaparte's Gull (p. 357), and diagnostic underwing pattern.

---

228 GREY-HEADED GULL
Larus cirrocephalus

PLATE 65 Figs 228a-228e
MAP 228

Length 41–43cm (16–17in.). Wingspan averages 102cm (40in.). Iris white, pupil dark, orbital ring red. Bill, legs/feet crimson.

Confined to Africa and South America, where range overlaps with Hartlaub's, Andean and Brown-hooded Gulls (p. 352, p. 351, p. 355). Sexes alike; slight seasonal variation. Juveniles separable from adults. Two subspecies listed; *L.c. cirrocephalus* breeding South America averages larger than *L.c. poiocephalus* with larger mirrors, paler grey saddle and upperwings. Grey-headed × Hartlaub's Gull hybrids have occurred.
JUVENILE: Iris brown; bill yellowish or pink, tip dark. **Head** Whitish, with partial hood separated from mantle by white hindcollar. **Body** Upperparts: saddle brown fringed paler; rump pale grey. Underparts white; sides of breast brownish-grey (from mantle). **Wings** Upperwing: outer 2–3 primaries mostly blackish-brown, innermost greyer with blackish tips and white bases uniting with primary-coverts to form white patch in middle of outer wing; dusky secondaries join with inner primaries, forming dark trailing edge. Greater coverts grey, tipped brown, contrasting slightly with browner median coverts. Underwing mostly grey, with blackish outer primaries. **Tail** White; narrow black subterminal band.
FIRST-WINTER: As juvenile except head white with greyish-brown mottling over crown and dusky ear spot; saddle mostly clear grey. Wings and tail unmoulted, faded through wear.

FIRST-SUMMER: As first-winter except for partial grey hood, concentrated posteriorly; wings and tail further faded.
SECOND-WINTER: As adult non-breeding except bare parts duller; outer primaries blacker, mirrors smaller, with dusky secondaries forming indistinct trailing edge to wing.
SECOND-SUMMER: As second-winter except for partial or full grey hood.
THIRD-WINTER/ADULT NON-BREEDING: As breeding adult but hood paler, darker ear-coverts sometimes visible.
ADULT BREEDING: Head Pale grey hood; whitish on forehead and chin, darker at posterior margin. **Body** Upperparts: saddle grey; rump white. Underparts white, occasionally flushed pink. **Wings** Upperwing: outer primaries mostly black decreasing in extent inwards; outer 2 with white mirrors. Bases of innermost primaries, their coverts, and alula white, forming prominent white leading edge to outer wing; remainder grey. Underwing mostly dusky, primaries blackish with white mirrors. **Tail** White.
FHJ: Compared with Eurasian Black-headed Gull (p. 356), present species larger, with darker saddle and upperwings and grey, not brown, hood. In flight wings noticeably broader and held flatter and straighter, with more gliding, less flapping. When perched bill longer and heavier, with sloping forehead, upright posture and longer legs. More inland than coastal, frequenting freshwater lakes and wetlands though often coastal too, especially in South America. Call a long drawn-out 'caw-caw', rather crow-like.
DM: Two races geographically isolated. *L.c. cirrocephalus* breeds Brazil, Argentina, Uruguay, Paraguay and Bolivia. Status in western South America not precisely known: has yet to be found breeding there but commonest gull of the Guayas River (Ecuador), whilst further south R Hughes (pers. comm.) regards it as regular visitor in small numbers to Mollendo, Peru, mainly May–Nov (breeding suspected for first time in Jun/Jul 1969 at lagoon near Mejia, Peru). In Africa *L.c. poiocephalus* has fragmented distribution from Gambia and Abyssinia S to South Africa, including Rift Valley lakes where some colonies are numbered in thousands (Britton 1980).
SS: See notes under Silver Gull (p. 352). Andean and Brown-hooded Gulls (p. 351, p. 355) occur within South American range but both have distinctive upperwing patterns and brown, not grey, hoods (breeding adults only). See also Eurasian Black-headed, Franklin's and Bonaparte's Gulls (p. 356, p. 352, p. 357).

229 ANDEAN GULL
other: Mountain Gull
Larus serranus

PLATE 66 Figs 229a-229d

MAP 229

Length 48cm (19in.). Wingspan not recorded. Iris brown. Bill, legs/feet dark red.

Breeds in high Andes, some dispersing to coasts of western South America, where Laughing, Grey-headed and Franklin's Gulls also occur (p. 349, p. 350, p. 352). Sexes alike; seasonal variation. Juveniles separable from adults. No subspecies.
JUVENILE: Iris brown, bare parts blackish. **Head** Mostly greyish-brown; forehead, lores and nape paler, ear spot brown. **Body** Upperparts: saddle ash-brown fringed whitish; rump grey, uppertail-coverts white. Underparts white, sides of breast brownish. **Wings** Upperwing pattern resembles adult's but outer webs of alula, outer primary-coverts, most primaries and their tips black; secondaries dusky, uniting with inner primaries to form trailing edge; lesser coverts grey; remainder as saddle. **Tail** White, black subterminal band.
FIRST-WINTER: As juvenile except head white with dark ear spot; saddle and upperwing-coverts mostly grey; wings and tail unmoulted, faded through wear.
FIRST-SUMMER: As first-winter but with partial hood.
SECOND-WINTER/ADULT NON-BREEDING: As breeding adult except head white, eye-crescent and ear spot dusky-grey; underparts occasionally rosy.
ADULT BREEDING: Head Dark brown hood; crescents, nape and hindneck white. **Body** Upperparts: saddle mostly grey, rump white. Underparts white, occasionally with rosy cast. **Wings** Upperwing: secondaries and coverts mostly grey, with conspicuous white forewing broken by black subterminal crescent across primaries. Underwing pale grey except for dusky primaries, outer 3 of which have elongated white mirror forming distinctive oval patch. **Tail** White.
FHJ: Rather large, stocky hooded gull frequenting inland river courses and lakes in Andes. Habits little known. Call a hoarse 'aagh-aagh-kee-aagh'.
DM: Breeds mountain lakes in high Andes from Ecuador through Peru to Bolivia and Chile, S to NW Argentina. Egg-dates Nov–Jan. Although many remain in Andes throughout winter, some visit coasts of western South America from Ecuador S to Valparaiso, Chile; non-breeders occasionally remain throughout year.
SS: Laughing and Franklin's Gulls (p. 349, p. 352) frequent same coasts during austral summer but differ in size and wing patterns. In winter plumage confusion also possible with Grey-headed Gull (p. 350), which is smaller and lacks ear spot, three elongated mirrors on upperwing and white oval patch on outer primaries of underwing. Brown-hooded Gull (p. 355) smaller with different wing pattern.

230 FRANKLIN'S GULL

Larus pipixcan

PLATE 64 Figs 230a-230c
MAP 230

Length 33–38cm (13–15in.). Wingspan 86–94cm (34–37in.). Iris blackish, orbital ring red. Bill red, thin subterminal blackish band. Legs/feet red.

North American inland species, migrating S to winter on coasts of western South America; range overlaps with several gull spp., see especially Laughing Gull (p. 349). Sexes alike; seasonal variation. Juveniles separable from adults. No subspecies. NOTE Unusual in that it appears to have a complete moult in both spring and autumn (see Grant 1979, 1982).

JUVENILE: Bill and legs blackish. **Head** Partial dark brown hood; forehead, chin and crescents white. **Body** Upperparts: saddle brownish fringed grey, giving scaly pattern; rump white. Underparts whitish. **Wings** Upperwing: outer primaries and their coverts black, decreasing in extent inwards to subterminal band on 6th or 7th, innermost greyer; secondaries dark grey-brown with darker centres and white tips which, with tips of inner primaries, form white trailing edge; remaining coverts brownish-grey with paler fringes. Underwing mainly greyish-white, tip smudgy-black. **Tail** Centre pale grey with black subterminal band, widest in centre; base, outer feathers and extreme tip white.

FIRST-WINTER: Bill and legs dull blackish-red. Much as juvenile except: **Head** Partial blackish-brown hood extending well below eye-level to ear-coverts; prominent white crescents. **Body** Upperparts: saddle uniform dark grey. **Wings** Upperwing: white fringes reduced or lacking, dark areas faded browner.

FIRST-SUMMER: Bill red at base. **Head** Incomplete blackish hood; forehead, chin and crescents white. **Body** Upperparts: saddle dark grey, rump white. Underparts white. **Wings** Upperwing mostly dark grey with broad white trailing edge, outer 5–6 primaries and their coverts blackish, decreasing in extent inwards, primaries with white tips; inner secondaries faintly dusky. **Tail** Outer feathers white, centre pale grey; faint partial tail band.

SECOND-WINTER: Bill and legs dusky-red. Plumage as first-summer except: **Head** Partial hood as first-winter, perhaps blacker. **Wings** Upperwing: black on primaries less extensive with small white mirror on outermost; inner secondaries lack dusky tips.

SECOND-SUMMER/ADULT BREEDING: Head Sooty-black hood extending to hindneck and throat; white crescents. **Body** As first-summer; breast sometimes faintly pink. **Wings** Upperwing as second-winter, except black on outer primaries usually reduced and divided from grey-coloured remainder by subterminal white band across primaries; white primary tips larger. Underwing greyish with black tip divided from remainder by whitish band. **Tail** Outer feathers white, centre pale grey.

ADULT NON-BREEDING: Much as adult breeding except: **Head** Partial blackish hood.

FHJ: Inland prairie gull, small and graceful; follows plough, hawks for insects, scavenges. Noticeably smaller than Laughing Gull (p. 349), which has different head shape and bill proportions. Present species has proportionately shorter, more rounded wingtips, which, with short neck and tail, impart much more compact appearance in flight; when perched has rather squat, hunched jizz with horizontal posture and short legs; head rounded with rather short, stoutish bill. These structural differences enable separation from Laughing Gull at any age. Flight light and buoyant, recalling smaller Little Gull, dipping down to surface, legs trailing, picking at small organisms or snatching at offal. Gregarious throughout year, often migrates in flocks of many thousands. Call a soft 'krruk' at colonies; mostly non-vocal outside breeding.

DM: Prairie sloughs from southern Canada S to southern Dakota and SW Minnesota; numbers decreasing. Returns to colonies Apr; egg-dates May/Jun; fledging and dispersal begins early Aug with impressive movements across southern Great Plains to reach western coasts of America, and then S to Peru from late Aug. Main numbers arrive Oct, replacing Grey as commonest shoreline gull (Hughes, pers. comm.). Winter range extends S to Strait of Magellan, Chile. Vagrants have occurred W to Hawaii, and E to western Europe, Tristan da Cunha and South Africa.

SS: See notes above on structural differences, which allow any age to be separated from Laughing Gull (p. 349). First-winter birds of present species differ further in more clear-cut partial hood, whiter underparts and less extensive secondary bar and tail band. Second-calendar-year birds more difficult to separate by plumage features, but blacker, more defined partial hood, whiter crescents and larger white apical spots on primaries are useful characters. Adults separated by wingtip pattern. See also slightly larger, much paler (above) Eurasian Black-headed Gull (p. 356).

231 SILVER GULL
other: Red-billed Gull (includes Hartlaub's Gull, 231X)

Larus novaehollandiae

PLATE 65 Figs 231a-231c, 231X
MAP 231

Length 38–43cm (15–17in.). Wingspan 91–96cm (36–38in.). Iris white, pupil dark, orbital ring red. Bill, legs/feet dull red to crimson.

Subspecies occur in South Africa, Australia and New Zealand; range overlaps with Grey-headed and Black-billed Gulls (p. 351, p. 355). Sexes alike; slight seasonal variation. Juveniles separable from adults. Four subspecies listed, some differing only in proportion of bill, size and number of mirrors; *L.n. hartlaubi* breeding South Africa averages smaller with dark iris, more slender bill, two

white mirrors and, when breeding, pale lavender-grey cast to head concentrated round neck and nape in thin necklace (further research will almost certainly show this form to be a separate species). Hartlaub's × Grey-headed and Silver × Black-billed hybrids recorded.
JUVENILE: Iris brown, bill dark horn to black; legs brownish-red. **Head** Mainly white; eye-crescent dusky, nape greyish-brown (abrades to white). **Body** Upperparts: saddle brown, feathers subterminally darker brown with buff or white fringes; rump whitish. Underparts white. **Wings** Upperwing: primary pattern resembles adult's but all primaries tipped black, most with white apical spots (some subspecies also have two white mirrors). Secondaries grey with dusky subterminal trailing edge; median and lesser coverts as saddle; alula and primary-coverts edged brown. **Tail** White, narrow black subterminal band.
FIRST-WINTER: As juvenile except saddle mostly clear grey; wings and tail unmoulted, faded through wear.
FIRST-SUMMER: As first-winter except saddle clear grey; wings and tail further faded.
SECOND-WINTER/ADULT NON-BREEDING: Bare parts blackish in some subspecies. **Head** White. **Body** Upperparts: saddle pale grey, rump white. Underparts white. **Wings** Upperwing: outer 3–4 primaries mostly black decreasing in extent inwards to black subterminal marks on 7th or 8th primary; two or three white mirrors, dependent on subspecies; remainder pale grey except for distinctive white leading edge to outer wing. Underwing mostly dusky-grey with two or three white mirrors. **Tail** White.
ADULT BREEDING: As non-breeding adult; bare parts in some subspecies brighter.
FHJ: Opportunist scavenger, mainly coastal but occasionally far inland on rivers and dams in Australasian region. Call notes 'kwarr' and 'kek-kek-kek'.
DM: Southern hemisphere. *L.n. forsteri* breeds New Caledonia and N Australia; *L.n. novaehollandiae* S Australia and Tasmania; *L.n. scopulinus* New Zealand; *L.n. hartlaubii* South Africa from Walvis Bay S to Cape Infanta. Egg-dates vary between populations: Apr–Dec. All populations disperse after breeding (see Serventy *et al.* 1971).
SS: See notes in this section under Black-billed Gull if birding in New Zealand. Range of Hartlaub's overlaps considerably with Grey-headed on the Cape and Namibian coasts, South Africa, forming huge, mixed colonies at Walvis and Swakopmund where interbreeding fairly regular (Sinclair, pers. comm.).

---

232 MEDITERRANEAN GULL

Larus melanocephalus

PLATE 69 Figs 232a-232d
see also Fig. 22, p. 353
MAP 232

Length 38–43cm (15–17in.). Wingspan 91cm (36in.). Iris brown, orbital ring red. Bill scarlet, sometimes with dusky subterminal band and yellow tip. Legs/feet scarlet.

Confined to Europe, where range overlaps with many gull spp., see especially Black-headed and Common Gulls (p. 356, p. 336). Sexes alike; seasonal variation. Juveniles separable from adults. No subspecies. Taverner (1970) and others record Mediterranean × Black-headed hybrids.
JUVENILE: Bill/legs blackish. **Head** Mostly white, partial hood separated from brown hindneck by thin white collar. **Body** Upperparts: mantle, scapulars and back rich brown with whitish edges; rump white. Underparts mostly white; buff or greyish band across breast extending to flanks. **Wings** Upperwing: outer 5 primaries and their coverts blackish, inner primaries grey with black subterminal marks; secondaries black tipped white, forming noticeable trailing edge. Greater coverts mostly pale grey, forming midwing panel contrasting with rich brown carpal, median and lesser coverts. **Tail** White; broad black subterminal band.
FIRST-WINTER: As juvenile except: **Head** White; blackish eye-crescent and ear-coverts impart distinct face patch normally extending diffusely over crown. **Body** Upperparts: mantle, scapulars and back very pale grey. **Wings and Tail** Unmoulted, carpal faded browner, but outer primaries remaining conspicuously black.
FIRST-SUMMER: As first-winter except bare parts often as or near adult coloration. Partial black hood; wings and tail somewhat faded.
SECOND-WINTER: As non-breeding adult except bare parts dull reddish-black; outer 3–6 primaries with black subterminal marks.
SECOND-SUMMER: As second-winter except bare parts as or near adult coloration; imperfect black hood.
THIRD-WINTER/ADULT NON-BREEDING: As breeding adult except bare parts dull blackish-red to orange; head as first-winter.

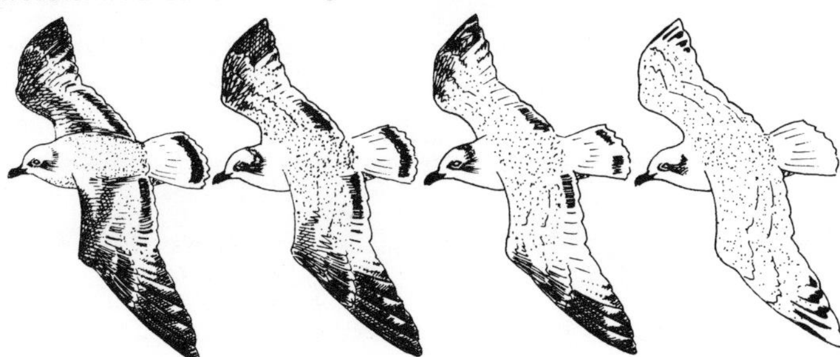

Fig. 22. Mediterranean Gull

ADULT BREEDING: Head Jet-black hood extending to nape and throat; white crescents. **Body** Upperparts very pale grey shading to white on rump. Underparts pure white. **Wings** Upperwing very pale grey shading to pure white on primaries and along secondaries; outermost primary shows variable black line along outer web. **Tail** White.

FHJ: Compared with Black-headed Gull (p. 356), flight heavier and more powerful due to thickset body, bull-necked jizz, broader less angled wings with rounded tips, and robust, drooping bill. When perched crown shape and heavy bill impart fierce facial expression; aggressive, often approaching similarly-sized gulls in 'hunched aggressive' posture and strutting gait, pecking or lurching to establish authority. Call as Black-headed Gull but deeper, more rasping.

DM: Breeds mainly on islands in Black and Aegean Seas N to Crimea and Dobruja, Romania; also Greece. Has bred sporadically England, West Germany, Austria, Holland, Belgium and France. Egg-dates May/Jun. Principal wintering grounds in Mediterranean, centred in Tyrrhenian Sea, coasts of Sicily, Adriatic and northern coast of Tunisia and Libya, where peak daily figures for Tripoli harbour 250, Sep–Apr (Bundy 1950). Winter range extends S to Mauritania and N to British Isles, where now regular in small numbers. Occurs elsewhere in Europe as irregular visitor or vagrant.

SS: First-calendar-year birds most likely to be confused with corresponding Common Gulls (p. 336), especially at long range when differences in bare parts colours and structure harder to judge. Present species differs further in dusky sides of face, more contrasting upperwing pattern and narrower tail band. Subsequent stages more likely to be confused with Black-headed Gull (p. 356) but present species at all ages larger, more robust, with longer, slightly drooping bill; plumage differs in wing pattern, and colour and extent of hood.

233 RELICT GULL
other: Mongolian Gull
Larus relictus

PLATE 68 Fig. 233

MAP 233

Length and wingspan not known. See Kitson (1980) for other measurements, which are larger in all respects than Mediterranean Gull (p. 353). Iris blackish, orbital ring red. Bill, legs/feet dark blood-red.

Recently rediscovered breeding central Asia; range overlaps with Eurasian, Indian and Great Black-headed Gulls (p. 356, p. 350, p. 348). Sexes alike; seasonal variation. Juveniles separable from adults, immature stages not yet known. No subspecies. The following descriptions and notes are based largely on the review by Kitson (1980) and photographs, notes and sketches supplied by SC Madge (pers. comm.).

JUVENILE (from Auezov 1971): **Head** White; nape reddish-brown. **Body** Upperparts: saddle reddish-brown fringed white; rump white. Underparts white. **Wings** Upperwing: outer webs and tips of outer primaries mostly black decreasing in extent inwards to small subterminal tips on 5th and 6th primaries; coverts as saddle. **Tail** White, all except outer two feathers subterminally tipped blackish-brown.

ADULT NON-BREEDING: Not described; presumably as for breeding adult but head probably white with dusky ear spot and perhaps a dusky wash over crown and nape (see Fig. 23 below).

ADULT BREEDING: Head Blackish-brown hood extending to hindcrown and throat; nape white. **Body** Upperparts: saddle pearl-grey, rump white. Underparts white. **Wings** Upperwing mostly pearl-grey shading to white on secondaries and primaries, latter with subterminal black crescent, decreasing in extent from outer primary to small subterminal band on 5th or 6th primary. Underwing mostly white; outer primaries as upperwing. **Tail** White.

FHJ: Superficially recalls miniature Great Black-headed Gull (p. 348). Compared with Mediterranean Gull (p. 353), present species larger with longer wings, tail and legs; bill slightly longer and deeper. Madge (pers. comm.) reports that when perched appears 'chunky, with fat, hunched, leggy look whilst feeding'. Call a laughing 'ka-ka, ka-ka, kee-aa' (Kitson 1980).

DM: Species fully recognised only after Auezov (1970) discovered nesting colony on Lake Alakul, Kazakhstan, USSR. Nine breeding sites since discovered in central, eastern and southeastern Asia (see Kitson 1980). Returns to colonies Apr/May; egg-dates May/Jun; fledging Aug, movements/winter quarters still unknown. A single specimen taken late Sep 1971 at Lake Bai-ti-long, N Vietnam, supports Kitson's (1980) tentative suggestion that wintering quarters probably lie between T'ien-ching and Vietnam in East and South China Seas.

SS: Distinguished from Chinese and Indian Black-headed Gulls (p. 358, p. 350) by its greater size, upperwing pattern and lack of black on underwing (excepting wingtip). In many respects adult Relict Gull recalls second-summer Mediterranean Gull (p. 353) but their known ranges lie some 5,000km apart.

Fig. 23. RELICT GULL (top two figures on left based on slides supplied by SC Madge)

234 BLACK-BILLED GULL
other: Buller's Gull
Larus bulleri

PLATE 65 Figs 234a-234c

MAP 234

Length 35–38cm (14–15in.). Wingspan not recorded. Iris white, pupil dark, orbital ring red. Bill black, reddish at base. Legs/feet black or brownish-red.

Restricted to New Zealand, where range overlaps with Silver (Red-billed) Gull (p. 352). No seasonal variation. Juveniles separable from adults. No subspecies. Black-billed × Silver Gull hybrids have been recorded.

JUVENILE: Iris brown; bill pinkish or orange with dark tip; legs/feet flesh-pink. **Head** Mainly white; grey-brown mottling over crown, ear-coverts and nape. **Body** Upperparts: saddle grey with brown subterminal spots and paler grey edges; rump pale grey shading to white on uppertail-coverts. Underparts white. **Wings** Upperwing as adult's but blackish shaft-streaks on outer primaries, dusky trailing edge along secondaries and brownish edges or tips to all coverts and alula. **Tail** White; indistinct brownish smudge on central feathers.

FIRST-WINTER: As juvenile but head whiter; saddle mostly clear grey; wings unmoulted, faded through wear.

FIRST-SUMMER: As first-winter but brown tips reduced through wear.

SECOND-WINTER/ADULT NON-BREEDING: As breeding adult, some with faint grey wash over crown and breast.

ADULT BREEDING: Head White. **Body** Upperparts: saddle pale silvery-grey; rump and uppertail-coverts white. Underparts white, some with rosy tinge. **Wings** Upperwing: outer primaries and their coverts white with black subterminal tips to most primaries; remainder grey (wing pattern thus recalls Eurasian Black-headed Gull, p. 356). Underwing: coverts pale grey, primaries blackish with two or three mirrors. **Tail** White.

FHJ: An inland gull superficially resembling more widespread Silver Gull (p. 352) but with thinner blackish bill and distinctive white leading edge to wing. Frequents larger lakes and rivers; often attends plough. Call as Silver Gull but higher-pitched.

DM: Confined to New Zealand, chiefly to South I., with smaller colonies North I.; usually nests along inland rivers and lakes but also within Silver Gull colonies at mouths of larger rivers. Egg-dates Dec/Jan. After breeding disperses to coasts and larger estuaries of both islands.

SS: Adult wing pattern distinctive, but immatures often confused with corresponding Silver Gulls (p. 352) due to their pink or reddish bills with black tips. Situation further complicated due to immature Silver Gulls having a blackish bill. Separation, however, straightforward if differences in head and wing patterns looked for.

235 BROWN-HOODED GULL
other: Patagonian Black-headed Gull
Larus maculipennis

PLATE 68 Figs 235a-235c

MAP 235

Length 36–38cm (14–15in.). Wingspan not recorded. Iris brown, orbital ring dull red. Bill, legs/feet dark crimson.

Confined to coasts of southern South America, where range overlaps with Andean and Grey-headed Gulls (p. 351, p. 350). All stages readily separable from those species by wingtip pattern. Sexes alike; seasonal variation. Juveniles separable from adults. No subspecies.

JUVENILE: Bill orange-red, tip blackish; legs/feet yellowish-brown. **Head** Mostly white; crown, nape and ear-coverts pale brownish-grey. **Body** Upperparts: saddle mainly drab greyish-brown, edges buff and brown; rump whitish. Underparts mostly white; sides of breast (occasionally all of breast) washed with grey-brown but this soon fades to white. **Wings** Upperwing: outer 2 primaries blackish except for small white mirror; remainder with greyish-white outer webs and black inner webs decreasing in extent inwards to small black subterminal bands and white apical spots. Primary-coverts and alula white, often edged grey; secondaries dull brownish-black with broad grey margins and tips, tertials similar but edged brown. Coverts mostly grey with brownish edges. **Tail** White; narrow black subterminal band.

FIRST-WINTER: As juvenile except head whiter, ear spot more pronounced; upperparts mostly clear grey, underparts white. Wings and tail unmoulted, faded through wear.

FIRST-SUMMER: As first-winter except bare parts redder; partial brown hood; wings further faded. Some or all tail feathers replaced to give wholly white tail (the only gull regularly moulting tail feathers at pre-nuptial moult, Dwight 1925).

Fig. 24. Upperwing variation of adult *L. maculipennis*

SECOND-WINTER/ADULT NON-BREEDING: Head Much as first-winter. **Body** Upperparts: saddle mostly pale grey, rump white. **Wings** Upperwing: mostly grey, with white leading edge to outer wing extending back to include 5th or 6th primaries (see Fig. 24 above for variation in markings on these outer primaries). Underwing: coverts pale grey, remainder whitish with variably marked primaries as upperwing. **Tail** White.

ADULT BREEDING: As non-breeding adult except for chocolate-brown hood.

FHJ: Size, jizz and call resemble Eurasian Black-headed Gull (p. 356).
DM: Confined to South America, breeding on coasts and inland pampas from Tierra del Fuego N to about 33°S in Uruguay on Atlantic Coast and to Valdivia, Chile, 40°S on Pacific coast; also Falkland Is. Returns to colonies Nov/Dec; egg-dates Dec/Jan. During winter months disperses N to about 10°S in Brazil and to about 18°S in Chile. Unconfirmed records of vagrants N to Peru.
SS: Range overlaps with Grey-headed Gull (p. 351). Adults separable by head and wingtip pattern. Most confusion arises between juvenile/first-winter birds. Present species differs in darker head markings and white mirror on outer 2 primaries. In all subsequent stages wingtip of present species shows progressively more white.

236 BLACK-HEADED GULL
Larus ridibundus

PLATE 63 Figs 236a-236d
MAP 236

Length 38–43cm (15–17in.). Wingspan 91–94cm (36–37in.). Iris brown, orbital ring red. Bill, legs/feet dark red.

Eurasian, a few have recently bred NE North America; winters S to Africa and southern Asia. Range overlaps with Little, Slender-billed, Mediterranean, Indian Black-headed and (rarely) Bonaparte's Gulls (p. 357, p. 356, p. 353, p. 350, p. 357). Sexes alike; seasonal variation. Juveniles separable from adults. No subspecies. See Mediterranean Gull (p. 353) for notes on hybrids.
JUVENILE: Bill/legs dull orange-flesh, former tipped black. **Head** White with partial ginger-buff hood. **Body** Upperparts: saddle ginger-brown fringed buff-white, imparting scaly appearance; rump whitish. Underparts white; ginger-brown wash on sides of breast. **Wings** Upperwing: outer webs of outer 3–4 primaries black, inner webs white; remaining primaries mostly grey tipped black, uniting with blackish secondaries to form subterminal trailing edge. Coverts grey except for brown carpal bar; tertials as scapulars. Underwing as adult except less white on outer primaries and dusky secondaries. **Tail** White; narrow subterminal band. NOTE Ginger-brown mantle and back retained for short period only (Jul/Aug) before start of head and body moult to first-winter plumage.
FIRST-WINTER: As juvenile except head whiter with pronounced blackish ear spot; saddle mostly clear grey. Wings and tail unmoulted, faded through wear.
FIRST-SUMMER: As first-winter except bare parts brighter orange; partial brown hood speckled and variable in extent. Wings and tail further faded.
SECOND-WINTER/ADULT WINTER: Bare parts dull red, tip of bill blackish. **Head and Body** as first-winter (some attain full brown hood from mid Dec). **Wings** Upperwing mainly pale grey, with prominent white leading edge to outer wing and blackish tips to outer 6 or 8 primaries. Underwing: coverts pale grey; outer primaries blackish, with white inner webs; secondaries whitish (in the field most of underwing often appears slaty). **Tail** White.
ADULT BREEDING: As non-breeding adult except for brighter bare parts, chocolate-brown hood and, occasionally, pinkish cast to underparts.
FHJ: The familiar small gull of Europe. Breeds mainly freshwater or tidal locations, dispersing in winter to scavenge on coasts, farmland and urban areas. Smaller than Common Gull (p. 336) with proportionately narrower, very angled and pointed wings; quicker wingbeats. Call: various harsh, rather high-pitched cries, most common 'kraah' (remains very vocal outside breeding season).
DM: Breeds Iceland, Faeroes, Britain and E through most of Europe (except S France and Spain) to Asia, including shores of Black and Caspian Seas, E to Sea of Okhotsk and Kamchatka Peninsula. Range expansion in N and W still in progress; first nested Iceland 1911 and a few pairs now reported breeding in NE North America. Returns to colonies Mar/Apr; egg-dates Apr–Jun; fledging and dispersal begin Jul. Many remain in or near breeding areas throughout winter; others, particularly juveniles, disperse quickly, wintering S to Mediterranean, coasts of Mauritania and occasionally Nigeria. In E Africa winters regularly Red Sea S to Kenya; also winters to Thailand, Philippines, China and Japan in Asia. Has wintered in small numbers on E coast of USA S to Florida since about 1930. On North American Pacific coast occurs as vagrant S to California (see Roberson 1980). Small numbers regular in southern Bering Sea during spring (Gibson, pers. comm.).
SS: Mediterranean Gull (p. 353) has different upperwing pattern at all ages, with heavier jizz and more extensive black (not brown) hood in breeding adults. In winter plumage resembles several species: Bonaparte's Gull (p. 357) is smaller, with finer black bill and different underwing pattern; Slender-billed Gull (p. 356) differs in diagnostic bill and head shape and lacks blackish ear spot; Grey-headed Gull (p. 350) is larger with different wing pattern. See also Indian Black-headed Gull (p. 350).

237 SLENDER-BILLED GULL
Larus genei

PLATE 69 Figs 237a-237d
MAP 237

Length 38–46cm (15–18in.). Wingspan 94cm (37in.). Iris pale straw, orbital ring red. Bill/legs dark scarlet.

Southern Europe S and E to N Africa and Arabian Sea; range overlaps with Black-headed Gull (p. 356). Sexes alike; slight seasonal variation. Juveniles separable from adults. No subspecies.
JUVENILE: Bill/legs pale orange, iris brown. **Head** Buffish-white; many show faint ear spot and clouding over crown; hindneck dark brown. **Body** Upperparts pale grey-brown; rump white. Underparts white. **Wings** Upperwing resembles adult's pattern except for indistinct brownish subterminal marks on secondaries, pale brown carpal, median and lesser coverts, and brown outer webs of primary-

coverts and innermost primaries. **Tail** White, blackish subterminal band.
FIRST-WINTER: As juvenile except head white; faint dusky ear spot; saddle pale grey. Wings and tail unmoulted, faded through wear.
FIRST-SUMMER: As first-winter except iris often paler, head usually lacks ear spot. Wings and tail further faded, brown areas sometimes lacking.
SECOND-WINTER/ADULT WINTER: As breeding adult except bill dark red to orange; legs orange-red; faint grey ear spot.
ADULT BREEDING: Head White. **Body** Upperparts pale grey; rump white. Underparts white, usually with strong pinkish cast. **Wings** Upperwing mainly pale grey, with white leading edge on outer wing and black tips to outer 6–7 primaries (recalls Black-headed Gull, p. 356, but white on outer primaries more extensive). **Tail** White.
FHJ: Although plumage at all ages resembles corresponding Eurasian Black-headed Gull, jizz of present species quite different: at rest longer bill with noticeably sloping crown and longer legs readily seen; in flight has distinctive long-necked, hump-backed profile.
DM: Breeds Black and Caspian Seas, Sea of Azov, several inland wetlands in Egypt, Turkey and Iran, Persian Gulf and Mekran coast E to Karachi, also locally in Romania, southern France, southern Spain, Tunisia and on islands of Arguin Bank, Mauritania, NW Africa; may also breed southern Senegal (Bannerman 1953). Egg-dates Apr–Jul; fledging and dispersal begin Jul/Aug. Most winter Mediterranean Basin, Egypt and Persian Gulf. Vagrant N to Britain, S to Nigeria (Wallace 1973) and Kenya (Britton 1980), S and E to Thailand (Redman & Murphy, in press).
SS: Resembles smaller Black-headed Gull (p. 356) at all ages, though juvenile and first-winter upperwing patterns paler, the head lacking conspicuous ear spot. Jizz and bill shape, as noted above, probably best distinction at all ages.

238 BONAPARTE'S GULL *Larus philadelphia*

PLATE 63 Figs 238a-238d
MAP 238

Length 33–36cm (13–14in.). Wingspan 81–84cm (32–33in.). Iris brown, orbital ring red. Bill black. Legs/feet orange-red.

Restricted to North America; winters S to central America, annual vagrant to western Europe. Range overlaps with (rare) Little and Black-headed Gulls (p. 357, p. 356). Sexes alike; seasonal variation. Juveniles separable from adults. No subspecies.
JUVENILE: Bill black, legs pale flesh. **Head** White; crown, eye-crescent and ear spot blackish, usually clearly defined. **Body** Upperparts: saddle brown, edged buff; rump white. Underparts white; sides of breast brownish. **Wings** Upperwing: outer webs of outer 3–4 primaries blackish, inner webs white; inner primaries pale grey tipped black, with small white apical spots from 3rd primary inwards. Secondaries mostly blackish, edged white, linking with primaries and forming subterminal trailing edge to wing. Coverts mainly grey except for blackish-brown carpal bar and edges to outer primary-coverts. Underwing: coverts grey; remainder mostly white except for neat black trailing edge along tips of primaries and secondaries, and translucent wedge on outer primaries (thus distinctly different from any stage of Black-headed Gull, p. 356).
FIRST-WINTER: As juvenile except head white, with blackish ear spot, pale dusky crown and grey nape. Upperparts mostly clear grey. Wings and tail unmoulted, faded through wear.
FIRST-SUMMER: As first-winter except for partial blackish-grey hood; wings and tail further faded.
SECOND-WINTER/ADULT NON-BREEDING: Head and Body Much as first-winter. **Wings** Upperwing mainly pale grey, with prominent white leading edge to outer wing and blackish tips to outer 6–9 primaries. Underwing as first-winter except black tips to outer 6–9 primaries only, secondaries wholly white. **Tail** White (backward examples may retain partial band).
ADULT BREEDING: As non-breeding adult except for blackish-grey hood and variable pinkish flush on underparts.
FHJ: Small and dainty; resembles miniature Black-headed Gull (p. 356) but flight lighter, more buoyant, recalling Little Gull, particularly when surface-picking with legs trailing. Occasionally dabbles when feeding, and during summer hawks for insects. Tree-nesting habits unusual in genus. Call a nasal 'cheer'.
DM: Breeds North America in boreal forest belt from western Alaska, Mackenzie District, southern Yukon, northern and central portions of British Columbia and Alberta, Saskatchewan and Ontario E to Hudson Bay. Returns to colonies May; egg-dates Jun/Jul; departure begins Aug, loose flocks moving along river systems, often forming large concentrations (peak figures at Niagara Falls in Oct up to 60,000). Winters on Atlantic, Gulf and Pacific coasts of USA from Maine and British Columbia S to Mexico, Cuba and Haiti. Regular Bermuda; annual vagrant Britain, western Europe; has also occurred Hawaii.
SS: Differs at all ages from Black-headed Gull (p. 356) in underwing pattern. Little Gull (p. 357) is smaller with darker hood, different wing pattern and distinctly different jizz.

239 LITTLE GULL *Larus minutus*

PLATE 63 Figs 239a-239d
MAP 239

Length 25–30cm (10–12in.). Wingspan 63–66cm (25–26in.). Iris and orbital ring blackish-brown. Bill reddish-brown. Legs/feet scarlet or dull red.

Eurasian, a few breed North America; range overlaps with Black-headed, and (less frequently) Ross's and Bonaparte's Gulls (p. 361, p. 365, p. 357). See also Kittiwake (p. 359). Sexes alike;

seasonal variation. Juveniles separable from adults. No subspecies.

JUVENILE: Bill black, legs/feet pale flesh. **Head** White; crown, hindneck and ear spot blackish-brown. **Body** Upperparts: mantle, scapulars and back blackish-brown edged white, imparting scaly appearance; rump white. Underparts mostly white except for blackish-brown patches on sides of breast. **Wings** Upperwing: outer webs of outer 5–6 primaries, their coverts, and alula blackish, forming dark leading edge to outer wing; inner primaries pale grey with dusky outer webs. Coverts and secondaries mostly grey, with prominent blackish-brown carpal bar and dusky grey centres to secondaries. Underwing white; tips of outer 5–6 and outer web of first primary black. **Tail** White, black subterminal band.

FIRST-WINTER: As juvenile except head whiter, crown and eye-crescent speckled dusky-grey, ear spot black; mantle, scapulars and back mostly pale grey, sides of breast grey. Wings and tail unmoulted, slightly faded through wear, but wings retain distinct M mark across upper surfaces.

FIRST-SUMMER: As first-winter except for partial or complete hood; saddle clear pale grey; underparts mostly white. Wings further faded. Tail band often broken in centre by newly grown white feathers.

SECOND-WINTER: As non-breeding adult except outer webs of outer 2–6 primaries with subterminal blackish marks; underwing variable, some as dark as adult but less uniform, others with axillaries and inner coverts white or pale grey.

SECOND-SUMMER: As breeding adult except wing pattern of second-winter retained.

THIRD-WINTER/ADULT NON-BREEDING: Bill black; legs dull red. **Head** As first-winter. **Body** Upperparts: saddle pale grey; rump white. Underparts white; sides of breast grey. **Wings** Upperwing pale grey, with broad white tips to all primaries and secondaries forming prominent trailing edge. Underwing mostly blackish except for prominent white trailing edge; axillaries and coverts greyer in tone. **Tail** White.

FHJ: World's smallest gull. Dainty, compact jizz, rounded crown and short legs can impart tern-like appearance when perched. Feeding flight hesitant and wavering, recalling Black Tern (p. 365) as it dips down, legs trailing, to pick small organisms from water. Occasionally hawks for insects; sometimes dabbles. Normal flight often direct and strong with deep wingbeats, particularly on downstroke. Call 'kek-kek', but mostly silent when not breeding.

DM: Main breeding areas eastern and western Siberia, locally in Baltic Basin, with isolated colonies Netherlands, Denmark, Sweden; also SE Europe, mainly Poland and northern Black Sea and Sea of Azov; has attempted to breed Britain. A few now nest in North America, with first recorded breeding near Toronto in 1962; these disperse through Great Lakes to winter along Atlantic states S to Long I., occasionally Florida. Egg-dates May/Jun. Dispersal of Eurasian population begins late Jul with most entering North Sea via Baltic; daily peaks in autumn off Netherlands exceeding 1,600 (Hutchinson & Neath 1978); smaller overland passage along principal European river systems to Black and Mediterranean Sea (Wouterson 1980). Winters from English Channel region S to NW Africa, occasionally Nigeria (Wallace 1973); vagrant Kenya (Britton 1980). Siberian population winters Japan Sea.

SS: See Kittiwake, Ross's and Bonaparte's Gulls (p. 359, p. 361, p. 357).

240 CHINESE BLACK-HEADED GULL
other: Saunders's Gull
Larus saundersi

PLATE 68 Figs 240a-240c

MAP 240

Length 30–33cm (12–13in.). Wingspan not recorded. Iris brown. Bill black. Legs/feet dark red.

Confined to inland lakes of northern China, dispersing to coasts of China and Korea during winter. Sexes alike; seasonal variation. Juveniles separable from adults. No subspecies.

JUVENILE: Legs dark brownish-red. **Head** Brownish-grey with duskier ear-coverts and hindcrown; forehead, chin and throat white. **Body** Upperparts: saddle mostly dull brownish-grey with clove-brown edgings; rump white. Underparts white. **Wings** Upperwing resembles adult but outer 2 primaries blacker; secondaries darker forming subterminal trailing edge; brown tips to lesser and some median coverts. **Tail** White, narrowly banded dull black; outer feathers white.

FIRST-WINTER: As juvenile except head whiter with blackish ear spot and greyish wash over crown; saddle mostly clear grey. Wings and tail unmoulted, faded through wear.

FIRST-SUMMER: As first-winter except for partial hood; wings and tail further faded.

SECOND-WINTER/ADULT NON-BREEDING: Head As first-winter. **Body** Upperparts: saddle mostly dark bluish-grey; rump and uppertail-coverts white. Underparts white. **Wings** Upperwing: outer 4–5 primaries, their coverts, and alula mostly white forming leading edge to outer wing; remainder mostly dark bluish-grey except for white trailing edge to secondaries and black subterminal tips along 2nd to 5th primaries. Underwing mainly grey; outermost 4–5 primaries mostly white, contrasting with blackish innermost primaries which form diagnostic blackish window. **Tail** White.

ADULT BREEDING: As non-breeding adult except for blackish hood extending to nape and throat.

FHJ: Much smaller than other hooded gulls of region. Size and jizz recall Bonaparte's Gull (p. 357), with heavier rather compressed black bill. Call unrecorded.

DM: Little known. Breeds inland lakes of northern China, dispersing to coasts of eastern Siberia, Korea and China, occasionally Japan, Formosa and Hong Kong.

SS: Small size, stubby blackish bill, dark grey saddle and upperwings, and wing pattern should prevent confusion with both Eurasian and Indian Black-headed Gulls (p. 356, p. 350). Black window on innermost primaries of underwing contrasting with white outer primaries diagnostic in adults.

241 BLACK-LEGGED KITTIWAKE

other: Kittiwake

Larus tridactyla

PLATE 71 Figs 241a-241d

MAP 241

Length 39–46cm (15½–18in.). Wingspan 90–92cm (35½–36in.). Iris blackish, orbital ring red/orange. Bill yellowish-green, mouth and gape orange. Legs/feet black.

Arctic Ocean and higher latitudes of North Pacific and Atlantic Oceans. Range overlaps with Red-legged Kittiwake and Sabine's Gull (p. 359, p. 361). Sexes alike; seasonal variation. Juveniles separable from adults. Two subspecies listed; adult *L.t. pollicaris* has darker grey upperparts with more extensive black on tips of outer primaries.

JUVENILE: Bill/legs blackish. **Head** Mostly white, eye-crescent dusky with blackish ear spot and conspicuous black cervical collar across lower hindneck. **Body** Upperparts: saddle dark grey; rump white. Underparts white. **Wings** Upperwing: outer 4–5 primaries, their coverts, alula and most of median coverts, some lesser and inner greater coverts blackish, forming conspicuous M mark across wing in flight. Inner primaries and most secondaries whitish-grey; remainder of coverts dark grey, paler on marginal coverts. Underwing mostly white, tips of outer primaries and leading edge of 1st black. **Tail** Mostly white except for black subterminal band, widest in centre.

FIRST-WINTER: As juvenile except rear of crown and hindneck greyer, cervical collar reduced.

FIRST-SUMMER: Bill black with yellowish base and grooves. Legs brownish-yellow or grey. Plumage highly variable especially in late summer due to wear and, in some cases, early moult of outer primaries. Plumage resembles first-winter except: **Head** White, hindneck grey, dusky cervical collar and ear spot sometimes lacking. **Wings** Upperwing: M pattern much faded and decomposed. Most retain dark outer primaries and leading edge but in Aug some show mostly white leading edge and tip to wing, including alula, primary-coverts and base of outer primary, only tips of 4–6 primaries showing any black; dark carpal bar also sometimes lacking. **Tail** Terminal band reduced, decomposed or lacking in late summer.

SECOND-WINTER/ADULT NON-BREEDING: As breeding adult except: **Head** Small dusky eye-crescent; blackish ear spot pronounced in some and extending on to hindneck. **Wings** Most as adult summer, some may retain faint first-winter markings on outer primary-coverts.

ADULT BREEDING: Head White. **Body** Upperparts: mantle and back deep grey, longer scapulars tipped white; rump white. Underparts white. **Wings** Upperwing: mostly deep grey shading to silvery on primaries, outermost 4 of which broadly tipped with black, subterminal black tip on 5th, sometimes 6th; secondaries and tertials edged white. Underwing mainly white, except for black outer web of 1st primary and tips of outer 4–6 primaries. **Tail** White.

FHJ: Small/medium-sized gull; black-tipped wings lack white mirrors. Tail slightly forked but difficult to discern in field, though more apparent in juveniles. Flight light and buoyant, particularly in calm conditions; in high winds wings often sharply angled, strokes deeper and decisive with much shearing. When perched has short legs and upright posture. More pelagic than most other gulls, particularly during northern winter; in rough weather often returns to roost on beaches and cliffs. A marine scavenger, especially at trawlers where call an aggressive 'kek-kek' and a thin 'zeep'; also 'Kitt-e-wake'.

DM: Almost circumpolar. *L.t. pollicaris* breeds USSR from NE Siberia S to Kamchatka and Commander Is, then eastwards through Bering Sea to Aleutian Is. *L.t. tridactyla* breeds along coast of Arctic Canada, including Prince Leopold, Bylot and Baffin Is, northern Labrador, Gulf of St Lawrence, Newfoundland and Nova Scotia (Cape Breton); also Greenland, Iceland, and Islands in Arctic Ocean including Spitsbergen, Jan Mayen, Faeroes, Novaya Zemlya and along N coast of USSR; in N Europe breeds from Murmansk S to Norway, British Isles, Baltic, and N France (Brittany). Returns to colonies Feb/Mar in S but Apr/May in N; egg-dates May–Jul; fledging Jul/Aug. In N Pacific winters S to Japan and Baja California; daily peak at Farallon Is, California, 4,000 (Desante & Ainley 1980). In W Atlantic winters S to New Jersey, USA, casual S to Gulf of Mexico. in E Atlantic most remain north of 40°N, occasionally S to Morocco and W Mediterranean. Peak daily passage figure off St Ives, England, during Nov gales 30,000 (Griffiths, pers. comm.). Vagrant E to Cyprus (Stewart & Christensen 1971) and, surprisingly, an uncommon winter visitor to Elat, N Red Sea, where recorded on 46 occasions with daily peak of five during winters of 1966–79 (Krabbe 1979). More surprising is a visual record 60km W of Cape Town, South Africa, Mar 1978 (Brooke & Sinclair 1978).

SS: See Red-legged Kittiwake, Sabine's, Little and Bonaparte's Gulls (p. 359, p. 361, p. 357, p. 357). Most confusion occurs with first-summer birds, which lack diagnostic black wingtips of adults and occasionally show little or no black on outer primaries—beware! Combination of size and bare parts colours, however, diagnostic. NOTE Some birds occasionally have reddish legs.

242 RED-LEGGED KITTIWAKE

Larus brevirostris

PLATE 71 Figs 242a-242d

MAP 242

Length 35–40cm (14–16in.). Wingspan 90–92cm (35½–36in.). Iris blackish, orbital ring red. Bill yellowish. Legs/feet red.

Bering Sea and adjacent waters; range overlaps with Black-legged Kittiwake (p. 359). Sexes alike; seasonal variation. Juveniles separable from adults; unique among small gulls in lacking a tail band. No subspecies.

JUVENILE: Bill black, legs dusky-brown or black.

Head Mostly white, indistinct dusky ear spot and cervical collar. **Body** Upperparts: saddle dark grey, faintly brown in certain lights; rump white. Underparts white. **Wings** Upperwing: outer 4–5 primaries mostly black, inner webs grey, 6th subterminally tipped black; innermost primaries grey, tipped white, shading to white on secondaries. Primary-coverts and alula dull black, coverts as back, variably tipped white (lacks diagonal bar of Black-legged Kittiwake, p. 359). Underwing: coverts and axillaries grey, secondaries and primaries darker, outermost 4–5 primaries tipped black. **Tail** Wholly white.

FIRST-WINTER: As juvenile except spotted cervical collar reduced or lacking. Wings and tail not moulted, faded through wear.

FIRST-SUMMER: Base of bill and grooves yellow, remainder black. Legs brownish-yellow. Plumage as first-winter except: **Head** Mostly white, hindneck grey. **Wings** Unmoulted; blackish outer primaries, their coverts, and alula much faded and decomposed.

SECOND-WINTER/ADULT NON-BREEDING: As breeding adult except: **Head** Eye-crescent, ear spot and nape dusky-grey. **Wings** Some may show blackish edging to primary-coverts and alula as in similar-stage Black-legged Kittiwake (p. 359).

ADULT BREEDING: Head White. **Body** Upperparts: saddle dark grey; rump white. Underparts white. **Wings** Upperwing: mostly dark grey above, including bases of primaries; outermost 4 primaries broadly tipped black, with black subterminal tip on 5th, innermost primaries and secondaries tipped white. Underwing: mostly grey (see Black-legged Kittiwake, p. 359); outer primaries tipped black.

FHJ: Slightly smaller than Black-legged Kittiwake, which it resembles in habits and flight; bill shorter, more stubby.

DM: Confined to Bering Sea and adjacent waters of N Pacific. Breeds off USSR on Copper I. in Commander Is. Main stronghold off Alaska, USA, at Pribilof Is, where largest colony at St George (220,000 birds); a smaller colony of some 2,200 birds at nearby St Paul I. Four other colonies in Aleutian chain, at Buldir, Bogoslof, Fire and Walrus Is. (All sites and numbers based on Sowls *et al.* 1978.) Egg-dates Jul. Pelagic dispersal largely unknown: recorded off natal islands throughout year in Bering Sea, suggesting that most probably disperse only to adjacent waters; RNBWS sightings at 51½°N, 141°W, and 39½°N, 163°W, during Feb/Mar. Vagrant record Nevada.

SS: Compared with adult Black-legged Kittiwake (p. 359), upperwing distinctly darker, more uniform grey without silvery bases to primaries; underwing mostly grey (not white) with black wingtip. Bright red legs usually diagnostic but some Black-legged Kittiwakes have brownish-red legs. Juveniles and immatures of present species differ from those of Black-legged Kittiwake in paler nape and lack of black on tail or carpal bar. At distance could be confused with non-breeding adult Sabine's Gull (p. 361), but latter has more striking upperwing pattern formed by blacker and more extensive wingtips, deeper grey wing-coverts, and white inner wing.

243 SWALLOW-TAILED GULL
Larus furcatus

PLATE 66 Figs 243a-243d
MAP 243

Length 55–60cm (21½–23½in.). Wingspan 124–139cm (49–55in.). Iris brown, orbital ring crimson. Bill black, tipped greenish-white, red at base. Legs/feet salmon-pink.

Unmistakable at Galapagos Is; disperses to W coast of South America, where range overlaps with smaller, similarly patterned Sabine's Gull (p. 361). Sexes outwardly alike, males average larger; seasonal variation. Juveniles separable from adults. No subspecies.

JUVENILE: Bill blackish, legs pale flesh. **Head** Mostly white; eye-crescent, ear spot and nape browner. **Body** Upperparts: saddle mainly greyish-brown fringed white; rump greyish, tipped brown. Underparts white. **Wings** Upperwing: outer primaries, their coverts, and alula white with dark brown outer webs and tips; secondaries white; remaining coverts as saddle. Underwing white, outer primaries dark brown. **Tail** Forked; white with black terminal band.

FIRST WINTER: As juvenile except head whiter, saddle grey; wings and tail unmoulted, faded through wear.

FIRST-SUMMER: Much as first-winter except for partial hood.

SECOND-WINTER/ADULT WINTER: As breeding adult except head mostly white with dusky eye patch and partial grey breast band.

ADULT BREEDING: Head Blackish-grey hood; white over base of bill. **Body** Upperparts: saddle deep grey, rump white. Underparts: vinaceous-grey breast merging to white on belly. **Wings** Upperwing: primaries and secondaries resemble juvenile's pattern but black outer webs of primaries less extensive; coverts as saddle, tertials narrowly edged white. **Tail** White.

FHJ: Large, striking species with long, broad wings and forked tail; unusual in being primarily nocturnal, catching fish and squid at night. Forages widely from natal islands, often met in small parties several hundred kilometres from landfall. Although confident on land, rather timid at sea, rarely approaching ships. Flight buoyant, long wings rising and falling well above and below body.

DM: Breeding confined mainly to Galapagos Is, where common on small islands and cliffs of larger islands; a few breed Malpelo I. off Colombia. Outside breeding season undertakes wide pelagic dispersal to Humboldt Current region, extending N to Panama (occasionally) and S to Mollendo, Peru (R Hughes, pers. comm.). Status further S uncertain, probably occurs northern Chile.

SS: Unlikely to be confused with other gulls at breeding islands. During pelagic dispersal range overlaps with much smaller, but similarly patterned Sabine's Gull (p. 361).

244 SABINE'S GULL *Larus sabini*

PLATE 61 Figs 244a-244c
MAP 244

Length 33–36cm (13–14in.). Wingspan 86–91cm (34–36in.). Iris blackish-brown, orbital ring red. Bill black, tip yellow. Legs/feet blackish-grey.

Circumpolar in high Arctic. Unusual among west Palearctic gulls in having complete moult in early spring and partial one in autumn, a feature no doubt linked to its migratory habits. Sexes alike; seasonal variation of head pattern. Juveniles separable from adults. Four subspecies listed.

JUVENILE: Iris brown; bill black; legs pinkish-grey. **Head** Clove-brown; forehead, chin and throat whiter. **Body** Upperparts: saddle clove-brown with prominent paler edges; rump white. Underparts white; sides of breast clove-brown (from mantle). **Wings** Upperwing: outer webs of outer 6 primaries, most of primary-coverts and alula black, inner primaries and outer secondaries mostly white; remainder as scapulars. Underwing mostly white except for narrow blackish tips to outer primaries, and diagnostic dusky bar across greater underwing-coverts (though this is a variable feature). **Tail** Forked; white with black subterminal band. (This plumage retained until Dec.)

FIRST-WINTER: As juvenile except head as non-breeding adult; saddle clear grey, rump white. Wings and tail much worn and faded, perhaps with some emergent grey feathers. (This plumage retained Nov–Apr.)

FIRST-SUMMER: As breeding adult except partial grey or blackish hood extending from ear-coverts to nape; wings resemble non-breeding adult; tail may show traces of tail band. (This plumage retained Mar–Sep.)

SECOND-WINTER: As first-summer except head as non-breeding adult.

SECOND-SUMMER/ADULT BREEDING: Head Grey hood shading to black at nape and forming faint necklace; nape white. **Body** Upperparts: saddle uniform grey; rump white. Underparts white. **Wings** Upperwing tricoloured: secondaries white, forming conspicuous white triangular patch contrasting with prominent black triangle on leading edge of outer wing and grey coverts. Underwing white; tips of outer primaries black, faint dusky bar across greater coverts. **Tail** Forked, white. (Plumage retained Mar–Oct but some, perhaps failed breeders, reach NW Europe during mid Aug in transitional plumage.)

ADULT NON-BREEDING: As breeding adult except legs flesh-grey; head mostly white with dark grey necklace over nape to ear-coverts; black areas on upperwing browner. (Plumage retained Sep–Mar.)

FHJ: Smaller than Kittiwake (p. 359), with proportionately longer, narrower wings. All plumages have distinctive tricoloured upperwing pattern and forked tail, latter often difficult to discern at distance. Flight buoyant, tern-like and, unlike Kittiwake, wings rise and fall well above and below body. Almost wholly pelagic outside breeding season. Call harsh and grating, similar to that of Arctic Tern (p. 370).

DM: Circumpolar; *L.s. wosnesenskii* breeds W Alaska, *L.s. sabini* Greenland, *L.s. palaearctica* in Taimyr-Lena delta (USSR) and *L.s. tschuktschorum* in Chuckchee Peninsula. Returns to colonies late May/Jun; egg-dates Jun/Jul. Departure of failed breeders begins Jul, most by mid Aug. Siberian and perhaps proportion of western Alaskan populations move SE across Pacific, with up to 2,000 peak daily count off Washington State during Sep en route to main Pacific wintering area off coasts of Colombia S to Peru; occasionally northern Chile (see Chapman 1969). Most juveniles probably remain in these latitudes during their first summer. Nearctic population migrates mainly SE across Atlantic to NW Europe, where now recorded annually including North Sea area, although numbers dependent to some extent on strong westerly winds; St Ives, England, perhaps best place to witness passage with daily peak during gales of up to 13 (Griffiths, pers. comm.). Records from RNBWS members indicate a staging area in northern Bay of Biscay with peak daily figure off Belle Isle, France, of up to 1,000 during late Aug; flocks also reported off Cape Finisterre, Spain, before moving S to winter off Namibia and South Africa where flocks of up to 1,000 off Cape Town (pers. obs.). Adults of both populations begin northwards migration late Apr/May. Stragglers have occurred S to Japan, Florida and Sinai.

SS: Beware juvenile Ross's Gull (p. 361) in high Arctic. Most confusion likely with first-calendar-year Kittiwakes (p. 359): juveniles of present species best separated by smaller size, darker head, and upperwing; at close range black bill of Sabine's also useful. Flight also different, present species appearing rather tern-like due to combination of pointed wings and more or less continuous wingbeats with very little gliding. See also juvenile Little Gull (p. 357).

Genus *RHODOSTETHIA*

Monotypic genus. Small, high Arctic species, adults with black necklace and pink suffusion to pale plumage. Differs from *Larus* in wedge-shaped tail, long, rather pointed wings and short, slender bill.

245 ROSS'S GULL *Rhodostethia rosea*

PLATE 71 Figs 245a-245d
MAP 245

Length 30–32cm (12–13in.). Wingspan not recorded. Iris blackish, orbital ring red. Bill black, mouth red. Legs/feet red.

A small high Arctic species which, due in part to increased observers/ability, now recorded annually in British Isles. Most likely to be confused with slightly smaller Little Gull (p. 357). In any plumage, however, tiny bill, long wedge-shaped tail and long pointed wings useful identification characters. See also Kittiwake (p. 359). Sexes alike; seasonal variation. Juveniles separable from adults. No subspecies.

JUVENILE: Orbital ring black. Bill blackish, mouth pink. Legs brown. **Head** Mostly white, except for blackish or brown eye-crescent, ear-coverts, crown and hindneck. **Body** Upperparts: saddle and upper rump dark brown fringed buff or golden, heaviest on scapulars creating scaly effect; lower rump white. Underparts mostly white except for noticeable dark brown sides of breast (extension of mantle). **Wings** Upperwing: outer web and half of inner web of outer 3 primaries mostly black, base of outer web of 4th to 6th or 7th blackish; remainder of primaries whitish, outer 4th to 8th tipped black, decreasing inwards. Secondaries white. Outer primary-coverts, alula and diagonal bar across coverts blackish-brown, some fringed white; remainder pearl-grey. Underwing mostly grey, axillaries whiter, outer web of 1st and tips of outer 8 black with conspicuous broad translucent trailing edge to inner primaries and secondaries. **Tail** Mainly white, central feathers subterminally tipped black, decreasing outwards; outermost wholly white.

FIRST-WINTER: As juvenile except: **Head** Mostly white; dusky eye-crescent extending below and enhancing largeness of dark eye (a conspicuous fieldmark); variable dusky ear-coverts and greyish wash to crown, nape and hindneck. **Body** Upperparts: saddle and upper rump pearl-grey, latter retaining small dark tips, scapulars tipped black and white; lower rump white. Underparts mainly white, sides of breast and flanks grey. **Wings and Tail** Unmoulted, somewhat faded.

FIRST-SUMMER: Orbital ring and legs sometimes reddish. As first-winter except: **Head** White; partial or complete, narrow necklace. **Body** Upperparts: blackish tips on upper rump and scapulars reduced or lacking. Underparts may show pink flush and lack grey wash on sides of breast and flanks. **Wings and Tail** Unmoulted, much worn; darker areas browner in hue.

SECOND-WINTER/ADULT NON-BREEDING: Legs dull orange. **Head** Mostly white except for variable dusky eye-crescent and ear spot; grey wash to crown, nape and hindneck sometimes lacking; partial or full necklace sometimes retained. **Body** Upperparts: saddle pearl-grey (paler than in Black-headed or Bonaparte's Gulls); rump white. Underparts white, often flushed pink. **Wings** Upperwing: mainly pale pearl-grey, except for black outer web of 1st primary and white tips increasing inwards from 6th primary to almost wholly white 10th primary; secondaries white. Underwing mostly pale grey on coverts and outer primaries; axillaries often appear whiter; conspicuous white trailing edge to inner primaries and all secondaries. NOTE Some show atypical dark grey underwings, further enhanced by shadow. **Tail** White.

ADULT BREEDING: Head Mostly white, with prominent black necklace, thickest on nape, extending narrowly across throat; crown sometimes greyish, hindneck pinkish-white. **Body** Upperparts: saddle pearl-grey; rump white, sometimes pinkish. Underparts white variably washed with pink, often intense. **Wings and Tail** As non-breeding adult.

FHJ: A small high Arctic species with chunky, compact body, longish wings and pigeon- or tern-like flight imparting distinctive jizz. Proportionately long, wedge-shaped tail not always easy to discern in field. When perched small dove-like head, large eye and short delicate bill, feathered at base, give distinctive facial expression. Often feeds along mudflats in phalarope or sandpiper fashion, when appears larger than its 31cm body length due to wings projecting well past tail point, accentuating attenuated jizz. Flight varies from pigeon-like, when wingbeats deep and rapid, to tern-like with more leisurely buoyant flight, dipping steeply to surface to pick from water or execute shallow surface-plunge. Occasionally hovers, often trails legs storm-petrel fashion.

DM: Confined to high Arctic. Only large breeding sites known are those listed by Buturlin (1906) in NE Siberia, USSR, from Khatanga river to Kolyma delta region; recently, however, small colonies have been located in Canadian Arctic at Bathurst I. and near Churchill, Manitoba, and also in Greenland and Spitsbergen. Returns to colonies May/Jun; egg-dates May/Jun; fledging and dispersal begin Jul/Aug. Some disperse E towards Chukchi and Bering Seas, where regular autumn visitor to Point Barrow, Alaska. Flocks usually arrive late Sep and continue through to late Oct. Numbers fluctuate annually, sometimes in thousands but dependent to some extent on strong NW winds. Very rare S of Bering Strait, only a few records S to Pribilof Is off Alaska. Others migrate in opposite direction, westwards along N USSR littoral towards New Siberian Is in Arctic Ocean and then progressing W through Kara Sea to Franz Josef Land and Spitsbergen. Winter range not precisely known, but Densley (1977) suggests many winter in Spitsbergen area with southwest drift of birds to NW Europe; the recent spate of sightings in northern Britain (where now an annual vagrant) would seem to confirm this theory. Peak count of four at Shetland Is, Scotland, during 1980/81 winter. Recent evidence (Meltofte *et al.* 1981) supports Densley's suggestion that Spitsbergen/Franz Josef Land area also an important feeding and moulting area during summer for non-breeders; large flocks of this species were noted in this area as long ago as 1828 (Parry 1828). Stragglers have occurred S to British Columbia, Massachusetts and Illinois, USA; to Sardinia, Mediterranean Sea, in Europe and to Japan in Asia.

SS: Breeding adults unmistakable. Non-breeders paler above than other small gulls which, coupled with long wings, wedge-shaped tail, small bill and large eye, should ensure ready identification. Other plumages could be confused with various plumage stages of both Little Gull and Kittiwake (p. 357, p. 359): first-year birds of both have similar flight pattern with blackish outer primaries and carpal bar forming distinctive M mark across upperwings; Kittiwakes, however, have black cervical collar and more black on head, wings and tail;

first-year Little Gulls also have more black on head, wings and tail and secondaries are grey (not whitish as in Ross's Gull). In autumn beware especially long-distance views of immature Little Gull in transitional plumage, when underwing may appear white (normally blackish).

Genus *PAGOPHILA*

Monotypic genus. Medium-sized species, adults wholly white. Usually confined to high Arctic seas. Differs from *Larus* mainly in greater extent of feathering on leg.

246 IVORY GULL *Pagophila eburnea*

PLATE 62 Figs 246a-246b
MAP 246

Length 40–46cm (16–18in.). Wingspan 104–117cm (41–46in.). Iris dark brown, orbital ring red. Bill greyish-green with yellow and orange tip. Legs/feet blackish.

High Arctic; unmistakable, and unlike any other species of region. Sexes alike; no marked seasonal variation. Juveniles separable from adults. No subspecies.

JUVENILE: Bill blue or black at base, tip yellow. **Head** Mostly white, variable blackish markings on forehead, lores and chin, sometimes ear-coverts, imparting dark-faced aspect. Crown and nape lightly spotted with black. **Body** Upperparts mainly white, sparsely flecked brown or black, heaviest on scapulars. Underparts similar. **Wings** Upperwing white; primaries tipped black, decreasing in size inwards, outer secondaries, tertials, alula and primary-coverts also tipped black, coverts faintly spotted. Underwing white, except for black tips of primaries and outer secondaries. **Tail** White with narrow black subterminal band.

FIRST-WINTER: As juvenile except fewer blackish tips on head and upperparts.

FIRST-SUMMER: Bill colour resembles adult's. Plumage as first-winter except face whiter, black confined to base of bill and chin; upperparts less spotted.

SECOND-WINTER/ADULT NON-BREEDING: Wholly ivory-white, shafts of primaries and tail yellowish.

ADULT BREEDING: As non-breeding adult except orbital ring and orange spot on lower mandible brighter.

FHJ: Strikingly white at all ages. When perched high domed crown, plump body and short legs impart pigeon-like gait and jizz. Flight buoyant, rather light and graceful for such a long, broad-winged and heavy-bodied gull. Often flies with legs trailing, patters feet on water. Contrary to most published literature, shows no aversion to resting on water (in temperate seas at least). An Arctic scavenger, quarrelsome and aggressive; attends Polar bear kills, dead cetaceans, seals etc., where uses bill to advantage, tearing and gulping large strips of flesh. During winter most frequent drift ice and edge of pack ice, feeding on fish and crustaceans.

DM: Breeds N to 85°N in Canadian Arctic, northern Greenland, Spitsbergen, Franz Josef Land, Novaya Zemlya and Severnaya Zemlya. Returns to colonies late May; egg-dates Jun–Aug; dispersal begins Jul–Sep. Winters mainly in Arctic waters within drift ice and along edge of pack ice in northern Atlantic and Chukchi and Beaufort Seas. Many hundreds, occasionally thousands, reported off northern Newfoundland late winter/early spring, a few straggling S to Nova Scotia. Regular vagrant in recent years S to Denmark, France, Britain, Ireland and Massachusetts, occasionally Japan.

SS: Glaucous and Iceland Gulls (p. 346, p. 347) larger with different bare parts coloration, and entirely different jizz. Beware albino gull spp.

Genus *CHLIDONIAS*

Three species; small to medium-sized, variably coloured 'marsh terns'. Migratory and dispersive. Marked seasonal variation in plumage.

Field identification of adult, breeding *Chlidonias* spp. straightforward given reasonable views. Non-breeding adults and immatures, however, difficult to separate; familiarisation with jizz and flight in breeding birds helpful when dealing with these more difficult stages. Whiskered Tern, at all seasons, is much closer in flight and jizz to *Sterna*. With comparative experience White-winged Black Tern will be seen to differ from Black Tern in shorter bill, thicker-set jizz, squarer tail and slower, shallower wingbeat. Plumage details to look for are extent of cap and degree of contrast on upperparts, especially presence of 'saddle' effect and whiteness of rump; the breast markings of Black Tern, whilst diagnostic, do vary in size (beware). Look too for carpal bar on upperwing. Moulting White-winged Black Terns may show some dark feathers at sides of breast but usually with black feather tips on underparts and underwing-coverts.

For further treatment see Williamson (1960).

247 WHISKERED TERN *Chlidonias hybridus*

PLATE 81 Figs 247a-247e
MAP 247

Length 25–26cm (10–10¼in.). Wingspan 69cm (27in.). Iris black. Bill, legs/feet dark blood-red.

Distributed throughout much of Old World, frequenting inland waterways; rare at sea. Breeding adults distinctive but non-breeding and immature plumages similar in pattern to juvenile Arctic and Common Terns (p. 370, p. 370); see also Black and White-winged Black Terns. Sexes similar; marked seasonal variation. Juveniles and subsequent stages separable from adults. Seven subspecies listed, some darker in tone than nominate race. (See Williamson 1960 for more thorough treatment of species.)

JUVENILE: Bill black, legs red-brown. **Head** As non-breeding adult but more extensive blackish hindcrown and nape, lobed at rear (almost reaching brown mantle). **Body** Upperparts: mantle and back sepia-brown edged blackish, lower back and scapulars broadly tipped buff; rump grey. Underparts mostly white; faint brown smudge on sides of breast recalls juvenile Black Tern (p. 365). **Wings** Upperwing: primaries and their coverts mainly grey, outer webs paler, bases of outer 5 primaries whitish; all primaries and secondaries tipped brownish-grey forming darker trailing edge to wing. Alula, tertials, lesser and inner median coverts have brownish-grey centres; outer median and greater coverts pearl-grey forming pale midwing panel. Underwing mostly white, trailing edge and lesser coverts grey. **Tail** Grey at base, indistinct dusky tip, sides narrowly edged white. NOTE In northern populations brown saddle quickly replaced during autumn by emerging grey first-winter feathers, most showing mainly grey saddle by Sep/Oct with brown edgings only to tertials and scapulars. Small brownish-grey mark on sides of breast usually absent after fledging.

FIRST-WINTER: As juvenile except saddle mostly clear grey, scapulars variably tipped brown. Wings unmoulted; brownish lesser and median coverts paler, may appear absent in strong sunlight.

FIRST-SUMMER: Little information available. Resembles breeding adult above, including dark cap and white facial streak; underparts mixed grey and white. Wings and tail more rounded, latter barely forked.

ADULT NON-BREEDING: Bill and legs dull red. **Head** Mostly white, eye-crescent and streak through eye blackish, extending back to join across nape; crown flecked with black, hindneck greyish. **Body** Upperparts wholly pale grey. Underparts white. **Wings and Tail** As breeding adult but paler.

ADULT BREEDING: Head Black cap divided from grey chin and throat by conspicuous white facial stripe. **Body** Upperparts wholly grey. Underparts mostly deep vinaceous-grey; ventral area and undertail-coverts white. **Wings** Upperwing grey with paler bases and darker tips to outermost primaries. **Tail** Grey, sides and tip narrowly edged white.

FHJ: Frequents inland freshwater areas, occasionally on coast. Usually patrols 5–10m over water, flying against wind in steady, direct flight with incisive wing action; rarely plunges like *Sterna*. Compared with Black and White-winged Black Terns (p. 365, p. 364) jizz closer to *Sterna*, but differs from 'commic' terns (p. 370, p. 370) in smaller size, shorter more rounded wings and lack of pronounced white collar; at rest legs proportionately longer. NOTE Only males have *Sterna*-like bills with pronounced gonys (Williamson 1960). Call note a harsh 'ki-ick'.

DM: Resident and migratory throughout much of Old World. *C.h. hybridus* breeds locally in southern Europe and North Africa from Spain and Morocco discontinuously E through Balkans and Tunisia to SW Asia, migrating to E and W Africa during northern winter with large autumn passage through Suez and Mediterranean beginning Jul; spring passage Apr/May. *C.h. sclateri* breeds South Africa and Madagascar; *C.h. delalandii* Kenya S to Tanzania; *C.h. indica* Iran to India; *C.h. swinhoei* southern China, Taiwan, Indo-China; *C.h. javanica* Sri Lanka, Malaysia, Java, Celebes; *C.h. fluviatilis* Moluccas, New Guinea, Australia.

SS: Unlikely to be confused in breeding plumage. Juvenile and adult non-breeding plumages closely resemble those of White-winged Black Tern, see notes opposite Plate 81. First-winter Arctic Tern (p. 370) has white secondaries and different underwing. First-winter Common Tern larger, longer-billed with distinct white collar and different wing pattern; at rest, when seen together, primaries of Common Tern always darker in autumn and black cap more extensive.

248 WHITE-WINGED BLACK TERN *Chlidonias leucopterus*

PLATE 81 Figs 248a-248e
MAP 248

Length 22–24cm (8½–9½in.). Wingspan 66cm (26in.). Iris black. Bill dull red. Legs/feet orange.

Old World; breeds inland marshes, moving S in northern winter to similar habitat but some also to coastal habitat. Breeding adults distinctive but separation of all other stages from those of Black Tern (p. 365) requires care. Males average darker; marked seasonal variation. Juveniles and subsequent stages separable from adults. No subspecies. See under Black Tern for hybrids.

JUVENILE: Bill black. Legs/feet reddish or flesh-grey. **Head** As non-breeding adult but dark cap more extensive. **Body** Upperparts: mantle, scapulars and back dark brownish-grey with darker feather edges (forming dark saddle); rump white (wears to pale grey by early winter). Underparts white. **Wings** Upperwing mostly pale brownish-grey; primaries and secondaries tipped darker forming indistinct trailing edge to wing, with paler midwing panel and indistinct carpal bar. Underwing white. **Tail** Pale grey.

FIRST-WINTER: As juvenile except saddle clear

Fig. 25. Head patterns of non-breeding Black and White-winged Black Terns.

grey; rump greyer (but noticeably paler than in Black Tern, p. 365). Wings unmoulted, faded through wear.

FIRST-SUMMER: (Based on Bundy 1982) Much as non-breeding adult except: **Wings** Upperwing: dark bar along secondaries; some show dark grey outer primaries forming narrow wedge along leading edge.

ADULT NON-BREEDING: Bill black, legs dull orange. **Head** Forehead white, extending narrowly over eye and forming partial or complete division between dark grey or blackish cap and black eye-stripe; remainder white. (NOTE Some examples show very little grey or black on crown, see Fig. 25.) **Body** Upperparts: mantle, scapulars and back grey; rump white becoming greyer with wear, but always distinctly paler than saddle (unlike Whiskered and Black Terns, p. 364, p. 365). Underparts white. **Wings** Upperwing mostly uniform grey; outer 3–5 primaries with darker outer webs; secondaries and marginal coverts slightly darker. Underwing variable: some wholly white, others with continuous or scattered dark tips across greater and primary underwing-coverts. **Tail** White or pale grey.

BREEDING ADULT: Head Black. **Body** Upperparts: mantle, scapulars and back blackish-brown; rump white. Underparts mostly black, ventral area and undertail-coverts white. **Wings** Upperwing: outer primaries blackish-grey, innermost and all of secondaries and greater coverts pale grey shading to white on lesser coverts. Underwing: coverts strikingly black, remainder pale grey, tips and outer primaries blackish. **Tail** White.

FHJ: Compared with Black Tern (p. 365) has slightly heavier jizz, wings proportionately shorter, broader, more rounded at tip, with normal flight slower, more leisurely, wingbeats shallower; shorter bill more evident when perched. During northern winter tends to disperse more to inland waters than to offshore waters (unlike Black Tern). Call 'krip-krip' and 'kree-ah—kik-kik'.

DM: Breeds irregularly western Europe in France, Germany, Belgium and Sweden; in eastern Europe recent increase and range expansion, breeding from Hungary E across Asia to central Russia and southern China. Most Eurasian populations winter central and southern Africa, mainly on inland lakes and rivers, where dense flocks of tens of thousands occur; uncommon on coast. Despite reports in some literature, is rare along coasts of West Africa although occurs commonly along rivers of central W Africa and further N at Lake Chad (pers. obs.). During spring and autumn many thousands move through Nile and Rift Valley. Further east, Asiatic population moves S through China, wintering India and Malay Archipelago S through Indonesia to northern Australia, where peaks of 1,500 at Darwin during Jan not uncommon (McKean 1981). Stragglers have reached Alaska, USA; West Indies; and New Zealand. A regular but scarce passage visitor, mostly in autumn, NW to British Isles and NE to Japan.

SS: See notes under Black and Whiskered Terns (p. 365, p. 364).

249 BLACK TERN *Chlidonias niger*

PLATE 81 Figs 249a-249e
MAP 249

Length 22–24cm ($8\frac{1}{2}$–$9\frac{1}{2}$in.). Wingspan 66cm (26in.). Iris black. Legs/feet blackish-red.

North America and Old World; breeds inland marshes, prairie sloughs; habits more maritime during winter. Breeding adults distinctive but separation of all other stages from those of White-winged Black Tern (p. 364) requires care. Sexes alike; marked seasonal variation. Juveniles and subsequent stages separable from adults. Two subspecies listed. Vinicombe (1980) described a possible Black × White-winged Black Tern hybrid, and van Ijzendoorn (1980) recorded an unsuccessful Black × White-winged Black Tern breeding attempt in Netherlands.

JUVENILE: Bill black; legs dark grey, sometimes fleshy. **Head** As non-breeding adult. **Body** Upperparts: mantle, scapulars and back brownish-grey edged black and buff; rump deep grey. Underparts mostly white except for greyish-brown smudge on sides of breast. **Wings** Upperwing mostly brownish-grey; primaries darker with paler outer webs; alula, marginal and lesser coverts almost black forming prominent carpal bar and contrasting with paler greater and median coverts. Tertials as back. **Tail** Grey.

FIRST-WINTER: Much as non-breeding adult except upperparts retain scattered brown tips; upperwing as juvenile but faded through wear.

FIRST-SUMMER: Highly variable. **Head** Forehead white, cap and sides of face black though some flecked white. **Body** Mantle, scapulars and back slate-grey, rump grey. Underparts wholly white or peppered black on throat, breast and belly. **Wings** Upperwing mostly uniform slate-grey, primary tips and secondaries slightly darker, bases of outer primaries whiter; alula, marginal and lesser coverts darker forming carpal bar.

ADULT NON-BREEDING: Head Forehead, chin, throat and narrow band across hindneck white. Blackish crown extends to nape, ear-coverts and through eye almost to bill (imparts darker-headed appearance than in corresponding White-winged Black Tern, p. 364). **Body** Upperparts pale brownish-grey. Underparts mostly white except for blackish-grey marks on sides of breast (a good field character lacking in both White-winged Black and Whiskered Terns). **Wings** As breeding adult but paler and greyer. **Tail** Greyish.

ADULT BREEDING: Head Blackish. **Body** Upperparts: mantle, scapulars and back vinaceous slate-grey; rump brownish-grey. Underparts mostly black in *C.n. surinamensis*, but vent and undertail-coverts white in *C.n. niger*. **Wings** Upperwing mostly as upperparts; primaries and secondaries tipped darker with base of outer primaries white. **Tail** Brownish-grey.

FHJ: Following comparisons are with White-winged Black Tern (p. 364). Slightly slimmer jizz, proportionately longer, more pointed wings with narrower bases; tail longer, more forked. When perched bill appears longer and slightly decurved. In flight wingbeats deeper and faster. Normal feeding flight erratic and buoyant, dipping down to surface; frequently hovers whilst hawking for insects over water, marsh or meadow, occasionally surface-dives. During migration and northern winter habits much more maritime than White-winged Black Tern. Normally silent outside breeding season. Call a shrill 'kik-kik-kik', or in alarm 'kreek'.

DM: North America and Old World. *C.n. surinamensis* breeds in North America throughout much of interior Canada from central British Columbia and Saskatchewan E to New Brunswick and S to Nevada, Colorado, Nebraska, Ohio and New York; formerly California (numbers apparently decreasing southern Great Plains region). Egg-dates May–Jul; dispersal begins Jul, peaking Aug/Sep. Winters along coasts from Panama S to Chile and Surinam, often congregating in flocks of several thousands offshore. In Old World *C.n. niger* breeds Europe and W Asia from Sweden and Spain E to Minusinsk, SW Siberia, and Caspian Sea. In Europe spring passage begins during Mar off Morocco, mostly Apr/May in Mediterranean, but numbers less impressive than autumn migration when flocks of many thousands pass W through Strait of Gibraltar Aug/Sep. Often associates with fish and dolphin shoals during these movements. Flocks of several thousands reported annually off NW Africa in transit to main wintering area along coasts of Ghana and Nigeria; some proceed S to Angola, Namibia and Cape Province, South Africa. Small numbers, possibly becoming mixed with migrating White-winged Black Terns (p. 364), pass through Red Sea, peak figures four at Elat, N Red Sea (Krabbe 1979), and should be looked for off NE Africa. Stragglers have reached Hawaii, Japan and Australia. Both populations feed mainly at sea during winter months (unlike White-winged Black Tern), returning to coast at nightfall to roost. Most first-summer birds of both populations remain in winter quarters throughout year.

SS: Confusion most likely during northern winter with immature and non-breeding White-winged Black Tern (p. 364). Non-breeding adults of present species differ in more maritime habits, longer bill, darker legs, darker more extensive cap, darker rump and conspicuous blackish-grey marks on sides of breast. Juveniles differ in lack of saddle effect, grey (not whitish) rump, dark sides of breast and darker upperwings.

Genus *PHAETUSA*

Monotypic genus; medium-sized species with strikingly patterned upperparts. Restricted mainly to NE South America.

250 LARGE-BILLED TERN *Phaetusa simplex*

PLATE 74 Figs 250a-250b
MAP 250

Length 37cm (14½in.). Wingspan 92cm (36in.). Iris blackish. Bill yellow, base greyer. Legs yellowish-grey, webs yellow.

Rivers and coasts of eastern and central South America. Sexes alike; slight seasonal variation. Juveniles separable from adults. Two subspecies listed; the southern race *P.s. chloropoda* differs from nominate in paler grey saddle and upperwings and brighter yellow bill.

JUVENILE: Bill duller. **Head** Mostly light grey with brownish streaks on crown and nape and indistinct blackish streak from eye to nape; lores, chin and throat white. **Body** Upperparts as adult but feathers tipped dull brown. Underparts mostly white except for grey sides of breast (extension from mantle). **Wings** Resemble adult but with brownish tips and edges. **Tail** Shorter than adult's with brownish tips.

FIRST-WINTER: As juvenile except forehead and crown paler, saddle clearer grey. Wings and tail unmoulted, faded through wear.

ADULT NON-BREEDING: As breeding adult except forehead and crown mottled with white.

ADULT BREEDING: Head Uncrested black cap divided from base of bill by narrow white band; remainder white. **Body** Upperparts dark grey. Underparts mostly white; sides of breast and flanks greyer. **Wings** Upperwing: primaries black, secondaries and inner primary-coverts white extending across wing to carpal; tertials and median coverts grey. Underwing mostly white. **Tail** Forked, rather short; grey above, white below.

FHJ: Distinctive; mainly a freshwater species with large bill and striking upperwing pattern.

DM: Confined to South America E of Andes, frequenting mouths of rivers, their courses and

larger lakes. *P.s. simplex* breeds from Colombia, Trinidad and Venezuela S throughout Amazonas to Brazil. *P.s. chloropoda* breeds Paraguay, Uruguay and northern Argentina; perhaps also further N. Vagrants occasionally reported from Ecuador and Peru, also Cuba (once), and USA twice (Ohio and Illinois, see McLaughlin 1979).
SS: Distinctive at all ages.

Genus *STERNA*

Typical terns; about 32 species. Generally white and grey with black on head; some, e.g. Sooty Tern, with dark upperparts. Size ranges from comparatively immense Caspian Tern to diminutive Little Tern. All have forked tails to some degree. Sexes alike; some species show seasonal variation, usually loss of complete black cap and dropping of outer tail streamers. Maturity usually reached second or third winter after fledging. Most immatures of migratory northern terns spend first, sometimes second, summers in winter quarters.

Field identification often difficult, particularly at long range or without comparative experience. Accurate identification made only by carefully noting colour(s) of all bare parts; extent of white forehead or cap; colour of body; upper- and underwing patterns, particularly on distal portion; colour of outer tail feathers. Given reasonable views, adults thus scrutinised should present few problems to careful birders. Juveniles and immatures more difficult: check for darker areas on upperwing, particularly for carpal bar (a feature also visible on closed wing), and colour of upperwing-coverts and secondaries. When perched, relative length of bill and legs are more easily judged. Note also whether tip of tail extends beyond wingtip. In flight look for jizz features: relative largeness of head and bill; length of tail compared with rest of body; translucent underwing panels; type of flight and feeding method; and relative overall whiteness or greyness.

For further notes on some European *Sterna* spp. refer to excellent pioneer identification paper by Grant & Scott (1980).

251 GULL-BILLED TERN *Sterna nilotica*

PLATE 76 Figs 251a-251d
MAP 251

Length 35–43cm (14–17in.). Wingspan 86–103cm (34–40½in.). Iris dark brown. Bill, legs/feet black.

Almost cosmopolitan. Recalls Sandwich Tern (p. 386) but gull-like bill, longer legs, broader wings and heavier body impart distinctive jizz; feeding habits also differ. Sexes alike; marked seasonal variation. Juveniles and first-summer types separable from adults. Six subspecies, none separable in the field.

JUVENILE: Head Mostly white with pale brown wash from crown to hindneck; dusky eye-crescent and ear-coverts form conspicuous dark mark on sides of face. **Body** Upperparts: as adult except brown edges to saddle feathers. **Wings** As adult except for brown tips to coverts and darker grey primaries. **Tail** White, tip brown.

FIRST-WINTER: As juvenile except brown tips to saddle and upperwing-coverts reduced or lacking.

ADULT NON-BREEDING: As breeding adult except: **Head** Mainly white with dusky eye-crescent; ear-coverts and streaks on nape form more or less continuous band from eye to eye. Pattern highly variable, however: in Ecuador one adult feeding young during Aug showed only faint ear spot with no smudging on hindcrown or nape (pers. obs.); see Fig. 26 below. **Wings** Outer webs of outermost primaries darker grey.

ADULT BREEDING: Head Black cap lacks crest; sides of face, chin and throat white. **Body** Upperparts, including rump, pale silvery-grey. Underparts white. **Wings** Upperwing as upperparts except for dusky-grey inner webs to outer 6–8 primaries, all of which are tipped dark greyish-black forming noticeable dark trailing edge to outer primaries. Underwing mainly white, dusky shafts and darker primary tips more apparent than when viewed from above. NOTE In northern spring some adults may show small white tips to outermost primaries (Tucker, pers. comm.).

FHJ: Appears white at distance with rather broad, rounded wings, heavy body and shallow-forked tail imparting gull-like jizz. Compared with Sandwich Tern (p. 386) flight less graceful with shallower wingbeats. Unlike latter species Gull-billed has wide habitat tolerance, feeding along coasts, over marshes, lakes, mudflats and even fields, dipping

Fig. 26. Variation in head patterns of Gull-billed Terns

swiftly to pluck prey from surface or seize insects in mid air. Although hawking over exposed flats is normal feeding technique, occasionally plunges into water but usually from no great height. At close range stout gull-like bill and longer, thicker legs than congeners are easily seen. Call 'kay-tih-did' or 'kay-did' accented on last syllable (Bent 1921); also a soft nasal 'kek-kek' (pers. obs.).

DM: Almost cosmopolitan. *S.n. vanrossemi* breeds western N America on Salton Sea, California, and on coasts of Sonora, Mexico, S to Ecuador; *S.n. aranea* breeds locally eastern N America from Long I., New York, S through Gulf States to Cuba and West Indies; *S.n. gronvoldi* breeds eastern S America on coasts of Brazil and Argentina. In Old World *S.n. nilotica* breeds Europe, discontinuously in Denmark, Holland, Spain, southern France and from eastern Europe across Asia Minor E to Mongolia, the Punjab, also N and E Africa. *S.n. macrotarsa* breeds Australia; *S.n. addenda* southern China S to Malay Archipelago. Egg-dates throughout year in scattered populations. A post-breeding dispersal occurs in all populations although northern ones more migratory; they occur S to Peru in western S America; to Lake Dow, Botswana, southern Africa; Japan and to South Island, New Zealand.

SS: Likely to be confused by the unwary with Sandwich Tern (p. 386) and, like that species, appears much whiter in flight than most other terns. At close range wholly dark, gull-like bill and 'long' legs diagnostic. At longer range, with practice, easily separated from Sandwich Tern by basic differences in structure, namely broader, more rounded wings, heavier body, larger more rounded head and broader, less forked tail. Flight and feeding habits also differ.

252 CASPIAN TERN *Sterna caspia*

PLATE 74 Figs 252a-252c
MAP 252

Length 48–59cm (19–23in.). Wingspan 127–140cm (50–55in.). Iris black. Bill mostly blood-red, distally black, tip often yellow, orange or white. Legs/feet black.

Almost cosmopolitan. Massive size and blood-red, dusky-tipped bill should prevent confusion with all but smaller Royal Tern (p. 383). Sexes alike; seasonal variation of head pattern. Juveniles separable from adults. Two subspecies listed, not separable in the field.

JUVENILE: Bill dull reddish-orange; legs blackish to dusky-yellow. **Head** More or less complete blackish cap, forehead and crown flecked with white; remainder white. **Body** Upperparts: saddle mostly pale grey with brown tips forming scaled pattern, heaviest on scapulars; rump unmarked greyish-white. Underparts white. **Wings** Upperwing: much as adult except for faint carpal bar, scattered brown tips across coverts, dusky secondaries and grey tertials with double brown bands at tip. **Tail** White, tip barred brown and grey.

FIRST-WINTER: As juvenile except saddle clearer grey; wings and tail unmoulted, faded through wear.

FIRST-SUMMER: As non-breeding adult except primaries and their coverts darker grey; faint brownish tips across remaining coverts and brownish tip to tail.

SECOND-WINTER: As non-breeding adult except some retain brownish tip to tail.

ADULT NON-BREEDING: As breeding adult except forehead and crown finely streaked white.

ADULT BREEDING: Black cap, slightly crested on nape; remainder white. **Body** Upperparts: saddle pale grey, rump white. Underparts white. **Wings** Upperwing: mostly pale grey; inner webs of outermost primaries slightly darker, secondaries tipped white. Underwing mainly white except for diagnostic blackish outer primaries decreasing in extent inwards (an excellent field character). **Tail** Pale greyish-white.

FHJ: Enormous; the largest tern (Herring Gull size). Flight strong, swift and graceful, though size and bulk rather gull-like. When fishing, patrols 3–15m above water with bill pointing downwards, pausing to hover before plunging—an impressive sight. In level flight, when not fishing, bill carried straight. Compared with Royal Tern (p. 383) is larger, more robust, with broader wings, the tail forked for a quarter of its length as opposed to half the length in Royal, and bill is dark-tipped where Royal's is orange throughout. Least sociable of all terns but often breeds in large, very tight colonies. Sometimes predatory, taking small birds, eggs and young of other terns etc. Call a hoarse 'kaaa' and shorter 'kowk'; juvenile beg note a high whistled 'pee-a-ee', in flight or perched.

DM: Almost cosmopolitan. *S.c. caspia* breeds North America along Atlantic coast from Virginia S to Gulf States, and locally on islands in interior lakes of North America W to interior California and S to Baja California. In Europe breeds along Baltic shores of Finland and Sweden; S Spain, then from northern Black Sea eastwards across Asia to Caspian Sea, Persian Gulf and interior lakes of E Siberia, USSR. Also breeds locally and discontinuously in Africa including Gulf of Suez and shores of Mozambique, South Africa and Namibia; status in W Africa uncertain. *S.c. strenua* breeds coasts of Australia and New Zealand. Egg-dates throughout year in tropical localities: Apr–Jul in north temperate regions, Nov–Jan in south temperate regions. Northern populations migratory and dispersive. In North America winters from southern California (rarely) S through Baja California, Gulf of Mexico and the Caribbean; may also occur Venezuela. In Europe winters coasts of Portugal, Spain and Mediterranean Basin S to Ghana, NW Africa, where relatively common. In E Africa winters locally Red Sea S to Arabian coasts and S Africa. In Asia a locally common winter visitor to Japan, especially Honshu, but less so in SE Asia where rare in winter to Thailand. In Australia and New Zealand mainly sedentary with local movements.

SS: Confusion possible only with smaller, narrower-winged Royal Tern (p. 383). Breeding adults of latter differ in unmarked orange-red bill, more prominent crest, underwing pattern and deeper fork to tail. Non-breeding Royal Tern has much whiter head than Caspian. Juveniles also differ in head pattern, underwing and leg colour.

253 INDIAN RIVER TERN *Sterna aurantia*

PLATE 77 Figs 253a-253b
MAP 253

Length 38–43cm (15–17in.). Wingspan not recorded. Iris black. Bill deep yellow. Legs orange-red.

Asiatic inland species, unlikely to be seen at sea. Sexes alike; seasonal variation. Juveniles separable from adults. No subspecies.

JUVENILE: Bill dusky-yellow with dark tip. **Head** Mostly brown, with white streaks forming indistinct cap; chin and throat greyish-white. **Body** Upperparts, including rump, grey, sullied with brown. Underparts white, sides of breast clouded grey-brown. **Wings** Upperwing as adult except primaries and coverts tipped brown with pale grey fringes. Underwing mostly white. **Tail** Grey, tipped brown with narrow white fringes.

ADULT NON-BREEDING: As breeding adult except black tip to bill; forehead and crown whitish.

ADULT BREEDING: Head Black cap, remainder white. **Body** Upperparts deep grey paling to light grey on rump. Underparts pearl-grey. **Wings** Upperwing deep grey, inner webs of primaries silvery-grey. Underwing white. **Tail** Long, deeply forked; mostly grey, outermost feathers white.

FHJ: Freshwater species occurring singly or in small parties along rivers; rarely strays to tidal creeks. Flight purposeful and strong though often jerky; long wings and streamered tail impart distinctive jizz.

DM: Found along inland rivers of Asia from Iran E through India, Burma and Malay Peninsula, where an uncommon resident in Thailand; does not apparently occur in Sri Lanka (Ali 1979). Egg-dates Mar–May.

SS: See Black-bellied Tern (p. 376).

254 SOUTH AMERICAN TERN *Sterna hirundinacea*

PLATE 78 Figs 254a-254d
MAP 254

Length 40–44cm (16–17½in.). Wingspan 84–86cm (33–34in.). Iris brown. Bill, legs/feet bright red.

Confined to South America; range overlaps with Arctic, Common and Antarctic Terns (p. 370, p. 370, p. 371). The former two visit South America in non-breeding dress; care required to separate from all stages of latter. Sexes alike; marked seasonal variation. Juveniles separable from adults. No subspecies.

JUVENILE: Bill blackish, legs/feet dull orange. **Head** Forehead brownish-white, crown, nape and ear-coverts brown streaked black, eye-crescent dusky; chin and throat buff, remainder, including hindneck, white. **Body** Upperparts: saddle grey, boldly barred blackish-brown; rump and uppertail-coverts white. Underparts white except buffish sides of breast and flanks. **Wings** Upperwing: outer 4–6 primaries mainly dusky-grey, outer web of 1st black, innermost and secondaries grey, tipped white. Remainder of upperwing grey, boldly barred blackish-brown. Underwing mostly white, tips of outermost primaries faintly greyer. **Tail** Grey, barred brown on outer webs.

FIRST-WINTER: Bill black, legs/feet dull red. **Head** Mostly white; streak through eye, hindcrown and nape blackish. **Body** Upperparts: saddle pale grey with scattered brownish tips; rump and uppertail-coverts white. Underparts white. **Wings** As juvenile except most median and greater coverts grey, carpal and lesser coverts edged darker forming noticeable carpal bar. **Tail** Grey, brown barring reduced or lacking.

ADULT NON-BREEDING: As breeding adult except: Bill/legs duller red. **Head** Forehead and forecrown mostly white. **Body** Underparts mostly white.

ADULT BREEDING: Head Black cap separated from grey chin and throat by whitish border. **Body** Upperparts: saddle pearl-grey; rump and uppertail-coverts white. Underparts pale grey, paling to white on lower belly and ventral area. **Wings** Upperwing pale pearl-grey, outer web of outermost primary black, innermost primaries and all secondaries edged white. Underwing mostly white, tips of outermost primaries slightly dusky. **Tail** White, deeply forked with long outer streamers.

FHJ: Slightly larger than Common and Antarctic Terns (p. 370, p. 371) with proportionately heavier, longer and slightly drooping bill. Gregarious, often fishes in large flocks, both over open water and kelp beds, plunge-diving from about 6m; occasionally hovers and picks from surface. Call a metallic 'kyick', also a screeching 'keer'.

DM: Confined to South America, migratory and dispersive, breeding on Falkland Is and both coasts of South America from Tierra del Fuego to about 25°S in Brazil and to about 15°S in Peru. In southern parts of range migratory, returning to Falkland colonies Sep/Oct; egg-dates Nov/Dec; departure begins Mar/Apr (Woods 1975), some dispersing only to adjacent waters. Recorded in Strait of Magellan all months except Sep and Apr (Humphrey *et al.* 1970). Many disperse N, reaching to about 5°S in Peru and 15°S in Brazil.

SS: Larger than both Arctic and Common Terns (p. 370, p. 370), which visit South America during austral summer in non-breeding plumage. Antarctic Tern (p. 371) occurs during austral winter on coasts of Brazil, Uruguay and Argentina (de Schauensee 1966). Breeding adults of latter species are darker grey above and below with proportionately shorter bills but require careful treatment to separate at sea; non-breeding adults also darker grey above whilst juveniles are browner and more finely barred above. Brown plumage is soon replaced by head and body moult, however, and may then be indistinguishable from first-winter and first-summer individuals of present species (identification criteria still evolving).

255 COMMON TERN *Sterna hirundo*

PLATE 75 Figs 255a-255d
MAP 255

Length 32–38cm (12½–15in.). Wingspan 79–81cm (31–32in.). Iris blackish. Bill usually scarlet with black tip; occasionally lacks dark tip. Legs/feet scarlet.

Breeds northern hemisphere, migrating to southern hemisphere. Range overlaps with Sandwich, Roseate, Arctic and Forster's Terns (p. 386, p. 373, p. 370, p. 372). Sexes similar; seasonal variation. Juveniles separable from adults. Four subspecies listed; *S.h. longipennis* differs from nominate in blackish bill and legs. Both Gray (1958) and Hays (1975) record Common × Arctic and Common × Roseate Tern hybrids, see also Robbins (1974).

JUVENILE: Bill pink or orange at base, distal half black; legs orange. **Head** Ginger-brown forehead of fledgling wears white by autumn; crown, nape and ear-coverts sooty-brown, remainder white. **Body** Upperparts: mantle, scapulars and back mostly pale grey with uniform ginger-brown wash and indistinct brown and white scaling; rump greyish, especially in centre. Underparts white. **Wings** Upperwing mostly pale grey with blackish carpal bar (very pronounced in recent fledglings) and blackish secondaries; tips of primaries blackish. Underwing as adult. **Tail** Lacks streamers; mostly greyish-white with blackish-grey outer web of outer tail feather.

FIRST-WINTER and FIRST-SUMMER: As non-breeding adult except for duskier crown; dark carpal bar and dusky trailing edge to secondaries: plumage often much worn and faded by first summer.

SECOND-WINTER: Much as non-breeding adult.

SECOND-SUMMER: As breeding adult, or with signs of immaturity (such as darker bill and white forehead.

ADULT NON-BREEDING: As breeding adult except bill all blackish, or with red base. **Head** Forehead and forecrown white. **Body** Underparts white. **Wings** Upperwing mostly pearl-grey. The distinctive dark wedge on outer primaries present during northern summer may be absent for short period in freshly moulted birds in their winter quarters; seems likely, however, that the inner unshed or older primaries would continue to show some colour degradation throughout year. **Tail** Lacks streamers.

ADULT BREEDING: Head Glossy black cap divided from whitish-grey chin and throat by indistinct whitish stripe (never as pronounced as in Arctic Tern, p. 370). **Body** Upperparts pearl-grey; rump off-white. Underparts greyish-white, variable in tone, some approaching greyness of Arctic Tern. **Wings** Upperwing mostly pearl-grey; wingtip shows distinct dark wedge from tip toward base of 5th or 6th primaries, but due to protracted moult process may be restricted to one or two inner primaries. Underwing mainly off-white with broad smudgy-black tips to outer 5–7 primaries; viewed against back light, when very close, only innermost primaries translucent. **Tail** Moderately streamered; mostly white, outer web of outer feather black.

FHJ: Compared with Arctic Tern (p. 370) appears longer-billed with longer and flatter crown. Flight silhouette of summer adult differs in proportionately broader, shorter wings, heavier body and shorter, broader tail: this makes part of bird in front of wings more or less same length as part projecting behind wings. For other comparisons see under this section in Arctic Tern (p. 370). Call a drawn-out 'kee-argh' and a rapidly repeated 'kik-kik-kik'.

DM: *S.h. hirundo* breeds eastern and central North America from Hudson Bay and Great Slave Lake S to islands off Gulf States, Bermuda, Bahamas, Virgin Is and islands off Venezuela; in eastern Atlantic on Azores and Madeira and in Africa coasts of Tunisia, Mauritania, Niger delta and across much of Europe. *S.h. tibetana* breeds Turkestan and Tibet. *S.h. minussensis* breeds central Asia, northern Mongolia. *S.h. longipennis* breeds NE Asia. Returns to colonies May; egg-dates May–Aug. American population migrates down both Pacific and Atlantic coasts, wintering from southern California and Florida S to Peru and Argentina. European population winters mainly from coasts of Mauritania S to Namibia and South Africa; Eurasian breeders winter south coast of Iran and NW India, whilst Asiatic population passes through Japan, Thailand and SW Pacific S to southern Australia. First-summer birds of all populations tend to remain in winter quarters; a few second-year types return to colonies after main arrival of adults.

SS: Separable in all but juvenile plumage from Arctic Tern (p. 370) by variably distinct dark wedge on primaries of upperwing (but beware distant views suggesting clear upperwing as in Arctic Tern). All ages show broad smudgy-black tips to outer primaries of underwing (much narrower and concise in Arctic Tern). For structural and other differences refer to main text above. See also Forster's, Roseate and White-cheeked Terns (p. 372, p. 373, p. 375).

256 ARCTIC TERN *Sterna paradisaea*

PLATE 75 Figs 256a-256d
MAP 256

Length 33–38cm (13–15in.). Wingspan 79–81cm (31–32in.). Iris blackish. Bill blood-red. Legs/feet red.

Breeds in northern hemisphere, migrating S to Antarctic. Range overlaps with Common, Roseate, Antarctic and South American Terns (p. 370, p. 373, p. 371, p. 369); all stages distinguishable from those species but easier with comparative experience. Sexes alike; seasonal variation. Juveniles separable from adults. No subspecies. Gray (1958) reported presumed Arctic × Common Tern hybrids.

JUVENILE: Bill varies: some have orange bases, by

autumn most have all-black bill. Legs/feet orange-red. **Head** Forehead, chin and throat white; blackish or brownish crown extends to nape and ear-coverts, hindneck white. **Body** Upperparts: dark grey, some with ginger-brown cast, but all usually without prominent scaling; rump pure white. **Wings** Upperwing mostly dark grey above; primaries tipped darker with only a faint carpal bar, secondaries pure white. Underwing as adult. **Tail** Shorter than adult's, lacks streamers; pure white except for grey outer web of outer feather.

FIRST-WINTER and FIRST-SUMMER: Much as non-breeding adult except for faint carpal bar and darker grey outer primaries; plumage often much faded and worn by first summer.

SECOND-WINTER: Much as non-breeding adult.

SECOND-SUMMER: As breeding adult, or with signs of immaturity (such as dark bill, white forehead and patchy grey underparts).

ADULT NON-BREEDING: As breeding adult except bill blackish, legs blackish-red; forehead and underparts white.

ADULT BREEDING: Head Glossy black cap divided from grey chin and throat by white facial stripe. **Body** Upperparts mostly grey; rump white. Underparts mainly grey; ventral area and undertail-coverts white. **Wings** Upperwing mostly grey; outer 7–8 primaries tipped darker, inner and all of secondaries narrowly edged white. Underwing pure white with narrow black tips forming thin trailing edge along outer primaries; most primaries translucent. **Tail** White; longish tail streamers.

FHJ: Compared with Common Tern (p. 370) breeding Arctic has shorter bill and more rounded head. In flight, combination of small head, narrow wings (particularly primaries) and long tail streamers imparts distinctive and characteristic attenuated jizz to rear end. Although varying with conditions, flight of Arctic usually more buoyant with slower, shallower more graceful strokes, with tail streamers tapering to wispy point. When perched Arctic shows shorter legs and tail streamers projecting well past wingtips (but apparent leg length often hard to determine). Juveniles and first-year birds have proportionately shorter, more rounded wings and tail than adults, giving jizz recalling that of marsh tern *Chlidonias* (p. 363) particularly when surface-feeding (see especially Whiskered Tern, p. 364). Call as Common Tern, perhaps harsher, more nasal.

DM: Circumpolar, breeding Arctic and sub-arctic regions of North America from Alaska and Canada S to British Columbia on W coast and Massachusetts on E coast. Also most of coastal Greenland north to about 83°N, Iceland, the Faeroes, Britain (mostly in north), Ireland, with small numbers in Brittany, France, and then from Baltic and Scandinavia E including Spitsbergen and N Russia to Bering Sea. Returns to colonies late May; egg-dates Jun/Jul; dispersal begins late Jul, most Aug. Undertakes remarkable migration, wintering S to Antarctic pack ice. Uncommon in western Atlantic during autumn or spring, indicating most move along western coasts of Europe and Africa. Abundant visitor in austral summer to southern Africa, particularly first-year birds, adults passing on to Antarctica. Similar passage occurs off western North and South America. During first and second summer most remain in southern hemisphere, dispersing throughout Southern Oceans.

SS: See Antarctic, Common, South American and Roseate Terns (p. 371, p. 370, p. 369, p. 373).

257 ANTARCTIC TERN
other: Wreathed Tern
Sterna vittata

PLATE 79 Figs 257a-257d

MAP 257

Length 41cm (16in.). Wingspan 79cm (31in.). Iris blackish. Bill bright red. Legs/feet dark red.

Southern Oceans. Resembles Arctic Tern (p. 370), from which difficult to separate although local Antarctic Terns are in breeding plumage when migrant Arctic Terns are in non-breeding plumage. Most confusion arises with South American and Kerguelen Terns (p. 369, p. 372). Sexes alike; seasonal variation. Juveniles and first-summer birds separable from adults. Four subspecies listed.

JUVENILE: Bill and legs black. **Head** Forehead brownish-white, crown and nape black mottled with white; remainder white. **Body** Upperparts: saddle grey strongly barred with black and washed with buff; rump white, uppertail-coverts finely barred brown. Underparts mostly white except for brown wash across breast and flanks. **Wings** Upperwing: primaries dark grey, subterminally tipped brown and fringed with white; secondaries grey; remainder as saddle. Underwing mostly white. **Tail** Shorter, less forked than adult, with darker grey outer webs and brownish tips.

NOTE Partial moult of head and body begins Mar, birds thus generally greyer on mantle and back with brownish tips; underparts white.

FIRST-SUMMER: Bill/legs blackish. Plumage much as non-breeding adult but with darker crown, scattered brownish tips on upperparts and dark carpal bar.

ADULT NON-BREEDING: As breeding adult except: Bare parts duller. **Head** Forehead, crown and lores white, merging well behind hindcrown into blackish nape and sides of face; remainder white. **Body** Underparts mostly white but many retain some grey (Fig. 257C, Plate 79). **Tail** Lacks streamers.

ADULT BREEDING: Black cap divided from grey chin and throat by white facial streak. **Body** Upperparts: saddle smoky-grey contrasting with white rump. Underparts mostly smoky-grey paling to white on undertail-coverts. **Wings** Upperwing grey; outer webs of outermost primaries darker forming faint wedge. Underwing white with narrow blackish line along trailing edge of primaries (as in Arctic Tern, p. 370). **Tail** Deeply forked; white.

FHJ: Resembles Arctic Tern though slightly larger and darker with heavier blood-red bill. Normally feeds by hovering 2–15m above sea and dipping to catch small prey over kelp beds and surf. When perched, legs longer than Arctic Tern. Call 'chit-chit-churr'.

DM: Almost circumpolar. *S.v. vittata* breeds Kerguelen, Crozets, Marion and Prince Edward Is; *S.v. tristanensis* Tristan da Cunha Is, Gough, St Paul and Amsterdam Is; *S.v. georgiae* South Georgia; *S.v. bethunei* sub-antarctic islands of New Zealand. Undetermined races also breed South Orkneys and South Shetlands. Returns to colonies Sep/Oct; egg-dates Oct–Jan; fledging and departure Jan–May. Movements not fully understood mainly due to confusion with other terns. Many populations appear to disperse widely to reach coasts of southern South America, and also to South Africa where flocks of up to 5,000 recorded near Cape Town Jul–Sep (Brooke & Sinclair, pers. comm.).

SS: Breeding adults distinguishable from South American Tern (p. 369) by darker grey underparts. Criteria for separation of other stages still evolving. See notes under Kerguelen Tern (p. 372). Non-breeders differ from non-breeding Arctic and Common Terns in brighter, heavier bill, larger size and thicker-set jizz; lores whiter than in either of those species, giving facial aspect recalling non-breeding Lesser Crested or Roseate Terns (p. 384, p. 373).

258 KERGUELEN TERN *Sterna virgata*

PLATE 79 Fig. 258
MAP 258

Length 33cm (13in.). Wingspan 71–79cm (28–31in.). Iris blackish. Bill red. Legs/feet orange-red.

Confined to a few islands in S Indian Ocean, one of world's rarest terns. Range overlaps with larger, much paler Antarctic Tern. Sexes alike; slight seasonal variation. Juveniles and first-summer types separable but plumage stages not well known. No subspecies.

JUVENILE: Bill/legs black. **Head** Forehead, crown and nape blackish-brown; remainder white, strongly tipped brown. **Body** Upperparts: saddle dark grey heavily barred brown and tan; rump whitish, uppertail-coverts lightly barred brown. Underparts: white, barred brown on breast and flanks; lower belly and ventral area whiter. **Wings** Upperwing: primaries grey, subterminally tipped brown and fringed tan; secondaries grey; remainder as saddle. Underwing mostly white (unlike adult). **Tail** Mostly grey, tip brownish.

FIRST-SUMMER: As non-breeding adult but mantle and upperwings retain brownish tips, forming carpal bar. Underwing white.

ADULT NON-BREEDING: Much as breeding adult except: Bill black, legs dark red; forehead grizzled white and black.

ADULT BREEDING: Head Black cap divided from dark grey chin and throat by white facial streak. **Body** Upperparts: saddle dark grey contrasting with white rump. Underparts dark grey. **Wings** Upperwing: dark grey, primaries darker. Underwing grey (see Antarctic Tern, p. 371). **Tail** Outer webs of all feathers grey; the whiter inner webs are visible only when tail spread.

FHJ: Smaller and darker than sympatric Antarctic Tern with smaller, rather thin, weak-looking bill and shorter, less forked tail. From the little information available, feeds both along tideline and inland. Call a high-pitched scream and a grinding chatter.

DM: Restricted to S Indian Ocean, small numbers breeding at Prince Edward, Marion, Crozet and Kerguelen Is (possibly also at Heard I.). Egg-dates Oct/Nov; fledging Dec/Jan. Apparently sedentary, dispersing only to seas adjacent to natal islands.

SS: Breeding adults distinguished from larger, sympatric Antarctic Tern by smaller bill, darker grey body and upperwing, grey underwing-coverts (except juveniles) and grey tail. Non-breeders differ in darker grey underparts and darker bill and legs.

259 FORSTER'S TERN *Sterna forsteri*

PLATE 75 Figs 259a-259d
MAP 259

Length 35–41cm (14–16in.). Wingspan 76–81cm (30–32in.). Iris blackish-brown. Bill orange-red, tip black. Legs/feet orange-red.

Confined to North America; winters S to northern South America. Range overlaps with Common, Arctic, Roseate and Sandwich Terns (p. 370, p. 370, p. 373, p. 386). Sexes alike; marked seasonal variation. Juveniles separable from adults. No subspecies.

JUVENILE: Bill blackish, base occasionally reddish; legs orange. **Head** Forehead, crown and nape brownish becoming whiter with wear, lores and ear-coverts blackish; chin, throat and hindneck white. **Body** Upperparts: saddle pale pearl-grey, all feathers heavily tipped buff-brown contrasting with whitish rump. Underparts white, sides of breast faintly clouded brown. **Wings** Upperwing as first-winter except for heavier brownish tips to greater and median coverts. **Tail** As first-winter.

FIRST-WINTER: Bare parts as juvenile. **Head** Mostly white; nape pale grey lightly spotted darker grey, with conspicuous black face mask from lores through eye to ear-coverts. **Body** Upperparts: saddle pale pearl-grey merging into greyish-white rump. Underparts white. **Wings** Upperwing mostly pale grey; outer webs and tips of outer 5–7 primaries blackish and contrast with silvery white inner primaries and outer secondaries which form a distinct paler triangle on rear of wing. At very close range dusky innermost secondaries, tertials and faint carpal bar. **Tail** Outer feathers white, remainder pale grey with dark tips to outer two or three pairs of feathers (appears white at distance).

FIRST-SUMMER: Much as non-breeding adult except base of bill red, extreme tip whitish; nape generally darker with more extensive eye patch; outer primaries darker with faint mottling on carpal, tertials and inner secondaries.

ADULT NON-BREEDING: As breeding adult except bill blackish, base often red; legs dull orange-red. Head pattern as first-winter but nape usually paler; lacks tail streamers.

ADULT BREEDING: Head Glossy black cap, remainder white. **Body** Upperparts: saddle pale pearl-grey merging, without contrast, into greyish-white rump. Underparts white. **Wings** Upperwing mostly pale pearl-grey; outer webs and tips of outer 3–5 primaries dark grey, remaining primaries silvery-white, often strikingly paler than rest of upperwing. Underwing uniform whitish-grey; outer web of 1st and tips of outer 3–5 primaries dusky-grey. **Tail** Deeply forked with long streamers; mostly grey with white outer web of outer tail feather.

FHJ: In summer closely resembles Common Tern (p. 370) in jizz, although bill longer, more robust and, when perched, legs noticeably longer, with tail streamers projecting past wingtip. Nests coastal and, more commonly, inland marshes, over which hawks for insects etc. Habits more maritime during winter, when it often dives for food from up to 9m, its pale plumage, head pattern and jizz recalling dainty Sandwich Tern (p. 386); at rest, however, bulk and jizz resemble Common Tern. Call a diagnostic 'tzaa-ap', also a shrill 'kit-kit-kit'.

DM: Breeds temperate North America from prairie provinces of Canada S to SE California and from SE Texas N along Atlantic coast to New Jersey. Returns to colonies May; egg-dates Jun/Jul. Winters on west coast from central California S to Guatemala, perhaps even to Panama; on eastern littoral from Virginia S through Florida, and West Indies (should be looked for in Venezuela). Vagrant to Iceland, and England (see Cave 1982).

SS: In summer adults separated from Common Tern (p. 370) by silvery primaries, white underparts, heavier bill, longer legs, tail streamers, and diagnostic call. In eastern Atlantic during winter could be overlooked as Sandwich Tern (p. 386).

260 TRUDEAU'S TERN
other: Snowy-crowned Tern
Sterna trudeaui

PLATE 77 Figs 260a-260c
MAP 260

Length 28–35cm (11–14in.). Wingspan 76–78cm (30–31in.). Iris blackish. Bill yellow with black subterminal band. Legs/feet orange.

Confined to southern South America. Sexes alike; marked seasonal difference. Juveniles separable from adults. No subspecies.

JUVENILE: Base of bill yellowish-brown, remainder black; legs dull yellow. Plumage as non-breeding adult except: **Head** Dusky eye-crescent and blackish streak across ear-coverts more extensive; faint brownish mottling on crown and nape. **Body** Upperparts: saddle mainly pale grey with indistinct brownish tips. **Wings** Upperwing: primaries and outermost primary-coverts mostly dark dusky-grey with fringes and inner webs of innermost primaries white; secondaries white with grey centres. Remaining coverts as upperparts. **Tail** Grey with brownish tips and white fringes.

FIRST-SUMMER: As non-breeding adult except outer webs of outer 3 primaries blackish-grey; alula and greater primary-coverts faintly mottled grey-brown.

ADULT NON-BREEDING: Bill mostly black, tip yellow; leg colour unrecorded, presumably blackish. Plumage as breeding adult except eye patch greyer; nape sometimes faintly grey; underparts white; silvery frosting on primaries more pronounced.

ADULT BREEDING: Head Mostly white, conspicuous black eye patch. **Body** Upperparts: saddle pale grey; rump white. **Wings** Upperwing pale grey shading to silvery on primaries; secondaries narrowly edged white. Underwing white. **Tail** Greyish-white; forked, but lacks long streamers.

FHJ: Flight and jizz recall Forster's Tern (p. 372) but tail averages shorter. Mainly a freshwater species but commonly occurs along coasts, over lagoons and at river mouths, especially in non-breeding season. Call rather like Forster's Tern, an explosive 'tik-tik-tik'.

DM: Confined to South America. Breeds coast and interior of Uruguay and Argentina casually S to Santa Cruz, occasionally Straits of Magellan. On western littoral in Chile from Aconcagua S to Llanquihue. Egg-dates Oct–Jan; dispersal not fully known. Type specimen was reputedly taken off Cape May, New Jersey, USA. More recently has been reported at several northerly locations on Pacific littoral, including Paracas, Peru (Donaghue & Peterson 1980).

SS: Breeding adults distinctive. Non-breeding adults closely resemble Forster's Tern (p. 372) in appearance but ranges do not normally overlap. Can be separated from latter species by yellow tip to black bill.

261 ROSEATE TERN
Sterna dougallii

PLATE 75 Figs 261a-261d
MAP 261

Length 35–43cm (14–17in.). Wingspan 76–79cm (30–31in.). Iris blackish-brown. Bill mostly black, base dull red. Legs/feet dark red.

Widespread throughout Old World, local in Americas. Range overlaps with Arctic, Common and Sandwich Terns (p. 370, p. 370, p. 386). Care needed to separate from those species at all ages but straightforward with comparative experience. Sexes alike; seasonal variation. Juveniles and subsequent stages separable from adult. Five subspecies listed. Possible Roseate × Common

Tern hybrids have been listed by Gray (1958), Hays (1975), with an account of possible interbreeding by Robbins (1974).

JUVENILE: Bill/legs black. **Head** Crown, nape and ear-coverts sooty-brown; forehead off-white or pale brown. Chin, throat and hindneck white. **Body** Saddle grey with buffish cast (richer in fledgling), most larger feathers with bold blackish bars producing scaly appearance; rump and uppertail-coverts white. Underparts white. **Wings** Upperwing mostly pale grey; primaries and secondaries tipped white forming noticeable trailing edge to wing; dark carpal bar. Underwing as adult. **Tail** White, lacks streamers.

FIRST-WINTER and FIRST-SUMMER: As juvenile except forehead whiter, upperparts mostly clear grey, carpal bar reduced or lacking; plumage much worn and faded by first summer.

ADULT NON-BREEDING: As breeding adult except: Bill black, legs brownish-orange. **Head** Forehead and crown white. **Body** Underparts mostly white; pinkish cast, if present, restricted to belly. **Wings** Upperwing: outer webs of outer 3–5 primaries blackish, forming dark leading edge on outer wing (valid until loss of outer primaries during moult).

ADULT BREEDING: Head Glossy black cap; remainder white. (Unlike congeners full black cap retained until late autumn, a useful field character.) **Body** Upperparts very pale grey; rump white. Underparts white, often rosy-pink in fresh plumage. **Wings** Upperwing mostly very pale grey; outer 3–5 primaries as non-breeding adult but paler, often appearing as dark grey leading edge to outer wing. Underwing, including primary tips, pure white (a useful field character). **Tail** White; very long streamers.

FHJ: Pale upperparts, often appearing white, slender body and long-streamered tail give distinctive appearance to summer adults. When perched, tail streamers extend well past wingtip. By autumn, however, some may lack streamers (probably due to moult, Tucker 1980). Bill longer and deeper than in Common Tern. Occasionally harries other terns; flight usually more graceful than congeners; habits almost exclusively marine. Call a soft wader-like 'chew-ick' and a grating 'aach'.

DM: Both sedentary and migratory throughout tropical and temperate regions. *S.d. dougallii* breeds locally in North America from Nova Scotia discontinuously S to West Indies, Central America and Venezuela. Also in Europe, mainly Britain and Ireland but small colonies in Brittany (France), with sporadic breeding reported from Denmark, Germany and off West Africa, Mauritania, perhaps Tunisia; locally in South Africa, but colonies up to 5,000 further N on Kiunga Is, off Kenya. *S.d. arideensis* breeds Seychelles, Mauritius and Cargados Carajos in Indian Ocean. *S.d. korustes* breeds Sri Lanka, Andaman Is and islands off W coasts of India. *S.d. gracilis* breeds Moluccas and northern Australia. *S.d. bangsi* Riukiu, Solomon, Philippine and Kei Is. Egg-dates Apr–Aug (N Atlantic), throughout year in tropics. Tropical populations probably resident. North American population winters S to Caribbean and adjacent Atlantic, occasionally S to Brazil. European population departs Aug/Sep and by late Sep most are in main wintering quarters off coast of NW Africa between Equator and 10°N. First-summer and some second-summer birds remain in these areas before returning N to breed, usually in their third calendar-year. NOTE Numbers apparently decreasing.

SS: In Queensland, Australia, beware White-fronted Tern (p. 374) which may occasionally occur. Breeding adults differ from Common and Arctic Terns (p. 370, p. 370) in much paler plumage, heavier darker bill, and long tail streamers projecting well beyond wingtips when perched. Juveniles and first-winter birds differ in head and wing patterns and, even at this age, outer tail feathers project beyond wingtips when perched (Tucker, pers. comm.). See also Sandwich Tern (p. 386).

262 WHITE-FRONTED TERN
Sterna striata

PLATE 79 Figs 262a-262d
MAP 262

Length 35–43cm (14–17in.). Wingspan not recorded. Iris brown. Bill black. Legs/feet dark burgundy.

Confined to New Zealand and SE Australia. Adults most likely to be confused with Common Tern (p. 370) but separated by almost white underwing. See also non-breeding Black-fronted Tern (p. 380). Sexes alike; seasonal variation. Juveniles separable. No subspecies.

JUVENILE: Bill/legs blackish-grey. **Head** Forehead narrowly white merging into dark clove-brown cap; remainder white. **Body** Upperparts: saddle grey, each feather edged brown forming chequered pattern; rump white. Underparts white. **Wings** Upperwing: outermost primaries and their coverts dark grey, subterminally brown, with white tips paling to grey on innermost primaries; remainder grey, tipped brown, heaviest along lesser and median coverts forming carpal bar. Underwing mostly white, tips of outermost primaries dusky-grey. **Tail** Mostly white, tips brown; lacks streamers of adult.

FIRST-SUMMER: Much as non-breeding adult except for darker head and primaries with pronounced carpal bar.

ADULT NON-BREEDING: As breeding adult except whiter crown; tail lacks streamers.

ADULT BREEDING (acquired midwinter by some individuals): **Head** Narrow white band over base of bill; cap black, hindneck, chin and throat white. **Body** Upperparts: saddle pale pearl-grey, rump white. Underparts white, some show faint pinkish cast. **Wings** Upperwing: outer web of outermost primary black, remainder pale pearl-grey. Underwing white except for blackish outer primary and faint dusky tips to outermost 3–5 primaries. **Tail** White; outer web of outer feather blackish.

FHJ: Appears very white in flight, recalling Roseate Tern (p. 373), though ranges do not normally overlap. Like that species, black bill longer and more robust than Common Tern's. In breeding plumage tail deeply forked with long streamers projecting up to 35mm beyond wingtip when perched. Streamers soon break (moult?) and many engaged in breeding have wingtips equal to or extending past tail. Feeds mainly over breaking surf, particularly over the backwash on outgoing tides of estuaries. Flight graceful and buoyant; dives from about 10m but when shoals of fish are close to surface from about 3m. Prefers to roost on rocks, shingle banks, even stone walls rather than sand or mudflats. Calls frequently in flight, 'keck-keck' and 'kee-eck-kee-eck'.

DM: Restricted to New Zealand and its outlying islands, where the commonest tern of coastal waters. A few breed Tasmania (Fullagar & van Tets, pers. comm.). Returns to colonies from Aug onwards; egg-dates Oct/Nov; fledging begins Dec/Jan. Many birds, perhaps mostly adults, disperse to seas around New Zealand whilst others, particularly juveniles, disperse NW across Tasman Sea to winter in SE Australia, where widespread, extending (rarely) N to Rockhampton, Queensland, and W to Adelaide, South Australia. Most first-summer birds apparently return to New Zealand during austral spring.

SS: Breeding adults differ from smaller Common Tern (p. 370) in whiter appearance, particularly underwing, and proportionately longer bill. At close range narrow white band over base of bill also useful, but non-breeding Roseate and Common Terns have white foreheads. Non-breeding White-fronted Terns retain whiter appearance and differ further from Common Tern in blacker lores and white underwing. Care required in separating from Roseate Tern (p. 374) but range overlaps (occasionally) only along Queensland coast. See also non-breeding Black-fronted Tern (p. 380). Overlaps with Antarctic Tern (p. 371) at Auckland I. (Fullagar & van Tets, pers. comm.).

263 WHITE-CHEEKED TERN *Sterna repressa*

PLATE 77 Figs 263a-263c
MAP 263

Length 30–35cm (12–14in.). Wingspan not recorded. Iris brownish-black. Bill red, tip blackish. Legs/feet red.

Endemic to NW Indian Ocean, where range overlaps with migratory Common Tern (p. 370). Sexes alike; marked seasonal variation. Juveniles separable from adults. No subspecies.

JUVENILE: Bill blackish-red; legs dusky-yellow. Plumage as first-winter except saddle feathers tipped brown with whitish fringes; darker brown tip to tail.

FIRST-WINTER: Forehead and forecrown white, crown and nape blackish extending forwards through eye; remainder, including hindneck and lores, white. **Body** Upperparts medium grey, paling to greyish-white on rump. Underparts white. **Wings** Upperwing: outer 2 primaries blackish, inner webs white; remaining primaries and secondaries dusky-grey, with indistinct brown tips, fringed with white, decreasing inwards. Coverts mostly grey but marginal, lesser, and outer primary-coverts blackish-grey forming carpal bar. Underwing mostly white, primaries and secondaries greyer. **Tail** Outer webs dusky-grey, inner webs white.

ADULT NON-BREEDING: Bill blackish-red. **Head and Body** As first-winter. **Wings** Upperwing: outer web of outermost primary and all primary tips dusky-grey forming narrow trailing edge to outer wing; outer webs of remaining primaries whitish-grey forming silvery-grey tip to otherwise deep grey upperwing. Underwing grey with blackish tips of primaries forming trailing edge. **Tail** Lacks streamers; mostly grey above with outermost feathers darkest; whiter below.

ADULT BREEDING: As non-breeding adult except black cap separated from dark vinaceous-grey underparts by white facial streak. Upperwing generally greyer (except primaries); longer tail streamers.

FHJ: Differs from Common Tern in shorter bill, smaller size, more compact jizz; flight jizz closer to *Chlidonias* than *Sterna*. Gregarious, often in large numbers.

DM: NW Indian Ocean. Breeds in Red Sea from Gulf of Suez, Gulf of Aden, Somaliland and Persian Gulf E to Malabar coast, western India and Laccadive Is. Also in E Africa S to Kiunga Is, Kenya. Return to colonies begins Apr/May; egg-dates May–Aug. Dispersal begins Aug, most apparently moving S along coasts towards western India, and perhaps to a lesser extent NE Africa, where Britton (1980) records it as rather local in Kenya. Stragglers have reached N to Elat, northern Red Sea, and S to Natal, South Africa.

SS: Breeding adults distinctive within range. In northern winter months non-breeders best separated from Common Tern (p. 370) by greyer rump and tail, and darker grey upperwing contrasting with silvery bases of primaries. Juvenile and first-winter White-cheeked Terns differ from similar stages of Common Tern in darker grey upperparts, rump and tail; carpal bar on upperwing also blacker and more extensive but, because of generally darker upperwing, may appear less apparent than in Common Tern. Arctic Tern (p. 370), which is rare along NE African coast, differs at all ages in white rump and tail.

264 BLACK-NAPED TERN *Sterna sumatrana*

PLATE 80 Figs 264a-264b
MAP 264

Length 30–32cm (12–12½in.). Wingspan 61cm (24in.). Iris brown. Bill black, occasionally with small yellowish or whitish tip. Legs/feet black.

Tropical Indian and Pacific Oceans. Adults distinctive but juveniles and immatures may be overlooked as Little or Fairy Terns (p. 382, p. 379) by inexperienced birders. Sexes alike; no seasonal variation. Juveniles and immatures separable. One subspecies.

JUVENILE: Bill dusky-yellow, shorter and proportionately thicker than adult's. **Head** Including hindneck mostly white, sides of head and nape mottled greyish-brown forming continuous band from eye to nape. **Body** Upperparts: saddle sepia-brown broadly edged buff and grey; rump and uppertail-coverts whitish. Underparts white. **Wings** Outermost primaries dark grey, subterminally brown with white tips; remainder of upperwing pale grey, coverts and tertials variably tipped buff-brown. Underwing white. **Tail** Rounded, not forked; mostly grey, subterminally brown, tip white.

IMMATURE (presumed first-winter): Bill and legs blackish. Resembles adult except: **Head** Crown mostly white, faintly tipped with brown; an incomplete blackish band runs from lores, through eye to nape. **Body** Upperparts: saddle mostly pale grey with scattered brownish tips. **Wings** Upperwing: mainly pale grey, tertials and some coverts indistinctly tipped pale brown. **Tail** White; lacks streamers.

ADULT: Head Mostly white except for triangular black spot before eye and continuing in broadening band to nape. **Body** Upperparts: pale dove-grey; underparts white, sometimes with rosy cast. **Wings** Upperwing: mainly pale dove-grey; outer web of outermost primary black, showing as dark edge on folded wing and in flight. Underwing mostly white. **Tail** Deeply forked; white.

FHJ: Appears almost white in the field except for black band from eye to nape. Feeds like a noddy, skimming low over open sea or shallow lagoons, snatching at prey, during which occasionally submerges. Call a short, sharp 'tsii-chee-chi-chip'; when excited a hurried 'chit-chit-chit-er'.

DM: Tropical Indian and Pacific Oceans. *S.s. mathewsi* breeds from Madagascar and Seychelles to Chagos Is, occasionally wandering S to Natal, South Africa (Brooke & Sinclair 1978), and N to Masirah I., where visually recorded (Strickland 1971) though status there uncertain. *S.s. sumatrana* breeds Andaman Is, Malay Archipelago, northeast Australia, southern China, Philippines, and from Amami Is, Japan, S through Liu Kiu Is to Samoa. Recorded at breeding stations throughout year, suggesting mainly sedentary habits; egg-dates probably throughout year in scattered populations.

SS: Confusion should not arise if properly seen, but see juveniles of Little (Least) and Fairy Terns (p. 382, p. 379), both of which differ in size, jizz and jerky or hovering flight. Beware also any small/medium-sized tern in non-breeding plumage, which would have similar head pattern to present species.

265 BLACK-BELLIED TERN
Sterna melanogastra

PLATE 79 Figs 265a-265b
MAP 265

Length 30–33cm (12–13in.). Wingspan not recorded. Iris blackish. Bill yellowish-orange. Legs/feet orange-red.

Asiatic freshwater tern. Unmistakable in breeding plumage; non-breeders could be confused with shorter-tailed Whiskered Tern but bill and legs yellowish or orange. See also larger Indian River Tern (p. 369). Sexes alike; seasonal variation.

JUVENILE: No specimen examined.

ADULT NON-BREEDING: As breeding adult except tip of bill dusky (in skins); forehead and crown white; underparts mostly white, many show traces of black on belly.

ADULT BREEDING: Head Black cap, remainder white. **Body** Upperparts pale dove-grey. Underparts: upper breast grey merging into blackish-brown belly. **Wings** Upperwing pale dove-grey. Underwing white. **Tail** Dove-grey, outer feathers white.

FHJ: Freshwater tern, frequenting rivers, jheels etc. Differs from Indian River Tern (p. 369) in smaller size, less robust bill and lighter jizz. Often hawks for insects. At rest tail of breeding birds extends well past wingtip.

DM: Restricted to Asia; breeds from Indus valley E and S through India, Burma, Sri Lanka and Thailand. Egg-dates Mar/Apr. Unlikely to be seen at sea.

SS: See Whiskered and Indian River Terns (p. 364, p. 369).

266 ALEUTIAN TERN
Sterna aleutica

PLATE 73 Figs 266a-266b
MAP 266

Length 33–38cm (13–15in.). Wingspan 76–81cm (30–32in.). Iris brown. Bill, legs/feet black.

Breeds eastern Siberia and western Alaska; wintering range unknown. Distinctive in N Pacific, where occurs alongside Arctic and Common Terns; winter range may overlap with Grey-backed Tern (p. 377). Sexes alike; seasonal variation unknown. Juveniles separable from adults but subsequent plumages to maturity poorly known. No subspecies.

JUVENILE: Head Forehead, lores and crown fawn-brown lightly streaked blackish merging into darker brown nape; sides of face, chin and throat white, variably washed with fawn-brown. **Body** Upperparts: saddle sepia-brown tipped buff-brown, heaviest on scapulars; rump pale grey. Underparts white, except sides of breast, flanks and belly variably washed with fawn-brown. **Wings** Upperwing: primaries slate-grey, subterminally tipped brown with narrow white fringes and inner webs; secondaries grey, tipped white; marginal coverts white, remainder as saddle. Underwing as adult. **Tail** Pale grey, subterminally brown, fringed white.

FIRST-SUMMER: Head Much as breeding adult except crown flecked grey or white. **Body** Upperparts mostly grey, saddle fringed paler. Underparts whitish. **Tail** Shorter than adult. (Based on notes by Stallcup, pers. comm.)

ADULT NON-BREEDING: As breeding adult except white streaking to forecrown and almost white underparts. (Stallcup, pers. comm.)

ADULT BREEDING: Head Forehead broadly white, forming sharply defined V extending over black loral streak to just behind eye. Crown and nape black; sides of face, chin and throat bordering black cap white, shading to lead-grey on throat. **Body** Upperparts: saddle lead-grey, rump and uppertail-coverts conspicuously white. Underparts mainly grey, slightly paler than upperparts, shading to white on undertail-coverts. **Wings** Upperwing: outer webs of outermost 4–5 primaries grey, inner webs white; remaining inner primaries paler, forming pale inner window in some lights; remainder lead-grey, tips of secondaries and marginal coverts white. Underwing mostly pale greyish-white with diffuse black line on trailing edge of primaries and secondaries. **Tail** White, deeply forked.

FHJ: Size and streamered tail recall Arctic Tern (p. 370), although wing point projects over tail point when perched. Differs from Arctic in white forehead and much darker plumage. Flight graceful, strong and direct, often high over ocean, with slower, deeper wingbeats than in Arctic Tern. Feeding methods not described. Often calls in flight; soft, wader-like, three-syllable note so untern-like that a distinctive field character.

DM: Restricted to Siberia, USSR, and Alaska, USA, where nests along coasts and at river mouths and lagoons of Bering, Okhotsk and South Chukchi Seas. Breeds sporadically along far eastern shores of USSR, including eastern coasts of Kamchatka and Sakhalin, but status unknown. Nechaev (1977) described a mixed colony of about 500 pairs and 1,000 pairs of Common Terns on Lyarvo I., Dagi Bay, Sakhalin. More is known of its status in Alaska, where Sowls *et al.* (1978) estimated population of 10,000 birds. The following is based largely on Gill (pers. comm.). Returns to colonies on S and SW coasts of Alaska, early May; egg-dates Jun; fledging and dispersal Aug/Sep. Current N American breeding range extends over approximately four-fifths of Alaska's 56,400-km coastline from Kotzebue S and W to Alaska Peninsula and western Aleutian Is, and N and E through Gulf of Alaska to Dry Bay, possibly further S. Throughout its range nests either in pure colonies or in association with Common or Arctic Terns. Its wintering range remains a mystery. By analogy with other terns, seems likely that it moves S, but an exhaustive search of all available literature has failed to yield confirmed winter records anywhere. Not seen off natal islands or coasts during the winter months and this may indicate a wide pelagic dispersal into N Pacific. Has been recorded once at Sagami Bay, Honshu, Japan. More surprising was the appearance of one at an Arctic Tern colony on Farne Is, Britain, during May 1979 (the only west Palearctic record).

SS: Unlikely to be confused with either Arctic or Common Terns (p. 370, p. 370) if seen well. Grey-backed Tern (p. 377) bears closest resemblance and, if present species does migrate S in northern winter, their ranges may well overlap in N or central Pacific.

267 GREY-BACKED TERN
other: Spectacled Tern
Sterna lunata

PLATE 73 Figs 267a-267b

MAP 267

Length 35–38cm (14–15in.). Wingspan 73–76cm (29–30in.). Iris brown. Bill, legs/feet black.

Confined to tropical Pacific Ocean. Closely allied to Bridled Tern (p. 378), from which differs in greyer saddle and upperwings. Replaces that species in central and NE areas of tropical Pacific, but status and distribution poorly known in W and S parts of range. Sexes alike; slight seasonal variation. Juveniles and first-summer types separable from adults. No subspecies.

JUVENILE: Head Resembles adult's pattern; forehead, lower lores and streak over eye white, finely peppered grey and brown; forecrown similar but darker merging into blackish-brown hindcrown and nape. Hindneck narrowly whitish-grey; sides of face, chin and throat white. **Body** Upperparts wholly grey tipped buff-brown and white, heaviest on scapulars. Underparts mainly white, sides of breast and flanks variably washed with grey. **Wings** Upperwing: primaries greyish-black, inner webs white shading to grey secondaries; marginal coverts white, remainder grey tipped buff-brown. Underwing as adult. **Tail** Mostly dark grey, outer retrice white, tipped dusky.

FIRST-SUMMER: As breeding adult except crown and nape browner, streaked with white. Upperparts lack buff and white tips of juvenile.

ADULT NON-BREEDING: As breeding adult but forecrown faintly streaked with white.

ADULT BREEDING: Head Forehead narrowly white extending over black loral streak to behind eye as narrow supercilium; crown and nape black; sides of face, chin and throat white. **Body** Upperparts pale brownish-grey; underparts white. **Wings** Upperwing: primaries and secondaries blackish-grey, marginal coverts white; remainder grey with brownish cast. Underwing white, primaries and secondaries washed with brown. **Tail** Brownish-grey, long outermost streamer white.

FHJ: Closely resembles Bridled Tern (p. 378) in flight and appearance.

DM: Breeding restricted to central tropical Pacific Ocean but range poorly documented; occurs Samoa, Tonga, Fiji and Phoenix, rarer in Solomons, Bismarck Archipelago and Micronesia (Mayr 1945). Also occurs Hawaiian chain, breeding on Moku Manu off Oahu, and on Northwest Chain (Shallenberger 1978), S through Oceania to Gilbert, Society and Tuamotu Is; casual E to Easter I.

SS: Much greyer above than Sooty Tern (p. 378), narrow white forehead and supercilium resembling more closely Bridled Tern (p. 378). Differs from latter species in slighter, more slender bill, greyer upperparts, particularly saddle, whiter underparts and less white on outer tail feathers; winter adults have white flecking to forecrown, whilst juveniles greyer above. See also Aleutian Tern (p. 376), whose wintering quarters yet to be discovered.

268 BRIDLED TERN
other: Brown-winged Tern
Sterna anaethetus

PLATE 73 Figs 268a-268b

MAP 268

Length 35–38cm (14–15in.). Wingspan 76cm (30in.). Iris dark brown. Bill, legs/feet black.

Widespread throughout tropical oceans. Range overlaps with both Sooty and Grey-backed Terns (p. 378, p. 377), from which readily separable although extreme range can negate differences. Sexes alike; no marked seasonal variation. Juveniles and thus first-summer types separable from adults, although specimens of latter not examined. Seven subspecies listed, none of which separable at sea.

JUVENILE: Head Resembles adult's pattern; forehead, lower lores and streak over eye white, finely peppered brownish-grey; forecrown buff-brown merging evenly into blackish hindcrown and nape; sides of face, chin and throat white. **Body** Upperparts brownish-grey tipped with buff and white, heaviest on scapulars. Underparts mostly greyish white, sides of breast and flanks grey. **Wings** Upperwing dark brownish-grey, coverts and tertials tipped with buff. Underwing as adult. **Tail** Brownish-grey; undertail white.

FIRST-SUMMER: No specimen examined; presumably as adult, perhaps head pattern less defined, tail shorter, without streamers and lacking white outer tail feathers.

ADULT: Head Forehead narrowly white, extending over black loral streak to behind eye as a narrow supercilium; crown and nape black. Sides of face, chin and throat white. Hindneck has narrow whitish grey collar (this often hard to discern in both perched and flying birds). **Body** Upperparts brownish-black. Underparts white, lightly clouded with grey. **Wings** Upperwing: blackish-brown, darker on primaries and secondaries; marginal coverts white. Underwing white, primaries and secondaries mostly sepia-brown. **Tail** Blackish-brown above, outermost feathers white; undertail white.

FHJ: Smaller than Sooty Tern (p. 378) and less pelagic in habits, normally frequenting inshore waters; usually returns to landfall each night to roost. Flight often stated as being swifter and more graceful than that of Sooty Tern but much dependent on conditions; when seen together there is little difference (pers. obs.). Feeding method as described for Sooty Tern; occasionally rests on water. Call a harsh, yapping 'wep-wep' or 'wup-wup'.

DM: Circumequatorial distribution. *S.a. nelsoni* breeds Pacific coast of Mexico and Central America. *S.a. melanoptera* islets off coast of Honduras, Venezuela, West Indies and Bahamas; also off Africa in Gulf of Guinea at Annobon I., possibly also São Tomé and near Principe. *S.a. juligula* breeds Red Sea and Persian Gulf. *S.a. antarctica* Mauritius, Seychelles, Laccadive and Cocos (Keeling) Is. *S.a. rogersi* W Australia. *S.a. anaethetus* Philippines and Formosa. *S.a. novaehollandiae* Queensland, Australia. Migratory and dispersive, now recorded regularly in western Gulf of Mexico and in Gulf Stream north to N Carolina waters during warmer months (Booth & Lee 1979); also occurs elsewhere along N American Atlantic coasts, usually after hurricanes. Red Sea and Persian Gulf populations move mainly S in winter to Mozambique, occasionally Natal (Brooke & Sinclair 1978); also to India and occasionally to northern Red Sea (Krabbe, pers. comm.).

SS: Adults resemble slightly larger Sooty Tern (p. 378), but forehead narrowly white and extending over and behind eye in narrow supercilium. Upperparts much browner and usually separated from black nape by narrow greyish collar. Patterned head and pale underparts of juvenile distinctly different from mostly blackish juvenile Sooty Tern. See also Grey-backed Tern (p. 377).

269 SOOTY TERN
other: Wideawake
Sterna fuscata

PLATE 73 Figs 269a-269c

MAP 269

Length 43–45cm (17–18in.). Wingspan 86–94cm (34–37in.). Iris brown. Bill, legs/feet black.

Widespread throughout tropical oceans, where range overlaps with both Bridled and Grey-backed Terns (p. 378, p. 377). Separation difficult at long range but straightforward when perched or at closer range. Sexes alike; no marked seasonal variation. Juveniles and first-summer types separable from adults. Seven subspecies listed, none of which separable at sea.

JUVENILE: Bill smaller than adult's. **Head** Wholly blackish-brown. **Body** Upperparts mostly blackish-brown tipped buff-white, heaviest on scapulars. Underparts mostly blackish, lower belly tipped buff-white, ventral area and undertail-coverts whitish-grey. **Wings** Upperwing: blackish-brown, coverts and tertials tipped with white. Underwing as adult. **Tail** Shorter than adult's, lacks streamers; mainly black above, outer rectrice and tips grey; white below, innermost feathers tipped brown.

FIRST-SUMMER: Variable; resembles adult except chin, throat and upper breast blackish, remainder of underparts white; or with underparts mostly white, clouded dusky on chin, throat and upper breast.

ADULT BREEDING: Head Forehead broadly white separated from white chin and throat by black loral stripe running from base of bill to eye; crown and nape black. **Body** Upperparts blackish. Underparts white. **Wings** Upperwing: Mainly black, marginal coverts white. Underwing white, alula, primaries and secondaries brownish. **Tail** Black above, long outer streamers white. Appears mostly white from below, innermost feathers tipped brown (seen when fanned). NOTE Non-breeding plumage similar but generally dowdy and faded, particularly on nape.

FHJ: Tropical and subtropical pelagic tern, frequently encountered many hundreds of miles from landfall. Highly gregarious, often associates with other seabirds over shoaling fish but does not plunge-dive; obtains prey by swooping low over water and snatching from surface. Bruyns & Voous (1965) suggest that it also feeds at night. Rarely returns to landfall, except to breed or under severe climatic conditions; habits thus more pelagic than similar 'offshore' Bridled Tern (p. 378). Often circles high over ocean; rarely settles on water. (Presumably sleeps on wing.) Call note 'ker-wacky-wack'.

DM: Circumequatorial, often breeding in immense colonies. *S.f. oahuensis* Hawaiian and Bonin Is in N Pacific. *S.f. crissalis* W Mexican Is and Galapagos Is in central eastern Pacific S to San Felix I., Chile. In Atlantic Ocean *S.f. fuscata* breeds on scattered islets from Alacran Reef (Yucatan) to Gulf coast of Florida, occasionally Texas N to North Carolina; also at Bahamas, West Indies, Fernando de Noronha, Ascension, St Helena, and Tenhosas Is, Gulf of Guinea, off West Africa. In Indian Ocean *S.f. somaliensis* breeds Mait I., Gulf of Aden. *S.f. nubilosa* throughout Indian Ocean and China Sea islands. *S.f. serrata* Australia, New Guinea and N Caledonia. *S.f. kermadeci* in SW Pacific at Kermadec Is. The following notes are based on Dry Tortugas population: arrives Mar/Apr; departs Aug/Sep; Robertson (1969) has shown by ringing that most juveniles spend Jul/Aug in Gulf of Mexico, moving to southern Caribbean Sep/Oct, then dispersing across tropical Atlantic to Gulf of Guinea Oct/Nov where some remain till their sixth year. (Most do not breed until sixth–eighth year, the longest period to maturity for any member of the *Laridae*, Harrington 1974.) Adults disperse only to adjacent seas, although hurricanes occasionally push a few as far N as New England and Nova Scotia. Elsewhere they occur as vagrants N to Britain and western Europe; as non-breeding visitors to the Agulhas Current, South Africa (Brooke & Sinclair 1978); casual to southern Australia, New Zealand and Pacific coasts of South America.

SS: See notes under Bridled and Grey-backed Terns (p. 378, p. 377).

---

270 FAIRY TERN
other: Nereis Tern
Sterna nereis

PLATE 80 Figs 270a-270c

MAP 270

Length 22–27cm (8½–10½in.). Wingspan 50cm (19½in.). Iris brown. Bill, legs/feet orange or yellow.

Confined to Australasian region, where range overlaps with Little (Least) Tern. Breeding adults separable but non-breeding adult and juvenile plumages may be indistinguishable. Sexes alike; seasonal variation. Juveniles and immatures separable. Four subspecies, none separable at sea.

JUVENILE: Bill and legs brownish-black. **Head** As non-breeding adult except forehead dusky-white; crown and nape browner. **Body** Upperparts: saddle grey, strongly edged dark brown or black at first but quickly fades to pale grey with brownish tips; rump and uppertail-coverts white. Underparts white. **Wings** Outer web of 1st primary black, remaining primaries grey; coverts and tertials tipped brown, secondaries slightly paler. Underwing white. **Tail** Mostly white, tipped brown.

FIRST-WINTER: As juvenile except: **Head** White crown more extensive, loral stripe and hindcrown blackish-brown. **Wings** Brownish tips on coverts reduced.

FIRST-SUMMER: As breeding adult except: Bill and legs blackish. **Head** Crown mottled black and white. **Wings** Brownish tips to coverts further reduced.

ADULT NON-BREEDING: Bill yellow with dark tip (beware Little Tern, p. 382). Legs dull yellow. Plumage as breeding adult except crown mostly white.

ADULT BREEDING: Head Forehead, lores, sides of face, chin and throat white; triangular spot before eye, crown and nape black. **Body** Upperparts: saddle pale pearl-grey; rump and uppertail-coverts white. Underparts white. **Wings** Outer web of 1st primary black, forming dark edge on closed wing and in flight; otherwise pale pearl-grey, secondaries marginally paler. Underwing mostly white. **Tail** Forked; white.

FHJ: Flight and jizz recall Little Tern (p. 382) but appears paler, especially in flight. Differs in highly gregarious habits, often forms dense flocks. At Lacepede Is, W Australia, I observed large flocks departing each morning and returning at dusk (feeding far out at sea?); others formed compact groups of a hundred or more, feeding along the shoreline on the incoming tide, hovering much like Little Terns with similar hurried flight, but over deeper water plunge-dived in close contact without hovering. Some flocks off Point Cloates, W Australia, contain between 2,000 and 15,000 birds (Serventy *et al.* 1971). Call a grating 'kee-eck, kee-eck' and a chattering 'kee-ick, kee-ick'.

DM: *S.n. honi* breeds from Dampier Archipelago, W Australia, S to Cape Leeuwin; *S.n. nereis* southern Australia east to Victoria and Tasmania (where Little Terns also breed). *S.n. exsul*, which is slightly larger, breeds New Caledonia. *S.n. davisae* breeds Northland, New Zealand, but status uncertain, perhaps fewer than ten pairs (Falla *et al.* 1975). Probably sedentary although both Falla *et al.* (1975) and Storr (1960) state that some populations migratory, and this may help explain appearance of large flocks off W Australia during non-breeding season. Egg-dates Aug–Mar.

SS: Breeding adults readily distinguishable from Little Tern by unmarked bill, white lores and paler upperparts. Bill colour, however, not always reliable: 60% of all birds in W Australia showed a dark tip to yellowish bill during Aug–Oct (pers. obs.) but legs were bright orange. Winter adults should be distinguishable by whiter crown and lores, paler upperparts, and more gregarious habits with tendency to form dense feeding flocks.

See also Black-naped Tern (p. 375). Juveniles may be indistinguishable from juvenile Little Tern but ranges overlap only along coasts of Tasmania and Victoria.

271 BLACK-FRONTED TERN
Sterna albostriata

PLATE 79 Figs 271a-271b
MAP 271

Length 30–33cm (12–13in.). Wingspan not recorded. Iris black. Bill, legs/feet bright orange-red.

Restricted to New Zealand. Habits and appearance suggest that this species would be better placed within *Chlidonias*. Recalls Whiskered Tern, of which it may only be a race that has evolved into a river-bed breeder. Breeding adults distinctive; smaller size, jizz and darker grey underparts enable separation of non-breeders from White-fronted Tern (p. 374). Sexes alike; marked seasonal variation. Juveniles separable from adults. No subspecies but regarded as a race of Whiskered Tern (p. 364) by some authors.

JUVENILE: Bill yellow, tip black; legs dull yellow. **Head** Forehead white, spotted with grey on crown; lores black, extending through eye to nape as darker streak. Hindneck, sides of face, chin and throat white. **Body** Upperparts: saddle grey subterminally tipped brown, with narrow white fringes forming scaly pattern; rump conspicuously white. Underparts white. **Wings** Upperwing mostly grey; outermost primaries darker, lesser and median coverts tipped with brown forming prominent carpal bar. Underwing mostly greyish-white, tips of outermost primaries dusky-grey. **Tail** Grey, tip brownish.

FIRST-SUMMER: As juvenile except partial cap; upperparts greyer. Wings and tail unmoulted, faded through wear.

ADULT NON-BREEDING: As breeding adult except forehead, crown and lores white; underparts whitish.

ADULT BREEDING: Head Black cap separated from grey chin and throat by white facial streak. **Body** Upperparts: saddle deep grey; rump conspicuously white. Underparts mainly grey, undertail-coverts white. **Wings** Upperwing: primaries grey, the outer webs and tips darker with prominent white shafts; remainder deep grey. Underwing as juvenile. **Tail** Sides narrowly white, remainder grey.

FHJ: Largely an inland tern, hawking for insects over rivers, lakes and crops; occasionally follows plough. Call a high-pitched 'kit' and 'ki-ki-kit'.

DM: Confined to New Zealand, where breeds for certain only on South Island E of Southern Alps along dried river-beds and lake shores; formerly bred North Island. Egg-dates Sep–Jun. In winter disperses to estuaries and shores of South Island and N across Cook Strait, where several hundred regularly winter off Wellington coast; casual further N to Auckland.

SS: Breeding adults at inland locations distinctive but in winter may be confused with larger and much paler White-fronted Tern (p. 374) by the unwary.

272 AMAZON TERN
other: Yellow-billed Tern
Sterna superciliaris

PLATE 78 Figs 272a-272c
MAP 272

Length 23cm (9in.). Wingspan not recorded. Iris brown. Bill, legs/feet yellow.

Confined to South America E of Andes, where frequents coasts and larger river systems. Bill rather larger, otherwise jizz and habits recall Little/Least Tern (p. 382) of northern hemisphere. Sexes alike; marked seasonal variation. Juveniles and all stages of adult plumage separable. No subspecies.

JUVENILE: Bill dull yellow, brown at base and tip. Forehead, lores and crown greyish-brown; eye-crescent, streak through eye and nape blackish-brown, indistinct white supercilium; sides of face, chin and throat white. **Body** Upperparts medium grey, saddle tipped brown. Underparts mostly white, sides of breast mottled grey-brown. **Wings** Upperwing: outermost 3–4 primaries mostly black, inner webs narrowly white; inner primaries grey, browner at tips, decreasing inwards; remainder of upperwing medium grey, fringed brownish-grey. Underwing mostly white, outer primaries dusky-grey. **Tail** Grey, tips of inner rectrices mottled brown.

FIRST-WINTER: Bill dull yellow, tip brown. As non-breeding adult except: **Head** Whitish, crown mottled with brown. **Wings** Primaries tinged brown.

ADULT NON-BREEDING: As adult breeding except crown and lores largely white, flecked with black.

ADULT BREEDING: Forehead narrowly white extending backwards over eye in narrow supercilium; loral streak, crown and nape black, hindneck grey, sides of face, chin and throat white. **Body** Upperparts, including rump, pale grey; underparts white. **Wings** Upperwing: outer 3–4 primaries black, inner webs narrowly white; inner primaries medium grey with dusky grey-brown tips decreasing inwards; remainder of upperwing medium grey. **Tail** Grey, slightly forked.

FHJ: A small tern, following larger rivers thousands of kilometres inland; occasionally found on coasts and lagoons. Size, jizz and flight recall Little/Least Tern (p. 382) of northern hemisphere, but slightly larger with larger, more robust bill.

DM: Confined to South America, occurring along coasts and river systems E of Andes from Colombia, S through Venezuela, the Guianas to Uruguay and eastern Argentina. Egg-dates Jul–Sep. Probably mainly sedentary.

SS: Separated from Little Tern (p. 382), where range overlaps, by larger, wholly yellow bill, deeper grey upperparts, grey rump and uppertail-coverts.

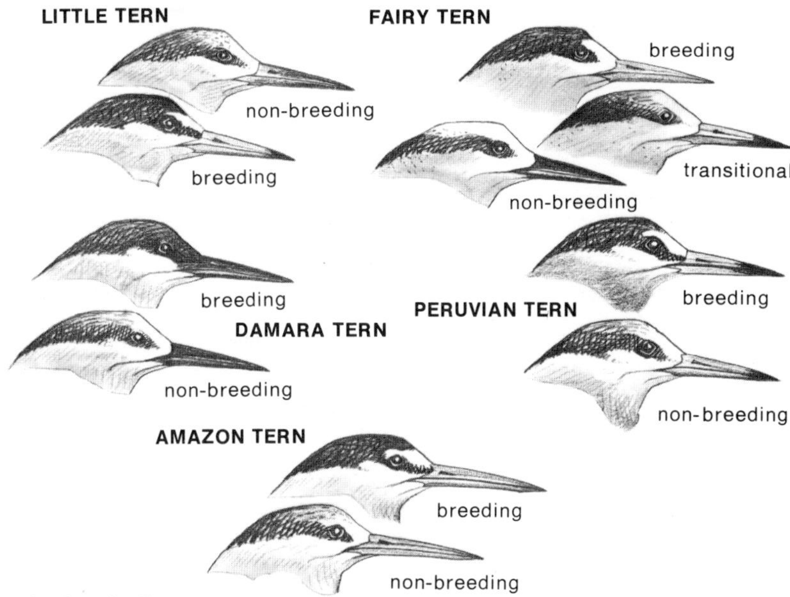

Fig. 27. Heads of smaller Terns

273 DAMARA TERN
Sterna balaenarum

PLATE 80 Figs 273a-273b
MAP 273

Length 23cm (9in.). Wingspan 51cm (20in.). Iris brown. Bill black, base sometimes yellowish. Legs/feet brownish or black.

Confined to western coasts of southern Africa; range overlaps with Little (Least) Tern (p. 382), from which adults readily separated; juveniles require more careful treatment. Sexes alike; seasonal variation of head pattern. Juveniles separable from adults; no data for immature plumages. No subspecies.

JUVENILE: (All based on notes supplied by Sinclair, pers. comm.) Bill and legs black. **Head** Mostly white; cap dark brown, flecked with white. **Body** Upperparts: saddle grey, heavily barred brown and buff; rump white. Underparts white. **Wings** Upperwing: outer primaries and their coverts blackish-grey, secondaries and remaining coverts grey, latter barred as for saddle. **Tail** White (perhaps tipped brown).

ADULT NON-BREEDING: As breeding adult except forehead white.

ADULT BREEDING: Head Black cap, including lores, extends from base of bill to nape; hindneck grey, chin and throat white. **Body** Upperparts, including rump, pale grey. Underparts mostly white, sides of breast faintly grey. **Wings** Upperwing: outer webs of outer 2–3 primaries blackish, inner webs white; remainder of upperwing grey. Underwing mostly white except for dusky outermost primaries. **Tail** Short, forked; mainly grey, outermost feathers white.

FHJ: Told from Little Tern (p. 382) in all plumages by long, thin, slightly decurved black bill (not short and spiky as in Little); body shape stockier and heavier; adults appear whiter in flight at all seasons. Flight similar to Little but more powerful, not so jerky; call note harsher. (All based on Sinclair, pers. comm.)

DM: Restricted as breeding species to western coasts of southern Africa from about 5°N south through Namibia and South Africa E to Mossel Bay. Clinning (1978) estimated total population between 3,500 and 4,000 birds; egg-dates Nov–Feb. Wallace's (1973) observations indicate that many winter in northern Gulf of Guinea mainly between Jul and Oct, peaking at about 250 during Aug, at Lighthouse Beach, Lagos. Extent of dispersal poorly known but certainly reaches W to Ghana. Some non-breeders may remain in winter quarters during austral summer.

SS: Breeding adults readily separable from Little Tern (p. 382) by black bill and wholly black cap. Non-breeders separable by structure, bill shape and colour, and generally paler saddle and upperwings which, at distance, can suggest miniature Sandwich Tern.

274 PERUVIAN TERN
other: Chilean Tern
Sterna lorata

PLATE 80 Figs 274a-274b
MAP 274

Length 23cm (9in.). Wingspan not recorded. Iris brown. Bill yellow, distal third tipped black. Legs/feet dull brownish-yellow.

The smallest tern of the Humboldt Current, restricted to desert coasts of western South America. Off western Colombia, Ecuador and Peru range may overlap with Little (Least) Tern (p. 382), from which readily separable. Sexes alike; seasonal variation. Juveniles and immatures not described (no specimens available).

ADULT NON-BREEDING: As breeding adult except: **Head** Crown streaked with white. **Body** Underparts: paler, almost white, with indistinct grey wash across breast.

ADULT BREEDING: Head Forehead and narrow stripe over eye white; crown, nape and loral stripe black, chin and throat greyish-white. **Body** Upperparts: saddle dusky slate-grey; rump and uppertail-coverts marginally paler. Underparts pale dusky-grey. **Wings** Upperwing: mostly grey, outer web of outermost primary black decreasing in extent inwards on 2nd and 3rd primary; secondaries narrowly tipped with white. **Tail** Short, forked; mostly slate-grey, outer feathers edged with white.

FHJ: Resembles Little Tern (p. 382). Feeds over open sea and lagoons. Call 'chick-chick', but when excited a chattering 'kerrick-kerrick' and 'churi-churi'.

DM: Confined to Humboldt Current. Murphy (1936) recorded breeding in Peru along coastal desert 2km from sea during Jan. Disperses N to Gulf of Guayaquil, Ecuador, where probably present in small numbers throughout year; status further N uncertain. Range in Chile unknown, but large numbers present Mollendo and Arica during Aug (pers. obs.); some presumably range southwards along desert coasts of Chile and may even breed there.

SS: Overall greyish plumage including tail, rump and underparts separates this species from Little Tern (p. 382), although ranges not yet definitely proved to overlap.

275 LITTLE TERN

other: Least Tern (includes Saunders's Tern, 275X)
Sterna albifrons (includes *S.a. saundersi*)

PLATE 80 Figs 275a-275c
MAP 275

Length 20–28cm (8–11in.). Wingspan 50–55cm (19½–21½in.). Iris black. Bill yellow with black tip. Legs/feet yellow.

Cosmopolitan; size normally diagnostic in northern hemisphere but range overlaps with Peruvian, Fairy and Damara Terns in southern hemisphere (p. 381, p. 379, p. 381). Breeding adults readily distinguishable but non-breeders and juveniles require careful treatment. Sexes outwardly alike, female averages smaller; seasonal variation. Juveniles and immatures separable. Nine subspecies listed, of which *S.a. saundersi* can be separated in the field and is described separately below; some authors treat it as separate species.

JUVENILE: Bill blackish, base yellow; legs/feet dusky-yellow or blackish. **Head** Forehead brownish-white, crown tipped brown and white, brownish streak from just before eye extending back to nape; remainder white. **Body** Upperparts: saddle grey, edged brown; rump and uppertail-coverts white. Underparts white. **Wings** Upperwing: outer 3–6 primaries and their coverts blackish-grey; marginal and some lesser coverts brownish-grey forming indistinct carpal bar; remainder grey, tipped brown, secondaries paler. Underwing mostly white. **Tail** White, tip faintly brown.

FIRST-WINTER: As juvenile but crown whiter; upperparts and upperwing clearer grey.

FIRST-SUMMER: As breeding adult except bill and legs dusky, crown mottled with white.

ADULT NON-BREEDING: As breeding adult except bill blackish, base often yellow; legs brownish-yellow. **Head** Crown and lores white, blackish streak through eye to nape.

ADULT BREEDING: Head Forehead white, extending a little over eye in shallow V; crown and nape black extending narrowly through eye to base of bill; remainder white. **Body** Upperparts: saddle pale grey, rump and uppertail-coverts whitish-grey. Underparts white. **Wings** Upperwing: outer 2–3 primaries and their coverts blackish, frosted with grey, remainder pale dove-grey. Underwing mostly white, except outermost primary dusky-grey decreasing inwards to small dusky mark on 4th or 5th. **Tail** Short, forked; white.

275X ADULT BREEDING (*S.a. saundersi*): As nominate race except: Legs brownish-yellow. **Body** Upperparts: rump and uppertail-coverts ash-grey. **Wings** Upperwing: outer 3–6 primaries and their coverts blackish, forming more definite dark edge to wingtip. **Tail** Ash-grey.

FHJ: Recognised throughout most of range by small size. Flight usually hurried with rapid wingbeats, rather wader-like; often hovers before plunge-diving from 3–6m. Mainly maritime but also occurs inland on larger rivers. Call a shrill 'kip-kip-kip' and a grating 'kid-ick—kid-ick'.

DM: In N America *S.a. browni* breeds along Pacific coast from central California S to southern Baja California. *S.a. antillarum* breeds interior USA from Iowa S, and on Atlantic coast from Maine and Massachusetts S to Florida, Gulf of Mexico, and Caribbean Sea through Bahamas and West Indies to Venezuela. *S.a. albifrons* breeds coasts and rivers of Europe from British Is and southern Baltic S to Mediterranean Basin, and from Morocco E discontinuously to Nile delta, Asia and NW India; perhaps also along northwest African coast S to Mauritania. *S.a. innominata* Persian Gulf islands. *S.a. saundersi* breeds southern half of Red Sea, to Seychelles and possibly Madagascar. *S.a. guineae* breeds coasts and rivers of tropical W Africa. *S.a. pusilla* breeds rivers of northern India S through Burma, Java and Sumatra. *S.a. sinensis* breeds from Japan and China through Liu Kiu Is and Malaysia S to New Guinea. *S.a. placens* breeds northern, eastern and southern Australia and Tasmania. Egg-dates: Mar–Jun northern hemisphere; May–Aug tropics; Nov southern hemisphere. American breeders disperse S to Brazil and Peru; Eurasian breeders S to South Africa; whilst Asiatic population may move as far S as Tasmania. Movements, however, not fully understood as migrating birds join local populations, but migratory tendencies strong and not limited to N–S movements, as shown in Serventy *et al.* (1971) by one ringed in Java 1949 and recovered in Ghana, West Africa, 1952.

SS: See notes under Peruvian, Damara and Fairy Terns (p. 381, p. 381, p. 379).

276 CRESTED TERN
other: Swift Tern, Great Crested Tern
Sterna bergii

PLATE 76 Figs 276a-276c
MAP 276

Length 43–48cm (17–19in.). Wingspan 99–109cm (39–43in.). Iris dark brown. Bill dull yellow, often with greenish cast. Legs/feet blackish.

Mainly Indian and Pacific Oceans, where range overlaps with smaller, neater and more graceful Lesser Crested Tern (p. 384) which differs also in its bright orange bill. In past literature emphasis has been placed on darker saddle and upperparts of present species and, whilst useful in Persian Gulf area, this feature by no means constant and in some populations is reversed. Main distinction lies in size, structure and head patterns (see Fig. 28). Sexes alike; marked seasonal variation. Juveniles and first-summer types separable from adults. Six subspecies listed (includes *S.b. enigma* described by Clancey 1979). Some races may be separable in field on tone of upperparts.

JUVENILE: Bill often darker than that of adult, sometimes with darker tip; legs occasionally orange or black. **Head** As non-breeding adult but cap duller, sides of face with darker streaks imparting scruffy appearance. **Body** Upperparts: saddle grey with scattered brown tips; rump paler, though occasionally as dark as back. Underparts white. **Wings** Upperwing: primaries and their coverts blackish-brown, secondaries dark brown, edged and tipped white; greater and median coverts pale greyish-brown, edged white, enhanced by wear, thus forming a pale wing panel both in flight and on closed wing; lesser coverts and carpal edged with brown. Underwing as adult. **Tail** Darker grey than rump, often blackish at tip and outer rectrices.

FIRST-WINTER: Bill and plumage resembles non-breeding adult except: **Body** Upperparts: saddle tipped with brown. **Wings** Upperwing: faint carpal bar and darker primary-coverts.

ADULT NON-BREEDING: As breeding adult except: Bill duller. **Head** Forehead and crown mostly white, hindcrown and nape black, streaked white. **Wings** Outermost primaries darker grey.

ADULT BREEDING: Head A narrow white band separates crested cap from base of bill; remainder white. **Body** Upperparts: saddle grey, rump paler. Underparts white. **Wings** Upperwing mostly pale grey, primaries silvery-white with dusky inner webs; secondaries tipped white forming pale trailing edge. Underwing white except for dark grey tips and shafts of outer primaries. **Tail** Pale grey.

FHJ: A large coastal tern with heavy, drooping bill, deeply forked tail and long scythe-like wings. Flight powerful, with long sweeping action of wings; feeds in typical *Sterna* manner. Juveniles utter a high-pitched 'see-see'; adults a harsh 'ke-eck' and a croaking 'krow'.

DM: Indian and Pacific Oceans. *S.b. bergii* breeds coasts of South Africa and Namibia; *S.b. enigma* Mozambique; *S.b. velox* Red Sea, Arabian Sea and Bay of Bengal; *S.b. thalassinus* Seychelles, Rodriguez and Chagos Is; *S.b. gwendolenae* northern and western Australia; *S.b. cristatus* southeast Australia, Tasmania and throughout SW Pacific Ocean N to Japan and E to Fiji. All populations disperse after breeding.

SS: Inexperienced birders are likely to confuse this large, yellow-billed tern with the smaller, orange-billed Lesser Crested Tern (p. 384). When seen together the two are distinctly different. Present species large and bulky with massive bill and long, rakish wings; in contrast Lesser Crested Tern much smaller with finer, more elegant proportions, and neater, unsullied plumage. In Red and Arabian Seas *S. bergii velox* has darker grey saddle and upperwings than *S. bengalensis par*, which is paler and bluer in tone. In Australia, however, position is reversed, *S. bengalensis torresii* showing much darker saddle and upperwings than the local *S. bergii cristatus* (refer to Plate 76 for differences in tone of upperparts). Juvenile and first-winter *S. bergii* have pronounced carpal bars and highly variegated plumage, whereas similar-stage *S. bengalensis* rarely show such pronounced contrast. See also Chinese Crested Tern, Royal Tern (p. 385, p. 383).

Fig. 28. Head patterns of winter Crested and Lesser-crested Terns. *S. bergii* *S. bengalensis*

277 ROYAL TERN
Sterna maxima

PLATE 74 Figs 277a-277c
MAP 277

Length 46–53cm (18–21in.). Wingspan 106–112cm (42–44in.). Iris black. Bill orange-red. Legs/feet black.

Coasts of Central America and equatorial West Africa. Range overlaps with larger Caspian Tern (p. 368). Sexes alike; seasonal variation of head pattern. Juveniles separable from adults. Two subspecies listed.

JUVENILE: Bill, legs/feet light orange or yellowish

occasionally black. **Head** Partial black cap (forehead and crown much whiter than in juvenile Caspian Tern, p. 368). **Body** Upperparts pale greyish-cream, each feather with brownish-grey centre and dusky shaft-streak. Underparts white. **Wings** Upperwing: outermost 4–6 primaries blackish, shafts and inner webs white; innermost primaries and all secondaries slate-grey, narrowly fringed with white forming slightly darker trailing edge to wing. Marginal and lesser coverts slate-grey forming conspicuous carpal bar; remaining coverts as upperparts. **Tail** Mostly dark grey, fringed white with brownish marks on tips of outer feathers.

FIRST-WINTER: As juvenile except saddle mostly clear grey; brown tips on upperwing reduced, producing distinctive creamy-white wing panel framed by slate-grey carpal bar and dusky-grey secondaries.

ADULT NON-BREEDING: As breeding adult except black cap reduced to black streak through eye and posterior margin over nape. Tail greyer, lacks streamers.

ADULT BREEDING: Head Shaggy black cap; remainder white. **Body** Upperparts pale grey. Underparts white. **Wings** Upperwing mostly pale grey; outer webs of outermost 4–5 primaries and most of primary tips blackish; secondaries slightly darker forming faint trailing edge. Underwing mostly white; outer primaries tipped blackish-grey. **Tail** White, deeply forked.

FHJ: Second largest tern. For comparison with Caspian Tern see under that species (p. 368). Unlike Caspian Tern, sociable, breeding in large colonies; often loafs in small flocks on sand bars etc. Call 'tourreee' and a bleating 'ee-ah'.

DM: Breeding confined to North and Central America, and shores of equatorial W Africa. *S.m. maxima* breeds North America on Pacific coast from San Diego, California (casual), S along NW Mexican coast, with major nesting area on Isla Raza, Gulf of California; also breeds Atlantic coast from Virginia S to Texas, E Mexico, the W Indies and perhaps also Venezuela. *S.m. albidorsalis* recently discovered breeding NW Africa (de Naurois 1959), where large colonies now known to exist on the Arguin Bank, northern Mauritania; outlying colonies discovered in Senegal and Gambia. Egg-dates Apr–Jul. North American population winters on Pacific coast from central California S to Mollendo, Peru, where regular but scarce (R Hughes, pers. comm.). On Atlantic coast winters from southern Carolina S through Caribbean to Argentina. NW African population appears to move in two directions: some move N along African coast to reach Morocco and W Mediterranean (where recently observed in two consecutive years and suspected of breeding alongside Caspian Terns on Coto Doñana, Spain); others move S to winter Gulf of Guinea, perhaps also further S as there is one record from Walvis Bay, Namibia (Sinclair & Turner 1981). In all populations first-summer birds and non-breeders remain in winter quarters throughout year.

SS: Confusion likely with Caspian Tern but winter head pattern and underwing pattern different at all ages; Royal never shows dusky subterminal tip to bill. Range overlap in West Africa with Lesser Crested Tern (p. 384) creates more of a problem, but latter much smaller and adults have darker grey saddle and upperparts. Plumage differences to enable separation between juveniles of the two species have yet to be formulated.

278 LESSER CRESTED TERN *Sterna bengalensis*

PLATE 76 Figs 278a-278e
MAP 278

Length 38–43cm (15–17in.). Wingspan 89–94cm (35–37in.). Iris dark brown. Bill bright orange. Legs/feet black.

Mainly Indian and Pacific Oceans, where range overlaps with larger, yellow-billed Crested Tern (p. 383). See also larger Royal Tern off NW Africa (p. 383). Sexes alike; marked seasonal variation. Juveniles and first-summer types separable from adults. Three subspecies listed; one, *S.b. torresii*, certainly separable in field though range does not overlap with other races.

JUVENILE: Bill greyish-yellow. **Head** As non-breeding adult. **Body** Upperparts: brownish tips to grey saddle fade quickly, revealing mostly clear grey upperparts. Underparts white. **Wings** Upperwing as adult except for brown outer primaries, their coverts, and indistinct brown tips to lesser coverts and secondaries. Greater coverts often edged white forming variegated wing panel. NOTE These features appear to fade rapidly, thus upperparts and upperwing resemble adult within a few months of fledging. **Tail** Pale grey, tip browner.

FIRST-WINTER: As non-breeding adult except bill duller; outer primaries brown, faint scattered brown edges to wing-coverts.

ADULT NON-BREEDING: As breeding adult except bill duller, forehead and most of crown white, extending well past peak of crown (thus whiter-headed than any stage of Crested Tern, see Fig. 28).

ADULT BREEDING: Head Black cap normally extends from base of bill to nape; sides of face, chin and throat white. **Body** Upperparts pale bluish-grey to deep steel-grey (varies geographically). Underparts white. **Wings** Upperwing as saddle except for silvery-grey primaries. Underwing mostly white; outermost, and tips of most primaries greyer.

FHJ: Compared with much larger Crested Tern (p. 383) present species has more slender, lighter jizz and proportionately shorter wings. Orange bill less massive, lacking noticeable droop. Flight graceful, buoyant. Call 'kek-kereck'.

DM: Mainly Indian and W Pacific Oceans. *S.b. par* breeds southern shores of Mediterranean Sea; exact status unknown but Moltoni (in Bundy 1950) estimated 2,000 breeding on islets off Zuwatina in Gulf of Sirte, Libya; also breeds coasts of Red Sea and East Africa S to Somalia. *S.b. bengalensis* breeds Persian Gulf E to Singapore. The darker-mantled *S.b. torresii* breeds Malay Archipelago and in Australia from Point Cloates in the W to

Heron I. in the E. Egg-dates Jun–Nov. Although Serventy *et al.* (1971) regard Australian population as mainly sedentary, others are certainly migratory. Mediterranean population moves mainly W in autumn, occurring commonly off Algeria and Morocco though less frequently at Gibraltar; exact wintering area unknown, presumably Atlantic coast of NW Africa. Red Sea birds disperse S, reaching Mozambique, and Natal, South Africa. Vagrants have occurred N to Britain and S to Cape Province, South Africa (pers. obs.).

SS: Most likely to be confused with Crested Tern (p. 383) in Indian Ocean and Australian regions. In western Mediterranean and NW Africa the much larger Royal Tern (p. 383) differs in longer, thicker, redder bill, with much paler upperparts recalling Sandwich Tern.

279 CHINESE CRESTED TERN
Sterna bernsteini

PLATE 77 Figs 279a-279b
MAP 279

Length 38cm (15in.). Wingspan not recorded. Iris dark brown. Bill yellow with broad black tip. Legs/feet black.

A rare and little-known species confined to coasts of China; ranges S to Philippine Is in winter. Sexes alike; seasonal variation of head pattern. Juvenile specimens as yet undescribed but, by analogy, probably resemble those of Crested Tern but smaller with black-tipped bill. No subspecies.

ADULT NON-BREEDING: As breeding adult except extreme tip of bill yellow; forehead and crown white, latter streaked black.

ADULT BREEDING: Head Crested black cap; remainder white. **Body** Upperparts: saddle pale pearl-grey, rump white. Underparts white. **Wings** Upperwing mostly pale pearl-grey; outer webs of outer 3–5 primaries blackish, secondaries narrowly tipped white. Underwing mostly white. **Tail** White, deeply forked.

FHJ: Little known. Compared with Crested Tern (p. 383), smaller with proportionately longer, more deeply forked tail.

DM: Breeding area apparently unknown (Alexander 1955). Frequents coasts of China N to Shantung in summer and S to Thailand and Philippines in winter.

SS: Resembles larger Crested Tern (p. 383), but black tip to bill, full black cap and paler grey upperparts. Juvenile and immature plumages little known.

280 CAYENNE TERN
other: Sandwich Tern (race of)
Sterna (sandvicensis) eurygnatha

PLATE 78 Figs 280a-280c
MAP 280

Length 40–43cm (16–17in.). Wingspan 94–97cm (37–38in.). Iris dark brown. Bill varies from black with yellow tip to wholly yellow. Legs/feet vary from wholly yellow to yellow spotted with black.

Confined to eastern South America; jizz recalls Sandwich Tern (p. 386) with which it appears to be involved in a cline and/or hybridisation all along Venezuelan coast (Alden, pers. comm.). Sexes alike; seasonal variation. Juveniles separable from adults. No subspecies but status under review, most authors now consider this to be a race of Sandwich Tern (p. 386).

JUVENILE: Bill/legs olive-brown. **Head** Mostly white, crown and hindneck streaked brownish-grey, heaviest on nape; eye-crescent dusky. **Body** Upperparts: mantle whitish, spotted with brown (extending to hindneck); scapulars and back grey edged with brown, heaviest on scapulars; rump white, faintly marked with grey. Underparts white. **Wings** Upperwing: outer 4–6 primaries dark grey, outer web of outermost black; innermost and secondaries grey, tipped white. Marginal coverts grey, carpal and most anterior lesser coverts tipped darker, forming conspicuous carpal bar; posterior lesser coverts white, medium and greater coverts grey fringed with white. Underwing mostly white, pale grey on outer primaries. **Tail** Ash-white, subterminally mottled brown.

FIRST-WINTER: No specimen examined; presumably as juvenile except mantle and back mostly clear grey, carpal bar and mottling on tail reduced.

ADULT NON-BREEDING: As breeding adult except: **Head** Forehead and lores white, black eye-crescent extends through eye to black nape; crown white, spotted black. **Wings** Outer webs of outermost 2–3 primaries blackish.

ADULT BREEDING: Black cap from base of bill to crested nape; remainder, including hindneck, white. **Body** Upperparts: saddle pale grey, rump and uppertail-coverts white. Underparts white. **Wings** Upperwing mainly pale grey; outer 3–5 primaries deeper grey tipped blackish, with darker grey stripe next to shaft; innermost primaries and secondaries fringed with white. **Tail** Forked, white.

FHJ: Resembles Elegant Tern (p. 386) but slightly smaller with pale yellow, not orange, bill. Call a shrill rasping 'kee-rack'.

DM: Breeding range poorly known; thought to breed from Venezuela S to Macaé Is, off Rio de Janeiro, Brazil. Occurs Caribbean and Atlantic coasts of South America from Colombia and Venezuela S to Puerto Deseado, Argentina. Movements largely unknown.

SS: The only medium-sized tern in South America with pale yellow bill. (Amazon Tern, p. 380, much smaller whilst Large-billed Tern, p. 366, larger with massive bill and patterned upperwings.) Bill and leg colour varies considerably however, some with wholly black bills. See Sandwich Tern (p. 386) of which present 'species' may only be a race.

281 ELEGANT TERN
Sterna elegans

PLATE 74 Figs 281a-281b
MAP 281

Length 40–43cm (16–17in.). Wingspan not recorded. Iris black. Bill yellow or yellow-orange, palest at tip. Legs/feet black.

Pacific coasts of California and Mexico, where range overlaps with larger, heavier-billed Royal and Caspian Terns (p. 383, p. 368). Sexes alike; seasonal variation. Juveniles separable from adults; immature plumages undescribed. No subspecies.

JUVENILE: (No specimens examined; following based on notes supplied by Stallcup, pers. comm.) Resembles Royal Tern in general appearance, but saddle and wing-covert feathers edged tan to buff giving more scaly appearance.

ADULT NON-BREEDING: As breeding adult except forehead and crown white, outer primaries and tail greyer.

ADULT BREEDING: Head Shaggy black cap, remainder white. **Body** Upperparts: saddle pale blue-grey, rump white. Underparts white, some with faint rosy tint. **Wings** Upperwing mostly pale blue-grey; outer webs of outer 1–3 primaries dusky. Underwing white, outer primaries tipped dusky. **Tail** Deeply forked, whitish.

FHJ: Recalls larger Royal Tern (p. 383) but smaller, with proportionately longer, finer, more drooping bill and prominently crested nape. Call a rasping 'karreek-karreek'.

DM: Confined to California and Mexico. First discovered breeding in southern California in spring 1959 at San Diego Bay with Royal Terns (Rand 1965); has bred there casually ever since. Elsewhere breeds along both coasts of Baja California and NW Mexico. Returns to colonies Mar/Apr; egg-dates Apr/May; fledging and departure begin Aug/Sep. Many range N in late summer and autumn, commonly to San Francisco and sparsely further N, some lingering until Nov/Dec. Most depart S, reaching Ecuador, Peru and Chile where a few remain throughout year. Vagrant E to Texas and Ireland.

SS: Resembles much larger Royal Tern (p. 383). Separable by difference in size, jizz, proportions of bill, underwing pattern and voice.

282 SANDWICH TERN
Sterna sandvicensis

PLATE 76 Figs 282a-282d
MAP 282

Length 40–45cm (16–18in.). Wingspan 91–94cm (36–37in.). Iris dark. Bill black, tip yellow. Legs/feet black.

North America and Eurasia. Confusion most likely with Gull-billed Tern (p. 367), which also appears very white in flight, but bill, jizz and habits of the two species differ. Sexes alike; marked seasonal variation. Juveniles and first-summer types separable from adults but precise plumages until maturity (third-summer) poorly known. Two subspecies, not separable at sea. Cayenne Tern (p. 385) may be conspecific.

JUVENILE: Bill often shorter than that of adult. **Head** Resembles non-breeding adult but browner in tone with paler streaks on crown. **Body** Upperparts: saddle grey with dull blackish bars, largest and most pronounced on scapulars. Rump white. Underparts white. **Wings** Upperwing: as non-breeding adult except for blackish arrowhead marks on wing-coverts and tips of primaries. **Tail** Greyish-white with black tip.

FIRST-WINTER: Similar to juvenile except saddle mostly clear grey; blackish marks on upperwing-coverts reduced.

ADULT NON-BREEDING: As breeding adult but with reduced crest and conspicuous white forehead; black crown and nape streaked with white.

ADULT BREEDING: Head Black cap extends from base of bill to nape, with crown feathers elongated forming erectile crest; remainder white. **Body** Upperparts pale grey, rump white. Underparts white or with pale cream or pinkish wash. **Wings** Pale silvery-grey above, inner webs of outer 3–6 primaries darker grey. Underwing white except for dusky inner webs and tips to outermost primaries. **Tail** White. NOTE Most adults show whiter tips to forehead by mid Jun and fully white foreheads by late Aug.

FHJ: A medium to large tern appearing wholly white at distance with a shorter, shallower-forked tail than most of its congeners. Crown rather flat and long, particularly noticeable when hunting with head held pointing downwards. Typical fishing habits of genus, though consistently dives from greater heights than smaller terns, with heavier, less graceful flight. In autumn juveniles often have more laboured flight with more rapid wingbeats. Call a harsh 'ki-ki-ki' or a rasping 'kir-rick'. In autumn juveniles utter sibilant 'kreak', sometimes repeated rapidly.

DM: Largest colonies of *S.s. sandvicensis* are in Britain, where over half NW European population now breeds following drastic decline in Netherlands' (Wadden Zee) population in early 1960s; other colonies France, W and E Germany, Denmark and Ireland. Status in Mediterranean not precisely known; small numbers have bred S Spain, Tunisia, Sicily and Sardinia. To the east breeds along northern shores of Black Sea and southern and eastern shores of Caspian Sea. In N America *S.s. acuflavidus* breeds locally along Atlantic and Gulf coasts from Virginia to Florida and Texas (population has increased recently in mid Atlantic states); also breeds Mexico, Yucatan and in Bahamas. In Britain some return to colonies late Mar, most Apr; egg-dates Apr/May. Post-breeding dispersal to adjacent coasts Jul/Aug where most remain till Oct, though some juveniles recovered NW Africa early Sep. NW European stock winters mainly NW Africa S to Cape of Good Hope, South Africa, occasionally E to Natal, but rare off Kenya. Movements of Black and Caspian Sea breeders not precisely known; ringing recoveries indicate that Black Sea population may winter in W Mediterranean; flocks of up to 300 off Oman, Indian Ocean,

during northern winter may have originated from Caspian Sea. In America winters from Florida S to Uruguay on Atlantic coast, and to S Peru on Pacific coast where annual in small numbers at Mollendo (Hughes, pers. comm.). Most juveniles of all populations spend first summer in or near wintering quarters, moving further N in their second summer with some occasionally reaching breeding colonies. Most breed in their third summer.
SS: Differs from all other large or medium-sized terns except Gull-billed (p. 367) in its mostly black bill. Separation from latter species confused in the past by overemphasis of differences in bill structure of the two. At close range the more slender and longer bill of Sandwich Tern with diagnostic pale yellow tip easily seen. At long range, before such critical factors can be ascertained, Sandwich Tern appears more elegant, with longer, slender, pointed wings, slim body and longer, more forked, whiter tail. In northern summer adult Sandwich Terns show a dark wedge on outer 3–4 primaries of upperwing, whereas adult Gull-billed show only dark tips to outermost 6–8 primaries, forming narrow trailing edge to wing. Gull-billed differs further in broader, less forked tail. Flight and feeding habits of the two species also differ. Beware especially juvenile Sandwich Terns in autumn with uncharacteristic flight, possibly unfamiliar calls and shorter, proportionately thicker bills.

Genus *LAROSTERNA*

Monotypic genus; large, dark, atypical tern with moustache-like facial plume. Restricted to coasts of western South America.

283 INCA TERN
Larosterna inca

PLATE 78 Figs 283a-283c
MAP 283

Length 40–42cm (16–17in.). Wingspan not recorded. Iris brown. Bill bright red, wattle at gape yellow. Legs/feet red.

Confined to Pacific coasts of South America; unmistakable at any age. Sexes alike; apparently no seasonal variation. Juveniles separable from adults. No subspecies.
JUVENILE: Bill/legs blackish-horn. Wholly dark purplish-brown above except for narrow grey-buff fringes, heaviest on scapulars and tertials; underparts slightly greyer. Primaries black, innermost 4 and all secondaries broadly tipped pale grey.
IMMATURE: Bill/legs dark horn, faintly red. **Head** Dark brownish-grey, chin and throat paler; short pale grey moustache-like plumes springing from gape. **Body and Wings** Dark brownish-grey; primaries and secondaries blackish, innermost 4 and all secondaries broadly tipped pale grey. **Tail** Black.
ADULT: Head Forehead, crown, nape and ear-coverts blue-black, separated from blue-grey chin and throat by conspicuous white moustache-like plumes springing from gape and curving downwards towards breast. **Body and Wings** Blue-grey except for blackish primaries and secondaries; innermost 4 primaries, all secondaries, tertials and scapulars broadly tipped with white. Underwing mostly blue-grey, coverts pale grey. **Tail** Black.
FHJ: Unmistakable; size of a small gull with dark plumage, massive red bill, rather long, rounded wings and a shallow-forked tail. Gregarious, often gathers in thousands (Beck, in Murphy 1936). Frequents rocky shores, also roosts within flocks of Grey and Franklin's Gulls on sandy beaches of Peru. Commonly observed in Peruvian harbours. Flight graceful and buoyant, hovers before dipping low to surface in quick, darting manoeuvres during which shows great agility. Frequently accompanies fishing cormorants, sea-lions and cetaceans. Coker (in Murphy 1936) likened call to that of a young kitten.
DM: Endemic to Humboldt Current, from Gulf of Guayaquil, Ecuador, S to Iquique, Chile. Ranges S to Valdivia, Chile.
SS: None.

Genus *PROCELSTERNA*

Monotypic genus, allied to noddies. Grey Noddy occurs in two morphs and is confined to tropical Pacific Ocean. Dark morphs generally occur S of 25°S. See Murphy (1936) for discussion on subspecies.

284 GREY NODDY
other: Blue-grey Noddy
Procelsterna cerulea

PLATE 72 Figs 284a-284c
MAP 284

Length 25–30cm (10–12in.). Wingspan 46–61cm (18–24in.). Iris black with black orbital ring round anterior portion. Bill black. Legs/feet black, webs yellow.

Tropical Pacific Ocean; unlikely to be confused with other species if seen properly. Sexes alike; no seasonal variation. Juveniles separable from adults. Seven subspecies listed, none separable at sea.
IMMATURE (PALE MORPH): As adult except: **Head** Including chin and throat streaked grey. **Body** Upperparts: brownish cast to saddle. **Wings** Upperwing: primaries and secondaries blackish forming dark trailing edge; coverts browner.

ADULT (PALE MORPH): **Head** Greyish-white. **Body** Upperparts: saddle blue-grey, rump and uppertail-coverts white. Underparts greyish-white. **Wings** Upperwing: mainly blue-grey, primaries and secondaries darker; lesser coverts, tertials and secondaries tipped white. Underwing mainly grey, coverts pure white. **Tail** Light grey.
ADULT (DARK MORPH): As pale morph except greyer head and grey underwing-coverts.
FHJ: Small distinctive species appearing mainly grey, although at long distances paler morphs look almost white-headed with grey wings and moderately forked tail. Flight graceful and buoyant; occasionally paddles on water.
DM: Occurs throughout tropical Pacific Ocean. *P.c. cerulea* breeds Christmas I.; *P.c. saxatilis* Hawaiian chain; *P.c. nebouxi* Phoenix, Ellice and Samoan Is; *P.c. teretirostris* Society, Marquesas and Tuamotu Is; *P.c. albivitta* Lord Howe, Norfolk, Kermadec and Friendly Is; *P.c. skottsbergii* Henderson and Easter Is; *P.c. imitatrix* San Ambrose and San Felix Is off Chile. A sedentary species, remaining at breeding grounds throughout year. Tropical storms often cause displacement; has reached Australia on several occasions (Serventy *et al.* 1971).
SS: A distinctive species; pale morphs at long range could be mistaken for White Terns (p. 390).

Genus *ANOUS*

Two species (formerly treated as three species). Almost wholly dark, pelagic terns of pantropical distribution. Characteristically, bill and legs black, cap pale, remaining plumage brown or blackish. Tail 'heavy', spatulated and slightly forked. Some authors now treat *A.(t.) minutus* as conspecific with *A. tenuirostris*. See Harrison (1981) for overlap in head patterns.

Unlike most other terns, noddies usually feed far out at sea, often congregating in dense flocks where predatory fish drive smaller prey to the surface. Like Sooty and Bridled Terns (p. 378, p. 378), do not plunge-dive but feed by hovering above surface before swooping down to pick up small fry, occasionally executing shallow belly-flops. Frequently settle on rigging of ships and readily alight on any flotsam, backs of turtles and even swimming pelicans. Occasionally roost on water, forming dense rafts. Noddies can regurgitate food, thus enabling them to forage more widely than typical terns, with fewer trips back to their fledgling. Their vernacular name stems from the behavioural habit of nodding and bowing to each other during courtship.

Flight swift, with rapid wingbeats, appearing as an atypical tern with heavy notched tail and brown plumage. Identification at breeding colonies should present few problems, as size, relative proportion of bill, and head pattern are easily seen. At sea identification can be problematic, particularly at long range. Unlike Sooty and Bridled Terns (p. 378, p. 378), almost never soar high over ocean; normal flight only about 3m above sea—a useful character.

285 BROWN NODDY
other: Common Noddy
Anous stolidus

PLATE 72 Figs 285a-285c

MAP 285

Length 40–45cm (16–18in.). Wingspan 79–86cm (31–34in.). Iris dark brown, white crescents above and below eye. Bill black. Legs/feet dark brown.

Pantropical; range overlaps with Black Noddy (p. 389). Distinguished by larger size, more robust bill, and paler underwing with dark margins. Sexes alike; no seasonal variation. Juveniles separable from adults. Five subspecies listed, none separable at sea.
JUVENILE: Bill shorter and finer. **Head** Mainly dark greyish-brown, forehead sometimes grey. **Body** Upperparts: saddle brown, tipped white; rump and uppertail-coverts brown. Underparts mainly brown, greyish cast on belly and undertail-coverts. **Wings** Upperwing: black primaries and secondaries show paler tips; remainder dark brown with pale tips to coverts and tertials. Underwing as adult. **Tail** Blackish, paler tips to some rectrices. (It is not known how long this spotted plumage is retained.)
IMMATURE: As adult but usually lacks well-defined cap.
ADULT: Head Ashy-white forehead and crown sharply demarcated from black lores, merge evenly into grey nape. **Body** Upperparts: almost wholly dull brown. Underparts: belly and undertail-coverts greyer. **Wings** Upperwing blackish-brown with browner coverts. Underwing shows dusky grey centre with darker margins (this can be useful in identification when coupled with heavier jizz and broader tail). **Tail** Blackish-brown.
FHJ: Largest, most heavily-built noddy; its broader wings and slower beats impart heavier jizz than other noddies. Refer to notes in Genus *Anous* for habits and flight. Call a guttural 'kark'.
DM: Breeds tropical and subtropical islands in Atlantic, Indian and Pacific Oceans. *A.s. stolidus* on islands in Gulf of Mexico, Caribbean Sea and tropical and subtropical Atlantic including Fernando de Noronha, Ascension, Trinidade, St Helena and Tristan da Cunha group. *A.s. plumbeigularis* Red Sea islands. *A.s. pileatus* islands in Indian Ocean, off Australia and greater part of tropical and subtropical Pacific Ocean. *A.s. galapagensis* Galapagos Is. *A.s. ridgwayi* islands off western Mexico and central America. Egg-dates throughout year in scattered populations. Watson (1910) showed this species' potential to navigate long distances, but its precise dispersal/migration throughout world range poorly known. Many island populations (e.g. Tristan da Cunha, Tortugas) pre-

sent only during breeding season; at other islands (Galapagos, St Paul's Rock) breeding birds present throughout year. Birds breeding Caribbean and Gulf of Mexico normally move S after breeding; casual in summer off Florida, usually associated with hurricanes which can push them as far N as Cape May. In Australian region summer storms can drive birds (Lord Howe I. breeders?) S to Sydney (pers. obs.).
SS: At breeding colonies, where birds are easily viewed, separation of the three 'brown noddies' straightforward. Present species largest, with heaviest bill and sharply demarcated lores; appears two-tone brown in flight. Broader wings and slower beats impart heavier jizz. Black Noddy (p. 389) also has sharply demarcated lores but differs in straight (not curved) demarcation, lack of narrow black line over base of bill, smaller size, more slender jizz, longer and finer bill; plumage also generally darker, particularly underwing. Appears one-tone smoky-black in flight. Lesser Noddy (p. 389) smaller, greyer and usually lacks demarcated lores. Identification at sea more complex; size difficult to judge and white caps often obscured by distance or poor conditions. Brown Noddies always show paler underwing with heavier jizz. White-capped Noddies appear much darker on upperparts and upperwings with lighter jizz, faster wing action. Lesser Noddies have slender jizz but, unless cap seen, appear featureless. Beware of confusing spotted juveniles with juvenile Sooty and Bridled Terns (p. 378, p. 378).

286 LESSER NODDY *Anous tenuirostris*

PLATE 72 Figs 286a-286b
MAP 286

Length 30–34cm (12–13½in.). Wingspan 58–63cm (23–25in.). Iris dark brown, white crescent above and below eye. Bill, legs/feet black.

Tropical Indian Ocean; range overlaps with Brown Noddy (p. 388). Distinguished by smaller size, greyer plumage and normally lacks sharply demarcated lores. Some authorities now regard this and Black Noddy (p. 389) as conspecific. Sexes alike; no seasonal variation. Juveniles separable from adults. Two subspecies listed, not separable at sea.
JUVENILE: Resembles adult, some show white caps (Serventy *et al.* 1971).
ADULT TYPICAL: Head Forehead greyish-white, merging evenly into grey nape and hindneck. **Body** Upperparts: mostly brown, mantle with greyish cast. Underparts greyer. **Wings** Upper and lower wings dark brown, blacker on primaries. **Tail** Blackish-brown.
ADULT ATYPICAL: Differs from typical in sharp demarcation between ash-grey forehead and dark lores (Harrison P, 1981).
FHJ: Differs from larger Brown Noddy in narrower wings, lighter jizz and faster wingbeats. On the wing appears paler than that species, particularly crown and nape, in which it resembles otherwise darker Black Noddy (p. 389).
DM: The two forms are hardly distinguishable. *A.t. tenuirostris* breeds Seychelles chain, Cargados Carajos Shoals (some 340km NNE of Mauritius), also Reunion and Maldives. *A.t. melanops* at Abrolhos Is off Western Australia. Egg-dates Sep–Jan. Pelagic range largely unknown, perhaps mainly sedentary, birds returning to breeding islands to roost during non-breeding season. Feeding range from islands probably extensive, seen feeding off Western Australia at 27°S, 112°E (pers. obs.). Gales can displace birds many hundreds of miles, wrecks having occurred S to Cape Naturaliste in W Australia.
SS: See notes under Brown Noddy (p. 388).

286X BLACK NODDY other: White-capped Noddy *Anous (t.) minutus*

PLATE 72 Figs 286Xa-286Xc
MAP 286X

Length 35–39cm (14–15½in.). Wingspan 66–72cm (26–28½in.). Iris dark brown, white crescent above and below eye. Bill black. Legs/feet brown (yellowish-orange in Hawaiian race).

Tropical Pacific and Atlantic Oceans; range overlaps with Brown Noddy (p. 388). Distinguished by smaller size, blacker plumage, finer and longer bill. Some authorities now consider Black Noddy as Pacific and Atlantic Ocean representative of Lesser Noddy (p. 389). Sexes alike; no seasonal variation. Juveniles separable from adults. Seven subspecies listed, none separable at sea.
JUVENILE: As adult except whitish forehead and crown sharply demarcated from blackish nape; upperwing-coverts and secondaries fringed with buff.
IMMATURE: As juvenile but without paler fringes.
ADULT: Head White forehead sharply demarcated from black lores; crown white, merging evenly into greyer nape and hindneck; remainder dull brown. **Body** Upperparts: blackish-brown. **Wings** Upper- and underwing dark brown, primaries blacker. **Tail** Blackish-brown.
FHJ: Bill relatively longer than other noddies. Smaller, more lightly built than Brown Noddy, with faster fluttering flight and more extensive white cap; tail marginally greyer.
DM: Tropical Pacific and Atlantic Oceans. In W Pacific *A.m. minutus* breeds from Tuamotu through New Guinea, Samoa, New Caledonia and Queensland, Australia, *A.m. worcesteri* islands off Philippines. In central Pacific *A.m. marcusi* breeds Marcus and Wake Is and throughout Micronesia to Caroline I.; *A.m melanogenys* Hawaiian Is; *A.m. diamesus* Clipperton and Cocos Is. In the Caribbean *A.m. americanus* breeds on islands off Belize. In the Atlantic *A.m. atlanticus* breeds on islands from St Pauls Rocks S to St Helena and

Ascension I. Egg-dates throughout year in scattered populations. Appears more sedentary in habits than other noddies, most populations roost at breeding locations throughout year, departing at dawn, returning at dusk. Regular in small numbers to Tortugas off Florida where several observed each year among masses of Brown Noddies (p. 388). Breeding not yet proved. Water temperature plays important part in pelagic distribution (see Murphy 1936), thus this species and Brown Noddy largely absent from cold-water upwellings off western coasts of South America and South Africa. A beached bird at Alexandria (Brooke & Sinclair 1978) is the only South African record.
SS: See notes above and under Brown Noddy (p. 388).

Genus *GYGIS*

Monotypic genus distributed throughout tropical and subtropical oceans. Bill rather straight with angled gonys giving slightly upturned impression when perched; tail resembles *Anous* in form, feathers sharp-pointed. Adults unique among terns in having wholly white plumage. Pelagic movements largely unknown.

287 WHITE TERN
other: Fairy Tern
Gygis alba

PLATE 82 Figs 287a-287b

MAP 287

Length 28–33cm (11–13in.). Wingspan 70–87cm ($27\frac{1}{2}$–$34\frac{1}{4}$in.). Iris brown (appears large and black at sea). Bill black, base often blue. Legs/feet slate-blue, webs white or yellow.

Wide-ranging throughout tropical oceans; distinctive, confusion should not arise with other species. Sexes alike; no seasonal variation. Juveniles separable. Six subspecies listed.
JUVENILE: Resembles adult except: **Head** Mainly white, except for black spot behind eye and brownish mottling over nape. **Body** Upperparts: saddle mostly greyish-white with variable brownish tips wearing to clear greyish-white; rump white. Underparts white. **Wings** Upperwing whitish-grey with black shafts to outer 3–5 primaries. Underwing white. **Tail** Pale grey, outer webs often brownish.
ADULT: Mainly white with faint ivory cast, except for narrow black ring around eye. Murphy (1936) records some individuals with brownish or dusky primary and tail shafts.
FHJ: Small, delicate, wholly white tern with large black eyes and slightly uptilted bill. In flight wings appear broad and rather rounded which, with large head and eye, imparts distinctive 'chunky' jizz whilst remaining buoyant and graceful. This ethereal quality further enhanced by translucent quality of wings when directly overhead. Inquisitive and tame.
DM: Circumequatorial, occurring throughout tropical and subtropical Atlantic, Indian and Pacific Oceans. *G.a. alba* breeds in Atlantic at Fernando de Noronha, South Trinidade, Martin Vaz, Ascension and St Helena. *G.a. monte* breeds Indian Ocean at Seychelles, Madagascar and Mascarene Is. *G.a. royana* breeds off Australia at Norfolk and Kermadec Is. *G.a. candida* breeds throughout SW Pacific Is. *G.a. rothschildi* at Laysan I. *G.a. microrhyncha* breeds Marquesas Is. *G.a. pacifica* throughout S Pacific islands E to Easter I. Disperses to pelagic waters outside breeding season but movements largely unknown. Egg-dates throughout year.
SS: Unmistakable; at long range Grey Noddy (p. 387) may appear white in bright sunlight.

Family *RYNCHOPIDAE* skimmers

Three species, one each in the Americas, Africa and Asia; not closely related to gulls and terns as once thought (Sears *et al.* 1976).

Genus *RYNCHOPS*

All three species have long bills, the knife-like mandibles compressed to thin blades with the lower longer than upper, a feature unique to skimmers. Wings long and pointed; tails short, moderately forked; legs rather short. Habits partially nocturnal, most feeding taking place in early morning or towards dusk when waters usually calm and prey rises to surface. When feeding they fly low over water with tip of longer, lower, mandible shallowly ploughing water. When lower mandible strikes prey bill snaps shut (see Zusi 1962). Occasionally feeds by standing in shallow water and sifting with bill. Sociable, nesting, feeding and loafing together. Ranges of the three species do not overlap, thus locality of sighting usually diagnostic. Skimmers frequent coastal regions and larger inland rivers and lakes.

288 BLACK SKIMMER *Rynchops niger*

PLATE 82 Figs 288a-288c
MAP 288

Length 40–50cm (16–19½in.). Wingspan 107–127cm (42–50in.). Iris dark brown with vertical pupil. Bill bright vermilion, terminal half of upper and most of longer, lower, mandible black. Legs/feet bright vermilion.

Only skimmer in the Americas; range usually diagnostic. Sexes alike; seasonal variation. Juveniles separable. Three subspecies listed.

JUVENILE: Bill dusky-red with blackish tip, lower mandible shorter than adult's; legs dull orange. **Head** Hindcrown, nape and hindneck brown, tipped black and white; remainder, including forehead, white. **Body** Upperparts: saddle mostly dark fawn-brown, each feather darker centrally and fringed white or fawnish-white; rump and uppertail-coverts whiter (wears to brownish with dingy, mottled effect, Bent 1921). Underparts white. **Wings** Upperwing: primaries mostly blackish, innermost tipped buff-white; coverts as saddle, secondaries broadly tipped white. Underwing as adult. **Tail** White; centre and outer webs of rectrices dusky-brown or grey.

ADULT NON-BREEDING: As breeding adult but upperparts paler and browner with broad whitish collar across lower hindneck.

ADULT BREEDING: Crown, nape and hindneck black, remainder, including forehead, white. **Body** Upperparts mostly black; rump and uppertail-coverts white with blackish stripe down centre. Underparts white. **Wings** Upperwing mostly black; inner 3–4 primaries and all secondaries broadly tipped white. Underwing coloration varies geographically, some mostly white except for darker primaries, others largely dusky-grey with blackish primaries (both forms illustrated Plate 82). **Tail** Mainly white, central rectrices greyish-black (*R.n. cinerascens* has darker tail than nominate).

FHJ: Unmistakable. Flight graceful and buoyant with measured beats of long, pointed wings. Often flies in flocks, when movements synchronous, twisting, turning, wheeling in unison. Spends much of day loafing on beaches. Call a barking 'kak-kak-kak' (well described by Murphy 1936 as 'like dogs baying in a dream').

DM: Restricted to the Americas. *R.n. niger* breeds locally along Atlantic coasts of North America from Massachusetts S through Gulf coasts to northern Brazil, and (presumably this race) from NW Mexico, where recent range expansion N to Salton Sea and San Diego Bay, California, southwards to Ecuador, though uncommon S of Gulf of Guayaquil. *R.n. cinerascens* breeds coasts and rivers of N and NE South America, including Amazonian Basin. *R.n. intercedens* breeds coasts and rivers of E and SE South America S to Rio de la Plata and central Argentina. Egg-dates May–Jul (N America), Sep (S America). Northern populations winter from San Diego Bay S to Chile, and on Atlantic coasts from northern shores of Gulf of Mexico and E Florida southwards, but exact movements complicated by presence of resident birds. In South America movements linked with annual floods on most of the rivers, when many disperse to feed over shallow, flooded areas. Wind-blown stragglers have occurred far N of normal range in North America and S to Tierra del Fuego (de Schauensee 1966), although not listed by Humphrey *et al.* (1970).

SS: None within range.

289 AFRICAN SKIMMER *Rynchops flavirostris*

PLATE 82 Figs 289a-289b
MAP 289

Length 38cm (15in.). Wingspan 106cm (42in.). Iris brown. Bill vermilion to deep orange; longer, lower mandible usually paler. Legs/feet vermilion.

Only skimmer in Africa; ranges from Senegal and Sudan S to South Africa. Sexes alike, seasonal variation. Juveniles separable. No subspecies.

JUVENILE: Bill blackish, base yellow, lower mandible shorter than adults. Legs dull yellow. **Head** Hindcrown, nape and hindneck pale brown faintly tipped black and white; remainder, including forehead, white. **Body** Upperparts mostly brown, each feather fringed buff or white. Underparts white, some specimens with brownish cast on chin and throat. **Wings** Upperwing: primaries mostly black, innermost tipped buffish-white; secondaries broadly tipped white; coverts as upperparts. Underwing mainly greyish, primaries black, secondaries tipped white. **Tail** Brown, outer feathers edged buff.

ADULT NON-BREEDING: As breeding adult except upperparts paler and browner with broad, whitish collar across lower hindneck.

ADULT BREEDING: Head Crown, nape and hindneck black; remainder, including forehead, white. **Body** Upperparts black; underparts white. **Wings** Upperwing mostly black; inner 3–4 primaries and all secondaries broadly tipped white. Underwing greyish-white; primaries blackish, secondaries tipped white. **Tail** Mainly black, sides white.

FHJ: As for Black Skimmer (p. 391) but smaller. See also notes on p. 390. Call a loud, sharp 'kik-kik-kik'.

DM: Coasts and rivers of Africa from the Sudan S to Natal and the Zambesi and W across central Africa below 15°S parallel to Senegal. Partial migrant within range, movements dependent on local rains and on requirement of smooth surface water and exposed sand banks for loafing/nesting. Egg-dates Apr–sep.

SS: None within range.

290 INDIAN SKIMMER
Rhychops albicollis

PLATE 82 Fig. 290
MAP 290

Length 43cm (17in.). Wingspan 102–114cm (42–45in.). Iris brown. Bill deep orange, tip yellow. Legs vermilion.

Only skimmer in Asia. Sexes alike; slight seasonal variation. Juveniles separable from adults. No subspecies.

JUVENILE: Bill dusky-yellow, tip black, lower mandible shorter than adult's; legs dull orange. **Head** Hindcrown, nape and hindneck brown, faintly tipped black and white; remainder, including forehead, white. **Body** Upperparts: saddle mostly brown, each feather fringed buff; rump and uppertail-coverts whiter, faintly tipped brown. Underparts white. **Wings** Upperwing: primaries mainly black, innermost tipped buff-white; secondaries broadly tipped white, coverts as saddle. Underwing as adult. **Tail** White except for narrow blackish line through centre.

ADULT NON-BREEDING: As breeding adult except upperparts browner and duller.

ADULT BREEDING: Head Crown and nape black; remainder, including forehead and lower hindneck, white. **Body** Upperparts: saddle black; rump and uppertail-coverts white except for narrow black line through centre. Underparts white. **Wings** Upperwing mostly black, innermost primaries and all secondaries broadly edged white. Underwing white, primaries blackish. **Tail** White, central feathers black.

FHJ: As for Black Skimmer (p. 391) but mainly on freshwater locations.

DM: Restricted to larger rivers and lakes of Asia from Persian Baluchistan E through India, Burma and Indo-China. Partial migrant throughout range, movements linked with local rains and requirement of smooth surface water. Egg-dates Mar–May.

SS: None within range.

Family *ALCIDAE* auks

Twenty-two species in 13 genera; confined to northern hemisphere. The ecological counterparts of Southern Oceans penguins. They have dense, waterproof plumage; mostly black and white, many with colourful bare parts and/or nuptial head ornaments. Characteristically, head proportionately large with legs set well back toward rear of thickset body; tail short. Sexes outwardly alike; most show seasonal variation.

All alcids are skilful divers and swimmers, using their wings to 'fly' under water. Larger forms feed on fish whilst smaller forms, i.e. auklets, feed chiefly on plankton. Breeding biology varies: some breed in huge colonies, others in loose colonies, a few solitarily. Nesting-habitat tolerance also wide-ranging, from mountain scree slopes some miles from coast, sea cliffs and burrows to tree holes and even on branches of large trees. Whilst many alcids attend flightless, partly-grown chicks at sea and in some species feed them, a few species give birth to nidifugous young which join their parents at sea within 2–3 days of hatching.

Identification of all alcids at sea often difficult at long range and, in some cases, may be impossible. Relative size, flight and distribution of black on head and body should be accurately noted. At close range bill structure and obvious features, e.g. nuptial crests or facial ornaments, often diagnostic.

Genus *ALLE*

Monotypic genus; small, short-necked alcid confined to higher latitudes of northern hemisphere. Abundant, occurs in millions at colonies.

291 LITTLE AUK
other: Dovekie
Alle alle

PLATE 83 Figs 291a-291b
MAP 291

Length 20–25cm (8–10in.). Wingspan 31–33cm (12–13in.). Iris black. Bill short, black. Legs/feet blackish-grey.

Arctic and N Atlantic Oceans, recently recorded Bering and Beaufort Seas. Unlike any other bird in high Arctic; confusion always possible with poor or distant views of Puffin (p. 404). Sexes alike; marked seasonal variation. Two subspecies, not separable at sea. Juveniles separable from adults. Albinism rare (Sealy 1969).

JUVENILE: As breeding adult except: Bill smaller and weaker. **Head** Including neck and throat clove-brown, paler on chin. **Body** Upperparts slightly browner.

FIRST-WINTER: Resembles non-breeding adult but upperparts, including upperwings, duller and browner.

ADULT NON-BREEDING (acquired Aug/Sep): Resembles breeding adult except: **Head** Ear-coverts, chin and throat white. **Body** Upper breast white, sometimes with brownish cast.

ADULT BREEDING (acquired late winter/early spring): **Head** Black. **Body** Upperparts black; underparts mainly white except for blackish upper breast. **Wings** Upperwing mostly black, secondaries tipped white, scapulars streaked white. Underwing varies; generally appears dark, with

variable whitish coverts sometimes concentrated in a narrow bar along tips of median and lesser underwing-coverts. **Tail** Black above, white below.
FHJ: Smallest Atlantic alcid, appears neckless; sometimes sits very low in water. Combination of small size, short bill, chunky outline and whirring wings imparts distinctive chubby jizz. Occasionally forms immense flocks at sea.
DM: Confined to high Arctic for much of the year. *A.a. alle* breeds Greenland, Iceland, Novaya Zemlya, Spitsbergen and Jan Mayen. According to Gabrielson (in Johnson *et al.* 1975) nests in Canada, probably on Ellesmere I. NWT, although Godfrey (1966) mentions only possibility of breeding. *A.a. polaris*, which is larger than nominate, breeds Franz Josef Land. Egg-dates Jun/Jul; fledging Aug/Sep; some birds winter within breeding range at edge of pack ice, but most move S into oceanic habitat. Movements begin Baffin Bay and Davis Strait Jul/Aug, reaching Newfoundland as early as Sep in some years; many reach New England late Oct/early Nov; casual S to Long I., New York. Proportionately few winter eastern Atlantic off S Ireland and SW England; arrivals begin Sep but numbers largely dependent on gales. Stragglers have reached Madeira, Bermuda, Cuba and the Mediterranean though winter range normally extends only to about 42°N, most remaining well to N. In N America spring passage begins Mar, with annual concentration of about 1 million in Lancaster Sound, Baffin Bay, during last weeks of May. Both races have recently been reported in Beaufort, Chukchi and Bering Seas (Johnson *et al.* 1975), suggesting hitherto unknown circumpolar range in high Arctic during summer.
SS: If seen well, confusion should not arise, although young alcids of any species, but particularly Puffins, may cause problems for the unwary. See Plate 84 for illustration of juvenile Guillemot about to depart from ledge.

Genus *ALCA*

Monotypic genus; large-sized black and white alcid with diagnostic bill markings.

292 RAZORBILL *Alca torda*

PLATE 83 Figs 292a-292c
MAP 292

Length 40–45cm (15½–17½in.). Wingspan 63–66cm (25–26in.). Iris brown. Bill large and deep, mostly black with transverse white bar on distal portion and narrow white line stretching from base to eye. Legs/feet blackish-grey.

Confined to N Atlantic Ocean. Bill diagnostic, but at long range or under poor conditions confusion possible with Guillemot and Puffin (p. 395, p. 404). Sexes alike; seasonal variation. Juveniles separable from adults. Three subspecies, none separable at sea. Albinism rare.
JUVENILE/FIRST-WINTER: As non-breeding adult; bill smaller without white bands, sides of breast sometimes dusky.
IMMATURE/FIRST-SUMMER: Resembles non-breeding adult but: bill has faint white bar. **Head** Differs in whitish chin and throat; grey (not black) sides of face. **Body** Upperparts slightly browner. Underparts: sides of breast often dusky.
ADULT NON-BREEDING: As adult breeding but: bill lacks white line from culmen to eye. **Head** Differs in white chin, throat and ear-coverts extending upwards behind eye.
ADULT BREEDING: Head Black. **Body** Upperparts mostly black except for white sides of lower back (conspicuous in flight). Underparts white. **Wings** Upperwing: black except for narrow white trailing edge along secondaries. Underwing-coverts white, primaries and secondaries mostly black. **Tail** Black.
FHJ: A large alcid with heavy head and deep, blunt bill. In flight, longish pointed tail, white sides to rump and plump torpedo-shaped body impart distinctive jizz. Usually appears blacker above than most of its congeners. Wingbeats slower than smaller Puffin (p. 404).
DM: Restricted to N Atlantic region. *A.t. torda* breeds N America, Greenland, Norway, Sweden, Finland, Bear I. and USSR. The smaller *A.t. islandica* breeds Iceland, Faeroes, British Is, Heligoland and NW France. Returns to inspect colonies Jan/Feb; egg-dates May–Jul; juveniles (incapable of flight) vacate ledges Jul/Aug. Both adults accompany juvenile to sea where they undergo a complete wing moult, rendering them flightless for short period. Winter dispersal poorly understood. N American population extends S to Long I., New York, casual further S. In E Atlantic some winter North Sea and coasts of Britain, Ireland and S Norway. Others, perhaps mostly young birds, move S in late autumn joining with other alcids to form spectacular flights off NW Europe; peak daily counts 40,000–60,000 off St Ives, SW England. Range extends S to Iberian Peninsula, W Mediterranean and NW Morocco; vagrant Canary Is. Large spring movements occur off NW Spain and S Ireland.
SS: See notes under Puffin (p. 404). From Guillemot (p. 395) by large head, deep bill, pointed tail and much blacker upperparts. Flightless juveniles normally half the size of their robust parents, could be mistaken for Little Auks or Puffins (p. 392, p. 404). Immatures and non-breeding-plumage adults differ from Brünnich's Guillemot (p. 394) in jizz, shape of bill, and the white sides of face extending above and beyind eye.

Genus *URIA*

Two species; medium to large-sized alcids confined to higher latitudes of northern hemisphere. Characteristically, with dark bill and upperparts, white underparts.

Separation of the two *Uria* spp. difficult at any stage. Whilst past literature has often emphasised the differences in 'weight' and colour of bill, juveniles have weaker and shorter bills and some overlap between the two species occurs. Differences in timing of moult and distribution of black on head are discussed in species account below.

293 BRÜNNICH'S GUILLEMOT
other: Thick-billed Murre
Uria lomvia

PLATE 84 Figs 293a-293c
MAP 293

Length 43–48cm (17–19in.). Wingspan 71–81cm (28–32in.). Iris black. Bill black with white stripe along basal cutting edge of tomium. Legs/feet yellowish-brown.

Higher latitudes of North Pacific and Atlantic Oceans; range overlaps with Razorbill and Guillemot (p. 393, p. 395). Sexes alike; seasonal variation. Juveniles separable from adults. Two subspecies listed, not separable at sea. Albinism and melanism occasionally recorded (see Terres 1980).

JUVENILE: Length about 20cm, bulk about one-third that of adult. Bill smaller, rather deep at base. Plumage resembles non-breeding adult except: **Head** Chin and throat grey. **Body** Upper breast grey, shading to white on middle of breast and belly (Bent 1919).

FIRST-WINTER: Bill smaller than adult's but otherwise as non-breeding adult, although chin and throat usually more mottled and dusky.

ADULT NON-BREEDING: Bill may lack white stripe on tomium. **Head** Mostly blackish-brown, merging evenly under eye into whitish chin and throat. Hindneck blackish-brown extending as narrow, incomplete collar at base of whitish foreneck. **Body** Upperparts blackish-brown (head and upperparts become browner with wear). Underparts mostly white. **Wings** Upperwing blackish-brown, secondaries narrowly tipped white. Underwing mainly blackish, coverts white. **Tail** As upperparts.

ADULT BREEDING: As non-breeding adult except: **Head** Including neck blackish-brown, terminating on throat in sharply pointed, inverted V (see Guillemot, p. 395).

FHJ: Flight strong and direct on proportionately short, fast-beating wings. Breeding adults, in flight, have stockier jizz than Guillemot (p. 395), heavier bill, and somewhat shorter-necked appearance which with blacker upperparts recalls longer-tailed Razorbill (p. 393). For further differences see under SS.

DM: Arctic and Bering Seas S to higher latitudes of Atlantic and Pacific Oceans. Tuck (1961) estimated world population of both guillemots as 56 million, with Brünnich's outnumbering Guillemot (p. 395) by 3:1 but in southern parts of range outnumbered at breeding colonies by Guillemot. *U.l. arra* breeds as far N in Siberia as Wrangel I. and along Chukchi Sea coast from Cape Lisburn S throughout Bering Sea to Aleutian Is, Gulf of Alaska and Commander Is. A small colony also occurs Canada, NWT at Cape Parry. *U.l. lomvia* breeds Canada, Gulf of St Lawrence, Labrador and Hudson Bay to Greenland, Iceland, Jan Mayen Land, Spitsbergen, Franz Josef Land and Novaya Zemlya. Recently proved to breed Norway in 1964, and since then found in small numbers at eight localities (Brun 1979). Return to colonies begins May, most Jun; egg-dates Jun–Aug. Chicks leave ledges before they can fly, to join adults on water; many colonies depleted by mid Aug. Winter dispersal of all populations governed by ice conditions. Regularly winters Chukchi Sea N to Point Hope and Cape Thompson, the Cape Parry population apparently migrating W to winter in Bering Sea (Johnson *et al.* 1975). In N Pacific winters commonly S to Hokkaido, scarcer Honshu (Japan), and in east to SE Alaska and British Columbia; occasionally Washington S to California (see Roberson 1980). In Atlantic winters from Greenland S to Hudson Bay and along Atlantic coast to Long I.; occasionally to S Carolina. In N Europe winters mainly in open water of breeding areas, with casual records S to Britain and Holland, one record France. Probably overlooked in these areas, occurring more frequently than records suggest.

SS: Adult Razorbill (p. 393) in summer has diagnostic bill but winter adults and juveniles (which have smaller bills than adults) could be confused by the unwary. Both adult and juvenile Razorbills in winter plumage have white extending upwards on ear-coverts behind eye, giving whiter-headed aspect than in present species which, combined with longer more pointed tail and critical examination of bill, enables ready separation. At any age or plumage present species resembles more closely Guillemot (p. 395). Best means of separation is bill shape (but see juveniles below). In adult Brünnich's Guillemot, bill not only deeper but shorter with an evenly decurving culmen throughout its length; the white tomium stripe may be absent in some specimens (Stallcup 1976). By comparison Guillemot has longer, thinner bill which is straight for most of its length and, due to angle at gonys, appears slightly upturned in the field. Some specimens show a faint tomium stripe; Kinnear (1980) points out that Guillemots carrying sand-eels often appear to have thicker bill with white line along it. Observations by Forsell & Gould (1980) and confirmed by research (personal) indicate that Guillemots begin a post-nuptial head moult from late Jul onwards, and by mid Aug most populations have the diagnostic white sides to face and dark post-ocular stripes. By contrast

Brünnich's Guillemot does not appear to begin post-nuptial head moult until Nov, so that head remains mostly dark throughout autumn. This difference in timing of post-nuptial moult is clearly illustrated in Roberson (1980, p. 210), which shows a photograph of both species swimming side by side, taken on 2 Oct; present species is in breeding plumage whereas Guillemot is in non-breeding plumage. Thus any dark-headed alcid in autumn or early winter should be scrutinised. The differences are reversed later in year, when Guillemots begin a pre-nuptial head moult during Dec–Feb. Any pale-headed alcids in Mar are therefore worth investigating, although first-year birds of both species would still have whitish chins and throats. Even in Jun or Jul some Brünnich's show traces of winter plumage, normally as a white patch at base of lower mandible. Juvenile and first-winter Guillemots are even more difficult to distinguish from similarly-aged Brünnich's, due mainly to combination of their dark ear-coverts and short bill, which proportionately resembles that of present species. The striking similarity is well shown by Van den Berg (1980).

294 GUILLEMOT
other: Common Murre
Uria aalge

PLATE 84 Figs 294a-294e

MAP 294

Length 40–43cm (16–17in.). Wingspan 71cm (28in.). Iris blackish. Bill black. Legs/feet grey with faintly yellowish cast.

N Atlantic and Pacific Oceans; confusion always possible at any distance with Razorbill and Brünnich's Guillemot (p. 393, p. 394). Sexes alike; seasonal variation. The bridled form, a genetic variation showing white eye-ring and post-ocular stripe, occurs only in North Atlantic. Juveniles separable from adults. Seven subspecies listed, of which *U.a. albionis* probably separable at sea due to browner (not blackish) upperparts. Albinism and melanism occasionally reported (Andrews, pers. comm.; see also Terres 1980).

JUVENILE: Length about 20cm, bulk only one-third of adult; bill smaller, rather deep at base. **Head** Forehead, crown and hindneck dark brown extending to just below eye, ear-coverts faintly mottled white; chin and throat white. **Body** Upperparts dark brown; underparts mostly white. **Wings** Not fully formed, incapable of flight; secondaries lack white trailing edge of adults.

FIRST-WINTER: Bill proportionately shorter and deeper than adults. Plumage as non-breeding adult except: **Head** Lacks post-ocular stripe, ear-coverts mostly dark extending to below level of eye (beware Brünnich's Guillemot, p. 394).

ADULT NON-BREEDING: (acquired late Jul onwards, see Brünnich's Guillemot, p. 394): As breeding adult except: **Head** Chin, throat and cheeks white, latter extending upwards behind eye and crossed by diagnostic black post-ocular stripe. Hindneck dark, extending as partial collar at base of white foreneck.

ADULT BREEDING: Head Including neck dark brown, ending on throat in shallow, rounded, inverted U (see Brünnich's Guillemot, p. 394). **Body** Upperparts dark greyish-brown or blackish (varies geographically). Underparts mostly white, flanks and thighs striated with brown (diagnostic, never found in Brünnich's Guillemot, although difficult to observe at sea). **Wings** Upperwing mostly brown, secondaries tipped white; underwing dark grey with whitish coverts and tips of secondaries. **Tail** As upperparts. NOTE Bridled form occurs more frequently in northern populations.

FHJ: Bill longer, more pointed than other alcids, giving head distinctive attenuated appearance. Differs further from Brünnich's Guillemot (p. 394) in slimmer body imparting longer, more slender appearance when sitting on water; crown more rounded and, in southern *U.a. albionis*, upperparts paler and browner, particularly back. Flight fast, usually low over water, turning from side to side, wings beating rapidly. Social, breeding and to some extent feeding together throughout year.

DM: N Atlantic and Pacific Oceans. *U.a. inornata* breeds Bering Sea and N Pacific Ocean S to Hokkaido, Japan. *U.a. californica* breeds along Californian coast S to Hurricane Point. In North Atlantic, *U.a. aalge* breeds Labrador and Greenland to Norway and N Scotland; *U.a. hyperborea* breeds Bear I.; *U.a. spiloptera* breeds Faeroe Is; *U.a. intermedia* breeds Baltic Sea; and *U.a. albionis* breeds S Scotland, British Isles, NW France S to Portugal (Berlenga Is). In Britain returns to inspect colonies from late Nov onwards, when some already in nuptial dress. Egg-dates May–Aug; juveniles, incapable of flight, depart from ledges 18–25 days after hatching when only third to half size of parent (beware Little Auk and Marbled and *Endomychura* murrelets in N Pacific). Adults flightless for short period during wing moult Aug–early Oct, prior to winter dispersal. Winter dispersal throughout range governed by gales and ice conditions; many remain at ice front and, in N Pacific, mixed flocks of this species and Brünnich's Guillemot form aggregations of up to 250,000 with densities up to 10,000 per km^2 (Divotky 1979). Elsewhere winters at sea within breeding range, extending S to Korea and N Honshu, Japan, in N Pacific and to W Mediterranean in N Atlantic.

SS: In Alaska breeding Guillemot separable from Brünnich's by their 'hershey-chocolate' (not black) upperparts. See fuller notes under Brünnich's (p. 394). Given reasonable views all ages readily separated from blacker-plumaged, heavier-billed Razorbill (p. 393) but at long range or under poor conditions, particularly distant views of auk flights during autumn/winter, separation of the two often impossible. At close range, browner upperparts plus bill and head shape enable ready separation, even between juveniles. Tail relatively short and rounded, not 'long' and tapering to a point as found in Razorbill which tends to cock its tail more whilst swimming. See also notes under Puffin (p. 404).

Genus *CEPPHUS*

Three species. Medium-sized alcids with marked seasonal difference in plumages; confined to higher latitudes of Pacific and Atlantic Oceans.

Throughout most of year the plumages of all three *Cepphus* spp. are distinctly different from other sympatric alcids. During winter months in North Pacific non-breeding Pigeon Guillemots may be confused with Marbled Murrelets (p. 398). Ranges of Pigeon and Black Guillemots now known to overlap in Bering Sea area. Separation should be possible by difference in colour of underwing-coverts.

295 BLACK GUILLEMOT
other: Tystie
Cepphus grylle

PLATE 83 Figs 295a-295c

MAP 295

Length 30–36cm (12–14in.). Wingspan 58cm (23in.). Iris brown. Bill black, mouth red. Legs/feet crimson.

Circumpolar; unlikely to be confused with other alcids throughout much of range, but overlaps with Pigeon Guillemot (p. 396) Bering and Chukchi Seas. Sexes alike, although Asbirk (1979) records most males as having smaller amounts of white on underwing; marked seasonal variation. Juveniles separable from adults. Seven subspecies listed (Asbirk 1980) but probably none separable at sea. Albinism and melanism occasionally recorded.

JUVENILE: Legs orange. **Head** Forehead, crown, lores, streak through eye, nape and hindneck blackish-grey; chin, throat and sides of face white, lightly tipped greyish-brown. **Body** Upperparts: mantle mostly uniform blackish-grey; scapulars, back and rump similar but with irregular whitish tips. Underparts mostly white with brownish-grey tips, heaviest along flanks. **Wings** As non-breeding adult but brownish tips scattered through white upperwing patch. Underwing-coverts white (see juvenile Pigeon Guillemot, p. 396).

FIRST-WINTER: Resembles non-breeding adult except: **Head** Crown and nape darker. **Body** Upperparts: pale tips on mantle and back probably less pronounced.

FIRST-SUMMER: As breeding adult except: **Body** Scattered white feather tips to upper- and underparts. **Wings** Unmoulted but white wing patch often reduced through wear.

ADULT NON-BREEDING: Head Mostly white except for dusky crown, nape, rear of neck and small patch in front of and below eye. **Body** Upperparts greyish-brown, narrowly barred white; underparts mostly white except for greyish bars along flanks. **Wings** As adult breeding, but faded, often with brownish edges. **Tail** Black.

ADULT BREEDING: Wholly blackish, except for conspicuous white upperwing patches and white axillaries and coverts on underwing. NOTE Nominate form described above. *C.g. islandicus* has irregular brown stripe through white upperwing patch. *C.g. mandtii* has larger white upperwing patch. Adults with wholly black wings occasionally occur in all populations.

FHJ: A striking species in all plumages, midway in size between Puffin and Guillemot. On water sits rather high; the combination of long, thick neck and pointed tail (often held slightly raised) gives distinctive jizz. Flight low over water with rapid wingbeats and distinctive pot-bellied jizz. Prefers shallower water, unlike most of its congeners.

DM: Circumpolar. Sowls *et al.* (1978) have recently published records of small numbers breeding at 12 sites in Alaska, presumably *C.g. mandtii*, which also breeds westwards along Siberian and high Arctic coasts to Spitsbergen. Elsewhere *C.g. ultimus* breeds mainly along high Arctic Canadian coast; *C.g. arcticus* Greenland and Labrador; *C.g. islandicus* Iceland; *C.g. faeroensis* Faeroe Is; *C.g. atlantis* along E coast of N Atlantic Ocean; and *C.g. grylle* Baltic Sea area. Egg-dates May–Jul; fledging Jul/Aug. Rather sedentary, disperses mainly to adjacent waters. A few occasionally wander S of breeding range during winter; casual S to Long I. and New Jersey in NW Atlantic and S to N France in Europe.

SS: Throughout much of its range unlikely to be confused with any other alcid. Complications arise in Bering and Chukchi Seas, where range overlaps with Pigeon Guillemot (p. 396) at Cape Lisburne and Cape Thompson, Little Diomede I. and possibly St Lawrence I. (see Sowls *et al.* 1978). Adult Pigeon Guillemot differs in blackish bar cutting part-way across white patch on upperwing, and brownish-grey underwing-coverts. Juveniles of the two species and adults in winter or transitional plumages are very similar and some overlap in colour and pattern of upperparts and upperwing-coverts may occur. The darker, greyish-brown underwing-coverts of Pigeon Guillemot would seem the most reliable way of separating the two species at these stages. See also winter-plumage Marbled Murrelet (p. 398).

296 PIGEON GUILLEMOT
Cepphus columba

PLATE 85 Figs 296a-296e

MAP 296

Length 30–35cm (12–14in.). Wingspan not recorded. Iris blackish. Bill blackish, mouth red. Legs/feet red.

North Pacific Ocean S to Kamchatka Peninsula and California; range overlaps with Black Guillemot and Marbled Murrelet (p. 396, p. 398). Sexes alike; marked seasonal variation. Juveniles separable from adults. Two subspecies listed; *C.c. snowi* differs in almost black wing-coverts in both juvenile and adult plumages (some appearing much like Spectacled Guillemot, p. 397, but without white eye patch).

JUVENILE: Legs orange. **Head** Forehead, crown,

lores, streak through eye and hindneck blackish-grey; remainder dusky-white variably speckled brownish or blackish-grey (heaviest on lower fore-neck). **Body** Upperparts: mostly fuscous-black above with indistinct whitish tips (usually darker than in corresponding Black Guillemot, p. 396). Underparts dull dusky-white with greyish feather tips, heaviest on upper breast and along flanks. **Wings** Upperwing: as non-breeding adult except white wing patch sometimes whiter (see Fig. 296d, Plate 85, for extreme). Underwing as adult. **Tail** Blackish.

FIRST-WINTER: Resembles non-breeding adult except: **Head** Crown and nape darker. **Body** Upper-parts darker, apparently with fewer white feather edges (Bent 1919). **Wings** Upperwing as juvenile.

FIRST-SUMMER: As breeding adult except: **Body** Underparts may show scattered white tips. **Wings** Upperwing: white coverts variably marked with black.

NON-BREEDING ADULT: Head Mostly white except for dusky crown, nape, hindneck and streak through eye. **Body** Upperparts greyish, narrowly barred white. Underparts mostly white, except for barring and striations along flanks. **Wings** Un-moulted but white wing patch often reduced through wear.

TRANSITIONAL: From Jan onwards adults begin prolonged moult sometimes lasting through to Jun. During initial stages dark crown and cheeks contrasting with whitish chin, throat and underparts cause superficial resemblance to non-breeding Marbled Murrelet (p. 398)—beware!

ADULT BREEDING: Plumage mostly dull, sooty-black except: **Wings** Upperwing: white patch on coverts broken by blackish bars (bars sometimes obscured when swimming). Underwing-coverts dusky greyish- or brownish-white (pure white in Black Guillemot, p. 396).

FHJ: Much as for Black Guillemot. A well-known North Pacific species, often nesting in or under man-made structures such as wharves etc. and, during breeding season, commonly seen close to shore in kelp-beds, harbours etc. Loosely gregar-ious but nests singly or in small groups, not large colonies. Like the closely related Black Guillemot, has a 'water-dance' in spring when several pairs may gather, forming lines, submerging and chas-ing each other, calling and presenting red mouths to each other.

DM: North Pacific. *C.c. columba* breeds from NE Siberia and Cape Lisburne, Chukchi Sea, S through Bering Sea along northern coasts of Kamchatka Peninsula, Aleutian Is and eastwards through Gulf of Alaska S to southern California. *C.c. snowi* breeds south Kamchatka and Kurile Is. Returns to nesting areas mid Mar onwards; egg-dates May–Jul; fledging and dispersal begin Aug–Sep. Wintering area/movements of this near-shore species something of a mystery; they are largely absent from many breeding areas (e.g. California) during winter months, not reappearing in any numbers until about Mar. Ringing recoveries of Farallon Is breeders show that they may move N after breeding (Desante & Ainley 1980).

SS: Breeding adults distinctive throughout much of range; see notes under Black Guillemot (p. 396) for separation where ranges overlap in Chukchi Sea. Elsewhere beware of confusing transitional stages with local murrelets, see especially non-breeding Marbled Murrelet (p. 398) which can look similar but has white scapulars, not coverts; jizz different when viewed critically. See notes under Spec-tacled Guillemot (p. 397).

---

297 SPECTACLED GUILLEMOT
other: Sooty Guillemot
Cepphus carbo

PLATE 85 Figs 297a-297c

MAP 297

Length 38cm (15in.). Wingspan not recorded. Iris blackish. Bill black. Legs red.

Restricted to NW Pacific Ocean; range overlaps with Pigeon, Brünnich's and common Guillemots (p. 396, p. 394, p. 395). Sexes alike; marked seasonal variation. Juveniles separable from adults. No subspecies.

FIRST-WINTER: As non-breeding adult except: **Head** Chin and throat paler. **Body** Underparts mostly pure white; sides and flanks narrowly brownish. **Wings** Underwing-coverts a little paler.

ADULT NON-BREEDING: As breeding adult except: **Head** Chin and throat paler brown ending in line across lower throat. **Body** Underparts mostly white, uniformly tipped very pale grey-brown; ap-pears whitish at distance. (NOTE See illustration of transitional on Plate 85.)

ADULT BREEDING: Mostly dull blackish-brown except: **Head** Conspicuous white patch around eye, smaller white area at base of bill. **Wings** Under-wing: coverts and axillaries brownish.

FHJ: Little known; jizz resembles widespread Black Guillemot (p. 396), with rather plump outline and whirring flight low over water but larger, with more robust bill. Swims buoyantly, the combination of long, thick neck, pointed bill and sloping crown imparting grebe-like quality.

DM: Confined to NW Pacific Ocean, breeding along shores of Kamchatka Peninsula, Okhotsk and Japan Seas and Kurile Is S to Japan. Breeding biology and movements little known; probably disperses only to adjacent seas.

SS: Beware of confusing Pigeon Guillemot (*C.c. snowi*), which may lack any traces of a white wing patch; that species, however, has wholly dark face and smaller, slimmer bill.

Genus *BRACHYRAMPHUS*

Two species; enigmatic medium-sized North Pacific alcids with slender bill, marked seasonal variation in plumage.

At sea separation of *Brachyramphus* spp. can be difficult without comparative experience or at long range. Breeding adults differ in tone of upperparts whilst non-breeders show distinct difference in extent of black on head. At all ages relative length of bill an important character to record accurately (much shorter in Kittlitz's Murrelet).

298 MARBLED MURRELET *Brachyramphus marmoratus*

PLATE 88 Figs 298a-298b
MAP 298

Length 24–25cm ($9\frac{1}{2}$–10in.). Wingspan not recorded. Iris blackish-brown. Bill blackish. Legs/feet flesh, webs blackish.

Enigmatic North Pacific species; range overlaps with Kittlitz's Murrelet and Least Auklet (p. 398, p. 403). See also winter/transitional Pigeon Guillemot (p. 396). Sexes alike; marked seasonal variation. Little is known of breeding habits. Juveniles differ from non-breeding adults only in clearer, blackish-brown upperparts and dusky-brown barring on underparts, but by about Nov differences negligible (Bent 1919). Two subspecies; *B.m. perdix* differs from nominate in larger size, white eye-ring and, in breeding plumage, lacks rufous tones on upperparts.

ADULT NON-BREEDING: Head Cap blackish, extending below level of eye; chin, throat and lower sides of face white, extending upwards towards nape on sides of neck. **Body** Upperparts mostly blackish-grey, indistinctly scaled grey; scapulars white forming horizontal band when swimming. Underparts mostly white except for narrow blackish collar on sides of breast and indistinct greyish mottling on flanks and thighs. **Wings** Upperwing brownish-grey or blackish-grey. Underwing dusky. **Tail** Blackish.

ADULT BREEDING (assumed Jan onwards): **Head** Mostly dark vinaceous-brown, including ear-coverts and hindneck, forming indistinct cap; chin and throat paler brown, marbled with buff and white. **Body** Upperparts mostly dark vinaceous-brown with richer red-brown barring visible at close range (when wet, at distance, appears wholly brown). Scapulars occasionally tipped greyer (forming indistinct horizontal stripe when swimming). Underparts pale olive-brown marbled with buff and white, darkest across breast forming indistinct breast band. **Wings** Upperwing as upperparts. Underwing dusky-brown. **Tail** Brown, narrowly fringed white.

FHJ: Small, chunky, 'neckless' alcid with rather long, slightly downcurved bill. Flight swift and direct, usually rising from water quickly and skimming low over surface on whirring wings, but at great height when commuting overland to nesting areas. Calls both in flight and when resting at sea: 'meer-meer-meer'. Breeding biology little known but unusual in non-colonial habits, apparently nesting either in hollows of, or on large limbs of, coniferous trees, where flightless juveniles presumably sit until they fledge (see details in Stallcup & Greenberg 1974); eggs have also been found on the tundra of treeless Alaskan islands. At sea feeds mainly inshore, rarely venturing more than a few kilometres offshore, visiting sheltered bays and harbours during winter.

DM: Despite local abundance, occurring in hundreds of thousands off Alaska and in smaller numbers S to California and Japan, only four nests have ever been found; breeding biology remains a mystery. One nest found in Siberia (Kuzyakin 1963); one in California (Binford *et al.* 1975); and two on East Amatuli I., Barren Is (Simon 1980). Two of the 'nests' were in trees, two on open ground. Precise limits of breeding areas unknown, only evidence being adults feeding offshore by day prior to flying inland at dusk. Range thought to extend in NE Pacific from northern California N to Adak I. in central Aleutians (Sowls *et al.* 1978); and in Asia probably from Kamchatka Peninsula S through Kuriles to northern Japan, where a few regularly seen off Akkeshi district, Hokkaido, but, as elsewhere in range, confirmation of breeding lacking. Egg-dates Apr–Jun?; fledglings appear at sea from end of Jun onwards (Sealy 1974); winters S to Japan and California. Of especial interest are sightings of birds over breeding habitat during winter (Strachan, in Sowls *et al.* 1980), suggesting that species may roost in coastal forests during winter. There are two inland North American records of Asiatic *B.m. perdix* (see Jehl & Jehl 1981).

SS: See notes under Kittlitz's Murrelet (p. 398).

299 KITTLITZ'S MURRELET *Brachyramphus brevirostris*

PLATE 88 Figs 299a-299b
MAP 299

Length 23cm (9in.). Wingspan not recorded. Iris blackish-brown. Bill brownish, tipped white. Legs/feet brownish.

Enigmatic North Pacific species; range overlaps with many alcid spp., see especially Marbled Murrelet and Least Auklet (p. 398, p. 403). See also winter/transitional Pigeon Guillemot (p. 396). Sexes alike; marked seasonal variation. Little is known of breeding habits; first-winter plumage similar to non-breeding adult but with fine barring on face, nape, underparts and tail (see Devillers 1972).

ADULT NON-BREEDING: Head Mostly white except for narrow blackish forehead, crown and nape; eye-crescent dusky. **Body** Upperparts mostly blackish-grey, tipped and spotted whitish; scapulars fringed white (forming horizontal stripe when swimming). Underparts white, except for narrow blackish breast band (extension from mantle) and dusky barring along flanks. **Wings** Upperwing blackish-grey. Underwing dusky. **Tail** Brownish, broadly tipped and edged white.

ADULT BREEDING: Head Wholly brown, marbled buff and fawn. **Body** Upperparts and upper breast as head, merging into imperfect white belly. **Wings** Upperwing: coverts as head; primaries and secondaries blackish. Underwing dusky-brown. **Tail** Dark brown, narrowly fringed white.

FHJ: Little known. Compared with more widespread Marbled Murrelet (p. 398), has much shorter, less apparent bill but otherwise resembles it in shape and jizz. A non-colonial species, nesting in alpine habitat usually some distance inland; the few eggs found suggest that it nests on open, stony ground, between snow fields. At sea may be more gregarious: Dixon (in Bent 1919) states that he saw 500 in one flock off Glacier Bay and that their flight was quicker and wilder than the other murrelets; they appeared to get off the water far more rapidly.

DM: During breeding season occurs in tens of thousands in Prince William Sound, Alaska, but few nests found and breeding biology remains virtually unknown. Sowls *et al.* (1978) regard Kittlitz's Murrelet as largely endemic to Alaska, probably breeding locally in NE Siberia and in Commander Is. Their centre of abundance, however, appears to be from SE Alaska to Kodiak I., where they are locally abundant, but they are also common along Alaskan Peninsula and throughout Aleutian Is with reported nests as far N as Cape Lisburne. Seldom, however, do they reach the numerical strength of the similar, closely related Marbled Murrelet. Egg-dates May/Jun. Thought to winter on adjacent open seas from southern parts of breeding range and SE Siberia S to Kurile Is. See Roberson (1980) for west coast record from Washington, Jan 1974.

SS: Breeding adults differ from Marbled Murrelet (p. 398) in much shorter bill, more marbled, sandy-brown upperparts, whiter belly and white outer rectrices (easily seen when birds are landing). In winter appears much whiter-headed than that species, the white extending well above eye and on sides of neck forming seemingly continuous collar. Least Auklet (p. 403) also has whitish scapulars but is smaller with darker head and white auricular plume. See also Pigeon Guillemot (p. 396).

Genus *ENDOMYCHURA*

Two species; small, thin-billed alcids, mostly blackish above and white below. Both species confined to eastern North Pacific.

At sea separation of the two *Endomychura* spp. difficult at anything but close range. Positive identification can be made only by accurately recording proportions of bill, extent of cap on sides of face, tone of upperparts, and colour of underwing-coverts.

300 XANTUS' MURRELET *Endomychura hypoleuca*

PLATE 87 Figs 300a-300b
MAP 300

Length 24–26cm (9½–10¼in.). Wingspan not recorded. Iris blackish-brown. Bill black. Legs/feet bluish.

North America, restricted to Channel Is and west coast of Baja California, Mexico; range overlaps with very similar Craveri's Murrelet (p. 400). Sexes alike; no appreciable seasonal variation. Juveniles and adults alike. Two subspecies listed; nominate *hypoleuca* differs in white crescents above and below eye (reasonably conspicuous at sea). Following notes refer to *E.h. scrippsi*.

PLUMAGE: Head Blackish cap extends only to level of gape; chin, throat and lower sides of face white. **Body** Upperparts blackish with faint greyish cast. Underparts mostly white, except blackish flanks extending back along body to thighs. **Wings** Upperwing blackish. Underwing mostly white with dusky-grey trailing edge. **Tail** Blackish (appears as short tuft at sea).

FHJ: Small black and white alcid with slender black bill. Characteristically, swims low in water showing little if any white on flanks but, like Craveri's and unlike all other murrelets, head is held high on extended neck while swimming (all others slouch) (Stallcup, pers. comm.). Flight low and extremely fast on whirring wings; thus differences in colour between underwing-coverts of this species and Craveri's Murrelet often difficult to ascertain at sea (see other differences under SS).

DM: Restricted to islands off Baja California and Mexico; breeds on Anacapa and Santa Barbara islands in the Channel Is off coast of southern California, and on Los Coronados, Todos Santos, San Benito and Natividad Is off western Baja California. Egg-dates Mar–Jul. Precocial juveniles, unable to fly, join adults at sea 2–4 days after hatching. Winters offshore in seas adjacent to breeding islands, wandering N during autumn, small numbers regularly reaching Monterey Bay with peak counts of up to 16 during Aug–Oct (see Roberson 1980, Stallcup 1976). Most records are of northern *E.h. scrippsi*. Although rare N of California, there are a number of records N to Oregon and Washington, most sightings being of 'pairs' (see Roberson 1980 for further details).

SS: Both species of *Endomychura* murrelets difficult to identify at sea without comparative experience or when at long range. Craveri's Murrelet (p. 400) differs from present species in longer bill; dark cap extending down sides of face to bottom edge of bill; darker, slightly browner upperparts; more extensive dark spur on sides of breast (more noticeable in flight); and dusky grey and white underwing-coverts. Southern form of present species (*E.h. hypoleuca*) differs further in prominent white crescents above and below eye. For more information see Dunn (1978) and Jehl & Bond (1975).

301 CRAVERI'S MURRELET
Endomychura craveri

PLATE 87 Fig. 301
MAP 301

Length 21cm (8¼in.). Wingspan not recorded. Iris blackish-brown. Bill black. Legs/feet bluish.

North America, restricted to islands off Baja California, and in Gulf of California, Mexico; range overlaps with Xantus' Murrelet (see differences under that species, p. 399). Sexes alike; no seasonal variation. Juveniles differ from adults only in shorter bill, blacker upperparts and by presence of numerous fine but rather conspicuous blackish spots or bars on sides of breast and body (Bent 1919). No subspecies.

PLUMAGE: Head Blackish cap extends to bottom edge of lower mandible; chin, throat and lower sides of face white. **Body** Upperparts brownish-black. Underparts mostly white, except for narrow black spur on side of breast and blackish flanks extending back along body and thighs. **Wings** Upperwing blackish. Underwing: coverts blotched dusky-grey, axillaries whitish, primaries and secondaries blackish-grey. **Tail** Blackish (appears as short tuft at sea).

FHJ: See Xantu's Murrelet (p. 399) for swimming posture; differs from latter species in slightly smaller size and longer bill. In flight the more extensive dark spur on side of breast and, if seen, the dusky underwing-coverts useful field characters.

DM: Restricted to islands in Gulf of California from Cape San Jose I., Ildefonso I. N to Isla Raza. Egg-dates Feb–Jul. Disperses to adjacent waters after breeding: some S along W coast of Mexico, others N reaching seas off southern California regularly during Aug–Oct, and N to Monterey Bay during warm-water years; one record from Oregon. (For further details see Roberson 1980, Stallcup 1976.)

SS: See notes in this section under Xantu's Murrelet (p. 399).

Genus *SYNTHLIBORAMPHUS*

Two species; small to medium-sized North Pacific alcids. Seasonal variation in plumage.

302 ANCIENT MURRELET
Synthliboramphus antiquum

PLATE 88 Figs 302a-302c
MAP 302

Length 24–27cm (9½–10½in.). Wingspan not recorded. Iris blackish-brown. Bill pale horn to whitish, tip and culmen blackish. Legs/feet greyish.

North Pacific; range overlaps with many alcid spp., but see especially Crested and non-breeding Marbled Murrelet (p. 401, p. 398). Sexes alike; marked seasonal variation. Juveniles separable from adults, see illustration Plate 88. No subspecies.

FIRST-WINTER: Bill duskier and smaller than in non-breeding adult; plumage similar except black on head extends only to gape (not to chin and lower sides of face).

ADULT NON-BREEDING: Head Mostly blackish, extending downwards below gape to chin; throat often dusky; lower throat and sides of neck white, extending upwards towards nape. (Some may retain traces of white plumes over eye, Bent 1919.) **Body** Upperparts pale slate-grey (contrasting with head). Underparts mostly white; sides of breast black forming narrow collar, flanks mottled blackish. **Wings** Upperwing: coverts as upperparts; primaries and secondaries blackish-grey forming trailing edge in flight. Underwing: coverts white, margins blackish. **Tail** Blackish.

ADULT BREEDING: Resembles non-breeding adult except: **Head** White stripe over and behind eye to nape; clearly defined black chin and throat extending narrowly toward breast; scattered white filoplumes on sides of neck and over dark half-collar.

FHJ: A small stocky alcid, about half size of Guillemot (Murre) with proportionately shorter neck and wings enhancing dumpy, rather rounded jizz. Unlike congeners, contrast in plumage between black head and bib, white head plumes and blue-grey back a useful field character both in flight and on water. Sits low when swimming and, during pursuit-dives, springs clear of water in lunging arc. Flight low and direct, usually for only short distances, seemingly stopping in mid flight and dropping into ocean.

DM: Breeds in Asia from Commander Is and Kamchatka S through Kurile Is to Korea; present in summer off Hokkaido, Japan, but breeding not proved. Breeds in USA from Aleutian Is eastwards to Alaskan Peninsula and then to Graham and Langara Is in Queen Charlotte group, British Columbia. Sowls *et al.* (1978) list about 40 Alaskan colonies, largest at Forrester Is (60,000), with total Alaskan population estimated at about 400,000. Does not apparently nest on islands in Bering Sea N of Aleutian Is. Returns to colonies Apr/May; egg-dates May/Jun; precocial juveniles, unable to fly, join adults at sea within a few days of hatching, where they complete their development under care of adults. Some winter at sea near breeding areas but most appear to disperse S, often occurring offshore in small, irregular movements S to California and Korea. In North America wind-blown derelicts occasionally occur far inland, peaking about Nov/Dec with smaller peak in Mar.

SS: No other small alcid has combination of uncrested black head contrasting with blue-grey back and white underparts. See also Crested Murrelet (p. 401).

303 CRESTED MURRELET
other: Japanese Murrelet
Synthliboramphus wumizusume

PLATE 87 Fig. 303
MAP 303

Length 26cm (10¼in.). Wingspan not recorded. Iris blackish. Bill pale horn to whitish. Legs/feet yellowish-grey.

Restricted to islands off Japan, dispersing N after breeding; range overlaps with Ancient Murrelet (p. 400). Sexes alike; seasonal variation. Juveniles differ from non-breeding adults only in browner cast to head and upperparts. No subspecies.
ADULT NON-BREEDING: Mostly as breeding adult except lacks crest and white stripe on head.
ADULT BREEDING: Head Crested; mostly blackish, extending from chin to nape; a narrow white stripe on sides of head meeting on upper nape. **Body** Upperparts greyish-black (contrasting with head). Underparts mostly white, flanks greyish-black. **Wings** Upperwing as upperparts. Underwing whitish; secondaries and primaries greyer.
FHJ: Little known; presumably much as Ancient Murrelet (p. 400).
DM: Rare and little known. Breeds at Izu-shictito Is, Japan, dispersing to mainland coasts from Sakhalin S to Korea (Dementiev and Gladkov 1951.).
SS: Breeding adults distinctive; beware Ancient Murrelet during winter months.

Genus *PTYCHORAMPHUS*

Monotypic genus; small-sized, small-billed Pacific alcid. No appreciable seasonal difference in plumage.

304 CASSIN'S AUKLET
Ptychoramphus aleuticus

PLATE 87 Fig. 304
MAP 304

Length 20–23cm (8–9in.). Wingspan not recorded. Iris white. Bill blackish-grey, small white spot at base of lower mandible. Legs/feet blue.

Wide-ranging in NE Pacific Ocean; range overlaps with many alcid spp., but see especially Rhinoceros Auklet, breeding Marbled Murrelet, and immature Crested and Whiskered Auklets (p. 404, p. 398, p. 402, p. 403). Sexes alike; no marked seasonal variation. Juveniles differ only in dark eye, whiter throat, browner wings and tail. No subspecies.
PLUMAGE: Head Dark greyish-brown; at close range a faintly paler, imperfect grey streak sometimes extends from rear of eye towards nape; chin and throat paler brown; white crescent above eye. **Body** Upperparts dark slate-blue (become browner with wear). Underparts: upper breast, flanks and lateral undertail-coverts greyish-brown, belly white. **Wings** Upperwing: coverts as upperparts, primaries and secondaries blackish-brown. Underwing: coverts greyish-brown, primaries and secondaries blackish-brown.
FHJ: Small, plump alcid with dusky plumage at all seasons. Gregarious throughout year, feeding far offshore in large flocks, usually on planktonic shrimp. Rises swiftly from surface, skipping across waves on short, rounded wings with low, direct flight. Appears generally greyish-brown at sea, with slightly darker head and upperparts; in flight dusky plumage and small white belly patch can recall much larger Rhinoceros Auklet (p. 404). Nocturnal at colonies.
DM: One of the most widespread Pacific alcids, breeding from Buldir I. in Aleutians eastwards through Gulf of Alaska, then S to Guadalupe I., Baja California. In Alaska Sowls *et al.* (1978) list 21 sites, with probable total Alaskan population of about 600,000. On Farallon Is off San Francisco, where 105,000 nest, is the commonest breeding bird (that population unusual in returning to roost on islands throughout winter, see further details in Sowls *et al.* 1980). Returns to colonies about Mar; egg-dates Mar–Jul. Apparently absent from Asian shores. Begins winter dispersal Aug onwards, moving generally southwards to winter from about Washington S to Baja California; feeds far offshore in winter, many returning to night roosts in sheltered bays (see especially Stallcup 1976).
SS: In southern parts of range, during winter months, is the only small, dusky, greyish-brown alcid. In summer Marbled Murrelet (p. 398) browner, with longer bill, more pointed wings and darker belly. In north could be confused with immatures of both Crested and Whiskered Auklets (p. 402, p. 403). Differs from former in white belly and dark bill; from latter (which also has whitish belly) in lack of three white facial streaks and brownish-yellowish bill.

Genus *CYCLORRHYNCHUS*

Monotypic genus; small-sized, red-billed North Pacific alcid with white nuptial facial plume.

305 PARAKEET AUKLET *Cyclorrhynchus psittacula*

PLATE 88 Figs 305a-305b
MAP 305

Length 23–25cm (9–10in.). Wingspan not recorded. Iris yellowish. Bill coral-red; yellow at gape. Legs/feet greyish-yellow, webs blackish.

North Pacific Ocean; range overlaps with many alcid spp., see especially Crested and Least Auklets (p. 402, p. 403). Sexes alike; marked seasonal variation. Juveniles and non-breeding adults probably alike. No subspecies.

ADULT NON-BREEDING: Bill dull brownish-red. Plumage much as breeding adult except chin and throat mottled white, whitish auricular streak less defined.

ADULT BREEDING: Head Mostly sooty-black; chin, throat and foreneck mottled whitish, auricular streak yellowish. **Body** Upperparts sooty-black. Underparts mostly white; upper breast and flanks mottled grey. **Wings** Upperwing sooty-black. Underwing dusky. **Tail** Black.

FHJ: Large, white-breasted auklet with upturned red bill. Flight strong and direct, normally higher than in many other alcids, rolling from side to side. Swims buoyantly. Less gregarious than most auklets, rarely flying about in dense swarms or roosting in such enormous rafts. Nests in small colonies or scattered groups under boulders, in holes etc.

DM: Breeds from Cape Lisburne, Bering Strait, S through Bering Sea including St Lawrence, Pribilofs and Aleutian Is W to Commander Is and E through Kodiak Archipelago to Prince William Sound. Sowls *et al.* (1978) record breeding at 90 sites in Alaska, where combined groups on St George I. number about 150,000 with estimated Alaskan population at about 800,000. Returns to colonies Apr/May; egg-dates Jun–Aug; fledging and dispersal begin late Aug/Sep. Precise wintering movements unknown. Sowls *et al.* (1978) suggest that majority probably remain in ice-free areas within breeding range, but Stejneger (1885, in Bent 1919) reported it as never seen or heard of at Commander Is during winter. Forsell & Gould (1980) did not record them off their Kodiak colonies during an extensive winter survey. It seems more likely that they disperse southwards to pelagic habitat (rather like Horned Puffin) as suggested by Roberson (1980), extending S in some years as far as Japan and California, movements and numbers dependent on salinity and temperature fluctuations.

SS: In breeding plumage white-breasted adults with red, upturned bills readily identified. In winter some Rhinoceros Auklets (p. 404) have bright orange bill which can appear reddish at sea (Roberson 1980), but differ in larger size, two white facial streaks and dark upper breast.

Genus *AETHIA*

Three species; small, red-billed, North Pacific alcids with conspicuous facial ornaments.

At colonies breeding adults distinctive; see notes under each species for non-breeding plumages and comparisons with sympatric alcids.

306 CRESTED AUKLET *Aethia cristatella*

PLATE 86 Figs 306a-306c
MAP 306

Length 23cm (9in.). Wingspan not recorded. Iris yellowish-white. Bill reddish-orange, tip yellowish. Legs/feet greyish-black.

North Pacific, primarily Bering Sea, dispersing S to northern Japan during winter; range overlaps with many alcids, see especially Whiskered and Cassin's Auklets (p. 403, p. 401). Sexes alike; seasonal variation. Juveniles separable from adults. No subspecies.

JUVENILE: Much as non-breeding adult except: Bill smaller, dull brownish-yellow. **Head** Crest and auricular plumes lacking.

ADULT NON-BREEDING: Bill-sheath shed; bill thus smaller, and dull yellowish. Plumage much as breeding adult but crest shorter; white auricular plumes less apparent.

ADULT BREEDING: Head Sooty-grey with thin white auricular plumes from eye across ear-coverts and conspicuous, forward-drooping crest on forehead. **Body** Wholly sooty-grey above, merging without demarcation to deep brownish-grey underparts. **Wings and Tail** Sooty-grey.

FHJ: In breeding season stubby, swollen bill, conspicuously orange-red, with long recurved crest drooping over it imparts appearance shared only by smaller Whiskered Auklet (p. 403). Flight usually low and direct on fast, whirring wings, characteristically in small compact flocks. Over breeding areas flocks amalgamate forming huge concentrations, swirling and wheeling over ocean and cliffs like swarms of locusts.

DM: Distribution centred mainly Bering Sea and Aleutian Is, from Cape Prince of Wales and St Lawrence I. S through Pribilofs and Aleutian Is E to Shumagin Is in Alaska. Sowls *et al.* (1978) estimate Alaskan population at about 2 million, with largest colony probably that at Sirius Point (186,000). In Asia breeds from Chukotski Peninsula S through Diomede I., and Sakhalin to central Kurile Is in eastern Siberia. Returns to colonies May onwards; egg-dates Jun–Aug; fledging and dispersal Sep/Oct. Winters at sea in ice-free waters of breeding range S to Japan in the west and to Kodiak, Alaska, in the east. The Kodiak area appears to be an important wintering area, perhaps holding up to 50,000, flocks reaching 15,000 (see Forsell & Gould 1980). One has occurred California (see Roberson 1980).

SS: Breeding adults differ from smaller Whiskered

Auklet (p. 403) in only one, not three, white facial plumes. Juveniles of present species closely resemble Cassin's Auklet (p. 401) but latter has darker bill and, in flight, whiter belly.

307 LEAST AUKLET *Aethia pusilla*

PLATE 86 Figs 307a-307b
MAP 307

Length 15cm (6in.). Wingspan not recorded. Iris white. Bill red, tipped white. Legs/feet blue-grey, webs black.

Reputedly one of most abundant birds of North Pacific; range overlaps with many alcid spp., see especially non-breeding Ancient, Marbled and Kittlitz's Murrelets (p. 400, p. 398, p. 398). Sexes alike; marked seasonal variation. Juveniles separable from adults. No subspecies.

JUVENILE: As non-breeding adult except head lacks white plume, upperparts darker (Bent 1919).

ADULT NON-BREEDING: Bill blackish, extreme tip faintly yellowish. **Head** Mostly blackish-grey, forehead and lores grizzled white, with short white auricular streak; chin, throat and sides of neck white. **Body** Upperparts blackish-grey. Underparts white. **Wings** Upperwing mostly blackish-grey; scapulars white (forming horizontal bar when swimming). Underwing: margins blackish, coverts white. **Tail** Black.

ADULT BREEDING: Head Mostly blackish, forehead grizzled white with indistinct white stripe from gape backwards to below eye, and a longer white auricular streak behind eye; chin and throat white. **Body** Upperparts blackish. Underparts mostly white, with variable greyish mottling usually extending across upper breast as continuous, ill-defined band. **Wings and Tail** As non-breeding adult but scapulars wholly black or with only traces of white.

FHJ: Smallest alcid, sooty-black above with diagnostic white throat and ill-defined breast band. One of most abundant seabirds; occurs in countless thousands, some colonies nearly a million strong, the air filled with immense numbers of whirring forms passing like smoke or swarms of twittering bees—an unforgettable experience. Flight away from colonies low over waves, appearing tiny with chunky body and whirring wings, dropping into water and disappearing from view. Gregarious throughout year, forms large rafts at sea. During pursuit-dives from surface, springs clear of water with sudden jump (see also Whiskered Auklet, p. 403).

DM: Breeds islands of Bering Sea from Chukotski Peninsula, USSR, and Cape Lisburne, Alaska, S through Pribilofs to Aleutian Is and E to Semidi Is, Gulf of Alaska. Sowls *et al.* (1978) list 31 major colonies in Alaska, some numbering between 250,000 and 1 million; estimated Alaskan population 6 million. Returns to colonies early May; egg-dates Jun/Jul; fledging Aug onwards. Winters in seas within breeding range, with westwards dispersal to seas of eastern Siberia, USSR, S to northern Japan. Straggler to Beaufort Sea area; vagrant San Francisco, California.

SS: Small size, white throat and dark breast band diagnostic in breeding adults. Non-breeders bear superficial resemblance to larger Marbled and Kittlitz's Murrelets (p. 398, p. 398), both of which have whitish scapular patch. Present species, however, has darker head with whitish auricular streak. See also non-breeding Ancient Murrelet (p. 400).

308 WHISKERED AUKLET *Aethia pygmaea*

PLATE 86 Figs 308a-308b
MAP 308

Length 17–18cm ($6\frac{1}{2}$–7in.). Wingspan not recorded. Iris whitish. Bill coral-red, extreme tip white. Legs/feet greyish, webs blackish.

Rarest of the alcids in Alaska; range overlaps with many alcids, see especially Crested and Cassin's Auklet (p. 402, p. 401). Sexes alike; slight seasonal variation. Juveniles separable from adults. No subspecies.

JUVENILE: Bill dusky-brown. Plumage much as non-breeding adult except: **Head** Lacks loral tuft, with only faint suggestion of adult's three white facial plumes.

ADULT NON-BREEDING: Bill brownish, tip bluish; plumage resembles breeding adult except: **Head** Loral crest thinner and shorter; white facial plumes less distinct. **Wings** Upperwing: coverts greyer.

ADULT BREEDING: Head Mostly slate-grey, with three long white facial plumes and long, recurved crest springing from forehead and drooping over bill. **Body** Upperparts slate-grey. Underparts as upperparts but paler, merging to pale greyish-white at ventral area (at colonies underparts often soiled and stained, appearing wholly dark). **Wings** Upperwing mostly slate-grey; coverts sometimes paler. Underwing dusky-brown. **Tail** Slate-grey.

FHJ: Little-known species only slightly larger than ubiquitous Least Auklet and sharing with Crested Auklet (p. 402) a conspicuous forward-curving, quail-like crest. Compared with Crested Auklet has three white facial plumes, two of which fork outwards from gape, a proportionately smaller bill without wattles at base, and a longer, more wispy recurved crest. During pursuit-dives from surface, springs clear of water with sudden jump (see also Least Auklet, p. 403). Flight low and fast on whirring wings.

DM: Confined to Aleutian Is, and perhaps also Commander and Kurile Is where reported breeding in the past but present status requires clarification. Following notes on Alaskan population based on Sowls *et al.* (1978). Rarest alcid in Alaska, known or suspected of breeding on ten islands in Aleutian chain from Buldir E to at least the islands of Four Mountains; the largest known colony is at Buldir I. (3,000); total Alaskan population about 20,000. Returns to colonies Apr onwards; egg-dates Apr/May; fledging about mid Jul. During

winter appears to disperse only to adjacent seas; stragglers S to Japan.
SS: Unlike larger Crested Auklet, adults retain white facial plumes year round. Juveniles of present species also show suggestion of white plumes on sides of head (unlike juvenile Crested) and are smaller. See also Cassin's Auklet (p. 401).

Genus *CERORHINCA*

Monotypic genus; medium-sized, pale-billed North Pacific alcid with nuptial 'horn' at base of upper mandible.

309 RHINOCEROS AUKLET *Cerorhinca monocerata*

PLATE 86 Figs 309a-309c
MAP 309

Length 35–38cm (14–15in.). Wingspan not recorded. Iris yellowish. Bill yellowish-orange with short, erect, whitish horn at base of upper mandible. Legs/feet greyish-yellow, webs black.

North Pacific Ocean; range overlaps with many alcid spp., see especially Tufted Puffin (immature) and smaller Cassin's Auklet (p. 406, p. 401). Sexes alike; slight seasonal variation. Juveniles smaller but barely separable from non-breeding adults (at sea). No subspecies.
JUVENILE: Bill smaller than adult. Plumage as non-breeding adult except head lacks traces of white facial streaks.
ADULT NON-BREEDING: Bill horn shed. Plumage as breeding adult except head plumes shorter, much less defined.
ADULT BREEDING: Head Mostly brownish, except for two long white facial streaks, one from eye backwards to nape, the other from gape to upper throat. **Body** Upperparts brownish with paler, buffish edges imparting faint scaling. Underparts: upper breast as upperparts but paler, becoming mottled, merging into imperfect whitish belly and ventral area. **Wings** Upperwing brown; coverts scaled as upperparts. Underwing brownish-grey. **Tail** Brownish.
FHJ: A large alcid more closely related to puffins and, like those spp., nests in self-excavated burrows; usually avoids land by day, departing from colonies at dawn and returning at dusk. Usually feeds far out at sea throughout year and, in winter, returns to roost in rafts of many thousands in sheltered bays (see Stallcup 1976). In flight almost as large as Horned Puffin (p. 405), but wings more pointed, appearing generally dark with light belly. Flight strong and direct. Sits rather low in water, appearing squat and chunky, with head tucked well down revealing little apparent neck.
DM: North Pacific, breeding discontinuously from Korea, Japan, Sakhalin, Kurile and Aleutian Is to southern Alaska S through British Columbia (uncommon) to California at Farallon Is, Castle Rock and Prince I. (Sowls *et al.* 1980). In Alaska Sowls *et al.* (1978) list fragmented distribution of twelve sites, with largest at Forrester I. (108,000); elsewhere occurs in much smaller numbers, total Alaskan population about 200,000. Returns to colonies Apr; egg-dates Apr–Jun; fledging late Jul/Aug onwards. Winters in seas adjacent to breeding areas, with general movement S on both sides of Pacific forming dense night-roosting flocks in suitable sheltered bays, e.g. Monterey where up to several thousand roost during winter (Stallcup 1976).
SS: The much smaller Cassin's Auklet (p. 401) has a dark bill. Flight and size of present species more suggestive of immature Tufted Puffin (p. 406) but latter has more rounded wingtips and larger, more triangular bill. Some Rhinoceros Auklets may have orange-red bills, which at range could suggest Parakeet Auklet (p. 402) but latter much whiter below.

Genus *FRATERCULA*

Two species; geographically isolated but of similar appearance, confined to North Pacific Ocean (*corniculata*) and North Atlantic Ocean (*arctica*). Characteristically, bill brightly coloured (breeding only); blackish upperparts, white below.

Unmistakable at breeding colonies, but care required at long range or when in non-breeding plumage; see notes in species account below.

310 ATLANTIC PUFFIN other: Puffin *Fratercula arctica*

PLATE 83 Figs 310a-310c
MAP 310

Length 28–30cm (11–12in.). Wingspan 53–58cm (21–23in.). Iris bluish-black, orbital ring red. Bill large, triangular-shaped, mainly blue grey at base, red on outer portion with transverse yellow bands and cere; gape yellow or orange (bill takes 4–5 years to develop fully, Harris 1981). Legs/feet orange to red.

North Atlantic Ocean; breeding adults unmistakable, but in non-breeding plumage size and jizz may suggest Little Auk (p. 392). Beware also Guillemot and Razorbill (p. 395, p. 393). Sexes alike; marked seasonal variation. Juveniles separable from adults. Three subspecies listed, none separable at sea. Albinism occasionally reported.
JUVENILE: Resembles non-breeding adult but greyish bill much smaller, not triangular; eye lacks ornaments; legs yellowish. **Head** Conspicuous

dark grey patch extends from base of bill to encircle eye; sides of face white. **Body** Upperparts browner in tone.

IMMATURE: Resembles adult; differs mainly in colour of bill and only one or two bill grooves (although variance between individuals renders exact aging impossible, Harris 1981).

ADULT NON-BREEDING: Bill and legs yellowish. As breeding adult except eye lacks ornaments, basal part of bill-sheath shed, distal portion yellower, grooves less distinct. Face dusky on lores and around eyes.

ADULT BREEDING: Head Forehead, crown and nape black, extending to form narrow collar across throat; sides of face greyish or white, extending in narrow line over nape; chin and throat dark grey. **Body** Upperparts black. Underparts mostly white, flanks narrowly black, broader on thighs. **Wings** Upperwing blackish. Underwing varies but mostly grey with paler area across coverts (in normal flight wingbeat so rapid and shallow that underwing rarely seen except when banking; at such times appears darker than in either Razorbill or Guillemot, p. 393, p. 395). **Tail** Black.

FHJ: Unmistakable, tame and confiding at colonies. A stubby, large-fronted alcid with conspicuous parrot-like bill, red legs, short tail and upright stance. Tends to spend more time on water than most other alcids. In flight appears black and white with dumpy jizz, short rounded wings and tail.

DM: Confined to N Atlantic; *F.a. naumanni* breeds northern Greenland, Spitsbergen, Novaya Zemlya and Jan Mayen; *F.a. arctica* southern Greenland, Iceland and in N America from about 55°N in Labrador S to Maine, and also in northern Norway; *F.a. grabae* southern Norway, Sweden, British Is and islands off NW France. Returns to colonies from mid Mar (later in northern populations); egg-dates May–Jul. Juveniles abandoned in burrows when adults return to sea Jul/Aug. Exact movements unknown. North American population appears to move only to offshore waters of breeding range; occasionally S to Long I., New York. Some British breeders winter in North Sea, others move S to Bay of Biscay and then Morocco and W Mediterranean. All populations normally winter far from land, where moult renders adults flightless immediately prior to moving back to colonies. Spring movements occur off NW Spain and Southern Ireland.

SS: At sea, particularly during winter, identification can be difficult, but Puffins much smaller than Razorbill (p. 393) or either guillemot species (p. 394, p. 395), and lack white trailing edge along secondaries of those species and the much smaller Little Auk (p. 392). In flight also lacks white sides to lower back of Razorbill and Guillemot, with shorter, more rounded wings.

---

311 HORNED PUFFIN
Fratercula corniculata

PLATE 84 Figs 311a-311b
MAP 311

Length 36–41cm (14–16in.). Wingspan 56–58cm (22–23in.). Iris blackish, eyelid red with small erectile horn of tissue over eye. Bill large, triangular-shaped, yellow with red tip and orange wattle at gape. Legs/feet orange or reddish.

N Pacific counterpart of closely related Atlantic Puffin (p. 404); similar in all plumages but ranges do not overlap. Most likely to be confused with Tufted Puffin (p. 406), but that species has black underparts and different head pattern. Sexes alike; marked seasonal variation. Juveniles separable from adults. No subspecies.

JUVENILE: As non-breeding adult except bill smaller and darker, less triangular-shaped.

ADULT NON-BREEDING: As breeding adult except: Bill-sheath shed (see account in Bent 1919) to reveal smaller, mainly dark bill with reddish tip. Eye lacks ornaments. **Head** Cheeks dusky-grey. **Body** Upperparts faintly browner.

ADULT BREEDING: Head Forehead, crown, nape and chin black, contrasting with whitish cheeks. Neck black forming continuous collar. **Body** Upperparts black; underparts mainly white, except flanks and thighs mottled with black. **Wings** Upperwing blackish. Underwing appears mostly dark (see notes under Atlantic Puffin, p. 404). **Tail** Black.

FHJ: Unmistakable at colonies; plumage mainly black above, white below, with conspicuous parrot-like bill and comic dignity. Flight strong, purposeful, usually high over water with fast-beating wings. Swims buoyantly, normally springing clear of water before diving under. In winter appears proportionately larger-headed with more rounded crown, heavier bill and deeper chest than either guillemot species, which also occur in N Pacific. Size and jizz smaller, less robust than Tufted Puffin (p. 406).

DM: Restricted to N Pacific, breeding along Siberian and Alaskan coasts of Chukchi Sea and throughout Bering Sea S to Kamchatka Peninsula and Kurile Is in Asia, and S and E to Glacier Bay, and Forrester Is in western N America (see Sowls *et al.* 1978). Small colony recently discovered Queen Charlotte I., British Columbia; adults also seen around Triangle I., off Vancouver I. during recent summers, suggesting breeding even further south (Roberson 1980). Spring arrival at colonies begins mid May; egg-dates Jun/Jul; fledging and dispersal Sep/Oct, to spend winter far out at sea, ranging from breeding area S to British Columbia; rarer further S off Washington and Oregon, with some S to California and N Baja, Mexico (see Roberson 1980 for detailed account).

SS: Separated at all ages from Tufted Puffin (p. 406) by clear white underparts; breeding adults lack head plumes of that species. In winter bill shape distinctly different from both guillemot species (p. 394, p. 395), but at long range or under poor conditions winter adults or juveniles could be mistaken for larger, white-chinned, winter-plumaged Brünnich's Guillemot (Thick-billed Murre, p. 394).

Genus *LUNDA*

Monotypic genus; medium-sized, mostly dark-plumaged alcid with conspicuously coloured bill and head ornaments. Confined to North Pacific.

312 TUFTED PUFFIN *Lunda cirrhata*

PLATE 85 Figs 312a-312c
MAP 312

Length 36–41cm (14–16in.). Wingspan not recorded. Iris yellow; orbital ring red. Bill reddish-orange, basal third of upper mandible yellowish or greenish-grey with yellow ridge. Legs/feet reddish-orange.

North Pacific; range overlaps with several alcids, see especially Rhinoceros Auklet and Horned Puffin (p. 404, p. 405). Sexes alike; seasonal variation. Juveniles separable from adults. No subspecies.

JUVENILE: Eye brown. Bill smaller than adult's, triangular-shaped, dull horn-yellow. **Head** Mostly blackish-brown, chin and throat paler. **Body** Upperparts blackish-brown, merging without contrast to dark brownish-grey on underparts; belly often tipped white. **Wings and Tail** Blackish-brown.

IMMATURE: As juvenile except: Iris whitish. **Head** Short, yellowish-brown tufts springing from behind eye. **Body** Underparts paler brownish-grey, some with scattered white tips on breast and belly.

ADULT NON-BREEDING: Bill-sheath shed; bill less triangular-shaped, reddish at tip, dusky-grey at base. **Head** Dull blackish, usually with obscure brownish plumes springing from behind eye. **Body** Upperparts dull blackish-grey, merging without demarcation to brownish-grey underparts; breast and belly perhaps with scattered white tips. **Wings and Tail** Dull blackish-grey.

ADULT BREEDING: Plumage wholly glossy black except: **Head** Narrow white forehead, conspicuous white sides of face, and shaggy, straw-white plumes springing from behind eye and down-curved to nape.

FHJ: One of most abundant and conspicuous seabirds of Alaska, where Sowls *et al.* (1978) estimate population to be about 4 million. Breeding adults with bizarre, parrot-like bills and tassled heads unmistakable. Stockier than Horned Puffin (p. 405) with heavy, rotund body and short rounded wings. Requires a long run-off to become airborne from water, but once aloft flight strong and direct, usually 20–30m above waves. More pelagic than congeners, foraging widely from colonies, often far out at sea. Occasionally attends trawlers and small boats.

DM: Restricted to North Pacific, breeding from NE Siberia and Cape Lisburne in Chukchi Sea S through Bering Sea and Aleutian Is to Farallon Is and Hurricane Point Rocks, California. Returns to colonies Apr/May; egg-dates Jun/Jul; fledging dates not certainly recorded. In winter disperses southwards into true oceanic habitat, rarely within sight of landfall unless sickly or injured, ranging S to Honshu, Japan; to about 35°S in mid ocean, and to offshore waters of California. Less gregarious during winter, usually seen singly or in pairs but precise movements unknown. Stragglers have reached Point Barrow, Beaufort Sea, and Maine (Atlantic).

SS: Breeding adults unmistakable. Non-breeding adults and immatures resemble similarly-sized Rhinoceros Auklet (p. 404) but bill shape diagnostic.

SEA-DUCKS

Order *ANSERIFORMES*

Medium to large-sized birds divided into two families: 1. *Anhimidae* (screamers). 2. *Anatidae* (wildfowl).

Family *ANATIDAE* ducks, geese, swans. About 140 species in three subfamilies. Cosmopolitan, ranging from huge swans to smaller dabbling ducks. All are aquatic, with proportionately long necks, and webs between the three front toes; most have short legs.

Whilst most ducks, at some time or other, will visit the coast, the following illustrations deal only with those species normally referred to as sea-ducks or bay-ducks. It is not within the scope of this guide to treat these in depth, but it is hoped that the following illustrations will be of some help in identifying the easier plumage stages of the species concerned. Female and immature stages of seafowl can be difficult to identify and readers are urged to consult their local bird guides, which afford more adequate information on identification techniques. In North America consult Peterson (1980); in Europe Cramp & Simmons (1977); in Australia Slater (1970); in South America Woods (1975) offers best but incomplete illustrations, alternatively see De Schauensee and Phelps (1978).

The following three pages have been divided into: 1. Mergansers and bay-ducks. 2. Sea-ducks. 3. South American seafowl.

Fig. 29. Merganser and Bay-ducks

Fig. 30. Sea-ducks

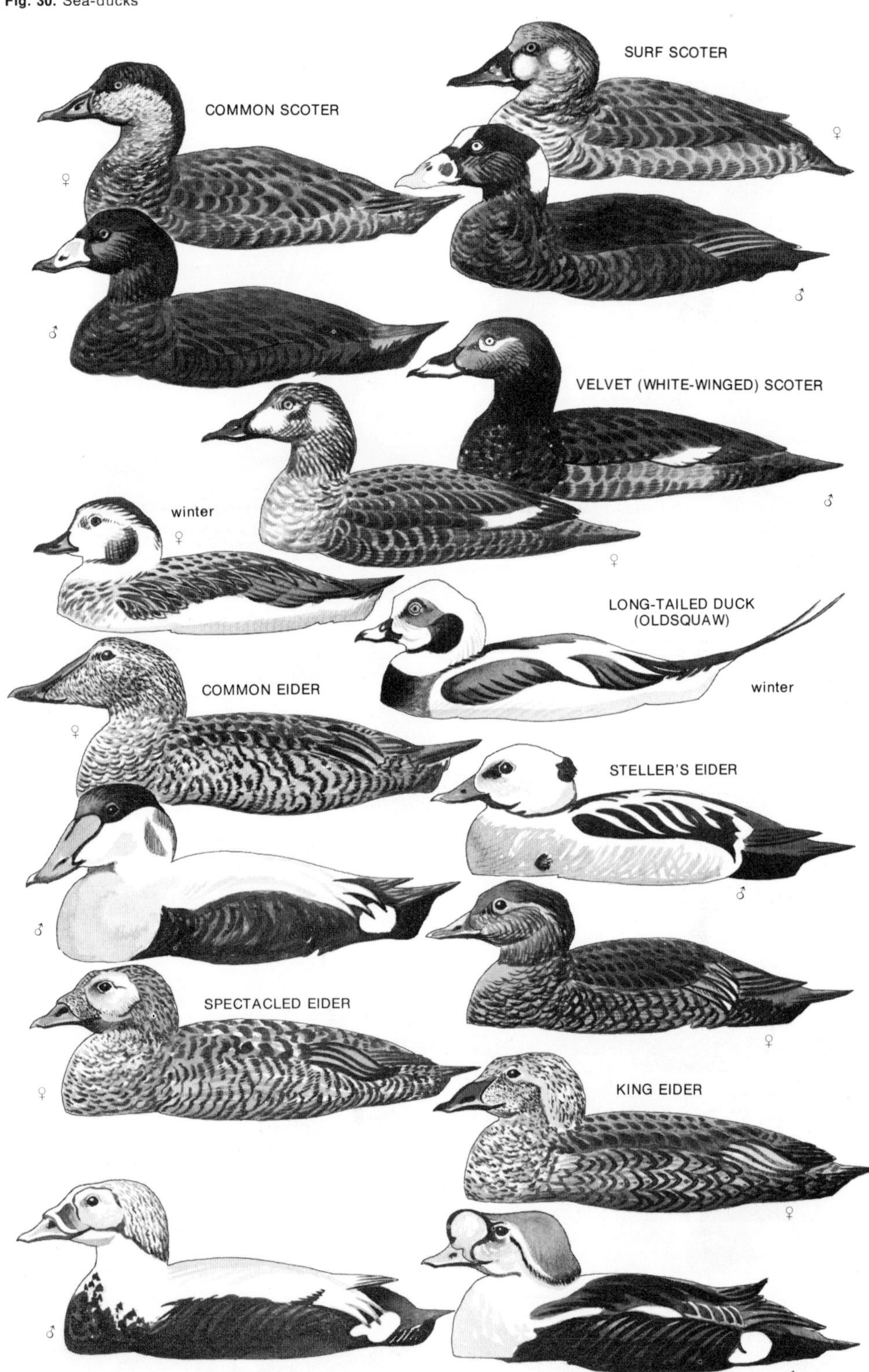

Fig. 31. South American Seafowl

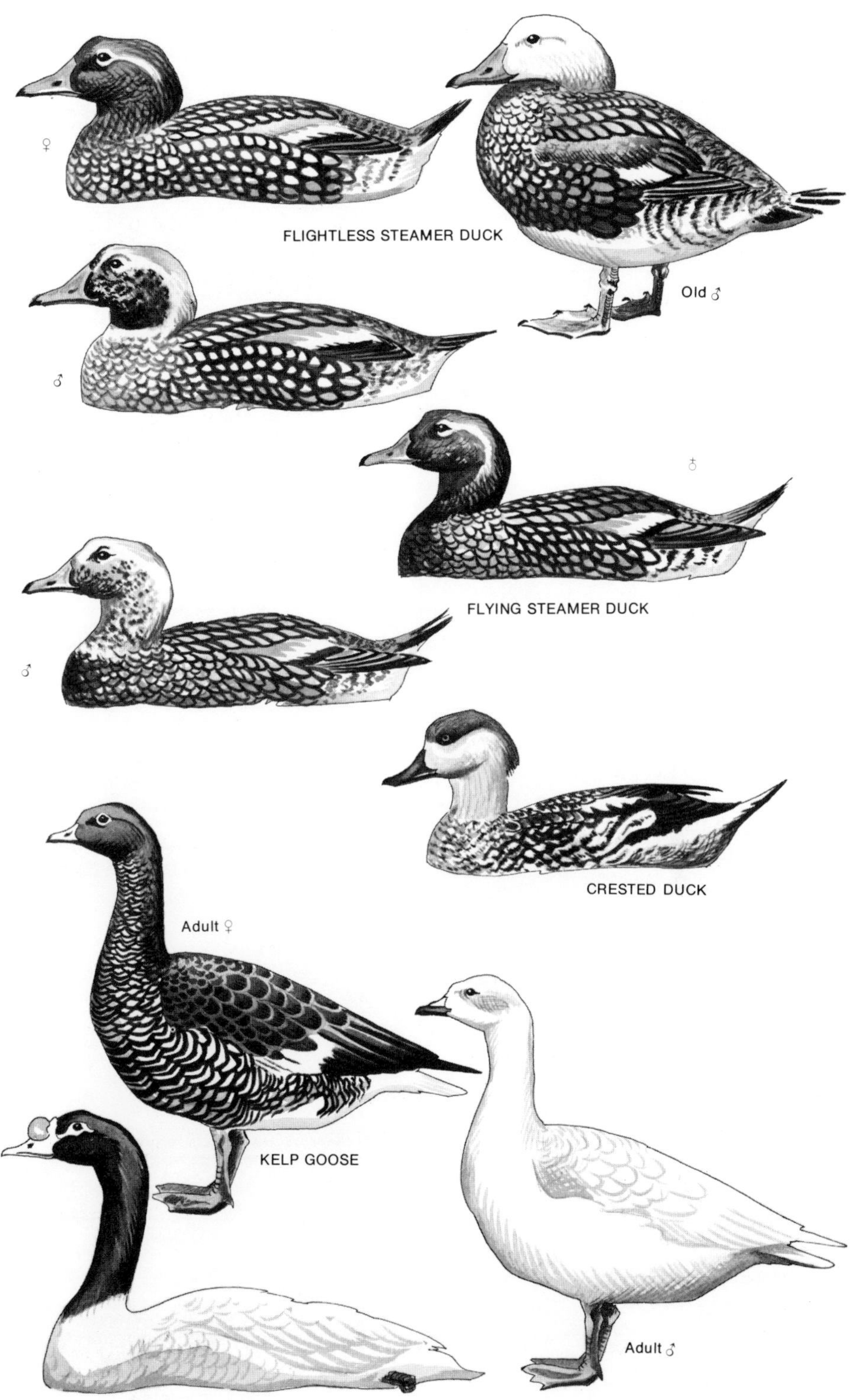

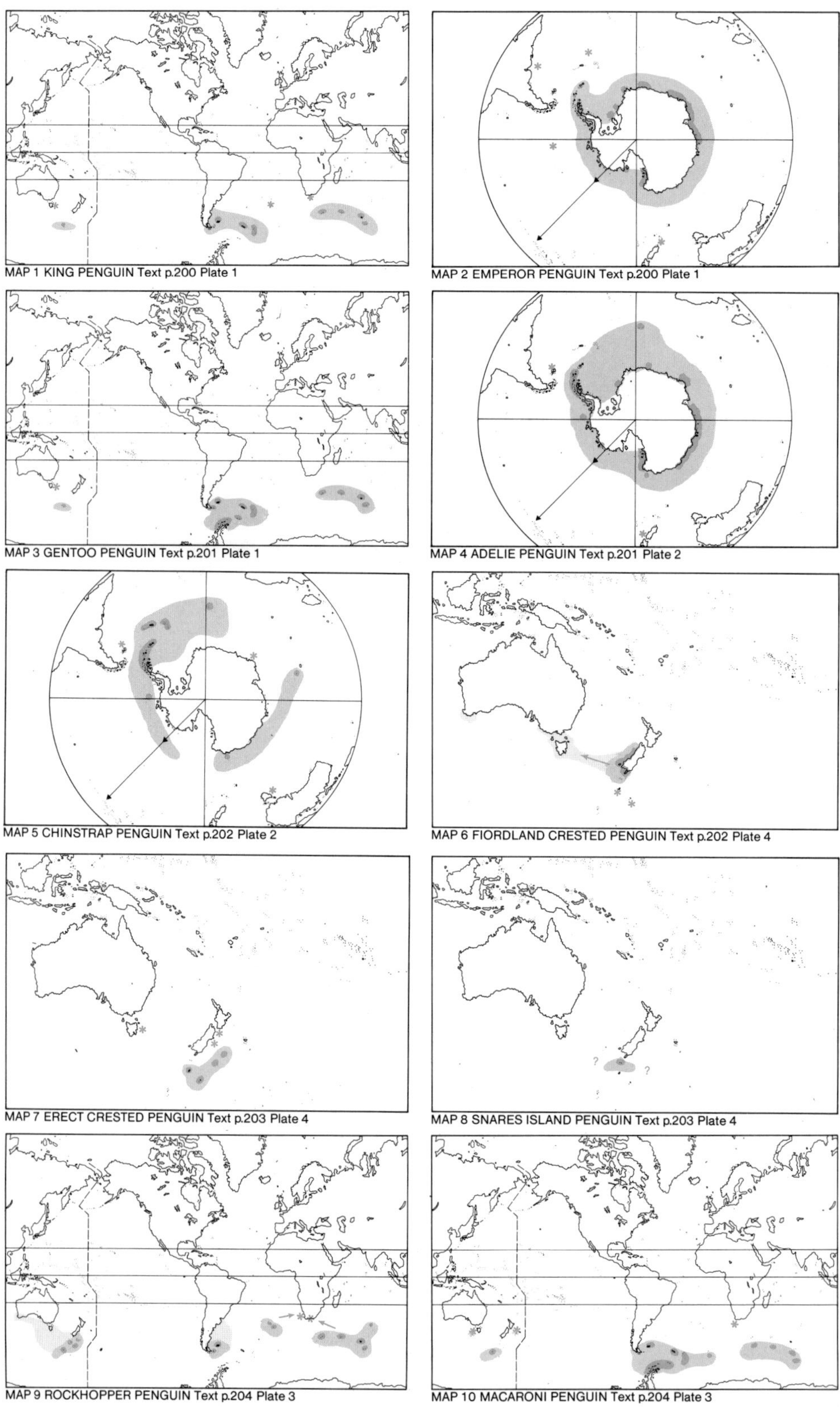

MAP 1 KING PENGUIN Text p.200 Plate 1

MAP 2 EMPEROR PENGUIN Text p.200 Plate 1

MAP 3 GENTOO PENGUIN Text p.201 Plate 1

MAP 4 ADELIE PENGUIN Text p.201 Plate 2

MAP 5 CHINSTRAP PENGUIN Text p.202 Plate 2

MAP 6 FIORDLAND CRESTED PENGUIN Text p.202 Plate 4

MAP 7 ERECT CRESTED PENGUIN Text p.203 Plate 4

MAP 8 SNARES ISLAND PENGUIN Text p.203 Plate 4

MAP 9 ROCKHOPPER PENGUIN Text p.204 Plate 3

MAP 10 MACARONI PENGUIN Text p.204 Plate 3

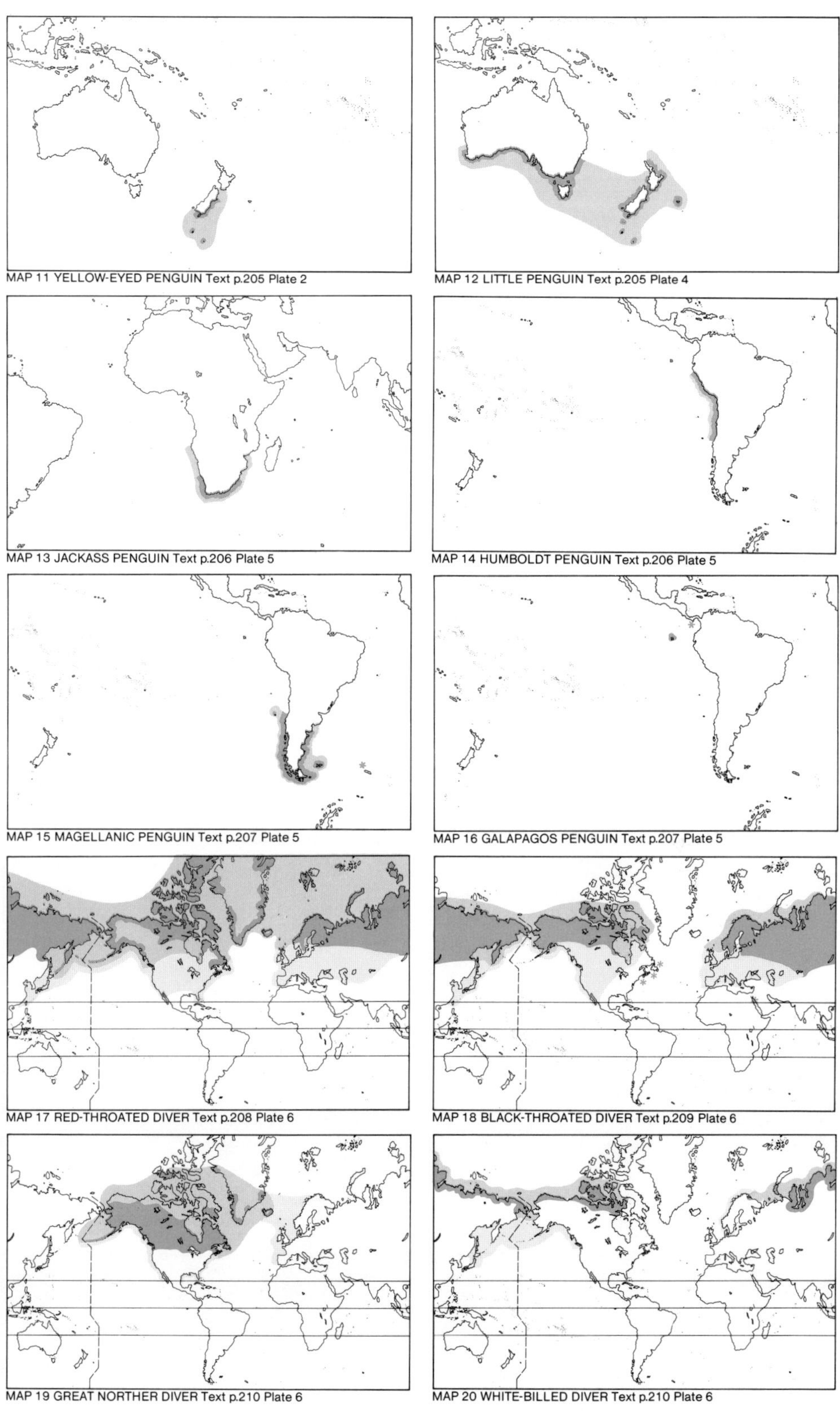

MAP 11 YELLOW-EYED PENGUIN Text p.205 Plate 2

MAP 12 LITTLE PENGUIN Text p.205 Plate 4

MAP 13 JACKASS PENGUIN Text p.206 Plate 5

MAP 14 HUMBOLDT PENGUIN Text p.206 Plate 5

MAP 15 MAGELLANIC PENGUIN Text p.207 Plate 5

MAP 16 GALAPAGOS PENGUIN Text p.207 Plate 5

MAP 17 RED-THROATED DIVER Text p.208 Plate 6

MAP 18 BLACK-THROATED DIVER Text p.209 Plate 6

MAP 19 GREAT NORTHER DIVER Text p.210 Plate 6

MAP 20 WHITE-BILLED DIVER Text p.210 Plate 6

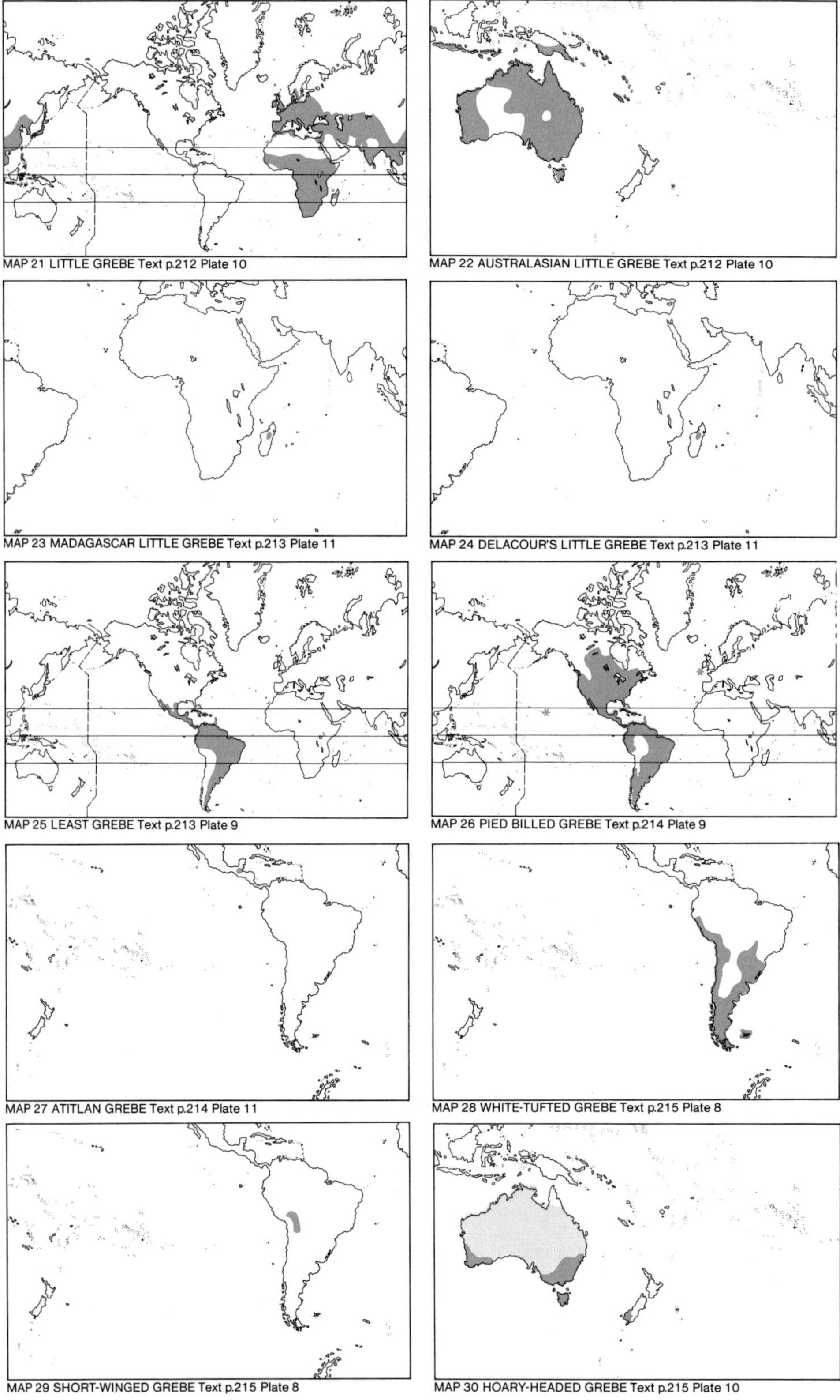

MAP 21 LITTLE GREBE Text p.212 Plate 10

MAP 22 AUSTRALASIAN LITTLE GREBE Text p.212 Plate 10

MAP 23 MADAGASCAR LITTLE GREBE Text p.213 Plate 11

MAP 24 DELACOUR'S LITTLE GREBE Text p.213 Plate 11

MAP 25 LEAST GREBE Text p.213 Plate 9

MAP 26 PIED BILLED GREBE Text p.214 Plate 9

MAP 27 ATITLAN GREBE Text p.214 Plate 11

MAP 28 WHITE-TUFTED GREBE Text p.215 Plate 8

MAP 29 SHORT-WINGED GREBE Text p.215 Plate 8

MAP 30 HOARY-HEADED GREBE Text p.215 Plate 10

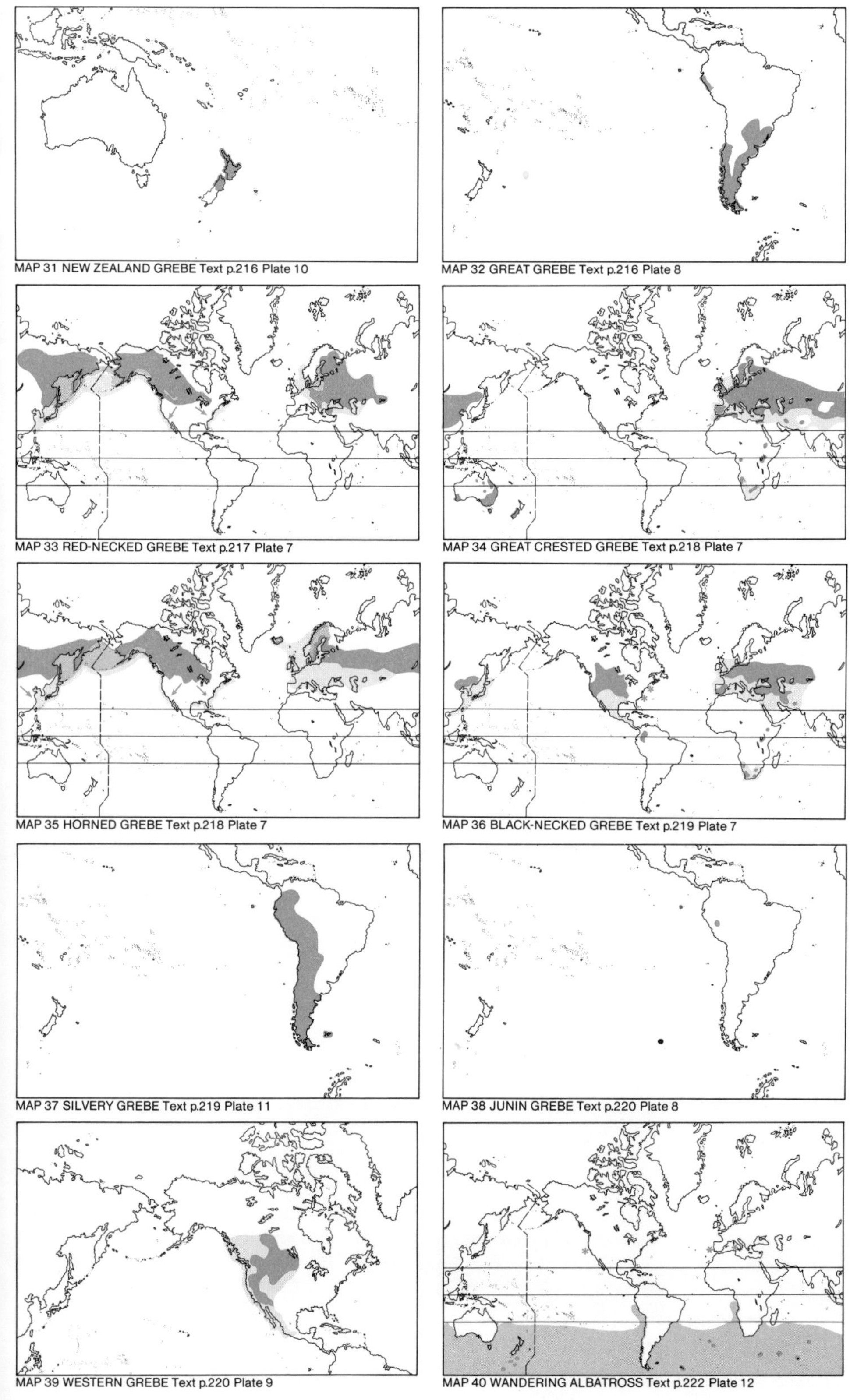

MAP 31 NEW ZEALAND GREBE Text p.216 Plate 10

MAP 32 GREAT GREBE Text p.216 Plate 8

MAP 33 RED-NECKED GREBE Text p.217 Plate 7

MAP 34 GREAT CRESTED GREBE Text p.218 Plate 7

MAP 35 HORNED GREBE Text p.218 Plate 7

MAP 36 BLACK-NECKED GREBE Text p.219 Plate 7

MAP 37 SILVERY GREBE Text p.219 Plate 11

MAP 38 JUNIN GREBE Text p.220 Plate 8

MAP 39 WESTERN GREBE Text p.220 Plate 9

MAP 40 WANDERING ALBATROSS Text p.222 Plate 12

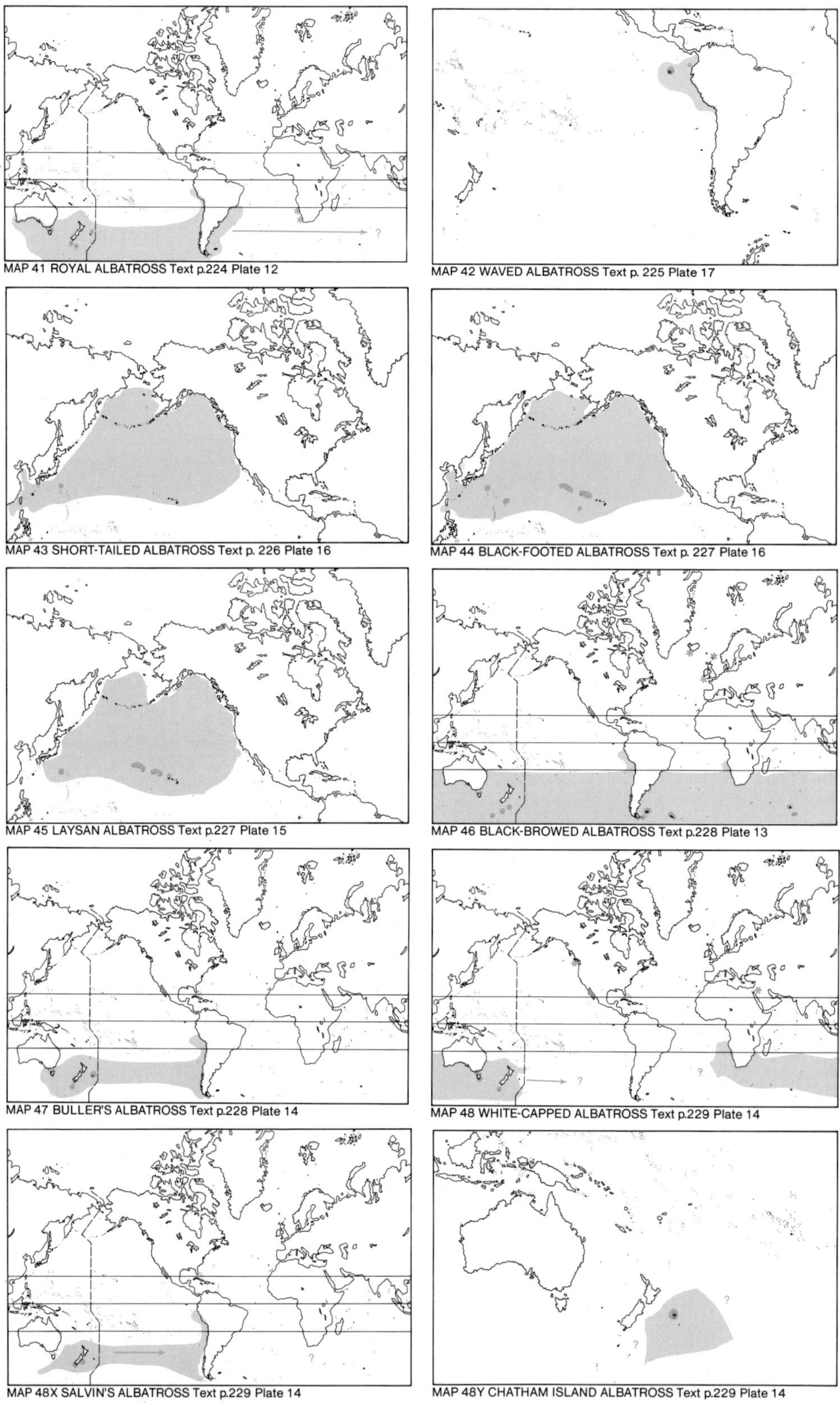

MAP 41 ROYAL ALBATROSS Text p.224 Plate 12

MAP 42 WAVED ALBATROSS Text p. 225 Plate 17

MAP 43 SHORT-TAILED ALBATROSS Text p. 226 Plate 16

MAP 44 BLACK-FOOTED ALBATROSS Text p. 227 Plate 16

MAP 45 LAYSAN ALBATROSS Text p.227 Plate 15

MAP 46 BLACK-BROWED ALBATROSS Text p.228 Plate 13

MAP 47 BULLER'S ALBATROSS Text p.228 Plate 14

MAP 48 WHITE-CAPPED ALBATROSS Text p.229 Plate 14

MAP 48X SALVIN'S ALBATROSS Text p.229 Plate 14

MAP 48Y CHATHAM ISLAND ALBATROSS Text p.229 Plate 14

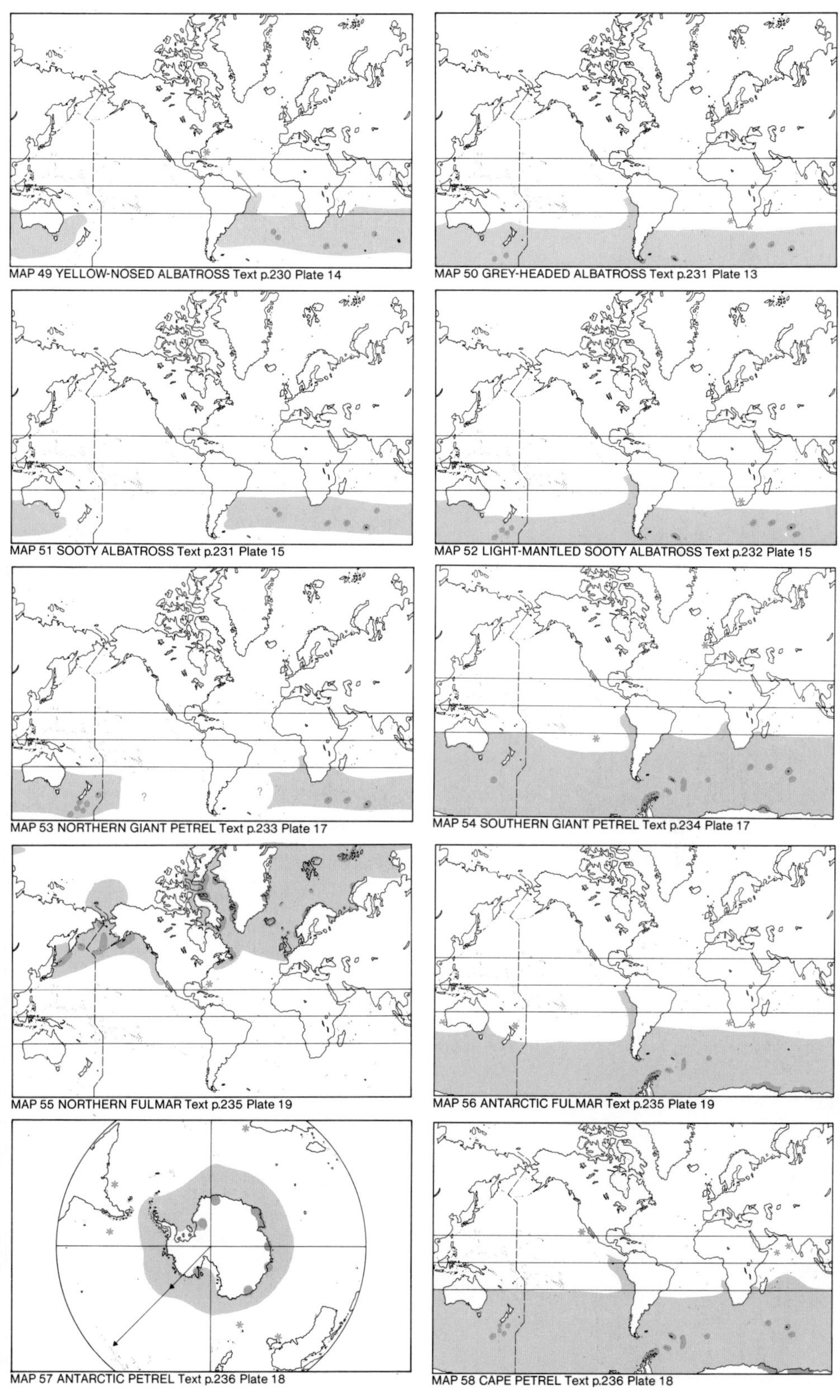

MAP 49 YELLOW-NOSED ALBATROSS Text p.230 Plate 14

MAP 50 GREY-HEADED ALBATROSS Text p.231 Plate 13

MAP 51 SOOTY ALBATROSS Text p.231 Plate 15

MAP 52 LIGHT-MANTLED SOOTY ALBATROSS Text p.232 Plate 15

MAP 53 NORTHERN GIANT PETREL Text p.233 Plate 17

MAP 54 SOUTHERN GIANT PETREL Text p.234 Plate 17

MAP 55 NORTHERN FULMAR Text p.235 Plate 19

MAP 56 ANTARCTIC FULMAR Text p.235 Plate 19

MAP 57 ANTARCTIC PETREL Text p.236 Plate 18

MAP 58 CAPE PETREL Text p.236 Plate 18

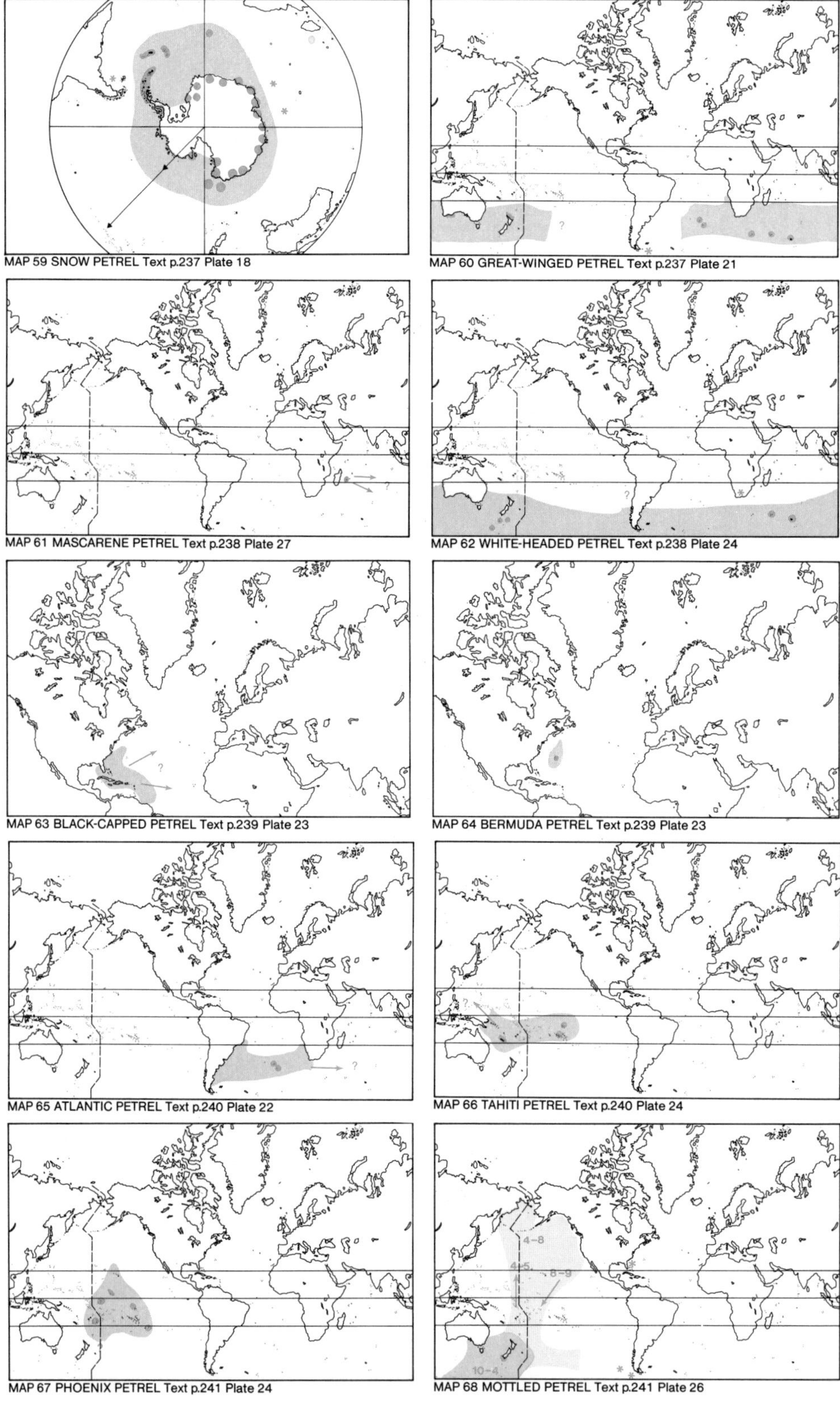

MAP 59 SNOW PETREL Text p.237 Plate 18

MAP 60 GREAT-WINGED PETREL Text p.237 Plate 21

MAP 61 MASCARENE PETREL Text p.238 Plate 27

MAP 62 WHITE-HEADED PETREL Text p.238 Plate 24

MAP 63 BLACK-CAPPED PETREL Text p.239 Plate 23

MAP 64 BERMUDA PETREL Text p.239 Plate 23

MAP 65 ATLANTIC PETREL Text p.240 Plate 22

MAP 66 TAHITI PETREL Text p.240 Plate 24

MAP 67 PHOENIX PETREL Text p.241 Plate 24

MAP 68 MOTTLED PETREL Text p.241 Plate 26

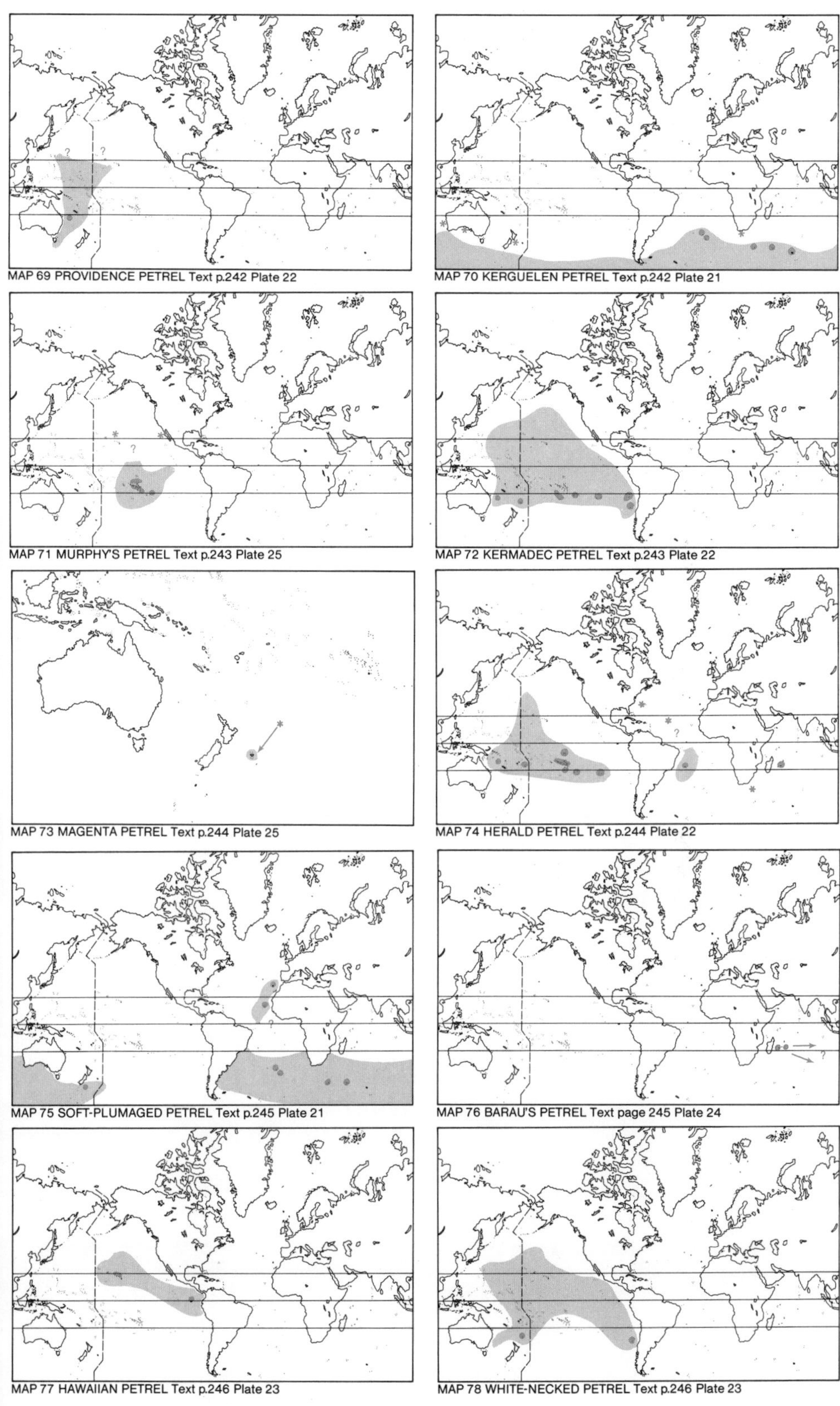

MAP 69 PROVIDENCE PETREL Text p.242 Plate 22

MAP 70 KERGUELEN PETREL Text p.242 Plate 21

MAP 71 MURPHY'S PETREL Text p.243 Plate 25

MAP 72 KERMADEC PETREL Text p.243 Plate 22

MAP 73 MAGENTA PETREL Text p.244 Plate 25

MAP 74 HERALD PETREL Text p.244 Plate 22

MAP 75 SOFT-PLUMAGED PETREL Text p.245 Plate 21

MAP 76 BARAU'S PETREL Text page 245 Plate 24

MAP 77 HAWAIIAN PETREL Text p.246 Plate 23

MAP 78 WHITE-NECKED PETREL Text p.246 Plate 23

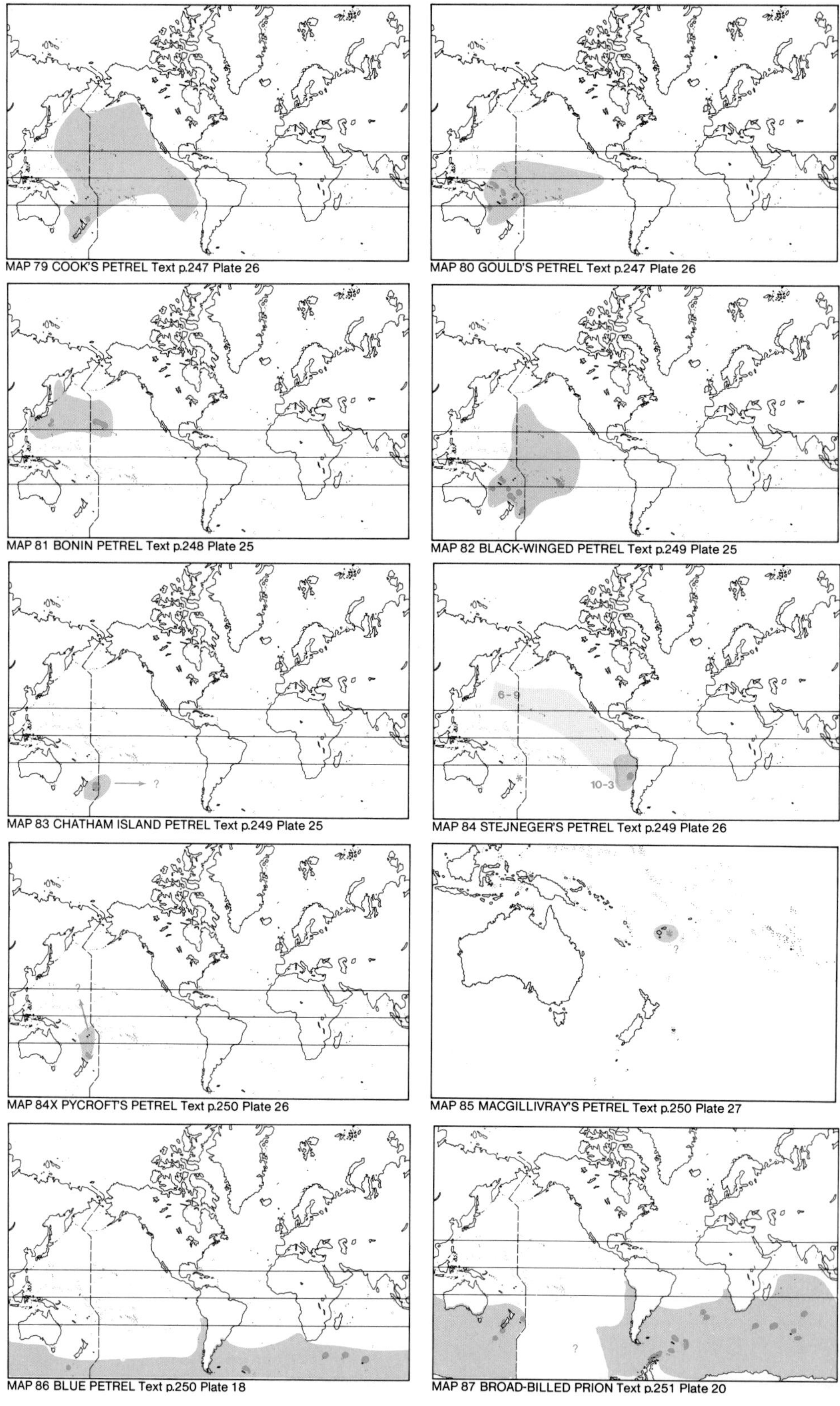

MAP 79 COOK'S PETREL Text p.247 Plate 26

MAP 80 GOULD'S PETREL Text p.247 Plate 26

MAP 81 BONIN PETREL Text p.248 Plate 25

MAP 82 BLACK-WINGED PETREL Text p.249 Plate 25

MAP 83 CHATHAM ISLAND PETREL Text p.249 Plate 25

MAP 84 STEJNEGER'S PETREL Text p.249 Plate 26

MAP 84X PYCROFT'S PETREL Text p.250 Plate 26

MAP 85 MACGILLIVRAY'S PETREL Text p.250 Plate 27

MAP 86 BLUE PETREL Text p.250 Plate 18

MAP 87 BROAD-BILLED PRION Text p.251 Plate 20

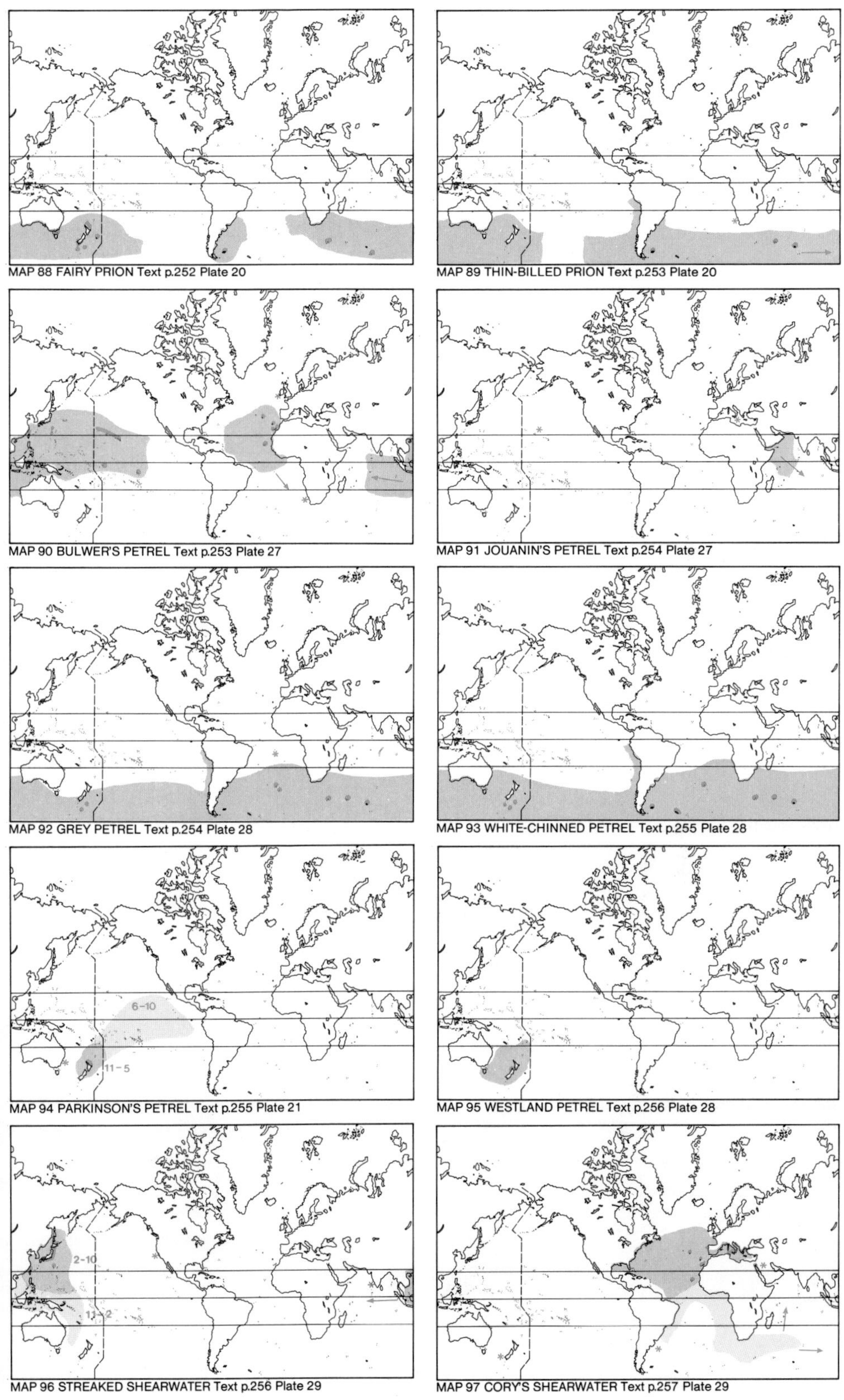

MAP 88 FAIRY PRION Text p.252 Plate 20

MAP 89 THIN-BILLED PRION Text p.253 Plate 20

MAP 90 BULWER'S PETREL Text p.253 Plate 27

MAP 91 JOUANIN'S PETREL Text p.254 Plate 27

MAP 92 GREY PETREL Text p.254 Plate 28

MAP 93 WHITE-CHINNED PETREL Text p.255 Plate 28

MAP 94 PARKINSON'S PETREL Text p.255 Plate 21

MAP 95 WESTLAND PETREL Text p.256 Plate 28

MAP 96 STREAKED SHEARWATER Text p.256 Plate 29

MAP 97 CORY'S SHEARWATER Text p.257 Plate 29

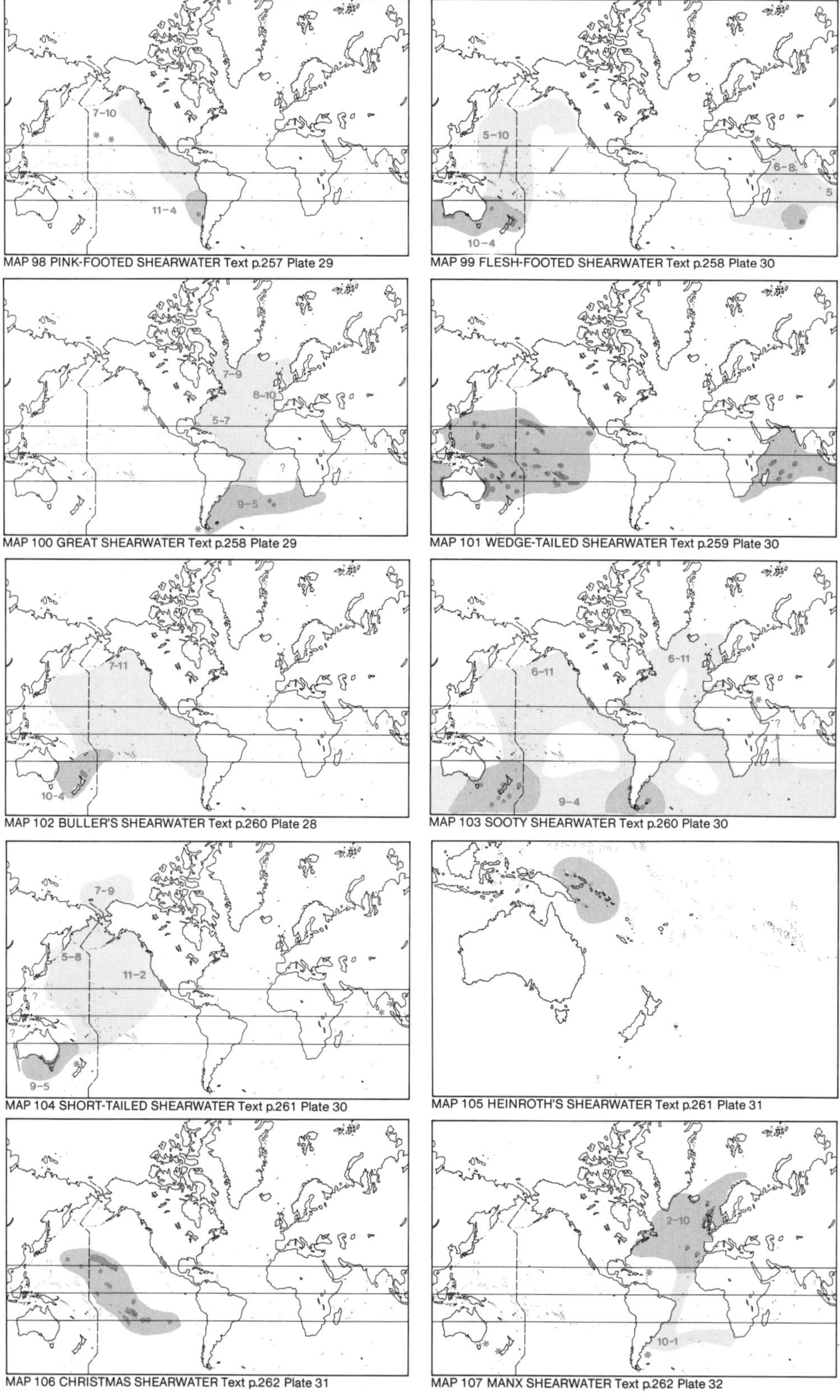

MAP 98 PINK-FOOTED SHEARWATER Text p.257 Plate 29

MAP 99 FLESH-FOOTED SHEARWATER Text p.258 Plate 30

MAP 100 GREAT SHEARWATER Text p.258 Plate 29

MAP 101 WEDGE-TAILED SHEARWATER Text p.259 Plate 30

MAP 102 BULLER'S SHEARWATER Text p.260 Plate 28

MAP 103 SOOTY SHEARWATER Text p.260 Plate 30

MAP 104 SHORT-TAILED SHEARWATER Text p.261 Plate 30

MAP 105 HEINROTH'S SHEARWATER Text p.261 Plate 31

MAP 106 CHRISTMAS SHEARWATER Text p.262 Plate 31

MAP 107 MANX SHEARWATER Text p.262 Plate 32

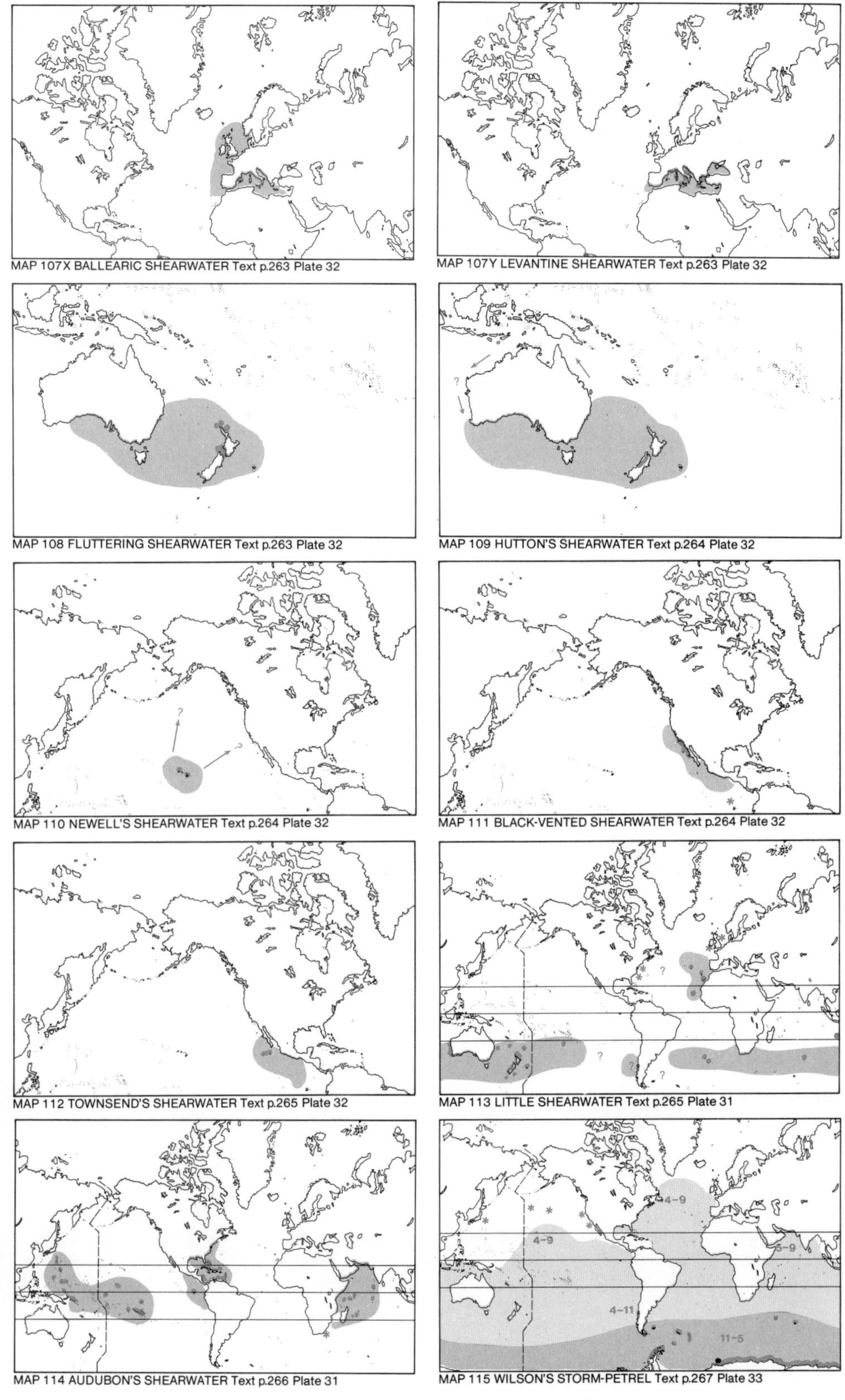

MAP 107X BALLEARIC SHEARWATER Text p.263 Plate 32

MAP 107Y LEVANTINE SHEARWATER Text p.263 Plate 32

MAP 108 FLUTTERING SHEARWATER Text p.263 Plate 32

MAP 109 HUTTON'S SHEARWATER Text p.264 Plate 32

MAP 110 NEWELL'S SHEARWATER Text p.264 Plate 32

MAP 111 BLACK-VENTED SHEARWATER Text p.264 Plate 32

MAP 112 TOWNSEND'S SHEARWATER Text p.265 Plate 32

MAP 113 LITTLE SHEARWATER Text p.265 Plate 31

MAP 114 AUDUBON'S SHEARWATER Text p.266 Plate 31

MAP 115 WILSON'S STORM-PETREL Text p.267 Plate 33

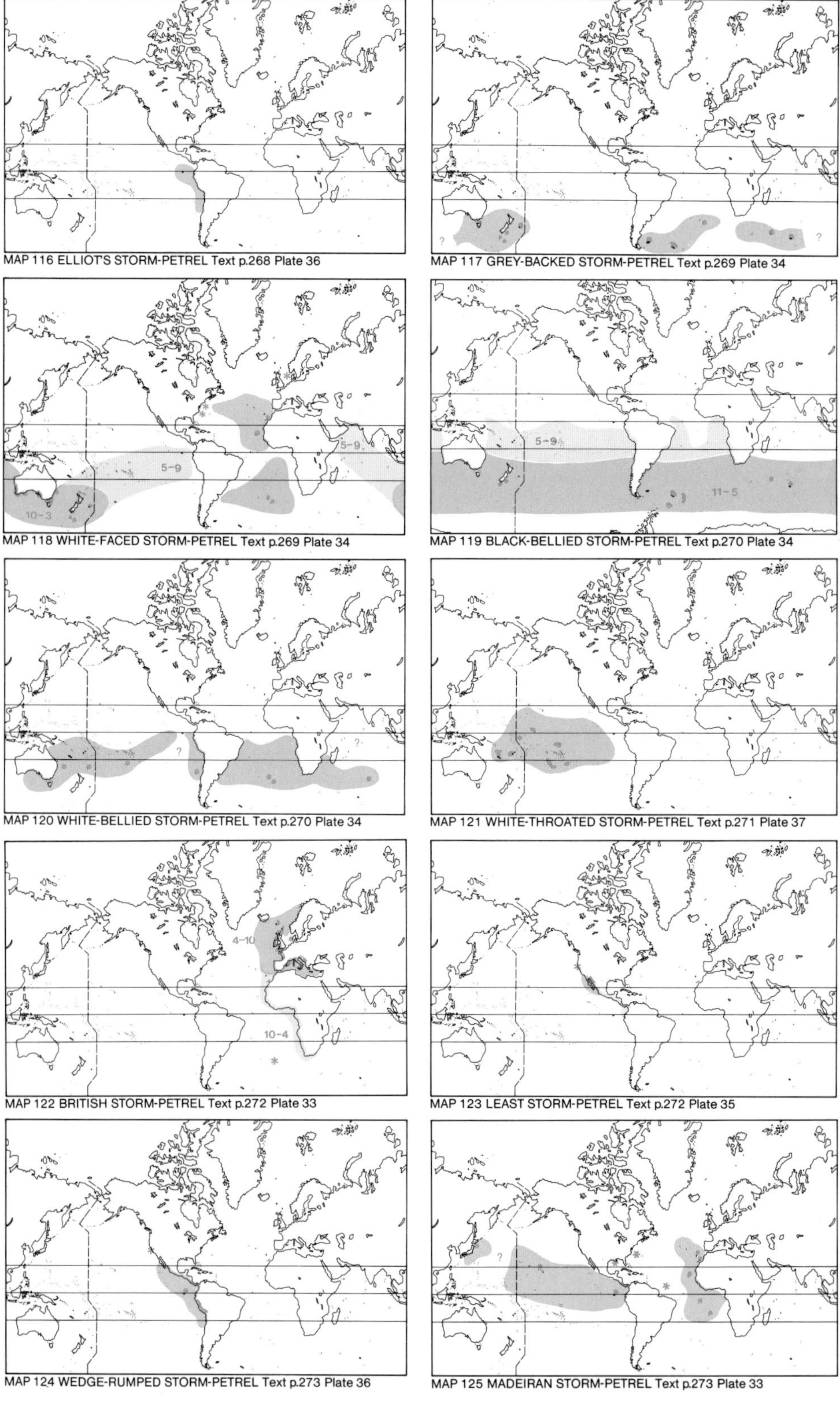

MAP 116 ELLIOT'S STORM-PETREL Text p.268 Plate 36

MAP 117 GREY-BACKED STORM-PETREL Text p.269 Plate 34

MAP 118 WHITE-FACED STORM-PETREL Text p.269 Plate 34

MAP 119 BLACK-BELLIED STORM-PETREL Text p.270 Plate 34

MAP 120 WHITE-BELLIED STORM-PETREL Text p.270 Plate 34

MAP 121 WHITE-THROATED STORM-PETREL Text p.271 Plate 37

MAP 122 BRITISH STORM-PETREL Text p.272 Plate 33

MAP 123 LEAST STORM-PETREL Text p.272 Plate 35

MAP 124 WEDGE-RUMPED STORM-PETREL Text p.273 Plate 36

MAP 125 MADEIRAN STORM-PETREL Text p.273 Plate 33

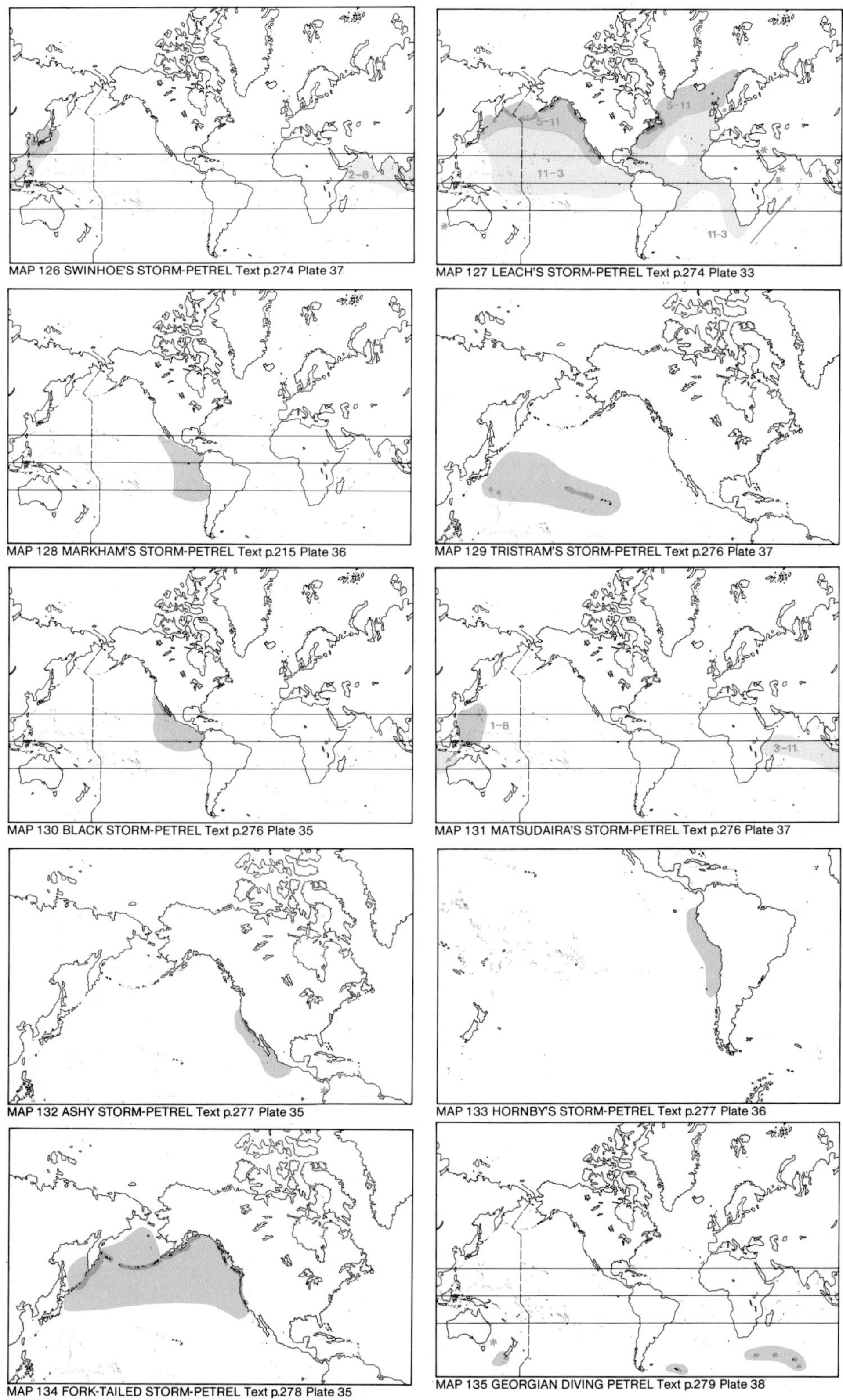

MAP 126 SWINHOE'S STORM-PETREL Text p.274 Plate 37

MAP 127 LEACH'S STORM-PETREL Text p.274 Plate 33

MAP 128 MARKHAM'S STORM-PETREL Text p.215 Plate 36

MAP 129 TRISTRAM'S STORM-PETREL Text p.276 Plate 37

MAP 130 BLACK STORM-PETREL Text p.276 Plate 35

MAP 131 MATSUDAIRA'S STORM-PETREL Text p.276 Plate 37

MAP 132 ASHY STORM-PETREL Text p.277 Plate 35

MAP 133 HORNBY'S STORM-PETREL Text p.277 Plate 36

MAP 134 FORK-TAILED STORM-PETREL Text p.278 Plate 35

MAP 135 GEORGIAN DIVING PETREL Text p.279 Plate 38

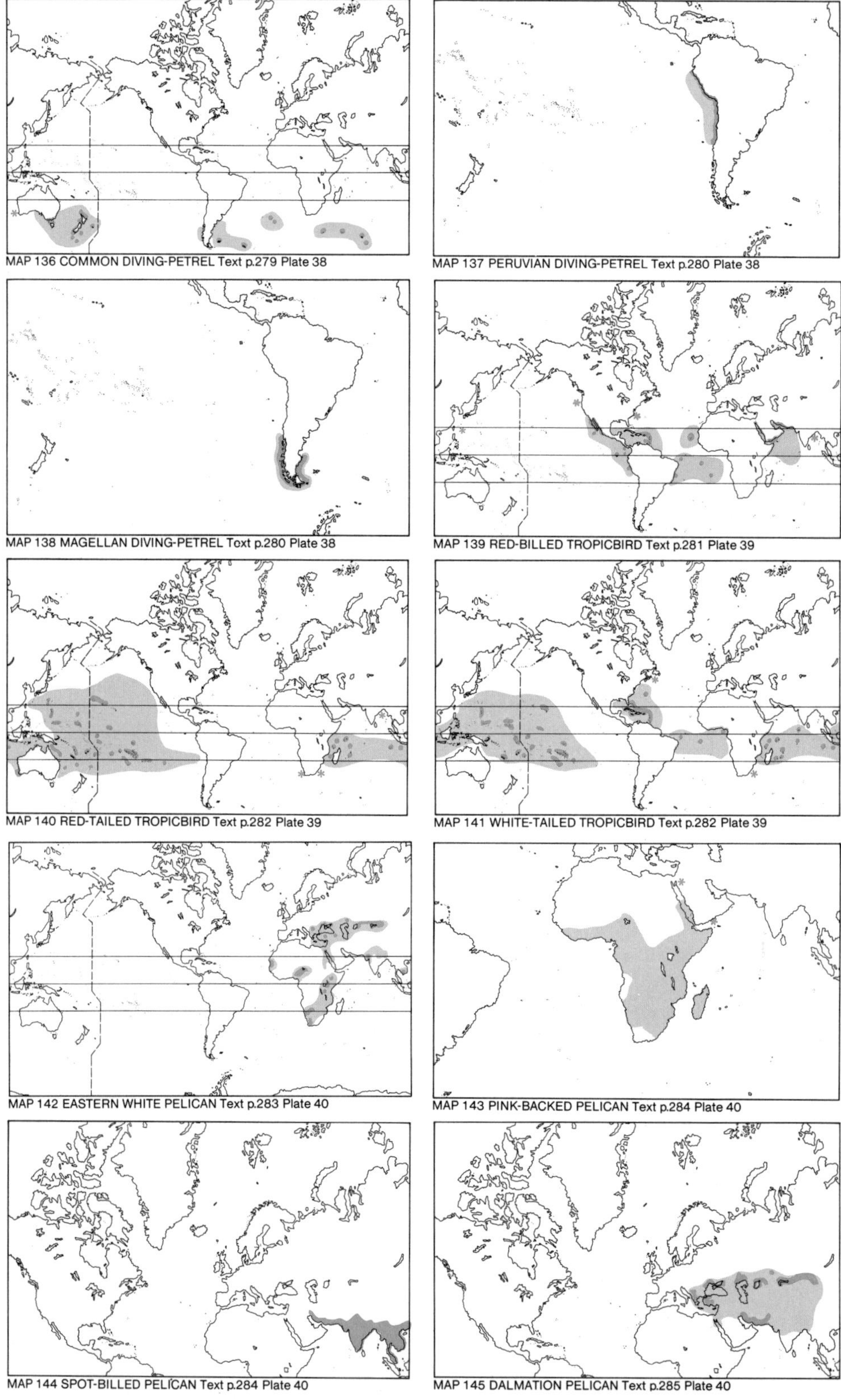

MAP 136 COMMON DIVING-PETREL Text p.279 Plate 38

MAP 137 PERUVIAN DIVING-PETREL Text p.280 Plate 38

MAP 138 MAGELLAN DIVING-PETREL Text p.280 Plate 38

MAP 139 RED-BILLED TROPICBIRD Text p.281 Plate 39

MAP 140 RED-TAILED TROPICBIRD Text p.282 Plate 39

MAP 141 WHITE-TAILED TROPICBIRD Text p.282 Plate 39

MAP 142 EASTERN WHITE PELICAN Text p.283 Plate 40

MAP 143 PINK-BACKED PELICAN Text p.284 Plate 40

MAP 144 SPOT-BILLED PELICAN Text p.284 Plate 40

MAP 145 DALMATION PELICAN Text p.285 Plate 40

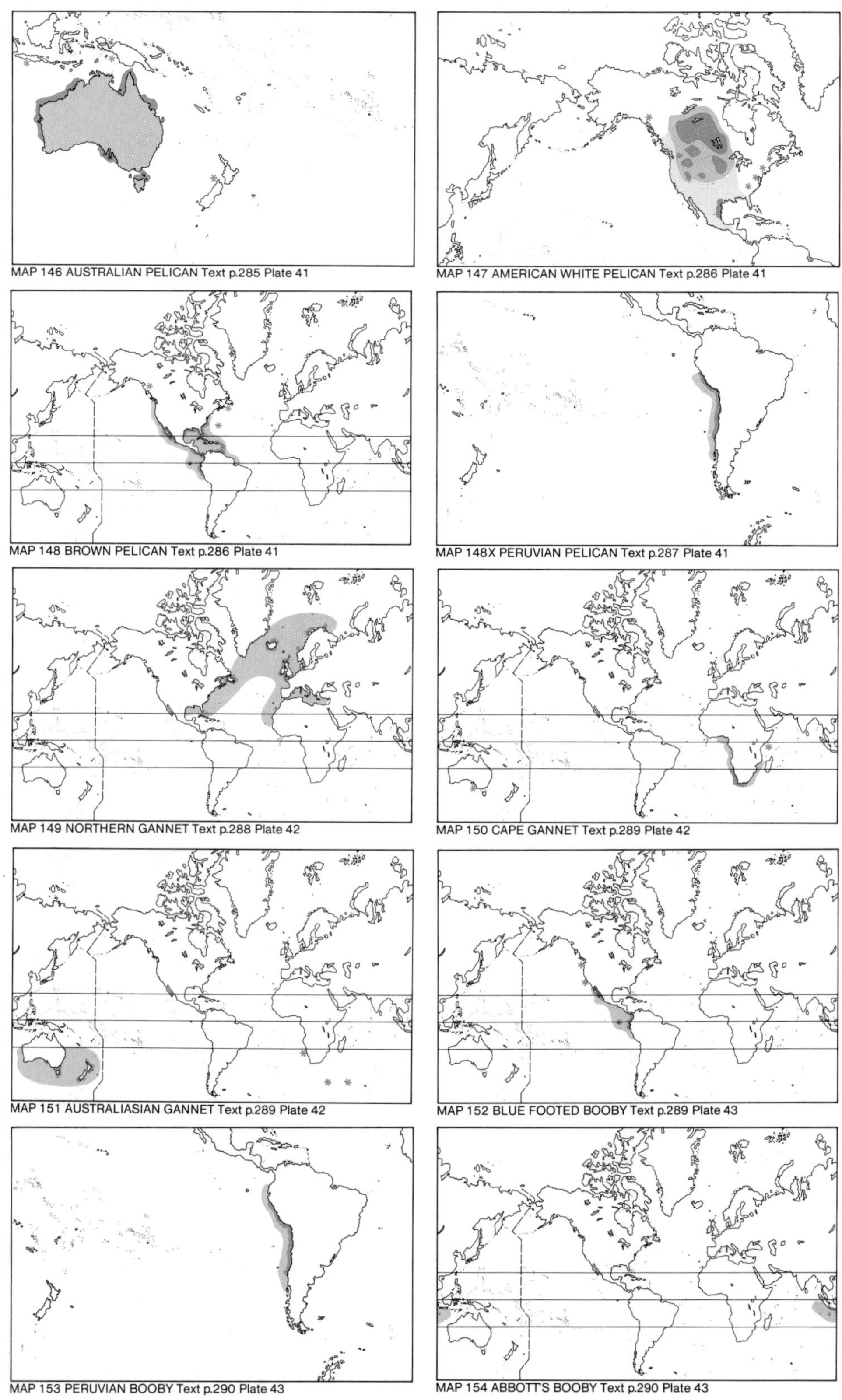

MAP 146 AUSTRALIAN PELICAN Text p.285 Plate 41

MAP 147 AMERICAN WHITE PELICAN Text p.286 Plate 41

MAP 148 BROWN PELICAN Text p.286 Plate 41

MAP 148X PERUVIAN PELICAN Text p.287 Plate 41

MAP 149 NORTHERN GANNET Text p.288 Plate 42

MAP 150 CAPE GANNET Text p.289 Plate 42

MAP 151 AUSTRALIASIAN GANNET Text p.289 Plate 42

MAP 152 BLUE FOOTED BOOBY Text p.289 Plate 43

MAP 153 PERUVIAN BOOBY Text p.290 Plate 43

MAP 154 ABBOTT'S BOOBY Text p.290 Plate 43

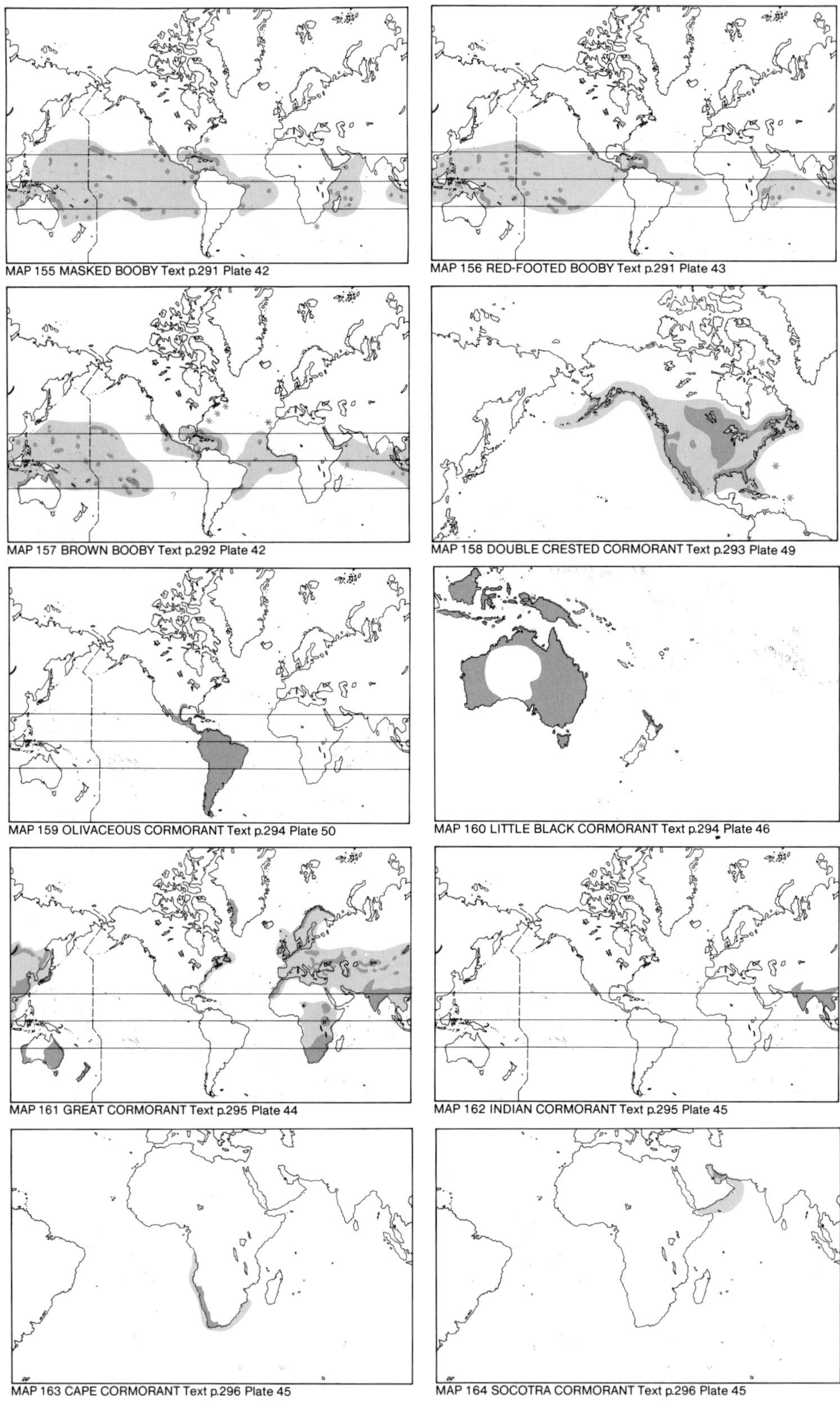

MAP 155 MASKED BOOBY Text p.291 Plate 42

MAP 156 RED-FOOTED BOOBY Text p.291 Plate 43

MAP 157 BROWN BOOBY Text p.292 Plate 42

MAP 158 DOUBLE CRESTED CORMORANT Text p.293 Plate 49

MAP 159 OLIVACEOUS CORMORANT Text p.294 Plate 50

MAP 160 LITTLE BLACK CORMORANT Text p.294 Plate 46

MAP 161 GREAT CORMORANT Text p.295 Plate 44

MAP 162 INDIAN CORMORANT Text p.295 Plate 45

MAP 163 CAPE CORMORANT Text p.296 Plate 45

MAP 164 SOCOTRA CORMORANT Text p.296 Plate 45

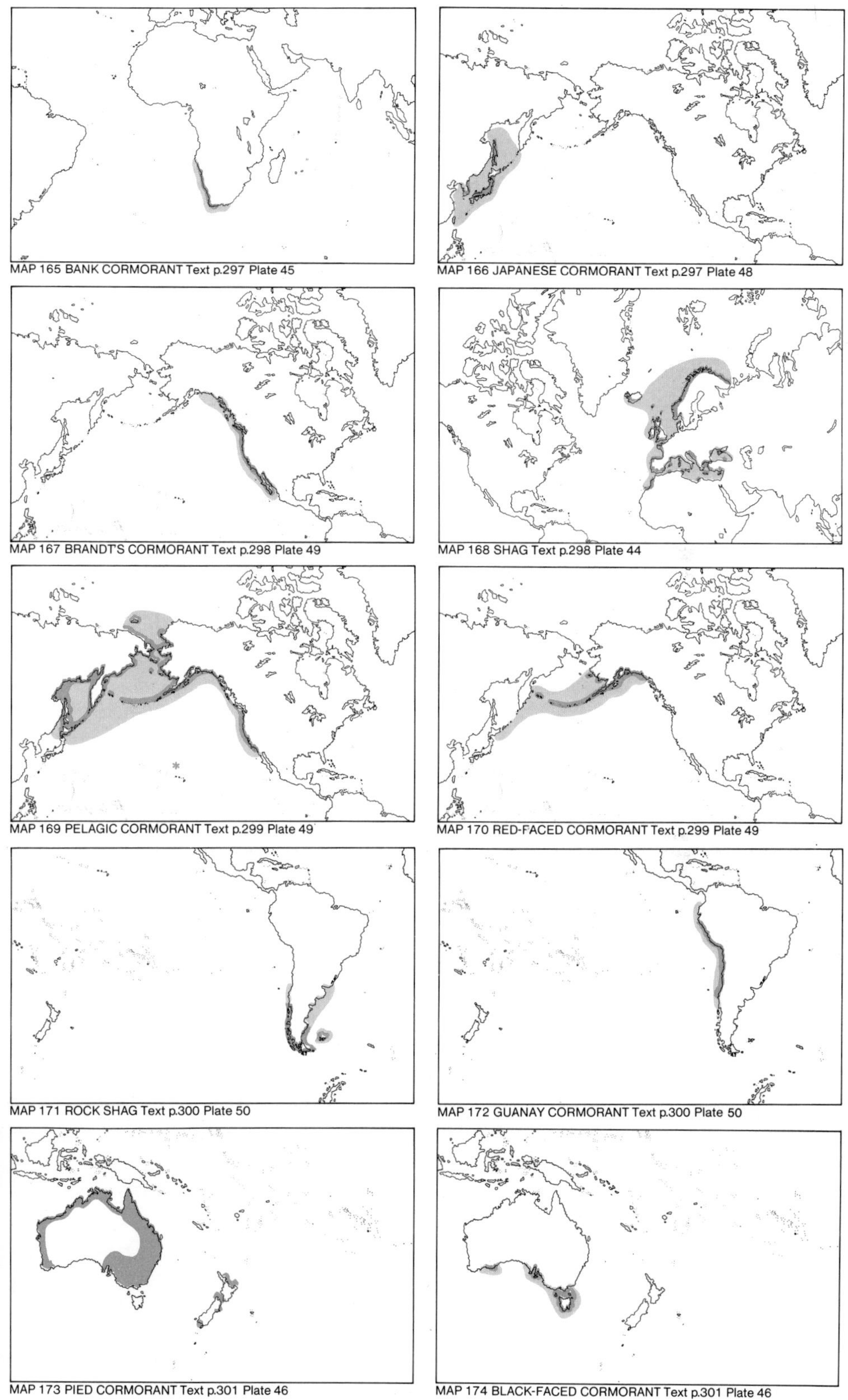

MAP 165 BANK CORMORANT Text p.297 Plate 45

MAP 166 JAPANESE CORMORANT Text p.297 Plate 48

MAP 167 BRANDT'S CORMORANT Text p.298 Plate 49

MAP 168 SHAG Text p.298 Plate 44

MAP 169 PELAGIC CORMORANT Text p.299 Plate 49

MAP 170 RED-FACED CORMORANT Text p.299 Plate 49

MAP 171 ROCK SHAG Text p.300 Plate 50

MAP 172 GUANAY CORMORANT Text p.300 Plate 50

MAP 173 PIED CORMORANT Text p.301 Plate 46

MAP 174 BLACK-FACED CORMORANT Text p.301 Plate 46

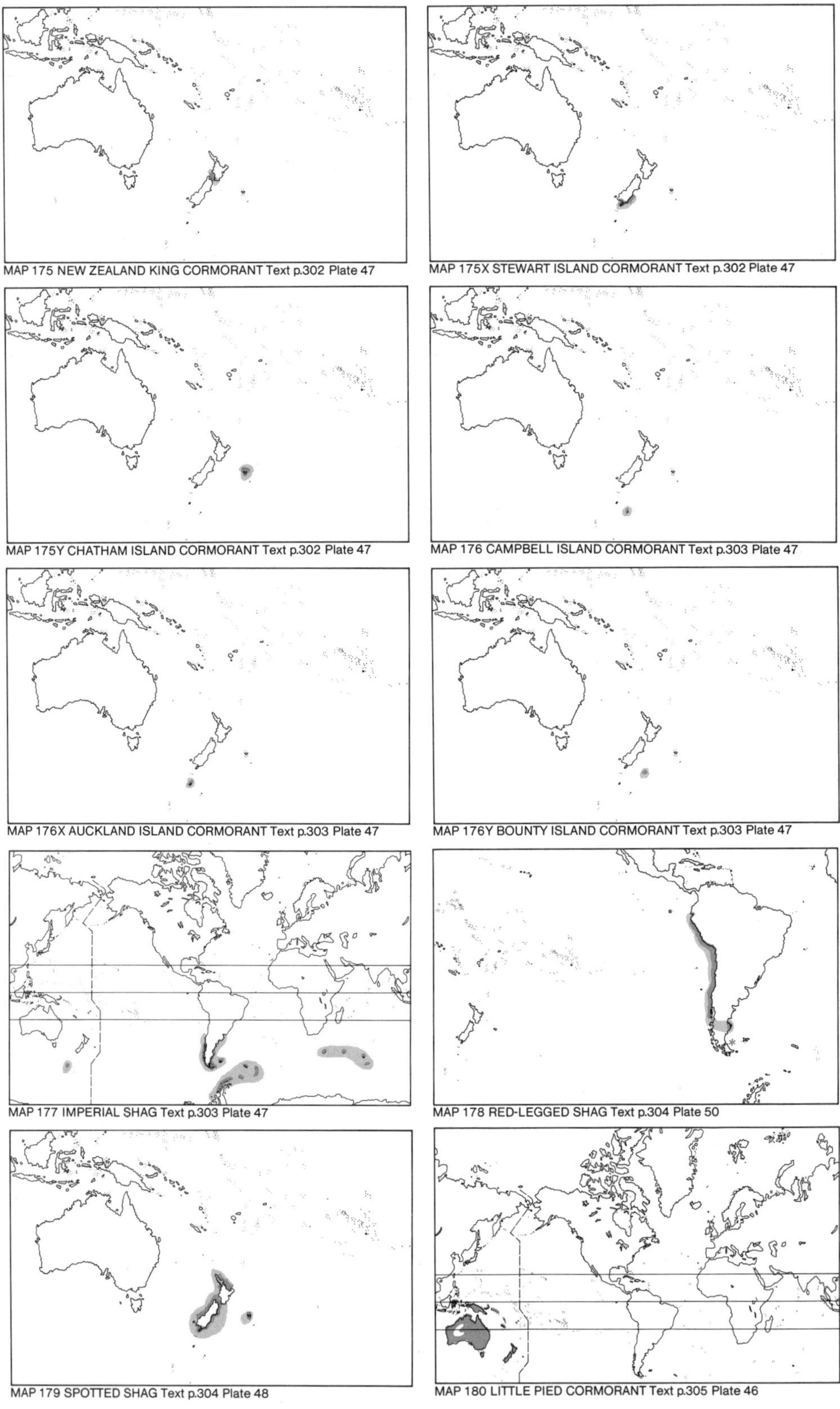

MAP 175 NEW ZEALAND KING CORMORANT Text p.302 Plate 47

MAP 175X STEWART ISLAND CORMORANT Text p.302 Plate 47

MAP 175Y CHATHAM ISLAND CORMORANT Text p.302 Plate 47

MAP 176 CAMPBELL ISLAND CORMORANT Text p.303 Plate 47

MAP 176X AUCKLAND ISLAND CORMORANT Text p.303 Plate 47

MAP 176Y BOUNTY ISLAND CORMORANT Text p.303 Plate 47

MAP 177 IMPERIAL SHAG Text p.303 Plate 47

MAP 178 RED-LEGGED SHAG Text p.304 Plate 50

MAP 179 SPOTTED SHAG Text p.304 Plate 48

MAP 180 LITTLE PIED CORMORANT Text p.305 Plate 46

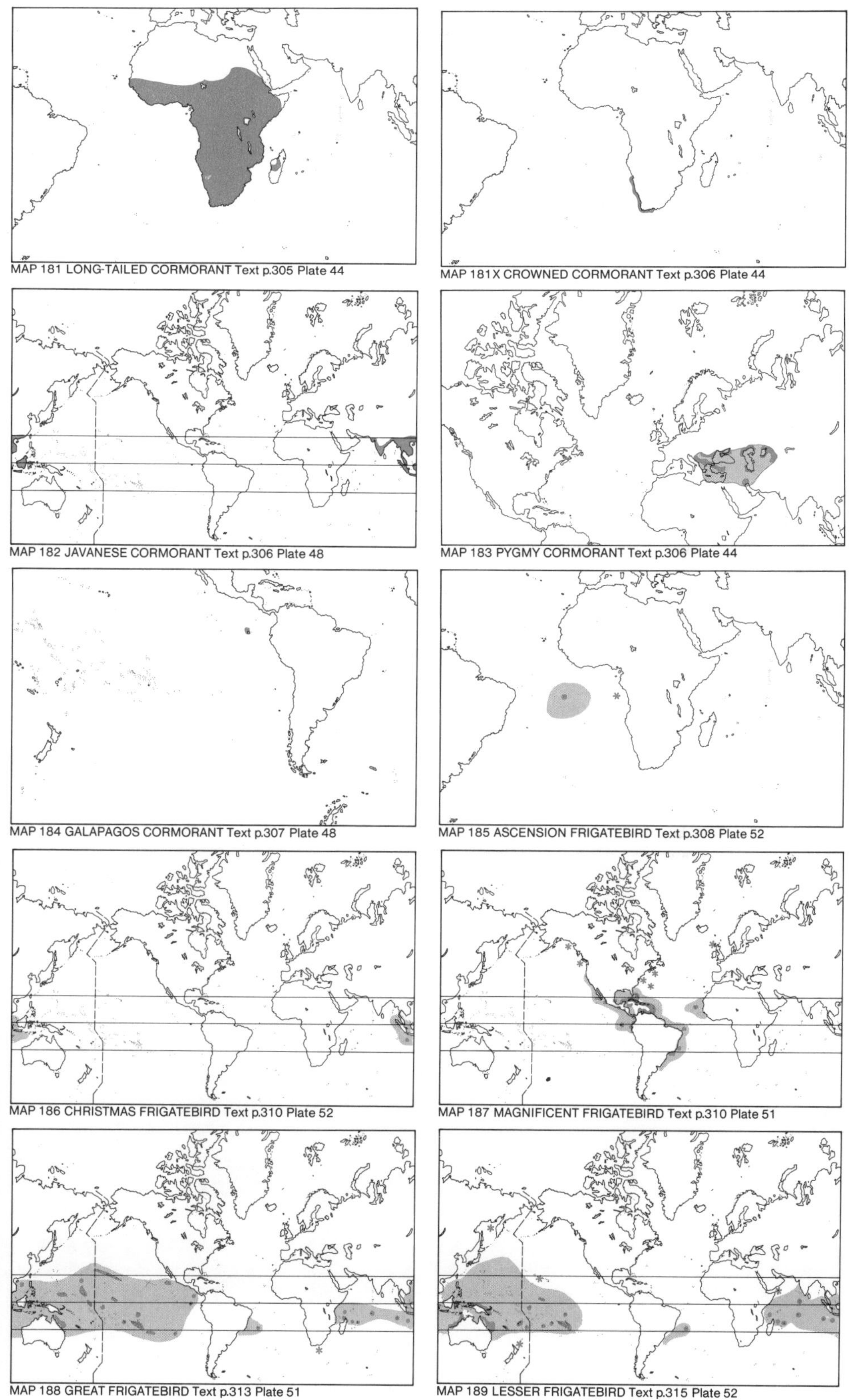

MAP 181 LONG-TAILED CORMORANT Text p.305 Plate 44

MAP 181X CROWNED CORMORANT Text p.306 Plate 44

MAP 182 JAVANESE CORMORANT Text p.306 Plate 48

MAP 183 PYGMY CORMORANT Text p.306 Plate 44

MAP 184 GALAPAGOS CORMORANT Text p.307 Plate 48

MAP 185 ASCENSION FRIGATEBIRD Text p.308 Plate 52

MAP 186 CHRISTMAS FRIGATEBIRD Text p.310 Plate 52

MAP 187 MAGNIFICENT FRIGATEBIRD Text p.310 Plate 51

MAP 188 GREAT FRIGATEBIRD Text p.313 Plate 51

MAP 189 LESSER FRIGATEBIRD Text p.315 Plate 52

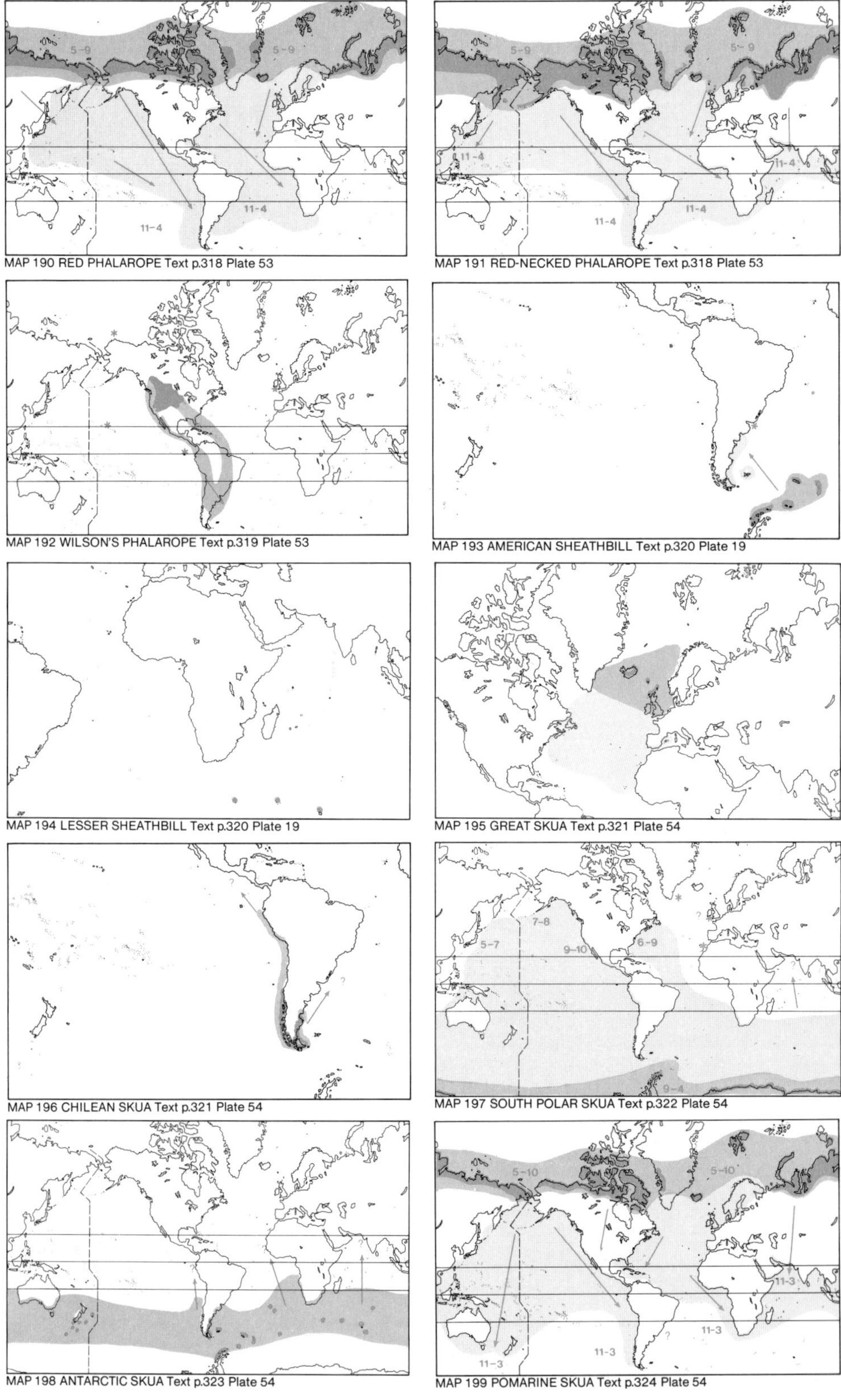

MAP 190 RED PHALAROPE Text p.318 Plate 53

MAP 191 RED-NECKED PHALAROPE Text p.318 Plate 53

MAP 192 WILSON'S PHALAROPE Text p.319 Plate 53

MAP 193 AMERICAN SHEATHBILL Text p.320 Plate 19

MAP 194 LESSER SHEATHBILL Text p.320 Plate 19

MAP 195 GREAT SKUA Text p.321 Plate 54

MAP 196 CHILEAN SKUA Text p.321 Plate 54

MAP 197 SOUTH POLAR SKUA Text p.322 Plate 54

MAP 198 ANTARCTIC SKUA Text p.323 Plate 54

MAP 199 POMARINE SKUA Text p.324 Plate 54

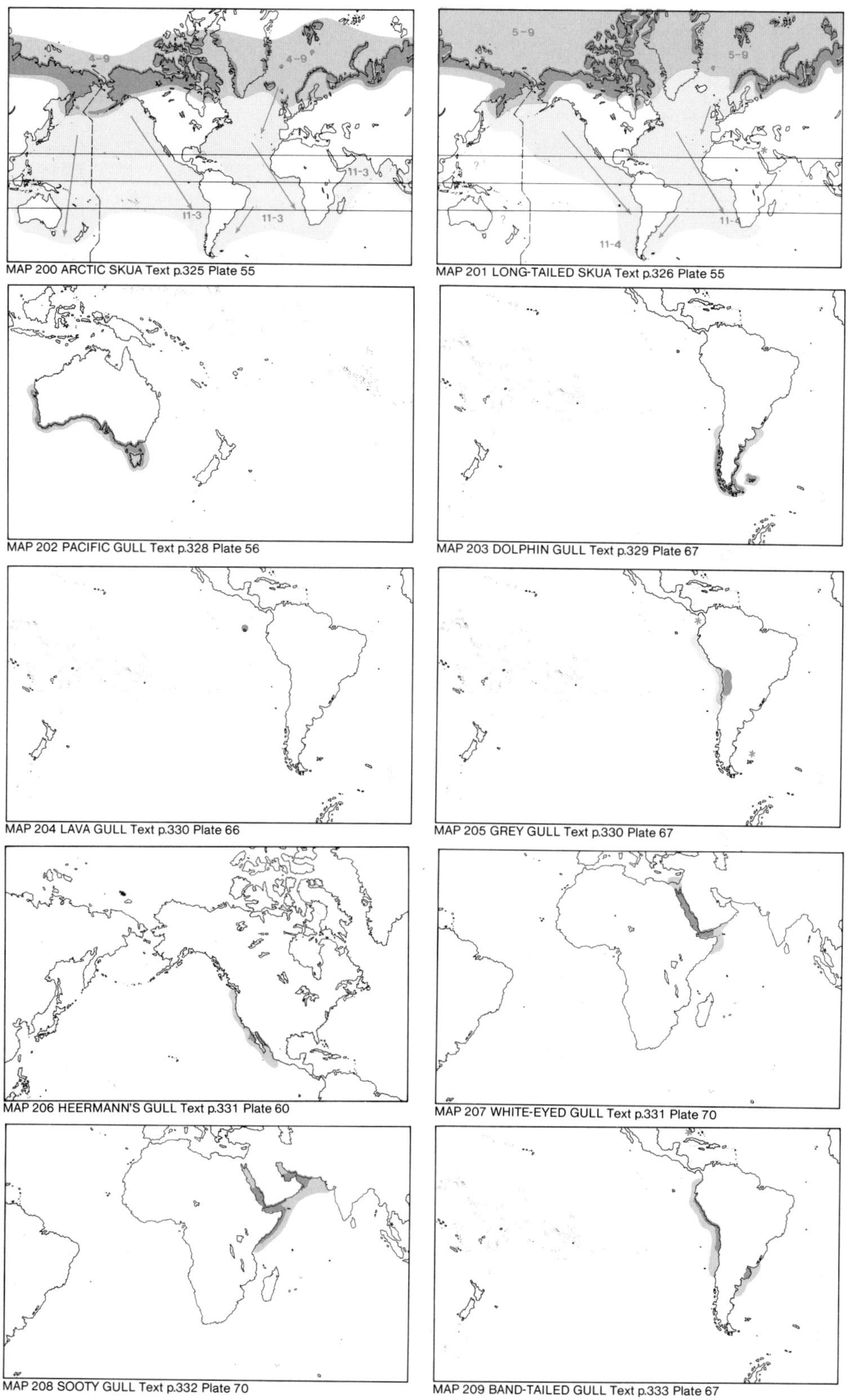

MAP 200 ARCTIC SKUA Text p.325 Plate 55

MAP 201 LONG-TAILED SKUA Text p.326 Plate 55

MAP 202 PACIFIC GULL Text p.328 Plate 56

MAP 203 DOLPHIN GULL Text p.329 Plate 67

MAP 204 LAVA GULL Text p.330 Plate 66

MAP 205 GREY GULL Text p.330 Plate 67

MAP 206 HEERMANN'S GULL Text p.331 Plate 60

MAP 207 WHITE-EYED GULL Text p.331 Plate 70

MAP 208 SOOTY GULL Text p.332 Plate 70

MAP 209 BAND-TAILED GULL Text p.333 Plate 67

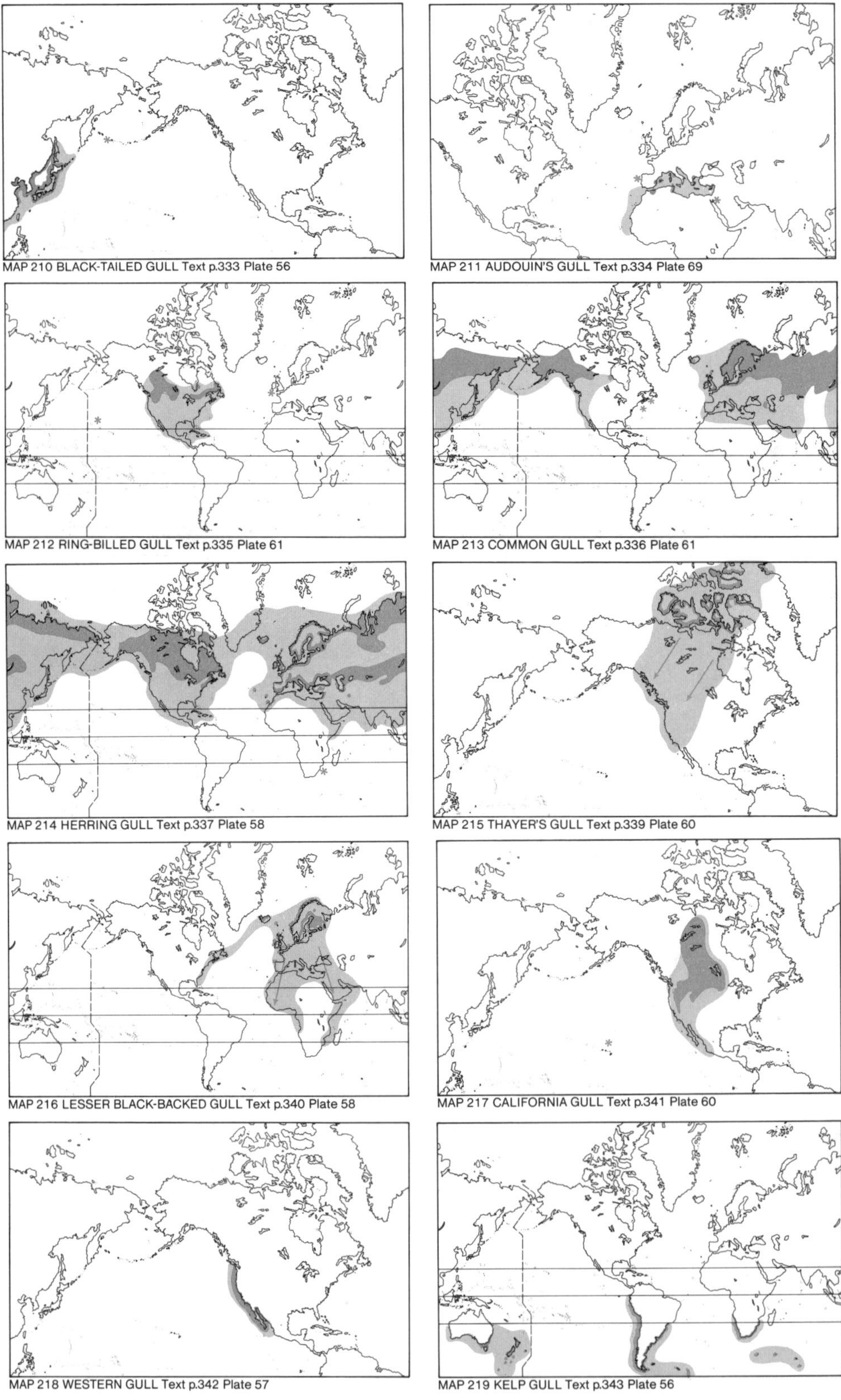

MAP 210 BLACK-TAILED GULL Text p.333 Plate 56

MAP 211 AUDOUIN'S GULL Text p.334 Plate 69

MAP 212 RING-BILLED GULL Text p.335 Plate 61

MAP 213 COMMON GULL Text p.336 Plate 61

MAP 214 HERRING GULL Text p.337 Plate 58

MAP 215 THAYER'S GULL Text p.339 Plate 60

MAP 216 LESSER BLACK-BACKED GULL Text p.340 Plate 58

MAP 217 CALIFORNIA GULL Text p.341 Plate 60

MAP 218 WESTERN GULL Text p.342 Plate 57

MAP 219 KELP GULL Text p.343 Plate 56

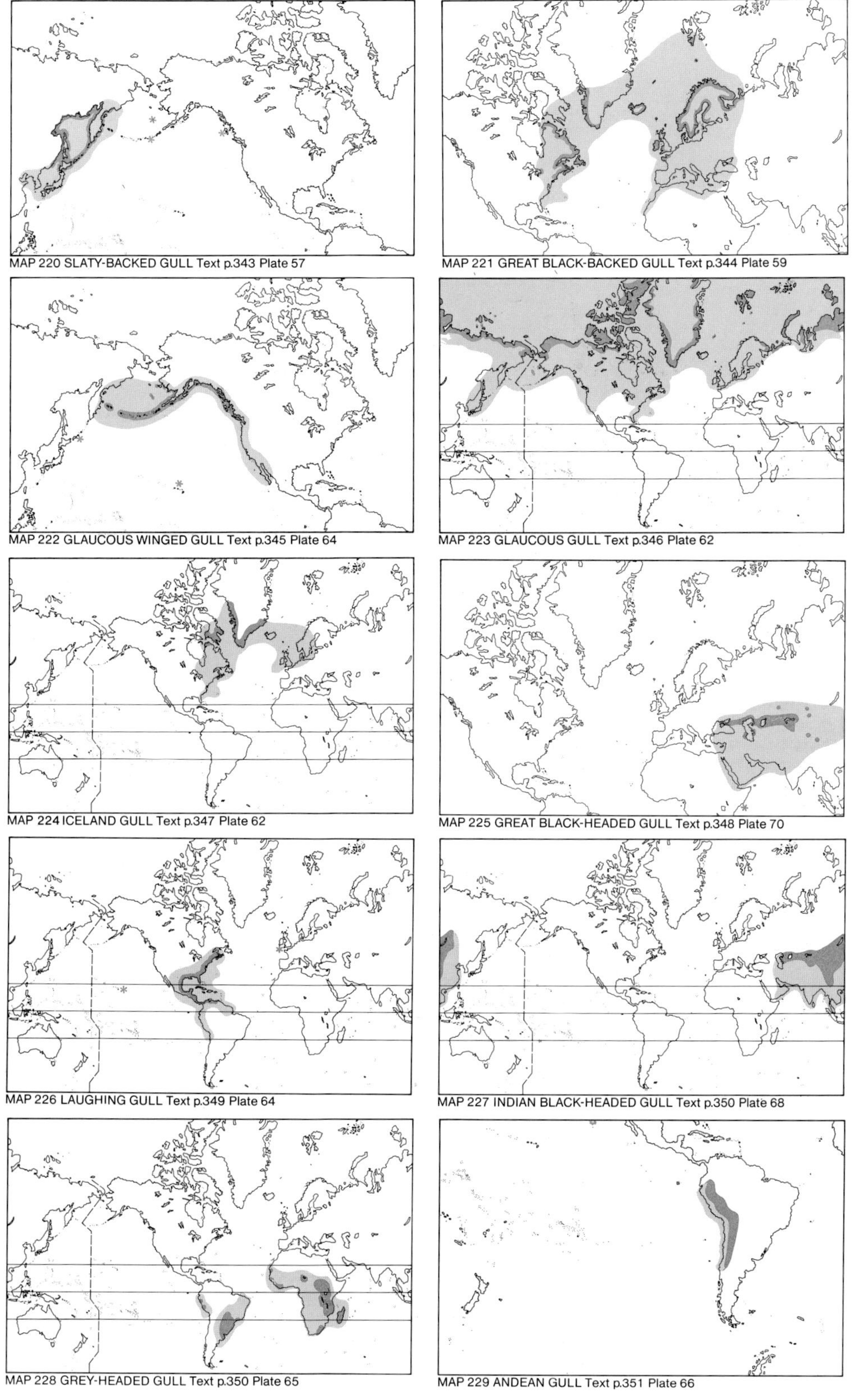

MAP 220 SLATY-BACKED GULL Text p.343 Plate 57

MAP 221 GREAT BLACK-BACKED GULL Text p.344 Plate 59

MAP 222 GLAUCOUS WINGED GULL Text p.345 Plate 64

MAP 223 GLAUCOUS GULL Text p.346 Plate 62

MAP 224 ICELAND GULL Text p.347 Plate 62

MAP 225 GREAT BLACK-HEADED GULL Text p.348 Plate 70

MAP 226 LAUGHING GULL Text p.349 Plate 64

MAP 227 INDIAN BLACK-HEADED GULL Text p.350 Plate 68

MAP 228 GREY-HEADED GULL Text p.350 Plate 65

MAP 229 ANDEAN GULL Text p.351 Plate 66

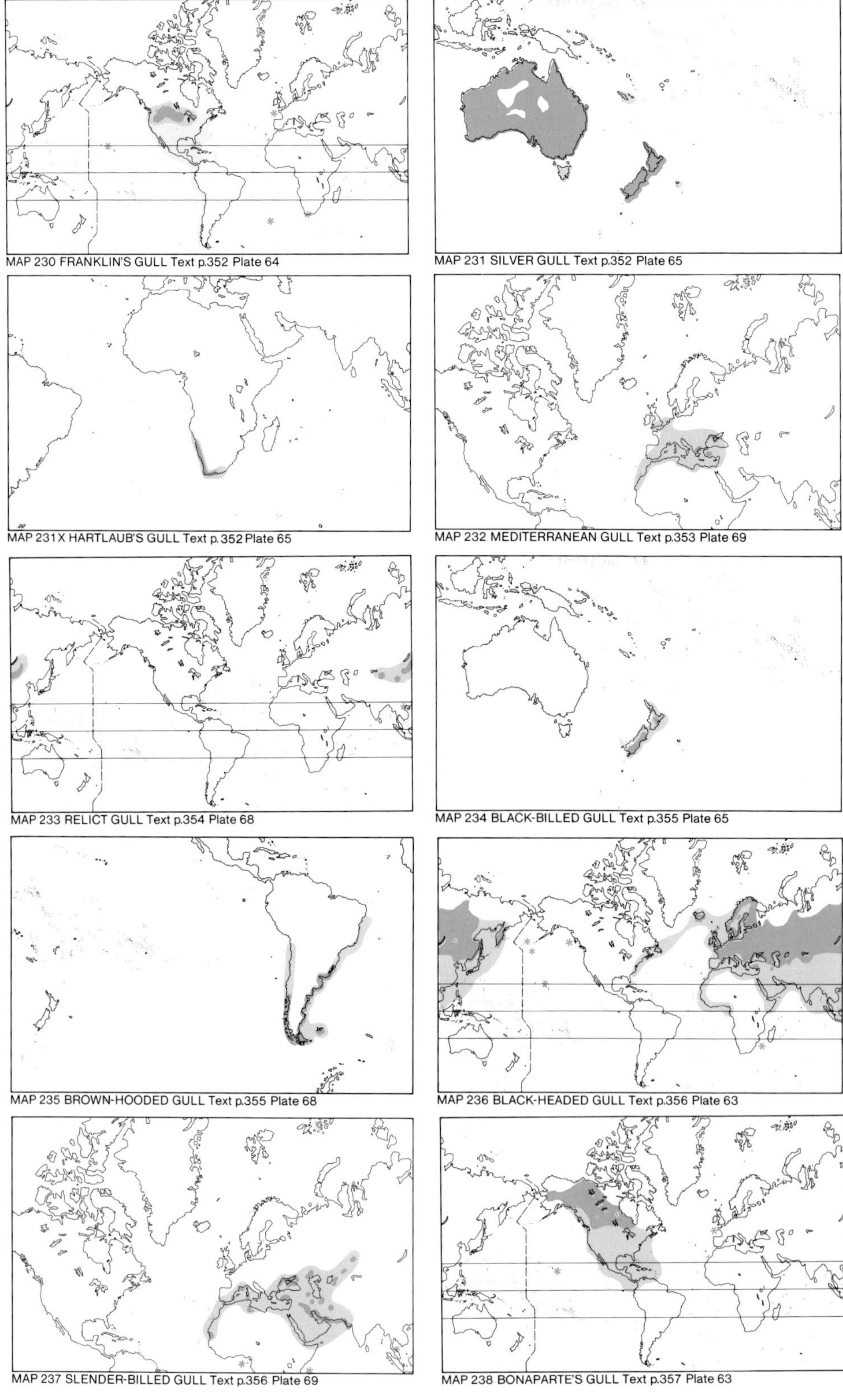

MAP 230 FRANKLIN'S GULL Text p.352 Plate 64

MAP 231 SILVER GULL Text p.352 Plate 65

MAP 231X HARTLAUB'S GULL Text p.352 Plate 65

MAP 232 MEDITERRANEAN GULL Text p.353 Plate 69

MAP 233 RELICT GULL Text p.354 Plate 68

MAP 234 BLACK-BILLED GULL Text p.355 Plate 65

MAP 235 BROWN-HOODED GULL Text p.355 Plate 68

MAP 236 BLACK-HEADED GULL Text p.356 Plate 63

MAP 237 SLENDER-BILLED GULL Text p.356 Plate 69

MAP 238 BONAPARTE'S GULL Text p.357 Plate 63

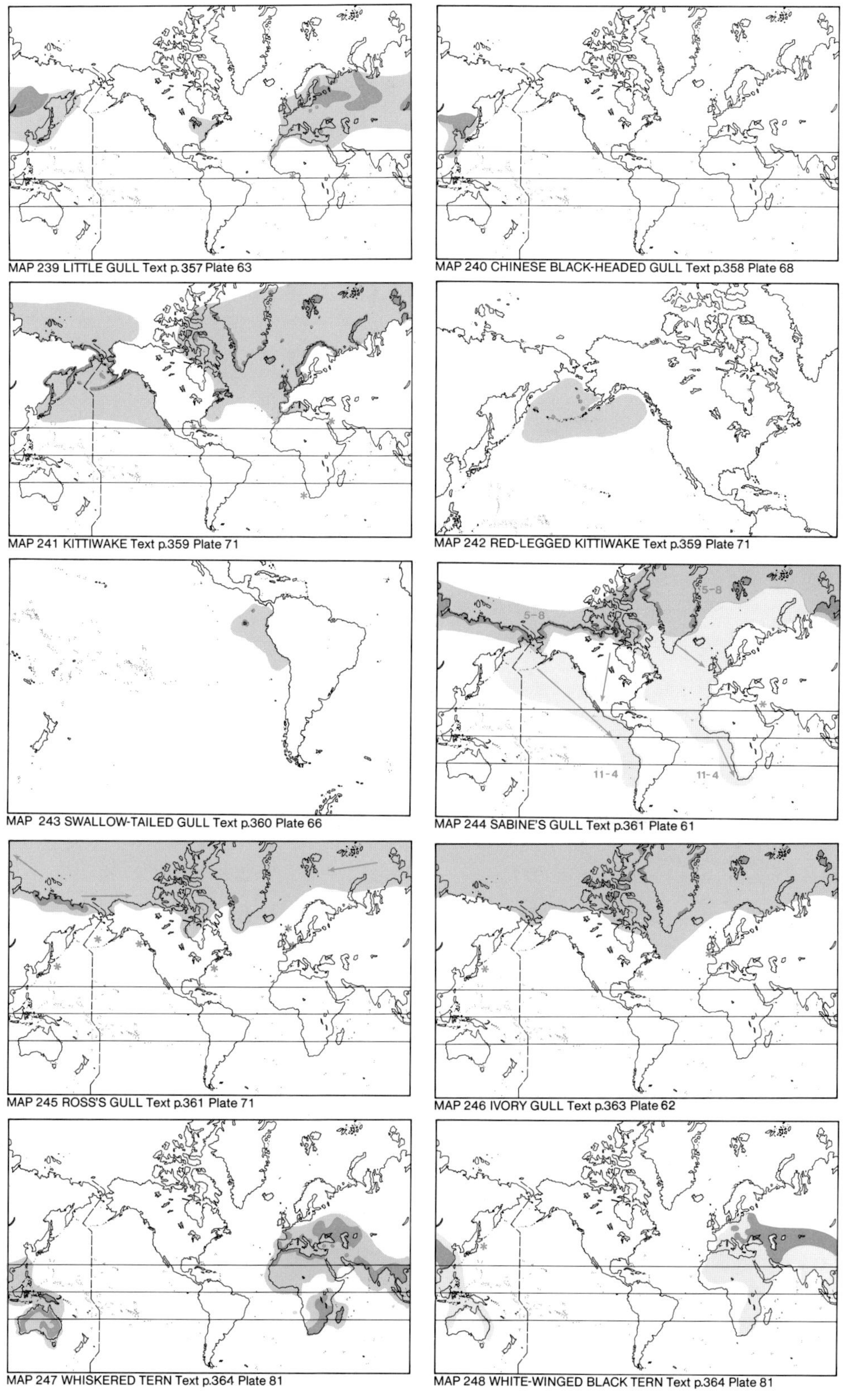

MAP 239 LITTLE GULL Text p.357 Plate 63

MAP 240 CHINESE BLACK-HEADED GULL Text p.358 Plate 68

MAP 241 KITTIWAKE Text p.359 Plate 71

MAP 242 RED-LEGGED KITTIWAKE Text p.359 Plate 71

MAP 243 SWALLOW-TAILED GULL Text p.360 Plate 66

MAP 244 SABINE'S GULL Text p.361 Plate 61

MAP 245 ROSS'S GULL Text p.361 Plate 71

MAP 246 IVORY GULL Text p.363 Plate 62

MAP 247 WHISKERED TERN Text p.364 Plate 81

MAP 248 WHITE-WINGED BLACK TERN Text p.364 Plate 81

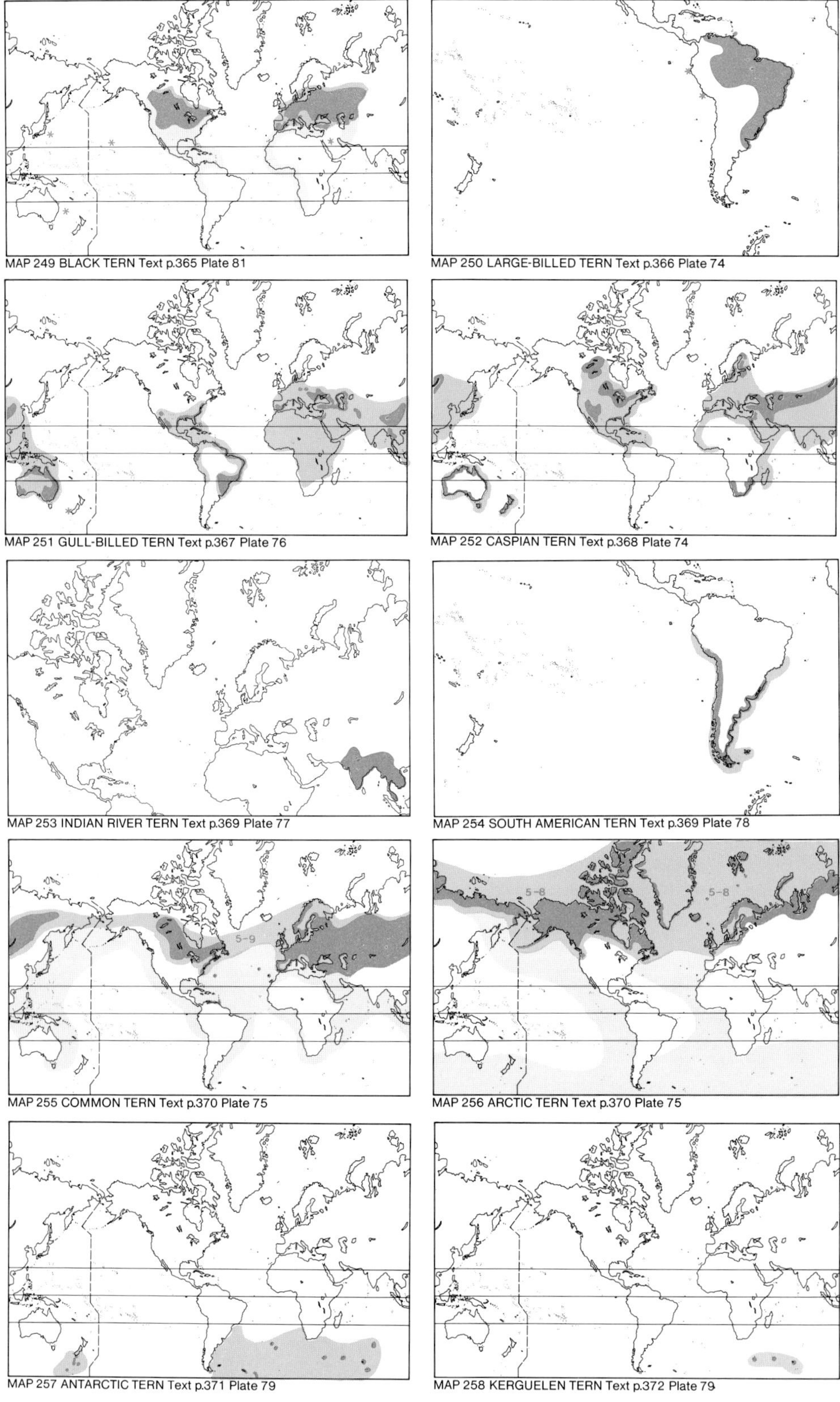

MAP 249 BLACK TERN Text p.365 Plate 81

MAP 250 LARGE-BILLED TERN Text p.366 Plate 74

MAP 251 GULL-BILLED TERN Text p.367 Plate 76

MAP 252 CASPIAN TERN Text p.368 Plate 74

MAP 253 INDIAN RIVER TERN Text p.369 Plate 77

MAP 254 SOUTH AMERICAN TERN Text p.369 Plate 78

MAP 255 COMMON TERN Text p.370 Plate 75

MAP 256 ARCTIC TERN Text p.370 Plate 75

MAP 257 ANTARCTIC TERN Text p.371 Plate 79

MAP 258 KERGUELEN TERN Text p.372 Plate 79

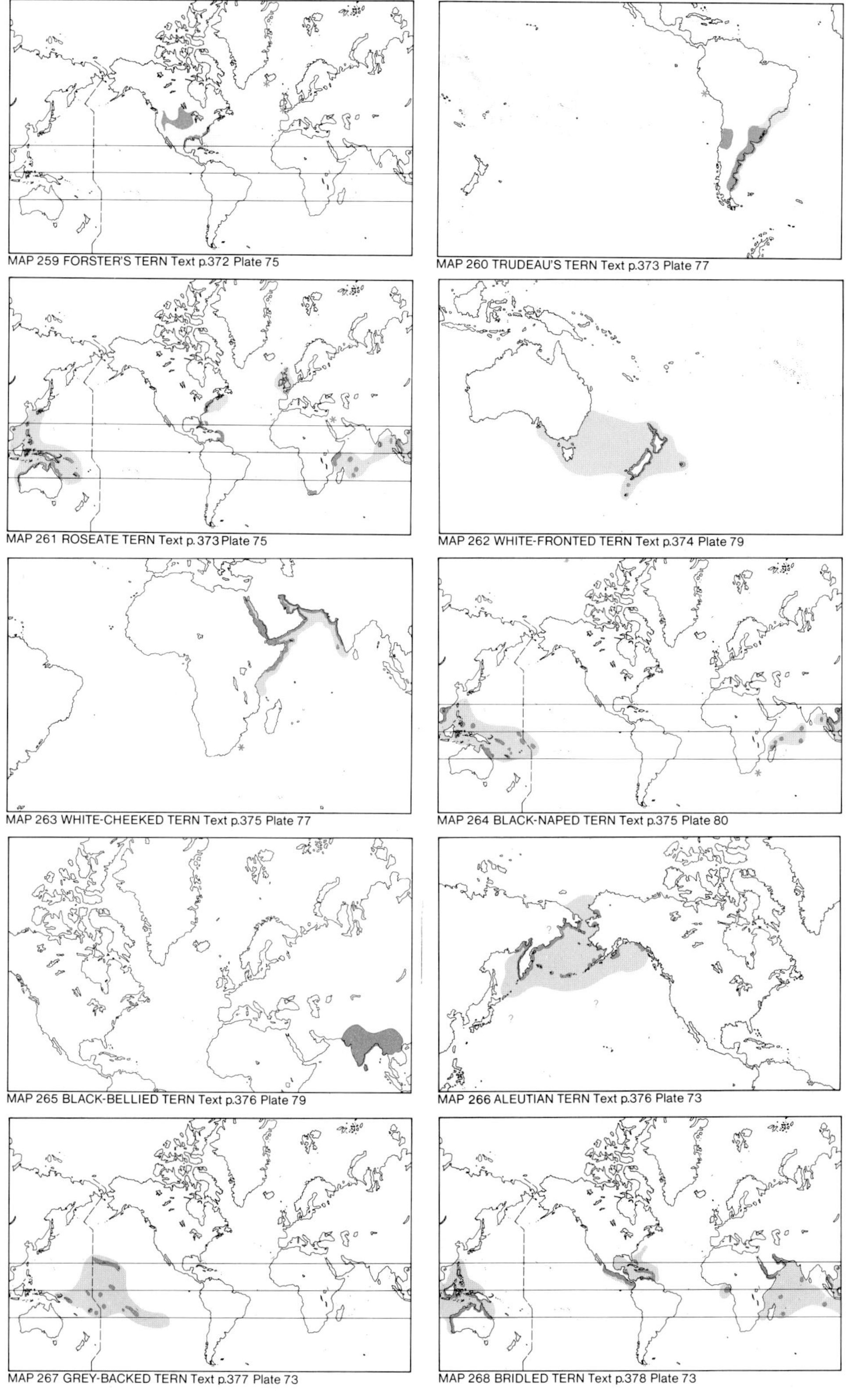

MAP 259 FORSTER'S TERN Text p.372 Plate 75

MAP 260 TRUDEAU'S TERN Text p.373 Plate 77

MAP 261 ROSEATE TERN Text p.373 Plate 75

MAP 262 WHITE-FRONTED TERN Text p.374 Plate 79

MAP 263 WHITE-CHEEKED TERN Text p.375 Plate 77

MAP 264 BLACK-NAPED TERN Text p.375 Plate 80

MAP 265 BLACK-BELLIED TERN Text p.376 Plate 79

MAP 266 ALEUTIAN TERN Text p.376 Plate 73

MAP 267 GREY-BACKED TERN Text p.377 Plate 73

MAP 268 BRIDLED TERN Text p.378 Plate 73

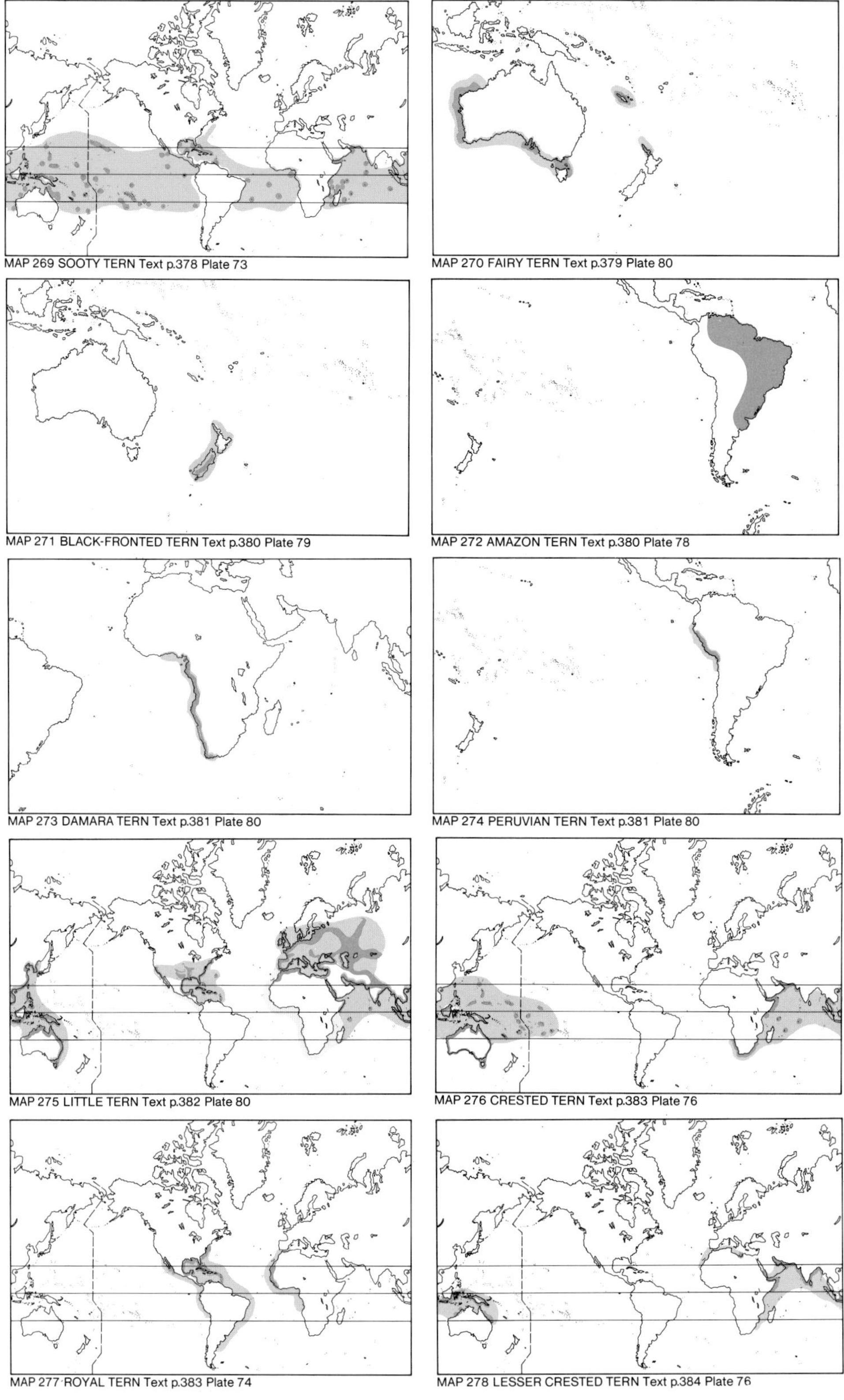

MAP 269 SOOTY TERN Text p.378 Plate 73

MAP 270 FAIRY TERN Text p.379 Plate 80

MAP 271 BLACK-FRONTED TERN Text p.380 Plate 79

MAP 272 AMAZON TERN Text p.380 Plate 78

MAP 273 DAMARA TERN Text p.381 Plate 80

MAP 274 PERUVIAN TERN Text p.381 Plate 80

MAP 275 LITTLE TERN Text p.382 Plate 80

MAP 276 CRESTED TERN Text p.383 Plate 76

MAP 277 ROYAL TERN Text p.383 Plate 74

MAP 278 LESSER CRESTED TERN Text p.384 Plate 76

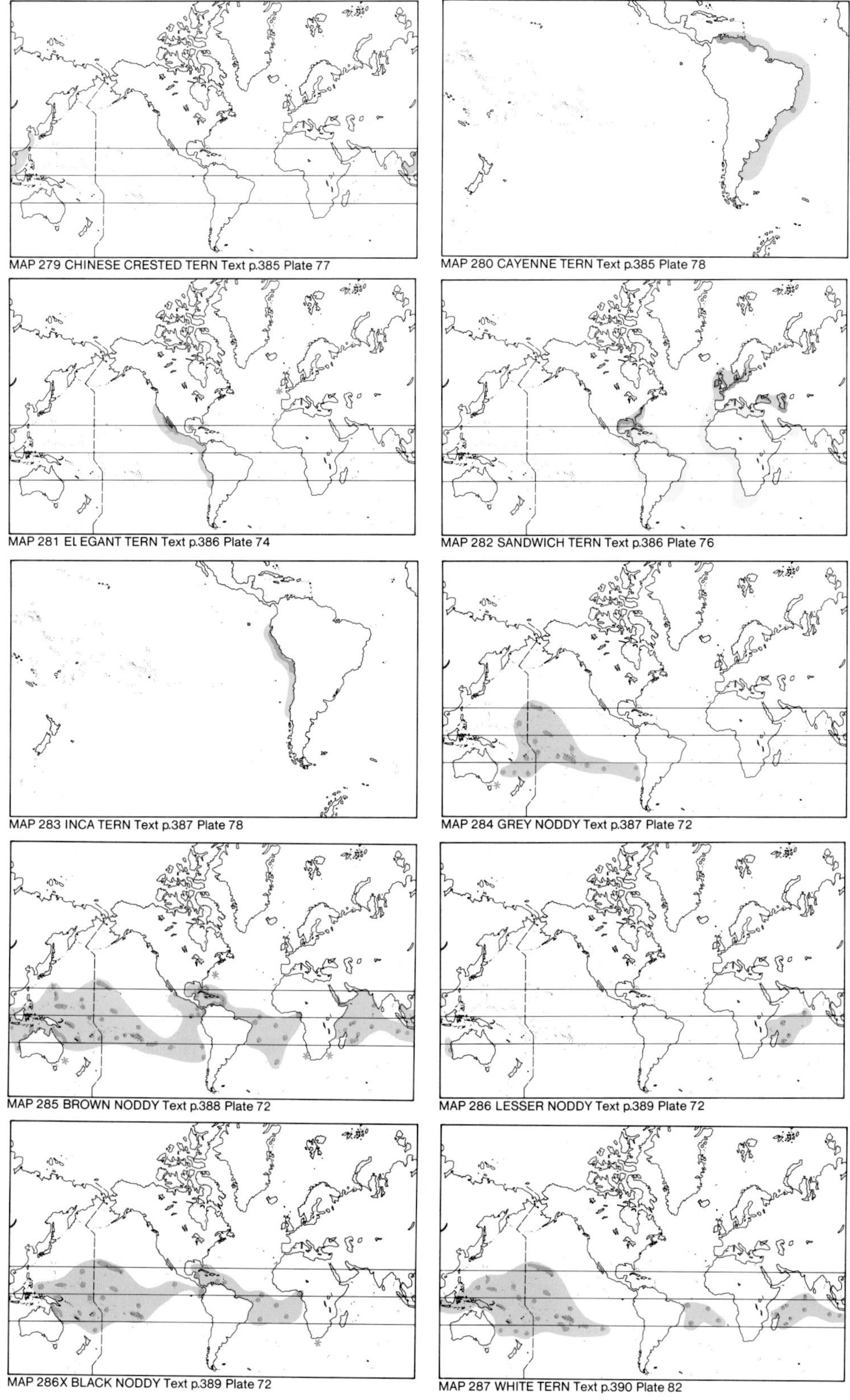

MAP 279 CHINESE CRESTED TERN Text p.385 Plate 77

MAP 280 CAYENNE TERN Text p.385 Plate 78

MAP 281 ELEGANT TERN Text p.386 Plate 74

MAP 282 SANDWICH TERN Text p.386 Plate 76

MAP 283 INCA TERN Text p.387 Plate 78

MAP 284 GREY NODDY Text p.387 Plate 72

MAP 285 BROWN NODDY Text p.388 Plate 72

MAP 286 LESSER NODDY Text p.389 Plate 72

MAP 286X BLACK NODDY Text p.389 Plate 72

MAP 287 WHITE TERN Text p.390 Plate 82

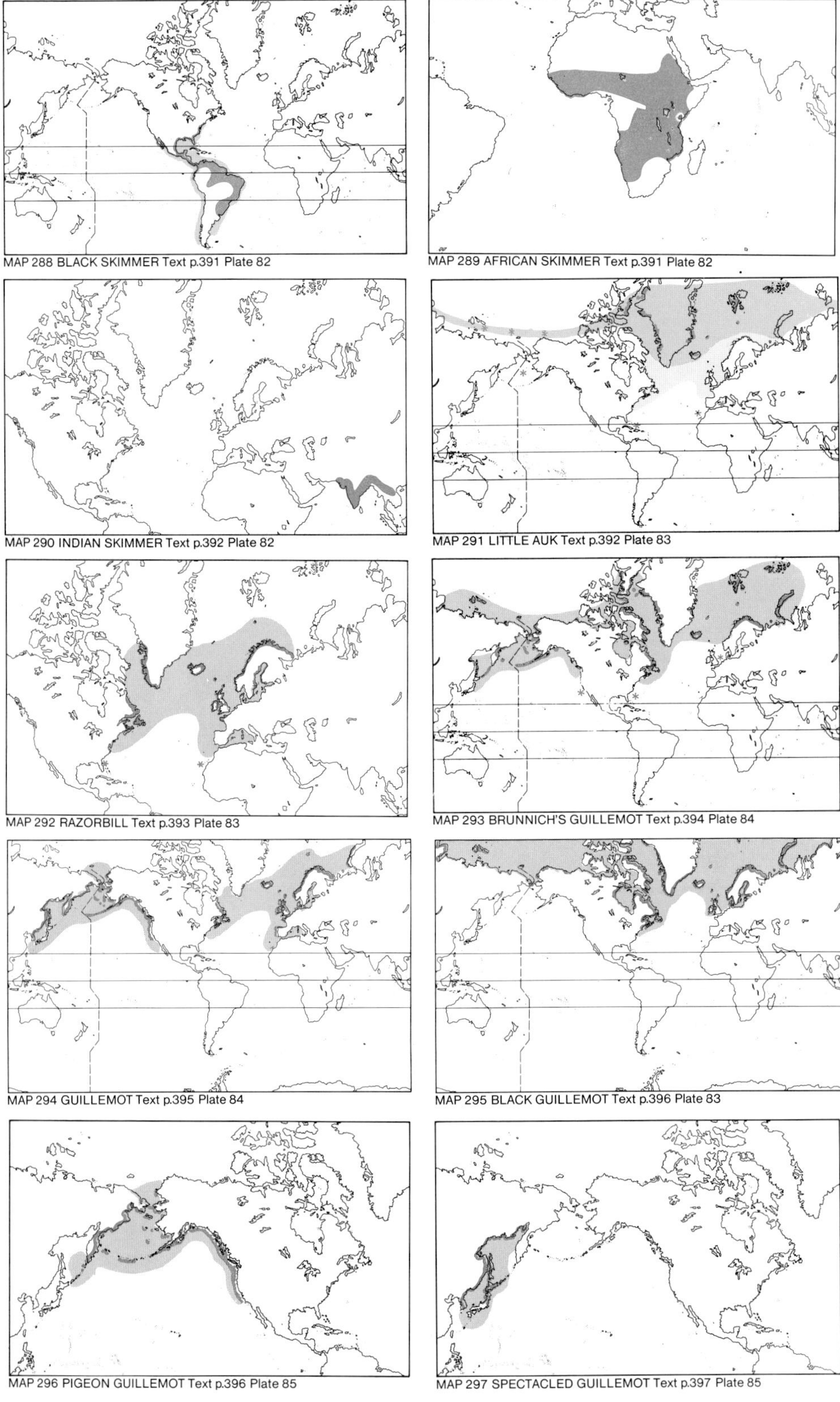

MAP 288 BLACK SKIMMER Text p.391 Plate 82

MAP 289 AFRICAN SKIMMER Text p.391 Plate 82

MAP 290 INDIAN SKIMMER Text p.392 Plate 82

MAP 291 LITTLE AUK Text p.392 Plate 83

MAP 292 RAZORBILL Text p.393 Plate 83

MAP 293 BRUNNICH'S GUILLEMOT Text p.394 Plate 84

MAP 294 GUILLEMOT Text p.395 Plate 84

MAP 295 BLACK GUILLEMOT Text p.396 Plate 83

MAP 296 PIGEON GUILLEMOT Text p.396 Plate 85

MAP 297 SPECTACLED GUILLEMOT Text p.397 Plate 85

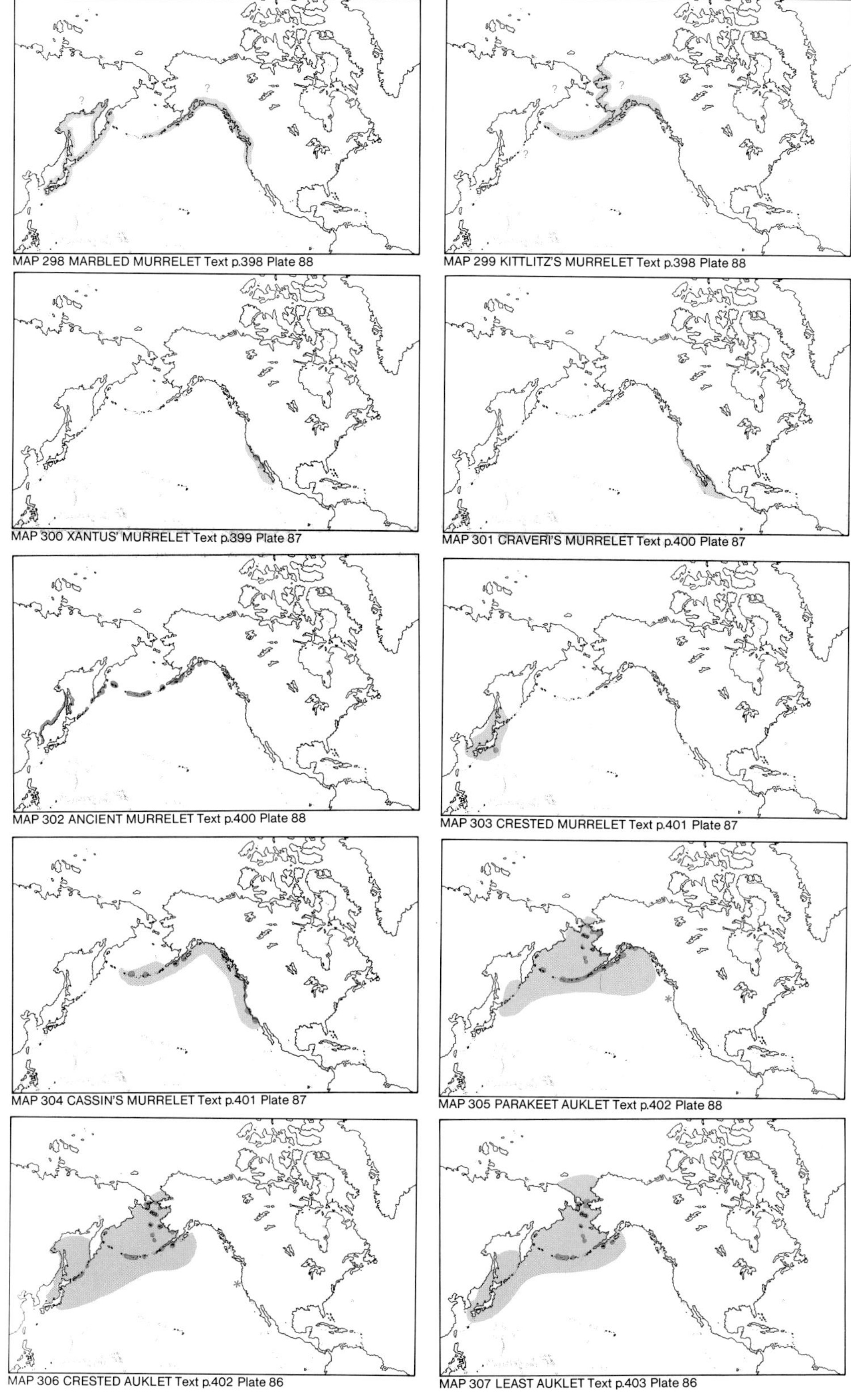

MAP 298 MARBLED MURRELET Text p.398 Plate 88

MAP 299 KITTLITZ'S MURRELET Text p.398 Plate 88

MAP 300 XANTUS' MURRELET Text p.399 Plate 87

MAP 301 CRAVERI'S MURRELET Text p.400 Plate 87

MAP 302 ANCIENT MURRELET Text p.400 Plate 88

MAP 303 CRESTED MURRELET Text p.401 Plate 87

MAP 304 CASSIN'S MURRELET Text p.401 Plate 87

MAP 305 PARAKEET AUKLET Text p.402 Plate 88

MAP 306 CRESTED AUKLET Text p.402 Plate 86

MAP 307 LEAST AUKLET Text p.403 Plate 86

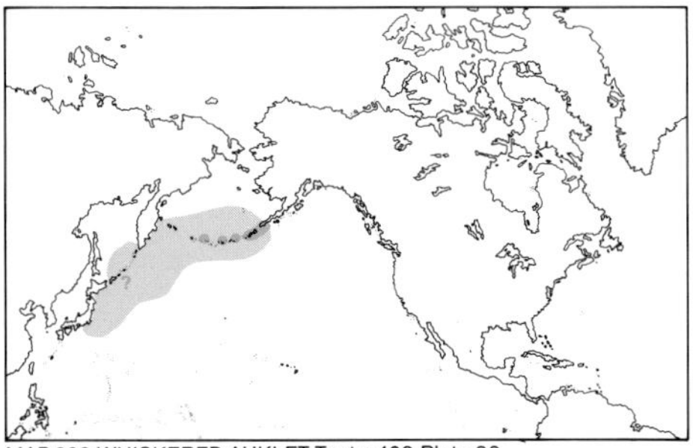

MAP 308 WHISKERED AUKLET Text p.403 Plate 86

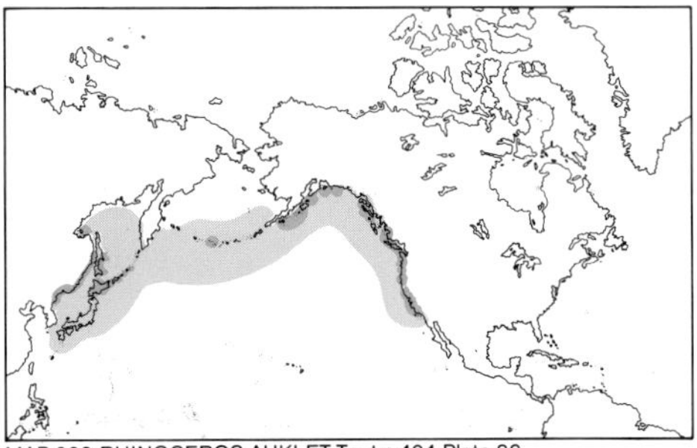

MAP 309 RHINOCEROS AUKLET Text p.404 Plate 86

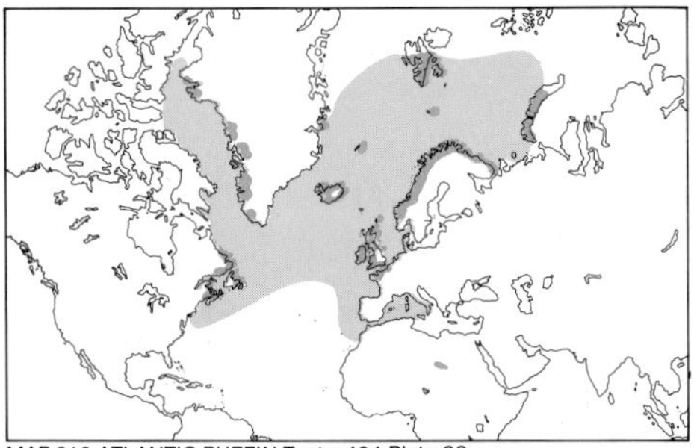

MAP 310 ATLANTIC PUFFIN Text p.404 Plate 83

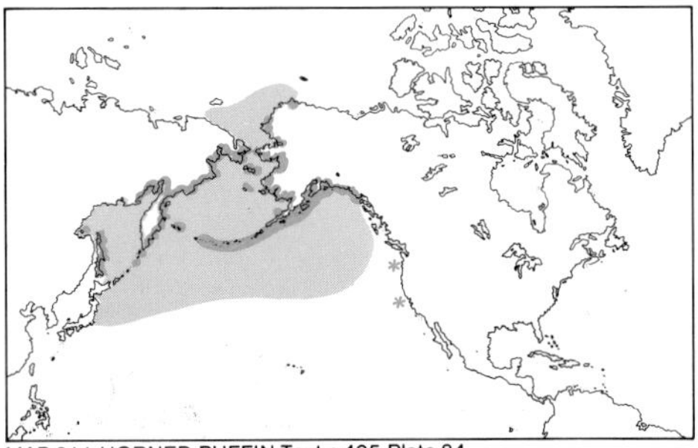

MAP 311 HORNED PUFFIN Text p.405 Plate 84

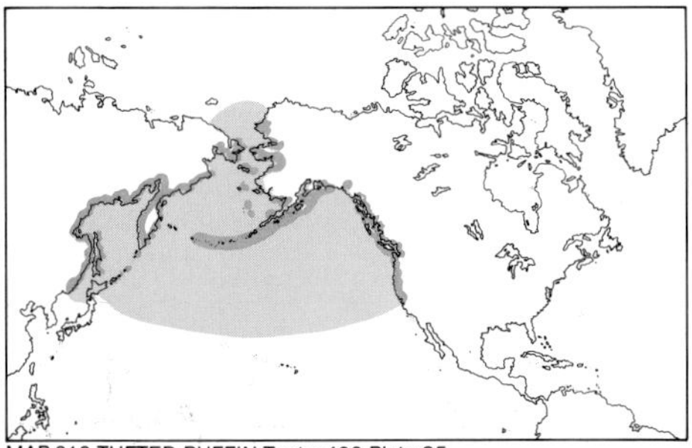

MAP 312 TUFTED PUFFIN Text p.406 Plate 85

MAP KEY

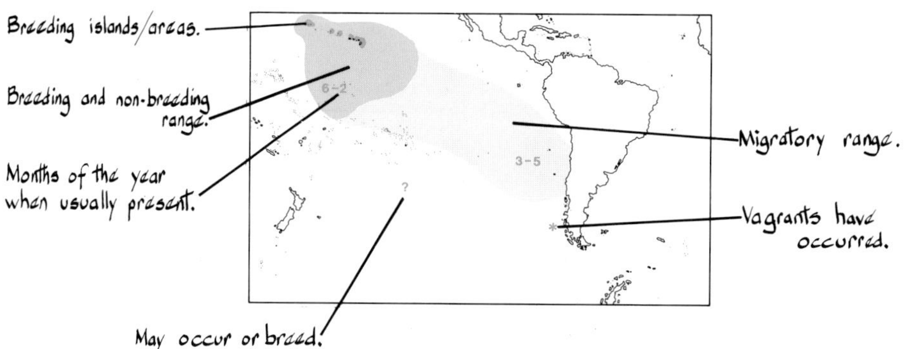

BIBLIOGRAPHY

The following is a list of selected reference material which is directly referred to in the main text.

Ainley, DG (1980) *Auk* 97:837–853.

Alden, P, and Gooders, J (1981) *Finding Birds Around the World*. Houghton Mifflin, Boston, and Andre Deutsch, London.

Alexander, WB (1955) *Birds of the Ocean*. New York.

Ali, S (1979) *The Book of Indian Birds*. Bombay.

American Ornithologists' Union (1973) *Auk* 90:411–419.

Anderson, M (1976) *J. Anim. Ecol.* 45:537–559.

Asbirk, S (1979) *Dansk Orn. Foren. Tidsskr.* 73:207–214.

Bailey, AM, & Sorensen, JH (1962) *Proc. No. 10*, Denver Mus. Nat. Hist.

Bailey, RS (1966) *Ibis* 108:224–264; (1968) *Ibis* 110:493–519; (1971) *Ibis* 113:29–41.

Bailey, RS, Pocklington, R, & Willis, PR (1968) *Ibis* 110:27–34.

Bannerman, DA (1953) *The Birds of West and Equatorial Africa*. Vol. 1. Edinburgh & London.

Barre, H, Derenne, P, Mougin, JL, & Voisin, JF (1976) *C.N.F.R.A.* 40:177–188.

Barth, EK (1975a) *Ornis Scand.* 6:49–63; (1975b) *Ibis* 117:384–387.

Barton, D (1978a) *Austr. Seabird Group Newsletter* 11:27–30; (1978b) *Austr. Seabird Group Newsletter* 12:27–30; (1980) *Austr. Seabird Group Newsletter* 14:8–13.

Beck, JR, & Brown, DW (1971) *Fregetta tropica. Ibis* 113:73–90.

Bent, AC (1919) Life histories of North American diving birds. *Bull. US Nat. Hist. Mus*; (1921) Life histories of North American gulls and terns. *Smithsonian Bull.* 113.

Best, HA, & Owen, KL (1976) *Notornis* 23:233–242.

Binford, LC, Elliot, BG, & Singer, SW (1975) *Wilson Bull.* 87:303–319.

Binford, LC, & Remsen, JV, Jnr (1974) *Western Birds* 5:111.

Blake, ER (1977) *Manual of Neotropical Birds*. V 1. Chicago: Univ. of Chicago Press.

Boonsong, L, & Cronin, E, Jnr (1974) *A Bird Guide of Thailand*. Bangkok.

Booth, J, Jnr, & Lee, DS (1979) *Amer. Birds* 33(5):715–721.

Bourne, WRP (1960) *Sea Swallow* 13:26–39; (1967a) *Sea Swallow* 19:51–76; (1967b) *Ibis* 109:141–167; (1977) *Cormorant* 2:5–7.

Bourne, WRP, & Dixon, TJ (1971/72) *Sea Swallow* 22:29–60; (1975) *Sea Swallow* 24:65–88.

Bourne, WRP, & Loveridge, A (1978) *Ibis* 120:65–66.

Bourne, WRP, & Warham, J (1966) *Ardea* 54:44–67.

Brattstrom, BH, & Howell, TR (1956) *Condor* 58:107–120.

Britton, PL (ed.) (1980) *Birds of East Africa: their habitat, status and distribution*. East Africa Nat. Hist. Soc.

Brooke, RK (1978) *Durban Mus. Nov.* 11:295–308; (1981) *Cormorant* 9:19–23.

Brooke, RK, & Cooper, J (1979) *Durban Mus. Nov.* 12:27–37.

Brooke, RK, & Sinclair, JC (1978) *Cormorant* 4:10–18; (1981)

Brothers, N (1978) *Austr. Seabird Group Newsletter* 11:6–8.

Brown, RGB, Cooke, F, Kinnear, PK, & Mills, EL (1975) *Ibis* 117:339–356.

Brun, E (1979) Present status and trends in population of seabirds in Norway. *Conservation of Marine Birds of Northern North America*. US Dept of Interior Report, Washington, DC.

Bruyns, WFJM, & Voous, KH (1965) *Ardea* 53(1–2):80–81.

Bundy, G (1950) *Birds of Libya*. BOU, London; (1982) *Brit. Birds* 75:129–131.

Burn, DM, & Mather, JR (1974) *Brit. Birds* 67:258–293.

Buturlin, SA (1906) *Ibis* (8) 6:131–139, 333–337, 661–666.

CarinsM (1974) *Emu*: 74 (1) 55–57.

Carter, MJ (1981) *Austr. Seabird Group Newsletter* 15:9–10.

Cave, B (1982) *Brit. Birds* 75:55–61.

Chapman, S (1969) *Ibis* 111:615–617.

Cheke, RA (1967) *Sea Swallow* 19:31–35.

Cheshire, N, & Jenkins, J (1981) *Austr. Seabird Group Newsletter* 15:5–6.

Clancey, PA (1979) *Durban Mus. Nov.* 12:6.

Clancey, PA, Brooke, RK, & Sinclair, JC (1981) *Durban Mus. Nov.* 12(18).

Clapp, RB (1973) *Condor* 73:490.

Clinning, CS (1978) *Madoqua* 11:31–39.

Conroy, JWH (1971) Wilson's Phalarope in the Antarctic. *Brit. Ant. Survey Bull.* 26:82–83.

Cooke, F, & Mills, EL (1972) *Ibis* 114:245–251.

Cox, JB (1980) *Rec. S. Austr. Mus.* 18:91–121.

Cramp, S, Bourne, WRP, & Saunders, D (1974) *The Seabirds of Britain and Ireland*. London.

Cramp, S, & Simmons, KEL (eds.) (1977) *The Birds of the Western Palearctic*. Vol. 1. Oxford.

Crossin, RS (1974) *Smith. Cont. Zool.* 158. Wash.

Davis, AH, & Vinicombe, KE (1980) *Brit. Birds* 73:31–32.

De Heer, P (1981) *Dutch Birding* 2:131–139.

Dementiev, GP, & Gladkov, NA (1951) *Birds of the Soviet Union*. Vol. 3. Moscow.

De Naurois, R (1959) *Alauda* 27:241–308.

Densley, M (1977) *Scot. Birds* 9:334–342.

Derenne, P, Lufbery, JX, & Tollu, B (1974) *Com. Nat. Fr. Rech. Antarctiques* 33:57–81.

Desante, D, & Ainley, DG (1980) *The Avifauna of the South Farallon Is.* Cooper Orn. Soc., Lawrence, Kansas.

De Schauensee, RM (1966) *The Species of Birds of South America and their Distribution*. Acad. of Nat. Sci.; (1971) *A Guide to the Birds of South America*. London & Edinburgh.

De Schauensee, RM, & Phelps, WH, Jnr (1978) *A Guide to the Birds of Venezuela*. Princeton.

Devillers, P (1972) *Western Birds* 3:33; (1977) *Auk* 94:417–429.

Devillers, P, & Terschuren, JA (1978) *Gerfaut* 68:53–86.

Diamond, AW (1972) *Ibis* 114:395–398; (1975) *Ibis* 117:302–323.

Divotky, GJ (1979) Sea ice as a factor in seabird distribution and ecology in the Beaufort, Chukchi and Bering Seas. *Conservation of Marine Birds of Northern North America*. US Dept of Interior, Washington, DC.

Donaghue, PK, & Petersen, WR (1980) *Amer. Birds* 34:213.

Dunn, J (1978) *Western Tanager* 44(8):8.

Dwight, J (1925) The gulls (Laridae) of the world: their plumages, moults, variations, relationships and distribution. *Bull. Amer. Mus. Nat. Hist.* 52:63–408.

Elliot, HFI (1954) *Brit. Orn. Club* 74:21–24.

Evans, PG (1970) Seabird Report 1970. *Seabird Group*: 35.

Falla, RA, Sibson, RB, & Tubott, EG (1975) *A Field Guide to the Birds of New Zealand*. London.

Finch, D (1973) *Amer. Birds* 27:26–27; (1978) *Amer. Birds* 32:281.

Fisher, HI (1965) *Condor* 67:355–357; (1972) *Auk* 89(2):381–402.

Fleming, CA (1950) *Emu* 49:169–188.

Flora, MD (1981) *Cormorant* 9(1):8–13.

Frith, CB (1978) *Emu* 1978(2):95–97.

Forsell, DJ, & Gould, PJ (1980) Distribution and abundance of seabirds wintering in the Kodiak area of Alaska. *US Fish and Wildlife Service.*

Foxall, RA (1979) *Amer. Birds* 33:838.

Fullagar, PJ (1976) Providence Petrel. In *Readers Digest Complete Book of Australian Birds*, p. 45. Sydney; (1978) *Austr. Seabird Group Newsletter* 11:4–5.

Fullagar, PJ, McKean, JC, & van Tets, GF (1974) Appendix F: Report on Birds. In *Environmental Survey of Lord Howe Is.* Sydney Govt Printers.

Fullagar, P, & van Tets, G (1976) *West Aus. Nat.* 13 (6):136–144.

Garcia, EFJ (1971) *Seabird Rep.* 1971:30–36.

Gibson, DD, & Kessell, B (1978) Studies in Avian Biol. 1. Cooper Orn. Soc.

Godfrey, WE (1966) *The Birds of Canada*. Ottawa.

Gosselin, M, & David, N (1975) *Amer. Birds* 29:1059–1066.

Grant, PJ (1978) *Brit. Birds* 71:145–176; (1979) *Brit. Birds* 72:142–182; (1980) *Brit. Birds* 73:113–158; (1981a) *Brit. Birds* 74:111–142; (1981b) *Brit. Birds* 74:363–394; (1982) *Gulls: a guide to identification*. Berkhamsted.

Grant, PJ, & Scott, RE (1980) Field Identification of juvenile Common, Arctic and Roseate Terns. In Sharrock, JTR (ed.) *The Frontiers of Bird Identification*, pp. 96–100.

Gray, AP (1958) *Bird Hybrids*. Tech. Communications no. 13, London.

Grinnell, J, & Miller, HA (1944) *Pacific Coast Avifauna*, no. 27.

Harper, PC (1980) *Notornis* 27(3):235–286

Harper, PC, & Kinsky, FC (1978) *Southern Albatrosses and Petrels: an identification guide*. Victoria.

Harrington, BA (1974) *Bird Banding* 45:115–144.

Harris, MP (1969) *Ibis* 108:17–33; (1973) *Ibis* 115:482–510; (1974) *A Field Guide to the Birds of the Galapagos*. London; (1981) *Brit. Birds* 74:246–256.

Harrison, C (1979) *Oceans* 12(5):25.

Harrison, P (1978a) *Cormorant* 5:19–21; (1978b) At sea identification of Wandering and Royal Albatrosses. *Austr. Seabird Group Newsletter* 11:14–21; (1978c) *Austr. Seabird Group Newsletter* 11:8–14; (1979) *Austr. Seabird Group Newsletter* 12:32–41; (1981) *Cormorant* 9(2):129.

Harrow, G (1965) *Notornis* 12(2):59–70.

Harvey, WG (1981) *Brit. Birds* 74:523–524.

Hasegawa, H (1978) *Pacific Seabird Group Bull.* 5(1):16–17.

Hays, H (1975) *Auk* 92(2):219–234.

Hoffman, W, Weins, JA, & Scott, JM (1978) *Auk* 95:441–458.

Holgersen, H (1957) Ornithology of the 'Brategg' Expedition. *Christensens Hvalfangstmuseum Bergen* 21:1–80.

Humphrey, PS, Bridge, D, Reynolds, PW, & Peterson, RT (1970) *Birds of Isla Grande (Tierra del Fuego)*. Smithsonian Institution Manual.

Hutchinson, CD, & Neath, B (1978) *Brit. Birds* 71:563–582.

Huyskens, G, & Maes, P (1971) La migracion de Aves Marimus en el NW de España.

Ingolfsson, A (1970) *Ibis*

112:340–362.
Jackson, R (1958) *Notornis* 7:230–233.
Jehl, JR, Jnr (1974) *Auk* 91:681–699.
Jehl, JR, Jnr, & Bond, S (1975) *Trans. San Diego Soc. Nat. Hist.* 18:9.
Jehl, DR, & Jehl, JR, Jnr (1981) *Amer. Birds* 35:911–912.
Jenkins, J (1981) *Austr. Seabird Group Newsletter* 16:3–16.
Johnson, SR, Adams, WJ, & Morrell, MR (1975) *The Birds of the Beaufort Sea*. Canadian Wildlife Service Pub.
Johnstone, GW (1974) *Emu* 74:209–218; (1980) *Austr. Seabird Group Newsletter* 14:17–18.
Johnstone, GW, Shaughnessy, PD, & Conroy, JWH (1976) *S. Afr. J. Antarctic Research* 6:19–23.
Jouanin, C (1957) *Oiseau* 27:12–27; (1969) *Oiseau* 40:48–60.
Jouanin, C, & Gill, (1965) *Oiseau* 37:1–19.
Jouanin, C, & Mougin, (1979) Procellariiformes. In Mayr, E, & Cottrell, GW (eds.) *Check-list of the Birds of the World*. Cambridge, Mass.
Kautesk, BM (1976) *Discovery* 5:18–20. (Vancouver Nat. Hist. Soc.)
Kessel, B, & Gibson, DD (1978) *Status and Distribution of Alaska Birds*. Studies in Avian Biology, Cooper Orn. Soc.
King, WB (1967) *Preliminary Smithsonian Identification Manual: Seabirds of the Tropical Pacific Ocean*. Washington; (1970) The Trade Wind Zone Oceanography Pilot Study Pt 7: Observations of Seabirds. *Spec. Sci. Rep.* Fisheries: no. 586. US Fish and Wildlife Service.
Kinnear, PK (1980) *Brit. Birds* 73:231–232.
Kinsky, FC, & Falla, RA (1976) *Nat. Mus. NZ Rec* 1:105–126.
Kitson, AR (1980) *Bull. BOC* 100(3):178–185.
Klapste, J (1981) *Austr. Bird Watcher* 9:88–92.
Krabbe, N (1979) *Checklist of the Birds of Elat*. BOU, London.
Kuroda, N (1955) *Condor* 57:290–300.
Kuzyakin, AP (1963) *Ornithologiia* 6:315–320.
Lapthorn, J, Griffiths, RG, & Bourne, WRP (1970) *Ibis* 112:260–261.
Lauro, AJ, & Spencer, BJ (1980) *Amer. Birds* 34:111–117.
Lee, DS (1979) *Amer. Birds* 33:138–139.
Lee, DS, & Booth, J (1979) *Amer. Birds* 33:715–721.
Lee, DS, Wingate, DB, & Kale, HW (1981) *Amer. Birds* 35:887–890.
Liversidge, R, & McLachlan, GR (1978) *Roberts Birds of South Africa*. Cape Town. 2nd edn.
Loomis, LM (1918) *Proc. Calif. Acad. Sci.* 4th Ser. 2:1–187.
Løppenthin, B (1943) *Medd. om Gronland* 131(12):1–26.
Marchant, S (1958) *Ibis* 100:349–387.
Mark, DM (1981) *Amer. Birds* 35(6):898–900.
Mayr, E (1945) *Birds of the Southwest Pacific*. New York.
Mayr, E, & Cottrell, GW (eds.) (1979) *Checklist of the Birds of the World*. Vol 1, 2nd ed. Museum of Comp. Zool. Cambridge, Mass.
McKean, JL (1981) *Austr. Seabird Group Newsletter* 15:11–16.
McLaughlin, VP (1979) *Amer. Birds* 33:727.
Meeth, P (1969) *Ardea* 57:92.
Meeth, P, & Meeth, K (1977) *Ardea* 65:90–91.
Meinertzhagen, R (1954) *The Birds of Arabia*. Edinburgh.
Meltofte, H, Edelstam, C, Granstrom, G, Hanmer, J, & Hjort, C (1981) *Brit. Birds* 74:316–320.
Mobberley, DH (1974) *Sea Swallow* 23:72–73.
Monaghan, P, & Duncan, N (1979) *Brit. Birds* 72:100–103.
Muller, A (1882) *J. Orn. Lpz.* 30(160):353–448.
Murphy, RC (1936) *Oceanic Birds of South America*. Vols. 1 & 2. New York; (1952) *Amer. Mus. Nov.* 1586.
Murphy, RC, & Harper, F (1921) *Bull. Amer. Mus. Nat. Hist.* 44(17):495–554.
Murphy, RC, & Pennoyer, JM (1952) *Amer. Mus. Nov.* 1580.
Murphy, RC, & Snyder, JP (1952) *Amer. Mus. Nov.* 1596:1–16.
Naveen, R (1981) *Birding* 13(6); 14(1–3).
Nechaev, VA (1977) In Voinstvenskii, MA (ed.) Proc. 7th All-Union Orn. Conf. part 1. Kiev.
Nelson, JB (1971) *Ibis* 103:429–467; (1976) *Living Bird* 14:113–155; (1978) *The Gannet*. Berkhamsted; (1980) *Seabirds: their biology and ecology*. Feltham, England.
Nicholls, GH (1978) *Cormorant* 5:29.
Norman, D, & Tucker, VR (1979) *Brit. Birds* 72:476.
Oliver, WRB (1955) *New Zealand Birds*. Wellington. 2nd Edn.
Ornithological Society of Turkey (1974) *Turkish Bird Report 1970–73*.
Owre, OT (1976) *Ibis* 118:419–420.
Palmer, RS (1962) *Handbook of North American Birds*. Vol. 1. Yale.
Parry, WE (1828) *Narrative of an attempt to reach the North Pole*. London.
Patten, SM, Jnr (1976) *Pacific Seabird Group Bulletin* 3(1):25–27.
Paulian, P (1953) *Mém. de l'Inst. Sci. Madagascar* 8:111–234.
Peterson, RT (1980) *A Field Guide to the Birds*. Boston.
Pocklington, R (1971) *Sea Swallow* 21:27–30.
Powers, KD, & van Os, JA (1979) *Amer. Birds* 33:253.
Prevost, J (1969) *Oiseau* 39:33–49.
Rand, AL (1965) Gulls and Terns. In Wetmore, A (ed.) *Water, Prey and Game Birds of North America*. Washington, DC.
Rand, RW (1963) *Ostrich* 34:122–128.
Robbins, CS (1974) *Brit. Birds* 67:168–170.
Roberson, D (1980) *Rare Birds of the West Coast of North America*. Woodcock Publications, California.
Robertson, CJR (1980) *Austr. Seabird Group Newsletter* 14:19.
Robertson, WB, Jnr (1969) *Nature* 225 (5194):632–634.
Rowan, AN, Elliott, HFI, & Rowan, MK (1951) *Ibis* 93:169–179.
Rumboll, MAE, & Jehl, JR, Jnr (1977) *Trans. San Diego Soc. Nat. Hist.* 19(1).
Sauppe, B (1979) *Amer. Birds* 33:802.
Scharf, WC, & Shugart, GW (1981) *Amer. Birds* 35:910.
Schramm, H (1982) *Cormorant* 10:3–6.
Schreiber, RW, & Ashmole, NP (1970) *Ibis* 112:363–392.
Sealy, SG (1969) *Wilson Bull.* 81(2):213–214; (1974) *Auk* 91:10–23.
Sears, HF, Moseley, LJ, & Mueller, HC (1976) *Auk* 93:100–104.
Serventy, DL, Serventy, V, & Warham, J (1971) *The Handbook of Australian Seabirds*. London.
Shallenberger, RJ (1978) *Hawaii's Birds*. Audubon Soc. Publication.
Shaughnessy, PD (1975) *Emu* 75:147–152; (1979) *Cormorant* 6:37–38.
Sibley, FC, & Clapp, RB (1967) *Ibis* 109:328–337.
Simon, TR (1980) *Condor* 82:1–9.
Sinclair, JC (1979) *Cormorant* 7:7–11; (1980) *Cormorant* 8(1):2–3.
Sinclair, JC, & Turner, CA (1981) *Cormorant* 9(1):41.
Sladen, WJL (1964) The distribution of the Adelie and Chinstrap Penguins. In Carrisk, R, Holdgate, MW, & Prevost, J (eds.) Biologie Antarctique, Proc. 1st SCAR Symposium on Antarctic Biology, pp. 359–365. Paris.
Slater, P (1970) *A Field Guide to Australian Birds, vol. 1: Non-passerines*. Sydney.
Smith, NG (1966) *Orn. Monog.* 4:1–99.
Snow, BK, & Snow, DW (1969) *Ibis* 111:30–35.
Sowls, AL, DeGange, AR, Nelson, JW, & Lester, GS (1980) *Catalog of California Seabird Colonies*. US Dept Int. Fish and Wildlife Serv. FWS/OBS 37/80 p. 371.
Sowls, AL, Hatch, SA, & Lensink, CJ (1978) *Catalog of Alaskan Seabird Colonies*. US Dept Int. Fish and Wildlife Serv. FWS/065 78/78.
Stallcup, R (1976) *Western Birds* 7:113–136.
Stallcup, R, & Greenberg, R (1974) *Amer. Birds* 28:945.
Stewart, PF, & Christensen, S (1971) *Checklist to the birds of Cyprus*. Privately published, England.
Stonehouse, B (1960) The King Penguin *Aptenodyptes patagonica* of South Georgia. *Falkland Islands Dependencies Survey Report* no. 23; (1971) *Ibis* 113:1–7; (1972) *Animals of the Antarctic: the ecology of the far south*. London.
Stonehouse, B, & Stonehouse, S (1963) *Ibis* 103(B):409–422.
Storer, RW (1965) *Living Bird* 4th annual: 59–63.
Storr, GM (1960) *Emu* 60(2):135–137.
Strickland, MJ (1971) *Sea Swallow* 22:16–19.
Taverner, JH (1970) *Brit. Birds* 63:380–382.
Tellería, JL (1980) *Bird Study* 27:21–26.
Terres, JK (1980) *The Audubon Society Encyclopedea of North American Birds*. New York.
Tickell, WLN (1973) *Sea Swallow* 23:21–25.
Tickell, WLN, & Gibson, JD (1968) *Emu* 68(1):7–20.
Tuck, GS, & Heinzel, H (1978) *A Field Guide to the Seabirds of Britain and the World*. London.
Tuck, LM (1961) The murres: their distribution, populations and biology. *Canadian Wildlife Service Rep. Series No 1*. Ottawa.
Tucker, VR (1980) *Brit. Birds* 73:264; (1981) *Brit. Birds* 74:299–301.
Van den Berg, AB (1980) *Dutch Birding* 2(1):19–21.
Van Ijzendoorn, EJ (1980) *Dutch Birding* 2:17–18.
Vaurie, C (1965) *The Birds of the Palearctic Fauna: Non-Passeriformes*. London.
Veit, RR (1978) *Amer. Birds* 32:300–302.
Vinicombe, KE (1980) *Brit. Birds* 73:223–225.
Voous, KH (1963) *Ardea* 51:251.
Wahl, TR, & Paulsen, DR (1974) *A Guide to Bird Finding in Washington*. Bellingham, Wash.
Wallace, DIM (1973) *Ibis* 115:559–571.
Wallace, DIM, & Bourne, WRP (1981) *Brit. Birds* 74:417–426.
Warham, J (1958) *Brit. Birds* 51:393–397; (1967) *Emu* 67:1–22; (1974) *J. Roy. Soc. New Zealand*: 63–108.
Watson, GE (1975) *Birds of the Antarctic and Sub-Antarctic*. Washington, DC.
Watson, GE, Zusi, LR, & Storer, RE (1963) *Preliminary Field Guide to the Birds of the Indian Ocean*. Smithsonian Inst.
Watson, JB (1910) *Science* 32(833): 470–473.
Weller, MW (1959) *Auk* 76(4):520–521.
Weston, FM (1934) *Auk* 51(1):82.
Wetmore, A (1945) *Auk* 62:577–586.

Williams, AJ, & Burger, AE (1978)*Cormorant* 5:11–14.
Williamson, K (1960) *Brit. Birds* 53:243.
Wingate, DB (1964) *Auk* 81:147–159.
Woods, RW (1975) *The Birds of the Falkland Islands*. Salisbury, Wilts, England.
Woutersen, K (1980) *Brit. Birds* 73:192–193.
Wynne-Edwards, VC (1935) *Proc. Boston Soc. Nat. Hist.* 15(4):307.
Yanagisawa (1973) *Yacho* 38:44.
Zusi, R (1962) Structural adaptations of the head and neck of the Black Skimmer, *Rynchops nigra*. L. Nuttall Orn. Club No. 3. Cambridge, Mass.

INDEX OF ENGLISH NAMES

References prefixed Pl refer to colour plate numbers; references in roman refer to text pages where the bird is described, references in italics refer to an illustration within main text; references prefixed M refer to Map number (between pages 410–442) Only those subspecies which can be separated under normal viewing conditions are indexed separately. For ranges of other subspecies refer to DM section under each species.

INDEX OF SCIENTIFIC NAMES

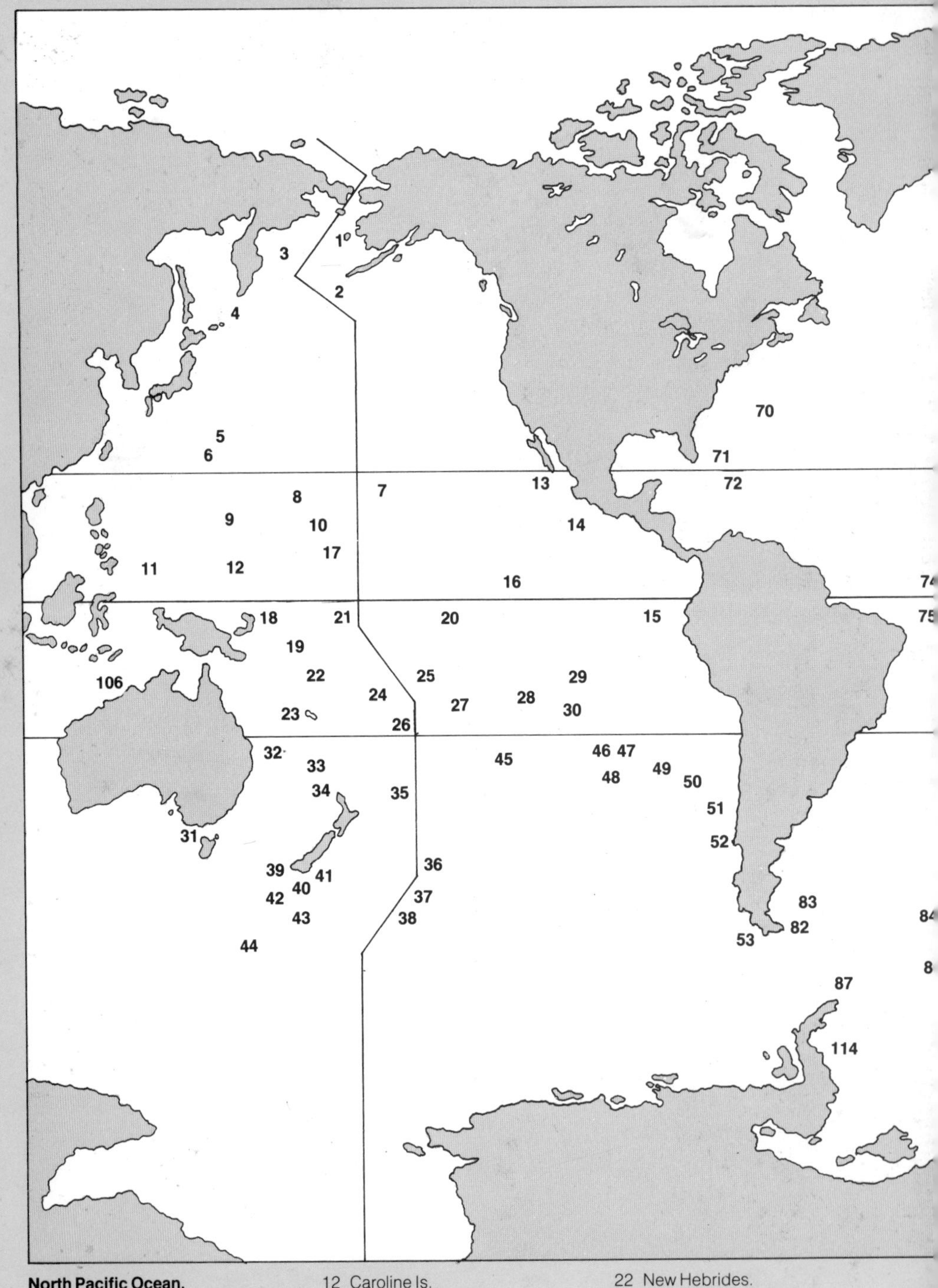

North Pacific Ocean.

1 Pribilof Is.
2 Aleutian Is.
3 Kommandu I.
4 Kunle Is.
5 Bonin Is.
6 Volcano I.
7 Hawaiian Is.
8 Wake I
9 Mariana – Guam.
10 Marshall Is.
11 Palau I.
12 Caroline Is.
13 Revilla Gigedo I.
14 Clipperton I.
15 Galapagos Is.
16 Line Is. – Christmas Is.
17 Gilbert Is.

South Pacific Ocean.

18 New Britain.
19 Solomon Is.
20 Phoenix Is.
21 Elice Is.
22 New Hebrides.
23 New Caledonia Is.
24 Fiji Is.
25 Samoan Is.
26 Tonga Is.
27 Cook Is.
28 Society Is.
29 Marquessa Is.
30 Tuamotu Archipelago.
31 Bass Straits.
32 Lord Howe I.
33 Norfolk I.